Footprint Sri Lanka

Edward Aves

Fourth edition

Travelling is almost like talking with men of other centuries.

Descartes, René (1596-1650), *Le Discours de la méthode*, 1637

Sri Lanka Highlights

See colour maps at back of book

1 Jaffna Peninsula
Eerie islands, half-submerged churches and a proud Tamil culture, open for the first time in two decades

2 Anuradhapura and Mihintale
Mighty *dagobas*, the holiest tree and Sri Lankan Buddhism's birthplace

3 Aukana
Exquisitely carved Buddha colossus hewn from a single rock

4 Kandy
Home to the worshipped Tooth and the island's grandest festival

5 Peradeniya
The finest botanical garden in Asia

6 Colombo
Buzzing capital and a foodie's paradise

7 Kitulgala
Prehistoric caves, white-water rafting and the location for the film, 'Bridge on the River Kwai'

8 Adam's Peak
Perfectly conical, a holy mountain worth climbing

9 Sinharaja Biosphere Reserve
This reserve, criss-crossed with trails, is filled with feathered friends

10 Galle
UNESCO-protected Dutch old town

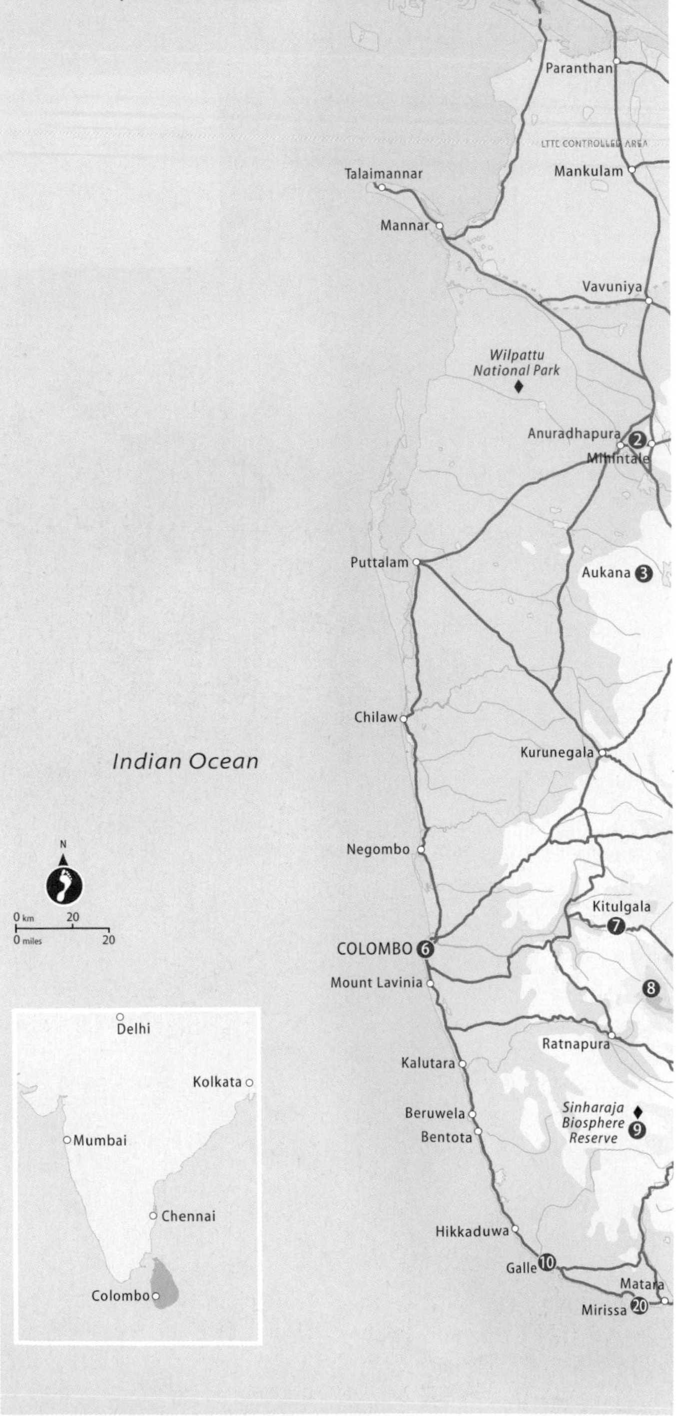

Jaffna 1
Paranthan
LTTE CONTROLLED AREA
Talaimannar
Mankulam
Mannar
Vavuniya
Wilpattu National Park
Anuradhapura 2
Mihintale
Puttalam
Aukana 3
Chilaw
Kurunegala
Indian Ocean
Negombo
N
0 km 20
0 miles 20
Kitulgala 7
COLOMBO 6
Mount Lavinia
8
Delhi
Ratnapura
Kolkata
Kalutara
Beruwela
Bentota
Sinharaja Biosphere Reserve 9
Mumbai
Chennai
Hikkaduwa
Galle 10
Matara
Colombo
Mirissa 20

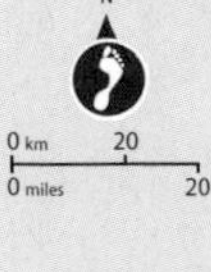

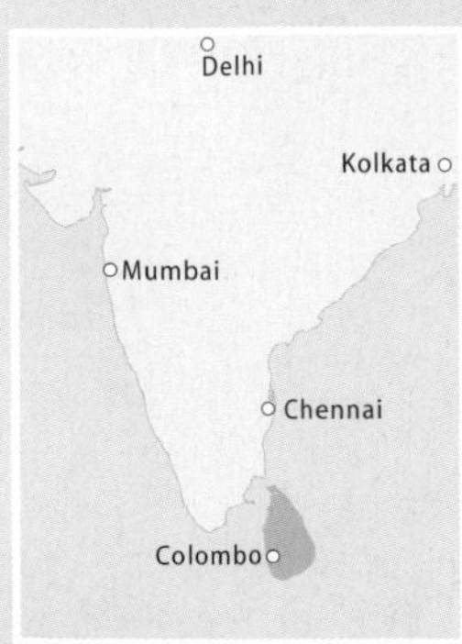

11 Uppuveli and Nilaveli
Beautiful beaches with hardly a soul around

12 Kaudulla National Park
An ancient tank where herds of elephants in their hundreds can be seen

13 Sigiriya
Spectacular 'Lion Rock', bare-breasted damsels and a fifth-century playboy's penthouse

14 Polonnaruwa
Well-preserved and compact ancient city in a peaceful shaded park

15 Nuwara Eliya
Eccentric former British hill station in the cool climes of tea-growing country

16 Ella
Mountain walks, waterfalls and vistas

17 Arugam Bay
The island's best surf and its latest beach hotspot

18 Kataragama
Hindu pilgrimage site famed for the water-cutting and fire-walking ceremonies

19 Yala West (Ruhuna) National Park
The best chance of spotting the elusive leopard

20 Mirissa
A picture perfect stretch of palm-backed sandy beach

Contents

Kandy and the Highlands

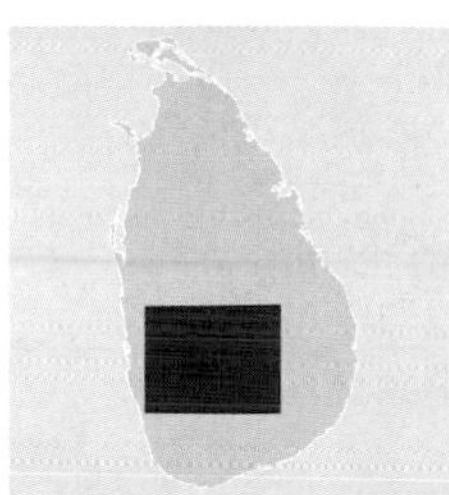

Ancient Cities

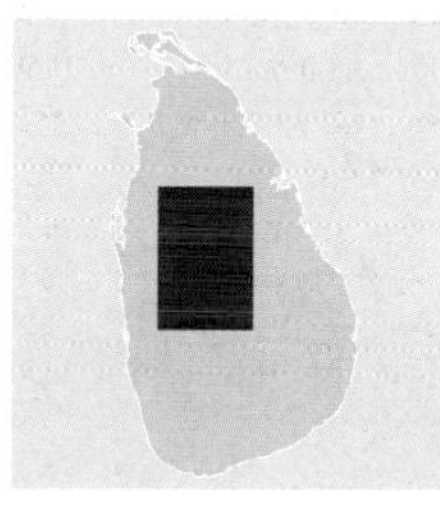

The East

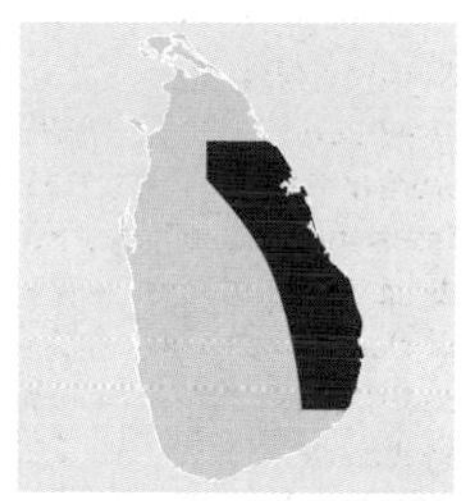

Jaffna and the North

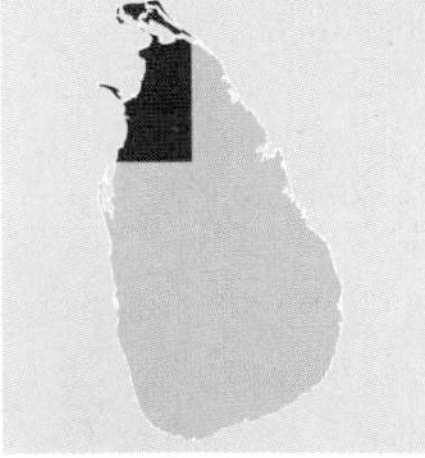

Background

A lion's den
The Lion's Paws half way up the 200 m high Sigiriya Rock, a royal citadel created in the fifth century.

Footnotes

Inside front cover

Inside back cover

Under cover
A stroll through the leafy back lanes in the coastal town of Koggala.

A foot in the door

Part of Sri Lanka's irresistible charm lies in the way it interweaves past and present. Whilst being forward-looking and progressive, this remains an island deeply imbued with a sense of pride in its traditions. Commuters and taxi drivers will stop on busy highways and queue at roadside temples to pay respects to their ancestors; businessmen will swap the comfort of their air-conditioned offices for an exhausting pilgrimage to the island's most sacred sites; and at special occasions, the timing of even the simplest events is governed by ritual and auspicious moments determined by astrology.

That Sri Lanka's diverse ethnic groups have clung fiercely on to their traditions is perhaps not surprising in the wake of centuries of invasion by foreign powers. The island's early settlers migrated from India, to which, recent evidence suggests, Sri Lanka was once linked by an ancient causeway. They established a 2,500-year old Buddhist tradition that survives here as a potent symbol of the national identity, despite having long since faded in its native land. Hinduism, too, made its mark, proudly protected by Tamils across the nation. Arab traders brought Islam, while in later years the colonial powers of Europe fought over the island's riches. Their legacy survives in the island's tumbledown forts and creaking railways, tea plantations and passion for cricket.

What gives Sri Lanka its edge, though, is that this intoxicating mix of cultures is so accessible. Marco Polo declared this the 'finest island of its size in the world.' Centuries later, it would be hard to disagree.

Pride and prejudice

Sri Lanka is cultivating a new image and one of which it's justifiably feeling rather proud. Beyond the tourist brochure hyperbole, there's always been much to celebrate: a developed world standard of literacy, for example, and the continent's greatest biodiversity, carefully protected by forward-looking ecological thinking. However, since the advent of large-scale tourism, the island has laboured under paradoxical misconceptions from outsiders. The package tourists who flock to the island's west coast resorts barely notice the cultural heritage beyond the palm-fringed beaches. For them Sri Lanka's appeal is limited to a popular, romanticized 'honeymoon isle', a sanitized Asia, a poor man's Bali. Others have been scared off by its war-torn image, swayed by the metaphor of the weeping 'teardrop in the Indian Ocean'.

Carved in stone
At Gal Vihara (Cave of the Spirits of Knowledge) in the ancient city of Polonnaruwa, this Buddha lies in a state of Parinirvana *(rather than death).*

But now Sri Lanka is confounding everyone. Rising above an international climate of mistrust, barely two years since a bomb at the international airport threatened to wipe out its tourist industry for good, Sri Lanka is dancing to a different drum. The sparks, of course, were the silencing of the guns, the peace talks and a renewed public zest for enmities to be put aside for the greater good.

The effects of the ceasefire are palpable, and nowhere more so than in the capital. Confidence is up and investment is flooding in as Colombo begins to looks east – to Singapore or even Sydney – for inspiration. Away from the capital the potential gains are even greater. The North and East, which saw the bulk of ethnic fighting, will take years to reconstruct, but saved from a generation of mass tourism, the area possesses a wildness that will prove irresistible to the adventurous traveller.

High life
Prayer flags at the summit of the island's holy mountain, Adam's Peak.

1 *Dancers in their fuchsia finery on Independence Day at Anuradhapura.* ▸▸ *See page 260.*

2 *The Temple of the Tooth at Kandy houses the Tooth Relic, believed to be that of the Buddha's, and worshipped by millions.* ▸▸ *See page 203.*

3 *Masks have been made in the town of Ambalangoda for generations. Their fearsome looks exorcise evil forces during Devil Dancing.* ▸▸ *See page 134.*

4 *Worshippers light scented oil lamps in the hope of receiving wisdom and enlightenment. Incense is burnt for purity.*

5 *A monk walks through a rice field near Sinharaja Biosphere Reserve.* ▸▸ *See page 123 .*

6 *At Mihintale 1840 granite steps lead the way to a mighty* dagoba *that is visible for miles around.* ▸▸ *See page 268.*

7 *Offerings of flowers on an altar at Weherahena on the south coast.* ▸▸ *See page 159.*

8 *The* gopurams *of a Hindu temple near Talawakele in the Highlands.*

9 *Along with Adam's Peak, the most important pilgrimage site in Sri Lanka is here at Kataragama. Platters of fruit are sold to pilgrims who offer them to the gods.* ▸▸ *See page 183.*

10 *At the Elephant Orphanage at Pinnawela, set up in 1972 to rescue four orphaned babies, you can watch elephants bathe and feed.* ▸▸ *See page 198.*

11 *Taking to the roads is an adventure in itself. Overtaking when approaching a blind bend is not uncommon. 'Fire and dust' may be a little too close to the bone!*

12 *A procession of monks is escorted by crowds bearing decorative parasols.*

An island of excess

The island is brimming with places to explore. Belying its size, there are no fewer than seven UNESCO World Heritage Sites, two dozen nature reserves, stands of pristine rainforest, mist-shrouded peaks, spice plantations, tea plantations, hill stations and gem mines. Surrounding it all, along the rim of its coastline, stretches a succession of white beaches that rank alongside the best in the world.

Cultural Triangle

The 'Triangle' of Sri Lanka's early capitals contains five of the seven heritage sites. Kandy, surrounded by verdant hills, is the repository of the precious casket holding the sacred Tooth Relic of the Buddha, drawing pilgrims in their thousands throughout the year. To the north, the enormous whitewashed *dagobas* of Anuradhapura and Mihintale are testament to the audacity and riches of the ancient kingdoms, while amongst the forested ruins at Polonnaruwa the serene expression of the recumbent monolithic Buddha at the Gal Vihara hints at the still calm of Buddhist meditation. In contrast, the natural fortress at Sigiriya rock nearby conceals a bloodthirsty epic tale as dramatic as its position.

There are over 3,000 elephants in Sri Lanka – this is eqivalent to about 10% of the world's Asian elephant population. Here, in the area around Nuwara Eliya, a mahout takes a step down.

A tropical treat awaits on one of the island's many beaches.

Birds and the beasts

Classical biogeographic theory predicts that small islands do not have large animals. Sri Lanka puts pay to that. Here, the largest terrestrial mammal, the elephant, roams the remaining wildernesses. Throughout the dry zone of the east, from Uda Walawe to Kaudulla and beyond, wild elephants can be seen, often in herds of several hundred, their migration corridors protected by an ever-growing network of national parks. Sri Lanka also offers one of the best opportunities in the world to see the leopard. Shy and elusive, the island's biggest cat still prowls the last stretches of forest, especially at Yala National Park in the southeast. And at Sinharaja Biosphere Reserve, virtually undisturbed by man, you can experience the thrill of exploring the primary rainforest. This is prime bird-watching territory too. The island's 230 resident bird species, from the yellow-eared bulbul to the red-faced malkoha, are joined in winter by flocks of migrants who find refuge in the coastal lagoons.

Palms, pampering and processions

If you just want to kick back and relax, the beautiful beaches of the south and east coasts offer coconut palms aplenty for tying your hammock. For diving and snorkelling, head to Unawatuna, Mirissa or Nilaveli, or for the island's best surf, strike out to Arugam Bay. Many resorts now offer spas and herbal cure centres, where you can dip into the science of Ayurveda, the ancient system of healing, for a massage with aromatic oils. To get a taste of the island at play, go to one of the festivals – Kataragama, Kelaniya, or most spectacular of all, Kandy, where the annual *Esala Perahera* features processions of hundreds of elephants decorated with jewels and flowers, drummers, dancing and thousands of pilgrims in procession.

There is rarely a time when a three-wheeler is hard to come by.

Essentials

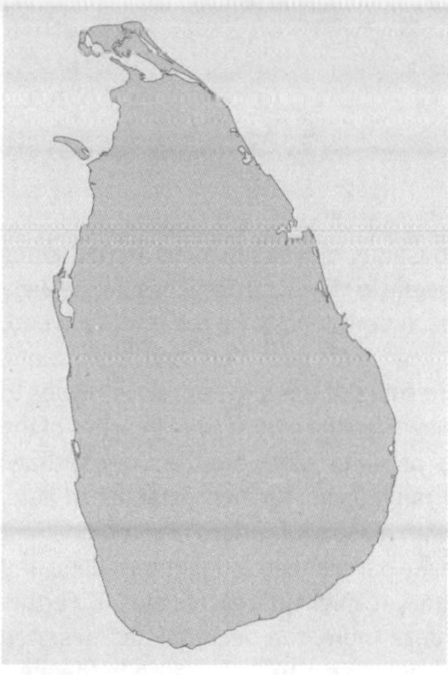

Planning your trip

Where to go

The island's superb beaches lie all along its coastline, with sandy coves and estuaries and long palm-fringed stretches. They vary greatly in character. Beaches on the west coast, conveniently close to Colombo and the airport, tend to be the most crowded, but offer opportunities for watersports and buzz with busy bars and restaurants. Here, also, away from the package hotels, are some of the most exquisite places to stay, notably in **Bentota**. For many travellers however, the picturesque beaches of the south coast, often with magnificent sweeps of white sand, are the biggest draw. Quieter than the west coast, **Unawatuna** and **Tangalla** are the best established here, offering opportunities for diving and packed with reasonably priced accommodation. Picture-perfect, laid-back **Mirissa** is increasingly popular with budget travellers, and there are plenty of other options in this area that you might just get to yourself. Further off the beaten track, but at last accessible once more, the beautiful and deserted beaches of the east coast are worth seeking out during the off-season in the west coast. **Arugam Bay**, Sri Lanka's surf capital, is the latest hotspot, while north of Trincomalee, **Nilaveli** and **Uppuveli**, with gentle clear waters perfect for swimming, are slowly beginning to wake up again.

However, most of Sri Lanka's most beautiful and interesting sights are away from the coast. By venturing a few hours inland you can explore the island's abundant cultural heritage. In the lush verdant hills, the last Buddhist capital of **Kandy** is found. To the north are the other two points of the cultural triangle – the ancient capitals of **Anuradhapura** and **Polonnaruwa** – and the extraordinary royal citadel atop the giant rocky outcrop of **Sigiriya**, decorated with its world famous frescoes. Close to Anuradhapura is **Mihintale** where the first royal conversion to Buddhism was inspired, while **Dambulla** has impressive paintings in its rock cave. While visiting Kandy you can also see baby elephants at bath time at the **Pinnawela Elephant Orphanage**. Nearby, are interesting spice plantations and several temples.

The central mountains with spectacular waterfalls and some great walking trails around **Nuwara Eliya**, surrounded by tea gardens, provide a refreshing break. To the east, the 'gaps' at **Ella** and **Haputale** provide spectacular views, while some travellers are lured by the attractive gem capital of **Ratnapura**.

Sri Lanka's varied wildlife can be explored in its impressive network of **national parks**, such as **Ruhuna-Yala** to the southeast where the fortunate may even spot a leopard, and **Uda Walawe**, famous for its herds of elephants. There is plenty of bird-watching along several shallow coastal lagoons, while **Sinharaja Biosphere Reserve** is the last significant stretch of pristine rainforest.

Choosing a route obviously depends on your interests, the time of year and to a certain extent your mode of travel. Hiring a car allows you greater flexibility. A good option can be to take the train to Kandy and then to take buses or hire a car for visiting the rest of the Cultural Triangle and the hill country. Even if you are staying at a beach hotel on the southwest or south coast it is easy to get up to Kandy and make that a base for further exploration.

One week

If you only have a week, you'd better get your skates on. A typical itinerary would head straight to Kandy, either on the scenic railway or by car (stopping at Pinnawela). On day two, after exploring the city and surrounds, travel north to Dambulla and overnight at Sigiriya. Climb the rock first thing the next morning, and then head east to explore Polonnaruwa in the afternoon. Those interested in Sri Lanka's ancient ruins could then head northwest to Anuradhapura and Mihintale, returning to Colombo on the Puttalam road, or for those who prefer relaxation on the beach return to Colombo and spend a couple of days on the west coast. An alternative one-week trip by car might head straight along the coast, via Galle, for a day on one of the south's beautiful beaches, then to Tissamaharama for a safari at Yala National Park, perhaps with a side trip to the temple town of Kataragama. It is a picturesque drive into the highlands, where you could explore the tea estates, walking trails and fading colonial grandeur of Nuwara Eliya, and return to Colombo via Kandy.

Two weeks

Two weeks gives you time for a 'classic' tour of Sri Lanka. You might start in Anuradhapura and take a few days covering the ancient cities, perhaps with a side trip to the east coast for the beaches north of Trincomalee, looping south to Kandy via Dambulla or Mahiyangana. From Kandy tour the Central Highlands, perhaps climbing Adam's Peak and continue east to Ella or Haputale and then south to the national parks at Yala or Uda Walawe for wildlife spotting. You could finish by flopping on a south coast beach for a couple of days, or return to Colombo via Sinharaja Reserve and Ratnapura.

Three weeks and over

Three weeks or longer gives you a chance to explore the above sites in greater depth and to get off the beaten track. You could easily spend a week exploring the villages of the south coast, or a few days trekking in the hill country, visiting some of lesser visited ancient sites of Northwest and North Central Provinces, or exploring the island's wildlife and birdlife in greater depth. Accessible once more, the unspoilt beaches and wild country of the East are an increasingly draw for travellers, with laid back Arugam Bay the island's latest 'cool' beach destination. Or you could see a very different side of Sri Lanka by visiting the Tamil heartland of Jaffna for a few days.

When to go

Climate → *The best times to visit Sri Lanka are between the two main rainy seasons.*

Because the island lies just north of the equator temperatures remain almost constant throughout the year. However, rainfall varies widely. In the southwest and the Central Highlands the best period is from late October to early March, after the southwest monsoon has finished. However, the north and east are affected by the northeast monsoon during this period and are dry but hot from June to October. The Central Highlands are much cooler throughout the year, but are very wet both during the southwest monsoon (June to October) and the northeast monsoon (October to December).

Festivals and events

In mid-April, the *Sinhala* and *Tamil New Year* celebrations are colourful and feature old traditional games. In May and June the *Wesak* and *Poson Poya* (full moon) days are marked with religious pageants. *Esala Perahera* (around July-August full moon) is the most striking of all, particularly in Kandy though major festivals are also held in Colombo, Kataragama and other major temples. Drummers, dancers, decorated elephants, torch-bearers and whip-crackers all add colour and drama to the 10 days of celebrations.

Tours and tour operators

If you don't wish to travel independently, you may choose to try an inclusive package holiday or let a specialist operator quote for a tailor-made tour. The lowest prices

quoted by package tour companies in late 2003 vary from about £700 for a fortnight (flights, hotel and breakfast) in the low season, to £1,200 plus during the peak season at Christmas and the New Year. For the cheaper hotels, you pay very little extra for an additional week. Package operators include: **JMC**, *T0870-5550440, www.jmc.com*; **Thomas Cook**, *T0870-010 9386, www.thomas cook.com*, and **First Choice**, *T0870-750001, www.firstchoice.co.uk*, all allow you to book a return flight with the first night's accommodation, leaving you free to arrange the rest yourself.

UK and Ireland

Abercrombie & Kent, *T0845-0700615, www.abercrombiekent.co.uk*
Ace Study Tours, *T01223-835055, ace@studytours.org*, cultural study tours, expert led.
Adventures Abroad, *T0114-2473400, www.adventures-abroad.com*, outward bound.
Andrew Brock (Coromandel), *T01572-821330, abrock3650@aol.com*, special interest including crafts, textiles, botany etc.
Audley Travel, *T01869-276222, www.audleytravel.com*, fairs, festivals, culture, religion.
Barefoot Traveller, *T020-8741 4319, www.barefoot-traveller.com*, diving specialist (with Maldives) plus Test match cricket.
Cox & Kings, *T020-7873 5000, www.coxandkings.co.uk*, ancient sites and tourist high spots.
Exodus Travels, *T020-8675 5550, www.exodus.co.uk*, includes cycling holidays.
Explore Worldwide, *T01252-319448, www.exploreworldwide.com*
Indus Tours, *T020-8901 7320, www.industours.com*
Gateway to Asia, *T0870-4423204, F4423205, www.gatewaytoasia.com*
Pettitts, *T01892-515966, F516615, www.pettits.co.uk*, upmarket, individual service.

 Sri Lanka Holidays, *4 Kingly St, London, T020-7439 0944, www.srilanka-holidays.co.uk*, country specialists.

Sri Lanka Insider Tours, *T01233-811771, www.srilanka-insider-tours.com*, cooperative tour organization stressing use of local transport, homestays or locally owned hotels.

Steppes East, *51 Castle St, Cirencester, Gloucestershire, T01285-651010, www.steppeseast.co.uk* Specialize in tailor-made tours.

Trans Indus, *T020-85793739, www.transindus.co.uk* Tailor-made tours in Southeast Asia and India.

North America

Absolute Asia, *180 Varick St, 16th floor, New York, NY10014, T800 736 8187, www.absoluteasia.com*, upmarket offering including Ayurveda and adventure travel.

Adventures Abroad, *T1-800-665-3998.*

Australia and New Zealand

Adventures Abroad, *T1-800 147 827, www.adventures-abroad.org*

Birding Worldwide, *T+613-9899 9303, www.birdingworldwide.com.au*

Passport Travel, *T+61 3 9867 3888, www.travelcentre.com.au*, for cycling holidays.

Sri Lanka

Lion Royale Tourisme, *Level 3, 110, Sir James Peiris Mawatha, Col 2, Colombo, T94-74-715996, lionroyal@slnet.lk*, for tailor-made tours. See also Colombo, page 92.

Finding out more

The Sri Lanka Tourist Board has offices in a number of countries around the world, which can help with planning an itinerary, and have plenty of information on finding accommodation, suitable tour operators etc. There is also a wealth of information on Sri Lanka on the internet.

Tourist offices overseas

Australia, *29 Lonsdale St, Braddon, ACT 2612, T62306002, F62306066.*

France, *19, Rue de Quatre Septembre, 75002 Paris, T42604999, F42860499, ctbparis@compuserve.com*

Germany, *Allerheililgentor 2-4, D-60311, Frankfurt, T287734, F288371, CTBFRA@T-online.de*

India, *c/o TRAC Representations India (P) Ltd, A-61, 6th floor, Himalaya House, Kasturba Gandhi Marg, New Delhi 110001, T3730477, F730476, ctbindia@tracrep.com*

Ireland, *59 Ranelagh Rd, Dublin 6, T149-69621, F65345, aelred@ireland.com*

Japan, *Dowa Building 7-2-22, Ginza Chuo-Ku, T332890771, F890772, ctb-toky@zaf.att.ne.jp; Nitto Ichi Building, 2F, Nanba 1-8-19, Chuo-Ku, Osaka City, T077-4452573, F4450523.*

New Zealand, *157, Somerville Rd, Howick, Auckland, T95340101, F95342355, dhane@ihug.co.nz*

Thailand, *5/105-6/105, Soi Rattanaprahm 2, Sukhumvit Soi 54/2, Bangkok 10250, T3329075, F3329076, inmark@ksc.th.com*

UK, *Clareville House, 26-27 Oxendon St, London SW1Y 4EL, T020-7930 2627, F7930 9070.*

USA, *111 Wood Avenue South, Iselin NJ 08330, T732-516 9800, F452 0087, ctbUSA@anlusa.com*

Sri Lanka representations overseas

Foreign diplomatic representations in Sri Lanka are listed on page 97.

Australia, 35 Empire Circuit, Forrest, Canberra, ACT 2603, T62397041, F62396166, slhc@atrax.net.au

Austria, Rainergasse 1/2/5, 1040, Vienna, T5037988, F5037993, embassy@sri.lanka.net

Belgium, Rue Jules Lejeune, 27, 1050 Brussels, T3445394, F3446737, sri.lanka@euronet.be

Canada, Suite 1204, 333 Laurier Ave West, Ottawa, Ontario K1P 1Cl, T2338449, F2388448, lankacom@magi.com

France, 15 Rue d'Astorg, 75008 Paris, T42663501, F40070011, sl.france@wanadoo.fr

Germany, Niklasstr 19, 14163 Berlin, T80909749, F80909757, info@srilanka-botschaft.de

India, 27 Kautilya Marg, Chanakyapuri, New Delhi 110021, T3010201, F3015295, lankacom@de 12.vsnl.net.in; 9 D Nawab Habibullah Ave, Anderson Rd, Chennai 600 006, T8270831, F8272387, sldehico@md3.vsnl.net.in; 34 Homi Modi St, Mumbai 400 023, T2045861, F2876132, slcon@bom5.vsnl.net.in

Indonesia, 70 Jalan Diponegoro, No 70, Jakarta-Pusat, T3141018, F3107962, lankaemb@vision.net.id

Italy, Via Adige No 2, 00198, Rome, T8554560, F84241670, MC7785@ mclink.it

Japan, 2-1-54, Takanawa, Minato-ku, Tokyo 108-0074, T03 3440 6911, F3440 6914, lankaemb@mba.sphere.ne.jp

Maldives, Sakeena Manzil, Medhuziayaaraiyh Magu, Male 20-05, T322845, F321652, highcom@dhivehinet.net.mv

The Netherlands, Jacob de Graefflaan, 2517 JM, The Hague, T3655910, F3465596, nlslmisn@bart.nl

Pakistan, House No 2C, Street No 55 F-6/4, Islamabad, T828743, F828751, srilanka@isb.comsats. net.pk

Singapore, 13-06/12 Goldhill Plaza, 51 Newton Rd, Singapore 308900, T2544595, F2507201, Slhcs@singnet.com.sg

South Africa, 410 Alexander St, Brooklyn, Pretoria 0181, T467690, F467702, srilanka@global.co.za

Sweden, Strandvagen 39, Box 24055, S-104 50, Stockholm, T6636523, F6600089, sl.emb@stockholm.mail.telia.com

Thailand, Ocean Tower 11, 13th Floor, BNo 75/6-7 Sukhumvit Soi 19, Bangkok 10110, T2611934, F6510059, slemb@ksc.net.th

UK 13 Hyde Park Gardens, London W2 2LU, T020-7262 1841, F7262 7970, mail@slhc.globlnet.co.uk

USA 2148 Wyoming Av, NW, Washington DC 20008, T4834025, F232 7181, slembassy@star power. net; 5371, Wilshire Boulevard, Suite #201, Los Angeles, CA 90036, T6340 479, F6341095, lacongen@pacbell.net

Useful websites

→ *Websites for specific areas or interests are listed throughout the text.*

www.srilankatourism.org is the official website of the Sri Lanka Tourist Board, with useful general tourist information.

www.infolanka.com has an extensive list of travel links, some useful articles, recipes and downloadable Sri Lankan music files.

www.lanka.net is a webserver with links to the major national newspapers and mags which have worthwhile and free (though this may change) websites daily updated.

www.peaceinsrilanka.org is a government website charting the progress of the peace process.

www.tamilnet.com has a fairly balanced Tamil perspective.

Language

→ *See page 384 for Sinhala and Tamil phrases.*

Sinhala and Tamil are the official languages, but English is widely spoken and understood in the main tourist areas though not by many in rural parts. Some German is spoken by a growing number of Sri Lankans in the southwestern beach resorts.

Disabled travellers

The country isn't geared up specially for making provisions for the physically handicapped or wheelchair bound traveller. Access to buildings, toilets, pavements and kerbs and public transport, can prove frustrating but it is easy to find people to give a hand with lifting and carrying. Provided there is an able-bodied companion to scout around and arrange help, and so long as you are prepared to spend on at least mid-price hotels or guesthouses, private car-hire and taxis, Sri Lanka should prove to be rewarding.

Some travel companies are now beginning to specialize in exciting holidays, tailor-made for individuals depending on their level of disability. **Global Access – Disabled Travel Network Site**, *www.geocities.com/Paris/1502*, is dedicated to providing information for 'disabled adventurers' and includes a number of reviews and tips from members of the public. You might want to read *Nothing Ventured* edited by Alison Walsh (Harper Collins), which gives personal accounts of world-wide journeys by disabled travellers, plus advice and listings.

Organizations in Sri Lanka include **Sri Lanka Confederation of Organisations of the Handicapped**, *20 Sir J Pieris Mawatha, Col 2, Colombo, T011-2302845*, and **Sri Lanka Federation of the Visually Handicapped (SLFVH)**, *74 Church St, Col 2, Colombo, T011-2437758, www.slfvh.org*

Gay and lesbian travellers

Homosexuality between men is illegal in Sri Lanka, even in private, and may lead to a prison sentence of up to 12 years. It is therefore wise to be discreet to avoid the attentions of over zealous and homophobic police officers.

Campaigning gay group **Companions on a Journey**, *46/50 Robert E Gunawardena Maw, Col 6, T2514680*, has a drop-in centre and arranges events. The internet is a good source of information: www.utopia-asia.com/tipssri lists some gay and lesbian friendly accommodation. A resource for lesbians is **Friendship Sri Lanka**, *c/o Shan Gunawardene, 1049 Pannipitiya Rd, Battaramulla. See also www.wsgsrilanka.org*

Student travellers

Full-time students qualify for an **ISIC** (International Student Identity Card) which is issued by student travel and specialist agencies at home (eg **STA Travel**). A card allows some few travel benefits (eg reduced prices) and acts as proof of student status. Only a few sites in Sri Lanka will offer concessions however.

Women travellers

Compared with many other countries it is relatively easy and safe for women to travel around Sri Lanka, even on their own. There are some problems to watch out for and some simple precautions to take which make it possible to avoid both personal harassment and giving offence. Modest dress for women is always advisable: loose-fitting, non-see through clothes, covering the shoulders, and skirts, dresses or shorts (at least knee-length). Unaccompanied women may find problems of harassment, though this is relatively rare, though you may need to get used to staring. It is always best to be accompanied when travelling by rickshaw or taxi at night. Do remember that what may be considered to be normal, innocent friendliness in a Western context may be misinterpreted by some Sri Lankan men.

Travelling with children

→ *It is advisable to keep children away from stray animals which may carry parasites. Monkeys too can be aggressive.*

Children of all ages are widely welcomed and greeted with warmth which is often extended to those accompanying them. Sri Lanka's beaches and wildlife are especially likely to appeal, and of course a visit to Pinnawela Elephant Orphanage.

Care should be taken when travelling to remote areas where **health** services are primitive since children can become ill more rapidly than adults. Extra care must be taken to protect children from the heat by creams, hats, umbrellas etc and by avoiding being out in the hottest part of the day. Cool showers or baths help if children get too hot. Dehydration may be counteracted with plenty of drinking water - bottled, boiled (furiously for five minutes) or purified with tablets. Preparations such as 'Dioralyte' may be given if the child suffers from diarrhoea. Moisturizer, zinc and castor oil (for sore bottoms due to change of diet) are worth taking. Mosquito nets or electric insect repellents at night may be provided in hotel rooms which are not air conditioned. To help young children to take anti-malarial tablets, one suggestion is to crush them between spoons and mix with a teaspoon of dessert chocolate (for cake-making) bought in a tube. Wet wipes and disposable nappies are not readily available in many areas.

In the big hotels there is no difficulty with obtaining safe baby **foods**. For older children, tourist restaurants will usually have a non-spicy alternative to Sri Lankan curries. Grilled or fried fish or chicken is a good standby, often served with boiled vegetables, as are eggs. Fruit is magnificent but should be peeled first. Toast and jam are usually served for breakfast, or hoppers (with bananas). Fizzy drinks are widely available, although king coconut is a healthier and cheaper alternative. Bottled water is available everywhere.

Many **hotels** and guesthouses have triple rooms, at little or no extra cost to the price of a double, or you can ask for an extra bed. The biggest hotels provide babysitting facilities.

Buses are often overcrowded and are probably worth avoiding with children. Train travel is generally better (under 12s travel half-price, under 3s free) but hiring a car hire is by far the most comfortable and flexible option; see page 43.

Working in Sri Lanka

All foreigners intending to work need **work permits**. No one is allowed to stay longer than six months in a calendar year, or to change their visa status. The employing organization should make formal arrangements. Apply to the Sri Lankan representative in your country of origin.

Voluntary work

UK and Ireland Major organizations include **International Voluntary Service**, *St John's Centre, Edinburgh, EH2 4BJ, www.sci-ivs.org* or **VSO**, *317 Putney Bridge Rd,*

London SW15 2PN, www.vso.org.uk; **i-to-i International projects**, *T0870-205 4620, www.i-to-i.com*, where students and young people may spend part of a 'year off' teaching English, or looking after the disabled and where there is also an option for some conservation work; **Teaching and Projects Abroad**, *T01903-8599911, www.teaching-abroad.co.uk*; **Link Overseas Exchange**, *T01382-203192, www.linkoverseas.org.uk*; or **Project Trust**, *T01879-230444, www.projecttrust.org.uk* The **World Service Enquiry directory** listing voluntary placements overseas can be obtained from www.wse.org.uk

USA and Canada Organizations include **Council for International Programs**, *1101 Wilson Blvd Ste 1708, Arlington, VA 22209*; **United Nations Volunteers**, *www.unv.org*, are usually mature, experienced people with special qualifications. For teaching English try **Projects Abroad**, *T-1-888-839-3535, www.projects-abroad.org*; **i-to-i** *T800 985 4864 (see above)*. **World University Service of Canada**, *T693 798 7477, www.wusc.ca*, runs a development project on a tea plantation.

Australia **Australian Volunteers International**, *T03 9279 1788, www.ozvol.org.au*

Before you travel

Getting in

Visas and permits → *Ask for a double entry visa if you are intending to visit another country (eg India or the Maldives), www.immigration.gov.lk*

All visitors to Sri Lanka require a valid passport. Nationals of the following countries are issued with a free, 30-day visa upon arrival: Albania, Australia, Austria, Bahrain, Bangladesh, Belgium, Bhutan, Bosnia-Herzegovina, Bulgaria, Canada, China, Croatia, Cyprus, Czech Republic, Denmark, Estonia, Finland, France, Germany, Greece, Hong Kong, Hungary, India, Indonesia, Iran, Ireland, Israel, Italy, Japan, Korea, Kuwait, Latvia, Lithuania, Luxembourg, Malaysia, Maldives, Moldova, Montenegro, Nepal, Netherlands, New Zealand, Norway, Oman, Pakistan, Philippines, Poland, Portugal, Qatar, Romania, Russia (plus most former republics), Saudi Arabia, Serbia, Singapore, Slovakia, Slovenia, Spain, Sweden, Switzerland, Taiwan, Thailand, Turkey, UAE, UK, USA. Nationals of all other countries need a prior visa. All tourists should also have a valid visa for the country that is their next destination (if a visa is necessary); check with your nearest Sri Lankan representative before travelling. It may sometimes be necessary to show proof of sufficient funds to support themselves (US$15 per day) and a return or onward ticket, although this is rarely checked on arrival. Transit passengers are issued with a Transit Visa.

A 60-day **extension** is available to nationals of all countries upon paying a fee, which varies according to the charge to Sri Lankans of entering your country. In order to qualify you may also need to show proof that you have exchanged at least US$15 for each day of your stay up to the time of application (bring all exchange certificates). In February 2003, the following fees applied: Australia, Rs 2,475; Canada, Rs 4,580; France, Rs 2,565; Germany, Rs 2,855; India, Rs 275; Ireland, Rs 1,470; Netherlands, Rs 4,490; New Zealand, Rs 3,100; Switzerland, Rs 2,490; UK, Rs 4,950. The most heavily targeted are the Americans who have to pay Rs 17,400. A further three-month extension is possible, though at swingeing cost. You have to pay the same fee again plus a 'Temporary Residence Tax' of Rs 10,000. Apply in person during office hours, to the **Department of Immigration and Emigration**, Tower Building, Bambalapitiya Station Road (immediately opposite the station), Colombo 4, T2597511. Bring passport, air ticket and exchange receipts. Enter by the side entrance (don't queue outside!) and go to the first floor. The whole process is fairly straightforward (allow one to two hours). Payment is accepted in Rupees, US dollars or by credit card. It is not necessary to wait until shortly before the expiry of your original visa. Extensions will be granted at any time within the original 30-day period.

Tourists from non-Commonwealth countries who have a visa for over 30 days (and those intending to extend their stay beyond 30 days) may need to **register** upon arrival at the Aliens Bureau, 5th Floor, New Secretariat Building, Colombo 1, although this does not appear to be always necessary.

Customs and import → *www.customs.gov.lk*

On arrival visitors to Sri Lanka are officially required to declare all currency, valuable equipment, jewellery and gems even though this is rarely checked. All personal effects should be taken back on departure. Visitors are not allowed to bring in goods in commercial quantities, or prohibited/restricted goods such as dangerous drugs, weapons, explosive devices or gold. Drug trafficking or possession carries the death penalty, although this is very rarely carried out on foreigners. In addition to completing Part II of the Immigration Landing Card, a tourist may be asked by the Customs Officer to complete a Baggage Declaration Form.

Professional photography or filming equipment must be declared and will be allowed entry on a valid carnet, bank guarantee or a refundable deposit of the duty payable on the items.

Duty free

You are allowed 1.5 litres of spirits, 2 bottles of wine, 200 cigarettes, 50 cigars or 250 g rolling tobacco, a small quantity of perfume and 250 ml of toilet water. You can also import a small quantity of travel souvenirs not exceeding US$250 in value.

Export restrictions → *It is illegal to buy items made from wild animals and reptiles.*

Up to 3 kg of tea is allowed to be exported duty free. Note that the 'Ceylon Tea' counter at the airport outer lobby accepts rupees; export duty is charged at Rs 2 per kilo for excess tea. The following are not permitted to be exported from Sri Lanka: all currencies in excess of that declared on arrival; any gems, jewellery or valuable items not declared on arrival or not purchased in Sri Lanka out of declared funds; gold (crude, bullion or coins); Sri Lankan currency in excess of Rs 250; firearms, explosives or dangerous weapons; antiques, statues, treasures, old books etc (antiques are considered to be any article over 50 years old); animals, birds, reptiles or their parts (dead or alive); tea, rubber or coconut plants; dangerous drugs.

Import of all the items listed above and in addition, Indian and Pakistani currency, obscene and seditious literature or pictures is prohibited.

Vaccinations

Vaccinations are recommended for hepatitis A, typhoid, tetanus and polio, and may be considered for rabies and Japanese encephalitis; and prophylaxis for malaria. See page 61 for more information.

Insurance

Although Sri Lanka does not suffer from being a crime-ridden society, accidents and delays can still occur. Full travel insurance is advised but at the very least get medical insurance and coverage for personal effects. There are a wide variety of policies to choose from, so it's best to shop around. Your local travel agent can also advise on the best and most reliable deals available. Always read the small print carefully.

Check that the policy covers the activities you intend or may end up doing. Also check exactly what your medical cover includes, eg ambulance, helicopter rescue or emergency flights back home. Also check the payment protocol. You may have to pay first before the insurance company reimburses you. In the UK, **Direct line**, *T0845 246 8744*, *www.directline.com*, offers a range of policies.

What to take → *Take twice as much money and half the clothes that you think you will need.*

Travel light. Most essentials are available in the cities, items are cheap and laundry services generally speedy. Take light cotton clothes – it is a good idea to have some very lightweight long sleeve cotton tops and trousers in pale colours for evenings, as they also give some protection against mosquitoes. It can be cool at night in the Central Highlands and some warm clothing is essential. Dress is usually informal, though one or two clubs and hotels expect guests to be formally dressed at evening meals. In Colombo short-sleeved shirts and ties are often worn for business. For travelling, loose clothes are most comfortable. Trainers or canvas shoes are good options for protecting feet against cuts and so on. Women should dress modestly. Even on the beach, very revealing swimwear attracts unnecessary attention.

Checklists

Here are some items you might find particularly useful: toiletries, including barrier contraceptives and tampons (available in the larger towns but you may prefer to take your own supply); personal medicines and inhalers and a copy of a prescription; camera films to be assured of quality (available in all major cities and tourist centres but always buy from a reputable shop); International driving licence; photocopies of essential documents (flight ticket, passport identification and visa pages); spare passport photographs; student (ISIC) card which can be used for discounts on some site entrance fees; hat and sunglasses; insect repellent; sun protection cream (factor 15 plus); Swiss army knife; torch; wet wipes; zip-lock bags; contact lens cleaning solutions (available in the larger towns and cities but it is best to bring your own).

Budget travellers may also want to take the following: sheet sleeping bag; earplugs; eyeshades; padlock (for room and baggage); alarm clock; soap; string (washing line); towel; washbasin plug; mosquito nets (standard in all but the very cheapest hotels). Mosquito mats/coils are readily available in Sri Lanka.

Money

→ *When agreeing a price make sure this includes all taxes and charges.*

Currency

→ *It is not possible to purchase Sri Lankan currency before arrival in Sri Lanka.*

The Sri Lankan rupee is made up of 100 cents. Notes in denominations of Rs 1000, 500, 200, 100, 50, 20, 10 and coins in general use are Rs 10, 5, 2 and 1. 50, 25, 10, while 5-cent coins are now rarely seen. Visitors bringing in excess of US$10,000 into Sri Lanka should declare the amount on arrival. All Sri Lankan rupees should be re-converted upon leaving Sri Lanka. It is also illegal to bring Indian or Pakistani rupees into Sri Lanka, although this is rarely, if ever, enforced.

Changing money

→ *If you cash sterling, make certain that you have been given rupees at the sterling and not at the dollar rate.*

There is an ATM and several 24-hour exchange counters at the airport which give good rates of exchange. Larger hotels often have a money exchange counter (sometimes open 24 hours), but offer substantially lower rates than banks. In the larger cities and resorts you will often find private dealers who will exchange cash notes or travellers' cheques. Rates are comparable to banks and are entirely above board. There is no black market money changing in Sri Lanka, although it may be useful to carry some small denomination foreign currency notes (eg £10, US$10) for emergencies.

Banking hours are generally 0900-1500 Monday to Friday, although some banks in Colombo have extended opening hours. Private banks (eg **Commercial Bank, Hatton National Bank, Sampath Bank**) are generally more efficient and offer a faster service than government owned banks like **Bank of Ceylon** and **People's Bank**.

Keep the **encashment receipts** you are given when exchanging money, as you may need them to prove that you are spending over US$15 per day for a visa extension. You will also need at least one to re-exchange any rupees upon leaving Sri Lanka. All foreign exchange transactions must be made through authorized banks and exchanges and entered on the Customs and Immigration form. Unspent rupees may be reconverted at a commercial bank when you leave Sri Lanka. Changing money through unauthorized dealers is illegal.

Travellers' cheques (TCs)

Travellers' cheques issued by reputable companies (eg **American Express, Thomas Cook**) are accepted without difficulty and give a slightly better exchange rate than currency notes in Sri Lanka. They also offer the security of replacement if lost or stolen assuming the case is straightforward. TCs in £ sterling, US$ and € are usually accepted without any problem and the process normally takes less than 15 minutes in private banks and moneychangers (longer in government-owned banks). Larger hotels will normally only exchange TCs for resident guests but will offer a substantially lower rate than banks or private dealers. A 1% stamp duty is payable on all TCs transactions plus a small commission which varies from bank to bank.

Take care to follow the advice given about keeping the proof of purchase slip and a note of TCs numbers separately from the cheques. In the case of loss, you will need to get a police report and inform the travellers' cheques company.

Credit cards

Major credit cards are increasingly accepted in the main centres of Sri Lanka both for shopping and for purchasing Sri Lankan rupees. Larger hotels also accept payment by credit card but this can sometimes take longer than using TCs since your credit rating will normally have to be checked. Cash can also be drawn from ATMs using credit cards (see below). No surcharge should be applied when making purchases but the 1% stamp duty is applicable when obtaining cash against a credit card.

Money matters

	Rs		Rs
Australian $	63	New Zealand $	71.50
Euro	110	UK £	155.50
Indian Rupee	2	USA $	97
Japanese Yen	0.80		

ATMs

Automated Telling Machines (ATMs) are now common in Sri Lanka, especially in Colombo and larger towns. A small fee (less than the commission charged for changing TCs) will be charged on your bill at home.

Commercial Bank and **Sampath Bank** have the most widespread networks, accepting Visa (including Plus and Electron cards), Mastercard and Cirrus, and are very user-friendly. **Seylan Bank** accepts Visa, as do an increasingly number of branches of **People's Bank**. In Colombo, **Citibank** and **HSBC** all accept Mastercard, Visa and Cirrus.

Transferring money to Sri Lanka

Thomas Cook, American Express and **Standard Chartered Bank** can make instant transfers to their offices in Sri Lanka but charge a high fee (about 8%). A bank draft (up to US$1,000) which you can post yourself (three to five days by Speedpost) is the cheapest option for which normal charges are between 1.5% and 2%.

Carrying money

It is best to carry TCs and credit cards in a money belt worn under clothing. Only carry enough cash for your daily needs, keeping the rest in your money belt or in a hotel safe. Keep plenty of small change and lower denomination notes, as it can be difficult to change large notes.

A service charge of 10% is applied to all accommodation, while most restaurants and hotels in category C and above also apply a further 10% Goods and Services Tax (GST). The 12.5% BTT (Business Turnover Tax) has been abolished so this should no longer appear on bills.

Cost of travelling

The Sri Lankan cost of living remains well below that in the industrialized world, although is rising quite sharply. Food and public transport, especially rail and bus, remain exceptionally cheap, and accommodation, though not as cheap as in India, costs much less than in the West. The expensive hotels and restaurants are also less expensive than their counterparts in Europe, Japan or the United States. Budget travellers (sharing a room) could expect to spend about Rs 1,500 (about US$15 or £10) each per day to cover cost of accommodation, food and travel. Those planning to stay in fairly comfortable hotels and use taxis or hired cars for travelling to sights should expect to spend at least Rs 6,000 (US$60 or £40) a day. Single rooms are rarely charged less than about 80% of the double room price.

Many travellers are irritated however by the Sri Lankan policy of **'dual pricing'** for foreigners – one price for locals, another for tourists. Sites which see a lot of tourists, particularly in Kandy and the Cultural Triangle, carry entrance charges comparable to those in the west, while National Park fees have grown exponentially in recent years and carry a catalogue of hidden extra taxes. In common with many other Asian countries, some shops and three-wheeler drivers will try to overcharge foreigners – experience is the only way to combat this!

Getting there

Air

All international flights arrive at Katunayake, about 30 km north of Colombo. International airlines flying to Sri Lanka include **Aeroflot, Cathay Pacific, El Al, Emirates, Gulf Air, Indian Airlines, Korean Airlines, Kuwait Airways, Lufthansa, Malaysia Airlines, Oman Air, Pakistan International Airways, Qatar Airways, Royal Jordanian, Saudi Arabian, Singapore Airlines** and **Thai International. Sri Lankan Airlines**, *www.srilankan.lk*, the national carrier, flies to over 20 countries worldwide, and has offices all over the world. A source of great national pride, it compares favourably with the best of the South East Asia airlines for comfort and service.

November to March is high season while Christmas, New Year and Easter are the most expensive. Shop around, book early and if using a 'bucket shop' confirm with the airline that your name appears on their list. It is possible to get a significant discount from a reputable travel agent especially outside European holiday times, most notably from London. The airlines invariably quote a higher price as they are not able to discount tickets but off-load surplus tickets on agents who choose to pass on part of their commission to passengers.

There are a number of charter companies which offer package tours, eg **Air Europe, Condor, Eurofly, Lauda, LTU,** operating mainly from Central Europe (Germany, Italy, Europe). These can work out cheaper than scheduled flight fares, but may have limitations. They are not available to Sri Lankan nationals and usually must include accommodation. You can also arrange a stop-over in Sri Lanka on a 'Round the World' and other long distance tickets.

From the UK and Ireland

Sri Lankan Airlines flies eight to nine times a week direct from London to Colombo. Quoted discounted fares in high season are around £540. It is usually cheaper to fly via the Middle East – **Royal Jordanian, Emirates, Kuwait Airways** and **Qatar Airways** tend to offer similar fares of around £500. Good deals are also occasionally possible on some Central European airlines, such as **Czech Airlines**.

There are various discount flight booking agencies which offer significantly better deals than the airlines oneself. The national press carry their advertisements as well as magazine like *TNT*. Many now have branches across the UK as well as in London. These include: **Bridge the World**, *T0870-443 2399, www.bridgetheworld.com*; **Flightbookers**, *T020-77573000, www.ebookers.com*; **North South Travel**, *T01245- 608291, www.northsouthtravel.co.uk*, donates its profits to charity; **Sri Lanka Tours**, *T020-743 43921, www.srilankatours.co.uk*, offer deals on flights with **Sri Lankan, Emirates** and **Kuwait Airways; STA**, *T0870-1600 599, www.statravel.co.uk*, with over 65 branches in the UK, offers special deals for under-26s; **Trailfinders**, *T020-7938 3939, www.trailfinders.com*, now has branches in 10 British cities and has a good range of tailor-made and Round-the-world deals; and **Travelbag**, *T0870-890 1456, www.travel bag.co.uk*, quotes competitive fares.

From USA and Canada

From the east coast, it is best to fly from New York via London or pick up a direct flight from the UK but this will usually involve a stopover in London. From the west coast, it is best to fly via Hong Kong, Singapore or Bangkok using one of those countries' national carriers. Discount travel agents include **STA Travel**, *T800-329 9537, www.statravel.com,* discount student/youth travel company with over 100 stores

Sites for flights

Flights from the UK:
Austrian Airlines www.austrianair.com
Czech Airlines www.czechairlines.co.uk
Emirates www.emirates.com
Gulf Air www.gulfairco.com
Kuwait Airways www.kuwait-airways.com
Qatar Airways www.qatarairways.com
Royal Jordanian www.rja.com.jo
Sri Lankan www.srilankan.lk
Swiss www.swiss.com

Flights from Australia/New Zealand:
Air New Zealand www.airnz.co.nz
Cathay Pacific www.cathaypacific.com
Emirates www.emirates.com
Malaysia Airlines www.malaysiaairlines.com
Qantas www.qantas.com.au
Singapore Airlines www.singaporeair.com
Sri Lankan www.srilankan.lk
Thai International www.thaiair.com

across North America; **Travel Cuts**, *T1-800 592 2887 (USA), T1-866-246 9762 (Canada), www.travelcuts.com*, specialist in student discount fares, IDs and other travel services. Branches in other Canadian cities and in the USA. **Discount Airfares Worldwide On-Line**, *www.etn.nl* is a hub of consolidator and discount agent links. Other online agents include **www.expedia.com**, **www.travelocity.com** and **www.orbitz.com**

From Australasia via the Far East

There are no direct flights to Colombo from Australia or New Zealand, but **Cathay Pacific**, **Malaysian Airlines**, **Singapore Airlines** and **Thai International** are the main linking airlines and usually offer the best deals. **Sri Lankan** also flies to the major South East Asian regional capitals. The cheapest deal quoted in August 2003 for a return from Sydney to Colombo in high season was around AUS$1,474; from Perth expect fares to be around AUS$100-150 cheaper. From Auckland, **Cathay Pacific** were quoting NZ$1,499.

Discount travel agents include: **Flight Centre**, *T133133, www.flightcentre.com.au*, and New Zealand, *T0800-243544, www.flightcentre.co.nz*, with branches in major towns and cities; **STA Travel**, *T1300733055, www.statravel.com.au*; New Zealand, *T0800-243544, www.statravel.co.nz*, branches in major towns and campuses around both countries; **travel.com.au**, *Sydney, T1300 130 482, www.travel.com.au*

From South Asia

Sri Lankan Airlines flies to a growing number of Indian destinations, including Bangalore, Bodhgaya, Chennai, Delhi, Kochi, Mumbai (Rs 17,400 one-way) Thiruvananthapuram (Trivandrum, Rs 6,000) and Tiruchirappalli (Trichy, Rs, 6500), as well as Karachi and Male in the Maldives. **Indian Airlines** flies to Colombo from Trivandrum (one way IND Rs 4,470), Mumbai (IND Rs 10,690), Chennai, Delhi (IND Rs 17,145) and Truchy.

Sea

→ *For further details, see page 94.*

The ceasefire and peace discussions have triggered serious moves towards re-establishing an official sea route to India, suspended in the mid 1980s. At the time of going to press, ferries were poised to begin between Colombo Harbour and

Tuticorin in Tamil Nadu, having been repeatedly put on hold. Other routes may also open. Once established, Indian visas will be obtainable at Colombo port.

Other than occasional cruise ships that stop at Colombo, it is virtually impossible to get to Sri Lankan by sea otherwise. You may be able to get a berth on a cargo or container ship from ports in the Gulf region or South East Asia but it is impossible to book trips in advance. Sailors in their own vessels may be able to berth in Galle, although it is possible that immigration formalities should be carried out in Colombo. Check with your nearest Sri Lankan representative in advance.

Touching down

Airport information → *www.airport.lk*

Disembarkation Cards are handed out to passengers during the inward flight. Complete parts 1 and 2 and hand them in at the immigration counter on arrival along with your passport. Keep your baggage identification tag safe as this must be handed in when leaving the Arrivals hall.

Bandaranaike International Airport, Sri Lanka's only international airport, is at Katunayake, 30 km north of Colombo. It has modern facilities including duty free shops (with a large selection of electrical goods) on arrival. Major banks are represented by branches in the Arrivals Hall, offering a good rate of exchange, and there is an ATM which accepts most cards. The tourist information counter has limited information although it is worth picking up copies of *Travel Lanka* and the *Sri Lanka Tourist Board Accommodation Guide*.

There is a pre-paid taxi stand and several hotel and tour company booths just after the Arrivals hall (see Transport below). Outside, porters will offer to transport your luggage – they will expect Rs 30 per item – or alternatively, the trolleys are free. There are several hotels and guesthouses within a few kilometres of the airport (see page 81), and a wider choice of accommodation at Negombo, 6 km away (see page 104). Stringent baggage and personal security checks are often carried out, especially on departure, so be prepared to repack your bags.

Visitors to Departures or Arrivals must buy an entrance permit for Rs 130 at the special booths before entering the terminal, but access is limited due to security controls.

A few flights each night arrive in Sri Lanka in the small hours. If you are going to arrive late, it is best to book a hotel or guesthouse in Negombo for the first night – given advance warning they will arrange a pick-up – and move to Colombo or another beach resort the following day. Avoid accommodation touts. At the airport bank exchange counters and taxis operate 24 hours, though public transport does not.

Public transport to and from the airport

A/c intercity **buses** (No 187) run every half an hour to Colombo's Bastian Mawatha Stand in the Pettah from 0430 until around 2200 (Rs 30, one hour) leaving from the bus stop immediately outside the Arrivals hall exit. To ensure a seat it may be worth walking towards the vehicular exit where the bus waits. Slower government (yellow) CTB buses also run the trip (Nos 187, 240, 300, 875). If you wish to go to Negombo, take the Colombo bus (or a taxi) to Katunayake Junction, 2 km away, from which the No 240 goes north to Negombo. Several hotels and guesthouses will arrange a pick-up; see page 104.

On the right of the Arrivals hall after you pass through customs, there is a **pre-paid taxi** counter close to the banks. The sign is only in Sinhalese but this a cheaper option than taking an a/c cab with the larger travel agents beyond the exit.

Touching down

Emergency services Police T2433333; Fire and ambulance T2422222; Hospital (Colombo) T2691111.
IDD code +94.
Official time GMT + 6 hours. Perception of time is sometimes rather vague in Sri Lanka (as in the rest of South Asia). Unpunctuality is common so you will need to be patient.
Official languages Sinhalese and Tamil, with English widely spoken in tourist areas.
Voltage 230-240 volts, 50 cycles AC. There may be pronounced variations in the voltage, and power cuts are common. Three-pin (round) sockets are the norm. Universal adaptors are widely available.
Business hours
Banks: 0900-1500 (some 1300) Monday-Friday; some open Saturday morning.
Post offices: 1000-1700, Monday-Friday; Saturday mornings.
Government offices: 0930-1700, Monday-Friday; 0930-1300, Saturday (some open alternate Saturday only).
Shops: 1000-1900 Monday-Friday, half-day Saturday; most close on Sunday. Sunday street bazaars in some areas.
Poya days (Full moon) are holidays.

Posted fares for non-a/c van taxis to the various postal areas in Colombo and nearby towns and resorts are: Rs 992 to Colombo 1-3 and 7-15; Rs 1,011 to Colombo 4; Rs 1,091 to Colombo 5 and 6; Rs 500-550 to Negombo; Rs 3,125 to Hikkaduwa; Rs 3,485 to Unawatuna; and Rs 2,695 to Kandy.

Alternatively, call an air-conditioned **radio cab company**. **GNTC**, T2688688, has a branch at the airport beyond the exit from the Arrivals Hall. This is a good, comfortable option, especially if you share one. Other radio cab companies include: **Ace Cabs**, T2501502 and **Quick Cabs**, T2502888. Travel agents such as **Europcar** also offer transport to the city though this tends to be more expensive (from Rs 1,200+). Colombo's hotels will also offer to meet you at the airport, though this is a very expensive option – they may charge up to US$25.

Some taxi drivers may try to persuade you that the hotel you have chosen is closed or full. Insist that you have a reservation. Others may still try to insist that Colombo is dangerous and coerce you to be taken to Kandy 'where it is safe'. Although there used to be curfews in the city, this is now simply a ruse to part you from extra money.

It is possible to **rent a car** at the airport (there is a branch of **Europcar** for example), though rates tend to be steep (around US$250 per week for car with driver) and it usually pays to shop around in Colombo. Moreover, if you wish to self-drive a Sri Lankan recognition permit is needed to accompany International Driving Permits, so it may not be possible to drive immediately. These are available from the AA or the Department of Motor Traffic in Colombo.

Katunayake **train** station is about 1 km (Rs 50 in a three-wheeler) from the airport, from which suburban commuter trains run north to Negombo (15 minutes, Rs 2.50) and south to Colombo (1¼ hours, Rs 8.50), although the bus is more convenient and comfortable.

Departure tax

A departure tax of Rs 1,000 is payable for all international departures including those to neighbouring SAARC countries. Even if you have already paid the foreign tax (denoted by FT in the bottom left hand corner of your flight ticket) the departure tax is sometimes demanded.

Tourist information

There are Sri Lanka Tourist Board offices in Colombo and a few major tourist centres, such as Kandy. They are listed in the relevant sections throughout the book.

Visiting archaeological sites

Trained registered English speaking tourist guides to sites (and sometimes one speaking a European language, Malay or Japanese) carry Sri Lanka Tourist Board cards. Fees vary according to the size of the group and language spoken. Contact **Travel Information Centre**, *T2437059*, an approved travel agent or **National Tourist Guide Lecturers' Association**, *409 RA de Mel Mawatha, Colombo 3, T2595212*.

If you intend to visit most of the major archaeological sites of the Ancient Cities, it is worth buying a **Cultural Triangle Round ticket**. This covers a single entry, valid for two weeks from the date of first use to Sigiriya, Polonnaruwa, most of Anuradhapura, Ritigala, Nalanda, Medirigiriya and the National Museum at Kandy, and includes the cost of a camera, though not normally a video camera. The tickets are available from Anuradhapura, Polonnaruwa and Sigiriya or less conveniently from Colombo, *Central Cultural Fund, 212/1 Bauddhaloka Mawatha, Colombo 7, T2587912*. The ticket price is US$32.50 (or Rs equivalent), US$16 for 5-12 year olds; there is not normally a student reduction. However, not all parts of these sites are included: there is a separate fee to visit Kandy's Dalada Maligawa (Temple of the Tooth), Aukana, Issurumuniya Museum (and occasionally Sri Maha Bodhi) at Anuradhapura and the Dambulla rock temple.

Alternatively, individual tickets to Sigiriya, Anuradhapura and Polonnaruwa cost US$15, children under 12 and sometimes students with an ISIC card half price (if you manage to persuade them!). Other sights are cheaper. Entry fees are much lower for Sri Lankans.

The sites are usually open 0600-1800; the ticket office often only opens at 0700. If you are keen to miss the crowds and visit a site early in the day, buying the triangle permit in advance enables you to avoid having to wait for the ticket office to open. If you visit a site during the heat of the day, it is best to take thick socks for protection against the hot stone.

Local customs and laws

Greeting

'Ayubowan' (may you have long life) is the traditional welcome greeting among the Sinhalese, said with the hands folded upwards in front of the chest. You should respond with the same gesture. The same gesture accompanies the word 'vanakkam' among Tamils.

Conduct

Cleanliness and modesty are appreciated even in informal situations. Nudity and topless bathing are prohibited and heavy fines can be imposed. Displays of intimacy are not considered suitable in public and will probably draw unwanted attention. Women in rural areas do not normally shake hands with men as this form of contact is not traditionally acceptable between acquaintances.

Use your right hand for giving, taking, eating or shaking hands as the left is considered to be unclean.

Sri Lanka's population at just under 20 million exceeds that of Australia with its population of just over 18 million, and exceeds that of the city of Mumbai (former Bombay, India) which has a population of around 18 million.

Visiting religious sites

Visitors to Buddhist and Hindu temples are welcome though the shrines of Hindu temples are sometimes closed to non-Hindus. Visitors should be dressed decently – skirts or long trousers – shorts and swimwear are not suitable. Shoes should be left at the entrance and heads should be uncovered. In some Hindu temples, especially in the North, men will be expected to remove their shirts.

Do not attempt to shake hands with Buddhist *bhikkus* (monks); see also Photography below. Monks are not permitted to touch money so donations should be put in temple offering boxes. Monks renounce all material possessions and so live on offerings. Visitors may offer flowers at the feet of the Buddha.

Mosques may be closed to non-Muslims shortly before prayers. In mosques women should be covered from head to ankle.

Begging

The sight of beggars especially near religious sites can be very disturbing. A coin to one child or a destitute woman on the street will make you the focus of demanding attention from a large number before long. Many Sri Lankans give alms to street beggars as a means of gaining spiritual merit or out of a sense of duty but the sum is often very small – Rs 10 or so. Some people find it appropriate to give food to beggars rather than money. Children sometimes offer to do 'jobs' such as call a taxi, show you the way or pose for a photo. You may want to give to a registered charity rather than individual handouts.

Tipping

A 10% service charge is now added to room rates and meals in virtually all hotels/guesthouses and restaurants. Therefore it is not necessary to give a further tip in most instances. In many smaller guesthouses staff are not always paid a realistic wage and have to rely on a share of the service charge for their basic income.

Tour companies sometimes make recommendations for 'suitable tips' for coach drivers and guides. Some of the figures may seem modest by European standards but are very inflated if compared with normal earnings. A tip of Rs 100 per day from each member of the group can safely be regarded as generous.

Taxi drivers do not expect to be tipped but a small extra amount over the fare is welcomed.

Photography

Do not attempt to be photographed with Buddhist *bhikkus* (monks) or to pose for photos with statues of the Buddha or other deities and paintings. Photography is prohibited in certain sections of the sacred sites as well as in sensitive areas such as airports, dams and military areas. It is best to take some film rolls and any specialist camera batteries although colour and black and white films are available cheaply at major tourist centres (check expiry date and seal). Only buy films from a reputable shop. Hawkers and roadside stalls may pass off out-of-date or used films as new.

Prohibitions

Penalties for possession of, use of, or trafficking in illegal drugs in Sri Lanka are strict, and convicted offenders may expect jail sentences and heavy fines.

Responsible tourism

The benefits of international travel are self-evident for both hosts and travellers – employment, increased understanding of different cultures, business and leisure

How big is your footprint?

The point of a holiday is, of course, to have a good time, but if it's relatively guilt-free as well, that's even better. Perfect eco tourism would ensure a good living for local inhabitants while not detracting from their traditional lifestyles, encroaching on their customs or spoiling their environment. Perfect eco tourism probably doesn't exist, but everyone can play their part. Here are a few points worth bearing in mind:

1 Think about where your money goes. Try and put money into local people's hands; drinking local beer or fruit juice rather than imported brands.
2 Haggle with humour and not aggressively. Remember that you are likely to be much wealthier than the person you're buying from.
3 Think about what happens to your rubbish. Take biodegradable products and a water bottle filter. Be sensitive to limited resources like water, fuel and electricity.
4 Help preserve local wildlife and habitats by respecting rules and regulations, such as sticking to footpaths, not standing on coral and not buying products made from endangered plants or animals.
5 Don't treat people as part of the landscape. Ask if you want a photo.
6 Learn the local language and be mindful of local customs and norms. It can enhance your experience and you'll earn respect of local people.

opportunities. At the same time there is clearly a downside to the industry. Where visitor pressure is high and/or poorly regulated, adverse impacts to society and the natural environment may be apparent. Paradoxically, this is as true in undeveloped and pristine areas – where culture and the natural environment are less 'prepared' for even small numbers of visitors – as in major resort destinations.

The travel industry is growing rapidly and increasingly the impacts of this supposedly 'smokeless' industry are becoming apparent. These impacts can seem remote and unrelated to an individual trip or holiday (eg air travel is clearly implicated in global warming and damage to the ozone layer, resort location and construction can destroy natural habitats and restrict traditional rights and activities) but, individual choice and awareness can make a difference in many instances (see below), and collectively, travellers are having a significant effect in shaping a more responsible and sustainable industry.

In an attempt to promote awareness of, and credibility for, responsible tourism, organizations such as **Green Globe**, *T61-2-6257 9102*, *www.greenglobe21.com*, and the **Center for Environmentally Sustainable Tourism (CERT)**, *T44-1268-795772*, *www.c-e-r-t.org*, now offer advice on destinations and sites that have achieved certain commitments to conservation and sustainable development. Generally these are larger mainstream destinations and resorts but they are still a useful guide and increasingly aim to provide information on smaller operations.

Of course travel can have beneficial impacts and this is something to which every traveller can contribute. Sri Lanka's national parks for example are part funded by receipts from visitors. Similarly, travellers can promote patronage and protection of important archaeological sites and heritage through their interest and contributions via entrance and performance fees. They can also support small-scale enterprises by staying in locally run hotels and hostels, eating in local restaurants and by purchasing local goods, supplies and arts and crafts.

There has been a phenomenal growth in tourism that promotes and supports the conservation of natural environments and is also fair and equitable to local communities. This ecotourism segment is probably the fastest growing sector of the travel industry and provides a vast and growing range of destinations and activities.

While the authenticity of some ecotourism operators claims need to be interpreted with care, there is clearly both a huge demand for this type of activity and also significant opportunities to support worthwhile conservation and social development initiatives.

International organizations such as **Tourism Concern**, *T44-20-7753 3330*, *www.tourismconcern.org.uk*, and **Conservation International**, *T1-202-4295660*, *www.ecotour.org*, have begun to develop and/or promote ecotourism projects and destinations and their web sites are an excellent source of information. **Ethical Consumer Research Assocation**, *www.ethicalconsumer.org*, publish a guide on ethical shopping. It is also worth picking up a copy of Mark Mann's *Good Alternative Tourism Guide* (London: Earthscan, 2002), published in association with Tourism Concern.

In Sri Lanka, the **Sri Lanka Ecotourism Foundation**, *www.srilankaecotourism.org*, is a non-profit making NGO dedicated to building sustainable community-based ecotourism. Visitors to Uva Province should contact the **Woodlands Network**, *www.woodlandsnetwork.org*, see page 243.

Safety

Restricted and protected areas

Since the ceasefire of February 2002, many roads have reopened in the North and East, and major towns and some tourists areas are once again accessible. Some areas however remain no-go or have limited access due to high security and/or land mines. Travel off road should not be undertaken. Local advice should be taken if travelling to the North and East, and you should be aware that the situation may change at any time.

Other areas with restricted access include certain archaeological sites, national parks and reserves which require permits before visiting. Refer to the relevant sections for details.

Confidence tricksters → *See also page 54.*

Con men and touts who aim to part you from your money are now found in most major towns and tourist sites. It is best to ignore them and carry on your own business while politely, but firmly, declining their offers of help.

Accommodation touts are common at rail and bus stations often boarding trains some distance before the destination. After engaging you in casual conversation to find out your plan one will often find you a taxi or a three-wheeler and try to persuade you that the hotel of your choice is closed, full or not good value. He will suggest an alternative where he will, no doubt, earn a commission (which you will end up having to pay). It is better to go to your preferred choice alone. Phone in advance to check if a place is full and make a reservation if necessary. If it is full then the hotelier/ guesthouse owner will usually advise you of a suitable alternative. Occasionally, touts operate in groups to confuse you or one may pose as the owner of the guesthouse you have in mind and tell you that it is sadly full but he able to 'help' you by taking you to a friend's place.

Another trick is to befriend you on a train (especially on the Colombo to Galle or Kandy routes), find out your ultimate destination and 'helpfully' use their mobile to phone for a three-wheeler in advance, telling you that none will be available at the station. Once at the other end, the three-wheeler driver may take you on an indirect route and charge up to 10 times the correct fee. In fact, three-wheeler drivers are nearly always waiting at major stations. It's worth checking the distance to your destination (usually given in the guidebook) and remember that the going rate for three-wheeler hire is around Rs 20-22 per km.

Another breed of tout is on the increase especially in towns attracting tourists (Kandy, Galle). One may approach you as you step out on the street, saying he recognizes you as he works in your hotel. Caught off-guard, you feel obliged to accept him as your guide for exploring the sights (and shops), and so are ripe for exploitation. Be polite, but firm, when refusing his offer of help.

A gem shop may try to persuade you to buy gems as a sample for a client in your home country – usually your home town (having found out which this is in casual conversation). A typical initial approach is to request that you help with translating something for the trader. The deal is that you buy the gems (maybe to the value of US$500 or US$1,000) and then sell them to the client for double the price, and keep the difference. Of course, there is no client at home and you are likely to have been sold poor quality gems or fakes! Only buy gems for yourself and be sure of what you are buying. This is a common trick in Galle and Ratnapura where various methods are employed. It is worth getting any purchase checked by the State Gem Corporation in Colombo. It is also essential to take care that credit cards are not 'run off' more than once when making a purchase.

Travel arrangements, especially for sightseeing, should only be made through reputable companies; bogus agents operate in popular seaside resorts.

Personal security

In general the threats to personal security for travellers in Sri Lanka are small. In most areas it is possible to travel without any risk of personal violence, though violent attacks, still very low by western standards, are on the increase. Women especially should avoid visiting remote areas of archaeological sites such as Polonnaruwa late in the day (ie after the tour groups have left) and care should be taken in certain lesser visited areas of popular beach resorts such as Hikkaduwa, Negombo and Mirissa – ask for advice locally.

Basic common sense needs to be used with respect to looking after valuables. Theft is not uncommon especially when travelling by train or crowded bus. It is essential to take good care of personal valuables both when you are carrying them, and when you have to leave them anywhere. You cannot regard hotel rooms as automatically safe. It is wise to use hotel safes for valuable items, though even they cannot guarantee security. It is best to keep travellers' cheques and passports with you at all times. Money belts worn under clothing are one of the safest options, although you should keep some cash easily accessible in a purse.

Police

Even after taking all reasonable precautions people do have valuables stolen. This can cause great inconvenience. You can minimize this by keeping a record of vital documents, including your passport number and travellers' cheques numbers in a separate place from the documents themselves. If you have items stolen, they should be reported to the police as soon as possible. Larger hotels will be able to help in contacting and dealing with the police.

Dealings with the police can be difficult, although many tourist resorts now have an English-speaking tourist police branch. The paper work involved in reporting losses can be time consuming and irritating, and your own documentation (eg passport and visas) will normally be demanded. Tourists should not assume that if procedures move slowly they are automatically being expected to offer a bribe. If you face really serious problems, for example in connection with a driving accident, you should contact your consular office as quickly as possible.

Where to stay

Sri Lanka has a surprisingly uneven range of accommodation. At the top end, there are international five-star hotels in Colombo and a handful of very exclusive 'boutique' hotels in some other areas. Below this level, you can stay safely and relatively cheaply in most major tourist areas, where there is a choice of quality hotels offering a full range of facilities (though their food can be bland and uninspired). At the lower end of the scale, there is an increasing range of family-run guesthouses in tourist areas offering bed and breakfast (and sometimes other meals) at reasonable prices. In smaller centres even the best hotels are far more variable and it may be necessary to accept much more modest accommodation. In the high season (December to March for much of the island) bookings can be extremely heavy. It is therefore best to reserve rooms well in advance if you are making your own arrangements, and to arrive reasonably early in the day.

Prices are highly inflated in Kandy during the *Esala Perahera* festival and in Nuwara Eliya during the April holiday season. 'Long weekends' (weekends when a public holiday or Poya Day falls on a Thursday, Friday, Monday or Tuesday) also attract a substantial increase in room rates in Nuwara Eliya. Many hotels charge the highest room rate over Christmas and New Year (between mid-December to mid-January). Large reductions are made by hotels in all categories out-of-season in many resorts. Always ask if any is available. During the monsoon rooms may sometimes feel damp and have a musty smell.

International class hotels

Mainly in the capital, these have a full range of facilities where prices and standards are sometimes comparable with the West. In Colombo, these are often genuinely luxurious.

Boutique hotels and villas

One of the fastest growing sectors of the market, these can be quite special offering a high degree of luxury, superb and very personal service, and a sense of privacy and exclusiveness lacking in resort-style hotels. Often they are innovatively designed with environmental sensitivity. Some sumptuous villas can also be rented by the day or week – see www.villasinsrilanka.com

Colonial-era hotels

The colonial period has left a legacy of very atmospheric colonial era hotels, notably in Colombo, Kandy and Nuwara Eliya. Some were purpose built, others converted from former governors' residences etc. A number have been carefully modernized without losing their period charm. Some very good deals are available.

Resort hotels

Catering mainly to tourists on packages, most larger tourist hotels on beaches and near important sites come into this category. Some are luxurious with a good range of facilities, others, notably in some west coast resorts, are rather tired and dated. Food served here tends to be of the 'all-you-can-eat' buffet variety. It pays to make bookings through tour operators, which offer large discounts on most resort-style hotels.

Guesthouses

Guesthouses are the staple of budget travellers, and are in plentiful supply in tourist haunts such as the west and south coasts, in Kandy, Nuwara Eliya, Anuradhapura and a few other towns. Some are effectively small hotels, usually at the upper end of

A bed for the night

Prices are for a double room excluding taxes during the high (not 'peak') season. Rates for hotels in categories C or above tend to be quoted in US dollars, or, in west coast package resorts, in euros. Prices are 'spot-rates' for individual travellers. Tour operators can get large discounts for 'package' clients in the top categories. Prices are exclusive of service charge and tax, both 10%. Single rooms are rare and single occupancy of a double room rarely attracts a significant discount.

LL US$200 and over This exclusive category consists mainly of 'boutique' hotels, small secluded properties often in magnificent positions with exquisite decor and superb service.
L US$150-200 Exceptional hotels in the larger cities or in an exclusive locations (eg, coastal promontory, lake side or hill top). Faultless, they have high-class business facilities, specialist restaurants, well-stocked bars, several pools and sports.
AL US$100-150 Major towns have at least one in this category. High international standards; good facilities for business and leisure travellers, but less exclusive.
A US$60-100 International class hotel with most facilities. Generous group discounts mean even budget package tours may use this category.
B US$35-60 Generally comfortable and good value except no pool. Several are converted colonial mansions where the 'experience' more than compensates for the antiquated facilities and furnishings.
C US$20-35 Often has a range of fairly comfortable rooms. Most should have some a/c rooms, TV and hot water.
D US$11-20 (Rs 1,200-1,800) This may be the highest category available in small towns (though not always best value). Rooms vary (most with hot water, some with a/c and TV). Many **D** Rest Houses are in idyllic locations, but lack investment and are sometimes run down.
E US$7-11 (Rs 800-1,200) Some are very good value, often noticeably better than F category with larger, cleaner rooms, more modern bathrooms etc. Towel, soap and toilet paper are usually provided. A/c often incurs a surcharge.
F US$5-7 (Rs 500- Rs 800) Backpacker's staple. Rooms are highly variable. Some are attractive and clean, others not. Inspect first. Expect a fan and mosquito net. Cheaper rooms may have shared facilities.
G Under US$5 (under Rs 500) In places with high demand, eg Colombo, Kandy, Nuwara Eliya. These may provide basic, and sometimes dirty, dormitory acco-mmodation with shared facilities. In some backpacker resorts (eg Hikkaduwa), however, you can find clean but simple private rooms, sometimes with attached toilet and shower.

the price bracket (**D** and **E**); others are simpler and more basic affairs. At their best, usually when family owned, they can be friendly, homely, and rich sources of local information. Those offering quality home cooking are well worth searching out. In addition, some private homes in Colombo, Kandy and some beach areas offer rooms, which can be very good value. Homestays in Uva province can be arranged via the Woodlands Network, see page 243.

Ayurdevic resorts

Mainly on the west coast, very popular with German-speaking tourists, these offer a

Best colonial hotels

Galle Face Hotel, Colombo, see page 82.
Mount Lavinia Hotel, Mount Lavinia, see page 83.
Hill Club, Nuwara Eliya, see page 233.
Bandarawela Hotel, Bandarawela, see page 247.
Closenburg Hotel, Galle, see page 163.

degree of luxury combined with ready or tailor-made programmes of Ayurvedic treatment. The authenticity of the treatments on offer tends to vary. **Ayurveda Pavilions** in Negombo, page 105, and **Siddhalepa Ayurveda Health Resort** in Kalutara, page 140, are two of the most highly regarded resorts, while more basic accommodation is offered with treatment at the Ayurvedic hospitals in Mount Lavinia, page 97.

Government rest houses

These are sometimes in converted colonial houses, often in superb locations, though compared to privately run enterprises are now often run down, overpriced with poor service. In some cases however they are the best (or only) option in town. **Ceylon Hotels Corporation (CHC)**, *411 Galle Rd, Colombo 4*, is responsible for management of several of the old Government Rest Houses across the island. Book through Central Reservations, Colombo, *T2503497, chc@sltnet.lk*, as occasionally an individual Rest House may not honour a direct booking. Prices charged by some on arrival may vary from what is quoted on the phone or the CHC's 'Official' typed list showing the tariff which only a few managers acknowledge exists. Rice and curry lunches at Rest Houses are often good, though at Rs 300-350 much more expensive than similar fare elsewhere.

National park accommodation

National park bungalows at all parks cost a hefty US$24 per person per night for foreigners (much less for locals) plus park fee of US$12, 'service charge' of US$30 for the group and linen charges (even if you bring your own) of US$2. If the bungalow is within the park boundaries then you will have to pay park entrance fees for two days for an overnight stay. Camping is possible in many national parks at US$6 per night, plus Rs 200 service charge. Accommodation must be booked at the Department of Wildlife Conservation in Colombo, though owing to excessive demand a complex lottery system at the time of writing made it difficult to book accommodation at popular parks such as Yala unless visiting the office in person well in advance. This was due to replaced by an online booking system: check www.dwlc.lk for details.

Plantation bungalows

Some attractive rubber and tea plantation bungalows in the hill country can be rented out by small or large groups and provide an interesting alternative place to stay. A caretaker/cook is often provided. There is no centralized booking agency, but see individual entries in the text or speak to the Tourist Board.

Circuit bungalows

Designed mainly for government workers, these may be the only option in areas well off the beaten track. They should be booked through the government offices in Colombo. Contact details are given under individual entries.

Railway Retiring Rooms

For people travelling by rail a few stations have Retiring Rooms which may be hired for up to 24 hours. However, there are only a few stations with rooms and they are generally rather poor value at Rs 300 for a double room. Some are open to people without rail tickets and can be useful in an emergency. Stations with rooms are: Anuradhapura, Galle, Kandy, Mihintale, Polgahawela, Maho and Trincomalee.

Getting around

Public transport in Sri Lanka is very cheap and, in the case of buses, island-wide. Due to overcrowding on buses, train is a (marginally) more comfortable alternative, although the network is limited. A majority of travellers choose to hire a car – whether self-drive or with a chauffeur – for at least part of their stay, especially if only here for a short time. Note that some areas of the north and east remain out of bounds.

Air

The ceasefire and peace talks brought about the lifting of the ban on internal air traffic in 2002. Flights resumed from Colombo's domestic airport at Ratmalana to Jaffna in late 2002, and in late 2003, Sri Lankan Airlines introduced a limited network of amphibious 'Air Taxis', shuttling on demand between Katunayake and Kandy (Victoria Lake), Koggala, Bentota, Trincomalee and Dambulla, though these have already proved prone to suspension. See www.srilankan.aero for further details.

Road

Roads in Sri Lanka are generally well maintained but traffic often moves very slowly, especially in Colombo and its surrounds. There has been some investment in recent years and there are now 'carpet' roads from Colombo to Kandy, Puttalam and Galle. Work began on the Colombo-Matara Expressway in March 2003.

Bus

Government-run CTB buses are generally yellow and are the cheapest, slowest and most uncomfortable of the options as they get very crowded at all times. Private buses follow the same routes, offer a higher degree of comfort (if you can get a seat) and cost a little more.

Private intercity buses are often a/c minibuses (sometimes coaches on popular routes). They cost about double the fare of ordinary buses but they are quicker and you are guaranteed a seat since they operate on a 'leave when full' basis. They can be quite cramped, especially if you have big luggage (if it takes up a whole seat you will probably have to pay for it) but on the whole they are the best option for travelling quickly to and from the main towns. They are generally non-stop but will let you off on request en route (ask the conductor in advance) although you will still have to pay the full fare to the end destination. If you do want to get off en route it is best to sit near the door since the aisle is used by passengers on fold-away seats. The fare is usually displayed on the front or side window.

In general it is best to board buses at the main bus stand in order to get a seat. Once out on the road it is normally standing room only.

Car hire

Many people choose to travel by car for at least part of their trip. This gives you greater flexibility if you want to tour, giving you the chance to see some places which are almost inaccessible any other way. Sharing a vehicle can make this occasionally possible for even those travelling on a small budget. On the downside however it cuts out some of the interaction with local people which can be one of the most rewarding aspects of travel by public transport, and may give you a lesser sense of 'achievement'.

There are several **self-drive** car hire firms based in Colombo including some linked to international firms. You have to be 25-65 years old and have an International Driving Permit (contact your local Automobile Association) in order to get a Sri Lankan driving permit through their AA. To get this free 'recognition permit', which is issued up to the expiry date of your International Driving Permit, is a simple process. Just call at the Automobile Association of Sri Lanka, *3rd floor, 40 Sir MM Markar Mawatha, Galle Face, Colombo 3, T2421528, F2446074. 0830-1630, Mon-Fri*. Some hire firms (eg **Avis**) will get this for you for Rs 50. If you do not have an International Driving Permit but do have your national licence, you must apply for a temporary Sri Lankan Driving Licence from the Register of Motor Vehicles, *Department of Motor Traffic, 341 Elvitigala Mawatha, Colombo 5, T2694331*. Temporary Driving Licences are issued on payment of Rs 600 plus GST per month up to a maximum of three months.

The rule of 'might is right' applies in Sri Lanka, and the standard of driving can be appalling. Many foreign visitors find the road conditions difficult, unfamiliar and sometimes dangerous. If you drive yourself it is essential to take great care and you should attempt to anticipate the mistakes that Sri Lankan road users might make. Most Sri Lankan drivers appear to take unbelievable risks, notably overtaking at inopportune times, such as when approaching a blind bend. Pedestrians often walk along, or in the middle of a narrow road in the absence of pavements and cattle and dogs roam at will. Never overtake a vehicle in front of you which indicates to the right. It usually means that it is unsafe for you to overtake and rarely means that they are about to turn right. Flashing headlights mean 'get out of the way, I'm not stopping'. In these circumstances it is best to give the oncoming vehicle space, since they usually approach at great speed. Roundabouts are generally a free-for-all, so take your chance cautiously. Horns are used as a matter of course, but most importantly when overtaking, to warn the driver being overtaken.

It may actually be safer (and more relaxing) to hire a **car with a driver**. These are available through travel agents and tour operators, or you can book with a freelance driver direct – this usually works out considerably cheaper. A driver may be helpful in being able to communicate with local people and also make a journey more interesting by telling you more about the places and local customs. Before setting off however, you should agree some ground rules, as there are a number of potential pitfalls: first, check that the driver is content for you to pick the route and accommodation, as some can be inflexible. It is best not to depend on the driver for suggestions of hotels, restaurants and gift shops since you may not get an unbiased opinion. Most large hotels have free driver accommodation and will provide a meal for him, but guesthouses and hotels off the beaten track often do not – in these instances you should agree in advance who will pay for drivers' accommodation (some will be happy to sleep in the car; others won't). It is also worth checking that the driver will stop for photographs; that his allowance will cover parking fees at sites; and, if you plan a long trip that he is prepared to spend the time away from home. Hire charges vary according to make and mileage and can be very high for luxury models. A tip to the driver at the end of the whole tour of about Rs 100 per day in addition to his inclusive daily allowance, is acceptable. The following rates quoted by **Quickshaw's** (see Colombo, page 93) for a/c cars were valid in April 2003. 20% tax is additional:

Self-drive Nissan Sunny: €19 per day (up to 100 km), €128 per week (up to 700 km), plus €0.17 per excess km. Mercedes Benz: €22 per day, €146 per week, plus €0.25 per km. A refundable deposit of Rs 15,000 is required, which covers insurance for accidental damage and loss (with a police report) up to this value. It is prohibited to drive in wildlife sanctuaries. Petrol costs, which are extra, are rising fast.

Car with driver Nissan Sunny: €27 per day (up to 100 km) or €178 per week (up to 700 km), plus €0.25 per excess km. Mini van: €31 per day, €206 per week, plus €0.30 per km. Mercedes Benz: €81 per day, €548 per week, plus €0.90 per km. Chauffeur's subsistence is an extra Rs 250 per day. Alternatively, some companies charge a flat rate of Rs 2,500-3,000, including mileage. Much cheaper rates are possible with freelance drivers.

Cycling

Cycling is very worthwhile in Sri Lanka as it gives you the opportunity to see authentic village life well off the beaten track. Foreign cyclists are usually greeted with cheers, waves and smiles. It is worth taking your own bike (contact your airline well in advance) or mountain bikes can be hired from **Adventure Sports Lanka** in Colombo and some other adventure tour companies, though they may not be up to international standards. They can be transported on trains, though you will need to arrive two hours ahead at Colombo Fort station. While cycling is fun on country byways, hazardous driving means that you should try to avoid the major highways (especially the Colombo-Galle road) as far as possible, and cycling after dark can be dangerous because of lack of street lighting and poor road surfaces. Take bungy cords (to strap down a backpack), spare parts and good lights from home, and take care not to leave your bike parked anywhere with your belongings. Repair shops are widespread and charges are nominal. Always bring plenty of water with you.

Local bikes tend to be heavy and often without gears but on the flat they offer a good way of exploring comparatively short distances outside towns. Many people choose to hire one to explore ancient city areas such as Polonnaruwa and Anuradhapura. Expect to pay Rs 100-175 per day for cycle hire from hotels and guesthouses, depending on the standard of hotel and condition of the bike. See also page 55.

Hitchhiking

This is rare in Sri Lanka, partly because public transport is so cheap.

Motorcycling

Motorcycles are popular locally and are convenient for visiting different beaches and also for longer distance sightseeing. Repairs are usually easy to arrange and quite cheap. Motorcycle hire is possible for around Rs 500 per day in some beach resorts (eg Hikkaduwa, Mirissa) or in towns nearby. You will generally need to leave a deposit or your passport. Check all bikes thoroughly for safety. If you have an accident you will usually be expected to pay for the damage. Potholes and speed-breakers add to the problems of a fast rider.

Taxi

Taxis have yellow tops with red numbers on white plates, and are available in most towns. Negotiate price for long journeys beforehand. **Radio cabs** (eg **Ace, Quick, GNTC**) are more expensive having a higher minimum charge, but are fixed price, very reliable, convenient and some accept credit cards. They are a/c, have digital meters and are available 24 hours at the airport, Colombo and Kandy. The cab usually arrives in 10-15 minutes of phoning (give exact location).

In tourist resorts, taxis are often Toyota **vans** which can carry up to 10 people. Ask at your hotel/guesthouse for an estimate of the fare to a particular destination. There is usually a 'going-rate', but you will probably have to bargain to reach this. Agree on the fare before getting in.

Three-wheeler

These three-wheeled motorised tricycles, the Indian auto-rickshaws made by Bajaj, move quickly through traffic but compare poorly against taxis for price. Sri Lanka's three-wheeler drivers are always keen to procure business, and you will be beeped constantly by any without a fare. An alarming 40% lack licences, and the driving is frequently of the kamikaze variety but they are often the only option available. Three-wheeler fares are negotiable as they are unmetered but fix a price before starting – the going rate is around Rs 20 per km. You can offer about 60% of the asking price though it is unlikely that you will get to pay the same rate as locals.

Train

Although the network is limited there are train services to a number of major destinations. Journeys are comparatively short, and very cheap by Western standards. Train journeys are leisurely (bar the Intercity between Colombo and Kandy) and an ideal way to see the countryside and meet the people without experiencing the downside of a congested bus journey through dusty crowded roads. You should be aware of touts on major train routes (especially Colombo to Kandy and Galle). There are three principal 'lines':

1 Northern Line This runs from Colombo up to Anuradhapura and continues north to Vavuniya, though no longer to Jaffna or Mannar. A line branches east at Maho (67 km south of Anuradhapura) towards Habarana, then splitting at Gal Oya junction, the northern section terminating at Trincomalee, the southern section continuing via Polonnaruwa to Batticaloa.

2 Main Line East from Colombo Fort to Kandy (with a branch line to Matale) with the ascent starting at Rambukkana. From Peradeniya the Main Line continues to Badulla through the hills, including stops at Nanu Oya (for Nuwara Eliya), Hatton (for Adam's Peak), Ohiya (for the Horton Plains) and Ella. This line is very scenic and a recommended way of travelling to the hill country, though book well in advance (up to 10 days).

3 Colombo-Matara Line South, originating at Maradana/Fort, and following the coast to Galle and as far as Matara, connecting all the popular coastal resorts. Running initially through the commuter belt south of the city, it can be crowded in the rush hour.

There are also the following lines: on the **Puttalam Line**, there are slow trains north from Fort to Puttalam via Katunayake (for the airport), Negombo and Chilaw. The **Kelani Valley Line** goes from Maradana to Avissawella.

Fares

Fares are worked out on a per km basis: first class is 99 cents per km, second class 57 cents per km, third class 21 cents per km. Children under 12 travel half-price (under 3s are free). Third class has hard seats; second has some thin cushioning; first class is fairly comfortable. Many slow trains may have second and third class coaches only, with first class only available on some express trains. You can pick up a rail timetable (Rs 100) at most major stations. The time of the next train in each direction is usually chalked onto a blackboard.

Reservations

Sleeping berth reservation charge in 1st class is Rs 75. In 2nd class and 3rd class 'sleeperettes' (reclining chairs) cost an extra Rs 25 and Rs 18 respectively. Reservation fees for 2nd and 3rd class are Rs 15 and Rs 12 respectively but seats cannot generally be reserved in advance. At Colombo's **Fort Station** there are different counters for different destinations and classes. Ask a local person to direct you to the correct counter. The Berth Reservation Office at Fort Station is open 0830-1530, Mondays- Saturdays, 0830-1200 on Sundays and public holidays. You can reserve at outstations with a refundable cash deposit.

Intercity trains

There are a/c intercity trains running to Kandy and Vavuniya (via Anuradhapura), which should be booked in advance. Kandy train also has a first-class observation car (extra Rs 50 on top of reservation fee), which must be booked well in advance as it is very popular. You will need to specify your return date at the time of booking the outward journey as tickets are not open-ended.

There are also some special through trains such as a weekly service from Matara all the way to Anuradhapura, and another from from Matara to Kandy, both via Colombo. Extra services are put on during festivals and holidays, eg from January for four months to Hatton (for the Adam's Peak pilgrimage season); April holiday season to the hills; in May and June for full moon days to Buddhist sites such as Kandy, Anuradhapura, Mihintale; and July/August for *Kandy Perahera*.

Maps

The Survey Department's *Road Atlas of Sri Lanka* (scale 1:500,000, around Rs 145), available at Survey Department branches in large towns, is useful, though printed in 1996 is now a little out-of-date. It has some street maps for larger towns. For more detail the department's four large sheet maps covering the island (scale 1:250,000) are the best available. These may not be available to buy for security reasons but you can ask to consult these at the Survey Department's Map Sales Branch in Colombo. *Arjuna's Atlas of Sri Lanka*. Arjuna, 1997 (see www.lankadotcom.com) is a comprehensive demographic survey of Sri Lanka. Sri Lanka Tourist Board branches both in Sri Lanka and abroad gives out a 1:800,000 Sri Lanka itinerary map plus several city and site guides with sketch maps free, but these are not particularly clear.

There are a number of user-friendly fold-out sheet maps produced abroad. These are mainly 1:500,000 scale and show tourist sights. Some have town street maps and some tourist information. Insight and Berndtson and Berndtson maps are both nicely laminated; Periplus's has some tourist information and clear street maps of Colombo, Kandy, Anuradhapura, Galle, Negombo, Nuwara Eliya and Polonnaruwa; Nelles Verlag also has some city insets; the Reise Know How map is probably the most detailed.

Keeping in touch

Communications

Internet

→ *See individual town and city directories for specific listings.*

Internet access is now widespread across Sri Lanka. Prices vary wildly however. In Colombo, Kandy and Trincomalee, there are now reliable internet cafés, with banks of reliable terminals and knowledgeable staff. They often other services such as internet phone (from around Rs 8 per minute) and CD writing. For internet, you shouldn't need to pay more than Rs 1 per minute. Internet cafés are also beginning to open up in some backpacker beach areas such as Unawatuna and Hikkaduwa, though expect to pay from Rs 2 per minute. Elsewhere, most major towns will usually have one or two communication centres where one or two terminals may be available. Connections

Digit demand

Owing to the ever-spiralling demand for new lines, all Sri Lankan telephone numbers (both fixed line and mobile) will be changing in stages during 2003 and early 2004. When completed, all numbers, previously of between 6 and 8 digits length, will be 10 digits long. New numbers will comprise a 3-digit STD code (previously in the case of Colombo (01), Kandy (08) and Galle (09) only two digits) and 7-digit main number, lengthened (from 5 or 6 digits) by the addition of extra 2s. For example, the Colombo number T01-123456 will change in October 2003 to T011-2123456. In the interests of keeping this guidebook up to date we have opted to list only new numbers. If a number has not been changed by the time you use this guidebook, dial the number without the two extra 2s and, in Colombo, Kandy and Galle, check the original code.

are usually much slower and less reliable and charges rise to Rs 8-10 per minute. Large hotels often offer internet service but usually at exorbitant rates. Sometimes post offices offer the cheapest internet connection in town, so it is worth dropping in to ask.

Post

Letters to Europe and Australasia cost Rs 26, to the USA, Rs 28 for the first 10 g (additional Rs 10 and Rs 15 respectively for each additional 10 g). Postcards to most countries beyond the Middle East cost Rs 17; aerogrammes to all countries (purchased over the counter at post offices) cost Rs 18; and small packets are Rs 80 to Europe, Rs 100 to the USA. Try to use a franking service in a post office when sending mail, or hand in your mail at a counter. Many towns often have private agencies which offer most postal services.

Air **parcel** rates to the UK are Rs 1,160 for the first 500 g, plus Rs 560 for each subsequent 500 g up to a maximum of 10 kg. To the USA the first 500 g will cost Rs 970 with an extra Rs 820 for each subsequent 500 g. For parcels by sea the rates to the UK are Rs 1,610 for the first kilogramme, Rs 2,105 up to 3 kg, Rs 2,600 for 3-5 kg and Rs 3,835 for 5-10 kg. To the USA it costs Rs 1,180 for the first kilogramme, Rs 1,670 up to 3 kg, Rs 2,180 for 3- 5 kg and Rs 3,385 for 5-10 kg.

For valuable items, it is best to use a **courier**, eg **DHL Parcel Service** in Colombo. Documents to UK cost Rs 1,700 for first 500 g, to USA Rs 1,820 for the first 500 g, and most of the EU Rs 2,522, plus Rs 530 for each additional 1 kg. Parcels cost for the first 500 g Rs 2,670 to the UK, Rs 3,200 to the USA and Rs 4,850 to the EU. It takes two to three working days to the UK or USA; three to four working days to mainland Europe.

Poste restante at the GPO in larger towns will keep your mail (letters and packages) for up to three months. American Express clients may have mail held at offices worldwide. Their website, www.americanexpress.com gives access to a list of offices with phone numbers and hours of opening.

Telephone

Dialling Sri Lanka from abroad: T+94. National operator: T100 to change to T1200. International operator: T101 to change to T1201. Directory enquiries: T161 to change to T1234 International directory enquiries T134 to change to T1236. See box.

Calls within Sri Lanka have a maximum charge of about Rs 3.50 per minute, the rate depending on time of day and distance. STD codes are listed for each town in the text. Dial the local number within the town but use the STD area code first (eg Kandy 081) when dialling from outside the town.

There are two private phone operators for whom at the time of writing a separate code (074 or 075) must be used wherever you call from. These are listed in the text, though the codes will change when numbers are standardised in 2004. Mobile prefixes are 071, 072, 077 and 078.

IDD (International Direct Dialling) is now straightforward in Sri Lanka with many private call offices throughout the country. It is best to use one with a computerised billing system rather than a stop-watch. Peak rate is between 0800-1800 Monday to Saturday; the cheapest rate is from 2200-0600 Monday to Saturday and all day Sundays. Calls to the UK, France, Germany, Canada and USA cost around Rs 40 per minute at cheap rate. Some places may allow you to accept incoming calls but may charge a nominal rate for each minute. Calls made from hotels usually cost a lot more (sometimes three times as much). They can be made cheaply from post offices though you may need to book. There are also IDD card-operated pay phones which connect you to many countries through satellite. Phone cards can be bought from post offices, kiosks near the pay phones and some shops. Pay phones can of course be used for local calls as well. Different companies issue cards which can be used for their own pay phones only and are not interchangeable – yellow and blue **Lanka** and the orange and black **Metrocard** are the most commonly used.

The cheapest way to phone abroad is by **internet phone**, with prices as low as Rs 8 per minute (to the UK), though quality may not always be good.

Mobile phone coverage is constantly improving across the island, and now extends across much of the west and south coasts, hill country, Ratnapura, Anuradhapura and the ancient cities and most other key towns including Jaffna, Trincomalee and Batticaloa. Most foreign networks are now able to roam within Sri Lanka; enquire at home before leaving. There are three networks: **Celltel**, *T011-541541, www.celltel.lk*; **Dialog GSM** (digital), *T011-678678, www.dialog.lk*; **Mobitel** (now run by SLT), *T0717-55777, www.mobitellanka.com* In early 2003, Dialog had the most comprehensive network, with coverage of most major towns in the western, central and southern regions, North Central Province as well and had extended to Jaffna, Trincomalee and Batticaloa; other networks were due to follow. It is possible to hire mobile phones. Expect to pay around Rs 100 a day plus connection charge (around Rs 1,000-1,500). Call charges vary according to package and network (eg Dialog pre-pay charge Rs 10 per minute peak, Rs 6 per minute off-peak; expect to pay around Rs 3 per minute for incoming calls too). If you are staying in Sri Lanka for a considerable period of time, another option is buy a mobile. Prices are upwards of Rs 7,000 for pre-pay – you can often sell it on for up to 75% of the original price – or alternatively pick up a second-hand mobile set (the Pettah is cheap but check the goods).

Media

Newspapers and magazines

It is well worth reading the newspapers, which give a good insight into Sri Lankan attitudes. *The Daily News* and *The Island* are national daily newspapers published in English; there are several Sunday papers including the *Sunday Observer* and *Sunday Times*. Each has a website with archive section which is worth investigating (see websites above). In Colombo and some other hotels a wide range of international daily and periodical newspapers and magazines is available. The *Lanka Guardian* is a respected fortnightly offering news and comment. *Lanka Monthly Digest* is aimed primarily at the business world but has some interesting articles.

Radio and television

Sri Lanka's national radio and television network, broadcasts in Sinhalese and English. **SLBC** operates between 0540 and 2300 on 95.6 FM in Colombo and 100.2 FM and 89.3 FM in Kandy. **BBC World Service** (1512khz/19m and 9720khz/31m from 2000 to 2130 GMT) has a large audience in both English and regional languages. Liberalization has opened the door to several private channels and an ever-growing number of private radio stations. **Yes FM** (89.5 FM), **TNL** (101.7 FM) and **Sun FM** (99.9 or 95.3 FM) broadcast western music in English 24 hours a day.

The two state TV channels are **Rupavahini** which now broadcasts 24 hours a day, and **ITN**. Many Sri Lankans now watch satellite TV with a choice of several channels: **Dynavision** for CNN, 24-hr **ETV-1** for BBC and **ETV-2** for StarPlus; **MTV**; **TNL**. These offer good coverage of world news and also foreign feature films and 'soaps'.

Food and drink

Although it shares some similarities with Indian cooking, Sri Lankan cuisine is distinct from its neighbour. While at its heart lies the island's enviable variety and bountiful supply of native vegetables, fruits and spices, Sri Lanka's history of trade and colonization has contributed to the remarkable range of dishes available today. Even before the arrival of the Europeans, Indians, Arabs, Malays and Moors had all left their mark. The Portuguese brought chilli from South America, perhaps the most significant change to food across the East, while the Dutch and even the British have also bequeathed a number of popular dishes. Sampling authentic Sri Lankan fare is undoubtedly a highlight of any trip.

Cuisine

Rice and curry is Sri Lanka's main 'dish', but the term 'curry' conceals an enormous variety of subtle flavours. Coriander, mustard seeds, cumin, fenugreek, peppercorns, cinnamon, cloves and cardamoms are just some of the spices that, roasted and blended, give a Sri Lankan curry its richness, while most cooks also add Maldive fish, or dried sprats. *Rampe* (screw-pine leaf) and tamarind pulp are also distinctive ingredients. The whole is then usually cooked in coconut milk.

Sri Lankan food is renowned for its fieriness, and **chilli** is the most noticeable – some would say intrusive – ingredient in some curries. While most tourist restaurants, aware of the sensitivity of many western palates to this most potent of spices, normally tone down its use, real home cooking will usually involve liberal quantities. If a dish is still too hot, a spoonful of rice or curd, or a sip of beer or milk (not water) will usually tone down its effects.

A typical Sri Lankan meal would comprise a large portion of rice, with a 'main curry' – for Buddhists usually fish, although chicken, beef and mutton are also often available – and several pulse and vegetable and (sometimes) salad dishes. *Dhal* is invariably one of these, and vegetable curries may be made from jackfruit, okra, breadfruit, beans, bananas, banana flowers or pumpkin, amongst others. Deliciously salty poppadums are also usually served, and the offering is completed by numerous side dishes: spicy pickles, sweet and sour chutneys and 'sambols', made of ground coconut (*pol sambol*) or onion mixed with Maldive fish, red chilli and lime juice (*seeni sambol*). *Mallung,* a milder dish prepared with grated coconut, shredded leaves, red onions and lime, is an alternative to try. *Kiri hodhi* is a mild 'white' curry prepared with coconut milk.

Rice-based alternatives to rice and curry include the Dutch-inspired *lamprais*, rice boiled in meat stock with curry, accompanied by dry meat and vegetable curries, fried meat and fish or meat balls (*frikkadels*), then parcelled in banana leaf and baked; and the ubiquitous *buriyani*, a Moorish dish of rice cooked in stock with pieces of chopped spiced meat and garnished with sliced egg.

The **rice** generally served is usually plain white boiled rice but it is worth searching out the healthier red rice. There are some tasty alternatives. **'String**

hoppers', a steamed nest of thin rice flour noodles, are often eaten with thin curries at breakfast but are often available at any time. **'Hoppers'** (*appam*), a breakfast speciality, are small cupped pancakes made from fermented rice flour, coconut milk and yeast. Crispy on the edges (like French crêpes), thick at the centre, they are often prepared with an egg broken into the middle of the pan ('egg hoppers'). *Pittu* is a crumbly mixture of flour and grated coconut steamed in a bamboo mould, usually served with coconut milk and sambol.

As befits a tropical island, Sri Lanka's **fish** and **seafood** is excellent. The succulent white seerfish, tuna and mullet, usually grilled and served with chips and salad, are widely available along the coast, while crab, lobster and prawns (often jumbo prawns) are magnificent and reasonably priced. Cuttlefish is very versatile and prepared a number of ways. Meat varies in quality; though it is cheap and is at least better than in India.

Unsurprisingly, **Indian** food is also popular, particularly from the south. Cheap filling traditional 'plate' meals (*thali*) are often available in Colombo, the north and east, as are *dosai*, crispy pancakes made from rice and lentil-flour batter, often served with a spiced potato filling.

Sri Lanka has a spectacular variety of superb tropical **fruit**, and this is reflected in the variety of juices on offer. Available throughout the year are pineapple, papaya (excellent with lime) and banana, of which there are dozens of varieties (red bananas are said to be the best). The extraordinarily rich jack (*jak*) fruit is also available all year. Seasonal fruit include the lusciously sweet mango (for which Jaffna is especially famous), the purplish mangosteen (July to September), wood-apple, avocado, the spiky and foul-smelling durian and hairy red rambutan from July to October. In addition to ordinary green coconuts, Sri Lanka has its own almost unique variety – the golden King Coconut (*thambili*); the milk is particularly sweet and nutritious.

Breakfast

The tendency amongst most smaller hotels and guesthouses is to serve a 'western breakfast' comprising fruit and white bread with some (often improbably coloured) jam. It is well worth ordering a Sri Lankan alternative in advance – ie the night before. This could comprise hoppers, string hoppers, kiribath (see below) or, best of all, the delicious **rotty** (roti), a flat circular unleavened bread cooked on a griddle.

Lunch

Lunch is the main meal of the day for many Sri Lankans. Rice and curry is the standard, often served in larger hotels as a buffet. The better rest houses are a good option for sampling a variety of authentic curries (usually around Rs 300). A cheaper and quicker alternative is to pick up a **'lunch packet'**, available from local restaurants and street vendors. This takeaway option usually comprises a portion of rice, a meat, fish or vegetable curry, plus *dhal*, all wrapped up in a paper parcel. Usually costing Rs 50-80, this is a cheap and filling meal. A lighter alternative still is a plate of **short eats**, a selection of meat and vegetable rolls, 'cutlets' (deep-fried in bread crumbs), *rotis* and *wadais*, a Tamil speciality of deep-fried savoury lentil doughnut rings, sometimes served in yoghurt (*thair vadai*). You will normally be given a full plate and charged for however many you eat.

Dinner

In larger hotels, dinner is usually the main meal of the day, often with enormous "all-you-can-eat" buffets on offer. Sri Lankans tend to eat late but light, and be aware that outside Colombo and the major tourist centres, the offering in guesthouses and restaurants may be limited unless you order in advance. It may not be possible to get rice and curry but Chinese food, ie fried rice, and devilled dishes are nearly always available.

Wedded bliss

The romantic palm-fringed beaches and exotic sights, sounds and flavours of this laid-back tropical island have made Sri Lanka an increasingly popular destination for weddings and honeymoons. A number of tour operators will tailor wedding packages with, for example, Kandyan dancing and drumming, decorated elephants for 'going away', and wedding blessings sung by Sri Lankan girls – or just about anything else you can think of – as well as the usual paraphernalia of planning, certificates, catering, photographs etc. UK tailor-made tour operators include: Cresta, T0870-1610909, Elite Vacations, www.elite-vacations.co.uk and Kuoni, www.kuoni.co.uk

Desserts

Sri Lankans tend to have a sweet tooth. Rice forms the basis of many Sri Lankan sweet dishes, palm treacle (*kitul*) being used as the main traditional sweetener. This is also served on curd as a delicious dessert (*kiri peni*) and boiled and set into *jaggery*. *Kavun* is an oil cake, made with rice flour and treacle and deep-fried until golden brown. Malay influence is evident in the popular *watalappam*, a steamed pudding made with coconut milk, eggs and jaggery, rather reminiscent of crème caramel. *Kiribath*, rice boiled in milk, is something of a national dish, often served at weddings and birthdays. It can be eaten with jaggery or as a breakfast dish with *seeni sambol*. Sri Lankan ice cream varies in quality; the best is made by soft drinks company Elephant House. Jaffna is also famous for its 'cream houses'.

Eating out

→ *Sri Lankans usually eat with their hands, mixing rice and curry together with the right thumb and forefingers. As a foreigner, however, you will always be supplied with a fork.*

Eating out in Sri Lanka is remarkably cheap. Most restaurants serve a choice of Indian, Chinese and continental dishes. Sadly, it is not easy to get good Sri Lankan food in most resort hotels which tend to concentrate on western dishes. The upmarket hotels in Colombo however serve first-class buffets at lunch and dinnertime, and there are an increasing number of excellent Sri Lankan restaurants in the city. Upcountry, home cooking in family-owned guesthouses is often unbeatable. It is however essential to order well in advance as Sri Lankan curries take a long time to prepare. This is one of the reasons for the universal popularity of Chinese and 'devilled' dishes available throughout the island, which can be knocked together in a few minutes! **Vegetarian** food is much less common in Sri Lanka than in India, and in places can be difficult to get.

Drinks

→ *Do not add ice cubes to drinks: the water from which the ice is made may not be pure.*

As they are year-round fruits, fresh papaya, pineapple and lime **juice** are always excellent. Sour-sop and wood-apple juice are two more unusual alternatives worth trying. One of the most popular and widespread drinks is King Coconut (the golden *thambili*). Always pure, straight from the nut, it is very refreshing. Mineral **water** is available everywhere, though is relatively expensive. There is a huge variety of bottled **soft drinks**, including international brands. Local favourites include ginger beer, cream soda, lemonade and Necto. These are perfectly safe but always check the seal. Elephant House is the main soft drinks manufacturer, and all their products are palatable. One potent soft drink is **Peyawa**, a ginger beer made with pepper and coriander for added kick.

The island's **coffee** harvest failed in 1869, and it would seem that Sri Lankans have never quite forgiven it, such are the crimes committed in the name of the drink.

Colombo's upmarket hotels do however serve decent coffee, and there are a couple of new western-style coffee bars opening up. As befits one of the world's great producers, **tea** is of course a much better option, although the highest quality varieties are generally exported.

Drinking **alcohol** in Sri Lanka is a no-nonsense male preserve and bars except in Colombo and tourist areas tend to be spit-and-sawdust affairs. **Beer** is strong (5%+), popular and served in large 660 ml bottles. **Lion, Carlsberg** and **Three Coins** are the three main brands, each producing a Pilsner style lager slightly thin to western tastes but quite palatable. **Three Coins** make some good specialist beers: their 8% **Sando stout** is smooth and chocolatey, and **Riva** is a more than passable wheat beer. The locally brewed **arrack**, distilled from palm toddy, is the most popular spirit and a cheaper option than beer. Superior brands include **Old Arrack, Double distilled**, the matured **VSOA** and **7-year old** arrack. The frothy, cloudy cider-like **toddy** is the other national drink, produced from the fermented sap of coconut, kitul (palm treacle) or palmyra palms. It is available from very basic toddy 'taverns', usually makeshift shacks that spring up in toddy-producing areas. Alcohol is not sold on *Poya* days (see page 59). Orders for alcoholic drinks in hotels are usually taken on the previous day!

Shopping

Local craft skills are still practised widely across the country. Pottery, coir fibre, carpentry, handloom weaving and metalwork all receive government assistance. Some of the crafts are concentrated in just a few villages.

What to buy

Of Indonesian origin but Sri Lankan design, good quality **batiks**, from wall hangings to *lungis* (sarongs), are widely available. **Handloom** has seen a major revival in recent years, and there is also a wide range of handwoven cotton and silk textiles in vibrant colours and textures.

The 'city of arts', Kalapura, has over 70 families of craftsmen making superb **brass**, wood, silver and gold items. Some specialise in fine carvings, inlays and damascene. Oil lamps are popular.

Ratnapura is Sri Lanka's **gem** capital, but they are sold throughout the country. Sapphires, rubies, cats eye, amethyst, topaz, moonstone and zircon are a few of the stones mined in the country.

A popular craft in the southwest of the island, especially around Ambalangoda, based on traditional **masks** used in dance dramas. Good quality masks in a range sizes can also be picked up in the craft outlets in Colombo. See box, page 135.

Another Kandyan specialism is **silverware**, with jewellery, tea sets, trays, candle stands and ornaments available. Inlay work is a further specialization. Fine gold and silver chain work is done in the Pettah area of Colombo.

Mlesna is a government run chain of **tea** shops, where good quality tea can be picked up. Tea is sometimes presented in attractive wooden or woven packages, and accessories such as teapots can make good gifts. Some tea and spice gardens welcome visitors and have retail outlets for their produce. Matale is noted for its spices.

Introduced by the Portuguese, Galle is famous for its **pillow lace** and crochet. Musical Instruments, especially **drums** are a popular gift. Matara is a good place to pick them up. **Coir and palm leaf** are made into mats, rugs, baskets and bags (see box page 348), while **reed, cane** and **rattan** are fashioned into attractive household goods, including mats, chairs, lampshades, bags and purses. **Lacquerware** is another craft centred on the Kandy region. The quality of **leather** goods especially bags, is often fairly high.

Where to buy

Craft department stores in the larger cities offer a range under one roof – **Lakpahana, Lanka Hands, Craft Link, Viskam Nivasa** are some you will come across. There are government **Laksala** shops in many towns, where prices are fixed. Private upmarket shops and top hotel arcades offer better quality, choice and service but at a price. Vibrant and colourful local bazaars (markets) are often a great experience but you must be prepared to bargain.

Bargaining

In some private shops and markets bargaining is normal and expected. It is best to get an idea of prices being asked by different stalls for items you are interested in before taking the plunge. Some shopkeepers will happily quote twice the actual price to a foreigner showing interest, so you might well start by halving the asking price. On the other hand it would be inappropriate to do the same in an established shop with price-tags, though a plea for the 'best price' or a 'special discount' might reap results even here. Remain good humoured throughout.

Tips and trends

Gem stones, gold jewellery and silver items are best bought in reputable shops. Taxi (and three-wheeler) drivers often receive commission when they take you to shops. If you arrive at a shop with a tout you may well end up paying absurdly high prices to cover the commission he earns. The quality of goods in a shop that needs to encourage touts may be questionable too. Try to select and enter a shop on your own and be aware that a tout may follow you in and pretend to the shopkeeper that he has brought you.

Batik 'factories', mask and handicrafts 'workshops', spice 'gardens', gem 'museums' across the island attract a traveller's attention by suggesting that a visit will be particularly interesting, but the main purpose of most is to get you into their shop where you may feel obliged to buy something in exchange for the free 'demonstration' or visit.

Export of certain items such as antiquities, ivory, furs and skins is controlled or banned, so it is essential to get a certificate of legitimate sale and permission for export.

Sport and special interest travel

Sport

Cricket

Many visitors come to Sri Lanka to support their touring cricket teams. Sri Lanka is the home of some of the most magnificently sited cricket grounds in the world, and the vibrant buzz at a Test or One-Day International is unforgettable. Internationals are played at the Premadasa Stadium at Khettarama in the north of Colombo (a day/night venue); the Asgiriya stadium in Kandy; at Galle, where the ground is backed by the ocean and fort; and most recently in the shadow of the rock at Dambulla. Another new ground, built at the cost of Rs 600 million, is scheduled to open at Pallekelle, east of Kandy, in 2004. Sri Lanka is hosting the following national cricket teams: November 2003, England; February 2004, Australia; August 2004, South Africa; July 2005, West Indies.

In the UK, **Gulliver Sports Travel**, *T01684-293175*, *www.gulliversports.co.uk*, are the official tour operators to the England Cricket Board; in Australia, **Australian Sports Tours**, *T1-800-026-668*, *www.astsports.com.au* It is also possible to organize playing tours with local teams; contact **Alps Travel**, *T01483-757660*.

One-day wonders

In a football-fixated world, the universal Sri Lankan passion for the gentler charms of cricket can seem both strange and refreshing. When the national team plays, everyone watches. The economy suffers as attendance at work drops dramatically with fans clustering around their radios and TVs without a care for anything else. Cricket is played on any spare patch of grass going, the fact that they may not have a bat or ball doesn't stop them. A plank and piece of fruit will do!

The Test team is one of the main focuses of national identity, and its players national icons – they become stars, politicians and sure-fire revenue-earners in the advertising world. Adoring schoolboys who speak no other word of English can reel off the names and batting averages of every international cricketer around the world.

Cricket's origins in Sri Lanka are of course colonial, but it wasn't until 1981 that the national team achieved Test status. Though they proved themselves far from minnows it was almost 20 years until 'senior' nations such as England finally agreed to play them in a full series. In the meantime, they transformed themselves with flair into kings of the one-day international, the game's shorter form, surprising everyone but themselves when they blasted their way to victory in the 1996 World Cup. The key to their success lay in the attacking batting of the openers, particularly Sanath Jayasuriya, who abandoned traditional caution at the start of an innings and smashed the opposition bowlers from the off, setting unassailable targets. Their success revolutionized the game as all teams adopted these tactics, transforming the one-day game forever.

Since then fortunes in both forms of the game have fluctuated, rising to third in the world Test rankings in 2002 despite facing the unusual embarrassment of losing to England both at home and away. It says much about expectations that despite reaching the semi-finals of the 2003 World Cup in South Africa an unhappy media and public bayed for blood from the board over selection policy. A marginalized Jayasuriya resigned the captaincy. Serious cricket starts at school in Sri Lanka, and though the game can be a great national unifier, there is undeniably bias towards privilege. Public schools cricket garners enormous media coverage, and its young players are idolised like their senior counterparts – for the outsider this is perhaps at its most bizarre in the Sunday Observer's Most Popular Schoolboy Cricketer of the Year competition! Until recently progress to the top flight, the Test team, was well nigh impossible without money. The national team's recent variable showing have prompted the game's administrators to spread cricket to the regions, setting up clinics, seminars and tournaments in the outstations to encourage talented youngsters from less wealthy backgrounds. A role model for many over the last decade, as well as a political bridge, has been the extraordinarily gifted Muttiah Muralitharan, one of the few Indian Tamils to play for Sri Lanka, who has won test matches almost single-handed with his sometimes unplayable off-spin bowling.

Cycling → *See also page 45.*

An increasing number of tour operators, both within Sri Lanka and abroad, are beginning to run tours by mountain bike of the island. A **National Cycling Trail,** much

Clear waters

Corals, invertebrates and dazzling fish – blue surgeon, comical parrot, butterfly, lion, large and small angels, snappers, groupers, barracudas and jackfish – enjoy Sri Lanka's warm coastal waters, yet the island has yet to become renowned as a diving destinaton. Much of the coastline, particularly in the southwest, was adversely affected by 'bleaching' in 1998. Although the reefs are slowly beginning to recover, it is a slow process. To avoid disappointment seek out clearer waters by taking a boat further out to sea. Questions have also been raised over some dive operations. Owing to the civil war, the use of radio equipment on boats is limited, essential of course in case of an emergency. Furthermore, there are only two decompression chambers, one in Colombo and the other at the naval base in Trincomalee's Fort Ostenburg.

There remain nonetheless some superb sites to explore. As long as you travel away from the coast, visibility up to 25 m is possible, especially in the morning, and a wealth of marine life can be seen at popular sites such as Negombo and Hikkaduwa. The south coast is even better and many rate the wrecks in the bays at Galle and Weligama. From April to June, Dondra to Tangalla are fine in calm seas, while the more adventurous should enquire about the Great and Little Basses off Kirinda, made famous by Arthur C Clarke, before setting sail. Some of Sri Lanka's most spectacular sites lay in areas off-limits due to the war, particularly on the east coast, where the wreck of HMS *Hermes*, a Second World War aircraft carrier, lies in good condition buried deep off Passekudah Bay, near Batticaloa.

of which will be along an existing infrastructure of dirt tracks, is currently being designed. The first stretch to open will be a 240 km coastal route from Wadduwa (near Kalutara) to Unwatuna, with trails through the hill country, Ancient Cities and parts of Sabaragamuwa province to follow. Contact **Adventure Sports Lanka**, see page 92, for more details.

Diving and watersports

The warm waters along Sri Lanka's palm-fringed coast are dotted with beach resorts ideal for **swimming**. December to March is the only suitable time to swim on the west coast, while November and April are usually also fine on the south. There are a number of drownings each year – avoid swimming outside these months, when the southwest monsoon batters the coast. Particular care should be taken of rip currents – check the situation locally. Many large hotels have excellent swimming pools and will usually accept non-residents for a small fee (around Rs 200), or even for free.

Dive centres on the west and south coasts have equipment for rent, and some offer a full range of PADI courses; an open water course usually costs US$300-330. Diving is best avoided during the monsoons. The best time in the southwest is the winter, from November to March when the sea is relatively calm and clear. The far south and the east coast are better from April to September (but avoid July). Specialist companies will advise you on good reefs. Also see box.

Several popular beach areas offer good **snorkelling** at reefs within walking distance of shore, notably Hikkaduwa, Unawatuna, Mirissa and Polhena (near Matara), while the clear waters of Pigeon Island, a short boat ride from Nilaveli near Trincomalee, are also once again accessible. The **surf** at Arugam Bay on the east coast is regarded as some of the best in Asia, though only between April and October.

Ayurvedic healing

Ayurveda (science of life/health) is the ancient Hindu system of medicine – a naturalistic system depending on diagnosis of the body's 'humours' (wind, mucus, gall and sometimes blood) to achieve a balance. In the early form, gods and demons were associated with cures and ailments; treatment was carried out by using herbs, minerals, formic acid (from ant hills) and water, and hence was limited in scope. Ayurveda classified substances and chemicals compounds in the theory of *panchabhutas* (five 'elements'). It also noted the action of food and drugs on the human body. Ayurvedic massage using aromatic and medicinal oils to tone up the nervous system has been practised for centuries.

This ancient system which developed in India over centuries before the Buddha's birth was written down as a *samhita* by Charaka. It probably flourished in Sri Lanka up to the 19th century when it was overshadowed by the western system of allopathic medicine. However, with the renewed interest in alternative forms of therapy in the West, Sri Lanka too considers it a serious subject for scientific research and has begun exploring its wealth of wild plants. The island has seen a regeneration of special Ayurvedic herbal cure centres which are increasingly attracting foreign, particularly German-speaking visitors. In addition, most large hotels now have special Ayurveda massage centres attached, and a number of specialist Ayurvedic 'resorts' have opened up, especially along the west coast.

In addition to the use of herbs as cures, many are used daily in the Sri Lankan kitchen (chilli, coriander, cumin, fennel, garlic, ginger), some of which will be familiar in the West, and have for centuries been used as beauty preparations.

Hikkaduwa is the main centre during the winter from November to March, sometimes attracting international tournaments, while Midigama and Mirissa are smaller and quieter. Surfing equipment can be bought or hired in these areas and cheap accommodation aimed at long-stay surfers is available.

Larger hotels on the west coast offer windsurfing, parasailing and water-skiing. Bentota is said to be the best spot.

Golf

A legacy from the British period, there are some excellently maintained courses in Colombo, Nuwara Eliya and on the banks of the Victoria Reservoir east of Kandy.

Hiking

There is little organized trekking in Sri Lanka, but some richly rewarding countryside to explore, especially in the hill country. Existing paths include ancient pilgrim routes and colonial-era bridal pathways. Moderately fit walkers should not miss climbing the sacred mountain of Adam's Peak, especially during pilgrimage season (December to May), while Horton Plains offers crisp mountain air and stunning views at World's End with the option of camping. The Knuckles range (Dumbara Hills) has some hard treks, while Nuwara Eliya, Ella and Haputale are particularly good bases for walkers.

White-water rafting and canoeing

Kelani River, which falls through a rocky gorge just above Kitulgala, is the most popular area for rafting and canoeing, offering grade 4-5 rapids. There are several operators in Colombo and Kitulgala. Gentle rafting is possible on the Walawe River in Uda Walawe, while the Mahaweli ganga, Sri Lanka's longest river, offers more challenging opportunities.

Special interest travel

Ayurveda → *See box, page 57.*

With the renewed interest in alternative forms of therapy in the West, Sri Lanka too considers Ayurvedic healing a serious subject for scientific research and has begun exploring its wealth of wild plants. There has been a regeneration of special Ayurvedic herbal cure centres, some of which are increasingly attracting foreign visitors, particularly to the southwest coast around Bentota. Some of those geared towards foreigners are 'resort' style complexes, regarded suspiciously by some Sri Lankans, though there are some exquisite and authentic retreats opening up (eg Ayurveda Pavilions in Negombo). Some day treatment centres can be found around Kandy.

Buddhism → *See page 353.*

The ancient Buddhist centres hold great attraction for all visitors and certainly for those interested in the living religion. Sri Lanka provides rewarding opportunities to discover more about the practice of Theravada (Hinanaya) Buddhism and meditation. Several centres offer courses on Buddhism in English (and occasionally in French and German). See page 97 and also www.buddhanet.net, for a list of addresses and websites of retreats which accept foreigners for teaching and meditation.

Wildlife → *www.dwlc.lk; see also page 373*

Sri Lanka's wildlife reserves are home to a wide range of native species, and wildlife 'safaris' offer the chance to see elephant, spotted deer, buffalo, wild pig, jackal, sambar and, with time and luck, the leopard and sloth bear. Around 24% of Sri Lanka's land area is covered by forest, most large tracts of which are protected by the government - the Forestry Department run the island's Forest Reserves (such as the **Knuckles range**) and Man and Biosphere Reserves (notably **Sinharaja**), while the national parks, sanctuaries and nature reserves, which offer the best chance of wildlife spotting, belong the Department of Wildlife Conservation. Most of Sri Lanka's national parks are in the Dry Zone areas of the north and east, the most frequently visited by tourists being **Ruhuna National Park** (also referred to as Yala), where a remarkable array of bird and animal life is easily visible; **Uda Walawe**, famous for its elephants; and **Minneriya** to the north. Closed for many years owing to the civil war, the island's largest reserve, **Wilpattu** reopened in early 2003.

All national parks are open 0630-1830. Entrance fees for most are US$12 for foreigners (Rs 20 for locals) and US$6 for children under 12 (though some charge US$6 for adults), plus fees for a compulsory tracker and taxes and service charge. These hidden charges totalled up make a visit quite expensive, though it should be remembered that (theoretically at least) the money is ploughed back into wildlife conservation. Most people choose to visit the parks on a day trip, though bungalows and campsites are available (see page 42). It is worth dropping in to the Wildlife Conservation Department's office in Colombo (see page 98) to pick up a copy of their *National Parks Guide* (Rs 210), although park permits can currently only be bought on the day of entry.

Bird-watching

Sri Lanka is also an ornithologist's paradise with 233 resident species, of which 26 (mainly in the Wet Zone) are endemic. Together with almost 200 migrant species recorded, bird-watching is highly rewarding.

Full moon festivities

Full Moon Poya days of each month are holidays. Buddhists visit temples with offerings of flowers, to worship and remind themselves of the precepts. Certain temples hold special celebrations in connection with a particular full moon, eg *Esala* at Kandy. Accommodation may be difficult to find and public transport is crowded during these festivals. No alcohol is sold (you can however order your drinks at your hotel the day before) and all places of entertainment are closed.

	2004	2005
January	7	25
February	6	23
March	6	25
April	5	24
May	4-5	23
June	3	22
July	2, 31	21
August	29	19
September	28	17
October	27	17
November	26	15
December	26	15

Sinharaja Forest Reserve, the Peak Wilderness Sanctuary and the Ruhuna-Yala National Park are particularly rewarding since they offer diverse habitats, while the reservoirs and coastal lagoons to the southeast (especially Bundala) attract a large variety of water birds. Local specialist tour operators are listed on page 92.

Holidays and festivals

Since the significant days of all four of its religions are respected, Sri Lanka has an remarkable number of festivals, and probably more public holidays – 29 – than anywhere else in the world, a matter of increasing consternation to the island's business leaders. All full moon (*poya*) days are holidays, as are Saturday and Sunday. There are also several secular holidays. Most religious festivals (Buddhist, Muslim and Hindu) are determined by the lunar calendar and therefore change from year to year. Check at the tourist office (www.srilankatourism.org) for exact dates.

January

Duruthu Poya – Sri Lankan Buddhists believe that the Buddha visited the island. There is a large annual festival at the **Kelaniya** Temple near Colombo. On **14th**, *Tamil Thai Pongal* is day observed by Hindus, celebrating the first grains of the rice harvest. In late January early February, *Navam Poya* is celebrated at Colombo's grandest *perahera* at Gangaramaya Temple, with caparisoned elephants, dancing, drummers and processions.

February and March

On **4th**, *National (Independence) Day* involves processions, dances, parades. In February/March, *Maha Sivarathri* marks the night when Siva danced his celestial dance of destruction (*Tandava*), celebrated with feasting and fairs at Siva temples, preceded by a night of devotional readings and hymn singing. March is the month of *Medin Poya Day*.

April

Bak Poya Day. Good Friday with Passion Plays in Negombo and other coastal areas, in particular on Duwa Island. The **13-14th** is Sinhala and Tamil *New Year Day*, marked with celebrations (originally harvest thanksgiving), by closure of many shops and restaurants. Many Colombo residents decamp to the highlands, see page 233.

May

1st, *May Day*. *Wesak Poya Day* and the day following is the most important *poya* in the calendar, celebrating the key events in the Buddha's life: his birth, Enlightenment and death. Clay oil-lamps are lit across the island and there are also folk theatre performances. Wayside stalls offer food and drink free to passers-by. These are special celebrations at Anuradhapura, Kelaniya (Colombo) and Kandy. **22**: *National Heroes' Day* (not a public holiday).

June

Poson Poya Day, marking Mahinda's arrival in Sri Lanka as the first Buddhist missionary; Mihintale and Anuradhapura hold special celebrations. *Bank Holiday* (**30**).

Around July and August

Esala Poya is the most important Sri Lankan festival. It takes place in July and early August with grand processions of elephants, dancers etc, honouring the Sacred Tooth of the Buddha in Kandy lasting 10 days, and elsewhere including Dewi Nuwara (Dondra) and Bellanwila Raja Maha Vihare, South Colombo. Culmination of the *Pada Yatra* pilgrimage to Kataragama, where purification rituals including firewalking are held. Munneswaram (Chilaw) *Vel Festival* and in Colombo from Sea St Hindu temple, procession to Bambalapitiya and Welawatta. *Nikini Poya Day* – celebrations at Bellanwila, Colombo.

September

Binara Poya Day A Perahera is held in Badulla.

October and November

In October is *Wap Poya Day* and in October/November is *Deepavali*, Festival of Lights, celebrated by Hindus with fireworks, commemorating Rama's return after his 14 years exile in the forest when citizens lit his way with earthen oil lamps. Also in November, *Il Poya Day*.

December

Unduwap Poya Day, marks the arrival of Emperor Asoka's daughter, Sanghamitta, with a sapling of the Bodhi Tree from India. Special celebrations at Anuradhapura, Bentota and Colombo. **25th**, *Christmas Day* and **31st**, *Special Bank Holiday*.

Muslim holy days

These are fixed according to the lunar calendar, see page 362. According to the Gregorian calendar, they tend to fall 11 days earlier each year, dependent on the sighting of the new moon.

Ramadan Start of the month of fasting when all Muslims (except young children, the very elderly, the sick, pregnant women and travellers) must abstain from food and drink from sunrise to sunset.

Id ul Fitr (November 2003, 2004) The three-day festival marks the end of Ramadan.
Id-ul-Zuha/Bakr-Id (February 2004; January 2005) Muslims commemorate Ibrahim's sacrifice of his son according to God's commandment; the main time of pilgrimage to Mecca (the Hajj). It is marked by the sacrifice of a goat, feasting and alms giving.
Muharram (March 2004, February 2005) when the killing of the Prophet's grandson, Hussain, is commemorated by Shi'a Muslims. Decorated *tazias* (replicas of the martyr's tomb) are carried in procession by devout wailing followers who beat their chests to express their grief! Shi'as fast for the 10 days.

Health

By Dr Charlie Easmon MBBS MRCP MSc Public Health DTM&H DOccMed Director of Travel Screening Services.

Medical care is generally of a poor standard throughout the country including in Colombo. In the event of serious medical conditions every effort should be made to go to Bangkok or Singapore. Hospital accommodations are inadequate throughout the country and advanced technology is lacking in most areas. However, health is a market and new clinics with aspirations to western standards are opening all the time.

As with all medical care, first impressions count. If a facility is grubby then be wary of the general standard of medicine and hygiene. It's worth contacting your embassy or consulate on arrival and asking where the recommended (ie those used by diplomats) clinics are. Providing embassies with information of your whereabouts can be also useful if a friend/relative gets ill at home and there is a desperate search for you around the globe. You can also ask them about locally recommended medical do's and don'ts. If you do get ill, and you have the opportunity, you should also ask your medical insurer whether they are satisfied that the medical centre or hospital that you have been referred to is of a suitable standard.

However, before discussing the disease-related health risks involved in travel within Sri Lanka remember to try to avoid road accidents. You can reduce the likelihood of accidents by not drinking and driving, wearing a seatbelt in cars and a helmet on motorbikes, but you should be aware that others on the road may think that they are in the remake of Death Race 2000.

Before you go

Ideally, you should see your GP or travel clinic at least six weeks before your departure for general advice on travel risks, malaria and vaccinations. Make sure you have travel insurance, get a dental check (especially if you are going to be away for more than a month), know your own blood group and if you suffer a long-term condition such as diabetes or epilepsy make sure someone knows or that you have a Medic Alert bracelet/necklace with this information on it.

Vaccinations recommended include **Polio** if none in last 10 years; **Tetanus** again if you haven't had one last 10 years (after five doses you have had enough for life); **Typhoid** if nil in last three years; **Hepatitis A** as the disease can be caught easily from food/water. **Yellow Fever** is not required unless you are coming directly from an infected country in Africa or South America. **Rabies** may be required if you are visiting rural areas. **Japanese Encephalitis** may be required for rural travel at certain times of the year (mainly rainy seasons). A **Malaria** risk exists throughout the year in the whole country, excluding the districts of Colombo, Kalutara, and Nuwara Eliya. Some of the malaria is resistant to chloroquine.

Items to take with you → *It is risky to buy medicinal tablets abroad because the doses may differ and there may be a trade in false drugs.*

Mosquito repellents. Remember that DEET (Di-ethyltoluamide) is the gold standard. Apply the repellent every four to six hours but more often if you are sweating heavily. If a non-DEET product is used check who tested it. Validated products (tested at the London School of Hygiene and Tropical Medicine) include Mosiguard, Non-DEET Jungle formula and non-DEET Autan. If you want to use citronella remember that it must be applied very frequently (ie hourly) to be effective. If you are popular target for insect bites or develop lumps quite soon after being bitten, carry an Aspivenin kit. This syringe suction device is available from many chemists and draws out some of the allergic materials and provides quick relief.

The Australians have a great campaign, which has reduced skin cancer. It is called Slip, Slap, Slop. Slip on a shirt, Slap on a hat, Slop on **sun screen**.

Pain killers. Paracetomol or a suitable painkiller can have multiple uses for symptoms but remember that more than eight paractemol a day can lead to liver failure.

Ciproxin (Ciprofloaxcin). A useful antibiotic for some forms of travellers diarrhoea.

Immodium. A great standby for those diarrhoeas that occur at awkward times (ie before a long coach/train journey or on a trek). It helps stop the flow of diarrhoea and in my view is of more benefit than harm. (It was believed that letting the bacteria or viruses flow out had to be more beneficial. However, with Immodium they still come out, just in a more solid form.)

Pepto-Bismol. Used a lot by Americans for diarrhoea. It certainly relieves symptoms but like Immodium it is not a cure for underlying disease. Be aware that it turns the stool black as well as making it more solid.

MedicAlert. These simple bracelets, or an equivalent, should be carried or worn by anyone with a significant medical condition.

For longer trips involving jungle treks taking a clean needle pack, clean dental pack and water filtration devices are common-sense measures.

On the road

Diarrhoea and intestinal upset → *One study showed that up to 70% of all travellers may suffer during their trip.*

Symptoms Diarrhoea can refer either to loose stools or an increased frequency; both of these can be a nuisance. It should be short lasting but persistence beyond two weeks, with blood or pain, require specialist medical attention.

Cures Ciproxin (Ciprofloaxcin) is a useful antibiotic for bacterial traveller's diarrhoea. It can be obtained by private prescription in the UK which is expensive, or bought over the counter in Sri Lankan pharmacies. You need to take one 500 mg tablet when the diarrhoea starts and if you do not feel better in 24 hours, the diarrhoea is likely to have a non-bacterial cause and may be viral (in which case there is little you can do apart from keep yourself rehydrated and wait for it to settle on its own). The key treatment with all diarrhoeas is rehydration. Try to keep hydrated by taking the right mixture of salt and water. This is available as Oral Rehydration Salts (ORS) in ready-made sachets or can be made up by adding a teaspoon of sugar and a half teaspoon of salt to a litre of clean water. Drink at least one large cup of this drink for each loose stool. You can also use flat carbonated drinks as an alternative. Immodium and Pepto-Bismol provide symptomatic relief.

Prevention The standard advice is to be careful with water and ice for drinking. Ask yourself where the water came from. If you have any doubts then boil it or filter and treat it. There are many filter/treatment devices now available on the market. Food can also transmit disease. Be wary of salads (what were they washed in, who handled them), re-heated foods or food that has been left out in the sun having been cooked

Leeches

When trekking in the monsoon be aware of leeches. They usually stay on the ground waiting for a passerby and get in boots when you are walking. Then when they are gorged with blood they drop off.

Don't try pulling one off as the head will be left behind and cause infection. Put some salt, or hold a lighted cigarette to it, which will make it quickly fall off. It helps to spray socks and bootlaces with an insect repellent before starting off in the morning.

earlier in the day. There is a simple adage that says wash it, peel it, boil it or forget it. Also be wary of unpasteurized dairy products, these can transmit a range of diseases from brucellosis (fevers and constipation), to listeria (meningitis) and tuberculosis of the gut (obstruction, constipation, fevers and weight loss).

Sun protection

Symptoms White Britons are notorious for becoming red in hot countries because they like to stay out longer than everyone else and do not use adequate sun protection. This can lead to sunburn, which is painful and followed by flaking of skin. Aloe vera gel is a good pain reliever for sunburn. Long-term sun damage leads to a loss of elasticity of skin and the development of pre-cancerous lesions. Years later a mild or a very malignant form of cancer may develop. The milder basal cell carcinoma, if detected early, can be treated by cutting it out or freezing it. The much nastier malignant melanoma may have already spread to bone and brain at the time that it is first noticed.

Prevention Sun screen. SPF stands for Sun Protection Factor. It is measured by determining how long a given person takes to 'burn' with and without the sunscreen product on. So, if it takes 10 times longer to burn with the sunscreen product applied, then that product has an SPF of 10. If it only takes twice as long then the SPF is 2. The higher the SPF the greater the protection. However, do not just use higher factors just to stay out in the sun longer. 'Flash frying' (desperate bursts of excessive exposure), as it is called, is known to increase the risks of skin cancer. Follow the Australians with their Slip, Slap, Slop campaign.

Hepatitis

Symptoms Hepatitis means inflammation of the liver. Viral causes of the disease can be acquired anywhere in Sri Lanka. The most obvious symptom is a yellowing of your skin or the whites of your eyes. However, prior to this all that you may notice is itching and tiredness.

Cures Early on, depending on the type of hepatitis, a vaccine or immunoglobulin may reduce the duration of the illness.

Prevention Pre-travel hepatitis A vaccine is the best bet. Hepatitis B (for which there is a vaccine) is spread through blood and unprotected sexual intercourse, both of these can be avoided. Unfortunately there is no vaccine for hepatitis C or the increasing alphabetical list of other Hepatitis viruses.

Dengue fever

Unfortunately there is no vaccine against this and the mosquitoes that carry it bite during the day. You will feel like a mule has kicked you for two to three days, you will then get better for a few days and then feel that the mule has kicked you again. It should all be over in seven to 10 days. Heed all the anti-mosquito measures that you can.

Sexual health

The range of visible and invisible diseases is awesome. Unprotected sex can spread HIV, Hepatitis B and C, Gonorrhea (green discharge), chlamydia (nothing to see but may cause painful urination and later female infertility), painful recurrent herpes, syphilis and warts, just to name a few. You can cut down the risk by using condoms, a femidom or avoiding sex altogether.

Further information

Websites

Foreign and Commonwealth Office (FCO) (UK), www.fco.gov.uk This is a key travel advice site, with useful information on the country, people, climate and lists the UK embassies/ consulates. The site also promotes the concept of 'Know Before You Go'. And encourages travel insurance and appropriate travel health advice. It has links to the Department of Health travel advice site, see below.

Department of Health Travel Advice (UK), www.doh.gov.uk/traveladvice This excellent site is also available as a free booklet, the T6, from Post Offices. It lists the vaccine advice requirements for each country.

Medic Alert (UK), www.medicalalert.co.uk This is the website of the foundation that produces bracelets and necklaces for those with existing medical problems. Once you have ordered your bracelet/necklace you write your key medical details on paper inside it, so that if you collapse, a medical person can identify you as someone with epilepsy or allergy to peanuts etc.

Blood Care Foundation (UK), www.bloodcare.org.uk The Blood Care Foundation is a Kent-based charity "dedicated to the provision of screened blood and resuscitation fluids in countries where these are not readily available". They will dispatch certified non-infected blood of the right type to your hospital/clinic. The blood is flown in from various centres around the world.

Public Health Laboratory Service (UK), www.phls.org.uk This site has up to date malaria advice guidelines for travel around the world. It gives specific advice about the right drugs for each location. It also has useful information for those who are pregnant, suffering from epilepsy or planning to travel with children.

World Health Organisation, www.who.int The WHO site has links to the WHO Blue Book (it was Yellow up to last year) on travel advice. This lists the diseases in different regions of the world. It describes vaccination schedules and makes clear which countries have Yellow Fever Vaccination certificate requirements and malarial risk.

Fit for Travel (UK), www.fitfortravel.scot.nhs.uk This site from Scotland provides a quick A-Z of vaccine and travel health advice requirements for each country.

British Travel Health Association (UK), wwwbtha.org This is the official website of an organization of travel health professionals.

Travel Screening Services (UK), www.travelscreening.co.uk This is the author's website. A private clinic dedicated to integrated travel health. The clinic gives vaccine, travel health advice, email and SMS text vaccine reminders and screens returned travellers for tropical diseases.

Books

The Travellers Good Health Guide by Dr Ted Lankester, ISBN 0-85969-827-0.
Expedition Medicine (The Royal Geographic Society) Editors David Warrell and Sarah Anderson ISBN 1 86197 040-4.
International Travel and Health World Health Organisation Geneva ISBN 92 4 158026 7.
The World's Most Dangerous Places by Robert Young Pelton, Coskun Aral and Wink Dulles ISBN 0-060011-60-2.

Colombo

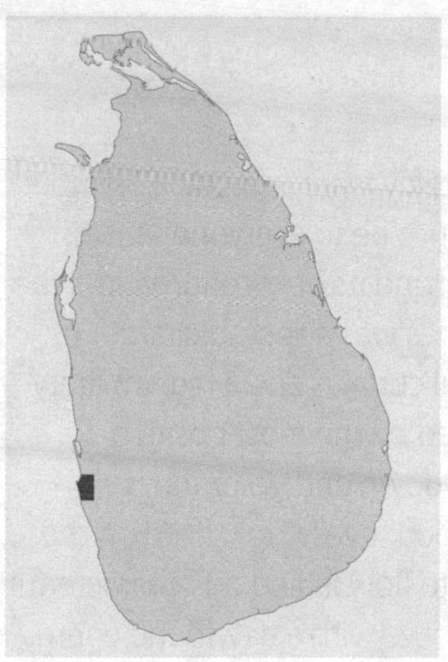

Introduction

Sprawling, choked with traffic and invariably chaotic, Colombo, like most large Asian cities, may not be to everyone's taste. As Sri Lanka's commercial capital and its only conurbation, the city centre in recent troubled times was a sporadic target of separatist targets with occasional curfews and a high military presence. Today however, buoyed by the most positive political climate, the barriers are down and Colombo is learning to breathe again. With both eyes firmly fixed on the future, investment is beginning to flow in and this characterful and diverse city is beginning to buzz with a newfound energy.

Although Colombo's origins pre-date the arrival of the Portuguese, culturally and architecturally it appears a modern city, with few established tourist sights. Close to the enormous **harbour**, to which Colombo owes its pre-eminence, the banking centre of **Fort** however still houses some impressive red brick and whitewashed buildings which give an impression of its colonial origins. To the east are the narrow lanes of the bustling **Pettah district** with its atmospheric and colourful bazaars and some reminders of the Dutch period.

Increasingly the heart of modern Colombo lies to the south of the old centre, where the city's wealthy young elite rub shoulders in the fashionable boutiques and restaurants of **Kollupitiya** and **Bambalapitiya**, while the broad avenues and elegant villas of **Cinnamon Gardens** nearby reveal the city's most exclusive residential district. Inland from here, or south to the predominantly Tamil suburb of **Wellawatta**, brings you to a more 'local' Colombo. Alternatively the pleasant colonial resort of **Mount Lavinia** with its narrow strip of beach is only a 30-minute train ride away from the centre, and a laid-back alternative base for exploring the city.

★ Don't miss...

1. **Galle Face Green** Wander across the green in the early evening and watch the city at play, page 73.
2. **Kollupitiya** Shop for handmade textiles at the stylish Barefoot boutique, then sample the epicurean delights of one of the chic restaurants, page 86.
3. **The Pettah** Explore the busy market of the Pettah, and capture the Dutch past at the Wolfendahl Church and Dutch Period Museum, page 72.
4. **Vihara Mahadevi Park** Enjoy the quiet stillness of the botanical garden at the Vihara Mahadevi Park, page 74.
5. **Kelaniya temple** Witness the colourful spectacle of decorated elephants, chariots and dancing during the annual perahera at the Kelaniya temple, page 80.
6. **Mount Lavinia** Transport yourself back to the 1870s to imagine the opulent lifestyle of Governor Barnes with a visit to the palatial Mount Lavinia Hotel, page 79.

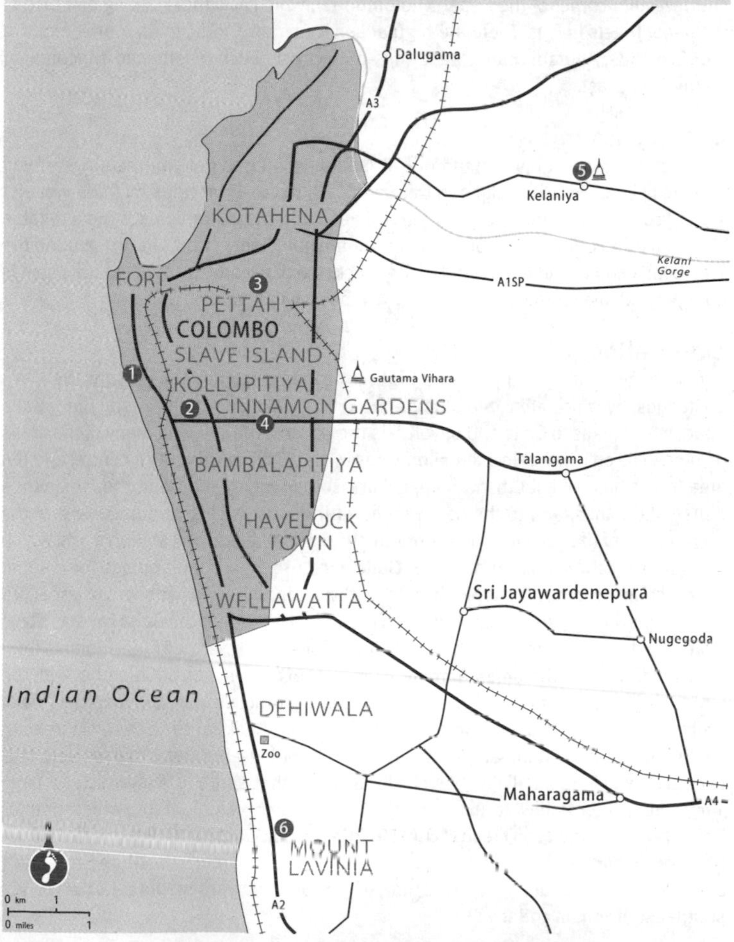

Ins and outs

→ *Phone code: 011. Colour map 3, grid A1. Population 650,000.*

Getting there

Air Almost all international visitors to Colombo arrive by air at Bandaranaike International Airport at Katunayake about 30 km north of the city and 6 km from Negombo. Available at the airport are regular buses to Colombo, which take an hour, as well as pre-paid van taxis, costing from Rs 1,000 depending on where in Colombo you wish to be dropped off, and more expensive a/c cabs, from around Rs 1,200. Trains leave from the station about 500 m away, see page 34. Domestic air passengers arrive at Ratmalana Airport to the south of the city. ▸▸ *For further details, see page 31.*

Bus Government and private buses run to Colombo from virtually every significant town in Sri Lanka. There are three bus stands, all close to each other, 1 km east of Fort station in the Pettah. There are regular bus services along Galle Road to Colombo's southern suburbs, where many visitors choose to stay.

Train Nearly all of Sri Lanka's railway lines originate in Fort Railway Station at the southwestern corner of the Pettah (Colombo 11), which is within walking distance of the major hotels in Fort. There are regular services from Kandy, main tourist areas in the Highlands, Anuradhapura, west and south coast beach resorts and Trincomalee on the east coast.

Getting around

Although the city is quite spread out, it is fairly simple to get your bearings. If you venture beyond Fort you will need transport to explore. Short hops by three-wheeler should cost no more than Rs 50 – you will need to bargain. Radio cabs are a reliable alternative and quite affordable if you can share one. Some streets in Fort, around the President's house and major banks, are blocked or have strict security checks so it is often impossible for transport to take the most obvious route.

Orientation

If you are going to spend any time here, it pays to become familiar with the city's postcodes, by which areas are often referred (see box). The main coastal road, Galle Road, which leads to Galle and beyond, is the spine of the city, and many of the areas of interest lie on it or within a few kilometres inland. Officially the city's centre, and the area from which all suburbs radiate, is **Fort**, containing the harbour, the President's house and banks, and to the south some of the most exclusive hotels. East is the busy bazaar of **the Pettah**, which contains the main train and bus stations, and which turns into **Kotahena**. South of Fort is **Galle Face Green**, a popular place for a stroll, which soon becomes **Kollupitiya**, a wealthy shopping area with many excellent restaurants. Inland, and separated from Fort and the Pettah by the Beira Lake, is **Slave Island** and the busy thoroughfare of Union Place. South of here (and inland from Kollupitiya) is leafy **Cinnamon Gardens**, the most exclusive area of Colombo, with the city's biggest park, main museums and some attractive guesthouses, so many visitors choose to stay here. To the east is **Borella**. Back on the coast, Galle Road continues south to **Bambalapitiya**, another shopping area but progressively less exclusive, which is parallel to **Havelock Town**. Further south is **Wellawatta**, a large Tamil area, then **Dehiwala** (not strictly speaking part of Colombo), which houses Colombo's zoo. Then you reach **Mount Lavinia**, a traditional bolt-hole from the city for both locals and tourists, see page 79. Yet none of these areas constitute Sri Lanka's administrative capital, which was moved to **Sri Jayawardenepura Kotte**, 11 km southeast of Fort, in 1982.

I'm in heaven ... Colombo Seven...

Even more than London, Colombo's citizens define their city by its postcodes. Aside from recognizing the snob value of having an office in Colombo 1 or a residence in Colombo 7 (and being suitably impressed), having a grasp of the most important postcodes will help you find your way around the city.

Colombo 1	Fort
Colombo 2	Slave Island
Colombo 3	Kollupitiya
Colombo 4	Bambalapitiya
Colombo 5	Havelock Town
Colombo 6	Wellawatta
Colombo 7	Cinnamon Gardens
Colombo 8	Borella
Colombo 9	Dermatagoda
Colombo 10	Maradana
Colombo 11	Pettah
Colombo 12	Hultsdorf
Colombo 13	Kotahena
Colombo 14	Grandpass
Colombo 15	Mutwal

Tourist information

Sri Lanka Tourist Board, *80 Galle Rd, Col 3, T2544534, ctb_ch@sri.lanka.net, 0830-1615 Mon-Fri, 0830-1230 Sat,* has free literature in English (and some in German, French, Italian, Swedish and Japanese) and will arrange guides, though not much information on transport (Cultural Triangle tickets are not sold here; best bought at sites). There is also an Information Counter at Katunayake airport, *T2452411.* **Railway Tourist Office,** *Fort Station, Col 11, T2440048, bluehavtravel@slt.net,* offers friendly, invaluable advice to anyone planning a rail journey. They will suggest an itinerary, book train tickets and hotels, and offer a car with driver. Special steam train excursions are offered on the *Viceroy Special* (usually groups of 30 are required, at around US$200 a head for a 2-day 1-night trip to Kandy).

Travel Lanka is a free monthly tourist guide available at larger tourist offices and in major hotels. It has some useful information and listings for Colombo and the main tourist areas, though much is out of date. For a more contemporary view, pick up a copy of *Leisure Times*. Also monthly, it has the latest restaurant, bar and nightclub openings, and a rundown of the month's events in Colombo. Free copies are available at the airport, big hotels, shopping complexes, and some bars and clubs.

History

Sheltered from the southwest monsoon by a barely perceptible promontory jutting out into the sea, Colombo's bay was an important site for Muslim traders long before the colonial period. Its name derives from 'Kotomtota', or port to the kingdom of Kotte founded in 1369, close to present-day Sri Jayawardenepura Kotte, see page 81.

However, Colombo is essentially a colonial city. Soon after arrival in Sri Lanka, the Portuguese set up a fortified trading post in modern-day Fort, captured in 1656 by the Dutch. The canals constructed to link up the coastal lagoons are a lasting legacy, as well as the churches and mansions of the Pettah, Kotahena and Hultsdorf. Colombo's rise to pre-eminence however did not start until the 19th century and the establishment of British power. When the British took control of Kandy and encouraged the development of commercial estates, the island's economic centre of gravity moved north, thereby lessening the importance of Galle as the major port. The town became the banking and commercial hub and benefited from its focal position on the rapidly expanding transport system within the island. From 1832 the British encouraged the rapid development of a road network which radiated from Colombo. In the late 19th century this was augmented by an expanding rail network. Since independence Colombo has retained its dominant position.

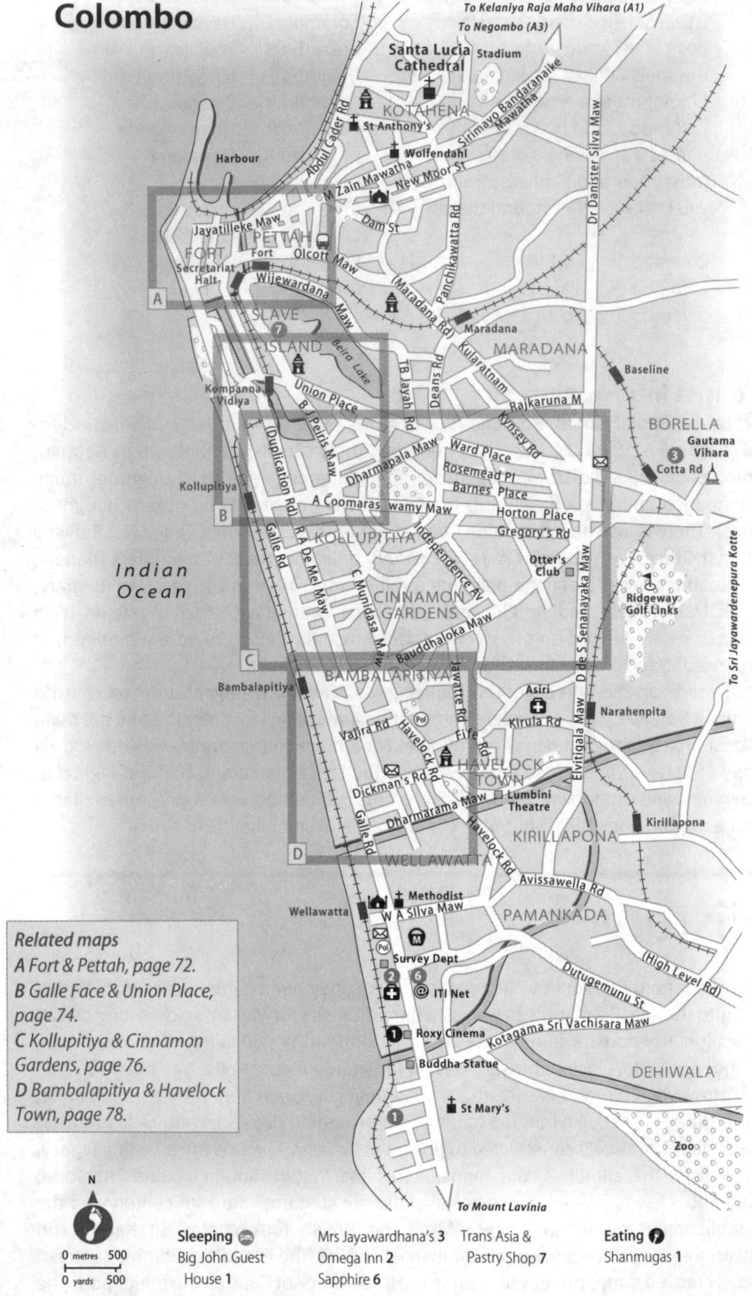

Sights

Colombo is a modern city with plenty of buzz but few 'must-see' sights. Its historical centre is the colonial Fort, which combined with a visit to the hectic bazaar and Dutch period legacy of the Pettah area to its east, can make for an interesting walking tour. Most of the rest of the city's sights are spread out in the southern suburbs, where the attractive wide boulevards of Cinnamon Gardens, the city's most exclusive district, are a highlight. Here you can visit the city's principal park and museums, and perhaps even more enticingly, sample some of the fare that is fast making Colombo one of the culinary capitals of Asia. » *For Sleeping, Eating and other listings, see pages 81-98.*

The city

Fort area

Lying immediately south of the harbour, the compact fort area, historically Colombo's commercial centre, is a curious blend of old and new, modern tower blocks rubbing shoulders with reminders of its colonial past. It can be an eerily quiet place outside office hours. Because it houses the Prime Minister's residence and the principal banking area, separatist targets during the war, it remains the only road-blocked area of the city and security continues to be high. The harbour and much of the northwest section remain off-limits. Though it houses many fine British colonial buildings (many of which are boarded up), little remains from either the Portuguese or Dutch periods, and the last traces of the fort itself were destroyed in the 19th century. Many offices have moved out of Fort, leaving it a rather empty shell, though it is still interesting to explore the accessible areas by foot.

The **Grand Oriental Hotel** is a good place to start a tour. Formerly the first port of call for all travellers arriving by steamship, it was once the finest hotel in Colombo. It used to be said that if you waited long enough in its hall, you would meet everyone worth meeting in the world. It is rather faded now, but you can get fascinating views of the harbour area from the hotel's third-floor restaurant. From here, **York Street**, Fort's main shopping area, runs due south, passing the brick-built colonial era department stores of **Cargill's** and **Miller's**, and the government emporium **Laksala**.

To the east on Bristol Street is the Central YMCA, next to the Moors Islamic Cultural Home. Across Duke Street is the Young Men's Buddhist Association. The shrine houses a noted modern image of the Buddha.

Sir Baron Jayatilleke Mawatha, once the main banking street, stretches west of York Street. Nearly all the buildings are in red brick. At the western end of Chatham Street to the south, past the Dutch period Fort Mosque, is the **Lighthouse Clock Tower**, now replaced as a lighthouse by the new tower on Chaithya Road. A modern clocktower (with Big Ben chimes) takes its place. The northern end of Janadhipathi Mawatha, which includes the **President's House** (*Janadhipathi Mandiraya*), is normally closed to the public.

Heading south along Janadhipathi Mawatha, a quite different, more vibrant Fort comes into view. The 1960s **Ceylon Continental Hotel** has magnificent views along the coast to Mount Lavinia, while on Bank of Ceylon Mawatha is Fort's modern day commercial hub, the twin steel and glass towers of the 39-floor **World Trade Centre** (1991), Sri Lanka's tallest building, along with some other high-rise offices. To the south, opposite the Galadari Hotel, the colonial **Old Parliament House** is now used as the President's Secretariat.

The Pettah and Kotahena

To the north and east of Fort Station is a busy market area with stalls lining Olcott Mawatha and Bodhiraja Mawatha, making pedestrian movement slow and tedious at times. The central area of the Pettah, with many wholesale outlets, bounded by these two roads as well as Main Street and Front Street, is frantic, dirty and noisy, the cries of the traders mingling with the endless traffic horns. It is fascinating and enervating in equal parts. Specialist streets house craftsmen and traders such as goldsmiths (Sea Street), fruit and vegetable dealers (the end of Main Street) and Ayurvedic herbs and medicines (Gabo's Lane). In the market area to the north, Arabs, Portuguese, Dutch and British once traded. Today, most of the traders are Tamil or Muslim, as evidenced by the many *kovils* and mosques.

About 100 m northeast of Fort Railway Station at the south western edge of the Pettah, the **Dutch Period Museum**, ⓘ *0900-1700, closed Fri, Rs 70 for foreigners, camera Rs 160, Prince St, T2448466,* was originally the residence of the Dutch governor, Thomas van Rhae (1692-97); it was sold to the VOC before becoming the Colombo seminary in 1696. Then in 1796 it was handed over to the British who turned it into a Military Hospital and later a Post Office. It has now been restored and offers a fascinating insight to the Dutch period. The museum surrounds a garden courtyard and has various rooms dedicated to different aspects of Dutch life including some interesting old tombstones. Upstairs, several rooms display Dutch period furniture.

To the north, half way along Main Street on the left-hand side after 2nd Cross Street is the **Jami-ul-Alfar Mosque** with its interesting white and red brick façade but

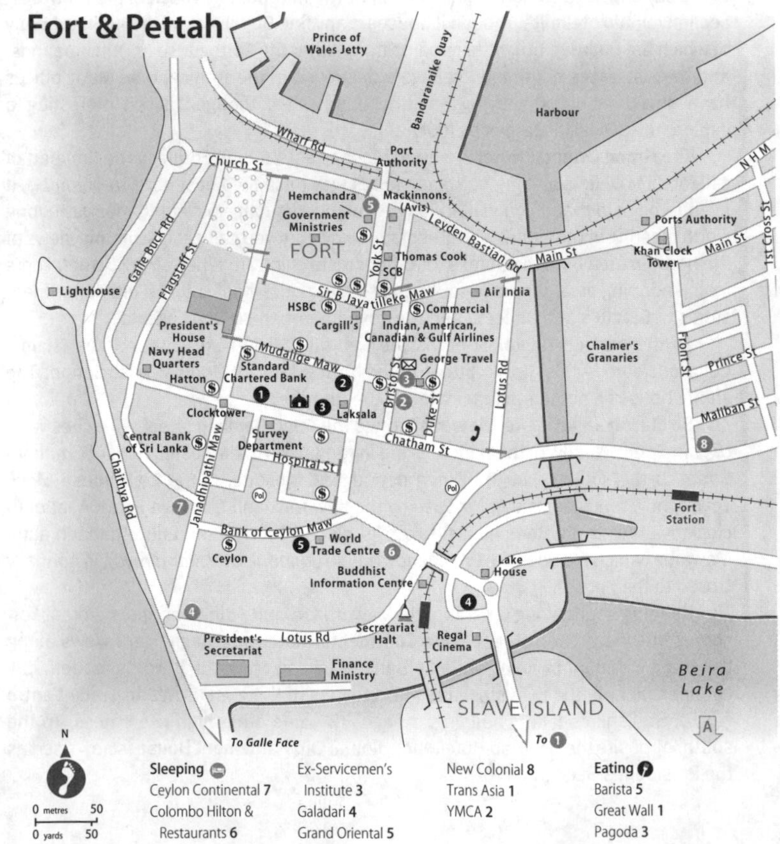

little of architectural interest inside. At the eastern end of Main Street, Mohamed Zain Mawatha (once Central Road) goes east from a large roundabout, just north of the market, and you enter **Kotahena**. A left turn off Mohamed Zain Mawatha immediately after the roundabout leads to a right fork, Ratnajothi Saravana Mawatha (formerly Wolfendahl Street). At the end (about 500 m) is the **Wolfendahl Church**. Built in 1749 on the site of an earlier Portuguese church, it is prominently placed on a hill, where its massive cruciform shape stands out, commanding a view over the harbour. Its Doric façade is solid and heavy, and inside it has many tombstones and memorial tablets to Dutch officials. It is the most interesting surviving Dutch monument in Sri Lanka. Some 200 m to the south in New Moor Street is the **Grand Mosque**, a modern building in the style, as one critic puts it, of a "modern international airport covered in metallic paint".

About 1 km to its northeast is **Santa Lucia**, the Roman Catholic cathedral, in some people's eyes the most remarkable church building in Sri Lanka. It is a huge grey structure with a classical façade and a large forecourt, begun in 1876, and completed in 1910. Inside are the tombs of three French bishops but little else of interest. The Pope conducted a service here during his visit in 1994. **Christ Church**, the Anglican Cathedral back towards the harbour, is a kilometre northwest of here and is the main church in a diocese which dates from 1845.

Also in the Pettah are three modest Hindu temples, of little architectural interest, but giving an insight into Hindu building style and worship. Perhaps the most striking is that of **Sri Ponnambula Vanesvara** at 38 Sri Ramanathan Road. The *gopuram* (gateway) has typical sculptures of gods from the Hindu pantheon. A Siva lingam is in the innermost shrine, with a Nandi bull in front and a dancing Siva (*Nataraja*) to one side, see page 360.

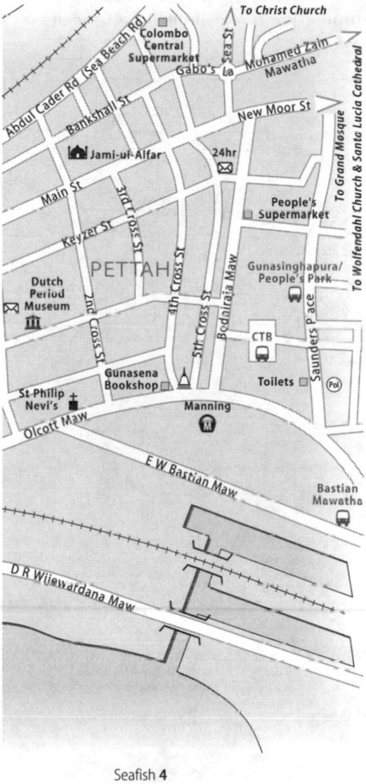

Galle Face, Union Place and Beira Lake

Heading south from Fort past the **Ceylon Continental Hotel** and Old Parliament, you reach **Galle Face Green**, to the south of the mouth of the canal feeding Beira Lake. Originally laid out in 1859, the area has been redeveloped and, green once more, is a pleasant place to wander and relax and very popular with Sri Lankans. There are lots of food stalls and hawkers selling knick-knacks, kites and children's toys. Speaker's Corner is at its southwestern corner opposite the historic **Galle Face Hotel**. Be on guard for pickpockets, especially at night when the whole area comes alive.

Cross Galle Road, and then the canal, and head into **Slave Island** (see box page 79). On Kew Street, near the **Nippon Hotel**, city tours often visit the **Sri Siva Subharamaniya Kovil**, with its enormous colourful *gopuram*. Along Sir James Pieris Mawatha to the south is the pea-green **Beira Lake**, where the internationally endangered spot billed pelican can often be seen. This potentially attractive area is due for redevelopment, some of which has been completed. At its northern end along Navam Mawatha is an important commercial zone, with some restaurants and bars, and a pavement now leads some of the way around the lake. There are jetties to two tiny islands, one a children's park, the other the tranquil **Seema Malakaya**, designed for meditation by Geoffrey Bawa with various Buddha statues. It belongs to the **Gangaramaya Temple** to the east, which has an interesting selection of rare curios, including an impressive set of gold Buddhas and some intricate carved ivory on show. You'll also see the temple elephant shackled up in the grounds. The temple comes alive during the *Navam Perahera* in January.

Kollupitiya, Cinnamon Gardens and Borella

Inland and parallel with Galle Road runs RA de Mel Mawatha (formerly Duplication Road), built up all the way south. Kollupitiya and, further south, Bambalapitiya have some of Colombo's best shopping areas, with some upmarket boutiques, notably **Barefoot**, see page 91. Wealthy locals also flock to the numerous excellent restaurants.

East of Kollupitiya station, Ananda Coomaraswamy Mawatha leads to the most prestigious residential area of Colombo, **Cinnamon Gardens** – widely referred to by its postal code, Colombo 7 – where cinnamon trees used to grow during colonial times. Broad roads and shaded avenues make it a very attractive area, more reminiscent of Singapore than South Asia, though an increasing number of offices and government buildings have moved here in recent years from Fort. Its centrepiece is the attractive **Vihara Mahadevi Park**, ⓘ *0600-1800, approach from the northeast, opposite the Town Hall,* with the museums and art gallery to its south. The park was re-named after the mother of the King Dutthagamenu. Early morning is an excellent time to visit.

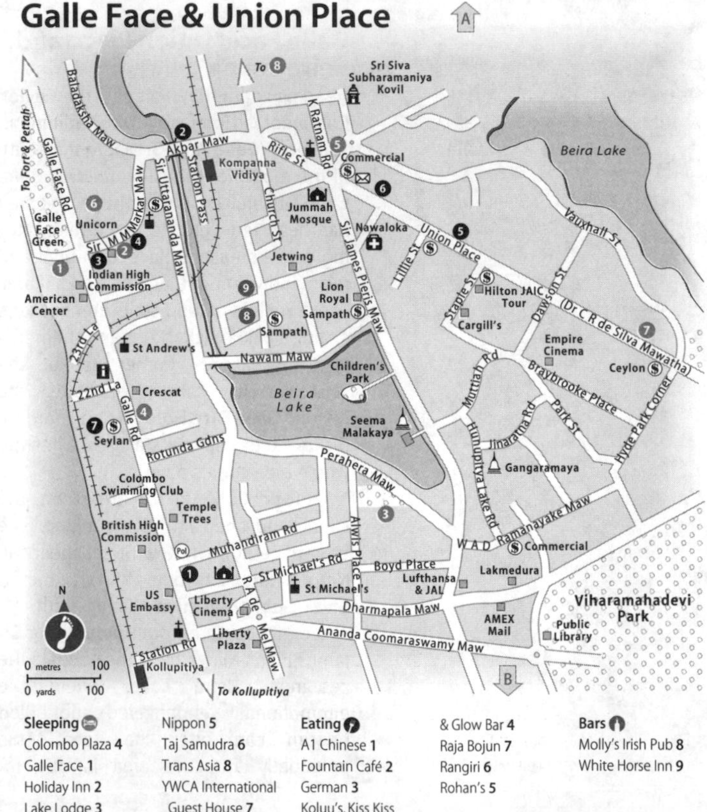

Colombo Harbour

Given Sri Lanka's historical reliance on trade, its harbours, of which Colombo is the most important, are a nerve centre of the economy. Colombo's success lay in its strategic position on the Indian Ocean sea route between Europe, the Far East and Australasia, almost equidistant between the Red Sea and the Straits of Malacca. Development did not begin until the late 19th century – the small promontory offered little protection for larger ships, so in 1875 the British started work on a series of breakwaters which were to provide an effective harbour round the year. By 1912, when the dockyard and fourth breakwater were completed, Colombo was recognized as one of the top seven harbours in the world.

Currently handling almost 4,000 ships a year, today Colombo is at the forefront of plans to make Sri Lanka the shipping hub of South Asia. Having developed its container terminals in recent years and refurbished its passenger terminal in anticipation of establishing ferry links with India and Maldives, the Sri Lankan Ports Authority is planning a new container terminal, the South Port, with 12 new berths and a new breakwater. The intention is to attract mega container vessels and double capacity within 20 years.

The best views of the harbour are offered at the Harbour Restaurant at the Grand Oriental Hotel.

In the southwest is a **botanical garden** with a range of tropical trees including a Bo tree, ebony, mahogany, *sal* and lemon eucalyptus which attract a wide variety of birds. There is also an enormous profusion of climbing and parasitic plants as well as rare orchids. The park is particularly colourful in the spring. You may catch sight of elephants which are bathed in the water tank to the southwest. A series of rectangular lakes to the east of the park leads to a golden statue of the seated Buddha. There is also a mini-railway line, now sadly fallen into disrepair, a boating area and an aquarium. The white cupola of the impressive **Town Hall** stands out on Kannangara Mawatha to the northeast corner of the park. It was completed in 1927. At the De Soysa Circus roundabout is an equally interesting red-brick building, the **Victoria Memorial Rooms**, built in 1903.

In **Borella**, the suburb east of Cinnamon Gardens, the modest shrine room of the **Gautama (Gotami) Vihara** contains impressive modern murals depicting the life of the Buddha by the Sri Lankan artist George Keyt, painted in 1939-40.

The **National Museum**, ⓘ *0900-1700, closed Fri and public holidays, Rs 65, children Rs 35, cameras Rs 160, 8 Marcus Fernando Mawatha (Albert Crescent), T2694768,* has a statue of Sir William Gregory, governor 1872-77, in front of the imposing façade. Opened in 1877, it has a very interesting collection of paintings, sculptures, furniture, porcelain and Kandyan regalia. The library houses a unique collection of over 4,000 *ola* (palm manuscripts) - an extremely rich archaeological and artistic collection. Very well labelled and organized, a visit is an excellent introduction to a tour of Sri Lanka. Exhibits include an outstanding collection of 10th-12th century bronzes from Polonnaruwa, and the lion throne of King Nissankamalla, which has become the symbol of Sri Lanka. There are interesting details and curiosities: for example the origin of Kolam dancing is traced back to the pregnancy craving of the Queen of the legendary King Maha Samnatha! The ground floor displays Buddhist and Hindu sculptures, including a striking 1,500 year old stone statue of the Buddha from Toluvila. 'Demon-dance' masks line the stairs to the first floor. One visitor noted, "These are more 'satire' than 'demon' in nature, with lots of characters of court officials, soldiers and 'outsiders' such as Muslims. Some were very elaborate and capable of moving their eyes etc. It is interesting to see how these evolved as different fashions swept the court." The first floor has superb scale reproductions of the wall paintings at Sigiriya and Polonnaruwa. Other exhibits include ancient jewellery and carvings in ivory and wood.

The **Natural History Museum**, ⓘ *0900-1700, closed Fri and public holidays, Rs 45, children Rs 25, no cameras, entered via the National Museum or from A Coomeraswamy Mawatha, T2694767,* is a Victorian-style array of ageing stuffed animals and lizards in formaldehyde, although the scope is quite impressive. The 'Applied botany' section introduces you to how various industries work, such as rubber,

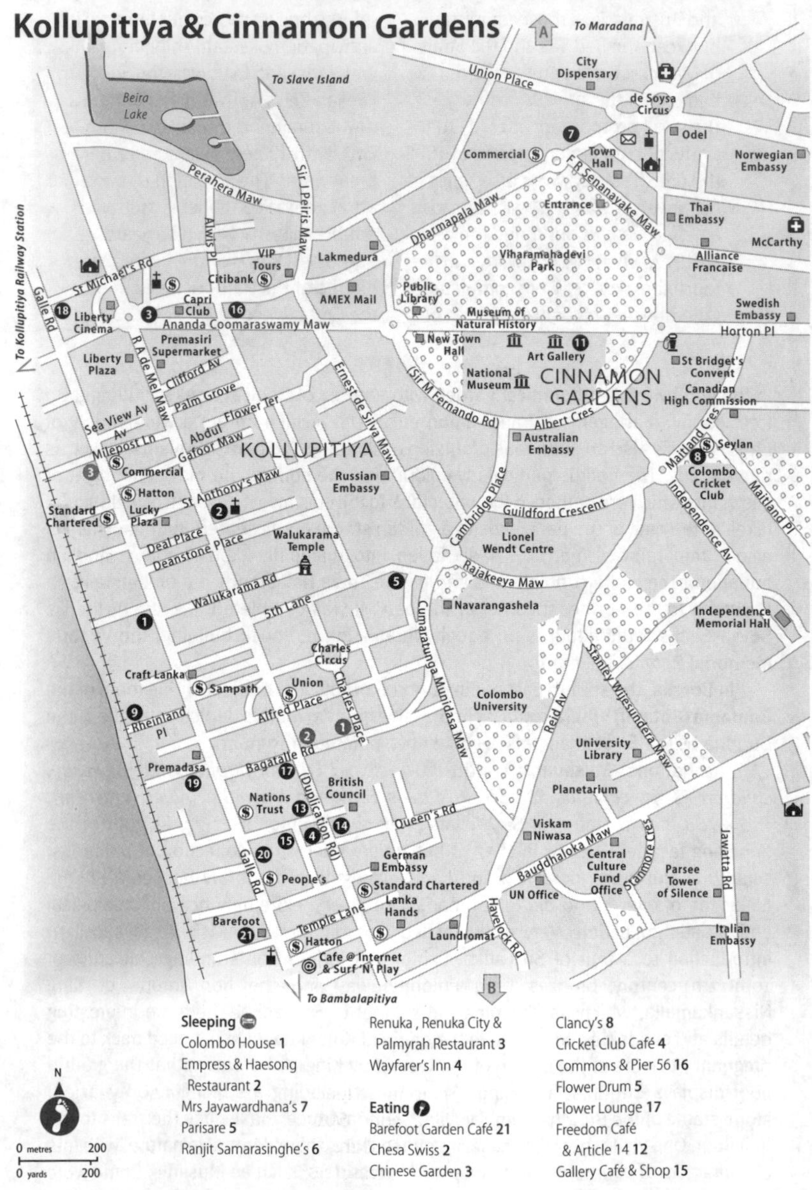

timber, tea and coconut (note the 13 different types), while there is also a collection of fossils found in Sri Lanka dating back to the Pleistocene age. The **National Art Gallery**, next door, a one-room collection by local artists, is disappointing.

Lionel Wendt Centre, ① *0900-1245 and 1400-1600, 19 Guildford Crescent,* a little further south, is a registered charity fostering the arts in Sri Lanka. Local artists are supported with temporary exhibitions, while there is a permanent exhibition of Wendt's pictures.

The well-presented **Bandaranaike Museum** ① *0900-1600, closed Mon and Poya holidays, Rs 3, Bauddhaloka Mawatha,* is housed inside the massive and imposing Bandaranaike Memorial International Conference Hall (BMICH), built by the Chinese government. As well as commemorating the life and times of the assassinated prime minister, with some interesting letters, diaries and personal effects on display, it offers a useful insight into Sri Lanka's steps into post-colonial nationhood. Opposite the BMICH is a replica statue of the Aukana Buddha.

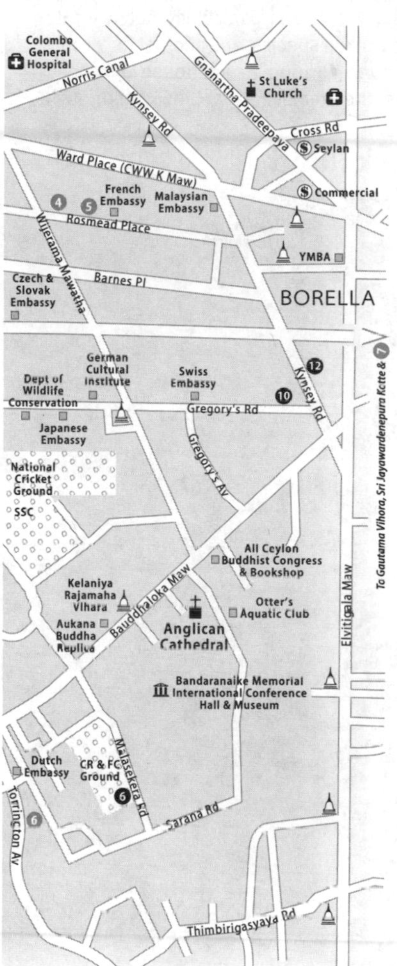

Green Cabin **20**
Le Palace **10**
Mandarin Palace **6**
Moshi Moshi **19**
Paradise Road **7**
Perera **18**
Queen's Café **14**
Sakura **9**
Summer Garden **11**
Thambapani **13**
The Fab **1**

South of the centre

Bambalapitiya and Havelock Town

South of Kollupitiya, Bambalapitiya extends south along Galle Road. This is a busy shopping area with two popular indoor malls at Majestic City and Liberty Plaza and some enticing eateries, but few interesting sights although the **Vajirarama Temple**, whose missionary monks have taken Buddhism to the west, is worth a look. To the east, south of Bauddhaloka Mawatha, **Havelock Road**, lined with some more excellent restaurants, is another traffic-filled thoroughfare, stretching south to Havelock Town. The **Isipathanaramaya Temple**, just north of Havelock Park, is famous for its beautiful frescoes.

Wellawatta and Dehiwala

South of Bambalapitiya, Wellawatta is the last busy suburb within the city limits. Home to many of Colombo's Tamils (and sometimes called 'Little Jaffna' as a result), it has a bustling charm away from the pretensions of wealthier suburbs further north.

Near the busy bazaar of Dehiwala, the **Subhodaramaya Temple** is a Buddhist complex with a shrine room dating from 1795. There is the usual *dagoba*, a Bo-tree and also a 'Seven-Week House' which illustrates the weeks following the Buddha's Enlightenment. There are several Buddha statues, some well preserved wall paintings and woodcarvings but the most arresting figure is the supremely serene 4.5 m reclining Buddha with eyes set in blue sapphires.

Dehiwala Zoo ⓘ *0830-1800, Rs 200 (foreigners), children Rs 100, video camera Rs 500 (professional Rs 1500), A Dharmapala Mawatha (Allan Ave), 10 km southeast from the centre, T2712751,* is one of the most attractive in Asia. Often very crowded on holidays. The 22 ha of undulating grounds is beautifully laid out with shrubs, flowering trees and plants, orchids, lakes and fountains. There are over 2,000 animals from all around the world, including big cats, crocodiles, bears and so on. The aquarium has over 500 species of fish. The zoo is particularly noted for its collection of birds – there is one aviary for Sri Lankan species, and another for 'exotic' (ie foreign) birds is planned. Sea-lions perform at 1600 and a troupe of trained elephants, around 1715. By Asian standards, the animals are well housed, though

Bambalapitiya & Havelock Road

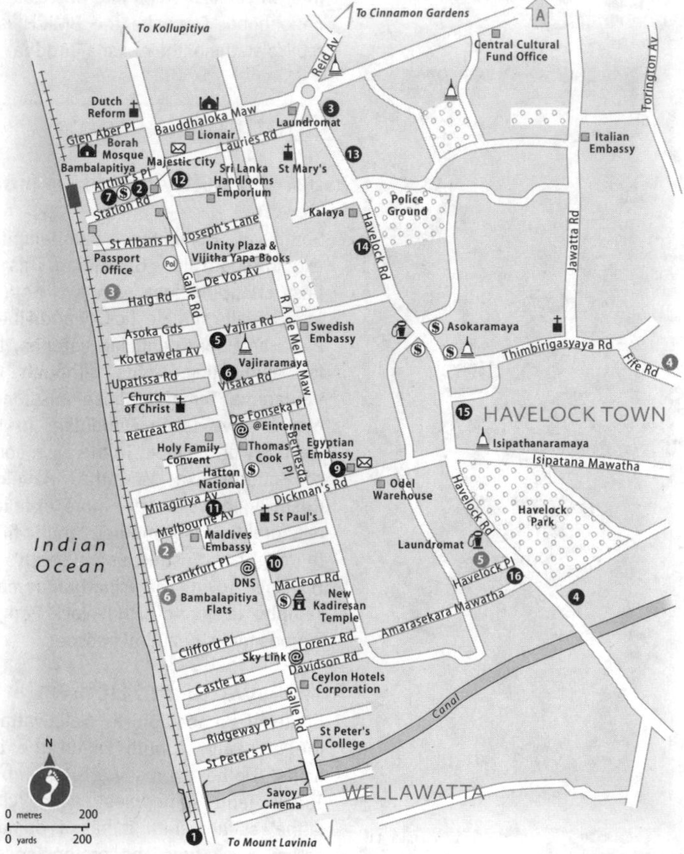

Sleeping
Havelock Bungalow **5**
Janaki **4**
Ottery Tourist Inn **2**
Sri Lanka Youth Council **3**
Westeern **6**

Eating
Beach Wadiya **1**
Caravan Bakery **10**
Chinese Dragon **11**
Curry Bowl & Perera **13**
Frangipani **14**
Hotel de Majestic **12**
Kinjou **16**
Malaysian Food Boutique **7**
Majesty City International Food Hall **2**
Mandarin Grill **15**
Mathura Madras Woodlands **4**
Sapid **5**
Saraswathie Lodge **6**
Shanti Vihar **3**
Sweet Chilli **9**

Slave Island

The high rise hotels and offices which have occupied the northward jutting peninsula in Beira Lake facing the fort now leave no trace of the earlier uses of what was known as Slave Island. 'Island' was a misnomer, but slaves played a very real part in the colonial history of Colombo.

During the Dutch period this tongue of open land was known as Kaffir Veldt. The Kaffirs – Africans from the East Coast around Mozambique – were brought to Sri Lanka for the first time by the Portuguese from Goa in 1630. When the Dutch ousted the Portuguese they made use of the slave labour force to build the fort in Colombo, when there may have been 4,000 of them. Their numbers grew, but after an unsuccessful insurrection in the 18th century the Dutch authorities decided to insist that all slave labour must be identifiably accommodated. The Kaffir Veldt was the nearest open space on which special shanty houses could be built, and a nightly roll call would be held to ensure that every slave was there.

By 1807, the number of slaves had fallen to 700, though the British did not abolish slavery in Sri Lanka until 1845. Nonetheless, the name Slave Island has persisted.

some, such as the big cats, have insufficient space. Partly to help ease this crowding, a new 36-acre site is planned near the Pinnawela Elephant Orphanage (see page 198). You can reach the zoo on bus Nos 100 or 155 to Dehiwala Junction and walk the last kilometre or take bus No 118. Trains also to Dehiwala Station.

Mount Lavinia → *12 km south of Fort. Many travellers choose to explore the city from here.*

Mount Lavinia is a pleasant place to stay away for those put off by the noise and congestion of the city. Once a fishing village, these days the drive along the busy Galle Road scarcely marks it apart from the rest of Colombo and the population has risen to around 220,000. The historic connection with British governors in the 19th century brings many seeking to sample something of that era in the famous **Mount Lavinia Hotel** here.

Some believe the town takes its name from a corruption of the Sinhalese 'Lihinia Kanda' – *gull rock*. The **Mount Lavinia Hotel** may contest the origins of the name. Their literature suggests that British Governor Sir Thomas Maitland established the original building on the headland here in 1806 for himself and his secret lover Lovina, an exotic and beautiful dancer of mixed Portuguese and Sinhalese race – hence the name. It is said that for seven years she trysted secretly with him by creeping through a tunnel connecting her garden to Maitland's wine cellar! Later, the original Mount Lavinia Hotel was Governor Edward Barnes' weekend retreat. He had the bungalow significantly extended in the 1820s ('Governor's Wing'), but was forced to sell it as the government in England approved neither of the expenditure nor his luxurious lifestyle.

Mount Lavinia is famous for its 'golden mile' of beach, from which the high-rise buildings of central Colombo are easily visible. The attractive colonial villas and lovely scent of frangipani and bougainvillea however mask a slightly seedier side. Easily accessible from the city, some of its cheaper guesthouses are used as brothels. Moreover, theft is more common than elsewhere and if visiting the beach do not take anything valuable with you.

The beach itself is cleanest south of **Mount Lavinia Hotel,** where it is 'private' for the use of the hotel residents only, although non-residents can pay for access as well as use of the pool. North of the hotel, it gets rather narrow and has a noticeable amount of litter especially at weekends and holidays. There are a number of bar/restaurant shacks here, mostly run by the hotels immediately behind them.

Hotels close to the beach are also close to the railway line, with trains passing at regular intervals from early morning to late at night, invariably using their horns to alert pedestrians on the track. Take care when crossing the railway en route to the beach.

Mount Lavinia

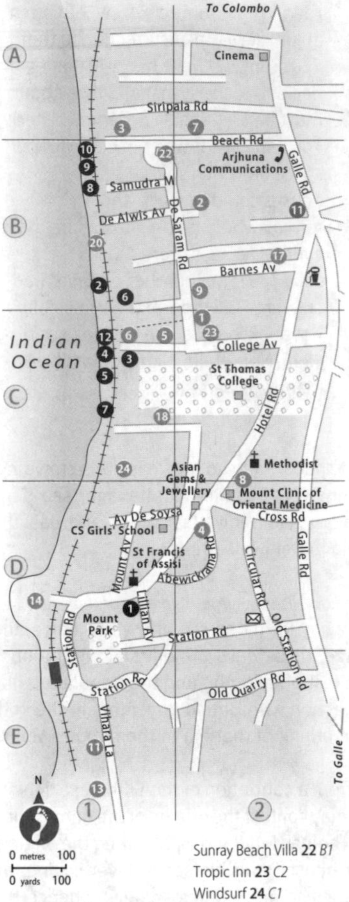

Sleeping
Berjaya Mount Royal Beach **6** *C1*
Beverley Hills & Hollywood Karaoke **1** *C2*
Blue Seas Guest House **2** *B2*
Cottage Gardens **5** *C1*
Green Shines **8** *C2*
Haus Chandra & Carrington Villa **3** *A1*
Ivory Inn **9** *B2*
Lak Mahal's Inn **11** *E1*
La Maison des Arts **7** *A2*
Mount Breeze Tourist Inn **13** *E1*
Mount Lavinia **14** *D1*
Ratna Inn **17** *B2*
Rivi Ras **18** *C1*
Sea Breeze **20** *B1*
Sunray Beach Villa **22** *B1*
Tropic Inn **23** *C2*
Windsurf **24** *C1*
YMCA **4** *D2*

Eating
Angler **1** *D1*
Beach shacks **2** *B1*
Boat Haus **10** *B1*
Connie's **3** *C1*
Fisherman's Villa **5** *C1*
Frankfurt Lavinia Beer Garden **6** *B1*
Golden Mile **4** *C1*
Happening **9** *B1*
La Langousterie **7** *C1*
La Lavinia **8** *B1*
Sea Spray Club **12** *C1*

Bars & clubs
Lion Pub **11** *B2*

North and east of the City

Kelaniya

Some 13 km northeast from Fort, across the Kelaniya River, is the **Raja Maha Vihara**, the most visited Buddhist temple in Sri Lanka after the Temple of the Tooth in Kandy. In the 13th century Kelaniya was an impressive city but for Buddhists its chief attraction today is the legendary visit of the Buddha to the site. The *Mahavansa* recorded that the original stupa enshrined a gem-studded throne on which the Buddha sat when he visited Sri Lanka. Ultimately destroyed by the Portuguese, the present *dagoba* is in the shape of a 'heap of paddy'. The first city on the site was believed to have been built by King Yatala Tissa. According to legend this was destroyed by a flood from the sea which was a punishment given to the king for mistreating the Buddhist *sangha*. He tried to placate the sea by setting his daughter afloat on a golden boat. Having drifted ashore in the south of the island she married King Kavan Tissa, and became the mother of one of Sri Lanka's great heroes, King Dutthagamenu. The city is subsequently believed to have been destroyed by Tamil invasions, and was only re-built in the 13th century by King Vijayabahu.

The present temple, which dates to the late 19th century, is set amongst attractive frangipani trees and has an impressive bell-tower. There is a famous image of the reclining Buddha, but there are also many images of Hindu deities. *Duruthu Perahera* each January draws thousands of pilgrims from all over the island. Take a Biyagama bus from Bastion Mawatha. They leave every half an hour and the trip takes 20-30 minutes.

Sri Jayawardenepura Kotte

Built in the shadow of the modern city of Colombo, most government offices have relocated in this new artificially planned capital 11 km southeast, but Colombo still retains its importance as the commercial capital. The decision to put the new 'Parliament' here was based partly on the fact that the site was formerly the almost sacred territory of Kotte, the ancient capital of Sri Lanka under Alakeswara who built a large fortress and defeated the Tamil leader Chakravarthi. Parakramabahu VI (ruled 1412-67) transformed the fortress into a prosperous modern city, building a magnificent three-storey temple to hold the Tooth relic which he had placed within several bejewelled gold caskets. However, subsequent weak rulers left the city relatively defenceless and it fell easy prey to the Portuguese. They destroyed the city so that there are no traces of its former glory left. Some panels from the old temple can be seen in the Colombo museum.

The impressive **Parliament Building** itself was designed by the renowned modern Sri Lankan architect Geoffrey Bawa, see box, page 367. It stands in the middle of a lake surrounded by parkland but is heavily fortified and not open to the public.

The **Gramodaya Folk Arts Centre** has craftsmen working with brass, silver, leather, coir and producing jewellery, pottery, natural silk, lace and reed baskets. There is a craft shop and a restaurant serving Sri Lankan specialities. Ask the tourist office for details.

The drive from Colombo's Fort area through the suburbs takes about 30 minutes. Buses run from the city or you can take a three-wheeler.

Sleeping

There are some very high quality hotels, mainly in Fort, Galle Face and Union Place, with luxurious rooms, first-class service, several restaurants, pool(s), bars, nightclub etc. Good quality mid-range accommodation however is rather thin on the ground. A good option for lower budgets is to stay at one of the many privately run guesthouses, especially in the southern suburbs. Sri Lanka Tourist Board's accommodation guide is a good source of information for these.

Close to the airport

Those arriving late or departing early may prefer to find a hotel close to the international airport at Katunayake (30 km north of Colombo). Another alternative is to stay at Negombo, some 6 km north of the airport, where the accommodation choice is much wider, see p104.

L **Taj Airport Garden**, *234 Negombo Rd, Seeduwa, 3.5 km from airport, T2252950, bizctr_1@airportgarden.com* Very attractive setting on lagoon (watersports possible), 120 rooms and suites, all with views, pool, plush and convenient

A-B **Tamarind Tree** (Jetwing), *1 Andiambalama Estate, Yatiyana, Minuwangoda (4 km from airport), T2254297, tamarind@eureka.lk* 22 a/c rooms, 35 self-catering apartments, attractive gardens, good pool, luxurious and well designed though service can be iffy.

C **Goodwood Plaza** and **Orient Pearl**, *Canada Friendship Rd, from terminal cross the road, and turn right towards Colombo, T2252356, hotelgoodwood@lanka.ccom.lk* 32 rooms in each, most a/c, twin hotels (former marginally better) with large rooms off long corridors, some refurbished to a good standard, reasonable restaurants, Colombo and Negombo buses pass the hotel, free airport transfer (driver may insist it is not free).

C-E **Airlink**, *580 Negombo Rd, Seeduwa, 5 km from airport towards Colombo, T2253607*. 16 simple rooms with bath, 8 a/c, 24-hr meals brought in. 12-hr and 24-hr rates available.

F **Mrs Pearl Jayatillake's**, *Minuwangoda Rd (5 km from airport), T2253031*. 3 simple rooms (Rs 500), meals on request.

Fort area and the Pettah

p71, map p72

There are several F and G hotels around Fort Railway Station though they are very basic.

L **Colombo Hilton**, *67 Lotus Rd, Echelon Sq, Col 1, T2344644, hilton@sri.lanka.net*

387 rooms fully refurbished, best views in the city, all facilities including 7 restaurants, sports, riding, nightclub (Rs 500 for non-members, ladies free), real sense of luxury.

AL Galadari, *64 Lotus Rd, Col 1, T2544544, F2449875 galadari@sri.lanka.net* 446 rooms with good views, all facilities, good nightclub.

A Ceylon Continental, *48 Janadhipathi Mawatha, Fort, Col 1, T2421221, hotel@ceylon continental.com* 250 fully equipped rooms with good views, good pool, open-air **Pearls seafood restaurant**, good bookshop.

A-B Grand Oriental, *2 York St, Fort, Col 1, T2320391, reserve@sltnet.lk* Colonial era hotel built to accommodate travellers arriving by sea and a Colombo legend (once advertised as "the largest and best equipped hotel in the East"), though faded now. Some rooms in need of renovation (ask for deluxe). Fascinating view of the docks from **Harbour Room** restaurant (no photos), nightclub (Fri and Sat Rs 300, ladies free), friendly staff.

F-G New Colonial, *opposite Fort Station, T232-3074*. 7 singles, 5 doubles, all common bath, fine for a night if catching an early train.

F-G YMCA (Central), *39 Bristol St, Fort, Col 1, T2325252*. 40 fairly clean rooms (Rs 450 common bath – 'filthy', Rs 700 attached), dorm (Rs 125), membership (returnable) Rs 350), cafeteria serving simple local food.

G Ex-Servicemen's Institute, *29 Bristol St, Fort, Col 1, T2422650*. 10-bed mixed dorm for foreigners only, Rs 200. Other rooms not recommended as they are often rented out to local couples by the hour; fans, safe, TV lounge/bar area, simple meals available.

Galle Face, Union Place and Beira Lake *p73, map p74*

LL-A Colombo Plaza (formerly **Oberoi**), *77 Steuart Place, off Galle Rd, Col 3, T2437437, F2449280*. 600 rooms in 2 wings including numerous luxury suites most with city views, some with sea or lake views. Beautiful, vast open spaces, all facilities, 2 restaurants, nightclub (Rs 350, ladies free), good pool (non-residents pay Rs 500).

AL Taj Samudra, *25 Galle Face Centre Rd, T2446622, taj@sri.lanka.net* Well situated overlooking Galle Face Green and the ocean, pleasant seating areas in lobby, attractive gardens behind, 315 comfortable rooms some with good views , 6 restaurants (excellent Chinese), nightclub (Thu, Fri and Sat Rs 250, ladies free). Good pool (non-residents against annual fee only), shops and friendly service.

AL Trans Asia, *115 Sir CA Gardiner Mawatha, Col 2, T2491000, tah_asia@sri.lanka.net* Slightly north of Galle Face in Slave Island, 358 rooms, 25 suites, 3 restaurants, superb food (try the lunchtime Sri Lankan buffet), excellent pool, nightclub, "exceptional".

A Holiday Inn, *30 Sir MM Markar Mawatha, Col 3, T2422001, holiday@sri.lanka.net* Modern hotel built in Moghul style. 94 reasonable rooms (US$90), executive floor, very good Mughlai food at Alhambra restaurant, large pool (open to non-residents).

A-B Galle Face Hotel, *2 Galle Rd, Col 3, T2541010, gfh@diamond.lanka.net* Originally built in 1864 and re-designed by Geoffrey Bawa (see box, p367), probably the most atmospheric place to stay in Colombo. Room price (some **L** suites) varies according to view, from none to ocean! Carefully maintained colonial atmosphere, with beautiful furniture. Friendly staff, 'superb' service, 30 m saltwater pool overlooking Indian Ocean (non- residents pay Rs 200), veranda bar best in Colombo for sunset drink, very competent travel desk.

C Nippon, *Manning Mansions, 123 Kumaran Ratnam Rd, Col 2, T2431887, F2332603*. Colonial style in attractive plant-lined colonnade. Spacious rooms, most with a/c. Bar and good Oriental restaurant.

D Lake Lodge, *20 Alwis Terrace, Col 3, T2326443, lakelodge@eureka.lk* 16 rooms with attached bath (Rs 1,650, a/c Rs 400 extra), good Sri Lankan food, breakfast included, quiet but complaints about cleanliness.

D YWCA International Guest House, *392 Union Place, Col 2, T2324181*. 20 rooms (Rs 1,340, breakfast included) in Dutch colonial mansion set in attractive gardens, accepts men, women and couples, large rooms with bath but a bit pricey, good meals available, friendly. Good fruit and spice garden.

Kollupitiya, Cinnamon Gardens and Borella *p74, map p76*

A-B Renuka & Renuka City, *328 Galle Rd, T2573598, renukaht@panlanka.net* Twin hotels with 80 comfortable a/c rooms (US$50-65), TV, fridge, IDD phone, 3 bars, pool, basement Palmyrah restaurant recommended for Sri Lankan curries.

C Empress, *383 RA de Mel Mawatha, Col 3, T2574930, haesong@sltnet.lk* 33 grubby a/c rooms with TV but good Korean restaurant, 24-hr internet facilities.

C-D Wayfarer's Inn, *77 Rosmead Place, Col 7, T2693936, wayfarer@slt.lk* 4 carpeted rooms (a/c US$20, non-a/c, US$16 including breakfast) with TV, tea making facilities, bath tubs and full kitchen facilities on request. Free swimming 5 mins walk away, restaurant, garden, table tennis, not as homely as other guesthouses though.

C-E Colombo House, *26 Charles Place, off Bagatelle Rd, Col 3, T2574900, colombohse@eureka.lk* Stylish 1939 mansion, 4 large rooms (Rs 950-1,450, a/c Rs 350 extra) with attached bath (2 with tub), some fine artwork (Picasso and George Keyts) and colonial furniture, handloom curtains, sunbathing terrace, email facilities, very quiet location. Recommended but reserve well in advance.

D Parisare, *97/1 Rosmead Place, Col 7 (no sign, next to UNHCR, ring on arrival), T2694749, sunsep@visualnet.lk* Exceptionally well-designed and beautiful house belonging to very welcoming and engaging couple, 3 extremely good value rooms, all with attached bath; best room (Rs 1,500) has 4 poster bed, bathtub, separate dressing room, desk, sofa and own (small) garden. 2 upstairs rooms (Rs 1,200) also excellent. Pleasant seating area with TV and roof-top sun terrace, all meals offered. Often booked up weeks in advance.

D Ranjit Samarasinghe's, *53/19 Torrington Ave, T/F2502403.* 3 rooms (Rs 1,500, a/c Rs 500 extra) in homely house with attractive terrace for (excellent) breakfasts. Ask about 3-room bungalow on edge of the city.

F Mrs Jayawardhana's, *42 Kuruppu Rd (off Cotta Rd), Col 8, T2693820.* 2 rooms (Rs 500-600) in charming family guesthouse owned by interesting older couple, library, garden, ideal for single females or long-stay visitors, meals on request, clean, good value.

Bambalapitiya and Havelock Town *p77, map p78*

A Havelock Bungalow, *6/8 Havelock Place, Col 5, T2585191, havelock.bungalow@mega.lk* Stylish designed modern house recently converted into luxury guesthouse. 6 suites (US$60), simple, beautiful individual furnishings, restaurant, gardens (some private), pool and jacuzzi. Homely and quiet.

C Janaki, *43 Fife Rd, Col 5, T2502169, F2589130, wim@sol.lk* 50 reasonable a/c rooms with TV and balcony, pool (open to non-residents).

C-D Westeern, *35 Frankurt Place, Col 4, T2507161, F2518481, info@hotelwesteern.com* 30 comfortable rooms (Rs 1,320, a/c Rs 220 extra), plus 5 suites with hot water, TV (up to Rs 2,475) in recently upgraded hotel by the sea (and railway line).

E-F Ottery Tourist Inn, *29 Melbourne Ave (off Galle Rd), Col 4, T2583727.* 8 large rooms, some with balcony, in colonial building (Rs 600-800), breakfasts, snooker table, rather run down but quiet location, friendly and helpful owner.

F-G Sri Lanka Youth Council, *50 Haig Rd, Col 4, T2581028, youthrights@visualnet.lk* 18-bed male dorm, 12-bed female dorm, bunk beds (Rs 125 with IYHF/ISIC cards, Rs 100 without), 1 triple with attached bath (Rs 500), kitchen facilities for self-caterers, maximum 3-day stay (flexible), internet, can get crowded but friendly and cheap.

Wellawatta and Dehiwala

p77, map p70

B Sapphire, *371 Galle Rd, Col 6, T2583306, sapphire@slt.lk* Ugly building but 40 comfortable a/c rooms, attached bath (TV and fridge available), rooftop Chinese restaurant, private beach **La Lavinia** restaurant, bar.

C Omega Inn, *324 Galle Rd, Col 6, T2582277, omegainn@pan.lk* 10 comfortable rooms with TV (a/c US$27.50, non-a/c US$17), **Regency Pub** next door, but noisy.

E-F Big John Guest House, *47 Albert Place, Dehiwala (by railway line; from Colombo take the first right after the 'wedding cake' church), T2715027, F2580108, bigjohn@slt.lk* 17 clean rooms with bath and fan (Rs 700-800), upstairs with balcony, close to (unappealing) beach, Chinese food available.

Mount Lavinia *p79, map p80*

AL-B Mount Lavinia, *102 Hotel Rd, T271-5221, lavinia@sri.lanka.net* Renovated and extended former governors' weekend retreat located on a small but prominent headland retaining a rich colonial atmosphere. 275 rooms, refurbished 'Sea' and 'Garden' wings plus 'Bay Wing' (US$90-110), good value non -a/c rooms in Governor's Wing (US$50) retaining olde worlde ambience, a 'must-stay'. Huge public areas and labyrinthine corridors, all facilities, range of restaurants, terrace bar (good for sunset drinks), nightclub (see Bars and clubs), shopping arcade, sports including tennis/mini golf, pool table, elephant rides (Sun 1000-1400), impressive terrace pool (non-residents Rs 300, Sun Rs 600 including brunch), peaceful private beach (cleaner than public beach to the north).

A-B Haus Chandra & Carrington Villa, *37 Beach Rd, T2730236, F2733173*. 28 small a/c rooms plus 5 suites and 1 excellent **AL** villa for 6 people (US$125) with piano, restaurants (on rooftop plus cheaper food at **Boat Haus Café** on beach), small but deep pool (non-residents Rs 115), acupuncture school on the first of every month, chauffeur-driven Rolls Royce available for hire! Ask about excellent hotels in Kitulgala.

B Berjaya Mount Royal Beach, *36 College Av, T2739610, berjaya@slt.lk* 95 large a/c rooms in comfortable resort hotel, private balconies, restaurants, pool (non-residents Rs 200), Sea Spray club, sloppy service though.

C Cottage Gardens, *42-48 College Av, T2719692, aquila@eureka.lk* 5 fully equipped bungalows with kitchenette (US$20) set in quiet, attractive garden, friendly, good value, available for monthly rental (Rs 30,000).

C Rivi Ras, *50/2 De Saram Rd, T2717786, rivirasph@eureka.lk* 50 rooms and suites, some non-a/c slightly cheaper in 2 storey villas with verandas set in attractive garden, some cheaper thatched huts, excellent **La Langousterie** seafood restaurant on beach.

Some of the cheaper guesthouses in Mount Lavinia (excluding those that are family run) are used as brothels

C Sea Breeze, *22/5a De Saram Rd, T2714017, F2733077*. 20 clean rooms (some a/c) with balcony, beach cabanas, bar, restaurant.

C-D Beverley Hills, *27 de Saram Rd, T2733555, bhills@eureka.lk* New ownership, 10 well laid out rooms, some a/c (US$15-25), very clean, Korean and Sri Lankan food, bar, beer garden, karaoke.

C-D La Maison des Arts, *20 Beach Rd, T2716203, pitupavel@dialogsl.net* Run by a French film director, an engagingly eccentric 'house of arts' with own mini-theatre and cinema. Charming villa, richly and colourfully decorated (eg a violet temple!) in a (mishmash) North Indian style, handmade furnishings, beautiful airy rooms, some a/c (Rs 1,500-1,800) with 4-poster beds. Recommended for those with artistic leanings.

D Ivory Inn, *21 De Saram Rd, T2715006*. 12 reasonable rooms with balcony (Rs 1,200 including breakfast), attractive garden front restaurant, open bar area, popular.

D Ratna Inn, *8 Barnes Av, T2716653, F273-2493*. 12 rooms with verandas, 2 a/c (non a/c Rs 1,200) in large colonial house, slightly dark and gloomy but quiet and friendly.

D Windsurf, *15a De Soysa Av, T/F2732299*. 15 large, simple rooms, clean, restaurant, rooftop beer garden, friendly, good value.

D-E Tropic Inn, *6 College Av, T2738653, F2344657*. 16 a/c and non-a/c rooms, sizes vary so check first, breakfast included, helpful management.

E Blue Seas Guest House, *9/6 De Saram Rd, T2716298*. 12 good clean rooms (US$9 including breakfast) in family run guest-house, quiet location, very friendly.

E Mount Breeze Tourist Inn, *38 Vihara Rd, T2718943*. 6 good sized, clean rooms in family guesthouse, rooftop garden, very friendly and interesting retired owner, meals on request, good value.

E Sunray Beach Villa, *3 De Saram Rd, T2716272*. 3 rooms with private entrances in family home (US$10 including breakfast), attached bath, quiet, friendly and knowledgeable, better for the mature visitor, discounts for singles, meals on request.

E-F Green Shines, *49 Hotel Rd, T4208487*. 5 simple rooms with attached bath (Rs 750-1,000) in private house, meals on request, friendly.

F Lak Mahal's Inn, *8 Vihara Lane*. Good value rooms with fan, attached bath, good rooftop restaurant, quiet and friendly.

G YMCA, *55 Hotel Rd, T2713786*. 7 rooms with attached bath (Rs 300, long-stay Rs 5,000 per month), tennis and badminton courts, restaurant planned. Very good value.

Eating

There are many excellent places to eat in Colombo. As well as Sri Lankan and Indian fare, most other types of Asian cuisine are very popular with Thai, Japanese, Korean and even Mongolian restaurants in particular popping up all over the place to add to ubiquitous Chinese offering.

Some of the best speciality restaurants are to be found in the upper category hotels, which also serve good western food. Their eat-all-you-want buffets are particularly recommended at lunchtime (Rs 400-600 plus tax), where you have the added benefit of sitting in cool comfort during the hottest part of the day. American/European-style venues are also becoming increasingly popular, particularly the 'Irish' pub.

For those on a tighter budget, lunch packets – available from street stalls all over the city – are a good idea. These normally comprise rice plus a meat, fish or vegetable curry, and cost Rs 50-80.

Fort area and the Pettah *p71, map p72*

RsRsRs **Crab Claw**, *Galadari Hotel, 64 Lotus Rd*, for Chinese.
RsRsRs **Harbour Room**, *Grand Oriental, 2 York St*, serves unexceptional food but the views over the harbour are spectacular.
RsRsRs **Il Ponte**, **Ginza Hohsen** and **Curry Leaf** restaurants, *Colombo Hilton.*
For 1st-class Italian, Japanese and Sri Lankan.
RsRs **Great Wall**, *77 Chatham St, Fort, Col 1.* Chinese, offers reasonable lunchtime set menus from Rs 200.
RsRs **Seafish**, *15 Sir CA Gardiner Mawatha, just behind Regal Cinema, Col 2, T2326915.* Excellent fish at reasonable prices, hoppers with curry (evenings).
Rs Lots of cheap 'rice and curry' places in Fort, the Pettah and along Galle Rd.
Rs **Crown's**, *next to Laksala, 54 York St (basement), 0630-1830.* South Indian style vegetarian, simple but good, friendly, cheap.
Rs **Pagoda**, *Chatham St, Fort, Col 1*, offers good value Chinese (main dishes Rs 50-95) plus Sri Lankan and Western.
Rs **Taj**, *54 York St, T2422812, 0700-2300.* Popular with local office workers at lunchtime, cheap rice and curry, kotthu rotty, short eats, a/c upstairs.
Rs **YMCA**, see Sleeping, has very cheap authentic Sri Lankan food, self-service.

Cafés

Barista, *3rd floor, World Trade Centre, Col 1, Mon-Fri 0800-2000, Sat 1100-1600.* Western-style coffee madness comes to Sri Lanka (via India). Cappuccinos, lattes etc, pastries and snacks for local office workers. Also branch next to **Galle Face Hotel**.
The luxury hotels in Fort and Galle Face have 24-hr coffee shops.

Galle Face, Union Place and Beira Lake *p73, map p74*

City dwellers take in the sea air on Galle Face Green while eating out off the street vendors.
RsRsRs **German Restaurant**, *11 Galle Face Court 2 (opposite Galle Face Hotel), Col 3, T2421577, 1800-0000.* German specialities in big portions, draught German beer on tap. Happy Hour 1800-1900.
RsRsRs **Golden Dragon**, *Taj Samudra, T2446622.* Excellent and moderately priced Chinese.
RsRsRs **Koluu's**, *32b MM Markar Mawatha (next to Holiday Inn), T2446589.* Wide and innovative menu of Asian fusion dishes, great desserts, 'heaps of atmosphere'.
RsRsRs **Molly's Irish Pub**, *46/38 Nawam Mawatha, Col 2, T2543966.* Western food including Irish specialities (main courses Rs 370-595, salads Rs 200-250). See also Bars and clubs, p88.
RsRsRs **Sea Spray**, Galle Face Hotel. Good seafood and western dishes in one of the city's most atmospheric locations.
RsRs **A1 Chinese**, *157 Galle Rd Col 3, T2332345.* Good Chinese.
RsRs **Raja Bojun**, *Seylan Towers, Galle Rd, Col 3, T4716171, 1200-2300.* Excellent lunchtime Sri Lankan buffet overlooking the ocean. Huge variety, very reasonably priced.
Rs **Crescat Food Court**. Not the most authentic surroundings (self-service in western-style shopping mall basement) but a good way to sample a wide range of Asian cuisines.

Rs Fountain Café, *1 Justice Akhbar Mawatha (Bridge St) opposite Kompanna station, Col 2, 1100-1830*. Excellent Sri Lankan dishes, full meal for under Rs 200; also European food.
Rs Rangiri, *67 Union Place, Col 2*. Eye-watering but tasty Sri Lankan curry plus full range of sambols for Rs 130. Friendly and popular with locals.
Rs Rohan's, *199 Union Place, Col 2, T2302679*. A branch of the North Indian chain popular with families. Also serves western food and juices for Rs 75.
Rs YWCA has very cheap authentic Lankan food, self-service.

Kollupitiya, Cinnamon Gardens and Borella *p74, map p76*

RsRsRs Chesa Swiss, *3 Deal Place, off RA de Mel Mawatha, Col 3, T2573433, 1900-2300*. Excellent Swiss food, though at a price (Rs 1,500+).
RsRsRs Cricket Club Café, *34 Queen's Rd (near British Council), Col 3, T2501384, 1100-2300*. International range of dishes, many named after famous cricketers (such as Murali's Mulligatawny or Gatting's Garlic Prawns), in a cricket-lover's heaven, though shows other sports on TV too. Local and touring teams usually visit. Good bar very popular with ex-pats.
RsRsRs Gallery Café, *2 Alfred House Rd, Col 3, T2582162, 1000-2200*. Once the office of famed Sri Lankan architect Geoffrey Bawa, see p367, (his old work table is still there), exclusive setting with unbeatable ambience, minimalist chic décor, good fusion food (black pork curry Rs 495, salmon with tuna aioli Rs 885), fabulous (chocolately) desserts, excellent wine list. Book in advance.
RsRsRs Moshi Moshi, *594/2 Galle Rd (3rd floor), Col 3, T2500312, 1100-0300*. Authentic Japanese, pricey though plentiful. Karaoke as well for full Japanese experience.
RsRsRs Le Palace, *79 Gregory's Rd, Col 7, T2695920, gegroup@sltnet.lk, 0700-0030*. Fine dining in beautiful colonial mansion (eg lobster and white wine soufflé Rs 525, escargots Rs 1,250, duck à l'orange Rs 825), good but very expensive wines, breakfast available and excellent patisseries too, so can drop in just for a drink. One of Colombo's most exclusive eating experiences.
RsRs Chinese Garden, *32 Dharmapala Mawatha, Col 3, 1200-1500, 1800-2100*. Wide range of Chinese dishes priced by size (Rs 105-400), unimpressive exterior and a bit grubby but popular with locals (may have to wait for table).
RsRs Clancy's, *29 Maitland Crescent, Col 7, overlooking Colombo Cricket Club, T2682945, 1100-0300*. Serves good western food. Snack menu plunders the names of Ireland's finest, from Bernard Shaw (chicken wings) to Ronan Keating's golden prawns (Rs 330). Main menu has meat and seafood platters for Rs 590. See also Bars and clubs, p89.
RsRs Flower Drum, *26 Thurstan Rd, Col 3, T2574216*. Excellent Chinese, extensive choice, quiet atmosphere, reasonable prices.
RsRs Flower Lounge, *18 Bagatelle Rd, Col 3, T2593032, 1130-1500, 1830-2300*. Good range of Chinese in salubrious surroundings.
RsRs Green Cabin, *453 Galle Rd, Col 3, T2588811, 1000-2300*. Good value authentic Sri Lankan food (curry and string hoppers) in pleasant surroundings owned by former Test cricketer Aravinda de Silva.
RsRs Haesong, Hotel Empress. Good Korean and Chinese food in stylish Japanese surroundings.
RsRs Palmyrah, Hotel Renuka, *0700-2200*, is widely praised for its Sri Lankan food.
RsRs Pier 56, *1st Floor, 74a Dharmapala Mawatha, Col 3, T2576509 (above The Commons Café), 1900-2300*. Good sushi and seafood in glass tank heaven.
RsRs Queen's Café, *417 RA de Mel Mawatha, Col 3, T2508345, 1100-0000 (closed Fri lunch-time)*. Indian and Chinese, curries, tandooris, snacks, plus milkshakes and juices, not much atmosphere but a/c and good value, pool lounge upstairs.
RsRs Sakura, *14 Rheinland Place, Col 3, T2573877, 1130-1400, 1730-0000*. Good Japanese.
RsRs Thambapani, *496/1 RA de Mel Mawatha, Col 3, T2500615, 1130-0000*. Upmarket and stylish with a 'Dry Zone' theme, interesting menu from across the island (eg Jaffna favourite Perattu rice, Rs 350), seafood a speciality, two dining rooms, attractive garden restaurant lit by oil torches and lanterns or colourful bar with modern paintings and batiks; art gallery too.
Rs Mandarin Palace, *near rugby and football grounds, Malalasekera Maw, Col 7, T2587740, 1130-1500, 1830-0000*. Wide range of good,

cheap Chinese in pleasant surroundings. Branch on Havelock Rd.

Rs Summer Garden, *110 Green Path, off A Coomaraswamy Mawatha, Col 7, 1030-2300*, has a selection of cheap Sri Lankan and Chinese dishes (fish curry Rs 65) in an open air setting, handy for museums.

Cafés

Barefoot Garden Café, *706 Galle Rd, Col 3, T2553075, 1000-1900 daily*. Wonderfully chic terrace café serving light meals, sandwiches (from Rs 250) and cakes in frangipani gardens next to bookshop and art gallery.

The Commons, *74a Dharmapala Mawatha, Col 7, T2574384, Mon-Fri 1000-1800 (open 1100 at weekends)*. Flavoured coffees (excellent frappuccinos), juices and snacks (bagels, wraps etc).

The Fab, *474 Galle Rd, Col 3, T2573348, 0800-2000*. Excellent patisserie.

Freedom Café, *155a Kynsey Rd, Col 8, T2681282, 1100-2100*. Stylish new place for coffee and cakes, also serves reasonably priced light dishes (eg wraps, burgers).

Paradise Road Café, *213 Dharmapala Mawatha, Col 7, T2686043, 1000-1900*. Beautiful old colonial mansion open daytime for light meals and drinks.

Perera, *17 Galle Rd, Col 3, T2323295*, for cakes, snacks, breads, mainly takeaway. Other branches around the city, off Pieris Maw, Col 2, and on Havelock Rd.

Bambalapitiya and Havelock Town *p77, map p78*

RsRsRs Frangipani, *126 Havelock Rd, Col 5, T2580678, 1200-0000*. A/c dining area or open air pavilion, excellent Mon-Fri rice and curry buffet lunch (Rs 400).

RsRs Chinese Dragon, *11 Milagiriya Ave, Col 4, T2503637, 1100-1500, 1800-2300*. Long-established local favourite, outside barbecues as well.

RsRs International Food Hall, Majestic City (basement), *Bambalapitiya, Col 4*. Great place to try out a range of different cuisines.

RsRs Kinjou, *33 Amarasekera Mawatha (off Havelock Rd), Col 5, T2589477, 1130-1430, 1830-2300*. Good Szechuan cooking in plush Japanese surroundings. Ask here about accommodation at Uda Walawe and Wagomuwa national parks.

RsRs Mandarin Grill, *117 Havelock Rd, Col 5*. A/c, rice and curry, Mongolian BBQ, Lankan rice and curry, string hoppers and kotthu, cheap lunch packets, night café.

RsRs Sweet Chilli, *2 RA de Mel Mawatha, Col 4, T2583901*. Halal, mainly Chinese in plush a/c surroundings, lunchtime buffets, pastry shop.

Rs Curry Bowl, *Havelock Rd, T2575157, 1000-2200*. Dosai and string hoppers, *Perera* bakers attached, takeaway available.

Rs Hotel de Majestic, *17 Galle Rd, Col 4 (opposite Majestic City), T5377760*. String hoppers and superb Pakistani and Singaporean curries.

Rs Malaysian Food Boutique, *Station Rd, Col 4, T2590581*. Packed with locals at lunchtime for excellent value curries and lunch packets.

Rs Mathura Madras Woodlands, *185 Havelock Rd, Col 5, T2582909, 1100-2300*. A/c, choice of good North and South Indian cuisine, good value lunch time buffets.

Rs Sapid, *junction off Vajira/Galle Rd, Col 4, 0600-2200*, offers very cheap 'hole in the wall' Chinese, Sri Lankan and Western dishes (halal meat), restaurant and pastry shop too.

Rs Saraswathie Lodge, *191 Galle Rd, Col 4, T2575226, 0700-2200*. Cheap vegetarian Sri Lankan food.

Rs Shanti Vihar, *3 Havelock Rd, Col 5, T2580224, 1200-1500, 1900-2200*. Good, simple 'Indian' veg food, *thalis* (Rs82) and *dosas* (Rs 75), buffet lunch and dinner.

Wellawatta and Dehiwala
p77, map p70

RsRs Beach Wadiya, *2 Station Ave, Col 6, T2588568, 1200-2300* (see map page 78). Very popular beach- side seafood restaurant, well-stocked bar, rustic surroundings, good food (grilled prawns Rs 375) but small portions and service can be slow.

Rs Caravan, *73/22 Saranankara Place, Sri Saranankara Rd, Dehiwala, 0600-2200*, is an excellent patisserie, various branches around town, including Galle Rd, Col 4.

Rs Shanmugas, *53/3 Ramakrishna Rd, Col 6, near Roxy Cinema, T2587629, 1100-2200*. Good a/c South Indian vegetarian restaurant boasting 15 varieties of dosai, plus some North Indian specialities, civilized atmosphere, close to beach.

Mount Lavinia *p79, map p80*

Most hotels and guesthouses in Mount Lavinia have a restaurant, though many serve fairly bland food (family guesthouses and private houses tend to be the exception, although lunch and dinner should be ordered in advance). Breakfast is often included. Most hotel restaurants are only open for breakfast, lunch and dinner. For other times head for the beach shacks which are open all day. Seafood is, naturally enough, the speciality. Restaurants on the beach tend to be quite expensive, but the views at sunset are magnificent.

RsRsRs **Governor's Restaurant**, *Mount Lavinia Hotel*, atmospheric colonial surroundings.

RsRsRs **Seafood Cove**, *also at Mount Lavina Hotel*, excellent seafood in great beachside position. Lunch US$11, dinner US$12.

RsRsRs **Frankfurt Lavinia Beer Garden**, *34/8 De Saram Rd.* German specialities, foreign and local beers plus a wide range of European and world wines.

RsRsRs **Golden Mile**, *43/14 Mount Beach (off College Av), T2733997.* Attractive timber constructed beachside restaurant, wide menu from around the world (lobster thermidor Rs 725, 'Aussie steak' Rs 825), expensive but atmospheric.

RsRsRs **La Langousterie** (part of Ravi Ras Hotel). One of the best for seafood.

RsRs **The Angler**, *71 Hotel Rd.* Family run, also 4 **E** rooms and apartment to let. Good Sri Lankan, Chinese and Western dishes.

RsRs **Boat Haus**, *Haus Chaudra*, tables in the sand, delicious seafood, pizzas and snacks.

RsRs **Connie's**, *College Rd.* Good Sri Lankan dishes, seafood, pizzas and pastas, cheaper than most; plus breakfast (Continental or Sri Lankan).

RsRs **Fisherman's Villa**, *College Av.* Reasonably priced Thai and Chinese, and recommended for barbecued seafood, service is friendly if occasionally inept.

RsRs **The Happening**, *43 A/1 Beach Rd.* Freshly caught seafood with the sea lapping at your feet!

Bars and clubs → *Some bars open until 0300, or even later.*

Once the preserve of the big hotels, new bars are opening up around the city all the time. Since drinking alcohol in Sri Lanka remains a predominantly male preserve, some of the older affairs may feel a little uncomfortable for some women, but the newer plusher bars possess a broader appeal Almost all **AL**, **A** and **B** hotels have pleasant, if expensive bars (local beer Rs 200+ for 625 ml, imported European and American brands upwards of Rs 350). On *poya* days alcohol is not generally available until midnight. The nightclub scene is largely restricted to top category hotels, most impose a hefty cover charge on non-residents at weekends (Rs 300-500, ladies often free) and expensive drinks (local beer Rs 200+). Some have early evening 'Happy Hours', though few get going much before midnight.

Fort, Galle Face and Union Place *p71, map p72*

Bars A sunset drink overlooking the sea at the Galle Face is a must.

Echelon Pub, *Colombo Hilton, 1100-0230.* Smarter than most.

Glow Bar, *3rd floor, AA Building, 42 Sir MM Markar Mawatha, Col 3.* Cocktails, fusion food and eclectic mix of music.

Kiss Kiss Bar at Koluu's (see page 85). Described as 'Vegas meets Swiss ski cabin', the height of kitsch (red neon lips behind the bar), popular with pre-clubbers.

Molly's Irish Pub, *1030-0330. Happy Hour 1730-1930*, local beers from Rs 220, pitchers Rs 630, Guinness (Rs 290) only canned, decent wine and cocktails, and MTV, DJs and pub quiz on Tue.

White Horse Inn, *2 Navam Mawatha, Col 2, T2304922.* Fairly inexpensive drinks, busy at weekends, otherwise quiet.

Sri Lanka Ex-Serviceman's Institute in Fort serves very cheap beer.

Clubs The following are hotel nightclubs.

Blue Elephant, *Colombo Hilton, 67 Lotus Rd.*

Blue Leopard, *Grand Oriental, 2 York St.*

The Boom, *Galadari Hotel, 64 Lotus Rd*, is rated highly.

Cascades, *Colombo Plaza, off Galle Rd.*

The Library, *Trans Asia*. Members and hotel guests only.
MKOP (My Kind of Place), *Tuj Samudra*.

Kollupitiya and Cinnamon Gardens *p74, map p76*

Bars Clancy's serves Draught Lion and Carlsberg (Rs 130), Happy Hour 1800-2000. Bands most nights, cover charge Rs 300-500.
Cricket Club Café serves draught Carlsberg by the pint (Rs 150) or Guinness (Rs 175), with a good selection of wines, good atmosphere, very popular with ex-pats.
Frangipani is where colonial meets retro. Psychedelic bar in colonial house, high ceilings and fuschia lights, good cocktail range.
Gallery Bar is an open-air (stone) bar in courtyard, very chic, cocktails Rs 485-900.

Mount Lavinia *p79, map p80*

The more expensive hotels often provide live music over dinner, especially at weekends. Almost all restaurants serve alcohol.
Bars Mount Lavinia Hotel for the terrace bar, probably the best setting for an end of day drink (although the beach bars will provide a cheaper option to enjoy the sunset).
Lion Pub, *corner of Galle and Beach rds*. You enter through a big lion's mouth, food nothing special but bar and gardens 'weird and wonderful'.
Clubs The Hut, *Mount Lavinia Hotel, has nightclub open Weds-Sun (2100-0200, till 0400 on Fri and Sat)*. A local, friendly crowd (Rs 1,000 'per couple', with 2 free drinks).
Hollywood Karaoke, *Beverley Hills Hotel, 1900-0130*.

Entertainment → *Karaoke is very popular in Colombo.*

Casinos

Bally's, *14 Dharmapala Maw, Col 3, 24 hrs*.
MGM Grand Club, *772 Galle Rd, Bambalapitiya, Col 4, T2502268, 1800-0500*. Offers banco, blackjack, roulette, baccarat, has VIP 'foreigners only' lounge.
Ritz Club, *5 Galle Face Terrace, Col 3 (behind Holiday Inn)*.

Cinemas

Films in English tend to be dire action or edited 'adult' films though the selection is beginning to improve. Check the *Leisure Times* for details.
Empire, *51 Braybrooke Place, Col 2, T2323250*.
Liberty, *35 Dharmapala Mawatha, Col 3*.
Majestic, *Level 4, Majestic City, Col 4*.
Regal, *8 Sir Chittamapalam Mawatha, Col 2*.
Savoy, *12 Savoy Building, Col 6, T2552877*, recently refurbished and more pleasant than most of the others.
Alternatively films are also shown at **Alliance Française**, **British Council** and **American Center**. See below for addresses.

Cultural shows

Some top hotels put on regular folk dance performances (also western floor shows/live music for dancing); open to non-residents.
YMBA Hall, *Borella, Navarangashala, C Munidasa Mawatha, Col 7*, for performances of Sinhala dance and music.
Lionel Wendt Centre, *19 Guildford Crescent, Col 7, T2695794*, for performances of Sinhala dance and music.
Lumbini Hall, *Havelock Town*, specializes in Sinhalese theatre.

Theatres

Lionel Wendt Centre, see above, has both western and local productions, and occasional classical music concerts. Box office 1000-1200, 1400-1700.
Tower Hall Theatre Foundation, *'Sausiripaya', 123 Wijerama Mawatha, Col 7, T2687993*.
Theatre Information Centre, *adjoining Elphinstone Theatre, Maradana, Col 10, T2433635*.

For an explanation of the sleeping and eating price codes used in this guide, see the inside front cover.

Festivals and events

Jan *Duruthu Perahera*, Kelaniya Temple, a 2-day festival with caparisoned elephants, acrobats and floats.
Feb *Navam Maha Perahera*, Gangaramaya Temple, celebrates the full-moon with processions around Beira Lake-Viharam ahadevi Park area. A large number of elephants, torch-bearers, drummers, dancers, acrobats, stilt walkers and pilgrims take part.

Shopping

Most shops are open 1000-1900 on weekdays and 0845-1500 on Sat, though tourist shops will be open for longer and sometimes on Sun. You can shop with confidence at government run shops although it is interesting to wander in the bazaars and look for good bargains. Shops in Fort tend to be good but more expensive than equally good quality items in Kollupitiya. Boutiques in the Pettah are worth a visit too. The top hotels have good shopping arcades selling quality goods but prices are often higher than elsewhere.

Bazaars

Sunday Bazaar, Main St, the Pettah and Duke St, Fort.

Bookshops

Colombo has plenty of good bookshops, especially along Galle Rd in Kollupitiya.
Barefoot, see Handlooms and handicrafts below, has an excellent selection with good coverage of Sri Lanka and books on design, photography, architecture and modern fiction, as well as cards and postcards.
Bookland, *430-432 Galle Rd, Col 3, T4714444.*
Buddhist Book Centre with branches at Buddhist Information Centre, *380 Sarana Rd (off Bauddhaloka Maw), Col 7, T2689786.*
Buddhist Cultural Centre, *125 Anderson Rd, Nedimala, Dehiwala, T2726234, bcc@sri.lanka.net Daily 0830-1730 including Poya and public holidays.*
Cultural Bookshop, *Ananda Cooraswam Mawatha, Col 7 (next to Art Gallery)*, has a wide selection.
Lakehouse, *100 Sir CA Gardiner Mawatha, Col 2, booklhb@sltnet.lk*. Branch upstairs at Liberty Plaza. Very good range.
MD Gunasena, *217 Olcott Mawatha, Col 11, T2323981, mdgunasena@mail.ewisl.net*, is the largest bookshop in Sri Lanka. Also branch at 27 Galle Rd, Col 4.
Odel (see below), good selection of books in English, especially lifestyle and cookery.
Sarasavi, *30 Stanley Thilakaratne Mawatha, Nugegoda, T2852519, sarasavi@slt.lk* Branches at YMBA Buildings in Fort and Borella.
Serendib, *36 Rosmead Place, Col 7.* Antiquarian books and maps.
Survey Department, *York St, Col 1, T2435328.* Maps of Colombo and Sri Lanka.
Vijitha Yapa, *Unity Plaza, Col 3, T2596960, vijiyapa@sri.lanka.net* Recommended for range. Branches at *Crescat, T5510100 and 32 Thurstan Rd, Col 3.*

Boutique shops

'Lifestyle' shops are becoming increasingly popular with Colombo's wealthy elite, and some high-quality gifts can be picked up amongst them.
Article 14, *downstairs from Freedom Café, Col 8, 1000-1900.* Well-crafted, chic furniture and gifts ideas.
Barefoot, see Handlooms and handicrafts .
Kalaya, *116 Havelock Rd.* Designer home store.
Paradise Rd, *213 Dharmapala Mawatha, Col 7*, also **Gallery Shop** at **Gallery Café** (*1000-2230*). Kitchen accessories, candles, beautiful leather diaries, address books etc, well-made sarongs.

Clothes

Textiles represent Sri Lanka's biggest industry, and clothes made here are exported to major brand names around the world. Very cheap clothes can be found in the Pettah, though don't buy off street stalls.
Barefoot, see Handlooms and handicrafts

below, has beautiful handmade cotton and silk sarongs, dresses, skirts, bags etc.
Cotton Collection, *40 Ernest de Silva Mawatha, Col 7*.
French Corner, *24 Hyde Park Corner, Col 2*.
House of Fashions, *28 RA de Mel Mawatha, Col 3*, is cheaper still and popular with locals.
Odel, see Department stores and complexes below, has designer labels, with a warehouse branch at *Dickman's Rd, Col 5*.

Department stores and complexes

Crescat, *Galle Rd, Col 3 (near Colombo Plaza)*, the most recent upmarket shopping mall.
JAIC Hilton Towers, *Col 2*.
Liberty Plaza on *Dharmapala Mawatha, Col 3* is slightly ageing now.
Majestic City, *Galle Rd, Col 4*, the largest mall.
Odel Unlimited, *5 Alexandra Place, Lipton Circus, Col 7, T2682712* (and a branch at **Majestic City**) is a classy department store with an eco-friendly edge and sells clothes, shoes, soaps, cosmetics, jewellery, music and homeware, and has a café and sushi bar.
Unity Plaza, opposite **Majestic City**.

Gemstones, silver and gold

These should only be bought at reputable shops; it is probably best to avoid the private jewellers in Sea St, the Pettah.
Sri Lanka Gem & Jewellery Exchange, *310 Galle Rd, Mon-Fri, 0830-1630 (closed for lunch)*, is a government institution with 34 wholesalers and retailers. Gem Testing Laboratory, 2nd floor, will test gems free for foreigners (you have to pay about US$2 for a certificate). Also customs, insurance, banking.
Premadasa, *560 Galle Rd, Col 3; 17 Sir Baron Jayatilleke Mawatha* and *20 Duke St, Col 1*.
Zam Gems, *81 Galle Rd, Col 4*, with a few branches at hotels: **Colombo Plaza**, **Trans Asia** and **Hilton**.
Hemachandra, *4 York St, Col 1 and 229 Galle Rd, Col 3*.
Colombo Jewellery Stores, *1 Alfred House Gardens, Col 3*.
Stone'N'String, *275 RA de Mel Mawatha, Col 4*.

Handloom and handicrafts

The government outlets offer good quality and reasonable prices, and the added bonus of not having to haggle. Here you can pick up masks, batiks, brasswork, silverwork etc. Government outlets include: **Laksala**, *Australia House, 60 York St, Col 1* which carries a wide range; **Lakmedura**, *113 Dharmapala Mawatha, Col 7, open until 1900*; **Lanka Hands**, *135 Bauddhaloka Mawatha, Col 4, 0930-1830;* **Lakpahana** *21 Reid Ave, Col 7*.
Craft Lanka, *403 Galle Rd, Col 3*.
Barefoot, *704 Galle Rd, Col 3, T2589305 sales@barefoot.lk* Very popular shop with tourists and wealthy locals. Started by Barbara Sansoni, the artist, excellent handloom fabrics, home furnishings, batiks, clothes; also toys, bookshop (see above).
Gallery 706, *next door*, exhibits and sells works of art.
Serendib, *100 Galle Rd, Col 4*, for batiks.
Fantasy Lanka, *302 (1st floor), Unity Plaza, 2 Galle Rd, Col 4*. Batiks.
Prasanna Batiks, *35 Main St, Col 11*. Batiks.

Supermarkets

Cargill's, *40 York St, Col 1; 407 Galle Rd, Col 3* (24-hour branch with pharmacy); *21 Staples St, Col 2*; and at Majestic City.
Keells at Crescat and Liberty Plaza.

Tea and spices

Mlesna Tea Centre, *44 Ward Place, Col 7, T2696348*. Excellent range of teas, pots etc. Several branches over town at Hilton, JAIC Towers, Crescat, Liberty Plaza, Majestic City and at the airport.
Sri Lanka Tea Board, *574 Galle Rd, Col 3*.
YWCA Spice Shop, *Union Place, Col 2*.

Sport and activities

Cricket

Colombo has several cricket stadiums.
Sinhalese Sports Club Ground (SSC), *Maitland Place, Col 7, T2695362*. Headquarters where Test matches and One-Day Internationals are played. Contact the Cricket Board here for tickets.
Colombo Cricket Club, which has a very attractive colonial style pavilion, and **Nondescript's Cricket Club** (NCC) are next door to each other.
R Premadasa Stadium, *Khettarama, Col 10*.

This large stadium hosts Tests and One-Days (sometimes day/night).

Diving

Though diving is possible off Colombo, most of the dive schools operate from coastal resorts, notably Hikkaduwa. **Lanka Sportreizen**, *29-b BS de S Jayasinghe Mawatha, Dehiwala, T2767500, lsr@sri.lanka.net* (also nature and wildlife). **Underwater Safaris**, *25c Barnes Place, Col 7, T2694012, F2694029, scuba@eureka.lk*, offer diving along the southwest coast. **Aqua Tours**, *108 Rosmead Place, Col 7, T2695170* (see under Hikkaduwa, page 147).

Football

Sugathadasa Stadium, *A de Silva Mawatha, Col 13*. For international matches. The 2002 Asian Games were also held here.

Golf

Royal Colombo Golf Club, *Ridgeway Golf Links, Col 8, T2695431*, offers temporary membership (a full round including club hire costs around Rs 2,000). There is a dress code.

Rowing

Colombo Rowing Club, *51 Sir CA Gardiner Mawatha, Col 2 (opposite Lake House Bookshop), T2433758*, offers temporary membership.

Tennis and squash

At the **Colombo Plaza**, **Ceylon Continental**, **Taj Samudra** and **Trans Asia** hotels. Also at: **Gymkhana Club**, *31 Maitland Crescent, Col 7, T2691025*, and **Sri Lanka Ladies Squash Association**, *T2696256*.

Swimming

Colombo Swimming Club, *148 Galle Rd, Col 3 (opposite Temple Trees, the President's Residence), T2421645*. Popular ex-pats' hang-out with pool, tennis, gym, bar, restaurant, initial membership Rs 35,000 (of which Rs 17,500 is refundable), annually thereafter Rs 865; you must be recommended by an existing member. Alternatively, many hotels allow non-residents to use their pool on a daily basis for a fee ranging from Rs 175-500 plus service charge/GST.

Yachting

Royal Colombo Yacht Club welcomes experienced sailors.

Tours and tour operators

Most tour operators offer half- or full-day city tours by car, typically visiting Kelaniya, Fort and the Pettah, the National Museum and usually Buddhist and Hindu temples. All tour operators will offer car hire and island tours. Some (eg **Aitken Spence, Confifi, Jetwing, Keells**) run a number of luxury hotels on the southwest coast and elsewhere. US$80-100 per day includes their hotel and breakfast (if you choose your own hotel, a large reservation fee may be added).

Adventure Sports Lanka, *Koswatte, T2791584, info@adventureslanka.com, www.adventureslanka.com* Recommended for adventure activities such as white water rafting, mountain biking, trekking.

Aitken Spence, *305 Vauxhall St, Col 2, T2308308, travel@aitkenspence.lk* One of Sri Lanka's largest operators, with some of Sri Lanka's finest hotels, full range of services, excellent if expensive tours.

A Baur, *5 Upper Chatham St, Col 1, T2448087, www.baurs.com* Includes bird-watching.

Confifi, *33 St Michael's Rd, Col 3, T2333320, F2333324, , www.confifigroup.com*

Cox & Kings, *315 Vauxhall St, Col 2, T2434295*.

Eco Adventure Travels, *58 Dudley Senanayaka Mawatha, Col 8, T2685601, www .ecotourism.srilanka.com*. Pioneering community-based ecotourism organization. Adventure sports, such as rafting, safaris, rock climbing, safaris, trekking, mountain biking, bird-watching.

George Travel, *2nd floor, 29 Ex-Serviceman's Building, Bristol St, Col 1, T2422345, F4223099*. Recommended for international flight tickets, very popular with budget travellers.

Hemtours, *75 Braybrooke Pl, Col 2, T2300001, F2300003, hemtours@sri.lanka.net www.hemas.com/leisure* Includes wildlife tours.

Jetwing, *46/26 Navam Mawatha, Col 2, T2345700, F2345725, www.jetwing.net* Highly recommended for personalized service, good car and driver/guide, excellent network of hotels.
Jetwing Eco Tours, *(as above), www.jetwingeco.com* Excellent nature and wildlife tours, personal service.
Keells, *130 Glennie St, Col 2, T2320862, F2447087, www.johnkeellshotels.com* Wide range of hotels, see also **Walkers Tours** below.
Lion Royal, *Level 3, 110 Sir James Peiris Maw, Col 2 (Sampath Tower), T4715996, lionroyal@sltnet.lk* Personal service, reliable fleet of drivers and generous discounts on a wide range of hotels.
Paradise Holidays, *160/2 Bauddhaloka Mawatha, Col 4, T/F502110, paradiseh@eureka.lk* Trekking, nature and weddings.
Quickshaw's, *www.quickshaws.com* Includes special tours for birders, cricketers, authors and honeymooners.
Thomas Cook, *15 Sir Baron Jayatilleke Mawatha, T2445971, F2436533*, and *245C Galle Rd, Col 4, T2580141, thomcook@slt.lk* Full range of services.
Walkers Tours, *130 Glennie St, Col 2, T2421101, www.walkerstours.com* Expensive but recommended for excellent service.

Transport → *Beware of pickpockets and avoid hotel touts at bus and railway stations. See pages 33 and 68 for more information.*

Local

Bus

Colombo has an extensive network of public and private buses competing on popular routes. Although the system can get very crowded, it is not difficult to use since the destinations are usually displayed in English. Useful services are those that run from Fort Railway Station down the Galle Rd (including nos 100, 101, 102, 106, 133). No 138 goes from Fort past the Town Hall and the National Museum (Glass House stop, across the road); no 187 between Fort and the International airport. Numerous buses run up and down Galle Rd to **Mount Lavinia**. Nos 100, 101, 102, 105, 106, 133 and 134 go to Fort. Local buses have white signs, while long distance have yellow. Details of the 3 bus stations near Fort Railway Station are given below. **Ceylon Transport Board** (CTB), T2581120.

Car hire

For general information on car hire, charges and self-drive versus being driven, see p. Most hotels and travel agents can arrange car hire (with or without driver). Agents include: **Avis**, *Mackinnons, 4 Leyden Bastion Rd, Col 1, T2448065 (24-hr garage T2524498) avis@ens.lk*, recommended; **Hertz** at *Galadari hotel, T4715550*; **Lion Royal** (see Tours above); **Mal Key**, *58 Pamankada Rd, Kirulapana, Col 6, T2584253, F2502494, malkey@pan.lk*; **Quickshaw's**, *3 Kalinga Place, Col 5, T2583133, cars@quickshaws.com*, with rates from chauffeur rates from €27 per day (€178 per week) for 100 km per day, plus Rs 250 for driver's subsistence; self-drive from €19 per day; and **Sudan's**, *Grand Oriental, T/F2320391 (ext 109), sudansint@lanka.com.lk*

Alternatively, you can book with a freelance driver direct which usually works out cheaper than an agency, though obviously some caution needs to be exercised. Two reliable drivers are **AG Kusumsiri Premalal ('Gamage')**, *T/F2519233, 077-7074722, koumlanka@sltnet.lk*, affable, knowledgeable, good rates. **Claude Fernando**, *T2538570*, 'knowledgeable, courteous, very honest', fair rates (Rs 17 per km, plus Rs 250 per night).

Motorbike/bike hire

Gold Wing Motors, *346 Deans Rd, Col 10, T2685750, F2698787*, rental on daily, weekly or monthly terms.

Taxi

Metered taxis have yellow tops and red-on-white number plates. Make certain that the driver has understood where you wish to go and fix a rate for long-distance travel. **Radio cabs** are very convenient and reliable (see p45), **Quick Cabs**, *T2502888, 501502*, GNTC, *T2688688, gntc@isplanka.lk*

Also branch at airport, *T2251688*. Recommended but pricey. **Unique Cabs**, *T2733733*. **Yellow Cabs**, *T2942942*. It'll cost about Rs 450-500 to Mount Lavinia from Fort in a taxi, less if you are lucky.

Three-wheeler

Three-wheelers are quick but you need to bargain hard (minimum usually Rs 20 per km). Trips around Fort will cost Rs 50; Fort to Cinnamon Gardens, Rs 180-200. Fort to Mount Lavinia will cost upwards of Rs 300, the exact fee depending upon your negotiating skills (see p45).

Train

Suburban train halts are Fort, Secretariat, Kompanna, Kollupitiya, Bambalapitiya, Wellawatta, Dehiwala, Mount Lavinia. To Mount Lavinia from Fort, buy ticket from counter no 13. Suburban services run regularly between Fort and Mount Lavinia (and beyond), approximately every 30 mins (less frequently at weekends and holidays) between 0436 and 2135, though they can get packed at rush hour. They take 30 mins. Timings of the next train are chalked up on a blackboard, Rs 3.50. If heading south after Mount Lavinia, it is quicker to change at Moratuwa than retrace your steps to Fort.

Long distance

Air

Bandaranaike International Airport (or Colombo), *T2452911*, is at Katunayake, about 6 km south of Negombo and 30 km north of Colombo. Aviation Services, *T2252861*. Flight Information, *T01973-32377*, at flight times, day and night. The helpful tourist information counter will give advice, brochures, maps, and the useful monthly *Travel Lanka* magazine. See p33 if arriving at night.

Domestic airport at Ratmalana, just south of Mount Lavinia (500 m off Galle Rd), is used for domestic flights. It remains primarily a military airport, security is high and there are few facilities. Airlines provide a free bus to and from the city. At the time of writing, flights were running only to Jaffna (1 hr).

International airlines include: **Aeroflot**, *7A Sir Ernest de Silva Mawatha, Col 7, T2671201*; **Air Canada**, *East Tower, World Trade Centre, Col 1, T2584975*; **Air France**, *Galle Face Hotel, Galle Rd, Col 3, T2327605*; **Air India**, *108 Sir Baron Jayatilleke Mawatha, Col 1, T2325832*; **American Airlines**, *5 York St, Col 1, T2348100*; **Balkan Airlines**, *6 York St, Col 1, T2325149*; **Bangladesh Biman**, *4 Milepost Ave, Col 3, T2565391*; **British Airways**, *Trans Asia Hotel, 115 Sir CA Gardiner Mawatha, T2320231, F2447906*; **Canadian Airlines**, *11a York St, Col 1, T2348101*; **Cathay Pacific**, *186 Vauxhall St, Col 1, T2334145*; **Czech Airlines**, *26/46 Navam Mawatha, Col 2, T2381200*; **Delta**, *45 Jandhipathi Mawatha, Col 1, T2338734*; **Emirates**, *Hemas Building 9th floor, 75 Braybrooke Place, Col 2, T2300200*; **Gulf Air**, *11 York St, Col 1, T2347857*; **Indian Airlines**, *4 Bristol St, Col 1, T2326844*; **Japan Airlines**, *61 WAD Ramanayake Mawatha, Col 2, T2300315*; **KLM**, *29 Braybrooke St, Col 2, T2439747*; **Korean Air**, *7th floor, East Tower, World Trade Centre, Echelon Sq, Col 1, T2422686*; **Kuwait Airways**, *69 Ceylinco House, 69 Janadhipathi Mawatha, Col 1, T2445531*; **Lufthansa**, *61 WAD Ramanyake Mawatha, Col 2, T2300501*; **Malaysian**, *Hemas, 81 York St, Col 1, T2342291*; **Oman Air**, *115 Sir CA Gardner Mawatha, Col 2, T2348495*; **PIA**, *342 Galle Rd, Col 3, T2573475*; **Qantas**, *Trans Asia Hotel, 115 Sir CA Gardiner Mawatha, Col 2, T2348490*; **Qatar**, *Galadari, 64 Lotus Rd, Col 1, T2341101*; **Royal Jordanian**, *40 A Kumaratunge Munidasa, T2301621*; **Royal Nepal Airlines**, *2 York St, Col 1, T2439319*; **Sahara India**, *Jetwing House, 46/26 Navam Mawatha, Col 2, T4715730*; **SAS**, *21 Janadhipathi Mawatha, Col 1, T2424973*; **Saudi Air**, *466 Galle Rd, Col 6, T4717747*; **Singapore Airlines**, *315 Vauxhall St, Col 2, T2300757*; **Sri Lankan Airlines**, *3rd floor, East Tower, World Trade Centre, Echelon Sq, Col 1, T01973-35555, F35500 (reconfirmations)*; **Swissair**, *25 Galle Face Centre, Col 3, T2435403*; **Tarom**, *18A York St, Col 1, T2448593*; **Thai Airways**, *JAIC Hilton, Union Place, Col 2, T2307100*; **United Airlines**, *06-02 East Tower, World Trade Centre, Echelon Sq, Col 1, T2346026*.

Domestic airlines are: **Expo Aviation**, *464 Galle Rd, Col 6, T2512666*; **Lionair**, *14 Trelawney Pla, Col 4, T4515615, lionairsales@sierra.lk;* branch at *2nd floor, Orchard Building, Col 6, T4515698*; **Serendib Express**, *500 Galle Rd, Col 6, T2505632*.

Boat

At the time of writing, services between

Colombo Harbour and Tuticorin, India, were under discussion. Several ships were poised to run the 9-hr trip, with a special visa counter of the Indian Embassy at the harbour. Contact **Unicorn**, *12 Galle Face Court 2, Col 3, T2302100*, around Rs 4,000 one way, Rs 6,000 return.

Bus

There is a good island-wide network and travel is cheap. Most major towns have an Express Service at least every 30 mins to 1 hr. There are 3 main bus stations in Colombo, all close to Fort Railway Station. All 3 are quite chaotic, choking with fumes, with services usually operating on a 'depart when full' basis.

CTB or Central, *Olcott Mawatha, southeast corner of the Pettah (right from Fort station, and across the road), T2328081*. Part private-part government owned buses, which are the cheapest, oldest and slowest, offer services to almost all island-wide destinations though the frequency of services has been cut back. Faster inter-city buses cost a third more. Left luggage here (Rs 8 per locker), is sometimes full.

Bastion Mawatha, *to the east of Manning Market. Transport Authority, T2421731*. The buses are privately run, with the cost and journey time depending on whether you get an ancient bone-shaker ('normal' bus), 'semi-luxury', 'luxury' (with a/c), or the wanton sensuousness of a 'super-luxury' coaster. It serves most destinations to the east, southeast and south, including **Kandy** (luxury bus 3½ hrs, Rs 94), **Nuwara Eliya** (6 hrs, Rs 152), **Ratnapura** (2 hrs, Rs 29), **Hikkaduwa** (2½ hrs, Rs 74), **Galle** (3 hrs, Rs 84), **Matara** (5 hrs, Rs 118), **Tangalla** (6 hrs, Rs 142), **Hambantota** (6½ hrs, Rs 166) and **Kataragama** (7½-8 hrs, Rs 200). Super luxury buses to **Badulla** cost Rs 250.

Gunasinghapura or People's Park, just to the north of the CTB bus station, which also offers private a/c coasters and bone-shakers to destinations to the north and northeast, including **Ampara** (9 hrs, Rs 176), **Anuradhapura** (5-6 hrs, a/c Rs 160), **Badulla** (7½ hrs, Rs 205), **Balangoda**, **Bandarawela** (7½ hrs, Rs 205), **Batticaloa** (7½ hrs, Rs 90), **Chilaw** (2 hrs, a/c Rs 84), **Dambulla** (4 hrs, Rs 130), **Embilipitiya** (for Uda Walawe), **Gampola**, **Hatton** (for Adam's Peak), **Kegalla** (for Pinnawela), **Kurunegala** (2½ hrs, Rs 64), **Negombo** (1½ hrs, Rs 30), **Polonnaruwa** (5-6 hrs, Rs 160), **Puttalam** (3 hrs, Rs 90), **Trincomalee** (7 hrs, Rs 180) and **Vavuniya** (6 hrs, Rs 190).

Private buses to **Jaffna** can be arranged in Wellawatta (around Rs 900).

Train

The main station is Fort, actually located at the southwestern corner of the Pettah, though many trains originate in Maradana. There are trains to most places of interest on four separate lines.

Enquiries (Express and Commuter trains), *T2434215*. Berths reservations, *T2432908*. For foreign travellers, the **Railway Tourist Office**, *Fort Station, T2435838*, is particularly useful (see p69). Left luggage ('Cloak Room'): Rs 15 per locker but is often full. The useful Railway Timetable is available from counter 4 at Fort (Rs 60).

There are special a/c **Hitachi** trains for day tours to Kandy and Hikkaduwa. Occasional tours are arranged on vintage steam trains – details from the Railway Tourist Office.

Intercity trains to **Kandy** leave Fort at 0700 and 1535 (1st class, including observation car reservation fee, Rs 170, 2nd class, reservation also required, Rs 72, 2½ hrs). Return tickets are valid for 10 days, but the return date must be booked in advance.

Normal trains to **Kandy** (2nd class Rs 69, 3rd class 25, 3¼ hrs), via **Gampaha** (for **Heneratogoda**) and **Rambukkana** (for **Pinnawela**) leave at 0555 (Podi Menike), 1030, 1240 (to **Hatton**), 1655, 1750 and 1940 (mail train). Trains to **Badulla** leave at 0555, 0945, 1940 (mail train) and 2200. The 0945 (Udarata Menike) is express (9 hrs) with observation car (1st class Rs 340 including reservation fee); the 2200 has 1st class sleeping berths (Rs 364), and 2nd (Rs 191) and 3rd (Rs 78) class sleeperettes. Normal trains take 10-11 hrs (2nd class Rs 166, 3rd class Rs 60). All trains call at **Hatton** (for **Adam's Peak**, 1st class Rs 173, 2nd class Rs 99, 3rd class Rs 36, 4½-5½ hrs), **Nanu Oya** (for **Nuwara Eliya**, Rs 205/118/43, 6-7 hrs), **Ohiya** (for **Horton Plains**, 7-8 hrs), **Haputale** (8½-9½ hrs), **Bandarawela** (Rs 258/147/54, 9-10 hrs) and **Ella** (9½-10½ hrs).

On the Northern line to **Anuradhapura** (4 hrs) and **Vavuniya** (for **Jaffna**, 5 hrs), an intercity train leaves Fort daily at 1630 (1st class a/c with reservation Rs 270, 2nd class Rs 150). Normal trains to **Vavuniya** at 0555 (1st class a/c available, Rs 277), 1040, 1405 and 2130 (4½-5 hrs to **Anuradhapura**, 2nd class Rs 116, 3rd class Rs 42), via **Kurunegala** (Rs 55/Rs 20, 2 hrs). For **Polonnaruwa**, take the 2230 (1st class Rs 331, 2nd class Rs 172, 3rd class Rs 72, 7½ hrs) or 0615 (2nd class Rs 147, 3rd class Rs 54, no 1st class, 9 hrs). To **Trincomalee**, take the 0615 or 2230 (2nd class Rs 168, 3rd class Rs 61). At the time of writing (Sep 03), trains on the **Batticaloa** line were terminating at **Valaichchenai**.

Trains run every 1-2 hrs from 0520 to 2020 on the Puttalam line to **Negombo** (Rs 10, 1½ hrs), via **Katunayake** (for the **airport**), a few continuing to **Chilaw** and **Puttalam** (4 hrs). Trains south to **Galle** (2nd class Rs 65, 3rd class Rs 23, 2½-3 hrs) leave Fort at 0710 (1st class available), 0900, 1030, 1405, 1600, 1700, 1720, 1750 and 1930. Most call at **Kalutara**, **Aluthgama**, **Ambalangoda** and **Hikkaduwa**, and continue to **Matara** (Rs 89/Rs 33, 3½-4 hrs), with stops at **Talpe** and **Weligama** and in some cases other south coast beach resorts.

Directory

Banks

Banks with 24-hr ATMs are widespread throughout Colombo. Banks usually open at 0900 and close at 1300 or 1500, though are keeping increasingly flexible hours. Some branches open for Sat morning and have an evening service; most are closed on Sun, *Poya* days and national holidays.

Bank of Ceylon, *Bureau de Change, York St, Fort*, is now open 24 hrs a day, including holidays for encashment of TCs and foreign currency. Cirrus ATMs are found mainly at private banks such as **Commercial Bank** and **Sampath Bank** and foreign banks in Fort. Most give cash advances on Visa and Mastercard. There are numerous licensed moneychangers in Fort area, notably on Mudalige Mawatha, offering marginally better rates for cash. Hotels generally offer a poor rate of exchange for cash and TCs, though they may be convenient for residents. Most banks now have ATMs for credit and debit card. See maps for details.

Communications

Couriers DHL, *Keells (Pvt) Ltd, 130 Glennie Street, Col 2, T2541285, tracing@cmb.co.lk, www.dhl.com* See p48 for details of rates.

Post GPO, *Bristol St, next to the Ex-Serviceman's Institute, Fort, T2326203, open 0700-1800, Mon-Sat (Poste Restante 0845-1645).*

American Express, *104, Dharmapala Mawatha, Red Cross Building; T2681215.* You can phone either office to check if any mail is waiting. Post office in Mount Lavinia is on *Station Rd*.

Internet Internet is widely available, though varies wildly in price: Fort and the Pettah are expensive (Rs 200+ per hr), while along Galle Rd you should never need to spend much more than Rs 1 per min. Some are 24 hrs, and offer internet phone. Wellawatta is cheapest. In Bambalapitiya it usually costs Rs 50 per hr.

Café@inter.net, *next door to Surf'n'Play (below), Kollupitiya, 0830-2300*. Rs 60/hr and quieter than Surf'n'Play.

DNS, *256 Galle Rd, Bambalapitiya, 0700-0000*.

Enternet, *241/1 Galle Rd, Bambalapitiya*, Rs 8 per min internet calls (to the UK).

ITI Net Café, *379 Galle Rd, Wellawatta, Col 6, 0830-2200*. Rs 40 per hr.

Sky Link, *339a Galle Rd, Bambalapitiya*, open 24 hrs.

Surf'n'Play, *483 Galle Rd (opposite Majestic City), Kollupitiya, 0900-0200*. Plenty of terminals (Rs 60-80 per hr) with huge screens but is principally designed for brattish teenage gamers.

Telephone Internet phones, the cheapest option for dialling abroad, are increasingly available (see above). Rates vary according to destination. Numerous private telephone offices offer more or less standard rates for IDD (International Direct Dialling) calls. Card Pay Phones (yellow and blue **Lanka Payphones** and orange and black **Metrocard**) offer 24-hr service and much lower rates than hotels. Phone cards of various denominations are sold in shops and kiosks near pay phones. Mobile phones can be hired by the day, see p48.

Cultural Centres

Most have a library and a reading room and have regular music and film programmes. **Alliance Française**, 11 Bomes Place, Col 7, T2694162, info@alliance.fr.lk, 0830-1230, 1300-1630. **American Center**, 44 Galle Rd, Col 3, T2332725, open Tue-Sat 1000-1800. **British Council**, 49 Alfred House Gardens, Col 3, T2581171, enquiries@britishcouncil.lk. Tue-Sat, 0900-1800. 2 week old newspapers, free internet on membership (Rs900 joing fee). **German (Goethe) Cultural Institute**, 39 Gregory's Rd, Col 7, T2694562, bibl-Goethe@eureka.lk. Open 0900-1300, 1500-1700 weekdays. **Indian Cultural Centre**, 133 Bauddhaloka Mawatha, Col 4, T2446892. **Russian Cultural Centre**, 10 Independence Ave, Col 10, T2685440. Open weekdays 0900-1700.

Embassies and consulates

Australia, *3 Cambridge Place, Col 7, T2698767.*
Canada, *6 Gregory's Rd, Col 7, T2695841.*
France, *89 Rosmead Place, Col 5, T2698815.*
Germany, *40 Alfred House Av, Col 3, T2580431.* Mon-Thu 0730-1630, Fri 0730-1400.
India, *36-38 Galle Rd (next to Galle Face Hotel), Col 3, T2421605.* Mon-Fri 0900-1730, visas (Rs 4,000) 0930-1200. Can take up to 5 working days to process visas, take 2 passport photos, expect a long wait; or go to Kandy where it is usually quicker.
Italy, *55 Jawathe Rd, Col 5, T2588388.*
Japan, *20 Gregory.'s Rd, Col 7, T2693831.*
New Zealand, *3rd floor 46/12 Navam Mawatha, T2479223.*
South Africa, *129 Reid Av, Col 4, T2597149.*
Spain, *130 Glennie St, Col 3, T2421101.*
UK, *190 Galle Rd, Col 3, T2437336.* Mon-Thu 0800-1630, Fri 0800 1300.
USA, *210 Galle Rd, Col 3, T2448007.* Mon-Fri 0800-1700.

Emergency services

Accident service, T2691111. Fire and ambulance, T2422222. Police, T2433333. Police stations, south of Maradana Railway Station, Kollupitiya, Bambalapitiya and Wellawatta. Tourist police, *Chatham St, Fort, T2433744.*

International agencies

ICRC, *29 Layard's Rd, Col 5, T2503346.*
UNDP, *T2580691.*
UNFPA, *T2580840.*
WFP, *T2586244. All at 202 Bauddhaloka Mawatha, Col 7.*
UNHCR, *97 Rosmead Place, Col 7, T2683968.*
UNICEF, *5 Gethanjali Place, T2551331.*
WHO, *135 Bauddhaloka Mawatha, Col 4, T2502319.*

Libraries

Colombo Public Library, *A Coomaraswamy Mawatha, Col 7, T2695156. Daily except Wed and public holidays, 0800-1845.* There is a small fee.

Medical services

Chemists A number on Galle Rd, Union Place and in the Pettah and Fort.
State Pharmaceutical outlets at Hospital Junction, Col 7 and Main St, Fort.
Keells Supermarket, *Liberty Plaza, Dharmapala Mawatha, Col 3* and at Cargill's, *Galle Rd, Col 3* (24 hrs). Pharmacies attached.
City Dispensary, *505 Union Place, Col 2.*
Ward Place Pharmacy, *24a Ward Place, Col 7.*
Herbal and Ayurvedic centres Mount Clinic of Oriental Medicine, *41 Hotel Rd, Mount Lavinia, T2723464,* offers acupuncture, Ayurvedic and Chinese medical massage, including 'milk rice massage'.
Siddhalepa Ayurveda Hospital, *106 Templer's Rd, Mount Lavinia, T2722524, F2725465.* Authentic herbal and Ayurvedic health programmes include herbal/steam baths and massage but fairly 'stark and institutional'; rooms available for longer stays.
Hospitals General Hospital, *10 Regent St, T2692222, T2691111* (24-hr A&E).
Dental Institute, *Ward Place, Col 10.* Poison information: *extn 350.* Ambulance *T2422222.*
Government Ayurvedic Hospital, *325 Cotta Rd, Borella, T2695855,* or see Mount Lavinia below. Homeopathy and herbal medicine. Foreigners often prefer to use the more expensive private hospitals: Asha Central, *37 Horton Place, Col 7, T2696412.* Asiri, *181 Kirula Rd, Col 5, T2500608;* Durdan's, *Col 3, T257-5205;* McCarthy's, *22 Wijerama Mawatha, Col 7, T697760;* Nawaloka, *23 Sri Saugathodaya Mawatha, Col 2, T2544444 (24-hr).*

Places of worship

Buddhist Contact The Buddhist Centre, *? Buddhist Centre Rd (near Hotel Sapphire) Col 10, T2695216;* Buddhist Information Centre,

50 A Coomaraswamy Mawatha, Col 7, T2573285; **International Buddhist Research and Information Centre**, *380/9 Bauddhaloka Mawatha, Col 7, T2689388*. **Buddhist Cultural Centre**, *125 Anderson Rd, Nedimala, Dehiwala, T2734256, F2723767*. Information, instruction and meditation. **Bhikku Training Centre**, *Gangaramaya, 61 Sri Jinaratana Rd, Col 2, T2327084, F2439508* (offers classes in English, French, German). **Hindu** Contact **Ramakrishna Mission International Culture Centre**, *Ramakrishna Rd, Col 6, T2584029*.
Christian St Peter's, *26 Church St, Col 1, T2422510*. Anglican. **Christ Church**, *Sir MM Markar Mawatha, Col 3, T325166*. Anglican. **St Michael's & All Angels**, *1 Cameron Place, Col 3, T2323456*. Anglican. **Baptist church**, *120 Dharmapala Mawatha, Cinnamon Gdns, Col 7, T2695153*.**Dutch Reform Church**, *724 Galle Rd, Col 3. 363 Galle Rd, Col 6, T2580454. Station Rd, Dehiwala, T2717122*. **St Andrew's**, *73 Galle Rd, Col 3, T2323765*. Interdenominational. **St Philip Neri's**, *157 Olcott Mawatha, Col 11, T2421367*. Roman Catholic. **St Mary's**, *Lauries Rd, Col 4, T2588745*. Roman Catholic. **St Lawrence's**, *Galle Rd, Col 6, T2581549*. Roman Catholic. **St Mary's**, *Galle Rd, Dehiwala*. Roman Catholic.
Muslim Grand Mosque, *New Moor St;* **Devatagaha Mosque**, *De Soysa Circus, Union Place, Col 7*; **Borah Mosque**, *4th Cross St, Col 11*; **Kollupitiya Mosque**, *Sir E de Silva Mawatha, Col 3*; **Bambalapitiya Mosque**, *Bauddhaloka Mawatha, Col 4*.

Useful addresses

Automobile Association of Ceylon, *40 Sir MM Markar Mawatha, Galle Face, Col 3,* T2421528, open Mon-Fri 0830-1630, for issue of temporary Sri Lankan driving permit (bring 2 photos, photocopy of your national licence and international driving permit).
Central Cultural Fund (Cultural Triangle Office), *212 Bauddhaloka Mawatha, Col 7 (to the right and half way to the back of building), T2500733, gen_ccf@sri.lanka.net* The 14-day Visitors' Permit is on sale (US$32.50) for entry to the sites and photography; information booklets are also available. The permits are easier and quicker to get at the sites (Anuradhapura, Kandy, Polonnaruwa or Sigiriya).
Ceylon Hotels Corporation (CHC), *411 Galle Rd, Col 4, T2503497, F2503504, chc@sltnet.lk*
Customs, *Customs House, Times of Ceylon Building, Col 1, T2421141*.
Department of Archaeology, *Marcus Fernando Mawatha, Col 7, T2694727*, for photography permit.
Department of Immigration, *Bambalapitiya Station Rd (right outside the station), 1st floor, Col 4, T2503629*, (allow 1-2 hrs); see p26.
Forestry Department, *Rajamalwatta Rd, Battaramulla (Colombo outskirts), T2566631*. Issues necessary entry permits for Sinharaja Biosphere Reserve and Knuckles, accommodation booked on ground floor.
National Aquatic Research Agency (NARA), *Crow Island, Col 15, T2522000*.
Wildlife Conservation Department, *18 Gregory's Rd, Col 7, T2694241, wildlife@slt net.lk, 0900-1630, for Wildlife Information and Bungalow Reservation*.
Wildlife and Nature Protection, *Chaithya Rd, Col 1, T2325248*.

West & Northwest

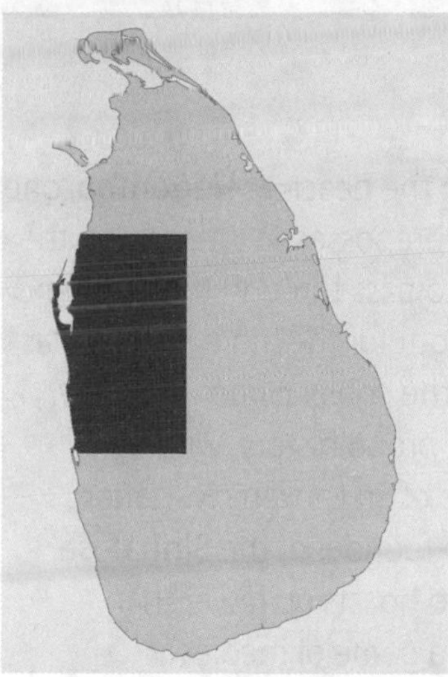

Introduction

Other than a day or two spent on the beach at **Negombo**, one of the most developed and least prepossessing resorts on the west coast, most travellers tend to pass through the West and Northwest regions, heading straight for the more spectacular sights of the Ancient Triangle or the cooler climes of Kandy. Yet this region possesses its own proud history, with a reasonable claim to be the cradle of Sri Lankan civilization. It was here that Prince Vijaya, the founder of the **Sinhalese race**, first landed in 543 AD. It also boasts no fewer than four ancient capitals, founded in a game of medieval cat-and-mouse to hide the sacred Tooth Relic from foreign invaders.

The area is also where the wet zone meets the dry. Around the densely populated northern suburbs of Colombo, closely packed coconut groves, occasional strands of forest and intensive cultivation contribute to the lush, evergreen landscape. A few kilometres north of **Chilaw**, however, the Deduru Oya marks the ancient boundary between the wet western hill country and the dry irrigated lands of the north. The landscape becomes increasingly barren and beyond the recently reopened **Wilpattu National Park**, Sri Lanka's largest protected area, the northern boundary of the region lie the arid wastes of the **Wanni**.

From west to east the landscape also undergoes a transformation. The wide shallow lagoons of the sand-fringed coast give way to the forest-clad hills and mountains of the highlands.

★ Don't miss...

1. **Negombo** Hire a fishing boat on the lagoon, cycle along the canals and then satisfy your appetite with the tastiest seafood on offer in the town's many beachside restaurants, page 102.
2. **Kalpitiya Peninsula** Venture well off the beaten track to explore the Dutch heritage, churches and traditional life of this remote peninsula, page 109.
3. **Yapahuwa** Climb up the beautifully sculpted ancient stairways of the vast granite rock palace and then enjoy the view from the top, page 114.

Negombo

→ *Phone code: T031. Colour map 2, grid C1. Population: 122,000.*

Owing to its proximity to the international airport, 6 km away, Negombo is the principal resort north of Colombo. Although it has a wide range of accommodation, and is a convenient place to end a holiday (or begin it if the flight schedules are unkind), the beach can be dirty – if you are looking for an unspoilt strip of white sand you are advised to head down south where the beaches are far superior. Moreover, some find Negombo seedy – Sri Lankans regard it as their vice capital, with visible evidence of prostitution and worse, though on an international scale its problems are fairly minor. Negombo town, although a little scruffy, does have a picturesque lagoon and a few interesting reminders of the Portuguese and Dutch periods. » *For Sleeping, Eating and other listings, see pages 104-108.*

Ins and outs

Getting there Negombo town is easily accessible from the airport by taxi, three-wheeler or bus. It takes about 20 minutes. Hotels often arrange transfer on request. From Colombo, take the no 240 bus (every 15-20 minutes) from Gunasinghapura bus stand in the Pettah which takes about an hour. The train from Fort Station also takes about an hour.

Getting around The main tourist area is 2-4 km north of the town itself. You can walk most of the way along the beach (which gets progressively more inviting), or take a three-wheeler (Rs 50-75) or the Kochchikade bus (no 905) from the bus station. Bicycles can be hired to explore area.

Best time to visit Swimming and watersports are only safe from November to April, outside the southwestern monsoon period. *Easter*, March/April, is celebrated with passion plays, particularly on Easter Saturday on Duwa island. In July the *Fishermen's festival* at St Mary's Church is a major regional festival.

Sights

The Portuguese originally built a **fort** on the headland guarding the lagoon in about 1600. Since the area was rich in spices and particularly the much prized cinnamon, it changed hands several times before the Portuguese were finally ousted by the Dutch in 1644. In attempting to make Negombo an important centre, the Dutch built a much stronger structure but this was largely destroyed by the British who pulled much of it down to build a jail. Today, only the gatehouse to the east (dated 1678) with its rather crooked clock tower survives. The place is still used as a prison and the District Court is tucked away in a corner of the grounds.

A more enduring monument to the Dutch is the **canal system**. Although originally explored in the 15th century, they were improved and expanded by the Dutch who saw their advantage in moving spices – cinnamon, cloves, pepper, cardamoms – and precious gems from the interior and along the coast to the port of Negombo for loading on to ships sailing for distant shores. Today you can see this if you follow St Joseph Road into Custom House Road and around the headland. It skirts the lagoon where mainly fishing boats are moored (witness to its thriving fishing industry). The junction of the canal is just past the bridge crossing the lagoon. Unfortunately at its mouth it is dirty and not that appealing.

St Mary's Church dominates the town. It is one of many churches that bears witness to the extent of Portuguese conversions to Roman Catholicism, especially

Catholicism and canals

The coastal road runs through the region most affected by Portuguese colonialism. Their imprint is clearly visible in the high proportion of Roman Catholics, and the number of Catholic churches in the numerous villages through which the road passes. Nearly a quarter of the population immediately inland from Negombo is Christian, increasing in the north to almost 40%. The common nature of names like Fernando and Perera gives one clue as to why their resolve to convert was so successful!

Dutch influence is also evident in the now unused canal which was built between Colombo and Negombo. Once it was busy with the flat-bottomed 'padda' boats which travelled the 120 km between Colombo and Puttalam. As the Rev James Cordimer wrote in 1807 "the top of the canal (near Colombo) is constantly crowded with large flat-bottomed boats, which come down from Negombo with dried fish and roes, shrimps, firewood, and other articles. These boats are covered with thatched roofs in the form of huts". The Dutch built canals extensively not just around Colombo but also around Galle in the south, but they were relatively minor works compared to the 1,000 km of irrigation canals already dug by the Sinhalese by the 12th century. The boats on these canals were often pulled by two men in harness. Now though the canal banks are largely the preserve of people strolling along the waterway. You can hire bikes at several points, including Negombo, and ride along a section of the banks.

among the fishermen in Negombo District. Work began in 1874 and was only completed in 1922. There are a number of alabaster statues of saints and of the Easter story as well as a colourfully painted ceiling.

There are three **Hindu temples** on Sea Street. The largest, Sri Muthu Mari Amman, has a colourful *gopuram* in the inner courtyard.

The area is very rich in marine life and although there is much evidence of a motorized fleet in the harbour, you can still see fishermen using catamarans and ancient outrigger canoes to bring up their catch onto the beach every day. The outrigger canoes known as *oruva* here are not made from hollowed-out tree trunks but rather the planks are sewn together and caulked to produce a fairly wide canoe with an exceptionally flat bottom. Look out for them as some are often beached in front of the hotels. You can usually see the fleet early in the morning returning to harbour, each canoe under a three-piece sail. Their catch includes seer, skipjack, herring, mullet, pomfret, amberjack, and sometimes sharks. Prawns and lobster are caught in the lagoon. There are a number of fish markets – one is near the bridge on Duwa Island across the lagoon and there is another beyond the fort.

The nearest **reef** is 3 km off the beach hotel area with corals within 10-20 metres, though the quality of this inner reef is poor. There are much better reefs further out, teeming with marine life including barracuda (even rare giant barracuda), blue-ringed angels and unusual starfish. Make sure you go with a registered (eg PADI) dive school.

Muthurajawela marsh in the lagoon is an estuarine wetland which harbours the salt-water crocodile, which can grow up to 9 m in length, as well as many species of birds such as the pied kingfisher. Sadly, however, the construction of the now aborted Peliyagoda-Katunayake highway has destroyed part of the marsh, and the visitor centre run by a conservation project protecting the crocodiles, has been forced to close.

Sleeping

Most people choose to stay in the beach area north of Negombo town. Hotels are spread out almost 2 km, mostly on Lewis Place and further north on Porutota Rd in Ethukala. The junction of Lewis Place, Porutota and Cemetery roads forms a convenient mid-point. To its south are most of the cheaper guesthouses while to the north are the more expensive package hotels. Some hotels don't allow Sri Lankans accompanying tourists to stay, partly because the area has been a suspect destination for shady practices. Most larger hotels offer watersports.

Negombo Town *p102*

E **New Rest House**, 14 Circular Rd, T2222299. 21 rooms (Rs 850-1,100), some with a veranda, half with a/c, spacious open areas with pleasant furnishings, bar, restaurant, attractive position though a little too close to the fish market.

Negombo Beach *p102, map p105*

A **Blue Oceanic** (Jetwing), *Porutota Rd, T2279000, blue1@sri.lanka.net* 110 large rooms with tub, not all with good views, typical resort hotel, all amenities and excellent service, good pool, sports,entertainment, German run Negombo Diving Centre.

A **Royal Oceanic** (Jetwing), *Porutota Rd, T2279000, roh2@sri.lanka.net* Geoffrey Bawa designed hotel, 91 a/c rooms with balcony, overlooking beach or garden, tubs, pool (open to non-residents when occupancy is low), sports (non-residents squash Rs 300, badminton Rs 250), busy resort hotel.

A-B **Brown's Beach** (Aitken Spence), *175 Lewis Place, T2222031, brownsbh@sltnet.lk* 140 a/c rooms (US$48), including 25 beachside rooms (US$68) plus 8 private cabanas (US$73) in busy resort hotel popular with families, full facilities, good reasonable restaurants, large pool (non-residents Rs 100), nightclub (2130, Rs 500, ladies free), karaoke bar, sports.

A-B **Rani Holiday Village**, *154/9 Porutota Rd, T2224803, ranihv@sltnet.lk* 25 very appealing self-contained a/c apartments (US$35) built around central courtyard, plus large bungalows (US$65 with breakfast), pleasant sitting area, fully equipped kitchen, fridge, TV.

B **Camelot Beach**, *345-7 Lewis Place, T2235881, camelot@itmin.com* 86 mainly a/c rooms (US$48), ugly modern exterior but attractive wood panelling inside, very friendly and helpful. Focus is around pool (non-residents, Rs 200), 2 bars, restaurant.

C **Hellmich Village**, *14/3 Porutota Rd, T2279052*. 3 nicely furnished a/c 'cabanas' (US$23), attached hot bath, quiet, breakfast to order, skin diving.

C **Sunflower Beach**, *289 Lewis Place, T/F2238154*. 66 rooms, some a/c with private balconies and sea views, restaurant/bar, pool (non-residents, Rs 100), unattractive building, popular with packages.

C **Sunset Beach** (Jetwing), *5 Seneviratne Mawatha, T2222350, F4870623*. 40 small non-a/c rooms in 3-storey block on the beach, upper floors more spacious, clean, light and airy, pool, visitors' book full of praise and useful local information.

C-E **Icebear**, *103 Lewis Place, T/F2233862 nicebear@ sltnet.lk* Attractively furnished bungalows and 'villas' (Rs 1,100-2,600) with spotless shared bath in well-kept Swiss-owned guesthouse, pleasant garden with wonderful secluded feel, personal attention, good home cooking.

D **Topaz Beach**, *21 Porutota Rd, T2279265, topaz@sltnet.lk* 30 good-sized rooms (non-a/c Rs 1,250), 7 a/c (Rs 1,650), views better from 2nd and 3rd floors, restaurant, post office, helpful owner, minor maintenance required but reasonable value.

D-E **Randiya Guest House**, *154/7 Porutota Rd, T2279568, F4871437*. 15 rooms with verandas in peaceful bird-filled setting, 10 fan only (US$10), 5 with a/c (US$15), breakfast included.

D-F **Coconut Grove**, *Porutota Rd, T4872375*. 15 decent rooms (2 a/c Rs 1,200, 13 non-a/c, Rs 600), good view upstairs , restaurant, also Ayurveda health centre.

E-F **De-phani**, *189/15 Lewis Place, T2234359, dephanie@slt.lk* 11 clean, comfortable rooms with nets (Rs 650-800), in very friendly family run guesthouse, small balconies (better upstairs), restaurant.

E-F **Ocean View**, *104 Lewis Place, T2238689, oceanview@ wow.lk* Upstairs rooms cleaner

For an explanation of the sleeping and eating price codes used in this guide, see the inside front cover.

and more spacious (Rs 800), lower ones small and grubby (Rs 500).

E-F Silver Sands, *95 Lewis Place, T2222880, F2237364, silversands@wow.lk* 15 large, well-kept, clean rooms, cheaper downstairs (Rs 650), best with large sea-facing balconies (Rs 900), nets, good restaurant, helpful owner, reliable taxi service, best value in this class, popular so book ahead.

F Beach Villa, *3/2 Senaviratne Mawatha, T2222833, F2234134, nissajet@sltnet.lk* 15 clean rooms with fan and net (Rs 600), restaurant next to the beach, owner Mr Nissanka organizes island tours. Also owns **The Villa** (C), a 4-roomed beach bungalow for long-term stay.

F Sea Sands, *7 Porutota Rd, T2279154*. 11 simple rooms with attached bath, friendly, reasonable.

F Sea-Drift, *2 Seneviratne Mawatha, T2222601*. 10 rooms in family guesthouse (one of the originals in Negombo), kitchen facilities available, friendly.

Ayurvedic resort

Ayurveda Pavilions (Jetwing), *Ethukala, T4870764, ayurvedapav@eureka.lk* 12 exquisitely, though deceptively simply furnished villas (King's villa US$425, Queen's villa US$375). Each villa has beautiful front garden with frangipani tree, open-air bath, own massage table, and DVD player. Very ecologically sound, attention to detail and personal service is breathtaking. Treatment packages from 3 days (US$165) to 30 (US$1350). The ultimate treat.

Towards the airport

F Srilal Fernando, *67 Parakrama Rd, Kurana, T2222481*. 5 rooms (Rs 585-685) set around a courtyard, with very clean bath and fan in spacious family home, excellent food, good value (phone for pick-up from airport, Rs 385; or take bus during daytime), German spoken.

Eating

Negombo Town p102

Rs Choys, *31 Custom House Rd, T2222807*, is in a pleasant location on the lagoon.

Rs Sapuna and **Wonshis**, *St Joseph's Rd*, serve reasonable Chinese.

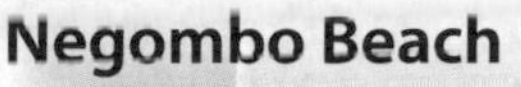

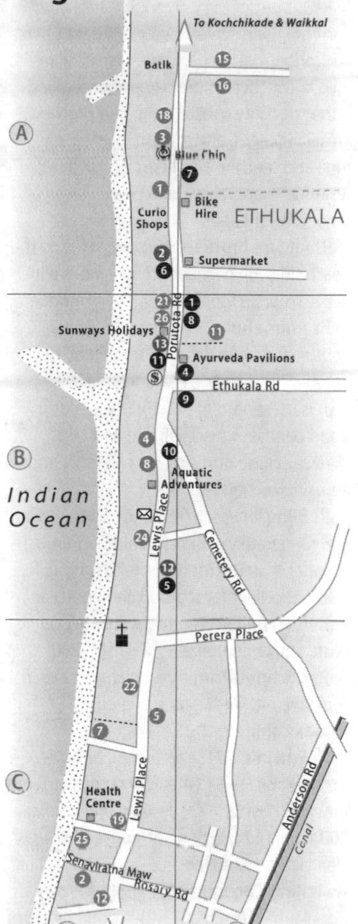

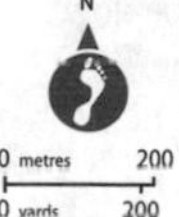

Sleeping
Beach Villa **2** *C1*
Blue Oceanic **3** *A1*
Brown's Beach **4** *B1*
Camelot Beach **8** *B1*
Coconut Grove **1** *A1*
De-phani **7** *C1*
Hellmich Village **11** *B2*
Icebear **12** *C1*
Ocean View **5** *C1*
Randiya Guest House **15** *A2*
Rani Holiday Village **16** *A2*
Royal Oceanic **18** *A1*
Sea-Drift **19** *C1*
Sea Sands **21** *B1*
Silver Sands **22** *C1*
Sunflower Beach **24** *B1*
Sunset Beach **25** *C1*
Topaz Beach **26** *B1*

Eating
Alt Saarbrucken **6** *A1*
Ammehula **10** *B1*
Bijou **1** *B2*
Ciao Bella **8** *B2*
Coconut-Primitive **9** *B1*
Edwin's **5** *B1*
Ocean Park **11** *B1*
Pri-Kin **4** *B2*
Sherryland **7** *A2*

Bars & clubs
King Coconut **13** *B1*
Player's Pub **11** *B1*
Rodeo Pub **2** *A1*

Negombo Beach *p102, map p105*
RsRsRs Most of the upmarket hotels in Porutota Road serve all-you-can-eat buffets. The tendency is towards western food or mild and rather insipid curries but seafood is the speciality: lobster, crab and prawns are all excellent, and the fish, particularly tuna and seer, are also first-class. The restaurants and bars along Lewis Place tend to be cheaper.
RsRs **Alt Saarbrucken**, *35 Porutota Rd*, on the beach side, Alpine influence is obvious with heavy wooden furniture and pricey fondue.
RsRs **Ammehula**, *286 Lewis Place, opposite Camelot Beach Resort*. Small but excellent restaurant, seafood speciality (fish is presented to you for inspection), good pancakes (Rs 150), rice and curry (Rs 200); huge portions, very friendly and amusing owner.
RsRs **Bijou**, *opposite Sea Sands*. Swiss-owned and moderately expensive (although much cheaper than the tourist hotels), fondue Rs 1,400, excellent for seafood and noodles.
RsRs **Ciao Bella**, *36 Porutota Rd*, seafood pasta and decent pizzas for Rs 180-280.
RsRs **Coconut-Primitive**, *on Browns Beach Junction, T4873441*. Same owners as King Coconut.
RsRs **Edwin's**, *204 Lewis Place, T2239164*. Excellent Sri Lankan meals (9 curries ordered previous day, Rs 200), devilled prawns, Rs 200. Generous portions, attentive host, very clean kitchen and loos.
RsRs **King Coconut**, *11 Porutota Rd*. Very popular bar/restaurant with a good range of freshly prepared food (main dishes Rs 280) in a relaxed setting (service can be slow).
RsRs **Ocean Park** has good Chinese (Rs 90-250), Sri Lankan, and western meals (pasta Rs 200, vegetarian Rs 175, pizza/steaks Rs 275), served in a pleasant environment.
RsRs **Pri-Kin**, *10 Porutota Rd, T2278646*, is friendly and offers excellent Chinese dishes (most Rs 250); try soups and prawn dishes.
RsRs **Sherryland**, *set back from the road in a garden*, most dishes under Rs 300 with attentive service, lively bar (*Lion* lager Rs 95) and good range of cocktails, good value.

Bars and clubs

Negombo *p102, map p105*
Most hotels have at least one bar, or serve alcohol in their restaurant. Some of the larger hotels have nightclubs (open 2130, dress 'smart but casual'). There is also an increasing number of western style bars.
King Coconut has Negombo's most popular bar, young crowd, popular with Aussies.
Players Pub has two billiard tables, is popular with Brits and boasts that it stays open longer than anywhere else in Negombo (0130 or when the last person left standing leaves!).
Rodeo Pub is very popular.

Festivals and events

Negombo *p102*
Easter, **Mar/Apr**, holds a special place in this strongly Catholic area. There are numerous passion plays usually held on Easter Sat, the most famous of which is on Duwa Island which involves the whole community. Station yourself between the 2 churches on Sea St (1 km south of Lewis Place) if short of time. Young girls in spotless white dresses are carried shoulder high by 4 men between the churches. This takes place in the afternoon but preparations take most of the day.

Shopping

Negombo *p102, map p105*
The curio stalls near the large hotels are handy for getting last-minute presents. Quality varies considerably and they are not nearly as good as when you buy direct up country. Visit them all before deciding and then bargain hard.
Tailors include: **Chandi**, *166 Lewis Place*, and **Gaffal**, *266 Lewis Place*, who will make suits etc (silk and cotton) in about 2 days.
Vijitha Yapa, *135 Rajapaksha Broadway*, books.

Sport and activities

Negombo *p102, map p105*
It is dangerous to swim, particularly during the southwest monsoon May-Oct. Warning notices are now posted on the beach.

Boat trips
Fishermen take tourists out to see the lagoon and canal. Each should cost around Rs 450s and Rs 550 respectively.

Diving

Only dive with a PADI-qualified operation and be careful of other dive operations. In January 2003, 5 people were stranded in the waters off Negombo after being abandoned by a dive boat on a trip led by an unqualified instructor. They were rescued the following day by a fisherman.

Aquatic Adventures Diving Centre, *321 Lewis Place, T077-7648459, www.divingandsafaris.com* The best place to learn to dive in Negombo. A professional joint British-Dutch owned operation, they visit more and further reefs (over 40) than other Negombo organizations. Purpose-built dive school, and post-dive bar; ask for Bobby or Marjolein.

Negombo Diving Centre, *T5318854, Blue Oceanic Resort*, one dive US$30, open water course US$375. PADI centre.

Fishing

Major hotels offer deep-sea fishing (For 4 people US$40 per hr for 4 hrs, or US$200 for 6 hrs), 'Leisure' fishing (US$40 per hr for 6 per person), rods (US$10-20).

Snorkelling

Fishermen offer boat trips for snorkelling.

Swimming

Most of the larger hotels allow non-residents to use their pools (Rs 100-200).

Tennis, badminton and squash

Brown's Beach Hotel, **Blue Oceanic** and **Royal Oceanic** hotels allow non-residents to use their tennis and squash facilities (Rs 300 per hr includes racquets).

Tour operators

Negombo *p102, map p105*

In addition to hotel travel desks, independent travel agents include:

Airwing Tours, *68 Colombo Rd, T2238116, F2238155, airwing@sri.lanka.net*, which offers several 'eco' tours for bird-watchers, photographers, trekkers etc (*UK T/F020-8503 6369*).

Jetwing, *opposite Blue Oceanic Hotel.*

Sunways Holidays, *next to Topaz Beach, T2277766.* Day trips offered to Kandy, Sigiriya, Dambulla and Galle. Also car hire with unlimited mileage.

Thomas Cook, *Green Rd shopping complex.*

Transport

Negombo *p102, map p105*

Transport is well regulated and hotel receptions should display a list of the agreed taxi rates.

From the airport

Frequent buses (no 240 to Colombo) stop close to the airport from early morning to late evening but can be crowded. Taxis cost Rs 500-550 (after bargaining) to/from Ethukala hotels. Expect to pay a little more at night. Most hotels/guesthouses can arrange taxis for you. Three-wheelers charge Rs 400.

Bus

Frequent buses run along the main beach road from the bus and railway stations. Bus to/from Negombo town Rs 5. Long-distance services depart from the bus stand. There are regular services to **Colombo** (no 240), both Intercity Express (Rs 30, 1-1½ hrs) and the cheaper, slower CTB buses. There are 16 buses a day to **Kandy**, which leave mainly early morning or mid-late afternoon. Also to **Kurunegala** (no 34), and **Chilaw** (no 907).

Car hire/taxi

Car hire/taxi is mostly through hotels; inspect vehicles carefully and expect to pay from about Rs 2,000 including driver and fuel for 80 km (some don't accept credit cards).

Sunways Holidays, *next to Topaz Beach, T2277766.* Unlimited mileage US$30 a day all inclusive. Also **Mr Lakshman Bolonghe**, *146 Lewis Place, T2233733.* A/c van, good English speaking guide.

Cycles

Available from many hotels/guesthouses; about Rs 150-200 per day. The flat roads make a short trip out of Negombo attractive.

Motorbike hire

For motorbike hire, expect to pay Rs 600 per day. Some hotels, eg Beach View, rent on daily/weekly terms.

Three wheeler

Drivers cruise the main beach road from Lewis Place to **Ethukala**. From Lewis Place to the bus or railway stations expect to pay around Rs 100, and up to Rs 150 from the hotels in Ethukala. Beware of touts.

Train

The regular commuter train (16 a day, 0515-2106) goes to **Colombo** via **Katunayake** (for the airport). Avoid this train during rush hours, and especially Mon morning, when it gets very crowded. Also 6 trains a day to **Chilaw** and **Puttalam**.

Directory

Negombo *p102, map p105*

Ayurvedic massage Many hotels now offer Ayurvedic massage. **Kräuter Shop**, *32 Porutota Rd, open daily 0930-1730*, offers massages from Rs 750 per 30 mins; also other herbal treatments offer relief from various allergies (including mosquito bites!), sunburn and rheumatism. **Ayurvedic Royal** Health Centre, *4 Seneviratne Mawatha*.

Banks Bank of Ceylon, *Main St nearly opposite St Mary's*. **Sampath Bank** and **Seylan** Bank, *Rajapasksha Broadway*. Sampath Bank has an ATM for Cirrus.

Communications **Post office**, *Main St towards the fort*. There is also an Agency post office, *Lewis Place*. There are numerous IDD phone outlets on Lewis Place and Porutota Rd. Many of these also have **internet** facilities (Rs 5-8 per min), and some are open 24 hrs. Much cheaper is **Bluechip Cybercafé** at Blue Oceanic, *0930-2230 (Sun 1330-2230)*, Rs 70 per hr. In Negombo town, **Mecarin** Enterprises, *100 Lewis Place (next to the bus station), T5310353*, has internet facilities for Rs 60 per hr.

Medical services Most hotels and guesthouses have doctors on call. **General** Hospital, *Colombo Rd, T2222261*.

Useful numbers **Tourist police**, *Ethukala, T2224287*.

Northwest coast

North of Negombo, you cross from the West to Northwest province, traditionally known as Wayamba province. It is an area of fishing hamlets and seemingly endless groves of coconut palms, while inland is a rich agricultural patchwork of paddy fields and plantations. The 'carpeting' of the coastal road to Puttalam in 2002 now makes this the quickest route from Colombo to Anuradhapura, and many pass through without stopping. However, there are some worthwhile attractions: secluded beaches, ancient Hindu temples, a 'forgotten' peninsula and Sri Lanka's recently reopened largest national park.

Beaches north of Negombo

→ *Phone code: Waikkal 031 and Marawila 032. Colour map 2, grid C1.*

There are two main beach areas which lack the bustle (and hassle) of Negombo but are still within easy reach of the airport. **Waikkal**, 12 km north of Negombo, is attractively sited on a meandering river but is quite remote so you are dependent on transport to get anywhere. It is however the site of one of the island's most impressive eco-resorts who organize a wide array of nature activities.

A further 11 km north is **Marawila** which has a large Roman Catholic church, curious Italianate houses and a reputation for producing good quality batiks. There are a growing number of resort-style hotels here, though the area has never really taken off in the way of resorts further south. The beach is good in places but sometimes gives way to breakwaters constructed of large rocks. » *For Sleeping, Eating and other listings, see pages 111-112.*

For an explanation of the sleeping and eating price codes used in this guide, see the inside front cover.

Along the west coast to Puttalam → *Phone code: 032. Colour map 2, grid B1/C1.*

Beyond Marawila and after crossing the estuary, the road passes between the lagoon and the railway through **Madampe** which is known for its Coconut Research Institute and **Taniwella Devale**, a colourful harvest festival held in August in which the whole farming community participates.

Chilaw, 75 km north of Colombo, is a small town with a large fish market, a shiny new branch of **Cargill's** and a big Roman Catholic church. Its shady claim to fame is as a smuggling centre though there is little in town to warrant a stop. However, 2 km east is **Munneswaram**, which is worth a detour, especially on Fridays, the busiest day for this Hindu temple complex of three shrines. The 1,500 year old inner sanctum of the main Siva temple has Tamil inscriptions and is an important pilgrimage centre. In August there is a month-long festival which includes firewalking.

A left turn at Battulu Oya leads to the prawn-fishing Tamil village of **Udappuwa** on the Kalpitiya Peninsula, 26 km north of Chilaw. As at Munneswaram, there is a festival with firewalking in July/August at its seaside three-temple shrine complex. Experiments in 1935-36 showed that the coals were heated to about 500°C.

Marshes and lagoons lie between the road and the sea for much of the route north, which crosses a series of minor rivers and a few major ones such as the Battulu Oya. The largely Muslim and Catholic town of **Puttalam**, 131 km north of Colombo, is a centre for prawn farming, dried fish and coconut plantations. It used to be famous for its ancient pearl fishery but is now better known for its donkeys, and is thus a target of many Sinhalese jokes. There is little to do here but the accommodation on offer can make it a useful base. The A12 continues northeast through to Anuradhapura. ⏩ *For Sleeping, Eating and other listings, see pages 111-112.*

Kalpitiya Peninsula → *Phone code: 032. Colour map 2, grid A1/B1.*

Though easily accessible by causeway from the main road, few travellers choose to explore this narrow, sandy spit of land – partly due to local skirmishes during the war, particularly at sea, it is also well off the beaten track. It has a quite distinctive, almost otherworldly landscape, and there are some important monuments to its history. Kalpitiya's position at the head of Puttalam's lagoon made it an important port for Arab traders from the seventh century and the peninsula remains predominantly Muslim to this day. Later, the Portuguese and the Dutch recognized its strategic use and the Dutch built a fort here in order to strangle King Rajasingha's trade with India. Today it is famous for its dried fish and prawn farming. Its sandy soil has also made its farmers some of Sri Lanka's richest. Despite its proximity to the sea, the land overlies an abundant supply of fresh, rather than brackish, water. Simple wells have been constructed for irrigation and crops including tobacco, shallots, chilli and even potatoes grow abundantly. The western side of the peninsula has some undeveloped beaches, though there is nowhere to stay. ⏩ *For Sleeping, Eating and other listings, see pages 111-112.*

Talawila → *Colour map 2, grid B1. 22 km from Puttalam, 5 km off the main road.*

Here, there is an important shrine at **St Anne's Church**. There are two accounts of its history. In one, a shipwrecked Portuguese sailor brought the image of St Anne to shore, placed it under a banyan tree and vowed to build a church here if his business prospered. In the other, a vision of St Anne appeared and left gold coins for the construction of a chapel. The present day church, set in extensive tree-lined grounds, was built in 1843 and has fine satinwood pillars. Remove shoes before you enter, and photography is not allowed. There is also a wide beach behind. There are two major festivals in March and June featuring huge processions, healing and a rural fair. These draw up to 50,000 people, with some pilgrims arriving by boat.

Kalpitiya → *Colour map 2, grid A1. 19 km beyond Talawila.*

The bustling, predominantly Muslim village of Kalpitiya, marks the end of the road. The small **Dutch fort**, built in 1676 on the site of a Portuguese stockade and Jesuit chapel, is one of the best preserved in Sri Lanka. It has a VoC gate (1760), an original wooden door, and inside the remains of the barracks, commander's house, chapel and prison. The navy has been *in situ* throughout the war and you will need to ask permission from the sentry to enter. In the modern base, you may be shown a number of rusting Indian trawlers, impounded for fishing in Sri Lankan waters. Two tunnels lead from the fort to St Peter's Kirk and a school, though these were blocked up during the war. Photography is prohibited and you may need to leave ID before entering. A naval officer will accompany you around the ramparts.

In contrast, the impressively gabled **St Peter's Kirk** nearby has lost many of its original features although inside a heavy stone font remains. There are some well-preserved 17th- and 18th-century Dutch gravestones inside. The church's columns and semi-circular porch date from a 19th-century renovation. Outside, there is a small, weathered cemetery.

Wilpattu National Park → *Colour map 2, grid A1/2.*

ⓘ *US$6 (due to increase to US$12 when facilities and roads are improved). 0600-1830. The park office, information centre and entrance are at Hunuwilagama, 7 km from the Wilpattu Junction turn-off at Maragahawewa on the A12.*

In March 2003 a clamour of excitement greeted the reopening of Wilpattu National Park, Sri Lanka's largest, oldest and – before the war – most popular wildlife sanctuary. The 131,693 ha park had been an important historical and archaeological site, as well as home to some of Sri Lanka's most visible populations of large mammals. The *Mahavansa* records that Prince Vijaya landed at Kudrimalai, to the southwest, married Kuveni, the local jungle princess, and founded the Sinhalese race.

The park was closed in 1985, immediately after an attack on its wardens and officers by a group of LTTE cadres. There were concerns that LTTE soldiers, army and local villagers had resorted to large-scale poaching. However, there is little physical evidence of significant such damage although animals such as leopard have fallen victim to poachers and the park's bungalows were destroyed by looting. Contrary to popular belief it is unlikely that any landmines have been laid. The road network is in poor condition.

Wilpattu has a unique topographical landscape of gently undulating terrain dominated by *villus*, natural sand-rimmed water basins, which fill up with rain and to which animals come to drink. These used to be the best placed to see leopards. Certain sections have a distinctive rich, red, loamy soil and there are also areas of dense forest. The western part of the park is reminiscent of Yala, see page 182, while out to sea Dutch and Portugal bays may still support populations of dugong. A further protected area, the Wilpattu Sanctuary, lies to the north within Northern Province.

The Wildlife Department had, at the time of writing, reopened a 51 km section of road into the park. This starts at the park entrance and leads northwest close to a number of *villus* up to the Moderagam River, terminating at Kokmotai. These days few animals are visible, many deer and water buffalo having been poached. A small population of leopard (around 8 in the core zone) remains but is hard to see, while elephants are more likely to be seen in the paddy farming areas to the south. The bird population of resident and migratory waterfowl and scrub and forest species has yet to be assessed but is said to be fairly healthy, as is the reptile population.

At the time of writing substantial rehabilitation work was planned, with further sections set to be reopened, and populations of deer and water buffalo brought in from other areas. ▸▸ *For Sleeping, Eating and other listings, see pages 111-112.*

Sleeping

Beaches north of Negombo *p108*

A **Clubhotel Dolphin**, *Kammala South, Waikkal, sandwiched between the sea and the old Dutch canal, T2233129, F2277788, dolphin@slt.lk* 76 a/c rooms and 50 non-a/c cottages, not all with sea views, popular with European packages, enormous swimming pool which zigzags between rooms, activity-based party hotel with plenty of sports and entertainment laid on, but no beach.

A **Ranweli Holiday Village**, *Waikkal, T2277359, F2277358, ranweli@slt.lk* 84 a/c chalets (from US$60) in award-winning eco-friendly resort reached via hand-punted ferry. Located in 9 ha mangrove peninsula, activities on offer include boat trips, bird-watching, guided nature walks and fishing. Well-designed and furnished rooms, plants in bathrooms, whole concept well thought out. Peaceful atmosphere, 'a naturalist's paradise'.

AL **Club Palm Bay**, *Thalawila Wella, Thoduwawa, near Marawila, T2254954, palmbay@lankacom.net* 104 well-furnished a/c cottages, plus 2 suites, in an attractive setting surrounded on 3 sides by a lagoon. Sports including fishing and boating, 9-hole golf, health centre, huge pool (rivalling **Clubhotel Dolphin** as Sri Lanka's largest). Good beach close by. Popular with Germans.

B **Aquarius Sports Resort**, *Beach Rd, Marawila, T2254998, www.ceylonhotel.com* German-run sports hotel with Sri Lanka's only indoor stadium, all-weather football pitch, many sports offered, small pool, weekly nightclub, good facilities for blind and disabled, 41 comfortable rooms.

B **Olenka Sunside Beach**, *Moderawella, near Marawila, T2252170, olenka@lanka.com.lk* New Swedish-run resort, 44 comfortable a/c rooms from US$42 (including 4 suites) with TV, balcony/terrace around small pool.

C **Sanmali Beach**, *Beach Rd, Marawila, T2254766, F2254768*. 20 rooms with balcony, close to beach (a/c US$30, fan US$25), small pool, restaurant, lower end package resort.

D **Palm Haven**, *Beach Rd, Marawila, T2251469, F011-2254557*. Refurbished by new management, 14 clean comfortable chalets with hot water (US$18), beach restaurant and small pool.

Along the west coast to Puttalam *p109*

D **Rest House**, *next to the Urban Council Park, Puttalam, T2265299*. 8 poorly maintained rooms (Rs 800-1,100), fan, attached bath, restaurant, poor service – watch your bill.

D-E **Senatilaka Guest Inn**, *81/a Kurunegala Rd, Puttalam, T2265403, F2265299*. 7 clean rooms with attached hot bath (Rs 800), some with balcony, a/c and TV (Rs 1500), open-air terrace, restaurant, good value.

D-F **Rest House**, *across the lagoon in Chilaw, close to the beach, T/F2222299*. 17 reasonable rooms (a/c Rs 1,300, fan Rs 750), some with balcony overlooking sea. Kitchens lack hygiene – avoid food.

G **Seven Eleven**, *5 Corea Av, near clocktower, Chilaw, T2222272*. 3 basic rooms, attached bath (Rs 400). Decent restaurant.

Kalpitiya Peninsula *p109*

G **Rest House**, *Main St, Kalpitiya, T2260705*. Fine old Dutch building but in poor state, 3 basic rooms (Rs 450). This is the only option. It is best to visit for the day only.

Wilpattu National Park *p110*

F **Preshamal Safari Hotel**, *Wilpattu Junction, Pahala Maragahawewa, T011-2521866, F2524469*. 4 basic, spartan rooms with fan and attached bath. Sri Lankan breakfast, rice and curry and breakfast packets for the park available. Two jeeps, Rs 2,000 for a tour.

Eating

For options see Sleeping above.

Tour operators

Wilpattu National Park *p110*

Jeeps base themselves at Wilpattu Junction, offering 4-hr safaris for Rs 2,000, or a full day for Rs 4,500. It is best to leave either at 0530 or 1500. Some hotels in Anuradhapura are also beginning to offer tours.

Transport

Along the west coast to Puttalam *p109*

Bus Frequent buses go along the coast between **Puttalam** and **Colombo** (3 hrs, Rs 90), some stopping at **Chilaw** (1 hr) and **Negombo** (2 hrs), and inland to **Anuradhapura** and **Kurunegala** (both 2 hrs).

Train The line can flood after heavy rain. 9 a day (about every 2 hrs) run from Colombo Fort station to **Chilaw**, via **Negombo** and **Madampe**, 3 of which continue to **Puttalam**, the end of the line.

Kalpitiya Peninsula *p109*

Bus Run along the main road from **Puttalam**.

Wilpattu National Park *p110*

Bus They ply the **Puttalam- Anuradhapura** road. Ask to be let out at Wilpattu Junction.

Kurunegala and around

As the chosen capital of four medieval kingdoms, the inland heart of Northwestern province contains some important archaeological ruins, the highlight of which, Yapahuwa, rivals the rock fortress at Sigiriya. They can be visited either as a detour en route to Anuradhapura or Dambulla, or they can make a rewarding day trip from the provincial capital of Kurunegala.

Kurunegala → *Phone code: 037. Colour map 2, grid C3. Population: 28,500. 93 km from Colombo.*

Kurunegala is an important crossroads town astride the route from Colombo to Anuradhapura and Kandy to Puttalam. It enjoys a pleasant location overlooked by huge rocky outcrops, some of which have been given names of the animals they resemble: elephant rock, tortoise rock etc. According to a legend, these 'animals' were magically turned into stone when they threatened the city's water supply during a drought. Situated at the foot of the 325-m black rock, Etagala, there are excellent views across the lake from the temple, where an enormous Buddha is being constructed.

Kurunegala was the royal capital for only half a century, starting with the reign of Bhuvanekabahu II (1293-1302) who was followed by Parakramabahu IV (ruled 1302-26). There is little left of the Tooth relic temple save a few stone steps and part of a doorway. Elsewhere in the town, you can drive up to Elephant Rock for wonderful views, or take a trip around the attractive lake. The town is best used though as a base to visit the deserted ruins in the surrounding countryside. » *For Sleeping, Eating and other listings, see pages 115-116.*

Arankele → *Colour map 2, grid B3. 24 km north of Kurunegala.*

Up a forested hillside is this sixth-century **cave** hermitage. Ancient Brahmi donative inscriptions have been found in some caves. Excavations have revealed meditation halls, stone-faced double platform structures and ambulatories for the *Tapovana* (forest-dwelling) sect of austere Buddhist hermits here. Typically, the platforms aligned east-west, with the entrance porch to the east, would be bridged by a large monolith. The smaller of the double-platform structure here was probably divided into nine 'cells' or monks' dwellings – the roof being supported on columns.

After travelling 14 km along the Kurunegala-Dambulla road, turn left on to the Ibbagamuwa-Moragollagama Road for 10 km. It is hard to reach by public transport. » *For Sleeping, Eating and other listings, see pages 115-116.*

Ridigama → *Colour map 2, grid C4. 18 km northeast of Kurunegala.*

The 'Silver Temple' marks the place where silver ore was discovered in the second century BC, during the reign of Dutthagamenu (Dutugemunu). It is an ancient Buddhist temple site with rock cave hermitages and an image house with Kandyan paintings. Among the finds, which mostly date from the 18th century, are Buddha statues (seated and reclining), a door frame beautifully carved and inlaid with ivory, and a curious altar with Dutch (Delft) tiles with Biblical figures gifted by a Dutch consul! There is an attractive artificial lake at the foot of the hills. The journey there is tricky. Head north from Kurunegala on the A6 (Dambulla road). Having passed Ibbagamuwa (11.5 km), take the first right onto the B409. At 7 km, turn right at the junction onto the B264; after 9 km you reach Ridigama. Turn left at the main junction, then right at the clocktower and follow the dirt track for 200 m. Turn left onto the sealed road, then turn right at the T-junction. Follow the road past the lake and go uphill for 1.5 km to the *vihara*. ▸▸ *For Sleeping, Eating and other listings, see pages 115-116.*

Dambadeniya → *Colour map 2, grid C2. 30 km southwest of Kurunegala.*

Dambadeniya became prominent in the mid-13th century when the capital was moved there by Parakramabahu II (ruled 1236-70) together with the Tooth Relic. Legend states that it was the site of a monumental battle with the Indian King Kalinga, during which 24,000 men were successfully repelled and the Tooth kept safe, though shortly afterwards it was moved to the more secure site of Yapahuwa. Little remains of the ancient rock palace buildings though six ponds, where the courts used to bathe, are still there. The 272-step climb to the top is nevertheless worth it for the panoramic views

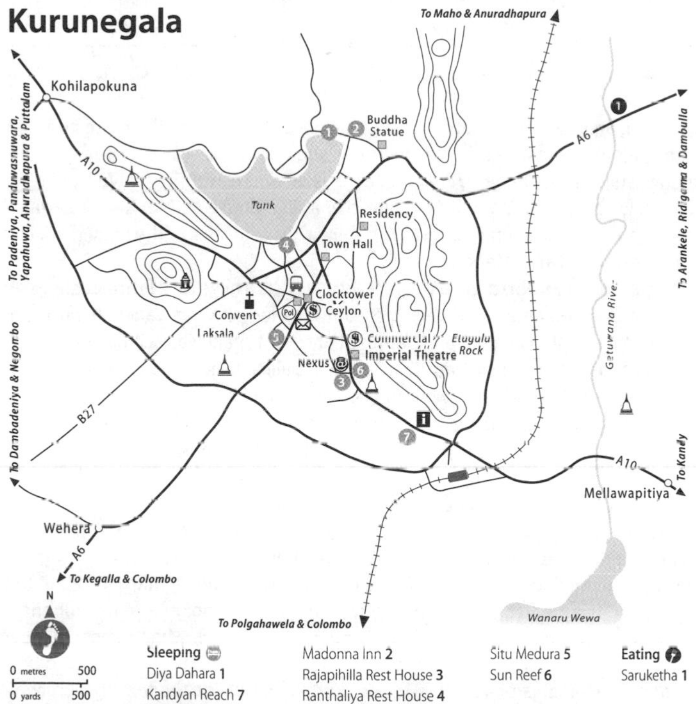

Sleeping
Diya Dahara 1
Kandyan Reach 7
Madonna Inn 2
Rajapihilla Rest House 3
Ranthaliya Rest House 4
Situ Medura 5
Sun Reef 6

Eating
Saruketha 1

of the surrounding rocks, and across to the ocean on a clear day. The two-storey temple (originally three) about 400 m south, which has Buddha images, is identified as the Vijayasundaramaya. It has some interesting wall paintings dating from the 18th century, when it was restored. It was used to exhibit the Tooth Relic which was normally housed in another temple near the palace. The site is just off the Kurunegala-Negombo road, along which buses ply. If coming from Colombo turn off at Ambepussa. » *For Sleeping, Eating and other listings, see pages 115-116.*

Panduwasnuwara → *Colour map 2, grid C2. 27 km northwest of Kurunegala.*

The oldest of the royal capitals in the district, Panduwasnuwara was used by King Parakramabahu I as a stepping stone to his great citadel at Polonnaruwa. Legend states that Panduwasdeva, Sri Lanka's second king, had his capital here in the fifth century BC. A forested mound has been identified as his predecessor King Vijaya's tomb.

The archaeological remains, in a sprawling, only part excavated, 20 ha site date to the 12th century AD. There is an impressive 1¼-km long ancient wall around the citadel with a moat in which crocodiles may have acted as an extra deterrent. Inside are the remains of a palace (once three-storey), audience hall and storehouses as well as a monastic complex and several bathing pools. A guide may show you around, though you can clamber at will around the ruins.

Nearby, a small Tooth temple reminiscent of the Tooth temple at Kandy has been restored, while back on the main road at the turn-off to the site is a small museum containing finds from local excavations, such as coins, images and jewellery, ⓘ *0800-1700.*

Follow the Kurunegala-Puttalam road for around 17 km, and turn left at Wariyapola towards Chilaw. The site is a kilometre from the main road. Buses run between Chilaw and Kurunegala. » *For Sleeping, Eating and other listings, see pages 115-116.*

Yapahuwa → *Colour map 2, grid B2. 47 km north of Kurunegala, 69 km south of Anuradhapura.*

Yapahuwa, arguably Wayamba's most impressive ruins, lies off the route north from Kurunegala to Anuradhapura. To reach the site follow the A10 past the turn-off to Panduwasnuwara to **Padeniya**. Here there is a *vihara* with 28 carved pillars, an elaborately carved door, and an ancient clay image house and library. At Padeniya, the A28 forks right to Anuradhapura. Yapahuwa lies 6 km east of the main road, close to the pleasant town of Maho.

Yapahuwa, ⓘ *Rs 200 and guide will expect a tip*, is a huge **rock fortress**, suggestive of Sigiriya, which stands on a very pleasant, shaded site. Bhuvanekabahu I (ruled 1272-84) moved his capital from Dambadeniya to Yapahuwa, seeing the need for stronger fortification against Tamil invaders, and built a palace and a temple where the Tooth and the Alms Bowl relics were housed for 11 years.

A vast granite rock, rising 100 m from the surrounding plain, is encircled by a 1-km long path rising to the top. The fort palace built of stone is surrounded by two moats and ramparts and there are signs of other ancient means of defence. The impressive ornamental stairway with some fine lions and guardstones is still well preserved, and somewhat reminiscent of Far Eastern art. The steps are fairly steep so can be tiring to climb. The ruins at the head of the remarkable flight of granite steps are unique and the views over the palms towards the highlands are not to be missed. The temple (restored in 1886) illustrates South Indian artistic influence in its fine carvings on the pillars, doorway and windows which show dancers, musicians and animals. One of the window frames is now exhibited in the Colombo Museum. The remains of a temple to the northeast, outside the fortification (which was thought at one time to have housed the Tooth Relic), has some sculptures visible. There is a small, fairly modern museum on site.

This fortress capital of the Sinhalese kings when abandoned was inhabited by Buddhist monks and religious ascetics. The relics were carried away from the temple here to South India by the Pandyas, and then recovered in 1288 by Parakramabahu III (ruled 1287-93), who temporarily placed them in safety at Polonnaruwa.

Yapahuwa is 5 km east of Maho, which is easily accessible by bus or train. Three-wheelers from here will cost Rs 200. Buses leave every two hours from Kurunegala and hourly from Anuradhapura. Since Maho lies on the Colombo-Vavuniya line, there are several trains a day from Kurunegala taking an hour and costing Rs 25 (second class), Rs 9 (third class). From Anuradhapura it takes two hours. » *For Sleeping, Eating and other listings, see pages 115-116.*

Sleeping

Kurunegala *p112, map p113*

C **Kandyan Reach**, *344-350 Kandy Rd, (1 km southeast from centre), T2224218, F2224541, athgiri@eureka.lk* Something of a white elephant – constructed with a dearth of tourists! 10 a/c rooms, 42 more being added one day, already dirty in parts though rooms are large with hot water, balcony and TV, restaurant and good (if rather shallow) pool.

D **Diya Dahara**, *7 North Lake Rd, T/F222-3452*. 3 a/c rooms (Rs 1,500), No 3 has large balcony, best located restaurant in town overlooking the lake, good buffet lunch (Rs 350) but very limited evening menu.

D **Madonna Inn**, *44 North Lake Rd, T5268888*. 7 good-sized rooms, clean and well-furnished, attached bath, nets, restaurant, quiet location close to the lake.

D **Situ Medura**, *21 Mihindu Mawatha, T2222335, F2223288*. 2 a/c if slightly gloomy rooms in large traditional mansion once belonging to local aristocrat, restaurant.

D-F **Ranthaliya Rest House**, *South Lake Rd (1 km from centre), T4690032*. 12 basic, cleanish rooms (fan only Rs 770), 2 a/c (Rs 1300), some with view overlooking the tank (with a bit of a stretch!), nets, restaurant.

F **Rajapihilla Rest House**, *Rajapihilla Rd, T2222299*. Colonial bungalow in need of a clean, 12 large, bare rooms, restaurant.

F **Sun Reef**, *51/1 Kandy Rd (by the Lion* lager sign), T/F2222433. 8 clean rooms with attached bath (Rs 750) including 1 larger a/c room (Rs 1,300), simple but comfortable, friendly, good English spoken, reasonably priced restaurant, towards the railway station.

Eating

Kurunegala *p112, map p113*

As well as the rest houses, there are a couple of Chinese places in town.

Rs-RsRs **Saruketha**, *2nd mile post, Dambulla Rd, T4691123*. The most popular is this tourist restaurant outside town. Attractive coconut thatch huts, own fruit and vegetables grown, excellent juices, seafood and Sri Lankan lunch (Rs 330) a speciality. Chalets planned here for 2004.

Shopping

Kurunegala *p112, map p113*

Folk Arts Centre, *141-145 Kandy Rd*, where you can watch craftsmen at work.

Laksala, *on the corner of Colombo and Puttalam rds*. One of the many branches selling handicrafts.

Transport

Kurunegala *p112, map p113*

Air Sri Lankan Airlines, *56 Colombo Rd, T4692518*.

Bus Frequent buses to **Colombo** (no 5 or no 6), Rs 31-35 (intercity Rs 62), takes 2-2½ hrs depending on route; to **Negombo** (no 34), Rs 22.50 (2 hrs); **Dambulla** every 15 mins, Rs 22 (2 hrs); **Anuradhapura** (no 57), Rs 42.50 (intercity Rs 75) (3 hrs), **Kandy**, Rs 20 (intercity Rs 40) (1½ hrs). A new stand is under construction.

Train The station is 1.5 km southeast of the town centre. Kurunegala is on the Northern line to **Anuradhapura** and **Vavuniya**. 5 trains to **Colombo Fort**, 0559, 1147, 1338,

1436 and 1714, takes 2 hrs. First class, Rs 95 if available; 2nd class, Rs 55, 3rd class, Rs 20. To **Anuradhapura** (Vavuniya train), takes 3 hrs. 0742 (1st class, Rs 109, available), 1303, 1611, 2343; (2nd class, Rs 63), (3rd class, Rs 23), plus Sat special to **Vavuniya** at 1220. To **Trincomalee**, 0818, Rs 199. To **Matara**, 0737, Rs 249 plus Sun special at 1859.

Directory

Kurunegala *p112, map p113*

Banks Plenty of banks in town including Commercial Bank and **Sampath Bank** with ATM facilities.

Communications **Internet** at several places on Kandy Rd. Try **Nexus**, *opposite Imperial Theatre, 0730-2100*, Rs 60 an hr.

The South

Introduction

Those who refer to Sri Lanka as a tropical paradise are usually describing the South. Here magnificent bays, beaches and rocky headlands line the coast while small-scale farms are scattered amongst the thick cover of trees in the interior.

The southwest region, from Colombo to Galle, is the most densely populated part of the island and its centre of industry. It is also its most developed with western sun-seekers packing into the island's major resorts, such as **Beruwela**, **Bentota** and **Hikkaduwa**. It requires little effort to escape the hordes however, with some short trips inland to explore the region's cultural riches and its tranquil rivers and lagoons.

Away from the palm-fringed coastal belt, dense forests and lush vegetation stretch inland. The heart of the Wet Zone is an undulating landscape of tea and rubber plantations, leading to **Ratnapura**, the centre of island's gem producing region. To its south lies the largest remaining tract of rainforest, **Sinharaja Biosphere Reserve**, a world heritage site.

Historic **Galle**, the province's unrivalled capital, is rich with colonial heritage. The outstandingly beautiful 80 km stretch of road between here and **Tangalla** is one of the most scenic routes in the country. Though no longer a secret, there are fewer package hotels, and amongst the popular and laid-back **Mirissa** and **Unawatuna**, a few idyllic beach hideaways remain.

East of Tangalla the landscape changes over just a few kilometres from lush to the comparatively barren. Here, in the ancient lands of the Ruhuna kingdom, are some of Sri Lanka's greatest national parks, in particular **Yala** and **Uda Walawe**, with magnificent opportunities for spotting wildlife and birdlife, as well as some of the island's most sacred pilgrimage sites.

★ Don't miss...

1. **Sinharaja Biosphere Reserve** Trek up to Lion Rock for unbeatable views over the forest canopy, page 123.
2. **Galle** Take an evening stroll around the fort's historic ramparts and, drink in hand, settle down to watch the sun set over the Indian Ocean, page 149.
3. **Weligama** Don your mask, fin and snorkel and head into the deep blue to explore the wrecks in the bay, page 156.
4. **Mirissa** Admire nature's bounty on these perfect palm-fringed sands , page 157.
   Yala National Park Hire a jeep and go tracking the elusive leopards in the otherworldly landscape of this park, page 182.
6. **Kataragama's Maha Devale** Revel in the bizarre sights, sounds and smells of *puja* at this temple, page 183.

Interior of the Wet Zone

Stretching inland away from Colombo and the west coast beaches towards the Central Highland ridge, Sabaragamuwa Province, with its luxuriantly verdant, gently hilly landscape, is one of Sri Lanka's most beautiful regions. Beyond the gem capital of Ratnapura, lies the wonderful UNESCO protected Sinharaja rainforest, while scattered around the region are some remarkable, if hardly ever visited, prehistoric cave sites.

Inland to Ratnapura

The most frequently used route inland to Ratnapura heads east from Colombo along the congested A4 through Nugegoda, though a more attractive route follows the B1 along the south bank of the Kelaniya River. This passes through the picturesque **Kaduwela**, 16 km from Colombo, where there is a large Buddhist temple and the irrigation tank of Mulleriyawa, where you can watch a constant succession of varied river traffic from the beautifully positioned rest house. The two routes converge near Hanwella (33 km), where the A4 traffic begins to clear. **Hanwella** is built on the site of a Portuguese fort, and is noted as the place where the last king of Kandy, Sri Vikrama Rajasinha, was defeated.

Avissawella (57 km), the ancient capital of the Sitawaka kings and now the centre of the rubber industry, is in beautiful wooded surroundings. The ruins of the royal palace of Rajasinha, a Buddhist king who converted to Hinduism, can still be seen. He was responsible for starting work on the unfinished **Berendi Kovil**, which still has some fine stonework despite the Portuguese attack. It is just off the Ginigathena road on the opposite bank of the river.

At Avissawella, the A4 turns south towards Ratnapura, while the A7 leads off east through Kitulgala, see page 231, Hatton and ultimately to Nuwara Eliya. The road to Ratnapura periodically crosses rivers that come tumbling down from the southwest Highlands. It passes through Pusella and crosses the Kuruwita River, running through a landscape that was the site of some of Sri Lanka's earliest settlements and is also a gem bearing area. At **Batadombalena Cave**, near Kuruwita, fragmentary human skeletal remains have been found, as well as those of several large mammal skeletons including elephants and cattle, dating back at least as far as 28,000 years ago, or possibly very much earlier. To reach the caves take the road towards Eratne, turn right after 2 km and follow it to the end (2 km). A path reaches the cave in 5 km.

An alternative route from Colombo to Ratnapura follows the coastal road south to **Panadura**, see page 130, turning inland along the A8 through **Horana**, where there is a rest house built in the remains of an ancient Buddhist monastery. On the opposite side of the road is a large Buddhist temple with a particularly noteworthy bronze candlestick, over 2 m tall. Heading east from here there are some good views of Adam's Peak. » *For Sleeping, Eating and other listings, see pages 127-129.*

Ratnapura → *Phone code: 045. Colour map 3, grid B3. Population: 47,000. 100 km from Colombo.*

The climate of Ratnapura has been likened to a Turkish bath. One of Sri Lanka's wettest towns, even February, the driest month, normally has nearly 100 mm of rain, while May, the wettest, has nearly 500 mm. Sadly, heavy rainfall led to tragedy in May 2003 when hundreds died in the island's worst floods in more than half a century. The vegetation is correspondingly luxuriant, and the city has a beautiful setting on the banks of the Kalu

A gem of a place

Sri Lanka's gems place it among the top five gem bearing nations of the world. Washed out from the ancient rocks of the Highlands themselves, the gems are found in pockets of alluvial gravel known as Illama, usually a metre or two below the surface. Ratnapura – the 'city of gems' – is still the heart of the industry, though new pits are being explored in other parts of the island.

The quality of Ratnapura's gems is legendary. In the seventh century Hiuen Tsang claimed that there was a ruby on the spire of the temple at Anuradhapura whose magnificence illuminated the sky. Marco Polo (1293) described the flawless ruby as 'a span long and quite as thick as a man's arm'! Today, sapphires are much more important.

Traditional gem mining makes use of only the simplest technology. Pits are dug in the gravel. Divided in two, one half is used for extracting water while the gravel is dug out from the other half. When after two or three days a large enough pile of gravel has been excavated it is systematically washed in a stream, sifting the gems and heavy minerals from the lighter material. The work is done in teams, everyone getting a share of the value of any gems found. The cutting and polishing is carried out largely in Ratnapura itself. Dressed, cut and then polished, the methods and materials used are still largely local. Hand-operated lathes, and polishing paste made from the ash of burnt paddy straw have been used for generations.

A number of precious stones are found nearby including sapphire, ruby, topaz, amethyst, cat's eye, alexandrite, aquamarine, tourmaline, garnet and zircon. Genuine stones are common. Valuable stones by definition are more rare. Advice given to travellers at the beginning of the century still holds: 'As regards buying stones, it is a risky business unless the passenger has expert knowledge or advice. It is absolute folly to buy stones from itinerant vendors. It is far better to go to one of the large Colombo jewellers and take the chance of paying more and obtaining a genuine stone.'

Ganga, with views of rubber plantations and paddies. When fine, its views of Adam's Peak are also unmatched elsewhere. This town is aptly named the 'City of Gems' as Ratnapura is best known for its gemstones that are washed down the riverbed. The gravel beds which contain the gemstones are also the source of evidence of some of Sri Lanka's earliest cultures and of the wildlife that is now extinct. Discoveries of animal bones as well as of a variety of stone tools have made it clear that the area is probably one of the first sites to have been occupied by humans in Sri Lanka. » *For Sleeping, Eating and other listings, see pages 127-129.*

Sights

Although people seem to trade gems all over town, there are certain areas that specialize in uncut and unpolished stones, polished stones, cut stones, while other streets will only deal in star sapphires or cat's eyes. From 0700-1000 the area around the clocktower is a fascinating place to visit, where you can watch hundreds of people buying and selling gems. If you do buy a gem, it is worth checking its authenticity at the State Gem Corporation, in the fort (① *0800-1630*). If the gem merchant is genuine, he should not mind if you check its authenticity before the transaction.

Gem traders usually wear a white sarong and white shirt to bring them luck. Most of the trading taking place early in the day.

There are around 200 working **gem mines**, in the Ratnapura area. The mines are around 30 m deep, each with a series of interconnecting tunnels. Travel agents can organize visits ⓘ *a tip of Rs 100-150 is expected*, or you can simply take a three-wheeler to Warallupa Road, where there are several working mines. At each mine there is a shack housing a generator, where you will be shown the mining process. Miners will demonstrate washing and sifting the stones, and it may also be possible to walk inside some mines – ask locally.

Ratnapura is surrounded by rubber and tea estates in a lush and beautiful setting, and gives better views of Adam's Peak than almost anywhere else on the island. The old **Fort** above the clocktower, currently under renovation, offers good views. Further afield, it is well worth going to the big **Buddha statue**, built by a wealthy young gem merchant, on a hill behind the Rest House, for the views. Driving up to **Gilimale** from the bridge gives you a chance to see the massive curtain wall of the central highlands to the north. The surrounding forests are rich in flowers, one of the most notable being the **Vesak Orchid**, which takes its name from the month of Vesak in which it flowers.

Maha Saman Dewale, some 4 km west of town, is the richest Buddhist temple in Sri Lanka. Dedicated to the guardian god of Adam's Peak, it is originally thought to date from the 13th century, but was rebuilt by Parakramabahu IV in the 15th century before being damaged by the Portuguese soldiers. The temple, which has been restored, has an ornamental doorway and fine wall paintings inside. Interesting features include the remains of a Portuguese fort. On the temple wall is a Portuguese soldier sculpted in stone while a slab bearing their coat of arms was also found here. There is a major Perahera procession during the July-August full moon, when decorated boats sail along the Kalu Ganga.

Ratnapura

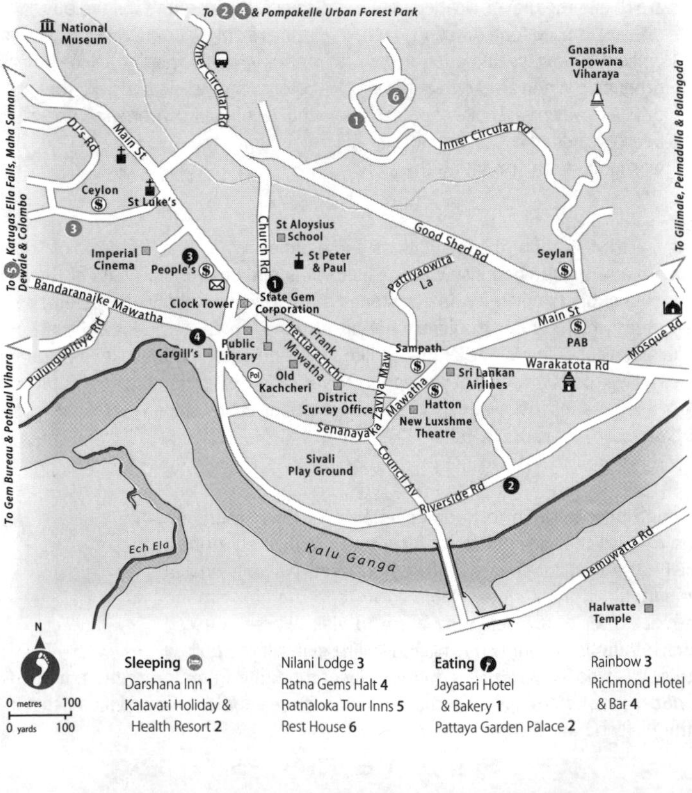

0 metres 100
0 yards 100

Sleeping
Darshana Inn 1
Kalavati Holiday & Health Resort 2
Nilani Lodge 3
Ratna Gems Halt 4
Ratnaloka Tour Inns 5
Rest House 6

Eating
Jayasari Hotel & Bakery 1
Pattaya Garden Palace 2
Rainbow 3
Richmond Hotel & Bar 4

There are a few museums in Ratnapura. Private museums tend to be primarily retail outlets for gems but at the same time demonstrate the craft of gem polishing. The **Gem Bureau and Museum**, ⓘ *Pothgul Vihara Rd, Getangama (2 km south) 0900-1700*, has gems from different parts of Sri Lanka, and an art gallery. The **Gem Bank Gemmological Museum**, ⓘ *6 Ehelepola Mawatha, Batugedera, 2 km along A4 towards Pelmadulla, T2222724, 0900-1700*, has an interesting private collection of gems and precious minerals and mining-related exhibits including a model of a pit. Don't miss the museum's rare elephant pearl. **Ratnapura National Museum**, ⓘ *Ehelapola Walauwa, Colombo Rd, T2222451, 0900-1700, closed Thu and Fri, Rs 45, children Rs 25*, has a small dated exhibition of pre-historic fossil skeletons of elephants, hippos and rhinoceros found in gem pits, plus stuffed animals and snakes in jars. Also arts and culture of the province: musical instruments, masks, jewellery, textiles and flags.

Excursions

Ratnapura is the base for the much steeper and more strenuous route which leads to **Adam's Peak** starting at Siripagama, 15 km away. The climb takes about seven hours, though the construction of new steps may shorten the time. Some pilgrims walk the 25 km from Ratnapura to Adam's Peak during the winter months. It begins at Malwala (8 km) on the Kalu Ganga to Palabadelle (11 km, 375 m), then follows a very steep path to Heramitipana (13 km, 1,100 m), and to the summit (5 km, 2,260m). Buses leave Ratnapura for Siripagama regularly until 1900. See page 230 for the shorter and more frequently used route.

A short walk northeast of town is **Pompakelle Urban Forest Park**, ⓘ *Rs 50, 0800-1700*. Signposted trails lead you through the surprisingly large 15 ha forest – a welcome change of pace from Main Street. Close to the entrance is a large, now defunct, natural swimming pool. Enclosed originally by the British as a reservoir for the town, the water is now muddy and polluted and swimming is prohibited, though a clean-up is planned.

Katugas Ella Falls, 2 km north from the centre, are attractive falls offering the opportunity to swim in the river. Avoid visiting on Sundays when it can get busy.

There are impressive **caves** at Kosgalla, 8 km from Ratnapura and at Eratna/Batatota, 19 km away.

Sinharaja Biosphere Reserve → *Phone code: 045; Colour map 3, grid B3.*

Sinharaja, as the last significant stretch of rainforest on the island to be left largely undisturbed, maintains enormous national importance. It is home to a remarkable array of endemic species. In 1989 it was recognized by UNESCO as an international Biosphere Reserve and became a World Heritage Site. 'Sinharaja' means 'Lion King' and is believed to have been the final refuge of the now extinct lion on the island. While it is managed by the Forestry Department with less than maximum efficiency, Sinharaja's ecotourism potential is now beginning to be recognized, with some good accommodation, including an enterprising new 'boutique' hotel, opening up in the area. While the wildlife is harder to see than at some of the big national parks, just being in the thick of the rainforest can be an exhilarating experience. ▸▸ *For Sleeping, Eating and other listings, see pages 127-129.*

Ins and outs → *For details of tours, see page 129.*

Getting there There are four entry points to the forest, though only two can be approached by car and possess any facilities. From Colombo, the west coast or Ratnapura, most people enter at the main gate at Kudawa at the northwestern edge of the reserve, where limited accommodation is available. East of Ratnapura, turn off the A4 at Tiruwanaketiya, head for Kalawana, and then turn right at Weddagala, 6 km from the park entrance. Alternatively you can approach from Rakwana through Pothupitiya, though the road may be impassable in the wet season. From the south coast it is best to enter at Mederipitiya, 12 km from Deniyaya, on the Galle-Ratnapura Road, which is also accessible by car from Embilipitiya to the southeast. The other two entrances are at Morningside (to the east) and Nelluwa (to the southwest), though a four-wheel drive is necessary, and you will need to buy your ticket in advance at the Forestry Departments in Battaramulla, see below, or Galle, *T091-2234306*.

Getting around There are several walking trails for exploring the forest by foot. Bring water, food, binoculars, rainwear and a lighter or salt to get rid of leeches.

Best time to visit December to early April and August and September, when rainfall tends to be lighter. The shaded forest, with an average temperature of 23.6°C, is fairly cool throughout the day, though afternoons are usually wet – come prepared.

Park information Rs 575 (children Rs 290), plus (compulsory) guide fee which varies according to the length of the trail: from Kudawa it costs Rs 500 to Singhagala, and Rs 300 for the Waturawa and Moulawella walks. There are about 30 guides, all local villagers, and though they are very knowledgeable don't always speak English. An entry ticket and a guide ticket (fee varies according to route) is purchased before entry. The guides will probably expect an additional tip. Video cameras costs Rs 500. The reserve is open 0600-1800 though guides rarely arrive before 0700-0730. If you wish to make an early start, make arrangements the previous day. Facilities and information at the park offices (Kudawa and Mederipitiya) are limited, and leaflets may not be available, so it is worth calling in at the Forestry Department, *82 Rajamalwatta Rd, Battaramulla (Colombo outskirts), T011-2866626*, for further information.

Background

The first records on Sinharaja date back to Portuguese time when detailed lists on not only names but also agricultural produce were collected for taxation purposes. Having been mapped first by the Dutch, the British made the forest Crown Property in 1840. Naturalist George Henry Thwaites undertook the first surveys in the 1850s, recording many plants found in Sinharaja, and in May 1875, 6,000 acres of the 'Sinharaja Mukalana' were recognized as reserved forest. Through the 20th century, numerous studies assessed the area's suitability as a source of wood, but owing to its inaccessibility the reserve remained untouched until 1968, when the government sanctioned selective logging. From 1971 to 1977, about 1,400 ha of forest was selectively logged, but pressure from conservation groups brought about a complete ban in 1978 when the area was designated a Man and Biosphere Reserve. In 1988 it was declared a National Heritage Area, and a World Heritage Site in 1989. Despite this, the forest remains an important source of income for inhabitants of the 22 villages surrounding the reserve. The sap from the kitul palm produces a fermented toddy and a treacle produced by heating it which in turn makes the dry brown sugar, jaggery. Rattan is collected to make baskets and mats, and also leaves and wood for construction and fuel. There is also some illicit gem-mining in some eastern areas of the reserve.

The Reserve

Sinharaja's importance lies not just in its pristine nature, but also in the high degree of endemism of its species. For example, 95% of the endemic birds of Sri Lanka, and more than half of its mammals and butterflies, have been recorded here. This said, in the dense forest animals can be hard to see, so don't expect game spotting on the level of Yala. The purple-faced leaf monkey is the most commonly seen mammal, and others include giant squirrel, dusky squirrel and sambar. The leopard population is estimated to be around 15 (very seldom seen) and there are no elephants. Birdlife, as ever, is the most rewarding to observe. Rare endemics include red-faced malkoha, Sri Lanka blue magpie, the white-headed starling and even the green-billed coucal, with plenty of others including orange minivets, orioles and babblers. An interesting and colourful spectacle is the presence of mixed flocks, sometimes comprising up to 80 species. The most commonly seen reptile is the green garden lizard, while snakes include the endemic Green pit viper and the Hump-nosed viper, and there are several endemic amphibian species, including the torrent toad, wrinkled frog and Sri Lankan reed frog. You will also be assured of feeling plenty of leeches, so come prepared.

Lying in the southwest lowland Wet Zone, the reserve's rolling hills with ridges and valleys between 200-1,300 m stretch 21 km from east to west, though north to south it only measures 3.7 km, bounded by the Kalu Ganga in the north and the Gin Ganga in the south. It spans the districts of Ratnapura, Kalutara, Galle and Matara. Vegetation consists of Tropical Wet Evergreen Forest and Tropical Lowland Forest, with lofty, very straight dominant trees a distinctive feature. As with its fauna, the forest's trees, ferns and epiphytes are also largely endemic.

There are three main **nature trails** from Kudawa. Guide leaflets are sometimes available. **Waturawa Trail** is 4.7-km long. It is about three hours of gentle walking. The path starts 250 m from the Camp and leads through the forest up to the visitors centre. From here, most guides will take you to the Giant Newada tree, some 43 m high. There are 14 observation posts which are marked on the guide leaflet and there are two good places for spotting birds and watching monkeys. This trail is a good introduction to the rainforest. **Moulawella Trail** is 7.5-km long. Taking about seven hours, this is a fairly strenuous trek. It takes you through primary forest up to Moulawella Peak (760 m) and from there you can see Adam's Peak and look over the forest canopy. The walk gives you a chance to see fascinating leaf-shaped frogs, lizards, tropical fish, snakes, crabs and a 300-year-old vine. **Sinhagala Trail** is 14-km long. This trek takes a full day. It leads through the heart of the rainforest to the 742-m 'Lion Rock' from where you can look out over the unbroken tree canopy of an undisturbed forest and see the various hill ranges – 'twice as good as Moulawella'.

Ratnapura to the Highlands

The recently relaid A4 between Ratnapura and Pelmadulla (18 km) continues across the fertile and undulating low country, while the hills on either side come closer and closer to the road. It is a major gem bearing area. **Pelmadulla** is a major junction, the road from Colombo running east and then northeast, curving round the southern flank of the Central Highland massif towards Haputale, while the A18 goes southeast to Madampe. From Pelmadulla the A4 continues to Balangoda and the caves beyond, through superb lush scenery all the way. This is the heart of the rubber producing area, and there are many rubber estates. Adam's Peak and the Maskeliya Range rise magnificently to the north, although during the southwest monsoon they are almost permanently covered in cloud. *For Sleeping, Eating and other listings, see pages 127-129.*

Balangoda and around → *Phone code: 045. Colour map 3, grid B4.*

Balangoda is one of an increasing number of towns overlooked by an enormous cement Buddha. The town itself has little of interest; most visitors use it as a base for excursions into the Peak Wilderness Sanctuary and to visit the nearby prehistoric cave sites. **Kuragala Cave,** with the Jailani Muslim shrine nearby, can be reached by following a path uphill from Taniantenna on the Kaltota Road. It is 25 km along the Kaltota Road. In August Muslims congregate here for a large festival. **Budugala Cave Temple,** 13 km away, is across a deep gully from the shrine. Take the road to Uggalkaltota, to the east, which follows the downward sloping ridge (buses go most of the way). The 3-km track from Uggalkaltota is safe for four-wheel drive in dry weather.

From Balangoda, after passing Rajawaka on the Kaltota Road, a track leads 4 km down to the south to **Diyainna Cave**, near the village of the same name, which was also inhabited between 8000 and 2500 BC. If you continue along the track southeast towards Uda Walawe Reservoir, you will reach **Handagiriya** on the river bank. It is claimed that the old Buddhist stupa once held the Tooth Relic, see page 203. This is close to **Bellan Bendi Pelessa**, the plain where large finds of prehistoric skeletons has confirmed it as an open-air site once used by *Homo sapiens Belangodensis*.

Belihuloya → *Phone code: 045. Colour map 3, grid B5.*

A small settlement on the Ratnapura-Badulla Road, Belihuloya is best known as a picturesque rest point on the banks of a gushing river, among tea estates. There is a track from here leading up to World's End on the Horton Plains, see page 227, though from this side it is a long uphill walk of some four hours.

Belihuloya to Haputale

Heading northeast for 16 km, you reach the **Non Pareil Tea Estate**, where a dirt track then winds 24 km up to World's End. Passing through **Halpe** (6 km), the road continues for a further 7 km to a turn off for the **Bambarakanda Falls**, which at 237 m – in three stages – is Sri Lanka's highest waterfall. The falls, which are impressive after the rains, are reached by a sealed road, 5 km off the A4. Just beyond the turn off for the falls is the settlement of Kalupahana. **Haldumulla**, nearby, has excellent views across to the sea. It is possible to visit an organic tea garden here, the **Bio Tea Project**, run by **Stassen Exports Ltd.** Their centre is signposted 3 km off the road. Further east from Kalpahana is **Beragala**, and then a further steep climb of 10 km is Haputale. For details of Haputale, Ella, Badulla etc, see page 238.

To the south coast

After Pelmadulla the A18 runs southeast through Kahawatta Ford. After 10 km, at **Madampe**, the A17 branches off to the right towards Galle and Matara. On the way you go through various towns and villages, of which **Rakwana** is the largest. The chief village of a tea-growing district, it has a large Tamil and Muslim population and a beautiful setting. There are many beautiful flowering trees in season and wild orchids, notably the large flowered *Dendrobium maccarthaie*. Three entrances to **Sinharaja Biosphere Reserve** are accessible from Rakwana. The road west out of town leads eventually close to the main entrance at **Kudawa**, via Pothupitiya and Weddagala. If you have a four-wheel drive it is quicker to follow the A18 south to **Suriyakanda**, from where it is 7 km along a track to the little used Morningside entrance. Alternatively you can continue south to **Deniyaya** for the Mederipitiya entrance.

The road south of Rakwana is very scenic, with fabulous views across to the mountains and valleys of the Peak Wilderness Sanctuary, numerous fine waterfalls and some grand, if rickety, old iron bridges. Tea and rubber plantations cover the landscape with *pinus* trees often lining the road. Crossing the Bulutota Pass there are ten hair-pin bends, marked by white markers, after which you pass just to the east of **Gongala Peak** (1,358 m). This is the easternmost edge of the Wet Zone. From Panilkande, where you can rent a well-situated tea plantation bungalow, the road continues west to Deniyaya, one of the centres of low-altitude tea production and a main gateway to Sinharaja (see page 123). Just south of **Akuressa** the road forks, the A24 turning left to Matara down the valley of the Nilwala Ganga, and passing from one of the wettest areas of Sri Lanka to one of the driest in under 20 km. The right fork continues as the A17 to Galle, remaining in typically Wet Zone vegetation and cultivation throughout. » *For Sleeping, Eating and other listings, see pages 127-129.*

Sleeping

Inland to Ratnapura *p120*

C-E **Rest House** (UDA), *Avissawella, T036-2222299*. Old rest house under refurbishment at the time of visit. Clean rooms with balcony, a/c rooms well-furnished but expensive (Rs 1,800-2,100), non a/c (Rs 950) are simpler. Popular lunch-time spot with fiery rice and curry, but overpriced (Rs 305).

D **Rest House** (CHC), *on the Kelaniya River, Hanwella, T011-2503497, F2503504*. 8 rooms (non-a/c US$17 with breakfast) with beautiful view along the river. Edward VII (then Prince of Wales) planted a jack tree in the garden here in 1875.

Ratnapura *p120, map p122*

C **Ratnaloka Tour Inns**, *Kosgala, Kahangama (6 km from town), T2222455*. 53 rooms (US$25 -35), deluxe carpeted with TV, bathtub and private balcony (views across to lotus pond and tea estates), all comfortable with a/c, good restaurant, exchange, long pool.

D-E **Kalavati Holiday and Health Resort**, *Polhengoda Village, Outer Circular Rd, 1.6 km from Bus Stand, T2222465, F2223657*. 18 rooms (Rs 1,175-1,335, depending on size), some a/c (Rs 400 supplement), no hot water, restaurant, house decorated with collector's pieces (antiques cabinets, palm leaf manuscripts, statues, betel cutters etc), beautiful tropical garden, some interesting tours (Dec to May only), natural therapy 'healing arts' practised here including oil baths and massage (Rs 1,000-1,200), herbal treatments (Rs 750-950), floral baths, 3-wheeler from Bus Stand, Rs 75.

D-E **Rest House**, *Rest House (Inner Circle) Rd, on a hill 1 km from centre, T2222299*. 11 large, simple rooms (Rs 1,000-1,500, best upstairs) though no hot water, food good value, peaceful, delightful site and outstanding views from atmospheric veranda.

E **Nilani Lodge**, *21 Dharmapala Mawatha, T2222170, hashani@sltnet.uk* 10 rooms with balcony and hot water, some a/c, in large modern white apartment-style building, restaurant and gem museum and shop on site, tours to mines and cutters– a gem shop with beds!

E-F **Darshana Inn**, *68/5 Rest House (Inner Circle) Rd, just below Rest House, T2222674*. 4 basic rooms (Rs 600), fan, rather damp attached bath, restaurant, popular bar, pleasant owner.

F-G **Ratna Gems Halt**, *153/5 Outer Circular Rd (short climb), T2223745*. Spotless, excellent value rooms, all with bath, in family house. 3 new upstairs rooms with shared veranda overlooking paddy fields and mines (Rs 550), 3 smaller box-like rooms downstairs (Rs 350). Good meals available (Rs 150 breakfast and dinner). Small gem centre (no pressure to buy) where you can watch stones being dressed, cut and polished.

Sinharaja Biosphere Reserve *p123*

There are a few options at the Kudawa entrance. Kudawa itself has only basic places to stay, and you should arrive in daylight. More luxury can be found at Kalawana, 17 km away. If entering from the Mederipitiya entrance, the nearest accommodation is at Deniyaya, 12 km away.

LL-L **Boulder Garden**, *Sinharaja Rd, Kalawana, Kudawa nearest entrance, T2255812, info@bouldergarden.com* Genuinely creative 'eco' concept, a sort of prehistoric luxury resort or upmarket hermitage, with 8 smart, though simple, rooms (plus 2 cave 'suites' used as a meditation area) built into a complex of 28 caves. Fully inclusive rates include a trip to Sinharaja, and also a 3-hr walk along cave route within grounds. Open-air haute cuisine restaurant in grotto (for residents only).

D **Sathmala Ella Rest**, *Deniyaya, 4 km towards Mederipitiya, 7 km from entrance, T041-2273481*. 10 clean rooms with balcony or terrace (Rs 1,200), restaurant, bar, pleasant position close to Ging Ganga, though no English spoken and rather disorganized. Transport to park Rs 1,200.

D-E **Singraj Rest**, *Koswatta, 1 km from Kalawana, for Kudawa entrance, T2255201*. 7 clean and comfortable rooms (Rs 1,000-1,500). Pleasant position between tea plantations and paddy fields, friendly, good food.

E-F **Martin Wijeysinghe's Lodge**, *200 m from park entrance, 3½ km by jeep (around Rs 1,000 to hire) from Kudawa village, 2 km shortcut on foot; no phone – to contact in advance phone or telegram Kudawa post office, T2225528*. Knowledgeable and highly respected former range officer, well worth calling on even if you don't stay. Magnificent forest views, 7 clean rooms, some with attached clean bath (Rs 750-1,000), breakfast Rs 75, lunch and dinner Rs 300.

F **Campsite**, *Pitadeniya in Dombagoda. Forest on the banks of Gin Ganga, near the Mederipitiya entrance. Contact the Forestry Department, T011-2866626.*

F **Rest House**, *Deniyaya, for Mederipitiya entrance, T041-2273600.* Fine position and very large, clean rooms, Rs 700. Popular lunch spot.

F **Singharaja Rest**, *Temple Rd, Deniyaya, T041-2273367, indika_1@sltnet.lk* 4 clean rooms (Rs 750), run by Bandula, Palitha's brother. Also runs good tours.

F **Sinharaja Rest**, *Temple Rd, Deniyaya, for Mederipitiya entrance, T041-2273368.* 4 clean rooms (Rs 750), run by Palitha Ratnayake, very knowledgeable and enthusiastic guide. Recommended trips to Sinharaja, good food (dinner Rs 200).

F-G **Sunil Handuwalage's**, 500 m along footpath from Weddagala-Kudawa Rd, 3 km before Kudawa, for Kudawa entrance, no phone. 1 basic room offered by 1 of the guides.

G **Forestry Department Bungalow**, *Kudawa, reserve at Forestry Department, T011-2866626.* None-too-clean 20-bed dormitory, Rs 350 per bed includes sheets and dinner. Mattresses OK if smelly but ask for sheets and pillowcases, western toilets but no showers. Alternatively, 2 rooms with attached bath, sleeping 8, which you have to rent in full (Rs 2,000 – not worth it unless several of you).

Ratnapura to the Highlands *p125*

C **Rest House** (CHC), *near the bridge, Belihuloya, T2280199, chc@sltnet.lk* 11 rooms (best in a newer extension) in over 100-year old building by an attractive though very noisy stream, rooms a little shabby though bed linen clean, attached hot bath, no nets or fan. At US$34 very overpriced. Restaurant on pleasant covered terrace (set lunch or dinner US$7-8) which can get overcrowded with tourists, a 'honeymooners' hotel.

D-E **River Garden Resort**, *Ratnapura side of the bridge, Belihuloya, T/F2280223, www.srilankaecotourism.com* Great position with attractive thatched huts on the hillside, fan, attached hot bath (US$15), in extensive gardens. Camping also available. Wide variety of sports offered include canoeing and mountain-biking, a 'natural pool' for bathing in the river (though take care). Good food.

E **Rest House**, *Rest House Rd, Balangoda, T2287299.* 5 large rooms (Rs 850), linen clean but rooms a bit shabby, fan, attached bath (no hot water), some with veranda, large dining hall, good location above town, ok value.

F **Pearl Tourist Inn**, *on hill above town, Belihuloya, T2280157.* Basic but moderately clean rooms with attached bath, fan, restaurant, bar, but no hot water. Decent food and not bad value.

F **Pelmadulla Guest House**, *82/12 Barnes Ratwatta Mawatha, Balangoda, T2287739.* 5 clean rooms (Rs 700), comfortable beds, attached bath, net, no fan, nice quiet setting, friendly family, good meals.

To the south coast *p126*

See Sinharaja, above, for sleeping at Deniyaya.

B **Panilkande Sinharaja Bungalow**, *14 km before Deniyaya, Panilkande, T041-2273297.* Rent whole bungalow (US$50), which sleeps 8-10. 4 enormous bedrooms plus living room and 3 bathrooms. Spartanly furnished, and the visitors' book urges better maintenance, but full of character. If you bring food, the caretaker will cook it for you. 1-1½ hrs from Sinharaja so could be used as a base.

F **Rest House**, *Rakwana, T045-2246299.* Large, clean rooms (Rs 750), some with own terrace, fine views.

Eating

Ratnapura *p120, map p122*

RsRs **Jayasiri Hotel & Bakery**, *198 Main St, 1030-2130.* Sri Lankan rice and curry downstairs, Chinese on 1st floor, bustling with activity, friendly staff, full of local colour.

RsRs **Pattaya Garden Palace**, *14 Senanayake Mawatha, T2223029.* Modern a/c restaurant with a wide choice of Chinese and Thai dishes.

RsRs **Rainbow**, *163 Main St*, good for Rice and Curry 'meals', large airy room looking onto part of gem traders street market.

RsRs **Rest House** is a good spot for lunch (excellent rice and curry Rs 225, reasonably priced drinks).

RsRs **Richmond Hotel**, *5 Bandaranaike Mawatha, T2222583, 1100-2330.* Second floor has the smartest new restaurant in town with lovely setting overlooking ganga. Good range of Thai dishes, with some Chinese. Cheaper restaurant on 1st floor and bar downstairs (see below).

Rs There are plenty of good bakeries near the bus station and in town.

Rs **Cargill's**, *Bandaranaike Mawatha, open 0800-2200*. For self-caterers.

Sinharaja Biosphere Reserve *p123*

Rs-RsRs You can arrange rice and curry meals by speaking to the **Camp Cook**. Day visitors should carry food and drink. If entering at Kudawa, even if not staying there it is worth breakfasting at **Martin's**. Limited snacks (bread, biscuits etc) are available from stalls in Kudawa.

Bars and clubs

Ratnapura *p120, map p122*

Richmond Hotel in the centre of town has a popular bar-restaurant on the ground floor. **Darshana Inn** is also popular, though only beer and arrack are available.

Tour operators

Sinharaja Biosphere Reserve *p123*

Palitha Ratnayaka, who runs **Sinharaja Rest** in Deniyaya is a long-established, experienced guide with excellent English. Tours range from 4 hrs to all day. The full day walk takes you to Lion Rock where you can look out over the forest canopy. A standard trip will cost Rs 500 each for guide, plus Rs 800 per group for transport, and include visits to waterfalls and swimming at a bathing hole. Walks can vary according to fitness. Palitha's brother, Bandula, also takes excursions.

Transport

Ratnapura *p120, map p122*

Air Sri Lankan Airlines, *Ramzi Gems Building, 1/1 Senanayake Mawatha, T2224813*.

Bus Ratnapura's new stand is one of the biggest in Sri Lanka, and handles both CTB and private buses. There are regular services to **Colombo** (2½-3 hrs), **Kalawana** (for Sinharaja) (2 hrs), and **Balangoda** (1 hr), 2 CTB buses a day at 0500 and 1400 to **Haputale** (4 hrs) via **Belihuloya** (2 hrs), 1 going on to **Badulla**, several buses to **Kandy** (4 hrs), via **Avissawella** and **Kegalla**; and 3 buses a day via **Embilipitiya** to **Hambantota** and **Matara** (1 hr). For **Galle**, take an a/c bus along the A8 to Panadura and change to a Colombo-Galle bus there.

Sinharaja Biosphere Reserve *p123*

Bus To **Kudawa**: buses from **Colombo**, 1 direct a day to Kalawana (1315, 4 hrs), otherwise change in Ratnapura (Rs 1½, 2 hrs). 4 buses from **Kalawana** to Kudawa from 0700 (45 mins). Walkers can ask locally for the short cut from Weddagala or use the 4 km track. At **Deniyaya** the smart new bus stand fields buses to **Colombo** (6 a day, 6½ hrs), **Ratnapura** (7 a day, 4½ hrs), and **Embilipitiya** (3 a day, 3½ hrs). For **Galle**, change at Akuressa (every 30 mins, 2½ hrs). Occasional buses also run to the Mederipitiya entrance (45 mins), though it is easier to take your own transport.

Ratnapura to the Highlands *p125*

Bus Buses run from Ratnapura east to **Balangoda** (1 hr) and **Belihuloya** (2 hrs) every 1-2 hrs, with 3 services running on to **Haputale** (4 hrs). From Pelmadulla and Balangoda hourly services to **Colombo** (3-4 hrs). For the south coast, buses run from Pelmadulla to **Tangalla** via **Embilitipiya** (2 hrs).

Directory

Ratnapura *p120, map p122*

Communications Main **post office**, *clocktower square, open Mon-Fri 0830-1900*. **International phone calls** can be made here, or through the IDD Metrocard and Lanka Payphones cardphone boxes.

Useful address **Tourist police**, *main police station, opposite clocktower, corner with Bandaranaike Mawatha*.

For an explanation of the sleeping and eating price codes used in this guide, see the inside front cover.

Beaches along the southwest coast

Beyond Colombo's urban sprawl lie the golden beaches that serve Sri Lanka's package tourism industry. To some, the coast's wealth of quality accommodation, beach restaurants and bars makes for a perfect indulgent holiday; to others it has been spoilt by overdevelopment. Yet away from the resorts traditional life continues. Many people still depend on fishing with fishermen bringing in their catch at numerous points along the coast. The coconut palms that line the shore also provide a livelihood for many. The road and railway line hug the ocean as they go south – an enjoyable journey.

South to Kalutara

Moratuwa, 23 km south of Colombo, has a large Catholic population, and some fine churches. The town is also noted for its furniture making and its college, and you will see by the side of the road furniture workshops carving wood into a wide variety of intricate designs. There is plenty of accommodation in Moratuwa, mainly on **Bolgoda Lake**, popular for local weddings and as a weekend escape from Colombo. Here you can fish for barramundi, or take boat trips out to the lake's islands.

Panadura, to the south of a wide estuary, has many fine colonial mansions. From here, the A8 road leads east to Ratnapura and beyond, hugging the southern edge of the Highlands. The town is known for producing some of the highest quality **batik** in Sri Lanka. It is well worth the small diversion to the workshop and showroom of Bandula Fernando, ⓘ *289/5 Noel Mendis Rd, just off the A2, T034-2233369*. One of the foremost batik designers in Sri Lanka, Bandula Fernando combines traditional and modern styles to produce some exceptionally vibrant and original batik designs. He is also credited with evolving mosaic art in batik, acknowledged as a uniquely individual style of batik. The designs on offer are quite different from those seen elsewhere on the island and are sold at fair prices considering the detail and excellence. » *For Sleeping, Eating and other listings, see pages 139-148.*

Kalutara → *Phone code: 034. Colour map 3, grid B2. 42 km from Colombo. Population 38,000.*

Kalutara is a busy district capital renowned for its basket making. Leaves of the wild date are dyed red, orange, green and black, and woven into hats, mats and baskets. To guard the spice trade the Portuguese built a fort on the site of a **Buddhist temple** here. The Dutch took it over and a British agent converted it into his residence. The site, ⓘ *free, though you may be asked for a donation for leaving your shoes*, by the bridge across the Kalu Ganga, now again has a modern Buddhist shrine, the **Gangatilaka Vihara**, with a sacred Bo tree outside. It is worth stopping to visit the hollow *dagoba* (actually a *dagoba* within a *dagoba*), as others on the island contain relics and are not accessible. Most remarkable is its extraordinary acoustics, which can be quite disorienting. There are 75 paintings inside, illustrating events from the Buddha's life.

Kalutara has a huge stretch of fine **sand** with **Wadduwa** to the north home to the area's top resorts. Kalutara itself divides into Mahawaskaduwa (Kalutara North) where the beach is more scenic, right down to Katukurunda (Kalutara South).

At Palatota, a little inland, is **Richmond Castle** ⓘ *0900-1730, Rs 100*. A fine country house in a 42-acre fruit garden estate, it is now used as an education centre

Sap tappers

Palm toddy is a universal favourite for Sri Lankans, as is the stronger distilled arrack, both of which are found throughout the island. They (as well as sweet palm juice, treacle or jaggery) are produced from the sap which is collected in earthen pots that you'll notice hanging at the base of the long green fronds at the crown of the palms which have been set aside for 'tapping'.

The sap flows when the apex of an unopened flower bunch is 'tapped' by slicing it off and tapping it with a stick to make the cells burst and the juice to flow. This usually starts in about three weeks of the first cut. From then on successive flower buds are tapped so that sap collecting can continue for half a year. Fruit production, of course, stops during this period, but tapping seems to result in an improved crop of nuts where the yield had previously been poor.

The sap is extracted from the crown of the palms by the *duravas* (toddy tappers). The skilful tapper usually ties a circle of rope around his ankles and shins up the tall smooth trunk two or three times a day to empty the sap pot into one he has tied around his waist. An agile man collecting from a group of palms will often get from tree to tree by using pairs of coconut fibre ropes tied from one tree top to the next, which saves the tapper time and energy wasted in climbing down and up again!

for underprivileged local children. Built in 1896, it originally belonged to landowner turned philanthropist NDA Silva Wijayasinghe, the local Padikara Mudah (village leader), and was used during the British period as a circuit bungalow for officials. Note the audience hall, with intricately carved pillars and beams (two shiploads of teak were brought from Burma for its construction) and a spiral staircase leading to a gallery. Another room shows some fascinating photographs from the time. Turn left immediately after the *vihara* along the Kalutara-Palatota Road. After 2 km, a track leads left to the house.

The large number of coconut palms along the coast road marks this as the centre of the arrack industry. The island's best quality mangosteen (introduced from Malaya in the early 19th century) and rubber are economically important. Graphite is also mined. Wild hog deer, introduced by the Dutch from the Ganga Delta, are reputedly still found nearby.

Beruwela, Aluthgama and Bentota

The coast at this point becomes more developed, with half a dozen villages indistinguishably joined together. Beruwela and its adjoining villages, with several large hotel resorts popular primarily with Germans, is at the north end, while Aluthgama, a little further south, is protected from the sea by a spit of land. Some characterful smaller guesthouses and restaurants can be found here, with a more peaceful riverside setting. The Bentota Bridge spans one of Sri Lanka's largest rivers, south of which Bentota, and particularly Walauwa, contain some sumptuous, and very expensive, places to stay. » *For Sleeping, Eating and other listings, see pages 139-148.*

Beruwela → *Phone code: 034. Colour map 3, grid B2. Population 34,000. 58 km from Colombo.*

The beach is notorious for its 'beach boys', who crowd around the beach entrances to the hotels

The name Beruwela is derived from the Sinhalese word *Baeruala* (the place where the sail is lowered). It marks the spot where the first Arab Muslim settlers are believed to have landed around the eighth century. **Kitchimalai Mosque**, on a headland 3 km north along the beach from the main hotel area, is worth seeing; it is a major pilgrimage centre at the end of Ramadan since there is also a shrine of a 10th-century Muslim saint, though guides that tell you that it is the oldest mosque in Sri Lanka are unlikely to be right. Looking east from the mosque, **Beruwela harbour** is an interesting place to watch the fishermen unload their catch. The harbour has over 600 boats, many of which are quite sizeable since the fishermen spend up to two months at sea. The fish market is busy early each morning – you may well see fresh shark or tuna change hands even before the sun is up. You can also hire a boat to the lighthouse raised on a small island offshore which offers an excellent view of the coastline from the top.

All the hotels listed in this section are actually in Moragalla, an adjoining settlement to the south of Beruwela, with some of the more upmarket hotels further south at Kaluwamodara. Fishermen offer to ferry holidaymakers across the narrow estuary to Bentota, the next resort.

Aluthgama → *Phone code: 034. Colour map 3, grid B2. 60 km from Colombo.*

Aluthgama, the principal town here, has a busy fish market and is famous for its oysters. The sand spit which separates the river from the sea where most of the hotels are built provides excellent waters for windsurfing and sailing. Many of the hotels referred to as being in Bentota are to the north of the Bentota Bridge and so are actually in Aluthgama.

Bentota → *Phone code: 034. Colour map 3, grid B2. 63 km from Colombo. The sea is rough during the monsoons – best between November and April.*

Bentota Bridge marks the border between the Western and Southern Provinces. The 100-acre **National Resort Complex** is built entirely for foreign tourists with shops, a bank and a post office. A full range of sports is available and the area is also gaining a reputation for providing first-class Ayurvedic healing centres, with more in the process of construction. South of Bentota, along Galle Road towards Induruwa, the area feels less of a tourist ghetto, and the natural beauty of the coastline returns. Here are some of the most sumptuous places to stay in the entire island. Unofficial 'guides' offer nearby river and lagoon trips and visits to temples, coir factories and woodcarvers. They are way overpriced.

The splendid **Brief Garden**, ⓘ *T2270462, daily 0800-1700, Rs 125*, at Kalawila was created between 1929 and 1989 by the late Bevis Bawa, the landscape architect, writer, sculptor, bon vivant and brother to Geoffrey (see box, page 367) – the name refers to a court brief! It is an enchanting garden in an

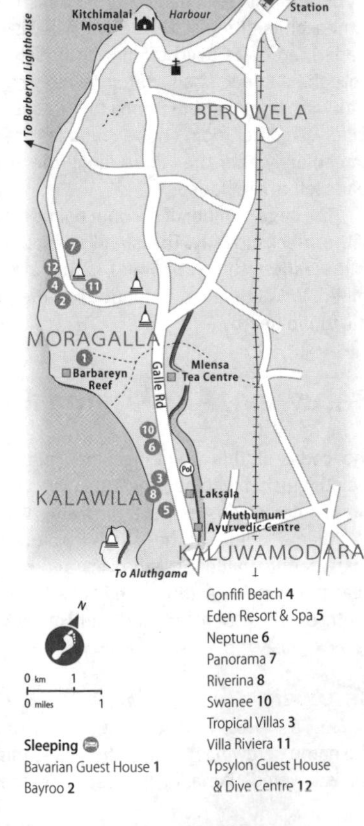

undulating landscape of paddies and scattered villages on a hillside. The five-acre garden with cool, shady paths and many mature specimen trees, was really created as a series of wonderfully composed views, designed in different moods. There are many references to European and Japanese style gardens, with shade-loving anthurium and alocasia plants common throughout. Bawa's house though is the highlight, with its eclectic private collection of paintings, sculptures, photographs (note Edward VIII and Lord Olivier, both of whom stayed here) and furniture (many colonial antiques), providing an added incentive to visit. Some of the paint- ings were composed by Australian artist Donald Friend, who came for a week and stayed for six years. Bawa himself appears in a number of forms, both in the house and garden, at one point representing Bacchus, holding a birdbath shaped as a giant clam-shell. In his outside bathroom, he appears again as a water-spouting gargoyle with wild hair and blue marble eyes. From Aluthgama, take the road inland to Matugama, and then Dhargatown (8 km). From here, a 2-km rough track (right at the first fork and left at the second) takes you to the gardens.

Aluthgama & Bentota

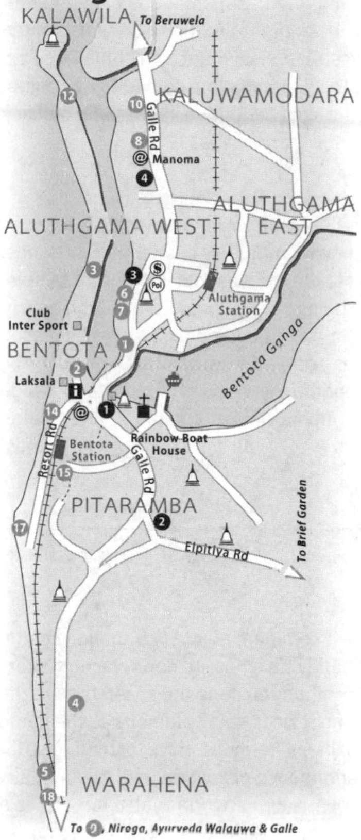

Kalawila, To Beruwela, Kaluwamodara, Galle Rd, Manoma, Aluthgama West, Aluthgama East, Aluthgama Station, Club Inter Sport, Bentota, Bentota Ganga, Laksala, Bentota Station, Rainbow Boat House, Resort Rd, Pitaramba, Elpitiya Rd, To Brief Garden, Warahena, To 9, Niroga, Ayurveda Walauwa & Galle

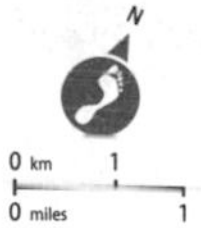

0 km 1
0 miles 1

Sleeping
Ayubowan 4
Bentota Beach 2
Ceysands 3
Club Bentota & Club Paradise Ayurvedic Centre 12
Club Villa 5
German Lanka Guest House 6
Hemadan 7
Nilwala 10
Saman Villas 9
Serendib 14
Sun and Moon 8
Susantha & Palm Restaurant 15
Taj Exotica 17
Terrena 1
The Villa 18

Eating
Aida 1
Refresh 2
Singharaja 4
Tropical Anushka River Inn 3

Induruwa to Ambalangoda

Induruwa → *Phone code: 034. Colour map 3, grid B2. 68 km from Colombo.*

Induruwa, with its pleasant stretch of beach, is being developed and some new hotels and guesthouses are opening up. Attractions in the area include several turtle hatcheries.

Visitors are welcome at the turtle hatchery here, ⓘ *Galle Rd, Bentota South, T2275850, Rs 100; donations appreciated.* Formerly part of the Victor Hasselblad Project, the hatchery has been running for about 20 years, buying eggs from local fishermen at a higher price (Rs 4 per egg) than they would get normally if sold for food. The eggs are buried as soon as possible in batches of 50. After hatching, the baby turtles are placed in holding tanks for two to three days before being released into the sea in the evening under supervision. Depending on the time of year (best November to April), you can see the hatchlings of up to five species – green, Olive Ridley, hawksbill, leatherback and loggerhead – at any one time. An example of each species is also held in separate tanks for research purposes At the time of writing (early 2003), the sanctuary also had a 1½-year old rare albino turtle (1:500,000 mutation), which would have little chance of surviving in the wild. » *For Sleeping, Eating and other listings, see pages 139-148.*

Kosgoda → *Phone code: 091. Colour map 3, grid B2. 73 km from Colombo.*

Kosgoda's 4-km stretch of beach has the highest density of turtle nesting in the country. In August 2003, the Turtle Conservation Project (TCP), an NGO formerly involved with the programme at Rekawa, see also box, page 160, launched a programme with the financial assistance of the UNDP to protect 1 km of the beach with the assistance of former nest poachers, retrained as 'nest-protectors' and tour guides. There is also a hatchery here, ⓘ *Rs 100*, similar to Induruwa. The fishermen are paid a slightly higher premium for the eggs than elsewhere, whilst the eggs are buried in the same batches as they were laid. The fishermen are paid a slightly higher premium for the eggs than elsewhere, whilst the eggs are buried in the same batches as they were laid. » *For Sleeping, Eating and other listings, see pages 139-148.*

Balapitiya → *Phone code: 091. Colour map 3, grid C2. 81 km from Colombo.*

A few kilometres north of Ambalangoda near the small town of Balapitiya, a bridge fords the Madu Ganga. The estuary is a major **wetlands**, famous for its 64 islands. Tours are offered which usually include a visit to the 150-year old **Koth Duwa temple**, and an island where you can watch cinnamon being cut and prepared, though bear in mind that the finished oil, bark and powder for sale is overpriced. You will also see some wildlife as the estuary is home to over 300 varieties of plant, including 95 families of mangrove, marshes and scrub supporting 17 species of birds, and a wide variety of amphibians and reptiles; water monitors are common. River safari operators leave from either side of the bridge. A 1½-hour trip, visiting two islands, costs around Rs 1,200 for a six-person boat.

Ambalangoda → *Phone code: 091. Colour map 3, grid C2. Population 20,000. 85 km from Colombo.*

The busy town of Ambalangoda is an important commercial and fish trading centre. With some local colour, and a fine sweep of sandy beach to its north, some visitors opt to stay here over its more touristy resort neighbours along the coast, though the accommodation options in town are limited. The town is chiefly famous as the home of **devil dancing** and **mask making** which many families have carried out for generations. It may be possible to watch a performance of *kolama* (folk theatre); ask at the museum or School of Dancing (see below). Ambalangoda is also famous as a major centre for cinnamon cultivation and production. Ask your hotel or guesthouse about visiting a plantation and factory. The colourful fish market is worth visiting early in the morning. » *For Sleeping, Eating and other listings, see pages 139-148.*

Sights

There are actually two **Ariyapala Mask Museums**, ⓘ *426 Patabendimulla, 0830-1730*, run by the two sons of the late mask-carver, who set up in competition. The museums are opposite one another: the smaller one houses the museum proper, while the other 'Mask Museum' is primarily a workshop and showroom. Some of the exhibits tracing the tradition of mask dancing are interesting and informative. The masks can be very elaborate. The *naga raksha* mask from the *Raksha Kolama*, for example, has a fearsome face with bulging eyes that roll around, a bloodthirsty tongue hanging from a mouth lined with fanglike teeth, all topped by a set of cobra hoods (see box). You can watch the odd craftsmen at work carving traditional masks

Dance of the sorcerers

The Devil Dance evolved from the rural people's need to appease malevolent forces in nature and seek blessing from good spirits when there was an evil spirit to be exorcised, such as a sickness to be cured. It takes the form of a ritual dance, full of high drama, with a sorcerer 'priest' and an altar. As evening approaches, the circular arena in the open air is lit by torches, and masked dancers appear to the beating of drums and chanting. During the exorcism ritual, which lasts all night, the 'priest' casts the evil spirit out of the sick. There are 18 demons associated with afflictions for which different fearsome *sanni* masks are worn. Although there is an element of awe and grotesqueness about the whole performance, the audience is treated to occasional light relief. These dances have a serious purpose and are, therefore, not on offer as 'performances'.

The **Kolam Dance** has its origins in folk theatre. The story tells of a queen, who, while expecting a child, had a deep craving to see a masked dance. This was satisfied by the Carpenter of the Gods, Visvakarma, who invented the dances.

The Kolam dances tell stories and again make full use of a wonderful variety of masks (often giant size) representing imaginary characters from folk tales, Buddhist jatakas, gods and devils, as well as well-known members of the royal court and more mundane figures from day-to-day life. Animals (lions, bears) too, feature as playful characters. This form of folk dance resembles the more serious Devil Dance in some ways – it is again performed during the night and in a similar circular, torch-lit, open-air 'stage' (originally Kolam was performed for several nights during New Year festivities). In spite of a serious or moral undertone, a sprinkling of cartoon characters is introduced to provide comic relief. The clever play on words can only be really appreciated by a Sinhalese.

from the light *kaduru* wood. The carvings on sale in the showroom are not of the best quality and are quite expensive. It is better to take your time to visit some of the smaller workshops around town on foot and compare prices and quality.

Traditional dancing shows take place about once a week at Bandu Wijesooriya School of Dancing ⓘ *417 Patabendimulla, T2258948, banduw@sri.lanka.net, dances normally take place 1830-1930 but check which day, Rs 500*. A typical show will include a kolam dance, followed by several ritual dances, a village folk dance, and end up with some short Indian dances. Courses are also possible at the school, from Rs 250 per day, where they teach dance, drumming and mask-carving.

Excursions

At **Karandeniya**, 208 steps lead up to the **Galabuddha temple**, which has a 33 m long lying Buddha, which a sign proudly proclaims to be the biggest in South Asia. The murals, currently under restoration, are worthy of note. The temple is 11 km inland from Ambalangoda, along the Elpitiya Road. Donations are welcome for restoring the Buddha, due to be completed in 2005.

At **Meetiyagoda**, 16 km inland, there is a moonstone quarry. The semi-precious stone, which often has a bluish milky tinge, is polished and set in silver or gold jewellery. The road sign claims that it's the 'only natural moonstone quarry in the world'.

Hikkaduwa → *Phone code: 091. Colour map 3, grid C2. 101 km from Colombo.*

Hikkaduwa is Sri Lanka's beach party capital, so if you are looking for peace and a beach to yourself, then you might wish to pass it by. A victim of its own success, the island's original surfers' hangout is now its most popular resort with mass tourism bringing pollution and overcrowding, as well a reputation for unsavoury activities and beach boys. Natural forces are also chipping away at Hikkaduwa's charm. The beach here is gradually disappearing with the sea noticeably encroaching inland year by year! This said, the resort still has some appeal. This coastal stretch has a vast number of high quality hotels and guesthouses of all price ranges. The food, especially seafood, is often excellent and with so much competition, reasonably priced. And the opportunities for watersports – swimming, snorkelling, scuba diving (as long as you don't expect living coral) and especially surfing – is probably unrivalled on the island. » *For Sleeping, Eating and other listings, see pages 139-148.*

Ins and outs

Getting there The bus station is in the centre of Hikkaduwa town. All accommodation lies to the south. The train station is about 200 m north of the bus station. Express trains and private buses are best for those travelling from or via Colombo.

Getting around There are four parts to what is known collectively as 'Hikkaduwa'. At the northern end is Hikkaduwa proper, the original settlement. The beach tends to be somewhat narrower here and less appealing. Further south is Wewala, where the beach is a bit wider and more attractive. Along with Narigama this is the main 'centre' with numerous beach bars and restaurants, and the cheapest accommodation. At the southern end is Thirangama, which is less frantic, but has good surfing waves and a wider beach. A major disadvantage though is the very busy main road which runs close to the beach. It is possible to walk uninterrupted along much of the beach. Three-wheelers can be stopped along the Galle Road (bus drivers are less obliging), but you will need to negotiate the price. Cycles and motorbikes can be hired.

Sights

Hikkaduwa's **'coral sanctuary'** is a shallow protected reef, close to the **Coral Gardens Hotel.** Once teeming with life, it was badly affected by 'bleaching' in early 1998, when sea temperatures rose causing the coral to reject the algae on which coral life fed. Recovery has been slow. The reef, and fish population, has also been degraded by tourism. Unregulated growth in the use of glass-bottomed boats to ferry visitors across the reef, dynamite fishing and the dumping of garbage from beach-side hotels have all contributed to the denigration of the habitat, prompting the Department of Wildlife to attempt to upgrade the area to full National Park status (with accompanying restrictions on visitor use), though these plans at the time of writing had stalled. However, it is

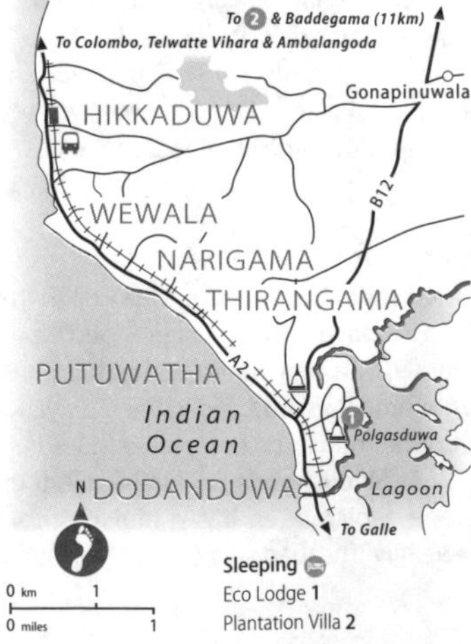

still possible to see reef fish which are fed by fishermen to provide an attraction for visitors. Glass-bottomed boats can be hired along the beach, though since the reef is shallow and close to shore, it is easy and less damaging to swim and snorkel to it. Despite the reduced diversity and population of coral and fish, Hikkaduwa is a good

Hikkaduwa & Wewala beach

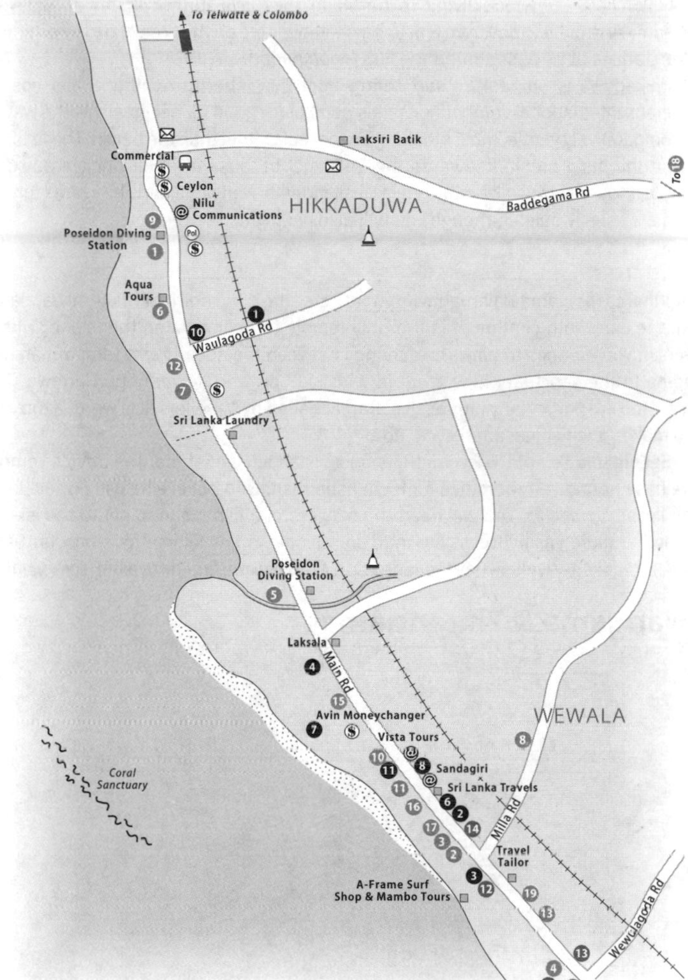

To Telwatte & Colombo
Laksiri Batik
Commercial
Ceylon
Nilu
Communications
HIKKADUWA
Baddegama Rd
To 18
Poseidon Diving Station
Aqua Tours
Waulagoda Rd
Sri Lanka Laundry
Poseidon Diving Station
Laksala
Main Rd
Avin Moneychanger
Vista Tours
Sandagiri
Sri Lanka Travels
WEWALA
Milla Rd
Travel Tailor
A-Frame Surf Shop & Mambo Tours
Wewalagoda Rd
Coral Sanctuary
To Narigama, Thirangama & Galle

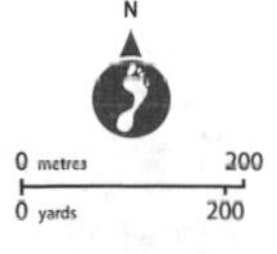

Sleeping
Blue Note Cabanas **2**
Blue Ocean Villa **3**
Casalanka **4**
Coral Gardens **5**
Coral Reef Beach **6**
Coral Rock **7**
Coral Sands **1**
El-Dorado **8**
Hikkaduwa Beach **9**
Lanka Super Corals **11**
Mama's Coral Beach **12**
Miga Villa **13**
Moon Beam **14**
Ozone Tourist Inn **15**
Plantation Villa **18**
Reefcomber **16**
Richard's Son's Beach Inn **17**
Tandem Guest House **19**
Whispering Palms Tourist Rest **10**

Eating
Abba's **1**
Blue Fox Cool Hut **2**
Budde's Beach **3**
Curry Bowl **4**
Hotel Francis & German Bakery **6**
JLH **7**
New Moon Beam **8**
Red Lobster **10**
Refresh **11**

Bars & clubs
Chill Space Surf Café **12**
Ranjith's Beach Hut **9**
Roger's Garage **14**
Vibration **13**

base for **scuba diving** and local operators run trips to up to 20 sites along the coast. Most rewarding close to Hikkaduwa are the rock formations, especially the deep Kirala Gala (21 m to 38 m), 10 minutes offshore, where there is also a wide range of pristine coral with groupers, barracuda and batfish. A number of wrecks, some in fairly shallow water, can also be visited, such as the *Earl of Shaftesbury*, though the wreck-diving is better in the bays further south at Galle or Weligama. Visibility varies from 8 m to 25 m, depending on the time of day (morning is better), and is at its best around the Full Moon period.

Sunday is market day in Hikkaduwa and it is well worth spending some time here exploring.

Hikkaduwa is Sri Lanka's **surf centre** from December to April, and has hosted numerous international competitions. It is particularly good for beginners as the waves are comparatively gentle, most breaking on the reefs rather than the beach. The focus is around the main break, known as the 'A-Frame' because of its distinctive apex, in Wewala, though this can be crowded in peak months. Narigama and Thiragama further south are usually quieter, though you will also need greater experience.

Excursions

Alut Vihara (Totagama Rajamahavihara) at Telwatta, 2 km north of Hikkaduwa, dates from the early 19th century. It is the only temple to Anangaya on the island, where lovers make offerings to him. The carvings between the fine *makara* (dragon) arches leading to the sanctuary hide a cupid with his bow and flower-tipped arrows. The murals too are particularly impressive. Rarely visited by travellers, it is worth a trip and also makes a very pleasant bicycle ride.

Seenigama Temple, 6 km north, is on an island just offshore. The Devil's Temple here has enormous importance for local fishermen, who believe he will protect both their lives and wealth. You will need the services of a fisherman to get to the island. At another more easily accessible roadside temple, a few kilometres north on Galle Road, Sri Lankan travellers pay their respects, bringing most traffic to a temporary halt.

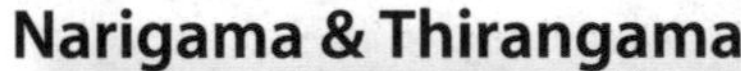

Narigama & Thirangama

Sleeping
Eco Lodge 8
Elephant Garden Beach Resort 1
Florida Inn 2
Hansa Surf 4
Hilda Guest House 10
Jupiter 6
Lotus Garden 7
Ocean View Cottage 9
Ranmal Rest & Tourist Home 11
Rita's Guesthouse 12
Sahra 13
Sarava Village 16
Suite Lanka 14
Sukhawathi 5
Sunbeach 3
Sunil's Beach 15

Eating
Rotty Stop 2

Bars & clubs
Baseline 5
Top Secret 4

At Dodanduwa, **Kumarakanda Rajamahavihara**, 4 km south of Hikkaduwa just before Km 103 post, has some murals and statues, though it is on the tourist trail so expect a dancing monkey and 'school pen' collectors. The temple is reached by a long steep and narrow flight of stone steps. Donations are expected. The beach opposite has a very small private **Turtle Research Centre,** ⓘ *Rs 50*, which works to protect this endangered species. You can see eggs and different stages of a turtle's development and a few posters under a shelter.

More relaxing as a break from the busy schedule at the beach is the picturesque **Ratgama Lake** which has abundant bird life and a large population of water monitors. There are three islands in the lagoon, one of which is Polgasduwa, where there is forest hermitage founded by a German monk. Touts offer trips from the beach. Once you are there you can explore the lagoon by paddleboat, ⓘ *Lal Jayasuriya, T077-7044057. Rs 500 per person, Rs 800 for 2.*

Baddegama, 11 km inland along the B153, is within easy reach of Hikkaduwa by bicycle or motorbike. The road is picturesque, cutting its way through coconut and banana groves, followed by several small plantations – rubber, tea and spices. About half way the road passes the Nigro Dharama Mahavihara (stupa) in Gonapinuwala. On a hill above the river in the grounds of Christ Church Girls College is the first Anglican church in Sri Lanka, built in 1818 and consecrated by Bishop Heber of Calcutta in 1825. Note the ironwood pillars.

Sleeping

South to Kalutara *p130*

C Ranmal Holiday Resort, *346/5 Galle Rd, Gorakana, Moratuwa, T038-2298921, F2298926, ranjithp39@yahoo.com* 30 large, fairly comfortable rooms, most with a/c and TV (US$20 includes breakfast), pool, plus option to sleep in a houseboat (which sounds better than it is), overall shabby but good position on the lake. Boat trips (either picnics or for overnight stay) offered to nearby islands and Kalutara.

Kalutara *p130*

LL-L Blue Water (Jetwing), *Thalpitiya, Wadduwa, T2235067, bluewater@eureka.lk* 100 excellent rooms (US$181, suite supplement US$100), in luxurious hotel with top facilities amidst palm groves, designed by Geoffrey Bawa, with spacious public areas, understated decor, ethnic feel (copied but not excelled by other hotels along the coast), large imaginative pool with resident monitor lizard.

L-AL Privilege, *260 Samanthura Rd, Molligoda, Wadduwa, T/F038-2295367, privilege@sltnet.lk* 24 luxurious, well-furnished suites (US$125-150), with TV, VCD, some with jacuzzi, jewellery shop with imaginative designs. Half board only (7-course dinner). Self-consciously 'boutiquey', though rather cramped.

AL Royal Palms Beach, *De Abrew Rd, Kalutara North, T2228113, tangerinetours@eureka.lk* 124 superb fully equipped rooms plus suites, private balcony or patio with sea or garden views, disco and pub, sports facilities shared with **Tangerine Beach Hotel**, huge pool (can almost swim around the hotel).

AL-A Golden Sun Resort, (Aitken Spence), *Kudawaskaduwa, Kalutara North, T2228484, F2228485, ashmres@aitkenspence.lk* 100 a/c rooms (US$95) including 32 cabanas (US$20 supplement), all sea-facing, in attractive gardens onto the beach, full facilities.

A Mermaid (Jetwing), *Mahawaskaduwa, T2222613, F2228572, hotels@jetwing.lk* 72 a/c rooms, split-level restaurant, bars, sports, excursions, mainly tour groups, beautiful location in coconut plantation, attractive lawn runs down to beach.

A Tangerine Beach, *De Abrews Rd, Waskaduwa, T2222982, tanbch@sltnet.lk* 166 a/c rooms (US$63-77), full facilities though reception can be slow, beautifully laid out with huge lawns and ponds stretching beneath coconut palms to the sea, popular with package groups.

B Kani Lanka Resort & Spa, (formerly **Hotel Sindbad**), *St Sebastians Rd, Katukurunda, T2226537, F2226530, info@kanilanka.com* 105 comfortable a/c rooms, some with private balcony and tub, in a good location sandwiched between sea and lagoon, floating restaurant, pool, mini-golf, watersports on lagoon, Ayurvedic health centre, traditional-style spa, cultural shows.

C **Hibiscus Beach**, *Mahawaskaduwa, T2222704, F5582271, hibiscus@isplanka.lk* 50 large rooms (US$35, a/c extra), pleasant balcony with sea view, lounge bar overlooks colourful hibiscus garden, pool, sports, good beach, helpful, friendly staff.

D-E **Garden Beach**, *21 Fonseka Lane, Kalutara North, T/F2224736*. 22 spacious and airy rooms (a/c Rs 1,800, non-a/c Rs 1,500), TV, hot bath, restaurant, pool, modest hotel.

F **Palm Beach**, *212/2 Sea Beach Rd, Kalutara North T2236194*. 3 clean large bright rooms (Rs 750) close to sea. Good value. Also own the slightly cheaper (Rs 650) and less clean **Dugong Beach** next door.

Ayurvedic resort

Siddhalepa Ayurveda Health Resort, *861 Samanthara Rd, Wadduwa, T038-2296967, siddalep@slt.lk* Siddhalepa is one of the most famous names in Sri Lankan Ayurvedic therapy, with a 200- year history, though resort is less 'authentic' than other new creations as it accepts non-Ayurveda guests and possesses a bar. 50 rooms, including 6 suites, in beautiful gardens full of Ayurveda plants. Suites are themed – 2 'caves', 2 made from clay and 2 Chandra Vasa, traditional Sri Lankan kabok and stone with furniture of magobe wood (recommended). Other rooms resemble a Dutch fort with mini canal system outside (kids can paddle boat). Packages range from a week (US$894) to 4 weeks (US$3,681) including consultation and all treatments for non-Ayurveda guests, US$98-140 per night, depending room.

Beruwela *p131, map p132*

AL **Confifi Beach**, *T2276217, F2276317, confifibeach@confifi.net* 73 rooms in either a/c garden view or non a/c 'deluxe' with sea view, 2 restaurants, bar, pool.

AL **Eden Resort & Spa** (Confifi), *Kaluwamodara, T2276075, F2276181, eden@confifi.net* 158 rooms in one of the newest and most luxurious of the top class hotels here (5-star), grand entrance, superb large pool, new spa, full entertainment and sports facilities.

AL **Neptune** (Aitken Spence), *T2276031, F2276033, ashmres@lanka.com.lk* 144 a/c rooms, including bungalows (from US$125 all-inclusive), Sri Lanka's first resort hotel so a little shabby, pleasant gardens and pool, beautiful beach with safe swimming (life-guard), floodlit tennis, Ayurvedic health centre, pleasant layout with shady trees.

AL **Riverina** (Confifi), *Kaluwamodara, T2276044, F2276047, riverina@confifi.net* 192 a/c rooms, full facilities including tennis, watersports, good indoor games room, cyber café, Ayurvedic centre, well organized.

AL-A **Bayroo** (Keells), *T2276297, F2276403, htlres@keells.com* 100 good a/c rooms, all with sea views, well laid out, wooded grounds, full facilities, not bad value. President Chandrika stays here on occasion.

A **Swanee** (Keells), *T2276006, F2276073, htlres@keells.com* 52 rooms, some a/c, balcony on upper floors, shady garden around pool, popular with tour groups although a bit grubby around the edges, free shuttle to **Club Inter Sport** at Bentota.

B **Tropical Villas** (Jetwing), *T2276780, F2276156, tropvilla@eureka.lk* 54 stylishly furnished split-level villas with sitting area, focused around small pool (with cascade) and fine gardens, personalized service. The lack of a beach (350 m through the Riverina) is regarded as an advantage by some as it cuts out the 'beach boys'. Good value.

B **Villa Riviera** (Jetwing), *T/F2276245, riviera@eureka.lk* 54 non a/c refurbished sea-facing rooms, buffet meals, a little old fashioned but cosy atmosphere.

C **Ypsylon Guest House**, *T2276132, F2276334, ypsylon@slt.lk* 25 rooms (Rs 2,100), hot bath, breakfast included, pool, German-run diving school (see Tour operators below).

D **Bavarian Guest House**, *92 Barberyn Rd, T/F2276129*. 6 large modern rooms around attractive courtyard with pool, hot bath, restaurant, bar.

E **Panorama**, *T2277091*. 10 simple, clean rooms (Rs 800) in small guesthouse, restaurant, good value for the area.

Ayurvedic resorts

Barberyn Reef, *T2276036, barbrese@slt.lk* Opened in 1982, the first Ayurvedic centre in Sri Lanka. 74 rooms (US$55), 24 beach cottages (US$95), some a/c, extensive Ayurvedic health centre, safe swimming enclosed by a reef, 95% German clientele.

Muthumuni, *16 Galle Rd, T2276766, F22289404, muthul@sltnet.lk* German-run resort in very peaceful setting on lagoon (own boat service to meditation temple). 1- to 2-week Ayurvedic packages cost US$1,200-1,500 depending on treatment. **White House**, opposite (near beach), has cheaper rates (from Rs 500 per night).

Aluthgama *p131, map p133*
A Ceysands (Keells), *T2275073, F2275895.* Located on a narrow spit of land between the sea and river reached by shuttle boat. 84 a/c rooms, fine beach, floating restaurant serving good food, marvellous setting, good choice despite looking a little frayed around the edges, discounted use of **Club Inter Sport** at Bentota.
A Club Bentota, 'Island Paradise', *T2275167, F2275172.* Recently taken over by the **Mount Lavinia Hotel**, 72 rooms and 78 bungalows in a maze of rooms on small spit of land accessible by shuttle boat, exclusively Austro-German clientele, full facilities.
C Nilwala, *Galle Rd (on the river), Kaluwamodara, T2275017, F2270408.* 14 clean a/c rooms (Rs 2000), although a/c units are noisy, overlooking river, watersports.
D German Lanka Guest House, *Riverside Rd, T2275622, F5581530.* 6 spotless, well-furnished, large rooms (Rs 1,200), in attractive setting overlooking river, hot bath, nets, restaurant (breakfast included), bar, watersports.
D Hemadan, *25 Riverside Rd (on the river bank), T/F2275320, hemadan@wow.lk* 10 good clean rooms (Rs 1634), some with balcony, though bigger without. Danish owned, quiet, hot bath, restaurant, watersports, free boat shuttle to beach, Internet Rs 8 per min.
D Terrena, *Riverside Rd, closest guesthouse to the bridge, T/F4289015.* 5 clean small but attractive rooms with hot bath (Rs 1,595, breakfast included), Austrian-owned, pleasant terrace and garden although location can be noisier than others. Family room for Rs 1800.
E Sun and Moon, *104/8 Galle Rd, T/F2275617, sunmoon@panworld.ws* New, decent-sized rooms with 4-poster beds Rs 1200. Good location on river, 3-hr riverboat trips Rs 1,000.

Bentota *p131, map p133*
Most of the accommodation in Bentota itself is close to the train station, on the beach side. It is worth visiting the top two hotels here, even if you are not staying.
LL-L Saman Villas (Jetwing), *Aturuwella, on a rocky headland 5 km south, T2275435, F2275433, samanvil@sri.lanka.net* 27 magnificent split level suites with sea views set on a spectacular rocky headland. Member of the Small Hotels of the World Association. All suites have attractive furnishings, remote-control curtains, 'astonishing' open-air baths. Superb pool high above sea which seems to merge with the ocean, panoramic views and access to long beaches either side. Good library. Expensive but worth every rupee.
LL-L The Villa (also known as Mohotti Walauwa), *138/18-22 Galle Rd (1.5 km south of Bentota), T2275311, reservation@the villa.eureka.lk* A former residence of Geoffrey Bawa, exquisite rooms in a large villa dated 1880, each individually designed, decorated and furnished with antique furniture. Superb bathrooms (open-air bath), beautiful shaded garden, understated pool. Sublime.
L Taj Exotica, *T2275650, ruwan.p@tajhotels.com* 162 large a/c rooms (higher floors best) in magnificent top-class hotel in a superb location on a headland, all with sea-facing balcony or terrace, good, varied buffets (à la carte disappointing), fantastic pool.
L-AL Club Villa, *138/15 Galle Rd (next to The Villa), T2275312, clubvilla@itmin.com* 16 beautiful, though simple rooms (1 suite) in a Dutch-style villa, restaurant (good Italian), wonderfully peaceful palm-shaded garden, small pool, beach a short walk across coastal railway line, friendly staff, superb ambience, mainly British.
AL Bentota Beach, *south of Bentota Bridge, T2275176, F2275179, htlres@keells.com* 133 comfortable a/c rooms (US$121), design reminiscent (and built on the site of) of a Dutch fort, luxurious layout in extensive gardens, good beach, full facilities including

For an explanation of the sleeping and eating price codes used in this guide, see the inside front cover.

hotel elephant, location of **Club Inter Sport** (see p146).

A **Serendib**, *T2275248, serenlti@sri.lanka.net* 90 a/c rooms (US$84) in ageing hotel which is still bearing up well, attractive rooms with balcony or terrace, directly on beach, fine gardens, friendly service, full facilities.

C **Ayubowan**, *171 Galle Rd, Bentota South, T/F2275913, info@ayubowan.ch* 5 bright, spacious and spotless bungalows (Rs 1,980 including tax and breakfast) with attractive furniture, in pleasant gardens. Restaurant has wide selection of food, including pizza (Rs 200-300). Swiss-owned.

C-D **Susantha**, *Resort Rd, Pitaramba, next to Bentota railway station (5 mins from beach, across from the rail track), T/F2275324, susantha@sltnet.lk* 18 spotless good-sized rooms with bath (US$20) in pleasant chalets. Bar, restaurant and badminton court. Suites also available (US$26).

Ayurvedic resorts

Ayurveda Walauwa, *Galle Rd, Warahena, T2753372, herbalhr@sltnet.lk* 20 a/c rooms in treatment centre (minimum stay 1 week although 2 weeks are advised for best effect). US$240 per day, including diagnosis, therapy, diet and treatments.

Bentota Aida Ayurveda and Holistic Health Resort, *12a Managala Mawatha, Bentota, T2271137, F2271140, aida@visual.lk* Spacious courtyards with good local furniture in great setting on Bentota river. 40 comfortable rooms for Ayurveda guests with TV, small balcony, minimum stay 1 week including treatment and all meals, from €200 per night. Also 1-day packages available for non-residents including consultation, massage or herbal bath/sauna.

Club Paradise, *near* Club Bentota, *Paradise Island, Aluthgama, T2275354, herbalhr@slt net.lk* Similar treatment to Ayurveda Walauwa, US$270 per night.

Niroga Ayurveda Health Centre, *next to Saman Villas, T/F2270312, chithral@slt.lk* 8 rooms, minimum 1 week (from Rs 10,000 depending on treatment). Also 1-day courses possible from Rs 3,000 (phone in advance).

Induruwa to Ambalangoda *p133*

L-AL **Triton** (Aitken Spence), *Ahungalla, 6 km south of Kosgoda, T2264041, F2264046, ashmres@aitkenspence.lk* 160 a/c rooms including 18 suites, excellent food, full sports and entertainment facilities, imaginative landscaping merging ponds into swimming pool into sea; you can virtually swim up to reception (pool open to non-residents who stay for a meal). Also another, quieter pool for those wanting a more peaceful holiday with separate eating facilities, excellent beach, well-run hotel.

A **Kosgoda Beach Resort**, *between the sea and lagoon, T2264017, cdchm@sltnet.lk* 52 comfortable and attractive a/c rooms including 12 deluxe, open-air tubs, large garden, lovely pool, boating, excellent restaurant, environmentally aware policy.

B **Induruwa Beach Resort**, *Galle Rd, T2275445, inbeachr@sltnet.lk* 90 a/c rooms (US$35), tubs, private balconies with sea view, breakfast included, pool with jacuzzi, full facilities, on good section of beach but large 4-storey block with uninspired architecture, mainly package groups, good value.

B **Royal Beach Resort**, *Galle Rd, Galaboda, Induruwa, T2274351, F2274350, rbeach@ sltnet.lk* British-owned, light and spacious if slightly tacky (map of Sri Lanka in the pond), gleamingly new hotel in colonial style. Attractive a/c rooms (US$50) with TV, tubs and veranda with great views of the ocean, clean stretch of beach.

F **Long Beach Cottage**, *Galle Rd, (next to Royal Beach Resort), T/F2275773, hanjayas@ sltnet.lk* 5 clean, sea-facing rooms with fan (Rs 770), local dishes and seafood to order, pleasant mangrove shaded garden with direct access to a fine beach, free pick up from Aluthgama station, friendly Sri Lankan/ German owners.

Ayurvedic resorts

Lotus Villa, *162/19 Wathuregama, south of Ahungalla, T2264082, ayulotus@sltnet.lk* 14 rooms in exclusive Ayurvedic herbal curative treatment centre. 13-day minimum stay, including transfer, all meals, consultations and treatment (€1,666 per person). For accompanying guest, rooms are €37.50.

Ambalangoda *p134*

C **Dream Beach Resort**, *509 Galle Rd, T2258873, dbra@sltnet.lk* 22 large comfortable a/c rooms (Rs 2,700), some with sea view, balcony, TV, restaurant, pool, small rocky beach, mainly German clientele.

D Sena's Lake View House (also known as Duwa Hotel), *Duwa, Maha Ambalangoda, about 2 km inland, T5450667*. Very quiet, by attractive lagoon (wonderful for swimming, and Sena will lend you a canoe if you want to explore the lake), watch wildlife from the balcony at dawn and dusk, excellent 3-hr trip arranged (sail on an outrigger and climb up to a large reclining Buddha).
D-F Samudra, *418 Main St, Patabendimulla, T2258832*. 5 rooms, good home cooking, pleasant atmosphere, good value.
E Shangrela Beach Resort, *38 Sea Beach Rd, T2258342, F2259421*. 25 clean, comfortable rooms, hot water (Rs 1,100), in an extension of former family guesthouse, though sometimes shut in off-season.
F-G Sunny's Guest House, *Akurella, T5451655*. 3 clean rooms (Rs 400-500), plans for 2 more, garden, quiet, friendly.
G Piya Nivasa, *Akurella, south of town, T2258146*. Light and airy rooms (Rs 350) in a lovely colonial house opposite the beach, good food, Rohana will arrange tours throughout the island. Proximity to the Galle Rd makes it noisy but nonetheless recommended for the warmth of the family.

Hikkaduwa *p136, map p137 and p138*
There are innumerable hotels lining the beach here, often with very little to distinguish between them. Places away from the beach side, understandably, tend to be cheaper than beachfront properties with similar facilities. Many prices drop by up to 50% out of season (May-Oct). Whatever season you visit, it is worth bargaining.

Hikkaduwa
A Coral Gardens (Keells), *T2277023, F2277189, htlres@keells.com* 154 a/c rooms in attractive building on small promontory though no balconies, nice pool (non-residents Rs 100), garden area, excellent restaurants (dinner buffet Rs 600, Sun lunch Rs 500), nightclub (Wed, Fri and Sun, Rs 100, ladies free), squash (Rs 250 for 45 mins), diving centre (glass- bottom boats Rs 100), Ayurvedic health centre, full of German groups, best hotel in town but not the most efficient.
B Coral Sands, *326 Galle Rd, T2277513, coralsands@stmail.lk* 50 clean and airy rooms with balcony (20 a/c), not all sea facing, restaurant, bar, tiny pool, diving school, friendly, reasonable value.
C Coral Rock, *340 Galle Rd, T2277021, F2277521, coralrock@sltnet.lk* New management, 40 rooms , bigger and better sea facing (US$32-35, latter with a/c), some with TV, restaurant (good fish), small pool (non-residents, Rs 100), nightclub. Landside rooms (US$25) close to noisy road.
C Hikkaduwa Beach, *298 Galle Rd, T2277327, hbhenr@sltnet.lk* 52 clean a/c rooms (top floor best), most with balcony and sea view, Rs 2,700 including breakfast, modern block, small pool (non-residents, Rs 75), hot bath, library, Ayurvedic centre.
D Coral Reef Beach, *336 Galle Rd (Km 99 post), T2277197, F2277453*. 32 rooms with sea view (Rs 1,500 with breakfast), although a bit spartan, bar, pool table, restaurant, **Aqua Tours Dive Centre** (see below).
E Mama's Coral Beach, *338 Galle Rd, T4383198*. 12 refurbished rooms (Rs 800-1,200) with balcony though a narrow property so most without views, rated seafood restaurant (with Rasta colours) the first in Hikkaduwa.

Wewala
B Reefcomber, *T2277377, reefcomber@slt.lk* 54 a/c rooms with terrace or balcony facing the sea though some face the road, nice beach garden, good pool (non-residents, Rs 100), restaurant, popular with package groups, a bit pricey.
B-C Lanka Super Corals, *390 Galle Rd, 1 km from Bus Stand, T2277387, supercor@pan.lk* 100 rooms ranging from non-a/c road-facing rooms, to deluxe a/c with hot tub, TV, minibar, sea view, from US$25-55, good pool (non-residents, Rs 150), Ayurveda centre, 24-hr coffee shop, a bit shabby in places, new wing nicer.
C-D Moon Beam, *T5450657, hotelmoon beam@hotmail.com* 18 clean rooms, Rs 1,600-2,600, better on upper floors with sea views, good restaurant (meals Rs 250 -300), but overpriced.
D Blue Note Cabanas, *424 Galle Rd, T/F2277016*. 9 very clean cabanas (Rs 1,440), well furnished, good restaurant but indifferent management and thefts from rooms have been reported.
D Blue Ocean Villa, *T/F2277566, blueocean @sltnet.lk* 9 large clean rooms, upstairs (Rs

1,500) better, downstairs Rs 1,200, restaurant, hot bath, good choice.

E **Casalanka**, *Galle Rd, T/F4383002.* 11 rooms (Rs 1,020) in barracks-style block, beachside restaurant, popular backpacker hangout.

E **Tandem Guest House**, *T4383019, F2277103, wewala@sltnet.lk* 9 reasonable rooms (Rs 1,000), nets, though not on beach.

F **Ozone Tourist Inn**, *374 Galle Rd, T4383008.* 5 simple, bare but clean rooms (Rs 500), attached bath, fan, friendly, good value.

F **Richard's Son's Beach Inn**, (no phone). 8 simple rooms (Rs 600), attached bath, fan, nice block though a little old, beach-side garden, very cheap out of season.

F **Whispering Palms Tourist Rest**, *382a Galle Rd, T4383275.* 4 large, clean rooms (Rs 600) in family guesthouse, attached bathroom, nets, good value.

F-G **Miga Villa**, *T5451559, migavilah@yahoo.com* 8 large, clean rooms (Rs 400-650) in beautiful old house, some family rooms, attached bath, friendly, family run, excellent value, despite requiring minor maintenance in places.

G **El-Dorado**, *Milla Rd, 200 m inland from Galle Rd, T2277091.* 6 rooms (Rs 350 shared bath, Rs 450 attached), in small family run guesthouse, use of kitchen, very clean, very peaceful setting away from busy road (but still only 10 mins from the beach), good value, good choice.

Narigama and Thirangama

B **Suite Lanka**, *T/F2277136, suitelanka@hotmail.com* 9 beautifully furnished standard rooms, deluxe rooms and suites (US$38-60), private verandas, pool, 2 bars (one on beach), very quiet and intimate, good fresh seafood.

B-C **Sunil's Beach**, *T2277186, F2277187.* 62 rooms (US$27-30, more expensive with sea-view), a/c (US$36), modern, pool, popular with German groups.

C **Ocean View Cottage**, *T2277237, oceanview@sltnet.lk* 9 attractive, clean rooms (Rs 2,200, upstairs better), with 5 more to come, shared balcony, fairly new and modern, good terrace restaurant, quiet, pleasant garden.

C-D **Sunbeach**, *T2277356, sunbeach@hotmail.com* 12 clean and cosy rooms (Rs 1,500-2,500, includes breakfast), 1 with a/c, plus a tree-house with great views (Rs 3,500).

C-F **Ranmal Rest and Tourist Home**, *T/F2277114, info@ranmal-rest.com* 19 rooms ranging from cheap non a/c rooms (Rs 500) to very clean luxury rooms with a/c (Rs 2,000), upper rooms with balcony (Rs 1,000), plus 2 cabanas (Rs 2,300), sea-facing 1st-floor restaurant with lovely sunset views, good section of beach, good food, pleasant staff, reserve ahead.

C-G **Hansa Surf**, *T2277039.* 26 rooms in most categories, from dark and basic (Rs 400) to bright and breezy (Rs 2,000), shady veranda, table tennis, friendly and helpful and popular with backpackers.

D **Florida Inn**, *T2257345.* 8 very clean, modern rooms, restaurant.

D-F **Lotus Garden**, *T2277779.* 9 clean and airy rooms with pleasant shared veranda (Rs 750-1,500), cheaper ones especially good value, friendly.

E **Rita's Guesthouse**, *T/F2277496.* 9 clean rooms (Rs 800-1,000), better on 1st floor, beach restaurant (with perennial Bob Marley) popular with American surfers.

E **Sahra**, *T2276093.* 6 spotless if small rooms in Swiss chalet style, nice terrace, friendly, not bad value at Rs 800.

E-F**Sukhawathi**, *T4383062, sukhawathi@wow.lk* Bright, large, spotless (and very green) rooms Rs 1,000 on ground floor, Rs 600 on first. Excellent food (see below) and Ayurveda clinic too.

F **Elephant Garden Beach Resort**, *T2276359.* 2 rooms with clean shared bath and 3 wooden cabanas, all (Rs 650) in quiet setting, nets, restaurant. Friendly owner.

F **Hilda Guest House**, *Uswatta, Wawala, 300 m from Galle Rd, T4383204.* 4 rooms (Rs 600) in an attractive house 10-min walk from the beach with a quiet, pleasant garden. A pleasant escape from the main drag.

F **Sarava Village**, *T4383268, sarava@wow.lk* Italian-owned and vaguely Italianate style, built around attractive courtyard, very clean rooms (Rs 600) and rated Italian food.

G **Jupiter**, *T2277498*, 6 very basic rooms (Rs 400), shared squat toilets, beach restaurant, popular, about as cheap and cheerful as you can get!

Baddegama

C **Plantation Villa**, *Halpatota, Baddegama, 15-min bus (no 186) or car drive inland from Hikkaduwa, T2292405.* 4 rooms (US$20) set in small tea estate surrounded by very peaceful wooded garden, excellent bird life, has the feel of an old planter's house although it is relatively new, excellent food (breakfast included) and Sri Lankan cookery courses offered, welcoming hosts, guest book repeatedly mentions 'paradise'. Very welcoming and highly recommended.

Dodanduwa
E **Eco Lodge**, *Sri Saranajothi Av, T2267350, ranmini@itmin.com (from Hikkaduwa take the next road after the turn-off to the vihara, before the bridge)*. On the lagoon, a former family holiday home, now converted to an Environmental Study Centre, with a plank walkway through mangrove swamp, and attractive water garden. Sleep in a house-boat or stilt house (€10 including breakfast). More accommodation planned.

Eating

Kalutara *p130*
Besides the hotel restaurants, see Sleeping p139, there are numerous, and cheaper, places to eat (and buy souvenirs) along the roads leading from Galle Rd to the hotels.

Beruwela *p131, map p132*
There are places to eat along the roads leading from Galle Rd. For further options see Sleeping, p140.

Aluthgama *p131, map p133*
There are numerous restaurants around Bentota Bridge and on the narrow lanes leading down to the hotels.
RsRs **Tropical Anushka River Inn**, *97 Riverside Rd, T2275377, 1100-1500 and 1900-2300*, has fine views. 'Special steak' Rs 330, and good seafood; fresh tuna Rs 200. Also has 3 guest rooms.
Rs **Singharaja Bakery and Restaurant**, *120 Galle Rd, Kaluwamodara*, is a good, clean establishment providing excellent Sri Lankan food including short eats, hoppers and curries. Popular as a roadside halt but worth visiting for a cheap and authentic alternative to hotel food.

Bentota *p131, map p133*
RsRs **Aida**, next to the **Aida Ayurvedic Resort**, has a restaurant upstairs (access from the back). Italian pasta dishes (upwards of Rs 300 for a meal), tasty curries are cheaper.
RsRs **Susantha Palm**, near the guesthouse, serves simple Sri Lankan and continental dishes for around Rs 250 and short eats.
Rs **Refresh**, *1 Galle Rd, T2271636, opposite Nilaveli Spice Garden*, has good cheap Chinese (Rs 100).

Induruwa to Ambalangoda *p133*
For options see Sleeping, p142.

Hikkaduwa *p136, map p137 and p138*
Most places listed are in Wewala offering plenty of choice, particularly for seafood. Prices are pretty much similar wherever you go; you can eat well for under Rs 200, though it is also possible to eat a good rice and curry for under Rs 70. For a change, opt for the cool of the plush a/c restaurant at the **Coral Gardens Hotel** for the excellent Rs 500 lunch time buffet. Crowded places may not necessarily be better; it could just be a mention in a guidebook!

Hikkaduwa
RsRs **Abba's**, *Waulagoda Rd, T2277110*. German (not Swedish) style, snacks and meals, good value, quiet setting.
RsRs **Red Lobster**, *Waulagoda Rd*. Excellent food, good value, friendly owners.

Wewala
RsRsRs **Refresh**, *384 Galle Rd, T2277810*. Classiest place in town, enormous and varied menu, pizzas Rs 490, jumbo prawns Rs 990, enormous mixed grill Rs 1,950, good choice of international vegetarian options, and impressive range of wines (Rs 1,400-1,800) and cocktails.
RsRs **Blue Fox Cool Hut**, *T2277029*. Nice setting, really good food, breakfast Rs 120, fish, steak, prawns and chicken Rs 150-200.
RsRs **Budde's Beach**, popular beach-side place, good food (fish, pasta, noodles).
RsRs **Curry Bowl**, good food and service, 'delicious garlic toasts', upmarket setting.
RsRs **Hotel Francis**, *T2277019*. Good international choice (under Rs 200), lobster Rs 1,200, devilled crab claws Rs 285, beers Rs 125-150.
RsRs **New Moon Beam**, seafood particularly good, most dishes Rs 240-280, lobster Rs 750-1,000, Lion lager Rs 120, pleasant ambience.

Rs **German Bakery**, *373 Galle Rd (opposite Reefcomber)*. Excellent bread and cakes. Breakfast all-day 0800-1800, closed Mon.
Rs **JLH**, *382 Galle Rd, T2277139*. Fresh seafood and ideal for breakfast, right by the water. Good cocktails too.

Narigama and Thirangama
RsRs **Sarava Village**, wide range of pasta dishes and a wood-fired pizza oven.
RsRs **Sukhawathi**, superb vegetarian food, (worth the wait!), special emphasis on South Indian, good value (rice and curry Rs 150), great breakfasts, evening menu (Rs 165-225) varies every day.
Rs **Rotty Stop**, Narigama. Tasty rice and curries, excellent rotties, local clientele.

Bars and clubs

Hikkaduwa *p136, map p137 and p138*
Baseline on Fri and **Top Secret** on Sat, both on Narigama beach, are the places for a boogie. On these nights they have live bands, with DJs the rest of the time. Reggae tends to figure highly on the playlist. They get going around 2130, and finish at sunrise.
Vibration is the newest place in town.
Chill Space Surf Café is a 24-hr café at the heart of surfland, with requisite reggae beats.
Ranjith's Beach Hut, *Wewala*, top spot to end the day with a few beers and late night music or table games. Hires out surfboards.
Roger's Garage, friendly owners, popular bar, nightly videos, pool table.

Shopping

Beruwela *p131, map p132*
There are branches of the excellent **Mlesna Tea Centre** and **Laksala** government handicrafts emporium along Galle Rd with prices more reasonable than the hotel shops.

Bentota *p131, map p133*
There is also a branch of **Laksala**, in the shopping arcade by **Bentota Beach Hotel**.

Ambalangoda *p134, map p*
Traditional masks worn for dancing, using vegetable colours instead of the brighter chemical paints, are available on the northern edge of the town. Masks sell from around Rs 500 to several thousand rupees. Traditional masks are more expensive. Antique shops often sell newly crafted items which have been 'aged'. It is illegal to take out any article over 50 years old without a government permit.

Hikkaduwa *p136, map p137 and p138*
There are numerous batik, handicraft, leather work, jewellery and clothing stores along the length of Galle Rd. Bargaining is expected.
Laksiri, *99 Baddegama Rd, T2277255*.
There are several book exchanges. Try opposite **Sunil's Beach Hotel** in Narigama.
There is a supermarket at Sandagiri where you can get photos developed within 24 hrs.

Sport and activities

Beruwela *p131, map p132*
Diving is best Dec-Mar.
Ypsylon Hotel, *T2276132, F2276334, ypsylon@slt.lk* German run dive centre here, PADI-registered. One dive US$25 (US$20 with own equipment), Open Water Course US$350, Advanced US$290.

Bentota *p131, map p133*
A range of activities is possible on the lagoon or the open sea.
Club Inter Sport (Keells), *within the grounds of Bentota Beach Hotel, T2275178, F2275179*. Watersports include windsurfing, water skiing, and banana boat, lessons possible. Also tennis, squash, archery, badminton. Sport passes available for discounted activities on 2-day (weekend) or weekly basis. Discounts for residents of any of the Keells hotels in the area.
Lihiniya Surf, *T2275126, lihiniya@slt.lk*, PADI diving centre and other watersports offered.
Confifi Marina, *T2242766 or T2276039 at Palm Garden Hotel*. PADI Open Water (US$380), single dive (US$32). Also sailing, canoeing or windsurfing (US$5 per hr), snorkelling (US$10), deep-sea fishing.
Rainbow Boat House, *by bridge next to Aida Restaurant, T2275383*, offers a 1-day river cruise up the Bentota Ganga. Early start for seeing mangrove birds and wildlife, including occasional crocodile, followed by visits to a rice mill and various plantations. Climb 'mini Adam's Peak' to see a temple (650 steps), and then, bizarrely, watch a re-enactment of a Sri

Lankan wedding, Rs 1,400 all-inclusive. Alternatively 1-2 hr boat cruises are available, overpriced at Rs 800.

Hikkaduwa *p136, map p137 and p138*
The diving season along the southwest coast is Nov-Apr, and Hikkaduwa has the best selection of diving schools on the island, though the not the best local sites. There are several other dive schools in addition to those listed here. Check that they are PADI qualified before agreeing to a dive or course. Snorkelling equipment can be hired from a number of places along the main street. Glass- bottomed boats can be hired from a number of places just north of the **Coral Gardens Hotel**. Rates are negotiable, though a 30-min viewing trip (without stops for snorkelling) is about Rs 350-400. Some travellers find there are too many boats chasing too few viewing spots, turtles are disturbed unnecessarily and that the glass is not as clear as you might expect.
A-Frame Surf Shop, *T4383216, open 0800-2100.* Surfing equipment is available for purchase from this Japanese-run shop.
Aqua Tours Diving Station, *Coral Reef Beach Hotel, T2277197.* PADI school, rates for dives and courses as *Poseidon* below.
Mambo Surf Centre, *T4380985, surfmambo50@hotmail.com* Surfboards can be rented for Rs 150 per hr or Rs 400 per day, and surfing lessons cost Rs 600.
Poseidon Diving Station, *just north of Coral Sands Hotel, T2277294, F2276607, poseidon@ divingsrilanka.com, also opposite Coral Garden Hotel, T2277447.* One of the longest established operations, set up in 1973, headquarters has an interesting selection of booty recovered by the school's Swedish founder. Single dive including equipment, US$22, or US$18 without; PADI Open Water Course, US$320; Advanced Course, US$220. Ask about diving expeditions to the east coast.

Tour operators

Hikkaduwa *p136, map p137 and p138*
Sri Lanka Travels, *opposite Reefcomber Hotel, T5451864.* Offers 1- to 5-day tours as well as longer island tours on request. Minimum 3-4 persons. Honest deals.
Travel Aid, *opposite Coral Gardens Hotel,* also offers tours and vehicle hire (for further details see Transport below).
Travel Tailor, *T4383007.* 1- to 5-day tours of the island, airport run, international air tickets, IDD.

Transport

Kalutara *p130*
Bus It is easiest to arrive by one of the buses (1-1½ hrs) that run between **Colombo** and **Galle** regularly.
Train Stop here on the **Colombo-Matara** railway line, with 5-6 intercity trains per day (1 hr, 2nd class Rs 24, 3rd class Rs 10.50).

Beruwela *p131, map p132*
Bus Ply the route between **Colombo** and **Galle**.
Train Stop on the main **Colombo-Matara** line, though only the slower ones (1¾ hrs). Best option is to take one of the express trains, get off at **Aluthgama** (see below) and take a 3-wheeler from there.

Aluthgama *p131, map p133*
Aluthgama is the main transport hub for Beruwela to the north and Bentota to the south.
Bus Those running between **Colombo** and **Galle** stop here.
Train Stop on the main **Colombo-Matara** line, Aluthgama can be reached by Express trains from **Colombo** (5-6 a day) in around 1½ hrs (2nd class Rs 34, 3rd class Rs 13).

Bentota *p131, map p133*
Bus Those passing through Bentota are often already full, so it is better to go to Aluthgama and take a bus that originates there.
Train Bentota's tiny station is on the main Colombo-Matara line but only the 'slow' trains stop here so it is better to travel on an Express train to/from Aluthgama.

Ambalangoda *p134*
Bus Regular buses run from **Colombo** and between **Ambalangoda** and **Hikkaduwa**, 13 km south (Rs 6.50).
Train 5 to 6 express trains a day run along the coast from **Colombo Fort** to Ambalangoda (2 hrs), and on to **Hikkaduwa** (15 mins).

Hikkaduwa *p136, map p137 and p138*
Bus The old, slow CTB variety that travel between **Colombo** and **Galle** via Hikkaduwa (Rs 36) can take up to 3 hrs+. Better option is private minibuses from Colombo's Bastian Mawatha bus station which take under 2 hrs. Frequent buses run from Hikkaduwa's bus station (at the north end of town) to **Ambalangoda** and **Galle** (both Rs 10). However, it is almost impossible to hail a bus on the Galle Rd (even from official bus shelters) so it is worth going to the bus station or taking a taxi or auto for short journeys.
Car and motor-bike hire From Sri Lanka Travels, *opposite Reefcomber Hotel, T5451864.* Motorbike hire, Rs 600 a day including helmet and insurance. Car hire from US$30 per day.
Taxi They wait outside the Coral Gardens and Reefcomber Hotels (more likely to be minibuses than cars).
Three-wheeler Available up and down Galle Rd. Short trips around town cost Rs 50.
Train To **Colombo Fort**, express trains (2-2½ hrs, 2nd class Rs 54.50, 3rd class Rs 20) at 0708, 0807, 0935 (weekdays only), 1110, 1433 (Sun only), 1509, 1835, most stopping at **Ambalangoda**, **Aluthgama** (for Bentota and Beruwela), **Panadura** and **Moratuwa**. Slow trains north run as far as **Aluthgama**. Frequent trains to **Galle** (45 mins, Rs 11/4) every 1-2 hrs up to 2050; the 0918, 1107, 1241, 1627, 1800 and 2021 continuing to **Matara** (1½ hrs, Rs 35.50/24), via **Talpe**, **Ahangama** and **Weligama**. **Kandy** train (via Colombo) leaves at 1509 (5¾ hrs, Rs 122.50/ 44.50). Vavuniya train, via **Anuradhapura** (8 hrs, Rs 170/61.50) leaves at 1110.

Directory

Kalutara *p130*
Medical services General Hospital *T2222261.*

Beruwela *p131, map p132*
Useful address Tourist police, *Galle Rd, Moragalla, opposite Neptune Hotel.*

Aluthgama *p131, map p133*
Banks Commercial Bank has a Cirrus/Visa/ Mastercard ATM and will change TCs.
Communications **Internet**, Manoma, next to Sun and Moon, 0900-2300, is the cheapest option, Rs 5 per min.
Useful address Tourist police, *Galle Rd, in Aluthgama town.*

Bentota *p131, map p133*
Communications **Internet** (Rs 7 per min) and **IDD calls** are available from the kiosk opposite the Bentota Beach, open 0900-2200.
Useful address **Tourist police**, in tourist complex by Bentota Beach Hotel, T2275022.

Hikkaduwa *p136, map p137 and p138*
Ayurveda Many places have 'Ayurveda clinics', though the treatments usually lack authenticity. Sukhawathi offers good treatments (Rs 800-2,250) by appointment only.
Banks *Open Mon-Fri, 0900-1500.* People's Bank, Commercial Bank and Bank of Ceylon all offer foreign exchange (cash and TCs), whilst the latter also has a Cirrus ATM. Avin Moneychanger just north of Hotel Lanka Super Coral charges no commission on cash or TCs, and will outbid the bank rate.
Communications **Internet** at Sandagiri and Sri Lankan Travels in Wewala are cheapest at Rs 2 per min. In Hikkaduwa itself, Nilu Communications, *7 Galle Rd, opposite Hikkaduwa Beach Hotel, open 0730-2130*, has 2 reliable terminals, Rs 5 per min. Vista Tours is open 24 hrs, Rs 5 per min. **Post office**, *0800-1900 (Sun 0800-1000)*. At the north end of town, a few mins walk inland from the bus station. Dimasha Agency Post Office, opposite the bus station to the north, sells stamps and arranges international calls, usually 0800-2100. There is a sub-post office at Thirangama. For **international phone calls**, it is best to use Lanka Payphones (yellow) and Metrocard (orange) card phones that are found all along Galle Rd. Most stores nearby sell the phonecards.
Useful address **Tourist police**, *Police Station, Galle Rd, T2277222.*

The south coast

Much less package oriented than the west coast, the spectacularly scenic bays and beaches of the south coast are a magnet for independently travelling sun and sea worshippers, with fewer crowds and some good-value accommodation. Unawatuna, Tangalla and, increasingly, Mirissa are the main beaches here, each with long sweeps of fine sand, while city life focuses on Matara and particularly Galle, whose colonial origins provide some historical interest. While you could pass along the south coast in under four hours, those with the time might easily spend a week here, hopping from village to village and enjoying the laid-back lifestyle.

Galle → *Phone code: 091. Colour map 3, grid C2. Population 93,000. 115 km from Colombo.*

Galle (pronounced in Sinhala as 'Gaal-le') is the most important town in the south and its fort area, with its mighty ramparts, encloses some wonderful examples of colonial architecture. A laid-back and enchanting place to wander, it was declared a UNESCO World Heritage Site in 1988. Rather removed from the busy modern town, the fort retains a villagey atmosphere, full of local gossip, and some find themselves staying far longer than they expected. Most however find that they have exhausted Galle's sites in a day or so. » *For Sleeping, Eating and other listings, see pages 163-176.*

Ins and outs → *Beware of touts who earn commission on accommodation and shopping (gems).*

Getting there Express trains are preferable to a crowded bus journey to or from Galle provided you avoid the rush hour. Both run frequently from Colombo (see page 174).
Getting around The train and bus stations are both in the new town, 10-15 mins walk north of the fort walls and cricket stadium. Galle Fort is so small and compact that most of the guesthouses are very easy to find. To get to the upmarket hotels outside Galle, you will need to hire a taxi or three-wheeler.
Tourist information There is a branch of the Ceylon Tourist Board, *Victoria Park opposite the railway station, 0900-1600.*

History

Galle's origins as a port go back well before the Portuguese. Ibn Batuta, the great Moroccan traveller, visited it in 1344. The historian of Ceylon Sir Emerson Tennant claimed that Galle was the ancient city of Tarshish, which had traded not only with Persians and Egyptians but with King Solomon. The origin of the name is disputed, some associating it with the Latin *gallus* (cock), so-called because the Portugese heard the crowing of cocks here at dusk, others with the Sinhala *gala* (cattle shed) or *gal* (rock).

The Portuguese Lorenzo de Almeida drifted into Galle by accident in 1505. It was a further 82 years before the Portuguese captured it from the Sinhala Kings, and they controlled the port until the Dutch laid siege in 1640. The old Portuguese Fort, on a promontory, was strengthened by the Dutch who remained there until the British captured Galle in 1796. Dutch East India Company, VOC (*Vereenigde Oost Indische Campagnie*) ruled the waves during the 17th and 18th centuries with over 150 ships trading from around 30 settlements in Asia.

A P&O liner called at Galle in 1842 marking the start of a regular service to Europe. In 1859, Captain Bailey, an agent for the shipping company, took a fancy to the spot where a small disused Dutch fort had stood in a commanding position, 3 km across the harbour. The villa he built, set in a tropical garden (now **Closenberg Hotel, see** page 163), was named 'Marina' after his wife. P&O's Rising Sun emblem can still be spotted on some of the old furniture.

Galle's gradual decline in importance dates back to 1875, when reconstruction of breakwaters and the enlarged harbour made Colombo the island's major port.

Old town and fort

The fort, enclosing about 200 houses, completely dominates the old town. You can easily spend a whole day in this area. Part of its charm is being able to wander around the streets; nothing is very far away and, by and large, there are only a few curio shops. The Dutch left their mark here, building brick-lined sewers which the tides automatically flushed twice a day. The fort's main streets run over these old sewers and you can still see the manhole covers every 20 m or so.

There are two entry points. The more impressive **gate** is under the clocktower. The ramparts just here are massive, partly because they are the oldest and have been

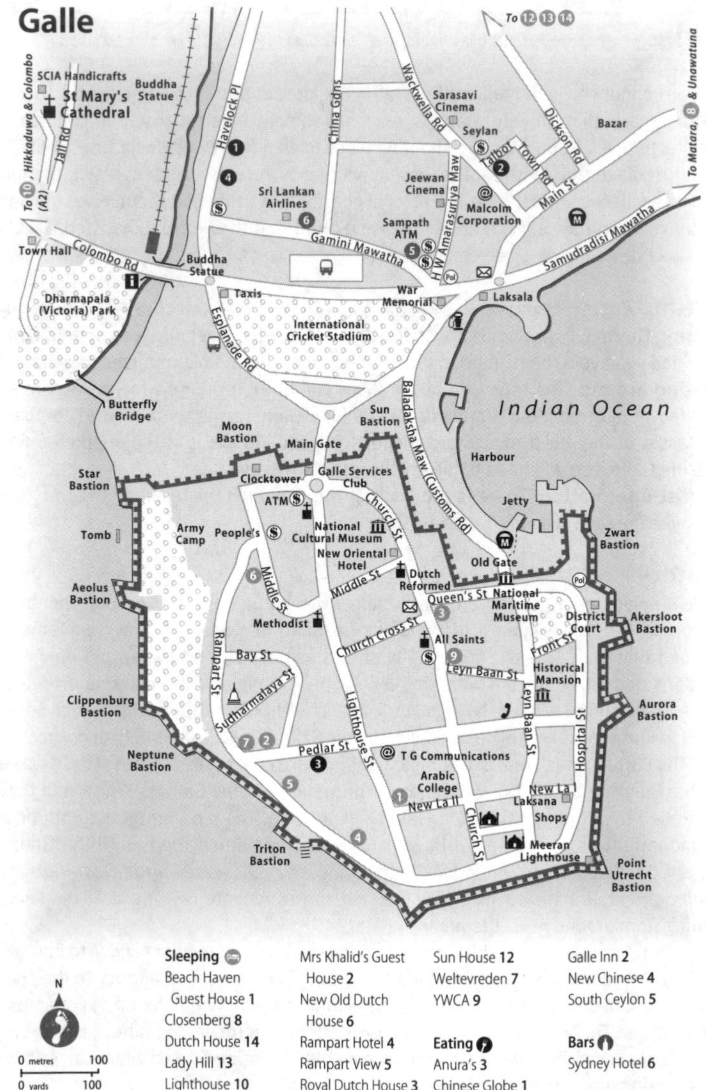

Sleeping
Beach Haven Guest House 1
Closenberg 8
Dutch House 14
Lady Hill 13
Lighthouse 10
Mrs Khalid's Guest House 2
New Old Dutch House 6
Rampart Hotel 4
Rampart View 5
Royal Dutch House 3
Sun House 12
Weltevreden 7
YWCA 9

Eating
Anura's 3
Chinese Globe 1
Galle Inn 2
New Chinese 4
South Ceylon 5

Bars
Sydney Hotel 6

reinforced over the years on many occasions. There are three quite distinct bastions (Star in the west, Moon and Sun in the east). The clocktower (1883) itself is quite modern and usually has a huge national flag flying from it. In Queen Street is the second and much older gate.

The **ramparts**, surrounded on three sides by the sea, are marked by a series of bastions covering the promontory. The two nearest to the harbour are Sun and Zwart, followed by Aurora and Point Utrecht bastions before the lighthouse, then Triton, Neptune, Clippenburg, Aeolus, Star and Moon. Those on the west side are more accessible and stand much as they were built, although there is evidence of a signals post built in the Second World War on top of Neptune. The Sri Lankan army still has a base in the fort and so have a use for the Aeolus bastion. Under the ramparts between Aeolus and Star bastions is the tomb of a Muslim saint neatly painted in green and white, said to cover an old fresh water spring. The open space between Rampart Street and the ramparts is used as a recreational area and there is often an unofficial game of cricket in progress in the evenings and at weekends. Also on the Green is a small shrine, the main one, Sri Sudharmalaya temple, being across the street.

The views from the ramparts over the roofs of the houses and the sunset out over the sea are unforgettable.

A **walking tour** around the ramparts is a must. You can try to do it on a clear evening and aim to reach the clocktower at sunset, starting at about 1630 and wandering slowly from the New Oriental clockwise. An interesting route is to walk south from the hotels, all along Church Street, then east to the 20-m high lighthouse which was built by the British in 1939, nearly on top of the old magazine with its inscription 'AJ Galle den 1st Zeber 1782'. You can get good views from the top, though you will need to get permission from the lighthouse keeper (ask in the gem store next door). You then return up Hospital Street past the Police Barracks (built in 1927 but failing to blend in with the older parts of the fort). The Government offices on Hospital Street were once the Dutch 'Factory' (warehouse). You then arrive at the square with the district court near the Zwart Bastion. Turn west along Queen Street which joins Church Street at the post office. The quiet fort streets are lined with substantial buildings, most with large rooms on the ground floor and an arched veranda to provide shade. The arched windows of the upper floors are covered by huge old louvered wooden shutters; the lower ones have glass nowadays. Unfortunately, quite a few of these fine houses are in need of restoration. **Dutch Reformed Church** (1754), next to the **New Oriental** (see box), is certainly worth visiting. It was built as a result of a vow taken by the Dutch Governor of Galle, Casparaus de Jong, and has a number of interesting memorials. Inside, the floor is covered by about 20 gravestones (some heavily embossed, others engraved), which originated in older graveyards which were closed in 1710 and 1804. The British moved them into this church in 1853. The organ loft has a lovely semicircular balustrade surrounding the organ while the pulpit, repaired in 1996, has an enormous canopy. The church is currently undergoing much needed conservation work (due to be completed in 2005), mainly to the roof and plasterwork, at the cost of Rs 12 million to the Dutch government. Opposite the church is the old bell tower erected in 1701, while the bell, open to the elements, is hung in a belfry with a large dome on top of it. The old **post office**, restored by the Galle Heritage Trust in 1992, is a long low building with a shallow red tiled roof supported by 13 columns. It is still functioning although it is very run down inside. Further down Church Street is the All Saints Church though it is not always open. This was built in 1868 (consecrated in 1871) after much pressure from the English population who had previously worshipped at the Dutch Reform Church. Its bell has an interesting history as it came from the Liberty ship *Ocean Liberty*. When the vicar asked the Clan Shipping Company whether they could help with the cost of a bell, the chief officer who had acquired the bell from the *Liberty* when it was scrapped (and named his daughter Liberty!), presented it to the church in its centenary year, 1968. There is a

New conquest of Galle

After many years languishing in apparently terminal decay, Galle Fort is due for a facelift. The current positive political climate has sparked a surge of interest in restoring it to the former glory of 'olden times'. *Time Asia* has called the city 'South Asia's latest boomtown'. But in keeping with its colonial tradition, the Galle of the future will have one foot firmly in the past. Europeans are once again beginning to colonize its bastions.

The declaration of the Fort as a UNESCO World Heritage site started the ball rolling, with the World Bank funding renovations to the town's courts. Now money from Europe and the Far East is flooding in. One of the biggest projects is the redevelopment of the desperately neglected 17th-century New Oriental Hotel, the former Dutch barracks and oldest registered hotel in Sri Lanka. The hotel was bought by the Indonesian luxury chain Amanresorts in 2002, and substantial restoration will, it's rumoured, turn it into one of the most expensive 'boutique' hotels in Sri Lanka.

Meanwhile the removal of a swingeing 100% tax on foreigners buying property on the island has caused prices in the Fort to treble in two years. Upwards of 50 (out of around 200) historic houses in the Fort have been snapped up for renovation, mainly by British bankers in the Far East, some to become guesthouses, art galleries, restaurants and cafés, and it is predicted that by 2008 half of local property will fall to foreign buyers. The newly formed Galle Heritage Foundation is to give local residents two years to restore their properties to the original Dutch architecture and ash white and samara colour scheme. The Dutch government is also providing funds for essential work on several public buildings, including the restoration of the Dutch Reformed Church, and the town of Welson in the Netherlands, with which Galle has been twinned since 1977, has recently provided Rs 200 million for, amongst other things, rubbish clearance. By the end of 2003, all government offices are due to have moved out of the Fort into a new high-rise complex in the new town. There will also be restrictions on traffic, which has contributed to the disintegration of the Fort's ramparts, and all unsightly electrical wires are to be moved underground.

The aim is to make Galle the South's cultural focus by 2010, as well as its biggest tourist draw. In 2003, the town was twinned with Graz in Austria, and several festivals, featuring traditional music, dance, puppetry, and lace-making, were organized throughout the year. Some of these crafts had been feared lost until practitioners came out of retirement and back into the limelight.

But amongst the buzz that the new investment in beginning to bring to the sleepy old town, there are critics of the new order. Some fear that as locals are priced out of the market, Galle Fort could become a 'little Europe', a spiritless enclave culturally detached from the surrounding area and devoid of local colour. Further expansion of its schools has already been prohibited, and local families, some of which have been here for centuries, may find it hard to resist the large sums they are offered to move.

particularly good view of the church with its red tin roof surmounted by a cockerel and four strange little turrets, from Cross Church Street. The old Dutch Government House, opposite the church, is now a hotel. Note the massive door in four sections at the Queen's Street entrance, so built for entry on horseback. At the end of Church Street lies the old **Arab Quarter** with a distinct Moorish atmosphere. Here you will find the Meeran Jumma Masjid in a tall white building which resembles a church with two square towers topped by shallow domes, but with the crescent clearly visible. Slender, tubular minarets are also topped by crescent moons. The mosque was rebuilt at the beginning of the 20th century where the original stood from the 1750s. The Muslim Cultural Association and Arabic College which was established in 1892, are here. It is still very active and you will see many Muslims in the distinctive skullcaps hurrying to prayer at the appointed hours.

Historical Mansion Museum, ⓘ *31-39 Leyn Bann St (well signed), T2234114. 0900-1800 (closed on Fri 1230-1400 for prayers), free,* is a restored old house. There are a number of rooms around a small courtyard containing his potentially worthwhile collection of colonial artefacts. There are several interesting and rare items which are simply 'stored' here. The real aim of the museum becomes apparent when visitors are led to the gems for sale in the adjoining shop.

National Maritime Museum, ⓘ *The Old Dutch Gate, Queen St, T2242261, 0900-1700 Sun-Thu, Rs 65,* the exhibition is housed in the basement of what were originally storehouses. There is much of interest inside the museum but regrettably it is not well exhibited. There is a small collection illustrating the island's maritime history including trade, spices, sea products (a pickled cuttlefish), fibreglass whales, models of different styles of catamarans. At the far end there is an interesting exhibit about fishermen making their annual pilgrimage to Kataragama to offer alms.

National Cultural Museum, ⓘ *Church St (next to New Oriental Hotel), T2232051, 0900-1700, closed Sun, Mon and public holidays, Rs 35,* in an old colonial stone warehouse. Exhibits include a model of Galle and the fort's Dutch and Portuguese inheritance.

New town

This area hasn't much to offer, though cricket fans will want to visit **Galle International Cricket Stadium**, where there is often a match going on. It is one of the finest set grounds in the world. You can clamber up on the ramparts of the fort to find the spot from which Jonathan Agnew, the BBC's cricket correspondent, was forced to broadcast after the famous incident in February 2001 when he wasn't allowed into the ground!

The new town is quite pleasant to wander through and its bustle contrasts with the more measured pace of the fort. It is an easy walk out of the old gate and along by the sea with its rows of fishing boats neatly drawn up on the beach. Near the main post office on Main Street there is however a splendid **equestrian statue**. You can walk alongside the old Dutch canal, which is very dirty at low tide. Monitor lizards can often be seen. You can cross the butterfly bridge into Victoria Park, which is quite well maintained. On the Colombo Road to the west of Victoria Park, are several gem shops. If you take the road opposite them you can walk up to **St Mary's Cathedral** which was built in 1874 and has a very good view over the town. There is little of interest inside, though.

Unawatuna

→ *Phone code: 091. Colour map 3, grid C3. 5 km south east of Galle.*

Unawatuna's picturesque beach along a sheltered bay was once considered one of the best in the world. Although rather narrow, it is more suitable for year-round swimming than say, Hikkaduwa, as the bay is enclosed by a double reef, which lessens the impact of the waves. For divers, it is a good base to explore some of the wrecks in Galle Bay, and there is some coral within safe snorkelling distance of shore (though you may be disappointed by their poor colour). Many find Unawatuna more appealing than its popular neighbour. However, this popularity has taken its toll. Beach restaurants have encroached to the point where the actual usable beach is very narrow, and the increasing number of visitors means that the beach is sometimes crowded, the western end of the bay particularly being popular with local day-trippers at weekends and public holidays. Petty theft has become a problem in recent years too as have drugs. During the week, however, if you are seeking somewhere with a beach safe for swimming, a wide range of clean accommodation and a variety of good beach-side restaurants, then Unawatuna is a good choice. ▸▸ *For Sleeping, Eating and other listings, see pages 163-176.*

Sights

Unawatuna's main attraction is unquestionably its beach but it isn't the only place worth visiting. There are some lovely walks in the area. Here are a couple.

Rumassala kanda (hillock), the rocky outcrop along the coast, has a large collection of unusual medicinal herbs. In the *Ramayana* epic, Hanuman, the monkey god was sent on an errand to collect a special herb to save Rama's wounded brother

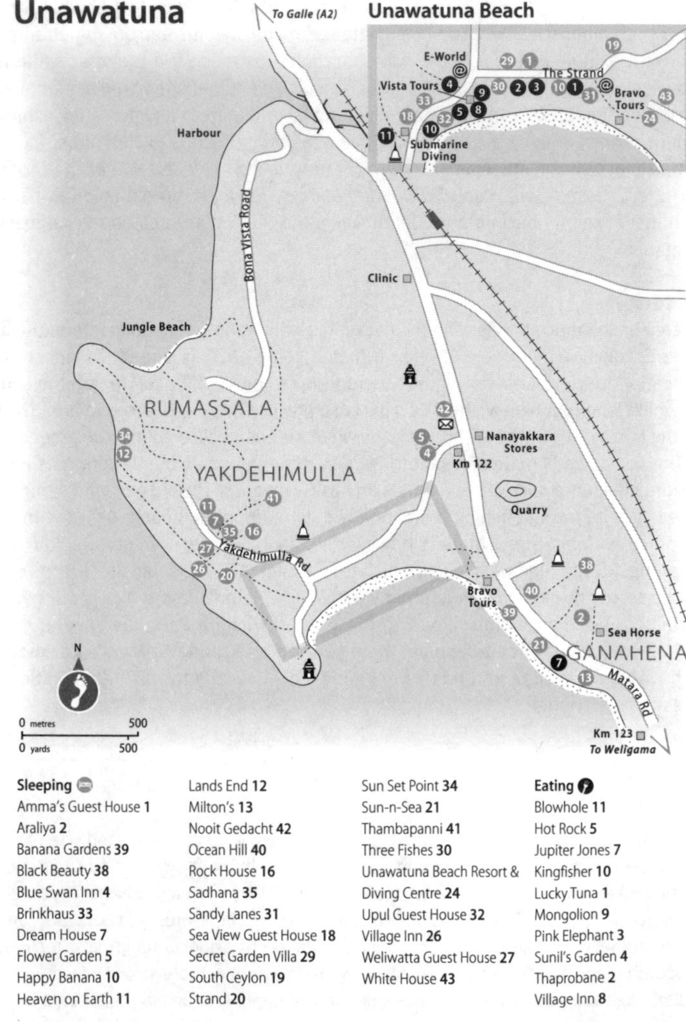

Lakshmana. Having failed to identify the plant, he returned with a herb-covered section of the great mountain range, dropping a part of what he was carrying here! Another part is said to have fallen in Ritigala (see page 281). This area of forest is now protected by the state to save the rare plants from being removed indiscriminately. It offers excellent views across Galle Harbour towards the fort. On a clear day look inland to catch sight of Adam's Peak. The sea bordering Rumassala has the **Bona Vista reef** which has some of the best preserved coral in Sri Lanka. Recovery from the 1998 bleaching has been faster than elsewhere on the coast.

Climb up to the temple at the western end of Unawatuna beach for fabulous views of the bay.

Jungle Beach, on the other side of the promontory, is pleasantly uncrowded and has some good snorkelling 'only slightly marred by the perfect view of Galle's cement works'. Boat trips from some of the guesthouses run here. Alternatively, you can walk (around 45 minutes) from Unawatuna beach. You will get lost but guides tend to appear as if by magic!

Unawatuna to Weligama → *Colour map 3, grid C3/4.*

The road running east from Unawatuna runs close to the sea offering wonderful views and linking a series of small attractive beaches. The area, with its white sandy beaches, attractive coves and first-class, well-priced accommodation, is no longer known to just a few, though there still aren't the crowds that are found at Unawatuna. The coast between Talpe and Weligama was best known for its remarkable fishermen who perched for hours on poles out in the bay. Nowadays, this is a dying tradition.
» *For Sleeping, Eating and other listings, see pages 163-176.*

Dalawella and Talpe → *Phone code: 091.*

The most likely place to spot 'stilt' fishermen working is from Dalawella to Ahangama early in the morning or sometimes, if they're hungry, in the evening. At other times they tend to arrive only when visitors with cameras appear, and they expect a small tip for a photograph! Dalawella is just east of Unawatuna. Though on the main road, it has a lovely undeveloped section of beach and a 'natural swimming pool' towards the eastern end. The fine beaches continue to picturesque Talpe, a short distance east, where an increasing number of upmarket hotels are beginning to open up. Many of the new hotels and guesthouses here are better value than in Unawatuna itself.

Koggala → *Phone code: 091.*

The coast road passes the old wartime airstrip, which is to be developed as a domestic airport. Nearby there is a small turtle hatchery, ① *0700-1830, Rs 70.* Opened in 1996, it gives Rs 5 to local fishermen to encourage them not to poach the turtle eggs and sell them on for food.

Koggala has an attractive, tranquil lake with rocky islets to the north, and a Free Trade Zone with some light industry. The lake, actually a lagoon, is lined with mangrove and rich with birdlife. Boat trips run to the **Ananda Spice Garden**, a temple and cinnamon island. ① *T2283805, for more details. One-hour boat trips cost Rs 600 for up to 7 people. Alternatively you can take a catamaran, Rs 250-300 per person.*

Just by the **Confifi Club Horizon Hotel** gate, a track leads left over the railway line to the **Martin Wickramasinghe Folk Museum**, ① *0900-1700; closed Mon and holidays. Rs 50 (with explanatory leaflet), children Rs 25, Sri Lankans Rs 15.* The museum houses the respected Sri Lankan writer's personal collection. His family home displays photographs and memorabilia, and some history about the area. Even if you are not a fan of Wickramasinghe, the museum is still worth visit as it contains some

By the entrance of the gardens is a sketch of a 2,000-year old irrigation system which proves how the ancient Sinhalese were light years ahead of the west in farming practices.

 fascinating exhibits from traditional Sri Lankan life. Religious items and agricultural and fishing tools are well displayed behind glass cabinets, with some traditional games (from before cricket obsessed the nation). There's a colourful selection of *kolam* masks and puppets from the Ambalangoda area, and 101 different utensils for treating coconuts. The house and museum are set in an attractive seven-acre garden with labelled trees, so you can mug up on your Sri Lankan flora.

Kataluva → *Phone code: 091.*

Purvarama Mahaviharaya, originally 18th-century with late 19th-century additions, is 3 km along a minor road turning off at Kataluva (Km 132 marker); you may need to ask directions locally. The ambulatory has excellent examples of temple paintings illustrating different styles of Kandyan art. Young monks will happily point out interesting sections of the *Jataka* stories depicted on the wall friezes. Note the musicians and dancers on the south side and the European figures illustrating an interesting piece of social history. The priest is very welcoming and keen to speak with strangers.

Midigama → *Phone code: 041.*

The coast from Ahangama to Midigama is regarded as the best surfing area on the south coast, and consequently it is popular with long-term surfers. However, unless you are into surfing it is probably best avoided. It is full of numerous very cheap and grotty guesthouses, catering for surfers on long stays.

Weligama → *Phone code: 041. Colour map 3, grid C3. Population 22,000. 29 km from Galle, 144 km from Colombo.*

Weligama is a busy centre for the surrounding fishing villages. Though the town itself is fairly unappealing, it has a picturesque location, with a magnificent sheltered and sandy bay safe for diving and snorkelling beyond the usual season on the southwest coast and some good surf to the eastern end of the beach, and is backed by the attractive Polwatte ganga. At the approach to the town there is a 4-m high statue of

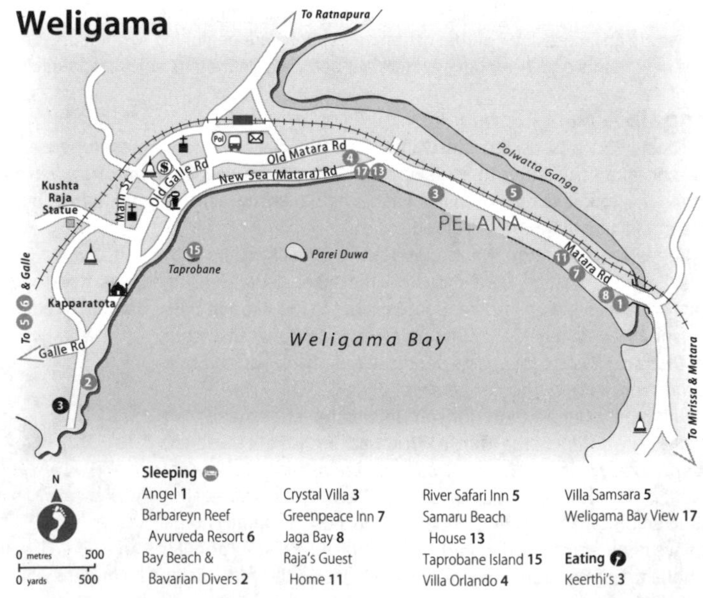

Tickling the ivories

Weligama's newest claim to fame is as the venue for the annual Taprobane Trophy, the world's only Beach Elephant Polo Championships, attended by Sri Lanka's rich and famous and the place to be seen over the long weekend. Elephant polo has a grizzly history, first played by the armies of the Mongol hordes, who celebrated their victories by playing polo with the severed heads of the vanquished. At the 2003 championships, the third in the tournament's history, staged on the anniversary of the signing of ceasefire agreement, teams arrived to do battle from as far afield as Sweden (Anantara Vikings) and Australia (the Tickle and the Ivories). In an uncharacteristic sporting success story for the country, it was the Scottish Chivas Regal team, featuring the Duke of Argyll, who challenged the Taprobane Tuskers, the local reigning champions, in the nail-biting climax. The Tuskers hammered a winner in the final minute, sealing the trophy and the glory.

Kushta Raja, sometimes known as the 'Leper King'. Various legends surround the statue believed by some to be of Bodhisattva Samantabhadra. Look out for the *mal lali* fretwork decorated houses along the road from the centre towards the statue. The area is also known for its handmade lace, see page 173. Devil Dances are held in neighbouring villages.

Weligama is most famous however for its tiny **Taprobane** island, walkable (at low tide) in the lovely bay. Once owned by the Frenchman, Count de Mauny, who built a magnificent house there, it was bought by American author Paul Bowles after his death. After a period of neglect, it was returned in the late 1990s to its former glory, and is now a luxury tourist retreat. » *For Sleeping, Eating and other listings, see pages 163-176.*

Mirissa → *Phone code: 041. Colour map 3, grid C3. 34 km from Galle, 149 km from Colombo.*

Of all the south coast beach resorts to have developed in recent years, Mirissa, with its beautiful wide stretch of golden sand backed by luxuriant vegetation, has received the greatest attention. For the moment the plaudits seems justified, as so far the relaxed little village, 5 km east across Weligama Bay, has been more sensitively developed than Hikkaduwa or Unawatuna, with the intrusion of guesthouses and restaurants on to the beach less obvious. Mirissa is no longer a secret hideaway though. Its popularity increases each year, prompting concerns about over-development. For the moment though, it is still one of the most idyllic places to relax along this stretch of coast.

The west end of the beach, very popular with surfers, is the most developed area and contains Mirissa's only 'resort' hotel. Further east, in the two beaches beyond the **Giragala Village**, is a reef where there is some good swimming and snorkelling. Giragala (or 'Parrot') Rock is a popular place to watch the sunset. Near here is a defile, known as Bandaramulla, where there is a Buddhist *vihara*.

Inland, you can explore the river, and there are some pleasant walks (or cycle trips) up into the jungle. Be on your guard in the forest at the western edge of the beach as a gruesome attack on a tourist couple was reported in 2002. Ask at your guesthouse about visiting rubber and tea factories, and a snake farm. » *For Sleeping, Eating, other listings and map, see pages 163-176.*

Matara

→ *Phone code: 041. Colour map 3, grid C4. Population 44,000. 42 km from Galle, 157 km from Colombo.*

Matara (pronounced locally as Maa-tre) is the south's second biggest town, after Galle. It is also an important transport hub, with the terminus of the railway line and an enormous bus station. Locals will tell you that the city is better than Galle as it has two Dutch forts to Galle's one! Though busy and full of traffic, it does have a rich history, and the old town with its narrow streets and colonial buildings is a pleasant place to explore. In the old marketplace you might still see the local wooden hackeries (oxcarts) that are sometimes used for races. Today, the Ruhuna University, 3 km east of town, has brought students into the town. Matara is also famous for its musical instruments, especially drums, and you can also pick up some good batik. Though the beach is attractive the waters are too rough for comfortable bathing much of the year. At **Polhena**, south of the town, is a good coral beach protected by a reef which offers year round swimming and some excellent snorkelling opportunities. There are also some good value guesthouses, a pleasant alternative to staying in Matara town. » *For Sleeping, Eating and other listings, see pages 163-176.*

Sights

An important Dutch possession on the south coast, controlling the trade in cinnamon and elephants, Matara was well fortified. **Star Fort**, which is faced with coral, was built in 1763. It has a moated double-wall and six points, and was designed to house ammunition, provisions and a small garrison. The gateway which shows the VOC arms and date is particularly picturesque. As in Galle, the Dutch government has recently invested money in restoring the Fort, formerly a library, and a museum is due to open in mid-2003. Across the **Nilawala Ganga** from the Fort, on the left-hand side is a gleaming and impressive **mosque**, a replica of the Meeran Jumma Masjid in Galle.

The **Main Fort**, south of the ganga, consists of a single rampart from which guns were fired. Its inadequacy as a defence was revealed during the 'Matara rebellion' of 1762, when a Kandyan army managed to take the town by bombarding it with cannonballs that simply went over the wall! The Dutch retook the town the following

year, and built the more successful **Star Fort**, ⓘ *generally closed, but keys to climb it can be obtained from the Municipal Council, T2222275,* to defend the town against siege from the river. There is a narrow gate, with an inscription of 1780, though it is in rather poor condition and covered in advertising stickers nowadays. Near the main bastion is the British clocktower (1883).

North of here, on Beach Road, is **St Mary's Church**. The date on the doorway (1769) refers to the repair work after the 'Matara rebellion'. Close by is St Servatius College, one of Matara's two exclusive public schools, whose most famous son is Sri Lankan batting hero and former cricket captain Sanath Jayasuriya.

At the western edge of town, the new **Ruhuna Cultural Centre** is built in the Dutch style next to the old market. Performances of music and dancing are held in the auditorium here.

Matara to Tangalla

Weherahena → *Phone code: 041.*

About 5 km beyond Matara, a left turn leads to this modern Buddhist sanctuary ⓘ *donation and tip for the guide*, which has a 40-m six-storey high painted Buddha statue. Much older is the *vihara*, whose 600 m of tunnels are lined with some 20,000 friezes, some dating back to Portuguese times, *Perahera* is at November/December full moon. Catch bus No 349 from Matara.

Dondra → *Phone code: 041. Colour map 3, grid C4. 6 km from Matara.*

Dondra or Devinuwara, which means 'City of Gods' (the British couldn't pronounce the name so rechristened the town!), is a fishing village famous for its Vishnu temple. The original temple, one of the most revered on the island, was destroyed by the Portuguese in a brutal attack in 1588. **Devi Nuwara Devale** retains, however, an ancient shrine possibly dating to the seventh century AD, which maybe the oldest stone built structure on the island. The modern temple, to the south, has old columns and a finely carved gate. Even today the Buddhist pilgrims continuing the ancient tradition venerate Vishnu of the Hindu trinity.

At the end of July/August is Esala Perahera, when there are 12 days of spectacular celebrations and processions which date back to 1258.

Some 2 km south of the town, the 50-m high lighthouse (1889) on the southern promontory at Dondra Head marks the southernmost point of Sri Lanka. It's immaculately maintained but security controls prevent visitors from climbing it.

Dikwella and Wewurukannala → *Phone code: 041.*

The marvellous bays and beaches continue across to Tangalla. There are some established resort hotels at the village of Dikwella offering diving and watersports in the bay, while 2 km inland at Wewuurukannala is **Buduraja Mahawehera**, ⓘ *Rs 100, a guide will approach (Rs 50 tip is acceptable)*. Until an even bigger one was built in Dambulla in 2002, this was the tallest statue on the island. The statues, tableaux and Buddhist temple are in a complex which has an impressively tacky 50-m high seated Buddha statue with a 'library' at the back. Some 635 paintings in cartoon strip form depict events from the Buddha's life covering every square centimetre of the interior. The artists are from all over the world but retain the same style throughout. There is also a garish 'Chamber of Horrors' with depictions of the punishments meted out to sinners, including some frighteningly graphic life-size models. One critic describes the site as looking 'more like an airport terminal than a temple'.

The upkeep of Dondra's historic lighthouse is provided by the British government. Everyone who works here draws their pensions direct from the UK!

Endangered turtles

Five of the world's seven species of turtle, the green, leatherback, olive ridley, loggerhead and the hawksbill all come ashore to nest on the beaches of Sri Lanka. All are listed by the World Conservation Union (IUCN) as either threatened or endangered. Despite the measures taken by the government, marine turtles are extensively exploited in Sri Lanka for their eggs and meat. In addition, turtle nesting beaches (rookeries) are being disturbed by tourism-related development, and feeding habitats, such as coral reefs, are being destroyed by pollution, especially polythene bags, and unsustainable harvesting. Around 13,000 turtles each year are caught, not always accidentally, in fishing gear while the illegal 'tortoise shell trade' continues to encourage hunting of the highly endangered hawksbill turtle's carapace.

Tourism has proved a double-edged sword in the fight to save the turtles. Since the early 1980s, the government has encouraged the setting up of tourist- friendly turtle hatcheries along the coast, from Induruwa on the west coast to Yala in the southeast, though the Wildlife Department acknowledges that these sometimes do more harm than good. In 1993, the Turtle Conservation Project was set up dedicated to pursuing sustainable marine turtle conservation strategies through education, research and community participation. Its *in situ* scientific project at Rekawa, where it used, in part, tourist cash to help monitor the turtles' hatching grounds, sadly ran out of funds in 1999 though a new scheme was scheduled to start at Kosgoda in late 2003. The Wildlife Department, who now manages the beach, remain committed however to finding a tourism-related solution to its protection.

Kudawella → *Colour map 3, grid C4. 6 km east of Dikwella.*

The natural blowhole at Kudawella, ⓘ *free (though you may be told otherwise)*, also known as **Hummanaya** due to the 'hoo' sound that you hear is one of the more bizarre attractions in Sri Lanka and worth the detour during the monsoon season. The water spray can rise to 25 m when the waves are strong. Take care when clambering on the rocks as they are wet and slippery in places. It is best to avoid weekends and go during school hours. The blowhole doesn't always 'perform' and is disappointing out of season, so check the situation locally before making the trip. The blowhole is 1½ km off the main road. If travelling by bus, ask the driver to drop you off at the turn-off. The route to the blowhole is well signposted by the Elephant House.

Mawella → *Colour map 3, grid C4. Phone code: 047.*

Mawella, 6 km west of Tangalla, has remained one of this stretch of coastline's best-kept secrets. It has a 3 km long, very wide beach, avoids the busy main road, and offers safe swimming. It's easy to miss – turn right at the Beach Cottage sign.

Tangalla → *Phone code: 047. Colour map 3, grid C5. 40 km from Matara, 198 km from Colombo.*

Tangalla (pronounced Tunn-gaa-le), famous for its turtles, is an attractive fishing port with a palm-fringed bay. In town, there are some distinctive colonial buildings and a picturesque ganga, while the surrounding bays have some some of the best beaches in the southern coastal belt. Even though there are a growing number of hotels and guesthouses, the beach remains mostly deserted despite good sand and safe swimming (when the sea is not rough). There isn't an enormous amount to see or do here except lie on the beach, but it does make a useful base for visiting the **turtles** at Rekawa, and the magnificent **Mulgirigala Rock Temple**. Sadly, Tangalla is rumoured to be one of the 'child-sex' destinations in Sri Lanka. The authorities have taken successful legal action against a number of offenders operating on some popular beaches. » *For Sleeping, Eating and other listings, see pages 163-176.*

Tangalla

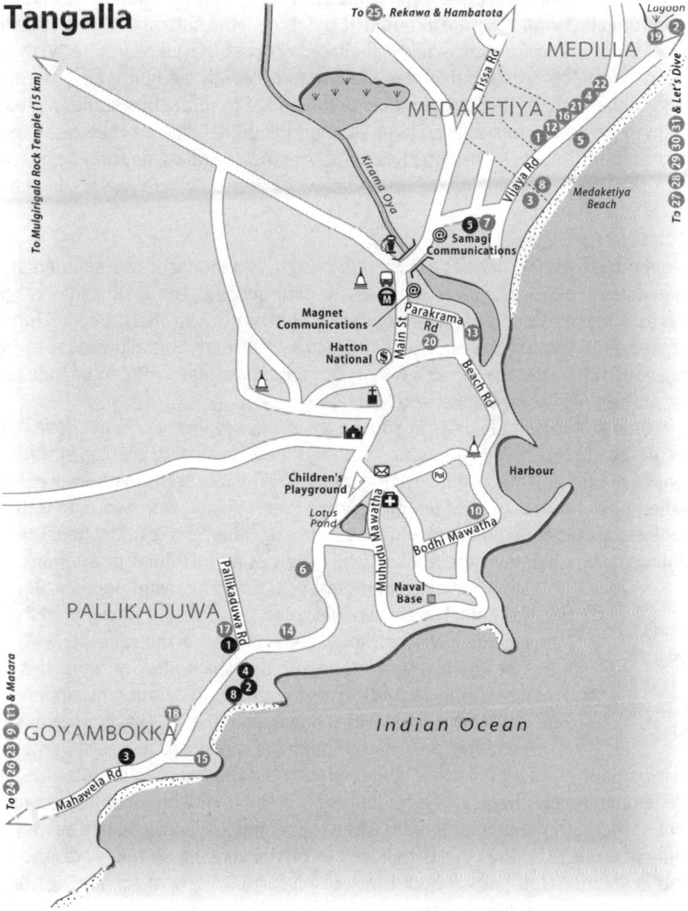

Sleeping
Anila Beach Inn **1**
Blue Horizon **2**
Catamaran Beach Home **3**
Darwins Beach Resort **25**
Dilena Beach Home **4**
Eva Lanka **24**
French Residence **6**
Ganesh Garden **29**
Gayana Guest House **5**
Goyambokka Guest House **23**
Green Jewel Cabanas **27**
Happy Bungalows & Ibis **28**
Namal Garden Beach **8**
Nature Resort **30**
Palm Paradise Cabanas **9**
Panorama Rock **31**
Rest House **10**
Rocky Point Beach Bungalows **11**
Samans **12**
Santana Guest House **13**
Sarath **7**
Sea Side Guest House **21**
Sea View Tourist Inn **14**
Seenimodera **26**
Shanika Beach Inn **6**
Tangalla Bay **15**
Touristen Gasthaus **17**
Tourist Guest House **18**
Villa Araliya **19**
Villa Ocean Waves **20**
Wavy Ocean **16**

Eating
Bay View **1**
Cactus Lounge **2**
Chanika's **3**
Green Garden **5**
Sea Beach **4**
Turtle's Landing **8**

Sights

There is a **Dutch fort** standing on the slope above the bay. Built of coral with two bastions in opposite corners, it was turned into a jail after a report in 1837 declared it was in sound condition and able to safely hold up to 100 men. The exterior has now been covered over by cement.

There are some lovely **beaches** with visitors having a choice of three main areas to stay. The settlements of **Goyambokka** and **Pallikaduwa** are on a series of bays to the south of town, and have clean and secluded beaches though some visitors have reported a terrible smell at the top end of the beach (near **Turtles' Landing** restaurant).

In **Tangalla town**, there are a couple of hotels near the harbour including the **Rest House**. The cove in front of is fairly sheltered so is consequently quite busy. The quietest locations are probably **Medaketiya** and **Medilla** along the long sweep of beach to the north of the harbour (across the bridge from the bus station). Medilla Beach, in particular, has a fine, clean sand and is quite idyllic as it also shelters a lagoon behind. Access to the latter two may be restricted and so may only be possible from Tissa Road. Some luxury accommodation is being built at **Rekawa**, 4 km east.

Excursions

Mulgirigala, ⓘ *Rs 100, guides ask for a fair Rs 50*, is a monastic site situated on an isolated 210 m high rock. It was occupied from the second century BC and was again used as a place of Buddhist learning in the 18th century. In 1826, George Turnour discovered the *Tika*, commentaries on the *Mahavansa*, here. This allowed the ancient texts, which chronicle the island's history from the third century BC, to be translated from the original Pali to English and Sinhala.

Although not a citadel, it is in some ways similar to Sigiriya. At the base of the rock there are monks' living quarters. The fairly steep paved path goes up in stages to the main temple and image house at the top. Along the way there are three platforms. The first platform has the twin temple, Padum Rahat Vihara, with two 14 m reclining Buddhas, images of Kataragama and Vishnu among others and a Bodhi tree. The wall paintings inside illustrate the *Jatakas* while the ceiling has floral decorations. The small second platform has a *vihara* with another Buddha (reclining) with two disciples. The murals show Hindu gods including Vishnu and Kataragama and the nine planets, and elsewhere, scenes from the Buddha's life. The third has four cave temples and a pond with a 12th-century inscription. The Raja Mahavihara with a fine door frame, has several statues and good wall paintings (though they are not as fine as at Dambulla), some partially hidden behind a cabinet which hold old *ola* manuscripts. The little cave temple, **Naga Vihara**, to the far left has a small door with a painted cobra – a cobra shielded the Buddha from rain when meditating, so is considered sacred and worthy of protection. The cave is believed to be a snake pit, so take care. The final climb is steeper. You pass a Bodhi tree believed to be one of 32 saplings of the second Bodhi tree at Anuradhapura, before reaching the summit with a renovated stupa, image house and temple. The site lies some 16 km north of Tangalla: take a bus to Beliatta, then change to a Wiraketiya-bound bus (Rs 7).

Although Mulgirigala is a fairly strenuous climb, it is well worth it as there are very good views across the surrounding countryside from the top.

It is estimated that up to 75% of Sri Lanka's female green turtles nest at **Rekawa**'s 2.5 km beach, ⓘ *Rs 350, from 1900*. A 'turtle night watch', a local community tourism project which employs ex-poachers as tourist guides, takes place each night. Visitors are encouraged to observe the females laying their eggs and returning to sea. The turtles could arrive at any time (often after midnight) so be prepared for a long wait. You will first visit a small 'museum' hut, where you can read about the turtles, and then be led on to the beach by a watcher. Sadly, without the direct control of the Turtle Conservation Project (see box, page 160), these watches have turned into something of a tourist trap, and the high-handed guides have been known to infringe conservation rules, with the turtles often disturbed by excessive shining of torches (no flash photography or torches are permitted on the beach). The government however, committed to long-term conservation, plans to develop the site and has earmarked Rekawa's lagoon for development as an Environmental Education Centre to highlight the mangroves and coastal birdlife. Rekawa's beach is 4 km east of Tangalla, then 3 km along Rekawa Road from Netolpitiya Junction. Taxis from Tangalla charge around Rs 600-650 including waiting. There are no facilities.

Sleeping

Galle *p149, map p150*

Beware of touts who may tell you that your guesthouse has hiked its prices or closed or that the fort itself is closed – it never shuts! If you accept a tout's recommendation, you'll be paying over the odds for their commission. A growing number of villas in the Galle area have been bought and renovated and can be let both short and long term. See the end of Galle sleeping section for details.

LL Dutch House, *opposite The Sun House (see below) and operated by the same people (contact for bookings)*, a former residence of a Dutch East India admiral built in 1712, with 4 magnificent suites (US$330) exquisitely decorated in colonial style, with personal library and CD player and a magnificent treetop pool.

LL Lighthouse Hotel (Jetwing), *Dadella, 4 km north of Galle, T2223744, F2224021, lighthousehotel@lanka.com.lk* Member of the Small Hotels of the World Association. 60 superbly furnished a/c rooms (US$205), panoramic views from sea-facing terrace, 2 restaurants including excellent **Cinnamon Room** for fine dining at a reasonable price for the quality, 2 pools, one salt water.

L-AL The Sun House, *18 Upper Dickson Rd, T/F2222624, sunhouse@sri.lanka.net* 5 superbly furnished rooms (US$120), with an excellent suite (US$180), all with different themes in 1860s spice merchant's house. Described as a '5-star boutique hotel' it is highly exclusive with discreet service, fine dining, pool, library, very atmospheric.

B Closenberg Hotel, *11 Closenberg Rd, Magalle, Unawatuna Rd (3 km, 3-wheeler from fort or bus stand, Rs 100), T/F2224313.* 20 comfortable rooms (US$40) in attractive colonial house built in 1858 on promontory overlooking Galle Bay (see above), modern wing (though in colonial style) has a/c rooms, minibar and balcony with good sea views; original rooms have high ceilings, beautiful antique furniture (beds have P&O Rising Sun crest) and are full of history. Attractive restaurant, bougainvillea garden, plenty of character and quiet ambience.

B Lady Hill, *Upper Dickson Rd (a little further up from The Sun House), T2244322, F2234855, ladyhill@sltnet.lk* A 19th-century mansion at the highest point of the city, with large veranda and teak ceiling. Modern extension has 15 well-furnished, if smallish, a/c rooms (US$48), with TV and balconies, **Rooftop Harbour Bar** which affords spectacular views of the Fort and the harbour, and some mornings as far inland as Adam's Peak! Also very good pool.

C-E New Old Dutch House, *21 Middle St, T4385032, F4384920.* 6 rooms in gleaming renovated house with Moorish-style decor, many arches and a great spiral staircase. Plans for Ayurvedic centre, restaurant, bar and pool, so prices (currently Rs 1,000-2,000) set to rise. Friendly.

D Rampart Hotel, *31 Rampart St, T4380103, F2242794.* 2 fairly simple rooms (Rs 1,400) in 200-year old building overlooking the walls, though rest of mansion is quite impressive. Hot bath, nets, good views from veranda restaurant although the jewellery and handicraft showroom is the main focus of business attention.

D Royal Dutch House, *15 Queen's St, T2247160, kengngse@sltnet.lk* 3 eerily vast, spartan rooms (Rs 1,500) with attached bath (free-standing tub) in the wonderfully antiquated old Dutch government house. Renovation planned under new owner, Amanresorts.

E Rampart View, *37 Rampart St, T4380566.* 6 sizeable, clean rooms (Rs 800-1,000) with attached bath in recently renovated colonial house. Also a family room with spiral staircase leading up to little den (Rs 1200). Wonderful views from the roof. Friendly, kind management.

E-F Mrs Shakira Khalid's Guest House, *102 Pedlar St, T2234907, khalid@dialogsl.net*

4 rooms (Rs 600-1,200) in a newly restored family home, good atmosphere, excellent home-cooked food, no commission to touts. A library planned, internet terminal. Phone ahead.
F **Weltevreden**, *104 Pedlar St, T2222650, piyasen2@sltnet.lk* 8 clean rooms (Rs 600) but only one bathroom, quiet lush garden, friendly family, very good food.
F-G **Beach Haven Guest House**, *65 Lighthouse St, T/F2234663, thalith@sri.lanka.net* 10 spotless rooms, Rs 400-700 (better upstairs), in a very friendly family- run guesthouse. Great atmosphere and the wonderful Mrs Wijenayake hasn't put her prices up for 7 years! No commission to touts.
F-G **YWCA**, *23 Church St, T2223109*, has rooms by day (Rs 500) or month (Rs 3,500 with meals).
Eden Villas, *65 Lighthouse St (above Beach Haven), T2232569, F2232568, www.villasinsrilanka.com*, is a British-run agency with upwards of 15 beautiful properties available for letting, many in Galle area, ranging from 2 person (from US$200 per night) to 23 person (US$1800). Contact Jack or Jo Eden.

Unawatuna *p153, map p154*
Book ahead at weekends as Unawatuna is a popular getaway from the city. Many cheaper shacks are being pulled down as Europeans buy up plots for development into sturdier (and more expensive) hotels and guesthouses.
A **Thambapanni**, *Yakdehimulla Rd, past Dream House, contact Thaprobane, T4381722, thaproban@wow.lk* Currently 6 large, splendidly furnished rooms in beautiful new building in peaceful setting on side of Rumassala hill. All rooms have mini-bar, balcony with hammock, some with tub, those on highest level have magnificent jungle views. Best room built into side of hill, with mini-temple and meditation area. 15 more to come, plus swimming pool.
A-B **Unawatuna Beach Resort** or UBR, *T4380549, ubr@sri.lanka.net* 62 light and spacious rooms with balcony (US$52-69, half-board), best in new annexe, large private garden, pool, various sports including PADI-qualified diving, boat trips, good restaurant, resort style hotel now fenced off from the crowded beach.
B **Dream House**, *T4381541, dreamhouse@libero.it* 4 beautifully furnished rooms (US$50 including breakfast) in Italian run old colonial-style house. Wonderful bougainvillea filled garden, very Italian ambience and authentic Italian food. Very peaceful.
B **Milton's**, *Ganahena, T2283312, miltons@isplanka.lk* 20 rooms, 10 a/c (US$56), 10 fan only (US$45) rooms, all with sea views, spotless, spacious and classily furnished. Large grounds, with bar and good terrace restaurant, but beach area (owned by hotel) is a bit of a disappointment.
B **Secret Garden Villa**, *T/F011-4721007, secretgardenvilla@msn.com* Tastefully decorated rooms (plenty of wood) in lovely gardens, US$35 (3 bed suites for US$50). Domed room in the middle for yoga lessons, 0800-1700, Rs 300-500. Owners run **Three Fishes** (see below).
B-D **Nooit Gedacht**, *T2223449, nooitged@sltnet.lk* Beautiful colonial mansion (1735), steeped in history. 12 simple rooms with period furniture (Rs 2,000-3,500), plus 1 apartment (Rs 4,000) in large, cool original building, 13 with attached bath and veranda in new wing (Rs 1,500). Also full, authentic Ayurveda centre (US$500 per week). Very peaceful and atmospheric.
C **Sun Set Point**, *Yakdehimulla, T2225939, lalwhitehouse@aol.com* 6 spacious, new gleaming and white rooms (Rs 2,500) with veranda in impressive house on headland, with great views, bar and restaurant.
C **Three Fishes**, *T2241857, F2224313*. 5 well-furnished sizeable rooms, one with separate bath tub (Rs 2,500). Good restaurant and atmosphere.
C-D **Lands End**, *Yakdehimulla, T2232593, srilankahotels@hotmail.com* 6 cool, comfortable rooms (US$10-20) in beautiful house with excellent location on rocky headland. Good views (especially at sunset) across to Galle, good restaurant/bar, snooker table.
C-D **Strand**, *Yakdehimulla Rd (set back from beach), T/F2224358, strand_u@sltnet.lk* 6 spacious rooms (Rs 2,000) plus 1 bungalow (Rs 2,500) and 1 apartment (Rs 3,000) in a 2- storey family apartment in 1920s colonial house in large grounds, private balcony/veranda, good food, friendly family, knowledgeable host, a little dark and frayed around the edges but recommended for atmosphere.
C-D **Sun-n-Sea**, *Ganahena, at east end of bay, T2283200, muharam@sltnet.lk* 8 clean

rooms, Rs 2,250 with a/c, Rs 1,750 without, good terrace restaurant overlooking the bay with excellent view, popular. Mrs Perera is a charming owner. Friendly, close to main rd.

C-F Banana Gardens, *T/F4381089*. Fabulous spot very close to the beach (feel the water lap your feet as you eat outside) with excellent views, and spotless rooms in wooden huts. 7 rooms on the beach (Rs 1,000-2,500), 5 well back from the road (Rs 700). Good Sri Lankan food, great atmosphere. If you want true seclusion, ask about new place being built (due autumn 2003) on deserted beach east of Matara.

D Blue Swan Inn, *Yakdehimulla Rd, T/F2224691*. 4 spotless comfortable rooms in English/Sri Lankan-run family guesthouse, well furnished. Rooftop restaurant.

D Flower Garden, *T/F2225286*. Pleasant cabanas, restaurant, laid-back quiet spot in pretty gardens, friendly and helpful owner.

D Sea View Guest House, *T/F2224376, seaview@sltnet.lk* 15 spacious, clean rooms (Rs 1,200) with large balcony in pleasant garden setting. Also a bungalow with 2 bedrooms and kitchen (Rs 1800). Restaurant, popular with local weekenders.

D-E Happy Banana, *T077-7151264*. 6 high-ceilinged, decent sized but variable rooms (upstairs better) with spotless bathrooms (Rs 1,000-1,500) in attractive 2-storey building, though no sea view. Popular bar and seafood restaurant.

D-F Rock House, *Yakdehimulla Rd, T2224949/8*. 20 rooms in 2 blocks with 2 owners (Rs 500-1800), all clean, some new, airy and spacious, lots of wildlife ('troop of mongooses'!). Good range, good value.

E Amma's Guest House, *T2225332*. 13 clean, spacious rooms, upstairs better, opening onto a lovely balcony, nets, clean. Arthur C Clarke was one of the first ever guests here.

E Sandy Lanes, *Welledevala Rd, T2223156, F2234010*. 8 rooms (Rs 1,000-1,200, breakfast included), with shared veranda.

E Upul Guesthouse, *T4384387, ajith999@hotmail.com* 4 rooms with bath plus 2 cabanas without, one with hammock on veranda overlooking beach (all Rs 800). Bit cramped. The restaurant specializes in pizza.

E Weliwatta Guest House, *T/F2242891, weliwatta@hotmail.com* 5 fairly plain rooms (Rs 1,100, including breakfast), quiet, good home-cooked food. Tours.

E-F Araliya, *T2283706, F380365*. 10 clean, large rooms (Rs 770-990) with shared veranda, away from road around a pleasant courtyard, restaurant, reasonable value.

E-F Brinkhaus, *Welledevala Rd, T2242245*. Quiet and peaceful, decent rooms Rs 600-800, in shaded gardens with family of monkeys in the trees. Lovely family, been here for decades.

E-F Ocean Hill, *T2224827*. Good value, clean and spacious rooms (Rs 600-900) with shared veranda in a friendly and youthful operation. Pleasant open areas, and a great view of Unawatuna beach from first floor terrace restaurant. Good food too (main dishes Rs 250-300).

E-F Village Inn, *T2225375, F380691*. 13 rooms in chalets and 1 bungalow (Rs 900), rooms with bath and balcony, no view Rs 500, with view Rs 800, lending library, good breakfast available, meals to order, quiet, friendly. Helpful owner has 3-wheeler and will take you on trips.

F Black Beauty, *Ganahena, T4384978*. Slightly eccentric set-up (signposted from Matara Rd in white script on a white background, then you have to ring the bell of a secret entrance in a wooden hut) but worth the effort. Very friendly, secluded laid-back atmosphere, and good value, clean and sparkling rooms at Rs 600.

F Sadhana, *Yakdehimulla Rd, T2224953, strand_u@sltnet.lk* 3 clean rooms back from the road. Roof terrace with hammock has birdbath, ideal for bird-watching. Good value.

F-G Heaven on Earth, 4 rooms (Rs 350 shared open-air bath, Rs 550-600 attached), rather simple but well furnished for the price.

F-G White House, *T4380638*. Very cheap family run guesthouse, rooms with bath Rs 500, shared bath Rs 300.

G South Ceylon, *sirig@sltnet.lk* 5 basic rooms with shared bath , good restaurant, meditation, ayurvedic treatment, laundry facilities, internet café. Ask about **Zen Rock Beach Retreat** at the eastern end of the beach, with en suite rooms and self-catering facilities.

Unawatuna to Weligama *p155*

C Point de Galle, *Matara Rd, Tulpe, T2283206, bindu@slt.lk* 12 airy rooms with beautiful beds, breakfast and balconies

(US$25) set in attractive gardens right on the beach, upmarket.

C Sri Gemunu, *Dalawella, T2283788, sgemunu@sltnet.lk* 20 comfortable sea-facing rooms (Rs 2,200) with veranda. Pleasant gardens and good restaurant overlooking attractive beach, but not as good value as others along here.

C Star Light, *T2282216, Talpe, starlight@sltnet.lk* Brand new, 16 very attractive a/c rooms with beautiful furniture and good attention to detail, TV, mini-bar and bath tubs (US$25). Lovely open areas, great pool and very smart restaurant. Theme nights run, and weekend barbecue packages. Free transfer to Unawatuna beach.

D Club Lanka, *Matara Rd, Ahangama (4 km east of Koggala), T2283296, F2283361.* Set in pleasant gardens and open, breezy feel with good beach but rooms in rather faceless main block (Rs 1,650 including breakfast). Sports, restaurant, bar and large pool.

D South Beach Resort, *Kataluva, T2283067, F5450048.* Very new, 2 clean, sizeable rooms with veranda (Rs 1,250), to become 10 by summer 2003, restaurant, bar and pleasant seating area in simple garden. Good spot with beach on one side and lagoon (can swim here, though the sea is too rough).

D Wijaya Beach Cottage, *Dalawella, T2283610.* 10 spotless rooms with verandas and 7 wooden cabanas bang on the beach (Rs 1,800 with breakfast). Good restaurant with great laid-back atmosphere, Ayurvedic massage offered, very friendly Sri Lankan/British management.

D-E Shanthi Guest House, *Dalawella, T2283550, mohan1@itmin.com* 6 rooms (Rs 1,000), 6 cabanas (Rs 1,000-1,500). Rooms are moderate size, shared balcony, facing beach. Cabanas closer to beach set amongst a series of ponds in attractive gardens. Stilt fishermen on beach, and salt water 'pool' nearby. Excellent restaurant and pleasant, friendly atmosphere.

E Blue Ocean Villa, *Dalawella, T/F2282242.* 6 comfortable rooms (Rs 1,000) with good position on beach, peaceful. Building 3 more very large rooms in peaceful gardens on other side of road at time of writing, which (same price) look to be good value.

E Villa Gaetano, *Denuwala, T2283968, vgaetano@sltnet.lk* Well-furnished clean rooms (Rs 900) in very friendly family guesthouse. Excellent food, internet (residents only) Rs 4 per min, body massage Rs 600. Lots of trips/advice available for visits to fresh fruit and vegetable markets, snake farm at Akuressa, good cheap batik shop. Airport pick-up possible. Bicycle hire Rs 175 per day (with guide).

F-G Hilten's Beach Resort, *Midigama, T041-2250156, surfcity@itmin.com* 17 rooms, some with attached bath (Rs 500, negotiable), some without (Rs 400) restaurant, idiosyncratic owner, popular.

G Surfers' Dream, *contact Villa Gaetano in Ahangama (above).* Probably the best option in Midigama, simple but clean, rooms Rs 350.

G Ram's Shack, *Midigama, T041-2252639.* 14 rooms in chaotic and communal hangout (Rs 250-350, with bath).

Weligama *p156, map p156*

The better value accommodation is in Pelana, a short bus or 3-wheeler ride from Weligama town.

LL Taprobane Island, *for reservations contact The Sun House, Galle, T091-2222624, www.taprobaneisland.com* Probably the most exclusive place to stay in Sri Lanka. Whole house available, from US$850.

A Villa Samsara, *2 km west at Kumalgama (140 km post), T/F2251144.* Beautiful colonial villa in lovely garden amongst coconut groves. 4 large, simply furnished rooms with 4 poster beds (US$77).

B Crystal Villa, *New Sea Rd, Pelana, T2250635, crystal@lanka.com.lk* 5 large, comfortable rooms, plus 2 bungalows with al fresco showers, good garden on the beach, pool, good restaurant.

C Bay Beach, *Kapparatota (west end of bay), T/F2250201, hashani@sltnet.lk* 60 a/c rooms (US$35), hot bath, private balcony/terrace, restaurant, bar, disco, pool, access to rather dirty beach, watersports at **Bavarian Divers** (see below). Overall rundown and unloved.

D-E Jaga Bay, *New Sea Rd, Pelana, T/F2250033, jagabay@sltnet.lk* 17 large, almost spotless chalets plus 3 cabanas with hot bath, nets, set in large garden on beach, good for swimming, very peaceful location, very good restaurant.

D-E Villa Orlando, *New Sea Rd, Pelana, T2251361, villa.orlando@weligama.info*

3 rooms, 1 with a/c and hot water (Rs 1,500), though simpler rooms (Rs 1,000) better value. Restaurant serves pasta.

F Angel, *New Sea Rd, Pelana, T/F2250475*. 6 spotless, airy rooms (Rs 1,200 including breakfast) in neo-colonial style building, garden stretches to the beach, reasonable restaurant.

E-F Samaru Beach House, *544 New Sea Rd, Pelana, T/F2251417*. 6 spotless rooms (Rs 600-800), each with own seating area, 3 more planned, good location on the beach, restaurant, friendly young management, good value.

F Greenpeace Inn, *New Sea Rd, Pelana, T2252957*. 6 attractively furnished rooms (Rs 650) with bath, painted every year, some nice touches, good views from some, clean, quiet location, garden, close to beach, friendly. Three-wheeler available for hire.

F River Safari Inn, *down track over railway line, and right 500 m), T077-7658165*. Peaceful spot on river, jungle as far as the eye can see, river trips (Rs 600 per person – a bit pricey), rooftop restaurant due, 5 rooms (Rs 500) nothing special but recommended for position.

F Weligama Bay View, *New Sea Rd, Pelana, T2251199*. Along good stretch of beach, 11 large rooms, attached bath, reasonably clean, good restaurant. Popular with surfer girls, and friendly management. Surfing equipment (Rs 150 per hr) and surfing lessons offered, plus surf shop and 'luxury cabanas' planned. Consistent good reports.

G Raja's Guest Home, *down track off New Sea Rd, Pelana, T2251750*. 4 simple, clean rooms (Rs 400), nets, attached bath, great location on clean section of beach, pleasant garden, wide menu with excellent seafood (especially lobster) but other tastes catered for, Raja is an exceptional host.

Barbareyn Beach Ayurveda Resort, *T2252994, F2252993, barbrese@slt.lk* New Ayurvedic centre (opened early 2003) run by respected Beruwela-based company. 45 simple but attractive rooms (3 classes €75-95), sea views and balconies, some split-level with bath-tub. Large Ayurveda clinic with full list of treatments, €350 per week. Yoga and meditation.

Mirissa *p157, map p167*

Between Nov and Apr, book ahead.

C Paradise Beach Club, *140 Gunasiri Mahime Mawatha, T2251206, mirissa@sltnet.lk* 'A winner', 40 bungalows (a/c Rs 2,300, non-a/c Rs 2,000), pool (Rs 100 non-residents), smart restaurant (mostly buffet), set in large rustic garden, tours, located on beach, not bad value but enforced half board tends to be restrictive.

D Ocean Moon, *Udupila Junction, T2252328*. 6 good cabanas (Rs 1500 with breakfast) on the beach, peaceful, good food, massage.

Mirissa

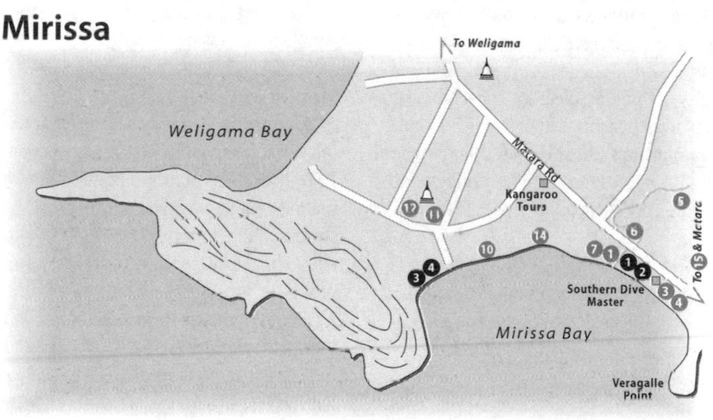

Sleeping
Amarasinghe's Guest House **5**
Calm Rest **12**
Central Beach Inn **14**
Damith Holiday Wings **11**
[illegible] Village **4**
Mirissa Beach Inn **1**
Ocean Moon **7**
Paradise Beach Club & Seafresh **10**
Samantha's Guest House **6**
[illegible] Traveller's Halt **15**
Sunset Inn **3**

Eating
Bay Moon **4**
Café Mirissa **1**
New Dealing **2**
[illegible]

D-E Calm Rest, *Sunanda Rd, T2252546.* 4 well-furnished wooden cabanas (Rs 1,500 with breakfast) and 3 rooms (Rs 900 with breakfast), spice garden. Very good restaurant. Run by Swiss Andy, who is a mine of information.

D-F Giragala Village, *eastern end of the beach, T2250496, nissanka.g@lycosmail.com* Well-established, 12 rooms ranging from Rs 500 (small and simple) to Rs 1400 (large spotless family rooms), pleasant gardens with swaying hammocks, good information about swimming and snorkelling.

E Sunset Inn, *T2251651.* 6 slightly overpriced rooms (Rs 950) but good swimming nearby.

E-F Central Beach Inn, *on beach, T2251699.* 6 simple rooms (Rs 600) and 2 bungalows (Rs 1,000), restaurant.

E-F Mirissa Beach Inn, *T2250410, F2250115, beachinn@sltnet.lk* 11 large rooms with veranda (Rs 800-1,000) plus 9 clean bungalows (Rs 500-750), restaurant, shaded gardens with good beach access.

F Damith Holiday Wings, *Gunasiri Mahime Mawatha, opposite Paradise Beach Club, T2251651, F2250115.* 6 clean rooms (Rs 550) and 3 bungalows (Rs 650), 'friendly and helpful owners', restaurant with enormous home cooked breakfasts.

F Summer Breeze Traveller's Halt, *Dandaramulla, T078-8514025.* Not on beach (rocky section between 2 bays), but 2 reasonable if dark rooms (Rs 700).

G Amarasinghe's Guest House, *T2251204, chana776@hotmail.com* 5 mins inland (follow signs). 6 large rooms (Rs 250-450) but grotty bathrooms, pleasant, quiet garden away from beach. Internet Rs 6-7 per min.

G Samantha's Guest House. 2 simple rooms (Rs 400) in forest setting by log bridge and lagoon. Very cheap food, free bike tours.

Matara *p158 map p158*

Most budget travellers choose to stay in Polhena. The Broadway is also known as Dharmapala Mawatha, Colombo Rd or New Galle Rd.

D-E Rest House, *main Fort area south of bus station, Matara, T2222299.* 14 rooms in colonial house by the sea. 2 wings, new wing Rs 900 (slightly plusher and with new furniture), old wing (grubbier but characterful), Rs 786, a/c Rs 1,800. Restaurant with good Sri Lankan breakfasts.

D-F Browns Beach Rest, *39b Beach Rd, Matara, T2226298.* 7 clean rooms (Rs 600), 2 sea view, a/c Rs 600 extra, popular restaurant .

F Sayuri, *on beach, Polhena, T2225529.* 6 simple but good value rooms overlooking fine stretch of beach, restaurant.

F-G Sunil Rest, *off Beach Rd, Polhena, T2221983, nilmiapo@sltnet.lk* 7 rooms, old Rs 350, brand new Rs 600 (very good value) with nets, in very friendly and helpful family guesthouse. 1 self-catering room with fridge, cooker and TV available (Rs 1,000). Restaurant. Snorkelling (Rs 200) and boat trips organized, free bicycle hire, motorbike (Rs 500/day) and even self-drive 3-wheeler for hire!

G Blue Ripples, *38 W Gunasekara Mawatha, Matara, T2222058.* 4 simple rooms (Rs 350-450) in wooden shacks, 2 in good location on the riverbank (plenty of birdlife) - you'll have the illusion you're in the middle of the jungle! No commission to touts.

G Sunny Lanka Guest House, *Polhena Rd, Polhena, T2223504.* 5 very clean rooms (Rs 400) in friendly guesthouse, modern building, nets, good restaurant, cycle rental (Rs 100), snorkelling (Rs 250) and day trips arranged (see below), visits to snake farm.

G TK Green Garden, *116/1 Polhena Beach Rd, Polhena, T2222603.* 11 good, clean rooms (Rs 200-400), some with shared veranda, though expensive restaurant (fried rice Rs 220), well-run, quiet, pleasant garden. Look out for Donald for good value batiks, and excellent snorkelling (Rs 300).

Matara to Tangalla *p159*

AL Claughton, *Kemagoda (3 km east of Dikwella), bookings to Russel Gray in Colombo, T/F011-2509134.* Sumptuous Italianate villa in magnificent setting overlooking a vast sweep of bay. 3 rooms (US$125 full board), whole house available for rent. The current president stays here so it must be good!

A Dikwella Village Resort, *Batheegama, 1 km west of Dikwella, T2255271, dickwella@mail.ewisl.net* 70 large a/c rooms (US$65 half-board only) in bungalows in 'Little Italy' luxury resort (Italian owned and patronised), guaranteed maximum 15 m distance from beach, all with sea views, pool, Ayurvedic massage, tennis, watersports, diving, excellent restaurants, very attractive location on rocky promontory. In-house dive school (courses US$380) and 7 sites (1 wreck) visited but Renato's English isn't very good, which may pose problems.

A-C Suriya Chandra Home, *Mawella, T077-7147818.* 4 cabanas, 2 private bungalows, 3 individually decorated rooms (1 with throne lavatory!) inside attractive house with beautiful large sofas for relaxing (€30-60), Ayurvedic treatments on offer, **Il Camino** restaurant serves authentic Italian food.

B Beach Cottage and Cabanas, *Mawella, T/F2240585.* 8 'eco-cabanas' and 2 rooms in large gardens, restaurant. Half-board, pricey.

C Kingdom Resort, *Kottegoda (5 km west of Dikwella) just before (from west) 175 km post, T/F2259364.* 8 spotless rooms, 6 with balcony, US$22, in attractive neo-colonial house with own stretch of beach. Italian- owned, with all furnishings Italian-made. Very pleasant.

D Kadolana Beach Resort, *Bandara Watta, Kemagoda (3 km east of Dikwella), T2256140.* 8 simple rooms with shared balcony (Rs 1,600 including breakfast), experienced owner, restaurant.

D Sunrise Beach Cabanas, *Mawella, T077-7653733.* 2 cabanas, 1 room, Rs 1,200.

F Dikwella Beach Hotel, *112 Mahwella Rd, just past the town, T2255326.* 10 comfortable, clean rooms, good value at Rs 750.

Tangalla *p160, map p161*

Rooms in some private houses in Medilla can be obtained for as little as Rs 200.

LL Seenimodera *(The Beach House), contact The Sun House in Galle for reservations, p163.* Nominated as one of the top 20 villas in the world, an exquisitely furnished 4-bedroom house (sleeping 7) on a fine stretch of beach, extensive library, stunning pool, open-air bathrooms, and an extraordinary collage about the poet Keats; from US$750 per night.

A-B Eva Lanka, *3 km west of Goyambokka, T/F2240940, eva.lanka@mail.ewisl.net* Italian family resort with 3 swimming pools, sports facilities, luxurious chalets, Ayurveda treatment and a fine beach.

B Nature Resort, *most easterly hotel, Medilla, T/F2240844, wickynr@sltnet.lk* 19 spotless rooms in German-run resort (US$36), lagoon terrace and restaurant, very attractive gardens, Ayurveda centre with steam bath, beach bar, large pool, good section of beach.

B-C Tangalla Bay, *Pallikudawa, T/F2240346, intence@sltnet.lk* 32 breezy rooms (US$32), including some unnecessary a/c (extra US$5) in unlikely 1970s kitsch 'truly eccentric' ship design which has seen better days, good position on headland, small pool, popular for weddings but "a sadly sinking ship".

C Darwins Beach Resort, *Rekawa Rd, Welleode Village, Ranna, 4 km along rough track, T077-7351489, darwins@itmin.com* Ecologically sound German-run resort on remote beach safe for swimming. Comfortable, well-furnished individual bungalows (US$27, plus US$5 supplement for a/c), good seafood (ingredients brought in on request), large pool. Own turtle hatchery – market rates paid to fishermen for eggs.

C Palm Paradise Cabanas, *Goyambokka, T/F2240338, ppcabanas@sltnet.lk* 20 comfortable cabanas set in a spacious and shady garden close to the beach, very peaceful (classical music at breakfast a welcome touch), but insipid food and mandatory half-board.

D French Residence, *260 Matara Rd, T2242231, deen.anver@wanadoo.fr* 3 comfortable rooms decorated in a bright Gallic style. Genuine French restaurant but since owner (and chef) divides his time between Sri Lanka and France, check before making the trek.

D Ganesh Garden, *Medilla Beach, T2242529, magnet@mail.ewisl.net* 8 cabanas, a bit overpriced (Rs 1,200) but in a quiet, secluded location, laid back atmosphere, hammocks in garden, cheap snorkelling equipment for hire, reasonable restaurant.

D Goyambokka Guest House, *Goyambokka, opposite Palm Paradise Cabanas, T/F2240838.* 4 comfortable, well sized, clean rooms (Rs 1,400 including breakfast) in colonial house, hot water, quiet, pleasant shaded garden, bamboo restaurant, good off-season discounts, good value.

D Rocky Point Beach Bungalows, *Goyambokka, T2240834, rockypointsl@hotmail.com* 3 bungalows (Rs 1,700) and 4 rooms (Rs 1,400), all large, clean with private veranda, pleasant gardens in quiet location overlooking rocky promontory, good food.

D Touristen Gasthaus/Tourist Guest House, *13 Pallikaduwa Rd, T/F2240370.* 2 bungalows, 4 rooms, 2 with hot water, all spotless plus an apartment with kitchen so you are spoilt for choice, friendly owner, extremely well run.

D Villa Araliya, *Medilla, T/F2242163.* 2 bungalows and 1 large room (Rs 1,200-1,500), beautiful antique furniture with 4-poster beds, pleasant gardens, friendly and helpful owner.

D-E Rest House, *on promontory overlooking harbour, Tangalla town, T2240299.* 23 clean rooms (Rs 850, plus Rs 400 for a/c) in rambling 18th-century Dutch building, recently refurbished, balcony/verandas, restaurant with lovely views, good value.

D-F Blue Horizon, *'Lakmal', Medilla, T2240721.* 5 rooms (Rs 500-1,500), one with 4-poster bed, very peaceful spot, friendly family, excellent food, pleasant first floor terrace overlooking sea, art gallery. Can be noisy in evenings due to generator but recommended as long as you like yellow.

D-F Green Jewel Cabanas, *Medilla, T/F2240827.* 7 cabanas (Rs 600) plus 3 rooms (Rs 1200), close to beach and lagoon, restaurant, catamaran service.

D-F Tourist Guest House, *Pallikaduwa, opposite Tangalla Bay Hotel, T2240389, tourist@sltnet.lk* Ingeniously named, 8 good-sized rooms, more expensive with hot water (Rs 1,700 with a/c, Rs450-1,200 fan only), clean, friendly, restaurant, internet Rs 7 per min, nice setting.

E Anila Beach Inn, *23 Vijaya Rd, Medaktiya, T2240446.* 7 airy, spotless rooms (Rs 800), garden restaurant, cycle hire, peaceful.

E Panorama Rock, *Medilla, T2240458.* 5 clean cabanas (Rs 800) on lagoon, good food.

E-F Gayana Guest House, *96 Medaketiya Beach, T2240659, F2240477.* 8 rooms of varying size (Rs 600-1,000), some fronting directly onto beach, good restaurant, friendly staff, secure, popular with backpackers, one of the best in this class, Wed evening slide presentation on turtle conservation.

E-F Happy Bungalows/Ibis, *Medilla, T077-7905480.* Spotless, attractive cabanas and brick built bungalows (Rs 700-1,000) in very peaceful location where beach meets lagoon, restaurant, friendly.

E-F Namal Garden Beach, *Medaketiya Rd, T078-8529576, F2223249.* 18 rooms (Rs 500-800), upstairs better with private balcony and sea views where you can watch the fishermen hauling up the nets, terrace restaurant, beach barbecues possible, rather block-like but breezy though recent reports of lack of cleanliness.

E-G Dilena Beach Home, *65 Wiyaya Rd, Medaketiya, T2242240.* 3 plain room (Rs 450) plus a cabana (Rs 900) , good location, friendly.

F Catamaran Beach Home, *Medaketiya Rd, T2240446.* 4 basic rooms (Rs 400-500), but cheap and friendly.

F Samans, *75 Wijaya Rd, Medaketiya, T224-0464.* 6 darkish clean rooms (Rs 400) set in lush garden, very good food, motorcycle hire Rs 500.

F Sarath, *Medaketiya Beach, T2242630.* Good double rooms (Rs 700) with modern bath, very clean, quiet, good food, friendly and helpful host, bike hire.

F Villa Ocean Waves, *67 Beach Rd, Tangalla town, T2240354.* 5 large rooms (Rs 550) in popular local watering hole but surprisingly good restaurant, friendly.

F Wavy Ocean, *Medaketiya, T2240629.* 8 new rooms (Rs 500-650), upstairs better, bicycle hire (Rs 150), seafood restaurant, friendly.

G Santana Guest House, *on lagoon close to town, T2240419.* Good value simple but clean rooms (Rs 250-300), quiet attractive location, restaurant on stilts in lagoon, but bridge to beach broken at time of visit. Friendly.

G Sea Side Guest House, *Medaketiya, T2242406.* New rooms with clean bathrooms (Rs 350-400), restaurant.

G Sea View Tourist Inn, *Mahawela Rd.* 3 large rooms with shared bath in friendly family home set in large garden.

G Shanika Beach Inn, *69 Medaketiya Beach, T2242079.* 6 simple rooms with bath (Rs 300), good cheap food. Good value.

Eating

Galle *p149, map p150*

There are currently very few places, other than guesthouses, to eat in Fort, though this will change as the area develops for tourists.

RsRsRs Lighthouse Hotel is highly recommended for a treat, especially in the **Cinnamon Room** (separate vegetarian menu), fine dining, superb attention to detail, order an Irish coffee just to see it being prepared; surprisingly, under US$10 per head. The **Cardamom Café** has lighter snacks.

RsRsRs South Ceylon, *Gamini Mawatha,* for good Chinese, Sri Lankan (try pineapple curry or cashew nut curry), Continental plus bakery. Also bar.

RsRs Anura's, *Pedlar St, 2224354, 0730-2330.* Mediocre pizzas and curries.

RsRs Closenberg Hotel. Tour groups mean service can be slow, but from under the pergola there are lovely views over the harbour, pleasant and quiet in the evenings, main courses from around Rs 300, beer Rs 120.

RsRs Rampart Hotel, *31 Rampart St, F2242794*. The veranda is 'a must for a sunset beer' though the food is average (main courses around Rs 225, lime soda Rs 100).

RsRs Royal Dutch House. Chinese (mixed fried rice Rs 280) and Sri Lankan dishes that seem to vary a lot in price but food is good.

Rs There are numerous cheap 'rice & curry' places around the train/bus stations, plus:

Chinese Globe, *38 Havelock Place.*

New Chinese, *14 Havelock Place.*

Galle Inn Chinese, *4 Talbot Town.*

Unawatuna *p153, map p154*

There are numerous restaurants along the beach, with very little to choose between them. Nearly all will serve good seafood, Chinese, Sri Lankan (full meal often only to order) and western dishes. Almost all serve alcohol (though those at the western end of the bay don't advertise it since the area close to the temple is officially 'dry').

RsRsRs Cocorumba Bar Rendezvous, *Unawatuna Beach Resort*. Popular place, wide menu including lunchtime buffet (US$6), authentic 'Aussie burgers', Sat night disco.

RsRs Blowhole in a great setting by the river (watch the wildlife), busy at night, good place to stop on the way up to Jungle Beach.

RsRs Happy Banana with lovely beach setting, good for seafood (seer with salad Rs 210), Fri night disco.

RsRs Jupiter Jones, good beach setting in ethnic decorated restaurant, good seafood.

RsRs Kingfisher has a party crowd at weekends, Sat night disco.

RsRs Lucky Tuna, grilled tuna (whose luck ran out) with chips Rs 220, Sri Lankan curry Rs 240. Cheaper rice and noodle dishes.

RsRs Mongolion, excellent fruit juices, friendly staff and reasonable prices.

RsRs Pink Elephant, great setting with views over both sides of the bay. Sri Lankan curries Rs 120-140.

RsRs South Ceylon, wide vegetarian menu, different themed international cuisine every night.

RsRs Sunil's Garden has the best sound system (plenty of Bob Marley), good food and juices.

RsRs Thaprobane with good selection of fish and western dishes in pleasant surroundings. Alcohol-packed cocktails Rs 150, Lion beer Rs 100.

Rs Hot Rock, probably the busiest and most popular partly because of its location, tables and loungers on beach outside, though food (mainly Chinese, Rs 80 for fried rice) not necessarily the best.

Rs Village Inn, *next to Hot Rock*, small vegetarian menu, but good laid-back atmosphere.

Unawatuna to Weligama *p155*

For further options see Sleeping, p165.

Rs-RsRs Garden Restaurant, *T077-907008, Talpe (opposite Star Light), sajeewan@wow.lk*, does a full Sri Lankan buffet every day in a pleasant shaded spot, 1100-1500. Very good value.

Weligama *p156, map p156*

Home cooking in the privately run guest-houses is difficult to beat, see p166.

RsRs Crystal Villa, good food and location.

RsRs Keerthi, close to the sea and peaceful, with large whale jaw in the garden to add interest. Wide range of good seafood, including mullet, snapper and sailfish, as well as usual seerfish and cuttlefish (Rs 210-230).

Mirissa *p157, map p167*

RsRs Bay Moon, the first in Mirissa and still one of the best, "nice beach bar ambience and they set a beach fire for effect".

RsRs Café Mirissa has a limited selection of food – seafood, curry, Chinese – but a perfect position to survey the beach.

RsRs Calm Rest is well worth going out of your way for, great food with specials every night. Banana curry soup and Swiss rösti very popular, as are diced shark and barracuda (if available).

For an explanation of the sleeping and eating price codes used in this guide, see the inside front cover.

RsRs New Dealing, new and eager, good seafood, plus usual Chinese (Rs 100-150), paean to the ghost of Bob Marley.
RsRs Seafresh, part of Paradise Beach Club, the smartest place in Mirissa.
RsRs Water Creatures, more Bob Marley and popular with surfers.

Matara *p158, map p158*
RsRs Chinese Dragon, *62 Tangalla Rd*, good meals for around Rs 150.
RsRs Golden Dish, *Station Rd*. Chinese.
RsRs Mayura Beach Resort, *33 Beach Rd* (next to **Brown's Beach Rest**), has a wide range of Chinese and curries and is popular with locals at lunchtime.
RsRs Samanmal, *next to the Hatton National Bank opposite the stadium*, good for Chinese.
RsRs Sawada does tasty Thai food.
Rs Cargill's Food Court.
Rs Fine Curd Food Cabin, amongst others, is recommended for the local delicacy of buffalo milk curd with honey or jaggery.
Rs Galle Oriental Bakery, *Dharmapala Mawatha*, does good Sri Lankan meals from Rs 50, as well as snacks.

Matara to Tangalla *p159*
For options see Sleeping, p168.

Tangalla *p160, map p161*
Along the beach towards the town, several restaurants and guesthouses prepare very good dishes, especially seafood. For options see p169.
RsRsRs Eva Lanka, *3 km west of Goyambokka*, if you're desperate for real wood-fired pizza (Rs 400-500) or authentic cappuccino.
RsRs Bay View is a lovely spot overlooking the bay, prawns Rs 480, lobster Rs 780.
RsRs Blue Horizon, *Medilla*, try the mixed seafood for Rs 350, and **Samans**, *Medaketiya*, are particularly recommended.
RsRs Cactus Lounge, *Pallikaduwa*, has a good setting on sheltered beach, fresh seafood (lobster Rs 750, prawns Rs 390), plus soups and snacks.
RsRs Chanika's, *Mahawela Rd, opposite entrance to Tangalla Bay Hotel*, small, an 'exceptional find', does excellent food, delicious and fresh (over 1 kg whole lobster for two, Rs 1,000!), if tired of tamed down 'European' dishes, ask for Sri Lankan style friendly and obliging, delightfully chatty hostess.
RsRs Green Garden, *Medaketiya Rd*. Rice and curry (Rs 250), seafood and pasta (Rs 225-275).
RsRs Panorama Rock Café for fine BBQs.
RsRs Rest House, *on promontory overlooking harbour, Tangalla town*. The terrace here overlooks the attractive harbour; does excellent lunch time rice and curry (Rs 250), or worth calling in just for a drink.
RsRs Sea Beach, *Pallikaduwa*. Good range of fish including seer, shark (Rs 320) and mullet.
RsRs Turtles' Landing, *next door to Cactus Lounge*, offers similar fare.
Rs Villa Ocean Waves is popular with locals and has a large, cheap menu.

Bars and clubs

Galle *p149, map p150*
There is little opportunity to go drinking in Galle Fort. Some of the guesthouses are Muslim, and don't appreciate alcohol on the premises. Locals drink at the **Sydney Hotel**, opposite the bus station, which serves Lion Beer at Rs 70, but it's pretty basic and you may find that you don't stay long. A better option is the bar at **South Ceylon**.

Unawatuna *p153, map p154*
The places listed in the eating section generally sell beer, see p171. A couple of places have discos at weekends, starting at 2130. Sat is the big night (at Kingfisher)!

Shopping

Galle *p149, map p150*
Galle is known for its lace-making, gem polishing and ebony carving. Several shops accept credit cards and foreign currency. In Galle town, on Colombo Rd, west of Victoria Park are several gem shops.
The following are recommended:
Star Jewellers, *41 Colombo Rd*; **Sapphire Gem Centre**, *5 Mosque Lane, Kandewatte*; **Universal Gems**, *42 A Jiffriya St (Cripps Rd)*; and for modern designs **Ubesiri & Co**, *Rampart Hotel, 31 Rampart St*.
Hatton Tea Stall, *31 Main St*. Good quality tea, loose or in more costly gift packs, very helpful proprietor helps you to choose without pressure.
Laksana, *30 Hospital St*, is recommended for handicrafts.

Lihinya Trades, by the lighthouse, has a good selection of handicrafts, knowledgeable, helpful owners.
Natural Silk Factory, *691/1 Colombo Rd, Gintota (north of Galle), T2234379, 0900-1830*, where you can watch silk worms (the silk being spun and weaved), showroom and shop with reasonable prices and little pressure to buy.
SCIA Handicraft Centre, *Kandewatte Rd, T2234304*. 5 workshops producing polished gems, carvings (ebony), batik, lace and leather bags etc employing about 50 people (approved by the State Gem Corporation and Tourist Board).
Vijitha Yapa, *170 Main Street*. New shop on 4-storeys, with a wide selection of English books, and internet planned for the top floor.

Unawatuna *p153, map p154*
There are various shops along The Strand selling provisions and tourist goods. Clothes are cheaper on Yakdehimulla Rd, but bargain.

Weligama *p156, map p156*
Weligama lace is available at several outlets and workshops along the road opposite Taprobane Island.

Matara *p158, map p158*
You'll find good batiks and citronella oil.
Art Batiks, *58/6 Udyana Rd, T/F2224488*. Shirley Dissanayake is a holder of the President's Honorary Gold Medal 'Kala Booshana' in arts. He produces top quality batiks from Rs 850, only available on site here in his workshop. Beware of imitations.
Laksala, by the temple, for handicrafts.
Sri Madura, *21 Dharmapala Mawatha*, specializes in locally made Pahatarata Biraya drums, which you can buy (Rs 3,000-5,000), or simply watch craftsmen producing.
Vijitha Yapa, *25a Dharmapala Mawatha, T2229777*, has English language books.

Sport and activities

Galle *p149, map p150*
There are a number of shipwrecks in Galle Bay but better diving is at Hikkaduwa, p136, and Unawatuna, below.

Unawatuna *p153, map p154*
The diving season runs from Nov to Apr here. Only about 30% of the coral in the immediate Unawatuna area is living, but there are 5 or 6 wrecks, some at a depth below 15 m, which you can visit. The best accessible wreck is the Rangoon in Galle Bay, though this is at a depth of 32 m.
Sea Horse, *off Matara Rd*, run by Rohana (12 years experience as a Divemaster), is the smallest operation in Unawatuna. 1 dive US$30, with own equipment US$25, 10 dives US$175. Open Water Courses US$300. Also runs fishing trips (Rs 2,100), to Jungle Beach (Rs 2,000) and for snorkelling (Rs 1,700). **F** range rooms with 20% off for divers.
Submarine Diving School, *T4380358, g.koralage@hotmail.com* US$25 (including equipment) for 1 dive, US$100 for 5. Also at **Unawatuna Beach Resort**. Check that a PADI-qualified instructor is on hand.
Unawatuna Diving Centre, *Matara Rd, T2244693, info@unawatunadiving.com* The largest and newest dive centre, with the best equipment, and soon to upgrade to PADI 5-star. Runs trips to about 15 dive sites. Open Water Courses US$330, Advanced US$225, single dives US$30 (US$20 with own equipment). Also shallow depth refresher courses (US$75), snorkelling trips (US$20), fishing (US$50) and glass-bottomed boat trips (US$40).
Most of the beach-side restaurants hire out snorkelling equipment (mask, snorkel, flippers Rs 100 per hr), and some run their own snorkelling trips.

Unawatuna to Weligama *p155*
For experienced surfers, the coast from Ahangama to Midigama has some excellent surf, at its best between Jan and Mar. There are various breaks at Midigama. The main (or 'left' break) is in front of **Hilten's Beach Resort**, and is good for beginners and longboarders. Further east, the 'right' breaks over a shallow reef close to **Ram's Shack**. 400 m east of here is a further break which is more suitable for beginners.

Weligama *p156, map p156*
There are plenty of fish in Weligama Bay (especially Yala Rock and Prinz Heinrich Patch) plus numerous wrecks here and further afield (*SS Rangoon* good but deep).
Bavarian Divers, *Bay Beach, T077-7858330, bbas@sltnet.lk, open Nov-Apr*, is highly

recommended. Captain Edgar K Rupprecht has 15 years experience in the Maldives. Good website, www.cbg.de/bavariandivers, gives details of sites and local places to stay. PADI Open Water Course (US$295 plus US$55 for certificate and logbook), plus courses up to Divemaster. One dive and check dive US$30 (including equipment). Deep-sea angling is available here mainly for marlin, yellowfin and sharks. A day's angling in a 24-ft Fjord with 200Hp engine (including outriggers, Penn equipment) is US$500.

Mirissa *p157, map p167*
Southern Dive Master, *contact Lakshmann Muthukuda, T077-7279672, info@southern divemaster.com* Small, new operation (needs to go to Unawatuna to fill tanks), but runs Open Water Courses (US$325), and will go up to Divemaster. Also runs trips to Kirinda (the Basses) and Trincomalee in season.

Matara *p158, map p158*
Nishantha, *T077-7600803*, **Blue Corals Restaurant**, organizes local diving excursions. Check qualifications.
Ask at **TK Guest House** or **Sunny Lanka Guest House** for Titus, an excellent snorkelling guide who knows the reef like the back of his hand having had over 30 years of experience. The reef is also good for first time snorkellers ("after 10 mins I felt like Jacques Cousteau!"), and there are night trips to see Moray eels.

Tangalla *p160, map p161*
Let's Dive, *50 m from Ganesh Gardens, Medilla, access best from Tissa Rd, T0777-902073, F2240401*. German-run dive school. 1 dive €25; PADI Open Water Course, €325; Advanced Course, €250. 15 sites visited including nearby coral reef, and 2 wrecks, a cargo ship (plenty of fish) and 200-year old steamer.

Tour operators

Galle *p149, map p150*
Southlink Travels, *2nd floor, Selaka Building, 34 Gamini Mawatha, next to the Bus Station.*

Unawatuna *p153, map p154*
Bravo Tours, 2-6 day tours (longer tours include Trincomalee) and safaris arranged. Car with driver Rs 3,500 per day, all-inclusive.
Vista Tours, *T4380258*, IDD calls (discounts on Sun and after 2200), airport minibus (Rs 450 per person, minimum 4), minibus with driver, plus a number of tours.
R Dharmadasa ('Harry'), *T077-7619371*, is a recommended driver, though negotiate all terms first. Flat rate Rs 2,500 per day for 8-person van. Safe and reliable.

Mirissa *p157, map p167*
Kangaroo Tours, *T/F2252404, camee-l@hot mail.com, 0900-2000*. Day tours Rs 3,000 (200 km, thereafter Rs 15 per km), motorbike rental Rs 500 per day, internet Rs 8 per min.

Transport

Galle *p149, map p150*
Air Sri Lankan Airlines, *3rd floor, 16a Gamini Mawatha (opposite bus station), T2246942.*
Bus There are regular services along the coast in both directions. Both CTB and private buses operate from the main bus stand. Frequent buses to **Colombo**: a/c Express recommended (Rs 84), 3 hrs, normal CTB (Rs 42) but avoid Sun as it can be very busy with queues of over an hour before you actually get onto a bus. Buses east to **Unawatuna** (15 mins), **Matara** (1-1½ hrs), **Tangalla** (2-3 hrs), **Tissamaharama** (4 hrs), **Kataragama** (4½ hrs) and **Wellawaya**.
Taxi Over Rs 3,000 for a Colombo trip.
Three-wheeler This would cost around Rs 100 to Unawatuna.
Train The station is a short walk from the bus station and the fort and town. Express trains to **Colombo** (3½ hrs, 2nd class Rs 64.50, 3rd class Rs 23), most via **Hikkaduwa**, **Ambalangoda**, **Aluthgama**, **Kalutara** and **Panadura** at 0645, 0740, 0905 (weekdays only), 1040 (Vavuniya train stopping at **Anuradhapura**, 7½ hrs, Rs 180/65.50), 1410 (Sun only), 1445 (**Kandy** train, 7 hrs, Rs 133/48) and 1805. Slow trains stop at other coastal destinations. To **Matara** trains (1½ hrs, Rs 35.50/24) leave every 1½-2 hrs, 0530 to 2055, stopping at **Talpe**, **Koggala**, **Ahangama** and **Weligama**. Slow trains (0530, 0730, 0920, 1430, 1715, 2055) stop at **Unawatuna** (10 mins) and **Mirissa** (1¼ hrs).

Unawatuna *p153, map p154*
It is very easy to miss Unawatuna when travelling by road. Look out for the Km 122 marker on the (sea) side of the road if coming from the east.
Bus Services between **Galle** and **Matara** will drop you at the main road on request.
Three-wheeler To/from **Hikkaduwa**, Rs 250-300, after bargaining. **Galle** Rs 100-125, takes 15 mins.
Train Trains pass through Unawatuna on the **Galle-Matara** line, though only the slow trains (7 a day – see Galle above) stop here. 10 mins to **Galle**, 1-1¼ hrs to **Matara**. If coming from **Colombo**, take the Express to Galle then change on to a Matara train. The station is to the east of the main Galle-Matara Rd, some 500 m north of the Km 122 marker (about 15-min walk to the beach). Touts and 3-wheeler drivers outside the station can be very persistent. Be sure of your destination to avoid caving in and arriving at a guesthouse of their choosing.

Unawatuna to Weligama *p153*
Many visitors to these beaches arrive by car but it is equally feasible to reach one of the resorts by public transport.
Bus Between Galle and Matara, local buses can be flagged down and stopped at any of these settlements.
Train Most trains between Galle and Matara stop at **Talpe**, **Ahangama** and **Weligama**, where there are 3-wheelers, and there are also local stations at **Habaraduwa**, **Kataluva**, **Midigama** and **Mirissa**.

Weligama *p156, map p156*
Bus Services between **Galle** and **Matara** will let you off on the New Sea (Matara) Rd, though some local buses will drop you at the bus yard on the Old Matara Rd. Buses from **Colombo** about 4 hrs; from **Galle**, 45 mins. Local buses run from **Weligama** to **Pelana**.
Train Weligama is on the Colombo-Galle-Matara railway line, though check to make sure the train stops here if it's an Express.

Mirissa *p157, map p167*
Bus Services between **Galle** and **Matara** pass through Mirissa. From **Weligama**, bus (Rs 3) or 3-wheeler (around Rs 100).
Three-wheeler Can be taken from Paradise Beach Club.
Train Slow trains from **Galle** or **Matara** stop at Mirissa, otherwise catch an Express to Weligama and then take a 3-wheeler.

Matara *p158, map p158*
Bus The station is in the Main Fort area with buses running on a 'depart when full' basis. A bone-shaker to **Colombo** costs Rs 57, and a/c coaster Rs 118, 4 hrs. There are regular buses to **Galle**, **Hambantota**, **Kataragama**, **Tangalla**, **Tissamaharama**, and all points along the coast, as well as inland to **Ratnapura** and **Wellawaya** for the eastern highlands. There is also at least one early morning departure to **Nuwara Eliya**, 8 hrs. Buses to **Mirissa** go regularly (Rs 6). Very irregular local buses run to the beach at **Polhena** (260, 350, 356). Alternatively a 3-wheeler will cost Rs 50.
Train Matara station, the terminus of this railway line, is 1 km away from town. Three-wheelers and taxis transfer passengers. To **Colombo** (4 hrs, Rs 89/32.50) at 0400, 0540, 0725 (weekdays only), 0910, 1315, 1650, plus slow trains as far as **Galle** (1½ hrs, Rs 24.50/13) at 0610, 0725 (Sat, Sun), 1155, 1430, 1715. **Kandy** train at 1315 (8 hrs, Rs 157/57), Vavuniya train via **Anuradhapura** (9 hrs, Rs 204.50/ 74.50) at 0910. From **Kandy** the early morning train at 0520 (7¼ hrs) is very busy (2nd and 3rd class only which doesn't guarantee a seat) but is still recommended if you can get on the train by 0500.

Matara to Tangalla *p159*
Buses running between Matara and Tangalla link the main villages strung along Matara Rd. To visit the sights inland it is best to have your own transport.

Tangalla *p160, map p161*
Bus The station is in the town centre close to the bridge. There are regular services along the coast to **Matara** (1 hr) and **Hambantota** (1 hr), with other services continuing on to **Tissamaharama** (2 hrs) and **Kataragama** (2¾ hrs). There are several morning departures for **Colombo** (5 hrs), plus some to **Wellawaya** and the Hill Country.
Three-wheeler From the bus station these ferry passengers to beaches nearby

Directory

Galle *p149, map p150*
Banks Bank of Ceylon, *Lighthouse St*, has a Visa ATM and will change TCs. **Commercial Bank** has a Cirrus ATM. **Hatton National Bank**, *HW Amarasuriya Mawatha*, exchanges currency, TCs and gives cash advances on Visa and Mastercard. **People's Bank**, *Middle St*.
Communications The huge **GPO** is on Main St. It also has Poste Restante and is the only place south of Colombo that offers EMS Speedpost (though you must call before 0900). There is a branch post office on Church St, within the Fort. **Internet** is expensive in Galle, with the few places available offering Rs 8-10 per min with unreliable connections. In the Fort, try **TG Communications**, *Pedlar St*. In the new town, **Malcolm Corporation**, *2 Main St*, is cheaper at Rs 6 per hr. There are numerous **IDD** Lanka Payphones and Metrocard cardphones scattered around, or you can use the various private offices on Havelock Place.
Medical services General Hospital, *T2222261*.
Useful addresses Forestry Department, *Lower Dickman Rd, T2234306*. For information and tickets for Sinharaja Biosphere Reserve (you will need to buy tickets in advance if using the minor entrances). Ask about Kanneliya here too. **Police station** is in the Zwart Bastion.

Unawatuna *p153, map p154*
Banks None here – head into Galle.
Communications **Internet** is widespread – facilities at Rs 5 per min. **Blue Fin Tours**, *next to Lucky Tuna*, has 24-hr internet. **E-World Internet Café**, a/c, internet Rs 5 per min, library exchange, free coffee, text messaging, 0900-0000. **Shehan Tours**, *Neptune Bay*, has internet, IDD and fax. **Vista Tours** (see above), IDD calls, internet Rs 5 per min, 0830-1130. **IDD** calls can be made from a number of private 'travel offices/reiseburos'.
Useful addresses **Tourist police** by Unatawatuna Beach Resort.

Weligama *p156, map p156*
Banks Bank of Ceylon and People's Bank.
Communications **Post office**, *Main St*, opposite the railway station.

Matara *p158, map p158*
Banks Amongst those around Sri Karothota Mawatha, east of the sports stadium, are **Sampath Bank**, with a Cirrus ATM, and **Hatton Bank**, changes TCs.
Communications **Internet** at Caddyshack, opposite Bank of Ceylon, has 24-hr facilities for Rs 7 per min. There is a **sub post office** in the Fort area, plus agency post offices on Station Rd and Dharmapala Mawatha.

Tangalla *p160, map p161*
Communications **Post office**, *just off the Main Rd opposite the mosque, is open Mon-Fri 0800-1700*. **Internet** is not cheap. **Magnet Communications**, *opposite the market, on Main St, open 0800-1730*, Rs 8 per min but slow. **Samagi Communication**, *6 Medaketiya Rd, open 0800-2200*, Rs 7 per min, restaurant, taxi and cycle hire planned.There are several **IDD** Lanka Payphones and Metrocard cardphones around town.

The dry southeast

The dry southeast offers a striking contrast with the lushness of the southwestern Wet Zone. In an astonishingly short space, east of Tangalla, everything changes. Open savanna and shallow wetlands take over from the dank forest and rich undergrowth and the increasingly frequent patches of bare earth have a burnt and arid look. From Nonagama, 25 km east of Tangalla, there are two choices of route through the Dry Zone. Both offer magnificent wildlife spotting opportunities. The road inland takes you close to Uda Walawe, famous for its elephants, from which you can travel to Ratnapura or the Sinharaja rainforest, or into the Highlands. Alternatively, you can continue east on the coastal road, visiting salt pans for some superb bird-watching, the remarkably varied wildlife of Yala, and on to the strange and wonderful pilgrimage site of Kataragama.

Inland to Uda Walawe

Kalametiya Bird Sanctuary → *Colour map 3, grid C5.*

A short distance off the coastal road, this is ideal for watching shorebirds in the brackish lagoons and mangrove swamps. It has a beautiful beach and lagoon, excellent for bird-watching undisturbed save for a few fishermen who might pester you for money. There are no facilities, nor entry fees, though there is accommodation nearby. To get there, turn right off the A2 after Hungama at the 214 km post and walk 2 km to the lagoon, or get off at the 218 km post and walk 300 m to the sanctuary. A three-wheeler from Tangalla should cost Rs 300. » *For Sleeping, Eating and other listings, see pages 187-191.*

Ridiyagama and around → *Colour map 3, grid C5. 24 km inland north from Ambalantota.*

Close to the Walawe Ganga, the **Madungala hermitage** is claimed to have remarkable paintings. In fact, all that remains of the old monument is a square white base and some writing engraved in the rock. There is a new concrete *dagoba* with murals on a hilltop. There are fine views of Ridiyagama Tank and Adam's Peak from there. A walk through the forest takes you to another new *dagoba*. Nearby, in an open space north of the tank, are the **Mahapalessa hot springs.** Believed to have healing powers, the bubbling water is collected in pools for bathers.

To the south, Ridiyagama Village is well known for its fine curd and honey. Nearby are the 100 or so ancient rocky **Karambagala Caves**, once occupied by Buddhist hermits, which were discovered in the scrub land. From the A18, take the road to the right (east) at **Siyambalagoda**, cross the Walawe Ganga River, and follow the track along the stream for about 5 km.

Uda Walawe National Park → *Phone code: 047. Colour map 3, grid B5.*

Easily accessible from the south coast, Uda Walawe is one of the island's most popular national parks. Mainly open parkland traversed by streams, it is best known for its elephants – large herds can be seen during the dry season. However, bird-watching is more rewarding than searching for any other wildlife. The 308 sq km park was set up in 1972 to protect the catchment of the Uda Walawe Reservoir which is at the south end of the Walawe Ganga. » *For Sleeping, Eating and other listings, see pages 187-191.*

Ins and outs

Getting there The park is accessible from the A18 Nonagama-Ratnapura Rd. Embilipitiya is the nearest major town, while there is also accommodation at Timbolketiya, close to the park office. To enter the park, you follow the road along a 4-km bund across the reservoir, and take a turn after 'Km 11' post.

Getting around 4WD vehicles only (from Rs 1,200, depending on where you start) are allowed to use the dry-weather roads and jeep tracks. These can be picked up at guesthouses or at the park gate.

Park information 0600-1800, US$12, ISIC holders and children under 12, US$6, Sri Lankans Rs 20, plus the usual moveable feast of extras – vehicle fee (Rs 120), with 'open hood' fee (another Rs 100), service charges for tracker (US$6), plus a couple

Current estimates suggest that there are about 3,500 wild elephant in Sri Lanka, with a further 800 domesticated.

more admin and tax charges. Tickets can be bought at the park entrance east of the reservoir, though the main park office is in front of the Elephant Transit Centre in Timbolketiya. Of the guides, Sanath Hewage has been recommended and speaks good English.

Best time to visit November to April when the resident population of water birds is joined by migrants from the north.

The Park

Along the river there is thick woodland of old teak trees, but the rest of the area is mainly open parkland traversed by streams, which makes elephant viewing easy. They number 400 to 450, and can be seen in herds of up to 100 or even more. They are best seen along the river and near the numerous streams and tanks. There are also healthy populations of macaque, langur, jackal and around 15 leopard, while increasing numbers of sambar, spotted deer, barking deer, wild boar and water buffalo are beginning to re-establish themselves. Recent reports suggest that there are no sloth bear. Some 189 species of avifauna have been recorded with bee-eaters, hornbills, peafowl, hawk eagles, ibis and Indian rollers frequently seen. Birds gather in large numbers around the tanks – the best ones are around Magam, Habarlu and Kiri Ibban.You may also be able to stop at the **Palugaswewa tank**, approached from the A18, about 8 km along a dry weather track from Galpaya to the west of the reservoir. **Timbirimankada**, 3 km from Sinnukgala, at the north end of the reservoir, is particularly good for bird-watching. These are not far from **Handagiriya village** which has a prehistoric site nearby (see page 126). **Ranagala**, which can be reached in dry weather, about 7 km from Sinnukgala is good for bird-watching. Elephants too may come to the river here.

Elephant Transit Centre → *Feeding time is every three hours from 0600-1800.*

Set up by the Department of Wildlife in 1995, the Elephant Transit Centre cares for abandoned calves, most of which have been injured, before returning them to the wild when they reach five years of age. Its successful reintroduction scheme, supported by the Born Free Foundation, contrasts directly with the orphanage at Pinnawela, where the animals have proved to become too domesticated to fend for themselves. Twenty of the centre's 32 animals are 'foster parented', which costs Rs 10,000 per elephant per month (half the required sum for food and medical treatment). Although visitors are not allowed to get as close to the animals as at Pinnawela, it is worth visiting at mealtimes. The site's facilities are limited at the moment, though a viewing platform for visitors is planned by 2004, along with a hospital and a new fenced 60-acre site for the elephants to roam. Entry at the time of writing was free, though a fee will be introduced in late 2003, as facilities improve. The centre is behind the main park office, 4 km east of the A18. Look for a left turn shortly after the big Safari Village sign.

Hambantota → *Phone code: 047. Colour map 3, grid C6. Population: 11,500. 41 km from Tangalla, 238 km from Colombo.*

Back on the coast, Hambantota is a small fishing port with a large Muslim population, predominantly of Malay descent. The town itself, with sand dunes immediately around it, has little to recommend it – the square has its usual clocktower and a curious statue of a 'coolie'. There is an interesting if neglected Catholic cemetery to explore. But for most visitors it is a base to visit the nearby *lewayas* (shallow lagoons) at **Bundala National Park**, excellent for bird-watching. The Karagan Lewaya and Maha Lewaya are easy to get to, where shore birds – flamingoes, gulls, plovers, terns etc – are attracted to the salt pans.

The town is at the centre of Sri Lanka's renewed interest in shipping and an international harbour, one of the deepest in the world, is planned. It is also the centre for producing salt from evaporated sea water. The *lewayas* are visible from the road and you can see the salt flats of Lanka Salt Ltd stretching away inland. To protect the salt pans and access to cinnamon plantations inland, the Dutch built a stockade or 'fort'. Today's circular 'Dutch' fort, on a hill overlooking the bay, is a run-down British **Martello Tower** (circa 1796), one of a twin – the other stands in Simonstown in South Africa.

The small bay offers some swimming, but the beaches, where you will see outriggers, are not attractive – the deserted eastern side, though, is great for jogging.

» *For Sleeping, Eating and other listings, see pages 187-191.*

Bundala National Park → *Colour map 3, grid C6.*

ⓘ 0600-1800, US$6, children under 12 and ISIC cards holders US$3, plus Rs 120 vehicle fee and taxes. A visitor centre has opened at the park entrance. From Weligatta, turn right for 2 km to the park entrance. To explore, you need to hire a jeep with a driver from Hambantota or Tissamaharama – the former is closer, and should cost around Rs 1,200. Guides, which are mandatory, are given on rotation, and their English may not be good. Gayan Prasanga has been recommended.

The area of open scrub around the coastal *lewayas* offers great opportunities for bird-watching with the added bonus of being able to spot the odd elephant and basking crocodile. The salt pans attract vast numbers of migratory shore birds,

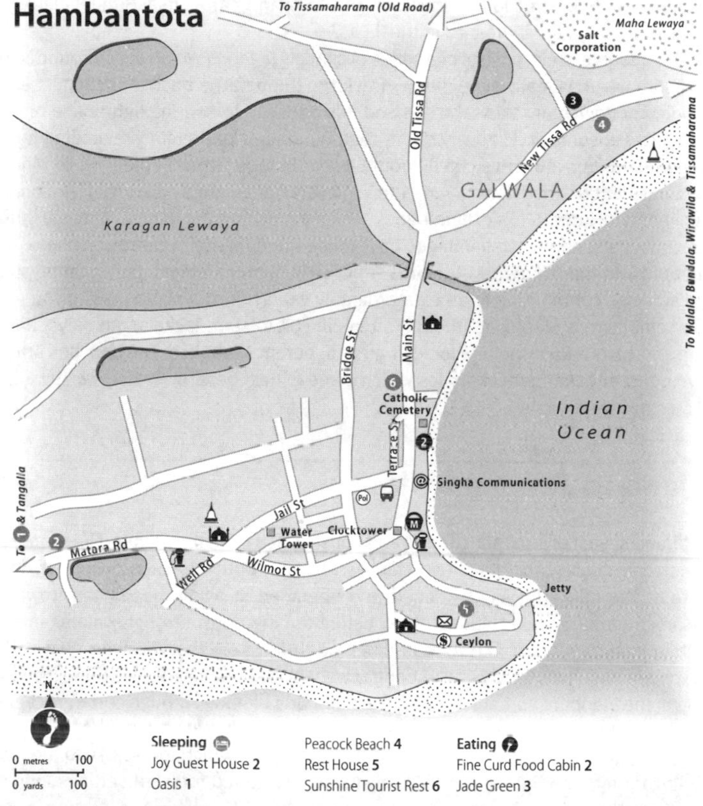

Going on safari

It seems as if every other vehicle in Tissamaharama is a jeep and you will be constantly offered a jeep safari to the national parks. Some words of advice to get the most out of a visit:
1 Ask to see the vehicle first – many are ancient and noisy, which will scare away any potential wildlife. It has even been known for a jeep to split into two during a safari!
2 Remember that it is obligatory to hire a tracker at the park gate. Thus don't pay extra for a driver and separate guide.
3 Make sure that the driver will stop on request, and that they will turn the engine off for photography.
4 Bring binoculars.
5 It is well worth investing in a bird spotting guide, as bird life is guaranteed to be rich.
6 Shop around – you needn't spend more than Rs 1,500-1,800 for a five-hour trip (including an hour each way to the gate).
7 Speak to other travellers who have already been on safari. They are often the best source of information.

accommodating tens of thousands at any one time, making it the most important wetlands in Sri Lanka outside the Northern Province.

Much of the park boundary is contiguous with the A2, so you do not necessarily need to go in to appreciate the wildlife. Before the park, the Malala lagoon, reached by following the Malala River from the main road, is a bird-watchers' paradise, where you might also see crocodiles. The Karagan, Maha and particularly Bundala *lewayas* are also excellent for shore-bird enthusiasts.

The **reserve** itself consists of a series of shallow lagoons which are surrounded by low scrub which is really quite dense. Tracks go through the bush and connect each lagoon. The sanctuary skirts the sea and it is possible to see the lighthouse on the Great Basses some 40 km away to the east. Bundala is particularly rewarding for its winter migrants, who arrive chiefly from Eastern Europe. From September to March, you can see abundant stints, sand pipers, plovers, terns, gulls and ducks. The park's highlight is its large flocks of flamingoes, which travel from the Rann of Kutch in India. In recent years, about 350 flamingos have made Bundala their year-round home. The migrants join the resident water birds – pelicans, herons, egrets, cormorants, stilts and storks – contributing to an extraordinarily variety. In the scrub jungle, you may also come across elephants (though often difficult to see), jackals, monkeys, hares (rare and carry a Rs 1,000 fine for killing!) and, perhaps, snakes. The beaches attract olive ridley and leatherback turtles which come to nest here. » *For Sleeping, Eating and other listings, see pages 187-191.*

Inland to Tanamalwila

At **Wirawila**, east of Bundala, there is an airbase which is being prepared for domestic commercial flights. You have two choices of route, both of which eventually lead north to the hills. The A32, widened and upgraded in 2003, heads east towards Tissamaharama to Yala National Park, before turning north through Kataragama to Buttala (see page 185). The A2 continues north crossing the **Wirawila Wewa Bird Sanctuary** and running close to **Lunuganwehera National Park**, set up in 1995 to protect the elephant corridor between Yala and Uda Walawe, though currently closed to tourists. There are good views along here of the sacred Kataragama Peak.

Lunuganwehera Reservoir is fed by the Kirindi Oya, which runs close to the road leading up into the Highlands. You can stay in a secluded forested setting along its banks, north of **Tanamalwila**, the largest settlement along this stretch, see page 187. This can also be used as a base to visit Uda Walawe to the west. From here, the road continues up to Wellawaya, passing the Handapangala tank and Buduruvagala shrine (see page 186).

Tissamaharama

→ *Phone code: 047. Colour map 3, grid C6. 32 km from Hambantota.*

Tissamaharama, or 'Tissa', is one of the oldest of the abandoned royal cities. King Dutthagamenu made it his capital before recapturing Anuradhapura. The ruins had been hidden in jungle for centuries and today there is little of interest visible. It does not, in any way, compare with the better preserved Polonnaruwa or Anuradhapura. The town is often used as a base for Yala National Park, though its plentiful accommodation is also popular with Kataragama pilgrims. If you arrive by bus, touts will probably pounce on you straight away to take you on 'safari' (see box). ▸▸ *For Sleeping, Eating and other listings, see pages 187-191.*

Sights

The **Tissa Wewa tank**, thought to have been created at the end of the third century BC, was restored with two others and attracts a lot of water birds. At dawn, the view of birds roosting on large trees and then moving over the tank is very beautiful.

Numerous **dagobas**, including one 50-m high built by King Kavantissa (second century BC) to hold a relic, had been lost under the sand, having been destroyed by the invading Dravidians. These have now been restored entirely by local Buddhists. Other buildings resemble a palace and a multi-storeyed monastery on the edge of Tissa Wewa. The Menik Wehera and Yatala Wehera are east of the clock tower. The latter, dating from the second century BC, has a moonstone and an 'elephant wall'. It also houses a **museum** with a collection of low-impact but charming Buddha and

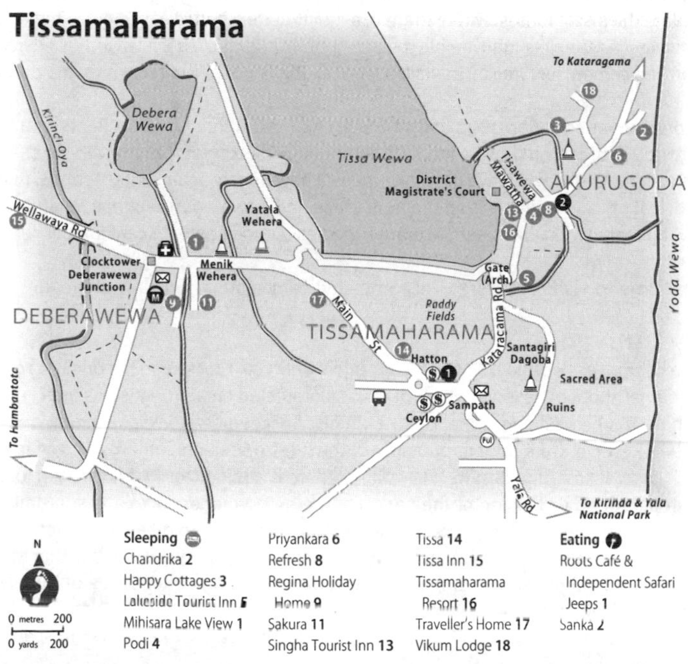

Bodhisattva statues and a 2,200 year-old monks' urinal. Excavations have been assisted by German archaeological groups.

A fishing port on the coast, 7 km south of Tissa, **Kirinda** has a good beach and an important Buddhist shrine on the rocks. Buses run regularly between Tissa and Kirinda. It is historically linked to the King Dutthagamenu. His mother, having been banished by her father, landed at the village and married the local king. Kirinda is popular with scuba divers who are attracted by the reefs at Great and Little Basses off the coast, but the currents are usually treacherous. You can see the Great Basses lighthouse from the temple on the rock. If you walk east along the coast towards Yala there is an area of Dry Zone scrubland along the coast, contiguous to Yala itself. It is a good place for bird-watching but keep a look out for elephants.

Yala West (Ruhuna) National Park → *Colour map 5, grid C5.*

Yala West, or Ruhuna as it alternatively known, is Sri Lanka's most popular national park. The 1,260 sq km park varies from open parkland to dense jungle on the plains. The scrub land is particularly distinctive with its enormous rocky outcrops, or *inselbergs*. There are also several streams, small lakes and lagoons, while the ocean to the east has wide beaches and high sand dunes. Such a varied terrain supports an extraordinary range of wildlife and vegetation.

Ins and outs

Getting there There are two entrances to the reserve. The main gate is at Palatupana, 20 km from Tissamaharama. Take the road from Tissa to Kirinda, 1 km before which a turn-off (12 km) is signposted. In early 2003, a second gate opened on the Kataragama-Situlpahuwa Road. Ask at the Wildlife Department for details.

Getting around Though the main tracks are accessible by car, a jeep enables you to explore the minor routes, where there is a much better chance of seeing animals. For the same reason, it is inadvisable to join a public bus tour (these leave Tissa twice a day) The compulsory tracker costs US$6. Walking is not permitted within the park.

Park information 0600-1800 daily. US$12, children under 12 (and students with ISIC cards), US$6, Sri Lankans Rs 20, plus compulsory tracker fee (US$6), vehicle charge (Rs 120) and tax. If you leave the park, you will have to pay again. Entry permits, maps and leaflets are available from the park office and information centre at Palatupana. GA Thushara Indika has been recommended as a good English-speaking tracker.

Best time to visit October to December and early morning and late afternoon.

Background

Yala comprises five 'blocks', of which tourists only visit Block One, the original 14,101 ha former shooting reserve, which became a protected area in 1938. This area is said to have the highest concentration of animals. Succeeding blocks, including a Strict Nature Reserve, were added, primarily in the late 1960s and early 1970s, giving the park its total area of 97,881 ha. In addition, there is a buffer zone which may in future form part of an expansion of the park. For the newly reopened Yala East (Kumana) National Park, reached from Pottuvil and Arugam Bay, see East Coast chapter.

There are a number of remains of ancient sites in the park, suggesting that many centuries ago the area was a part of the Ruhuna Kingdom. Thousands of Buddhist monks resided at the monastery at **Situlpahuwa**, now an important pilgrimage centre, while the restored **Magul Mahavihara** and **Akasa Chetiya** date to the first and second centuries BC.

In recent years, the park has drawn worldwide attention as having possibly the highest concentration of leopards in the world. They are elusive, but a sighting would be a highlight of your trip.

The Park

For many, the search for the one of the park's 30 or so elusive leopards is a major attraction. Though sightings remain quite rare, Yala's male leopards are nonetheless quite bold and may be seen walking along tracks in dry sandy or rocky areas during the day. **Vepandeniya** is considered a favourite spot. Elephants are another attraction and are easily seen especially near water sources from January to May, though not on the scale of Uda Walawe. Other animals seen throughout the park include macaque and langur monkeys, sambar, spotted deer, jackal, wild boar, buffaloes and crocodiles. Sloth bears are occasionally spotted, particularly in June, when they feed on local fruit.

The park is worth visiting for its birdlife alone, and a bird-watching focused day trip including the riverine forests of the **Menik Ganga** may yield over 100 species, during the migrating season. There are about 130 species overall, including barbets, hoopoes, malabar pied hornbills, orioles, Ceylon shamas, and paradise flycatchers, though pea and jungle fowl are the most frequently seen. The expanses of water attract eastern grey heron, painted stork, serpent-eagle and white-bellied sea-eagle, amongst many others. In addition a large number of migrant water-fowl arrive each winter to augment the resident population. You may be lucky enough to spot the rare black-necked stork near **Buttawa** on the coast. The **Palatupana salt pans** on the Tissa Road, 6 km before the park entrance, are one of the best sites in the world for watching waders.

Kataragama → *Colour map 5, grid C4. 16 km north of Tissamaharama.*

Kataragama (in Uva Province) is, along with Sri Pada (Adam's Peak), the most important pilgrimage site in Sri Lanka. Like Adam's Peak, it holds significance for Buddhists, Hindus and Muslims. It is most famous for its two-week Perehera in July and August, but is popular throughout the year. A small town with clean, tree-lined roads with rows of stalls selling garlands and platters of fruit – coconut, mango, watermelon – it attracts thousands from across the Island. The Hindu and Buddhist sanctuaries are quite separate. Buddhists visit the ancient **Kirivehera dagoba**, 500 m north of the plain white Hindu temple, but also consider the 'Kataragama Deviyo' here sacred. Sri Lankan Muslims associate the town with the prophet Moses, who was said to have taught here and come to pray at the Khizr Takya mosque nearby. ›› *For Sleeping, Eating and other listings, see pages 187-191.*

Approach

From the bus stand or car park, a short walk takes you to the Menik Ganga. Steps lead down to the water which is quite shallow in places allowing pilgrims to take their ritual bath almost in the middle of the river. It is a very attractive area with large trees on the banks providing plenty of shade. Cross the bridge to enter the main temple complex. The wide street lined with tulip trees leads to the Hindu temple (300 m).

Maha Devale

Maha Devale (Hindu Temple), dedicated to Skanda (Kataragama Deviyo), is itself not particularly impressive. A small gate with a large wrought iron peacock on the reverse, leads onto the rectangle where there is a small area where the pilgrims throw coconuts onto a stone slab to split them before making the offering. The breaking of the coconut signifies the purging of evil, so it is inauspicious if it fails to break. Trees in the rectangle are surrounded by brass railings and there are a number of places where pilgrims can light leaf-shaped candles. Here, you can see men in 'ritualistic trances': some are professionals, though, since you might see the same man, a little later, making his way to the Buddhist *dagoba*, carrying a briefcase and an umbrella!

Puja is spectacular. It is well worth timing your visit to coincide (ceremonies are held at 0430, 1030 and 1830) to witness the clamorous riot of bells, trumpets, drums and feverish dancing.

There is often a long queue to enter the shrine (particularly on Poya days) where platters are offered to the priests. The idea seems to be to 'hide' some money in the platter. Some say anything less than Rs 200 may be unacceptable and the gift might be refused by the deity. There is certainly evidence that the platters are 'recycled': men on bicycles can be seen returning them to the market, covered in garlands – nobody seems to mind though! There is no image of the god Skanda in the shrine – simply his vel or lance. There are separate small shrines to others in the Hindu pantheon, including Vishnu, Ganesh and Pattini, the last also linked to the fire-walking ceremony. Nearby are the two Bodhi trees.

The largest draw is the Esala (July/August) full moon festival which ends with fire-walking and 'water cutting' ceremonies. Thousands of pilgrims flock to the Hindu temple for the **Kataragama Festival**. They come to perform penance for sins they have committed and some of the scenes of self-mutilation, performed in a trance, are horrific. The water-cutting ceremony, in which the waters of the Manik Ganga are 'cut' with a sword at the moment of the full moon, symbolizes the separation of pure from impure.

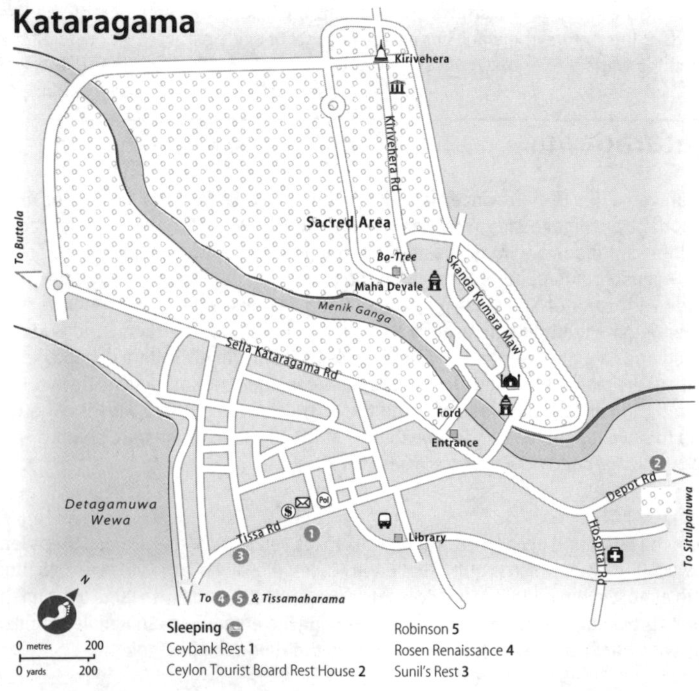

Mind over matter

Fire-walking takes place on the eve of the great procession, the culmination of the *Esala* festival. A long trench is prepared and filled with hardwood logs which are burnt to cinders. The worshippers, who will have refrained from meat or fish for a week, then walk barefoot across the burning embers shouting '*Haro hara*' in front of the crowds who cry in homage to the miracle. That most firewalkers emerge unhurt is a source of mystery, though many believe that the walkers are in the deepest state of self-hypnosis, in which the body can block out pain.

The origins of the tradition may hark back to the story of Sita in the epic *Ramayana*. Ravana, the King of Lanka, abducted Rama's wife Sita, an Indian princess, from the forest and carried her away to his island. After she is finally rescued by her husband, Sita proves her purity (chastity) by walking barefoot over fire and emerging unhurt. In southern Sri Lanka, devotees of Kataragama and Pattini follow her example and seek their blessing as they undergo the purification ritual.

To western eyes, an even more shocking act of self-mutilation are the carts carrying men suspended by steel hooks attached to their skin. These grotesque parades, accompanied by great crowd noise and excitement, are designed to purge the devotee of his sins.

You may see groups of pilgrims performing the Kavadi (peacock) dance when men, women and children hold semicircular blue arches above their heads as they slowly progress towards the temple.

Kirivehera

Beyond the Hindu shrine and a meeting hall on the north side of the square, starting from the east gate, there is another tulip tree avenue which leads to the milk-white Buddhist *dagoba*, about 500 m away. Stalls selling lotus buds, garlands and platters of fruit line the route but here there is competition with girls shouting out the bargains and pressing people to buy. You can often see the temple elephant shackled to the trees here, being fed a copious diet of palm leaves. The *dagoba* itself is a very peaceful place and, as usual, beautifully maintained. It is not especially large and its spire is quite squat compared with those farther north.

Museum

There is a small museum, ⓘ *closed on Tue*, near the Hindu temple, with Buddha statues, moonstones and ancient inscriptions.

North of Kataragama

The remote area north of Kataragama, fringing Yala National Park, is rarely visited by tourists, though the 35 km road to Buttala is one of the main pilgrimage routes. **Buttala** ('rice mound') was known as the rice bowl of the country, and is the main centre. This is a wilderness area, with plenty of opportunities for trekking, wildlife spotting, rock-climbing and even rafting.

At **Maligawila**, southeast of Buttala, is the largest monolithic Buddha statue in Sri Lanka and is regarded by some as the finest piece of all Sinhalese sculpture. Housed inside a brick *gedige*, the *Mahavansa* suggests the 10.5 m high, 3 m wide crystalline limestone Buddha was crafted by Prince Aggabodhi in the seventh century. The statue was originally part of a monastic complex which had a gateway, pillared hall and terraces. It had fallen and was 'lost' in the jungle until 1934, before being restored fully in 1991. One kilometre away, at **Dambegoda**, is a mound where the island's largest image of Avalokitesvara Bodhisvata, who is said to give succour to the helpless, has been found and restored. There are direct buses to the site from Wellawaya and Buttala via Okkampitiya. It is also accessible from Moneragala.

Wellawaya → *Phone code: 055. Colour map 3, grid B6.*

Wellawaya is a major transport junction with many buses leading up to the Hill Country from here. The A4 here is the main road, leading west skirting the southern highlands through Ratnapura and ultimately to Colombo, and east through Buttala and Moneragala to Pottuvil for Arugam Bay, while the A23 north climbs through picturesque country to Ella. The area is known for its sugar cane fields, and it is worth a brief stop to visit a factory and have a taste of the raw sugar cane and the resulting 'honey', which is also made into jaggery. The workers are usually very happy to show the production processes to tourists, though a tip is appreciated.

A beautiful road leads south of town past a dammed lake to the ancient Mahayana Buddhist rock carvings of **Buduruvagala**, ⓘ *Rs 100*. It is a short walk away past the monastery to the massive rock. Of the seven rock-cut figures in high relief, the 16-m high Buddha (Buduruvagala) in the centre, the tallest of its type in Sri Lanka, is flanked by possibly Avalokitesvara, to his right, who in turn has his consort Tara by his side, and an attendant. Traces of the original red and yellow paint remain on the Buddha itself. Close to the right foot of the Buddha is a hole in the shape of an oil lamp flame; a mustard-smelling oil is said miraculously to flow through periodically. To the Buddha's left, the figure is believed to be Maitreya who too is accompanied. The figure of Vajrayapani (or Sakra) holds a quartz implement similar to those found in Mahayana Buddhist countries such as Tibet. The quality of the carvings is more impressive close to, so it is worth removing your shoes and climbing up to the rock to view. The site itself is very peaceful and often deserted although unfortunately a pair of ugly concrete posts carrying lights have been erected in front of the carvings making photography of all seven images difficult. There is a small museum inside the meditation centre nearby. Take a Kataragama bus from Wellawaya and get off at Buduruvagala Junction (about 10 minutes). It's best to go in the morning as afternoon buses are scarce. The track to the site is an easy walk accompanied by a monk.

Some 6 km south of Buduruvagala along the A2 is a left turn for the **Handapangala Tank**, where elephants migrate from Yala for water during the summer months, a danger for villagers en route. There have been clashes in recent years between environmental groups and a local sugar factory, which has periodically attempted to drive the elephants away. These came to a head in October 2002 when two baby elephants were killed, prompting calls for the government to reopen a protected elephant corridor. There is a popular local bathing spot here, about 2 km off the main road, at which you can scramble up and see the elephants at a distance on the other side of the water. Alternatively, and more rewardingly, you can take a tour to see the elephants at close hand, for which you will need a boat and guide, not least since the area is dangerous if you don't know what you're doing! For details of tours, see page 190. **Diyaluma Falls** are also within easy reach of Wellawaya (see page 244).

Sleeping

Inland to Uda Walawe *p177*

D-E Ceylon Fisheries Holiday Resort, *5 km from 214 km post (essential to reserve with Fisheries Corporation, T011-2523689), Kalametiya*. Beautiful position overlooking lagoon. 3 rooms, a/c Rs 1,200, non-ac Rs 900. Caretaker prepares meals.

Uda Walawe National Park *p177*

The best accommodation is at Embilipitiya, though there is reasonable accommodation close to the park office at Timbolketiya and simple accommodation inside the park.

C Centauria, *New Town, Embilipitiya, T2230104, F2230514, centauria@sltnet.lk* Popular lunch spot (buffet Rs 350) and the most comfortable place near the park, good location next to Chandrika tank, pool, 51 fresh, clean and quiet rooms (US$22), mostly a/c, some with TV and balcony. Also in the grounds is **B Cottage** (called the bungalow even though it has 2 storeys!) with 4 bedrooms, 3 bathrooms and 'day' kitchen (US$50). Tours to Uda Walawe Rs 1,750, leaving 0545 and 1500; also boat trips on tank (Rs 2,000).

C-D Safari Village, *Dakuna Ela Rd, Timbolketiya, T2233201, kinjou@dialogsl.net* Best option in Timbolketiya, though a little overpriced. 15 musty rooms with hot water and fan (US$15 plus US$6 supplement for a/c), mainly Chinese food, undergoing some renovations and redecoration at time of visit. Park tours Rs 1,300.

D Circuit Bungalows, *inside the park at Thimbiriyamankada, Veheragolla, Seenukgala and Gonaviddagala*, are all near water sources, each hold 10 persons and provide good viewing opportunities; bring provisions for the camp cook. Contact the Wildlife Department, details below (Campsites).

D-E Kottawatta Village, *Colombage Ara, T2233215, 8 km from park*. 5 average rooms (Rs 900), but a well-furnished cabana with more planned (Rs 1,500) amidst pleasant gardens leading to an oya. Friendly management; jeep tours to Uda Walawe Rs 1,400.

F Campsites *inside the park, near the river at Pranshadara, Wehrankade and Allwudiyu. Reservations Wildlife Conservation Dept, T011-2694241, wildlife@slt.lk*

E Sarathchandra Tourist Guest House, *Pallegama, T2230044, F2230165*. 20 clean rooms with fan and balcony (Rs 900), one with a/c (extra Rs 300), same ownership as Centauria. Bar, restaurant.

Hambantota *p178, map p179*

A-B Oasis, *Sisilasagama, 6 km west, T/F2220651*. 40 a/c rooms, plus 10 bright, spacious chalets with TV and small tubs, set in large gardens between the sea and a lagoon, full facilities including a huge pool, good restaurant, service can be a bit slack at times, aimed at package groups, half day trip to Bundala Rs 2,500 (jeep only).

B Peacock Beach Resort, *New Tissa Rd, 1 km from bus stand at Galwala, T2220377, F2220387, peacock@sltnet.lk* Under ongoing, much needed renovation. 111 decent-sized a/c rooms (best ones US$50, comfortable, bath tubs), very pleasant gardens, pool (open to non-residents Rs 250 but sometimes demand more), popular with groups. Jeep to Bundala, Rs 2,000.

C-D Rest House, *T/F2220299*. 15 large rooms (1 a/c), situated in superb position on a promontory overlooking the harbour, old wing rooms (US$30), clean and carpeted, are better than new wing (US$20).

F Joy Guest House, *Matara Rd, T2220328*. 6 small, basic rooms (Rs 500) in well-run guesthouse with restaurant.

G Sunshine Tourist Rest, *47 Main St (150 m north of bus Station), T2220129*. 7 simple rooms (Rs 400 shared bath, Rs 450 attached), nets, friendly family guesthouse, good food available, not bad value.

Bundala National Park *p179*

Many visitors base themselves at Hambantota (above).

D Salt Corporation Circuit Bungalow, *turn right off track, passing park entrance, reserve in Colombo T2585840*. 3 rooms with attached bath, caretaker will cook (carry provisions).

F Campsites, *along Embilikala Kalapuwa (lagoon) and Goluwage Wadiya, reserve with Wildlife Conservation Dept, T011-2694241, wildlife@slt.lk* Recommended.

Inland to Tanamalwila *p180*

B Tasks Safari Camp, *Kithulkotte, Kudaoya, Tanamalwila, T060-2472346 (booking T011-4208578 tag@slt.lk)*. 18 spacious jungle tents with 'hollow log' showers, real frontier feel, picnics by riverside, elephants come close to drink, prices inclusive of nature walks and safaris.

Tissamaharama *p181, map p181*
There are plenty of options, so bargain hard. Tissa is plagued by touts who get a commission for the hotel room they 'fix' and also any 'safari' you may arrange through the hotel. Some places listed here are actually in **Deberawewa**, about 3 km west of Tissa, where touts sometimes jump on the bus and try to persuade you that it is Tissa. There is also accommodation at Kirinda and at Amaduwa, close to the park gate into Yala (see below).

B Tissamaharama Resort *(CHC), Kataragama Rd, T/F2237201, chc@sltnet.lk* 58 rooms, a/c new wing faces lake (US$43), non-a/c old wing (US$40), safari-style entrance but rest of hotel concrete and box-like, restaurant (limited menu but tasty curries), open-air bar, nice pool overlooking tank, gardens, pleasant staff but inefficient, excellent location but a bit scruffy inside, popular with pilgrims to Kataragama at weekends, virtually empty at other times.

C Priyankara, *Kataragama Rd, T2237206, F2237326, priyankara@sltnet.lk* 26 clean a/c rooms (Rs 2,500), deluxe with hot bath, all with private balcony overlooking paddy fields, bar, good restaurant with wide wine selection, pleasant atmosphere, friendly staff, reasonable deal, best in town.

C-F Happy Cottages, *off Kataragama Rd, T2237085*. 3 2-bedroomed bungalows with kitchen and living room (Rs 2,000) or rent individually (Rs 600-650), plus 8 new ones in separate block, some with a/c (Rs 1,200-1,800). Clean but, despite the name, a bit glum.

D Chandrika, *Kataragama Rd, T/F2237143, chandrikahotel@yahoo.com* 20 clean rooms (half a/c Rs 1,730, half non-a/c Rs 1,280) around a courtyard, good beds, fairly modern, bar, pricey restaurant, pleasant garden, good value.

D Refresh, *Kataragama Rd, Akurugoda, T2237357*. 5 attractive, clean rooms (Rs 1,700) including 2 a/c (Rs 1,900), including breakfast, excellent restaurant, friendly and welcoming, accepts Visa/Mastercard.

D-F Hotel Tissa, *Main St*, near bus stand, T2237104. 8 clean rooms (a/c Rs 1700, non-ac Rs 1200), popular bar/restaurant so can be noisy.

D-E Lakeside Tourist Inn, *Kataragama Rd, Akurugoda, opposite lake, T/F2237216*. 24 clean and comfortable rooms, most in new block (Rs 1,450 with breakfast) , others mustier but with views in old wing (Rs 950), pleasant sitting areas overlooking lake, lots of birdlife, good restaurant.

E Podi, *Punchi Akurugoda, T2237698, janewd23@sltnet.lk* New, friendly, Scottish-run, 5 clean rooms, 2 with balcony, Rs 1,000 (including breakfast), restaurant.

E-G Suduweli Garden Cabanas, *down track 2 km before Kirinda from Tissa, T072-2281059*. Joint German-Sri Lankan run, 5 simple but clean rooms (Rs 250-350), plus 2 cosy bungalows with idiosyncratic Dutch-style eaved roofs (Rs 600), own music system in room, friendly, good menu, jeep and cycle tours. Superb value.

E Vikum Lodge, *off Kataragama Rd, T2237585*. Clean and green, 10 spotless, comfortable rooms (Rs 800), plus one family room (Rs 1300) around attractive courtyard, quiet location, good food, friendly.

F Kirinda Beach, *down dirt track off main road, Kirinda, T2223405, F2223402*. Rooms Rs 600, rather forlorn, but with an eclectic collection of odds and ends decorating the place. Enquire about diving next door.

F Sakura, *off Main St, Deberawewa, just east of clocktower, T2237198*. 6 clean rooms (Rs 500) set in mango grove by canal plus one separate 'cottage' (a bit dirty, Rs 700), good food. Safaris have been recommended.

F Singha Tourist Inn, *Tissawewa Mawatha, off Kataragama Rd, Akurugoda, T2237090, F2237080*. 15 dark and musty rooms (Rs 600) in excellent location on the lake but potential not realised.

F Tissa Inn, *Wellawaya Rd, 1.3 km west of clocktower, Polgahawelana, T2237233, tissainn@sltnet.lk* 11 clean rooms (Rs 650-750), balcony upstairs, pleasant garden, restaurant, internet, rather pushy at selling tours but still one of the most popular.

F Traveller's Home, *195/4 Kachcheriya-*

For an explanation of the sleeping and eating price codes used in this guide, see the inside front cover.

gama, T2237958, supuncj@sltnet.lk 4 clean rooms (Rs 500 with separate bath, Rs 600 attached), nets, friendly, good food, pleasant patio, free bike hire and bus from town, good safaris, very popular with travellers.
F-G Regina Holiday Home, *off Main St, Deberawewa, just east of clocktower, T2237159*. 4 large, clean rooms in separate block (Rs 750) plus 4 very small rooms in house (Rs 250), safaris Rs 1,500, pleasant tree-lined setting next to canal, free 3-wheeler from town, restaurant planned.
G Mihisara Lake View, *Deberawewa, T2237322*. 2 clean, fresh rooms. Very friendly family home (Rs 300-400). Excellent food.

Yala West (Ruhana) National Park *p182*
Close to the entrance, Amaduwa, on the coast, is an easier and more comfortable option than sleeping inside the park itself (see below). It has a beautiful beach and lagoon.
AL Yala Village, *Palatupana (2km from park entrance) T/F072-2286224, yala@stlnet.lk* New, 40 luxurious chalets, fantastic position overlooking lagoon, observation deck, large pool, fishing, cycling.
A Yala Safari Game Lodge (Jetwing), *T/F047-2238015, yalasafari@eureka.lk* 63 comfortable a/c or non a/c rooms (US$70-90), restaurant facing lagoon, pool, new bird-watching hide, reference library, boats and bikes for hire, nightly film shown on Yala's leopards, guided nature walks with highly respected resident naturalist. Excellent eco-credentials.
C Brown's Beach Motel, *T060-2473216, F2674377*. 8 large simple rooms (Rs 2,250) with veranda overlooking beach, restaurant and bar, small (man-made) lake for bird watching, deep-sea fishing, watersports and tours of the park can be arranged.
C New Forest Circuit Bungalow, *opposite Rap's Lodge, book in Colombo T2786456*. 3 rooms, Rs 2,000, sleep 10 people.
C Rap's Lodge, *11 km from Yala, 1 Yala Rd, T078-8607171, tusker2@sltnet.lk* 2 very basic dormitory rooms, rent whole lodge (sleeps 10 people) for Rs 2,000. Jeeps to Yala Rs 1,500.
E-F Park Bungalows, *Wildlife Department, T2694241, wildlife@ slt.lk, for details*. 6 simple bungalows inside the park in scenic locations include New Buttawa, Mahaseelawa, Patanangala along the coast, Heenwewa by the tank, Ondatjee and Thalgasmankada on the Manik Ganga River. Meals are prepared by a cook, but there is no electricity. These are very popular and often booked up.
Camp sites at Jamburagala and Kosgasmankada (on the bank of the Manik Ganga River).

Kataragama *p183, map p184*
There are many other pilgrims' guesthouses and hotels for all budgets on Sella Kataragama Rd.
A-B Rosen Renaissance, *57 Detagamuwa, 2 km from Kataragama, T/F2236030, rosenr @sltnet.lk* 50 modern, comfortable rooms (US$50) including 2 luxurious suites (US$75) and 4 cabanas, full facilities including pool with underwater music system!
D-E Robinson Hotel, *Tissa Rd, Detagamuwa, T2235175, F2235471, anjulaj@sltnet.lk* 20 rooms with balcony in an attractive building with pleasant garden, Rs 1,250 a/c, Rs 850 non a/c. Good value.
E-F Ceylon Tourist Board Rest House, *T2235227*. Simple clean fan only rooms (Rs 550), or poor value a/c rooms (Rs 1175), very cheap vegetarian restaurant, rather prison-like but friendly.
F Ceybank Rest, *T2235229*. Attractive guesthouse. Good vegetarian meals.
F Sunil's Rest, *Tissa Rd, T2235300*. 3 very clean rooms with attached bath (Rs 600), attractive garden.

North of Kataragama *p185*
A Galapita Eco Lodge, *contact via www.i-escape.com/galapitaecolodge* Perched on rocks, 4 open-sided huts on stilts with own washing area, rent individually or whole property (sleeps 12), idyllic setting by ganga with natural pool and waterfall, activities include cycling, bird-watching and river-rafting by tyre tube.
C Treetops Farm, *Illukpitiya, Weliara Rd (9 km from Buttala, Rs 300 in a 3-wheeler or take 4WD), T011-2763806, www.treetopsfarm. tripod.com* Part of Woodlands Network, 2 traditional huts (1 wood, 1 clay) plus camping for 6-8 people, US$30 full board with discounts for longer stays. Genuine wild setting frequently visited by elephants (don't arrive beyond 1530), active ecological role including organic farming, replanting trees and preventing logging. Activities include

'awesome' local treks in Yala buffer zone, rock climbing, bird-watching. Aku is a knowledgeable host with excellent English.

Wellawaya *p186*
B Limetree House, *left turn out of town before Rest House, T057-2287406, F2274995, davidc@sltnet.lk* British-run, beautiful house in peaceful acre of gardens. 2 rooms (1 a/c) with interconnecting bathroom. Lots of goodies including massive DVD library, satellite TV, radio and phone, lovely shaded terrace, garden temple based on Borobodur, observation roof area with telescope and inviting pool.
D-E Rest House, *Ella Rd, T2274899*. 5 reasonably clean but musty and overpriced rooms (Rs 800-1,200), nets, restaurant, knowledgeable manager used to work for the Archaeological department.
E-F Saranga Holiday Inn, *Ambawatta, 1 km north of town, T2274904*. 9 rooms (Rs 750) including 1 a/c (Rs 950), quiet, good restaurant, grubby and overpriced but all right for a night.
G Little Rose Inn, *Tissa Rd (1km south of town), T2274410*. 4 simple clean rooms with basic washing facilities (Rs 450 but negotiate). Good home cooking.

Eating

Uda Walawe National Park *p177*
For options see Sleeping, p187.

Hambantota *p178, map p179*
For further options see Sleeping, p187.
RsRs Jade Green, *Galawala, opposite* Peacock Beach Resort, is smart, modern and western style with prices to match (though you may get hassled by 'safari' touts).
Rs Fine Curd, *Tissa Rd, opposite the Bus Station (beach side)*, does delicious curd and treacle and inexpensive meals (huge, tasty rice and curry meal plus drink for under Rs 50).

Tissamaharama *p181, map p181*
For further options see Sleeping, p188.
RsRs Refresh, a branch of the excellent Hikkaduwa based restaurant, does a variety of excellent food with big portions.
RsRs Sanka, *Kataragama Rd, T2237441, open 1100-2330*. Over 100 Chinese dishes.
Rs Root's Café, very cheap rice and curry and popular for a beer.

Yala West (Ruhana) National Park *p182*
For options see Sleeping, p189.

Kataragama *p183, map p184*
For further options see Sleeping, p189.
RsRs Nandana Hotel, *40b New Town*, near clocktower, does a good authentic rice and curry.

Wellawaya *p186*
For options see Sleeping, p190.

Festivals and events

Tissamaharama *p181, map p181*
In Jun, the Poson full moon commemorates the introduction of Buddhism with week-long festivities ending with colourful elephant processions accompanied by drummers and dancers.

Tour operators

Hambantota *p178, map p179*
Touts offer tours to Bundala, Yala and Uda Walawe, but it only makes sense to make Hambantota a base for the first of these. **Oasis Hotel** and **Peacock Beach Resort** offer the most reliable (and priciest) tours.

Tissamaharama *p181, map p181*
The following drivers have been recommended. **SP Chandrasiri**, *T2237522*, who has testimonials from satisfied customers; **Sunil** (Bindhu), *T072-2678735*; **Metthe** *of the Independent Safari Jeep Service, office in Main St next to Roots Café, T072-2687033*, can also arrange camping. Land Rover enthusiasts should contact **Nimal Premathilaka**, *T2237712*, who has 6!

Wellawaya *p186, map p156*
JP Wimalasooriya, *T071-2240376*, runs boat trips. Day tours run from 0830-1900 cost Rs 3,400 for up to 4 people.

Transport

Uda Walawe National Park *p177*
Bus There are direct services to Embilipitiya from **Colombo**, **Ratnapura**, **Tangalla** and **Matara**. Local buses will then take you to Timbolketiya.

Hambantota *p178, map p179*
Bus On a 'depart when full' basis sevices leave at regular intervals to **Tissamaharama** (1 hr) and **Tangalla** (1 hr 20 mins). Buses go to **Weligata** every 15 mins. Morning departures to **Colombo** (6 hrs). Services along the A18 via **Embilipitiya** to **Ratnapura** (4 hrs).

Tissamaharama *p181, map p181*
Bus To **Colombo**, (6 hrs), via Galle, or to Ratnapura, via Embilipitiya. There are plenty of buses to Kataragama.
Jeep To **Yala** should cost Rs 500, though touts will nearly always try for Rs 800.

Yala West (Ruhana) National Park *p182*
It is best to organize your own transport.
Bus Leave for the park leave at 0630 and 1530.
Jeep or **3-wheeler** From **Tissa** take 1 hr: jeep Rs 500, 3-wheelers which are inadvisable at night owing to the possibility of wild elephants along the road, Rs 350. From **Hambantota** (50 km) it can take nearly 2 hrs; from **Galle**, 4-5 hrs.

Kataragama *p183, map p184*
Bus Services in all directions including direct bus to **Nuwara Eliya**, **Galle** and **Colombo**.

North of Kataragama *p185*
Bus To Buttala twice daily from **Kataragama** (1 hr) and frequently from **Wellawaya** (30 mins). Take a 3-wheeler to the camps.

Wellawaya *p186*
An important **bus** terminus, direct buses go to **Colombo** via **Ratnapura**, **Tissamaharama** and **Kataragama** and a few to **Matara** via **Tangalla**. For buses east to **Pottuvil** (for Arugam Bay), change at **Monaragala**. For the hills, there are plenty of buses to **Badulla**, via **Ella**, and **Haputale**.

Directory

Hambantota *p178, map p179*
Banks Bank of Ceylon and Hatton National Bank deal in foreign exchange.
Communications Internet at Singhe Communications, 7 Thassim Mawatha, open 0800-2100, has IDD and internet at Rs 6 per min.

Kataragama *p183, map p184*
Banks Bank of Ceylon has a Visa ATM and changes TCs.

Tissamaharama *p181, map p181*
Banks Plenty of banks in town.

Wellawaya *p186*
Banks There is a Hatton National Bank.
Communications CTM Express, opposite the bus station, has internet (Rs 20 for 1st min, thereafter Rs 7 per min) and IDD facilities.

Kandy & the Highlands

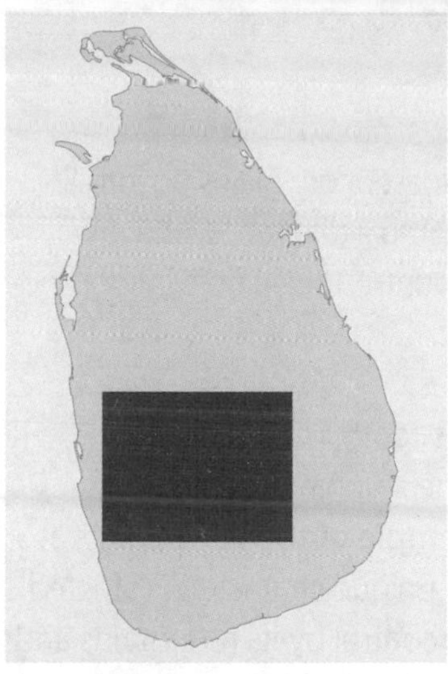

Introduction

The road or rail journey from the coast or dry plains up into Sri Lanka's lush hill country takes you into a different world. Away from the stifling heat of the low country, the air here is cool and crisp. This is great walking country.

Kandy, the home of the Buddha's tooth, is both capital and gateway to the highlands. The stunning view over its 18th-century lake towards the **Temple of the Tooth** hints at some of the reasons for the city's unique character. Protected for centuries from direct external control by its mountains and forests as well as by a fierce desire by a succession of leaders to protect its independence, Kandy and its region offers rich insights into Sri Lanka's cultural traditions. Designated a World Heritage Site in 1988, the city is at the southern corner of the Cultural Triangle.

South of Kandy, the Central Highland ridge, often shrouded in cloud, reaches its apex across the steep and spectacular **Ramboda Pass** at **Mount Pidurutalagala** near the eccentric former British hill resort of **Nuwara Eliya**. This is Sri Lanka's chief tea-growing region, and the hills are carpeted with the uniformly clipped bright green bushes of this crucial crop. To the south lies the hauntingly bleak isolated plateau of the **Horton Plains**, the source of most the island's major rivers, while to the west pilgrims flock to the sacred mountain of **Adam's Peak**.

Stretching east across dry zone lands, irrigated in both ancient and modern times, **Uva Province**, like Kandy, has a rich and defiant cultural history, associated in popular legend with two visits by the Buddha, and widely celebrated in the festivals at **Badulla** and **Mahiyangana**.

★ Don't miss...

❶ **Kandy** Experience the buzz at Kandy's Temple of the Tooth when the casket is displayed, then drop in at one of the city's Ayurvedic centres for a soothing massage, page 199.

❷ **Peradeniya** Brush up on your botany at the magnificent gardens at Peradeniya, and then ramble through the Kandyan countryside to some of the island's most colourful temples, page 206.

❸ **Nuwara Eliya** Hit a round on the immaculate green at Nuwara Eliya, afterwards slipping into something less comfortable for dinner and a game of snooker at the eccentric Hill Club, page 223.

❹ **Adam's Peak** Set your alarm early and join a group of pilgrims for the steep climb up to Adam's Peak in time for the first glimmer of dawn, page 230

❺ **Ella and Haputale** Hike a trail from one of the spectacular 'gap' towns, stopping for a tour of one of the area's organic tea factories and a well-earned brew, page 238.

❻ **Kitulgala** Don your helmet for a white-knuckle ride down the rapids of this river at Kitulgala, before relaxing in the beautiful natural pool at Edurella Resort, page 231.

Kandy and around

Kandy, Sri Lanka's second largest city and cultural capital, stands both as one of the most important symbols of Sinhalese national identity, and as the gateway to the higher hills and tea plantations. Although it has a reputation as something of a tourist trap, with a problem with touts, the clarity of the air and its verdant, hilly outlook around the sacred lake make it a pleasant escape from the heat of the coast. It is a laid-back place, and many visitors choose to base themselves here for a few days and explore the surrounding Kandyan countryside, before heading into the highlands or setting off for the ancient cities. The route northeast from Colombo across the coastal plain passes through lush scenery: paddy fields interspersed with coconut and areca nut palms, endless bananas and pineapples which are available graded by size and price from roadside stalls.

Colombo to Kandy

Taking 11 years to complete, the trunk road from Colombo to Kandy was the first modern road to be opened in Sri Lanka in 1932, when the first mail service ran between the two cities. Tour groups invariably stop to visit the baby elephants at Pinnawela, but there are some other lesser known sights along this busy route which are well worth a digression. Barely free of Colombo's suburbs, the road passes near the impressive temple at Kelaniya, the island's most popular, just 13 km from Colombo, see page 80. Although the road route is quicker, the train often gives better views, the last hour rattling through stunning scenery. » *For Sleeping, Eating and other listings, see pages 210-220.*

Sapugaskanda → *12 km north of Colombo.*

Situated on a low hill, there are beautiful views from the terrace of the small stupa here, but the temple is famous for its murals which show the arrival of the Burmese saint Jagara Hamuduruvo in Sri Lanka. It's 3 km along a side road, a right turn off the main A1.

Heneratgoda Botanical Gardens → *Colour map 3, grid A2.*

ⓘ 0830-1700. Rs 300, students Rs 200.

These beautiful gardens are particularly famous as the nursery of Asia's first rubber trees introduced from the Amazon basin over a century ago. Several of the early imports are now magnificent specimens. No 6, the first tree planted, is over 100 years old, but the most famous is No 2 because of its remarkable yield. The trees include *Hevea brasiliensis*, *Uncaria gambier*, rubber producing lianas (*Landolphia*), and the drug *ipecacuanha*. A female of the Coco de Mer was imported from the Seychelles and bore fruit in 1915. Turn off just before Yakkala. The gardens are well-signposted, 1 km beyond the sizeable town of Gampaha.

Bandaranaike family home and memorial → *Colour map 3, grid A2.*

The road passes through Yakkala, and then by the former estate of Sir Solomon Dias Bandaranaike, aide de camp to the British Governor at the time of the First World

Sri Lanka had the world's first female Prime Minister. Mrs Sirimavo Bandaranaike, widow of the assassinated Solomon Bandaranaike, became Prime Minister on 20 July 1960. Her daughter Chandrika Kumaratunge has been President since 1994.

War. His son, Solomon Western Ridgway Dias Bandaranaike, became Prime Minister of independent Ceylon in 1956 but was assassinated in 1959. His widow succeeded him becoming the world's first female Prime Minister. They are buried together at the memorial here. Their daughter, Mrs Chandrika Kumaratunga, was elected President in 1994. The family home, where visitors such as King George V and Jawaharlal Nehru stayed, is nearby, though it is private. The Bandaranaike memorial is by the side of the road at Nittambuwa, 39 km from Colombo. A broad walkway, about 10 m wide and 100 m long and flanked by frangipanis, leads to a raised plinth with five stone pillars behind it, the whole surrounded by a coconut grove. On the other side of the road, on a small hill, is a monument to Bandaranaike Senior.

Pasyala and around → *Colour map 3, grid A2.*

The area around Pasyala, 7 km further on, is noted for its *plumbago* (graphite) mines, betel nuts and above all, cashew. This is western edge of the central highland massif. Passing through Cadjugama ('village of cashew nuts'), you will see women in brightly coloured traditional dress selling cashew nuts from stalls lining the road. Sadly, the cashews offered here are not always of the highest quality – they are often 'seconds'. Inspect and taste before you buy.

Warakapola and Ambepussa → *Phone code: 035. Colour map 2, grid C2. 60 km from Colombo.*

This is a convenient and popular stop en route to Kandy or Kurunegala and beyond. The busy little village of Warakapola provides an outlet for locally made cane baskets and mats in its bazaar. It is also a popular halt for those with a sweet tooth searching for sesame seed *thalagulis* which are freshly made at Jinadisa's shop, among others.

Ambepussa, 2 km north, is just off the road to the west, with a train station. Its rest house is claimed to be Sri Lanka's oldest, built in 1822, and is a popular lunch stop. About 1.5 km behind the rest house, near the Devagiri Vihara, is a series of caves which at one time formed a hermitage.

Dedigama → *Colour map 2, grid C3. 3 km south of the A1, from Kegalla take the B21.*

Near Ambepussa, a turn off to the south before Kegalla takes you to the two 12th-century *dagobas* at Dedigama, built by King Parakramabahu I, who was born here. One has 10 relic chambers, including one a lower level. A gem studded golden reliquary has also been found here. The museum (ⓘ *closed Tue*) nearby is worth visiting.

Kegalla to Kandy → *See also page 206 for other sights around this area.*

Kegalla is a long straggling town in a picturesque setting. Most visitors take a detour here towards Rambukkana for the Pinnawela Elephant Orphanage (see below). After Kegalla, the hill scenery becomes increasingly beautiful, and the vegetation stunningly rich. About 1 km before Mawanella, a town surrounded by spice plantations, a sign points to the place where **Saradial** ('the local Robin Hood') lived, where there is a small monument. You then pass through **Molagoda**, a village devoted to pottery with both sides of the road lined with shops displaying a wide range of attractive pots. At the top of the Balana Pass is a precipice called **Sensation Point**.

At the km 107 mark is an outdoor museum displaying the original equipment used to lay the Colombo-Kandy road, such as steamrollers and bitumen boilers. Next to the museum is a replica of the 300-year old Bogoda Bridge, see page 240.

The railway goes through two tunnels to Peradeniya, where the road crosses the Mahaweli Ganga, Sri Lanka's longest river, and into the city.

Pinnawela → *Phone code: 035. Colour map 2, grid C3. 49 km from Kandy.*

Pinnawela, 6 km off the main Colombo-Kandy road, is the home of one of the most popular stops on the tourist circuit, the famous elephant orphanage. A number of spice gardens line the road. While most visitors are en route between Colombo and Kandy, travellers who choose to spend a night are delighted by the peace and beauty of this place with its river and jungle orphanage. The village becomes an oasis of natural quietness as calm descends when the tourist groups leave.

Pinnawela Elephant Orphanage

ⓘ *T2266116. 0830-1800. Rs 200, children Rs 100. Video camera Rs 500 (professional Rs 1500). Retain your ticket as may be checked again on the way to the elephant bath.*

The government-run Elephant Orphanage is a must for most visitors and although very popular, the place is not yet too commercialized. It was set up in 1975 to rescue four orphaned baby elephants when they could no longer be looked after at Dehiwala Zoo. Now there are almost 70, the largest group of captive elephants in the world. The animals, some only a few weeks old, very hairy and barely 1 m high, are kept in parkland where they are nursed by adult elephants. There has been a successful captive breeding project, which at the time of visiting had produced 22 second generation births.

The elephants, which roam freely in parkland, are 'herded' just before being taken to the feeding sheds, when they are very photogenic. They may occasionally 'charge', so to avoid getting hurt stand well back. The feeding, usually around 0915, 1315 and 1700, is done in a couple of large sheds. Each baby elephant is shackled and then bottle-fed with copious amounts of milk. Adults, which need around 250 kg of food each day, are fed mainly on palm leaves. Two special farms run by the National Zoological Gardens meet part of their needs. After feeding they are driven across the road, down to the river. You can usually watch them bathing there for an hour or so at 1000, 1200, 1400 and 1600, and sometimes being trained to work.

Although the park has capacity for up to 100 elephants, the authorities are beginning to realize that the programme cannot last forever in its current format. Since the elephants become so used to humans, it is impossible for them to be released back into the wild. Previous efforts have resulted in them returning to villages to find food. Following the success of the Elephant Transit Home scheme at Uda Walawe, see page 178, a new 36-acre safari park, which will also feature other Sri Lankan animals, is planned in the area, due to open in 2006. Another problem has been the lack of facilities and the proximity of humans to elephants to tourists, some of whom fail to realise that the elephants are still, at least in part, wild. This has led to a couple of incidents. A new tank and viewing platform, where humans will be kept at a distance from the animals, is planned for 2005. This may of course lessen the orphanage's appeal as it will prevent the direct contact which, although technically forbidden, has been a feature of the site. An education centre, library, accommodation and restaurant are also planned.

There is scope for up to 10 **foreign volunteers** to work at the Orphanage, on programmes lasting from two weeks to three months. If you're handy with a shovel, contact i-to-i, www.i-to-i.com or the National Zoological Gardens, T011-2729790, zoos1@slt.lk, direct for further information.

Millennium Elephant Foundation → *3 km before the Elephant Orphanage.*

ⓘ *Hiriwadunna, Randeniya, T2265377, elefound@sltnet.lk, 0800-1700, Rs 300 for an introductory talk and to help bathe the elephants, Rs 1,500 for a 15-min 'safari'.*

This registered charity, formerly Maximus Elephant Foundation, a member of WSPA, cares for elderly and disabled elephants. Although it has less of the 'aah' factor than Pinnawela, it is still worthwhile visiting. There are five elderly elephants which worked in the timber industry and are now pensioned off, and three younger ones. The scheme also runs a Mobile Veterinary Unit, established in 2000, which provides healthcare across the country for domesticated elephants. You can help bathe the elephants and also go on (very overpriced) rides around the village. As at the Elephant Orphanage, foreign volunteers can help with the project, and there is also an 'Adopt an elephant' scheme. US$22 (under-16s US$11) adopts an elephant for a year. Apply direct for voluntary work placements for up to three months.

Kandy → *Phone code: 081. Colour map 2, grid C4. Population 110,000.*

The last bastion of Buddhist political power against colonial forces, the home of the Temple of the Buddha's Tooth Relic, and the site of the island's most impressive annual festival, Kandy is also the capital of the Highlands. Its architectural monuments date mainly from a final surge of grandiose building by King Vikrama Rajasinha in the early 19th century. So extravagant were the edifices, and achieved only at enormous cost for the people of Kandy, that his nobles betrayed him to the British rather than continue enduring his excesses. The result is some extraordinary buildings, none of great architectural merit, but sustaining a Kandyan style going back to the 16th century, and rich in symbolic significance of the nature of the king's view of his world. » *For Sleeping, Eating and other listings, see pages 210-220.*

Ins and outs → *Beware of touts, see p211.*

Getting there

Kandy is fairly easily accessible from all parts of the country. Some travellers head here immediately on arrival at the international airport. Intercity buses leave every half an hour, taking 3½ hours, while the official taxi rate is Rs 2,695. There are also direct buses from Negombo. From Colombo, there are government buses from Central Bus Stand in the Pettah (intercity Rs 63, normal bus Rs 42), or private buses from Bastian Mawatha (luxury bus Rs 94, normal bus Rs 46.50).

Getting around

The bus (Goods Shed) terminus and railway station are close to each other about 1 km southwest of the centre. A three-wheeler into town will cost around Rs 50, and to the guesthouses in the Saranankara Rd area south of the lake, up to Rs 100, or radio cabs are available. Gopallawa Mawatha, the main road into town, is horribly choked with traffic, especially at rush hour. To avoid the fumes, it's a good idea to do as the locals do and walk north along the railway line into town. Local buses ply the routes to Peradeniya, Pinnawela etc.

Best time to visit

Kandy has a pleasant climate throughout the year, lacking the humidity of the coast. In July, *Esala Perahera* is a truly magnificent spectacle.

Tourist information

Hotel and guesthouse owners are usually the best source of information. Tourist Information Centre, *Headman's Lodge, 3 Deva Veediya (Temple St), opposite entrance to Temple of the Tooth, T2222661, open 0900-1645 Mon-Fri only, closed weekends and public holidays.* See also the stylish website, www.kandycity.org

Kandy

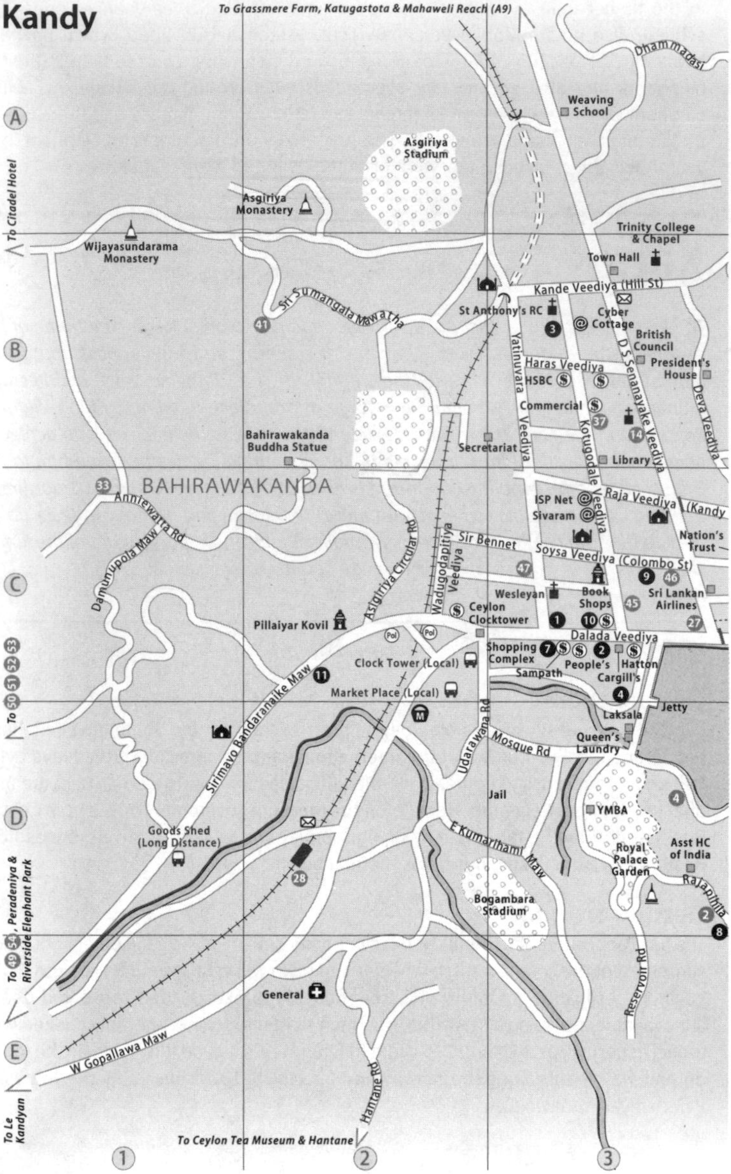

To Grassmere Farm, Katugastota & Mahaweli Reach (A9)
Dhammadasi
Weaving School
Asgiriya Stadium
Asgiriya Monastery
To Citadel Hotel
Wijayasundarama Monastery
Trinity College & Chapel
Town Hall
Kande Veediya (Hill St)
Sri Sumangala Mawatha
St Anthony's RC
Cyber Cottage
British Council
President's House
Haras Veediya
HSBC
Commercial
Yatinuvara Veediya
Kotugodale Veediya
D S Senanayake Veediya
Deva Veediya
Library
Secretariat
Bahirawakanda Buddha Statue
BAHIRAWAKANDA
Anniewatta Rd
Raja Veediya (Kandy
ISP Net
Sivaram
Nation's Trust
Sir Bennet
Soysa Veediya (Colombo St)
Damunupola Maw
Asgiriya Circular Rd
Wadugodapitiya Veediya
Wesleyan
Ceylon Clocktower
Book Shops
Sri Lankan Airlines
Pillaiyar Kovil
Dalada Veediya
Shopping Complex
Sampath
People's
Hatton
Cargill's
Clock Tower (Local)
Market Place (Local)
Laksala
Jetty
Sirimavo Bandaranaike Maw
Udarawana Rd
Mosque Rd
Queen's Laundry
Jail
YMBA
Goods Shed (Long Distance)
E Kumarihami Maw
Royal Palace Garden
Asst HC of India
Rajapihilla
Bogambara Stadium
To 49 54, Peradeniya & Riverside Elephant Park
General
Reservoir Rd
W Gopallawa Maw
Hantane Rd
To Le Kandyan
To Ceylon Tea Museum & Hantane
To 50 51 52 53
A
B
C
D
E
1
2
3

N
0 metres 200
0 yards 200

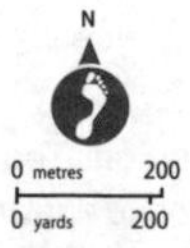

Sleeping

Blinkbonnie Tourist Inn **1** *E5*
Casamara **45** *C3*
Castle Hill Guest House **2** *D3*
Comfort Lodge **3** *E5*
Devon **55** *E6*
Devon Rest **4** *D3*
Expeditor Tourist Inn **6** *D4*
Freedom Lodge **7** *D4*
Golden View Rest **8** *D4*
Green Woods **9** *C5*
Helga's Folly **10** *E5*
Highest View **40** *E5*
Hill Top **49** *E1*
Ivy Banks Annexe **54** *E1*
Ivy Banks Guest House **12** *E6*
Ivy Banks Resort **48** *E5*
Kandy City Mission **14** *B3*
King's Park **16** *D5*
Lake Corner Rest Inn **18** *E6*
Lake Inn **19** *E4*
Lake Mount Tourist Inn **20** *E5*
Lakshmi **22** *E4*
Mcleod Inn **23** *E4*
Olde Empire **24** *C4*
Paiva's **47** *C3*
Peace Haven **25** *E6*
Pink House **26** *D4*

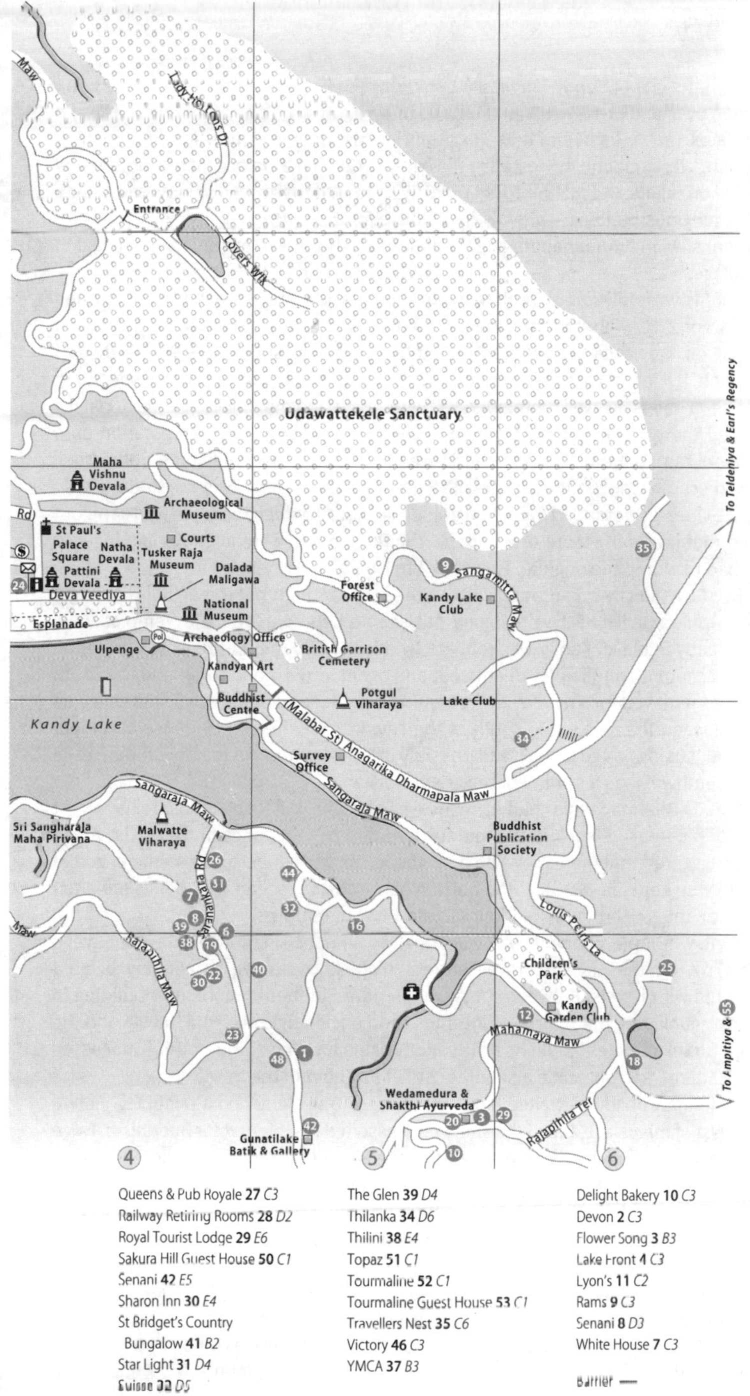

Queens & Pub Royale **27** *C3*
Railway Retiring Rooms **28** *D2*
Royal Tourist Lodge **29** *E6*
Sakura Hill Guest House **50** *C1*
Senani **42** *E5*
Sharon Inn **30** *E4*
St Bridget's Country Bungalow **41** *B2*
Star Light **31** *D4*
Suisse **32** *D5*
Swiss Residence **33** *C1*
Thambapanni Guest House **44** *D5*
The Glen **39** *D4*
Thilanka **34** *D6*
Thilini **38** *E4*
Topaz **51** *C1*
Tourmaline **52** *C1*
Tourmaline Guest House **53** *C1*
Travellers Nest **35** *C6*
Victory **46** *C3*
YMCA **37** *B3*

Eating

Bake House & The Pub **1** *C3*
Delight Bakery **10** *C3*
Devon **2** *C3*
Flower Song **3** *B3*
Lake Front **4** *C3*
Lyon's **11** *C2*
Rams **9** *C3*
Senani **8** *D3*
White House **7** *C3*

Barrier —

History

Although the city of Kandy (originally Senkadagala) is commonly held to have been founded by a general named Vikramabahu in 1472, there was a settlement on the site for at least 150 years before that. On asserting his independence from the reigning monarch, Vikramabahu made Kandy his capital. He built a palace for his mother and a shrine on pillars. In 1542 the Tooth Relic was brought to the city, stimulating a flurry of new religious building – a two-storey house for the relic itself, and 86 houses for the monks. As in Anuradhapura and Polonnaruwa, the Tooth temple was built next to the Palace.

Defensive fortifications probably came only when the Portuguese began their attacks. Forced to withdraw from the town in 1594, King Vimala Dharma Suriya set half the city on fire, a tactic that was repeated by several successors in the face of expulsion by foreign armies. However, he won it back, and promptly set about building a massive wall, interspersed with huge towers. Inside, a new palace replaced the one destroyed by fire, and the city rapidly gained a reputation as a cosmopolitan centre of splendour and wealth. As early as 1597 some Portuguese showed scepticism about the claims that the enshrined tooth was the Buddha's. In 1597 De Quezroy described the seven golden caskets in which the tooth was kept, but added that it was the tooth of a buffalo. The Portuguese were already claiming that they had captured the original, exported it to Goa and incinerated it.

By 1602 the city had probably taken the form (though not the actual buildings) which would survive to the beginning of the 19th century. The major temples were also already in place. Kandy was repeatedly attacked by the Portuguese. In 1611 the city was captured and largely destroyed, and again in 1629 and 1638, and the Tooth Relic was removed for a time by the retreating King Senarat. A new earth rampart was built between the hills in the south of the city. In 1681 there is evidence of a moat being built using forced labour, and possibly the first creation of the Bogambara Lake to the southwest, as a symbol of the cosmic ocean.

Vimala Dharma Suriya I had a practical use for the lake for he is said to have kept some of his treasure sunk in the middle, guarded by crocodiles in the water. It has been suggested that there was also a symbolic link with Kubera, the mythical god of wealth, who kept his wealth at the bottom of the cosmic ocean. Crocodiles are often shown on the *makara toranas* (dragon gateways) of temples.

A new Temple of the Tooth was built by Vimala Dharma Suriya II between 1687-1707, on the old site. Three storeys high, it contained a reliquary of gold encrusted with jewels. Between 1707-39 Narendra Sinha undertook new building in the city, renovating the Temple of the Tooth and enclosing the Natha Devala and the sacred Bodhi tree. He established the validity of his royal line by importing princesses from Madurai, and set aside a separate street for them in the town.

Major new building awaited King Kirti Sri (1747-82). He added a temple to Vishnu northwest of the palace, but at the same time asserted his support for Buddhism, twice bringing monks from Thailand to re-validate the Sinhalese order of monks. The Dutch, who captured the city in 1765, plundered the temples and palaces. The Palace and the Temple of the Tooth were destroyed and many other buildings were seriously damaged.

Kirti Sri started re-building, more opulently than ever, but it was the last king of Kandy, Sri Vikrama Rajasinha (1798-1815), who gave Kandy many of its present buildings. More interested in palaces and parks than temples, he set about demonstrating his kingly power with an exhibition of massive building works. Once again he had started almost from scratch, for in 1803 the city was taken by the British, but to avoid its desecration was once again burned to the ground. The British were thrown out, and between 1809-12 there was massive re-building. The palace was fully renovated by 1810 and a new octagonal structure added to the palace, the

Patthiruppuwa. Two years later the royal complex was surrounded by a moat and a single massive stone gateway replaced the earlier entrances.

In the west, Sri Vikrama Rajasinha built new shops and houses, at the same time building more houses in the east for his Tamil relatives. But by far the greatest work was the construction of the lake. Previously the low-lying marshy land in front of the palace had been drained for paddy fields. Between 1810-12 up to 3,000 men were forced to work on building the dam at the west end of the low ground, creating an artificial lake given the cosmically symbolic name of the Ocean of Milk. A pleasure house was built in the middle of the lake, connected by drawbridge to the palace. By now the city had taken virtually its present form.

Rajasinha's rule had been so tyrannical however, violating religious laws and committing brutal murders, that the terrorized Kandyan aristocracy allied themselves with the British invaders, who garnered support for a war against the king promising to protect the people and their property. The final fall of Kandy to the British in 1815 signalled the end of independence for the whole island.

Sights

The area with the Temple of the Tooth and associated buildings, a World Heritage Site, is the chief focus of interest. Sadly, it was the target of a bomb attack on 26 January 1998, which left over 20 dead, following which security has been upgraded, and some roadblocks remain. Repairs to the extensive damage of the temple were completed in 1999.

Temple of the Tooth

ⓘ *Foreigners Rs 200 (free for Sri Lankans). Cameras, Rs 100 (video cameras Rs 300). Guides will expect a donation. Wear a long skirt or trousers. Otherwise lungis (sarongs) must be worn over shorts. Remove shoes and hats before entering (a fee for looking after your shoes). The Cultural Triangle Permit does not cover the temple here. Museum, T2234226, Rs 100, 0900-1700.*

The entrance to the complex is in Palace Square opposite the Natha Devala. It is best to visit early in the morning before it gets too busy with tourist buses and pilgrims. Whilst visiting do be aware that the Temple of the Tooth (*Dalada Maligawa*) is a genuine place of worship and not simply a site of tourist interest.

The original dated from the 16th century, though most of the present building and the Patthiruppuwa or Octagon (which was badly damaged in the 1998 attack) were built in the early 19th century. The gilded roof over the Relic chamber is a recent addition. The oldest part is the inner shrine built by Kirti Sri after 1765. The drawbridge, moat and gateway were the work of Sri Vickrama Rajasinha. There is a moonstone step at the entrance to the archway, and a stone depicting Lakshmi against the wall facing the entrance. The main door to the temple is in the wall of the upper veranda, covered in restored frescoes depicting Buddhist conceptions of hell. The doorway is a typical *makara torana* showing mythical beasts. A second Kandyan style door leads into the courtyard, across which is the building housing the Tooth Relic. The door has ivory inlay work, with copper and gold handles.

The Udmale – upper storey – houses the Relic. Caged behind gilded iron bars is the large outer *karanduu* (casket), made of silver. Inside it are seven smaller caskets, each made of gold studded with jewels. Today the temple is controlled by a layman (the *Diyawadne*) elected by the high priests of the monasteries in Kandy and Asgiriya. The administrator holds the key to the iron cage, but there are three different keys to the caskets themselves, one held by the administrator and one each by the high priests of Malwatte and Asgiriya, so that the caskets can only be opened when all four are present.

Worship of the Tooth Relic

The eyewitness account of Bella Sidney Woolf in 1914 captures something of the atmosphere when the Tooth Relic could be viewed by pilgrims.

"The relic is only shown to royal visitors, or on certain occasions to Burmese and other pilgrims. If the passenger happens to be in Kandy at such a time he should try to see the Tooth, even though it may mean many hours of waiting. It is an amazing sight. The courtyard is crammed with worshippers of all ages, bearing offerings in their hands, leaves of young coconut, scent, flowers, fruit. As the door opens, they surge up the dark and narrow stairway to the silver and ivory doors behind which lies the Tooth.

The doors are opened and a flood of hot heavy scented air pours out. The golden 'Karandua' or outer casket of the Tooth stands revealed dimly behind gilded bars. In the weird uncertain light of candles in golden candelabra the yellow-robed priests move to and fro. The Tooth is enclosed in five Karanduas and slowly and solemnly each is removed in turn; some of them are encrusted with rubies, emeralds and diamonds.

At last the great moment approaches. The last Karandua is removed – in folds of red silk lies the wondrous Relic – the centre point of the faith of millions. It is a shock to see a tooth of discoloured ivory at least three inches long – unlike any human tooth ever known. The priest sets it in a golden lotus – the Temple Korala gives a sharp cry – the tom-toms and conches and pipes blare out – the kneeling worshippers, some with tears streaming down their faces, stretch out their hands in adoration."

The **sanctuary** is opened at dawn. Ceremonies start at 0530, 1000 and 1900. These are moments when the temple comes to life with pilgrims making offerings of flowers amidst clouds of incense and the beating of drums. The casket is displayed for only a part of the day. The Relic itself for many years has only been displayed to the most important of visitors. You can join pilgrims to see the casket but may well have to overcome pushing and jostling by those desperate to see the holy object. There is a separate enclosure in front of the Relic, which wealthy Sri Lankans pay to go into. The hall behind the Tooth Relic sanctuary has a number of golden Buddha statues from Thailand and and modern paintings depicting the Buddha's life and the arrival of Buddhism on the island.

The **Temple Museum** above is accessed from the rear. It contains bronze busts of the Kandyan kings, and displays some of their garments, as well as photocopies of documents detailing some of the history of the Temple. There is also a gallery of photographs showing the extent of the damage to the temple in the 1998 bomb.

The **Audience Hall** was rebuilt in the Kandyan style as a wooden pillared hall (1784). The historic document ending the Kandyan Kingdom was signed here, when the territory was handed over to the British. There is excellent carving on the pillars.

Around the Temple

Across from the complex is a working **monastery** and beyond its walls is **St Paul's Church** which was built in 1843 although the earliest minister, George Bisset, was here in 1816. The church was also damaged in the 1998 blast. There are various interesting memorials from 1822 to the 1870s in the British Garrison Cemetery, which is up a hill behind the National Museum. The caretaker is there daily and is very helpful (donation is expected). Behind the temple, in the area of the Law Courts, you can watch lawyers in black gowns and white wigs going about their business in open-sided halls.

The lake

On the lakeside, **Ulpenge**, opposite the Temple of the Tooth, was the bathing place of former queens. The Cultural Triangle Fund has undertaken to restore the Ulpenge. Further along to the east, is the Buddhist Publications Society, which has information on courses about Buddhism and meditation (see page 219). The **Royal Palace Park** (Wace Park), ⓘ *0830-1630, Rs 22.50 for foreigners*, is approached from the lake's southwest corner. There is a scenic 4 km path around the lake. Boat tours run from the jetty on the western side. They cost Rs 400 per person, with group discounts.

Malwatte and Asigiriya viharas

The 18th-century Malwatte Vihara, on the south side of the lake, where the important annual ordination of monks takes place in June, is decorated with ornate wood and metal work. Occasionally, a friendly monk shows visitors around the monastery and the small museum. This and the Asigiriya Vihara (northwest of town) are particularly important monasteries because of the senior position of their incumbents. The latter, which stands on a hill, has good wood carving and an impressive collection of old palm leaf manuscripts. There is a large recumbent Buddha statue and the mound of the old Royal Burial ground nearby.

Kandy National Museum

ⓘ *Within the Queen's Palace, behind the Temple of the Tooth, T2223867. 0900-1700, closed Fri, Sat. Rs 65, children Rs 35, camera Rs 160.*

The collection traces a vivid history of the development and culture of the Kandyan Kingdom. It features jewels, armaments, ritual objects, sculptures, metalwork, ivory, costumes, games, medical instruments, old maps – an enormous range of everyday and exceptional objects. There is much memorabilia, and the attendants will attempt to explain it all, sometimes pointing out the obvious in expectation of a tip!

Tusker Raja Museum

The much venerated elephant which carried the Tooth Relic casket in the Esala Perahera for many years, was offered to the temple by a pious Buddhist family when he was very young. Raja was 85 when he died in 1988. He was stuffed and placed in this separate museum north (left) of the Temple of the Tooth which is more easily visited before entering the Temple.

Archaeological Museum

ⓘ *Palace Sq. 0800-1700, closed Tue.*

Good sculptures in wood and stone housed in what remains of the old King's Palace. Some architectural pieces, notably columns and capitals from the Kandyan Kingdom. Three dusty rooms, disappointing.

Udawattekele Sanctuary

ⓘ *An expensive Rs 575 for foreigners, Rs 290 for children. Kande Veediya, past the post office leads to the entrance gate to the sanctuary.*

Once the 'forbidden forest' of the kings of Kandy, this is now the city's lung. Previously reserved for the use of the court, the British cleared vast areas soon after arrival, though declared it a 'reserved' area in 1856. The sanctuary now covers 257 acres, and contains several endemic species of flora and fauna, with over 150 species of birds (including Layard's parakeet, Sri Lankan hanging parrot, barbets, bulbuls, bee-eaters and kingfishers), monkeys, squirrels and porcupines. There are also a number of meditation centres here. Some interesting legends are attached to the forest. Look out for the trail with stone steps leading down to a cove, the Chittu Vishudi. This is where King Vickramabahu was said to have hidden here when his palace was under siege. The Pond is the original bathing place of the court. Gold coins are said to be concealed by its murky waters. Myth has it that a serpent with glowing red eyes guards the treasure, which surfaces once a year. Lady Horton's Drive takes you into the tropical rainforest, and further east offers good views of the Mahaweli River.

Trinity College

Trinity College, which is approached from DS Senanayake Veediya, has a chapel with some beautiful paintings which makes a quiet diversion from the busy part of town. It is also worth exploring the school's archives.

Around Kandy

Dotted around the lush Kandyan landscape are a number of important temples which make for a good day trip from the city. Thrill-seekers could head for the misty mountains of Knuckles, while for the green-fingered the magnificent botanical gardens at Peradeniya, arguably the finest of their kind in Asia, are an undoubted highlight. South of Kandy, the world's first tea museum has recently opened up in a disused factory. ⏩ *For Sleeping, Eating and other listings, see pages 210-220.*

West of Kandy

→ *Sights further west are covered on p196*

Beyond the wonderful Botanic Gardens at Peradeniya, is a group of 14th-century temples which display ancient artistic skills of the islanders. The traditions continue to be practised in the crafts villages nearby. If you have your own transport, you can combine a visit to the gardens and some temples with a visit to the Pinnawela Elephant Orphanage (see page 198). For a temple loop on foot, you could take the bus to Embekke, walk to Lankatilaka, finishing at Galadeniya, which is close to the main road.

Peradeniya

→ *Phone code: 035. Colour map 2, grid C4. 6 km southwest of Kandy*

ⓘ *Entry to the gardens is Rs 300 (Sri Lankans Rs 20), students and children (under 12) Rs 200. Useful map Rs 20.*

Peradeniya is famous for its magnificent **Botanic Gardens** justly earning the town a place on most itineraries. Conceived originally in 1371 as the Queen's pleasure garden, Peradeniya became the residence of a Kandyan Prince between 1747 and 1782 where royal visitors were entertained. The park was converted into a 60 ha Botanical Garden in 1821, six years after the fall of the last Kandyan King. There are extensive well-kept lawns, pavilions, an Orchid House with an outstanding collection, an Octagon Conservatory, fernery, banks of bamboo and numerous flower borders with cannas, hibiscus, chrysanthemums, croton and colourful bougainvillaea. The tank has water plants including the giant water lily and papyrus reeds. You will see unusual exotic species, especially palms (palmyra, talipot, royal, cabbage), and *Ficus elastica* (latex-bearing fig or 'Indian rubber tree' with buttress roots), an amazing avenue of drunken looking pines, and some magnificent old specimen trees. In all, there are about 4,000 labelled species. A signboard at the entrance, with a map, features a numbered circuit from 1-30. The corresponding numbers are placed at strategic points on the route, black on a yellow background. The suggested route below closely follows this in reverse. It is best to keep to the paths to avoid the invisible large holes in the rough grass.

> *Good lunches are available (reserve a table on arrival) at the Royal Park Cafeteria in the garden. Open 1000-1700.*

A **suggested walk** is to start at the Spice Garden (to the right of the entrance) which has many exotic spices (eg cardamom, cloves, pepper, vanilla). Follow the road to the right (east) to take in the Orchid House. Just off Palmyra Avenue there are

Javanese Almond trees with amazing roots. The palmyra leaf was used for ancient manuscripts. The Cabbage Palm Avenue from South America was planted in 1905. You can then walk along the Royal Palm Avenue (1885) – you will notice the fruit bats in quite large colonies hanging in many of the trees. This meets the River Drive which follows the course of the Mahaweli Ganga. Follow the drive to the Suspension Bridge which is about half way around the River Drive and you can if you wish go back via the Royal Palm Avenue. This goes through the Great Circle, a large grassy central area around which a remarkably diverse list of dignitaries have planted further specimens. Alongside generations of English royalty, there are trees planted by Indira Gandhi, Yuri Gagarin, Marshal Tito, U Thant and Harold Macmillan. Between the Great Circle and the Great Lawn is the Herbarium. Try not to miss one of the rarest plants in the gardens – the Coco de Mer. You will find it on the path leading to George Gardner's monument. This is on your right as you return to exit (left as you enter the park). This plant has the largest and heaviest fruit (or nut) in the plant kingdom, weighing on average some 10-20 kg. They take between five and eight years to mature and are surprisingly productive. It is not unusual to have over 20 nuts on a tree. They are all carefully numbered. Native Coco de Mer are only found on Praslin, an island in the Seychelles. Carry on along this path to get to the Memorial, a dome shaped structure. George Gardner was Superintendent of the gardens from 1844-49. From here you overlook the lily tank which is surrounded by giant bamboo, some 40 m tall (it grows at 2-3 cm a day!).

Outside the gardens a bridge across the Mahaweli River takes you to the **School of Tropical Agriculture** at Gannoruwa, where research is carried out into various important spices and medicinal herbs as well as into tea, coffee, cocoa, rubber, coconuts and varieties of rice and other cash crops. The **Economic Museum** has botanical and agricultural exhibits.

Peradeniya is also the home of the **Sri Lanka University** (1942), built in the old Kandyan style in an impressive setting of a large park with the Mahaweli Ganga running though it and the surrounding hillocks. It is worth visiting the small teaching collection museum in the Department of Archaeology. Call ahead, T2388345 ext 518.

Gadaladeniya Temple

ⓘ *Rs 100. Under restoration at the time of writing.*

The Buddhist temple is in a beautiful hilltop setting, built on a rock, 1 km from the main road. Built of stone, showing influence of Indian temple architecture, it has lacquered doors, carvings and frescoes and a moonstone at the entrance of the shrine. The brick superstructure, shaped like a stupa, has an octagonal base. The inscriptions on the rock by Dharmakirti date it to 1344. The principal gilded image of the Buddha (18th century, which replaced the original destroyed by the Portuguese) is framed by elaborate *makara* decoration. Unusually, there is also a shrine to Vishnu here. Outside, there is a covered stupa and a Bodhi tree. At **Kiriwavula village** nearby, craftsmen cast brass ornaments by the ancient lost-wax (*cire-perdu*) process. Some are for sale. Take a left turn off the A1 just after Pilimatalana.

Lankatilaka Mahaviharaya

The second monument of the group, 4 km away in Hiripitiya, sits on top of the rock Panhalgala. King Bhuvanekabahu IV (ruled 1341-51) moved the Sinhalese capital from Kurunegala to Gampola nearby. When a monk reported the extraordinary vision of an elusive golden pot on the water of the tank here, the King saw this as a sign and had the temple built. He appears among the wall paintings.

The present two storeyed blue-washed brick structure, ⓘ *donation requested*, was originally four storeys high. It was renovated and the tiled roof was added in 1845 after the two top storeys had fallen. You climb up a rock-cut stairway to the moonstone at the entrance, and the finely carved wooden doorway flanked by guardian *gajasinghas* (elephant-lions). The inner image house containing fine gold plated images of the Buddha is surrounded by a devale. The walls and ceiling have well preserved frescoes, some of the oldest and best examples of the Kandyan temple style. The west door has carved figures of Hindu gods (Saman, Skanda, Ganapathi and Vibhisena among others). There is a large rock inscription dating the temple to the thirteenth century. Craftsmen can be seen carving wood at the base of the rock.

Embekke Devale

The Hindu devale, ⓘ *Rs 100*, dedicated to God Kataragama (Skanda), is 1.5 km away along a track through pleasant cultivated fields. The temple with its sanctuary, Dancing Hall and the Drummers' Hall, is famous for its carved wooden pillars (which may have once adorned the Audience Hall in Kandy) with vibrant figures of soldiers, wrestlers, dancers, musicians, mythical animals and birds. You can see similar stone pillars at the remains of the old Pilgrim's Rest nearby. The patterned roof tiles are attractive too. The village has craftsmen working in silver, brass and copper.

Suriyagoda Vihare

If you have your own transport and wish to visit the Suriyagoda Vihare, turn off north from the A1 at Kiribatkumbura, signed to Murutalawa. The present 18th-century *vihara*, on a 15th-century site, has striking Kandyan wall paintings.

North of Embiligama (Km 105 post), the 17th-century **Dodanwala Temple** was built by Rajasinha II. It is where the king is believed to have offered the deity his crown

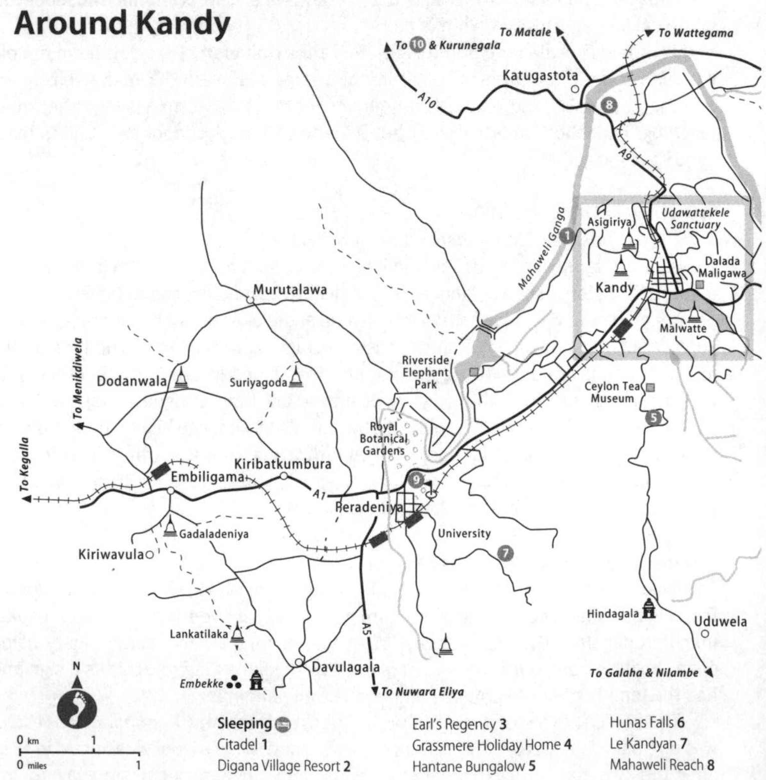

and sword after defeating the Portuguese. From Embiligama, to reach the textile weaving village of **Menikdiwela**, after a short distance along the Murutalawa road take the left fork for 6 km.

Riverside Elephant Park

① *0730-1630, Rs 150.*

Opposite the War Cemetery on Deveni Rajasinghe Mawatha, tame elephants are brought here at around 1200 after a morning of work. Their *mahouts* (elephant keeper/owner) brush, sponge and splash the elephants with water – essential for the animals' health.

East of Kandy

Medawela Temple → *10 km northeast of Kandy.*

This temple marked a Buddhist revival. It was built in the 18th century, where an older 14th-century temple stood. Interesting features include the small image house built in wood and wattle-and-daub, raised above the ground on stone pillars, similar to the old Kandyan grain stores. The railed balcony forms the Pradakshina Path. Inside, the marble Buddha image sits in front of a decoratively carved and painted wooden panel with representations of a Bodhi tree, protective gods, disciples and dragons. The fine Kandyan paintings on the side walls show a line of saints and disciples along the lower level and tales from the *jatakas* along the middle (unfolding from the back of the room, to the front). Above this, the murals on the left show the weeks after the Buddha's Enlightenment, and on the right, the 16 holiest places for Buddhists. Medawela, at the junction of B36 and B37, is a metalworkers village. The Kandyan Dance academy near Amunugama is 3 km south.

Nattarampota and around → *7 km east of Kandy.*

At Nattarampota, in the beautiful Dumbara Valley, you can watch traditional crafts-people at work. At **Kalapuraya Craft Village** artisans work in village homes with brass, copper, silver, wood, leather etc. Prices are better than elsewhere but not fixed. Take a left turn down a lane off the Digana road.

Degaldoruwa Cave Temple, at Gunnepana, 3 km north of Nattarampota, has vivid wall paintings of *Jataka* stories dating from the 18th century. There is a Dance Academy here.

About 1½ km along the Kalapura road from Nattarampota Junction on the Kandy-Kundasala road, the unusual incomplete 14th-century **Galmaduwa Temple** was an attempt to combine the features of Sinhalese, Indian, Islamic and Christian architectural styles.

Peradeniya Rest House **9**
Tree of Life **10**

Dumbara Hills (Knuckles Range) → *Colour map 2, grid C5. For tours, page 218.*

ⓘ *Rs 575, plus guide fees.* With peaks towering over above 1,500 m and an annual rainfall range of 2,500-5,000 mm it follows that a wide variety of forest types would exist here from Lowland Dry patana to Montane Wet Evergreen with their associated trees, shrubs, plants and epiphytes. These forests, in turn, harbour wildlife including leopard, sambar, barking deer, mouse deer, wild boar, giant squirrel, purple-faced langur, toque macaque and loris, as well as the otherwise rarely seen otter. Over 120 bird species recorded here include many endemic ones including the yellow-fronted barbet, dusky-blue flycatcher, Ceylon lorikeet, Ceylon grackle, yellow-eared bulbul and Layard's parakeet. In addition, endemic amphibians and reptiles include the Kirtisinghe's rock frog and leaf-nozed lizard, which are only found here.

The misty hills to the northeast were given the English name on account of the distinctive clenched-hand profile seen from a distance.

The importance of the range as a watershed for the Mahaweli River and the Victoria reservoir has led the government to designate the area over 1,500 m as a Conservation area. Soil and water conservation have become critical issues because of the way the area has been exploited so far. Cardamom cultivation, the removal of timber and fuelwood, the use of cane in basket making and the production of treacle from kitul have all been sources of concern.

South of Kandy

Ceylon Tea Museum

ⓘ *0815-1645 Tue-Sat, 0815-1600 Sun (closed Mon), Rs 250, students Rs 100, T060-2803204. 3 km south of town along Hantane Rd (past Hospital). Free guided tour.* Opened in December 2001, the government-backed Ceylon Tea Museum proudly claims to be the first of its kind in the world. Located in an old tea factory abandoned in 1986, it contains some impressive old machinery, polished up and laid out in manufacturing sequence, collected from various disused plantations around the Highlands. The first floor holds the archive of James Taylor who set up the first tea plantation at Loolecondera in 1867, with some interesting curios such as the oldest extant packet of Ceylon Tea (still in its original packaging) and a photograph of the largest tea bush in the world, as well as a history of Thomas Lipton. The top floor has been converted into a restaurant and has a telescope for viewing the surrounding hills.

Some 2 km further on is the working **Hantane Tea Factory**. Guided tours are available (morning is best) for Rs 100 (from Monday to Friday only), and there is a wonderfully located bungalow, see Sleeping, page 215. To the south, the **Hindagala Temple**, along the Galaha Road, has sixth-century rock inscriptions. The wall paintings date from different periods.

Sleeping

Colombo to Kandy *p196*

Warakapola and Ambepussa

D-F Rest House (CHC), *Ambepussa, T2267299, Reservations T011-2503497, F011-2503504*. Beautiful Dutch-style building with large teak veranda, close to a stream. 8 rooms, 1 (for 'ministers') with beautiful furniture, a/c, hot water and TV (Rs 1,500), others are simpler (Rs 750).

F Navimana Inn, *Kandy Rd, Warakapola, just south of clocktower junction at Weweldeniya, T2251339*. 10 rooms. There is a good restaurant/take away with good snacks indoors or on the veranda. Try the excellent breakfast (fish curry with hoppers). A nice atmosphere is aided by the small garden.

Pinnawela

Most line the Rambukkana Rd on the way to the Pinnawela Elephant Orphanage.

C **Pinnawela Village** and **Elephant View**, *next to and opposite the Orphanage, T2265383, eleview@sltnet.lk* 16 a/c rooms (Rs 1,950 at each), some with mini-bar.

Former has better value rooms,though no view, the latter's are overpriced, but you can see the elephants on their way to bathe.
D Raladiya, *100 m from Orphanage, T/F2264069, raliai@sltnet.lk* 3 clean and comfortable rooms with balcony (a/c Rs 1,750, non-a/c Rs 1,500) with good views over the river, restaurant. Good value.
D-F Green Land Guest House, *Elephant Bath Rd,T2265668, nandani@sltnet.lk* 5 clean rooms with nets and attached bath (Rs 700-1,500), upstairs better, excellent rice and curry dinner.

Kandy *p199, map p200*

It is best to reserve your accommodation before arriving here. Kandy is full of touts. Some board trains approaching the town. Others besiege newcomers at the bus and rail stations. They can be very persistent, will try to put you off going to certain hotels/ guesthouses and then direct you to one where they can get a large commission from your host, often demanding up to 20% of everything you spend (not just the room, but food and tours as well). Insist that you want to choose your own and have a confirmed reservation. Don't tell them which hotel you will be staying at and ignore stories that your hotel/guesthouse has closed or is no good. Some touts will follow you, if you are on foot, and pretend they have taken you to your hotel – make it clear to your host that you chose the hotel of your own accord. Many guesthouse owners refuse to pay touts. These are the ones that the touts will tell you are closed or no good. Ignore them! They will use all sorts of tricks – be on guard.

Saranankara Rd and Rajapihila Mawatha, a 10-20 minute walk southeast of the lake, are popular and have a good range of reasonably priced accommodation. This area offers a good balance. It far enough out of the centre to be peaceful though not too far out so that taxi fares bump up the costs during your stay. Some of the guesthouses at higher points here have fine views over the lake.
A Helga's Folly, *70 Frederick E de Silva Mawatha, T22234571, chalet@sltnet.lk* 40 individually decorated rooms (US$90) in eccentrically designed 'anti-hotel' full of character and quirkiness, uniqueness of interior and exterior design ('the Salvador Dali of hotels') has to be seen to be believed, set in quiet wooded hills, stylish restaurant, small pool (not well maintained). Far from town and prices have hiked since *Tatler* and *Condé Nast* features but recommended for imagination and romance.
A Swiss Residence (Jetwing), *23 Bahirawakanda, near Buddha statue, T4479055, swissres@ispkandyan.lk* 40 comfortable rooms (standard US$60, deluxe with TV (US$72), variable views, best towards Buddha Statue, all with balcony, 1 **AL** stylish suite with jacuzzi, pool, popular nightclub (Rs 350, ladies free).
A Topaz, *Anniewatta (1.6 km west of town), T2224150, topaz@eureka.lk* 76 well-kept rooms, 45 a/c with TV and tub (US$10 extra) in excellent location on high hill overlooking mountains, but rather remote, popular with package tours, balconies, good pool shared with sister hotel slightly lower down, regular shuttle to town.
A Tourmaline, *Anniewatte, sister hotel of Topaz, T2233099, F2232073.* 29 a/c rooms with similar facilities.
B Hill Top (Aitken Spence), *200/21 Bahirawakanda Peradeniya Rd, 2 km from centre, T2224162, ashmres@aitkenspence.lk* 81 rooms (US$40), a/c US$5 extra, in attractively designed hotel, comfortable and striking rooms, beautiful restaurant, poolside rooms better. Recommended though attention to detail could be improved.
B King's Park, *34 Sangaraja Mawatha, T/F2223620, kinpahot@slt.lk* 20 rooms (US$45), 5 a/c, fairly comfortable, TV in sitting area, smart restaurant, convenient quiet location but not quality finish, rather characterless, overpriced.
B Suisse, *30 Sangaraja Mawatha, T2233024, suisse@kandy.ccom.lk* 100 a/c rooms, best with balcony on lakeside (US$50). Limited views of lake but friendly and helpful staff, restaurant (some bored waiters), good pool (non-residents, Rs 100), tennis, snooker, herbal clinic, shopping arcade, good position, colonial style hotel (1920s), was Lord Mountbatten's wartime HQ.
B Thilanka, *3 Sangamitta Mawatha, T2232429, thilanka@ids.lk* 80 well-furnished rooms (US$55), including 35 deluxe which are worth the extra, private balconies with lake views, good restaurant though westernized (Rs 400 buffet lunch), good pool (non-residents Rs 100), very clean, good

service, retains parts of original house which began as a small guesthouse, helpful and friendly staff.

B-C Devon, *51 Ampitiya Rd, T2235164, F2235167*. 25 very comfortable rooms (4 categories, US$30-59), TV, minibar, a/c, some with tubs, 24-hr coffee shop and well-renowned Devon chain food.

B-C Queens, *45 Dalada Veediya, T2222813, F2232079, queens@kandy.ccom.lk* Full of colonial character (established 1844). 54 smallish but comfortable rooms, half a/c (US$35), but non-a/c rooms (US$25) have balcony and are better value, some with tub, avoid noisy front rooms, restaurant, good bar, super pool (non-residents, Rs 100), "hard to beat for slightly decaying colonial charm".

C Casamara, *12 Kotugodella Veediya, T/F2224688, casamara@sri.lanka.net* Unexceptional exterior but recently redecorated interior with a/c, good furniture, friendly and helpful staff, reasonable food.

C Castle Hill Guest House, *22 Rajapihilla Mawatha, T2224376, ayoni@sltnet.lk* 4 large beautifully decorated rooms (Rs 2,200), larger on garden-side, antique art-deco furniture, good food (breakfast included), lovely garden, magnificent views over town.

C Comfort Lodge, *197 Rajapihilla Mawatha, T2473707, comfort@sri.lanka.net* Clean, modern and rather characterless rooms (US$22) with TV, nice balconies, friendly and helpful staff. Free pick-up from station, internet Rs 3 per min.

C Senani, *167/1 Rajapihilla Mawatha, T2235118, senani@kandyan.net* Clean, spacious a/c rooms (US$25), helpful staff and good food.

C-D Royal Tourist Lodge, *93 Rajapihilla Mawatha, T2222534, royalxx@slt.lk* 2 very large well-furnished rooms (Rs 1,700-1,850 including breakfast) with own patio into garden in spacious family guesthouse, nets, clean, friendly, though quite pricey.

D-E Golden View Rest, *46 Saranankara Rd, T2239418, goldenviewrestkandy@hot mail.com* 12 clean, airy rooms, some with balcony (Rs 850-1,200). Good views of lake from rooftop, internet Rs 5 per min (much cheaper in town), Chinese restaurant, piano and CD player. Small massage room (Rs 1,200 for 1½ hrs for residents). Good atmosphere.

D-E Sharon Inn, *59 Saranankara Rd, T2222416, sharon@sltnet.lk* 15 spotless rooms with balcony (Rs 1,100-1,600), restaurant, internet Rs 125 for 30 mins, friendly, very popular.

D-E St Bridget's Country Bungalow, *125 Sri Sumangala Mawatha, Asgiriya (west of town), T2225689, stbridge@sltnet.lk* Pleasant rooms Rs 1,000-1,300, peaceful surroundings, spacious garden, good food.

D-F Expeditor Tourist Inn, *41 Saranankara Rd, T/F2238316, expeditorkandy@hotmail.com* Moving late 2003 to brand new plot, 8 comfortable rooms (Rs 600-1,200) with 4 more in 2004, some with private balcony, first floor with good views, friendly, excellent food, no touts, excellent wildlife tours (see p218). Consistent good reports.

D-F Highest View, *129/3 Saranankara Rd, T/F2233778*. 10 sparklingly clean rooms (owner worked in Switzerland), Rs 700-1,200 depending on view – the best are fantastic, solar powered. Restaurant with panoramic view over Kandy planned for late 2003.

E Blinkbonnie Tourist Inn, *69 Rajapihilla Mawatha, T2222007*. 9 clean rooms with balcony and good views (Rs 1,000), breakfast included, free pick-up from station.

E Devon Rest, *4e Sangaraja Mawatha, T/F2232392*. 10 comfortable if slightly squashed rooms, some overlooking lake, 3 a/c, 5 with hot water, Rs 880-990.

E Ivy Banks Annexe, *62/5 Anniewatta Rd (opposite Kalutara Kade), southwest of town, T2222875*. 4 quiet large rooms in modern house, immaculate garden, 'wonderful'.

E Ivy Banks Guest House, *52 Sangaraja Mawatha (opposite Kandy Gardens Club), T2234667*. 7 large rooms (Rs 1,000) in the original Ivy Banks.

E Ivy Banks Resort, *68 Rajapihilla Mawatha, T2234667*. 4 large rooms (Rs 1,000) in another annexe of the original Ivy, excellent views of lake and town from attractive and peaceful garden, meals on order but a bit isolated.

E Kandy City Mission, *125 DS Senanayake Veediya, T2223464*. 20 large clean rooms (Rs 1,000; half price for singles), though there have been complaints about noise, restaurant with good snacks, home made bread, lunch packets available, good tours – ask for Sunny (Henry Perera).

E Lake Inn, *43 Saranankara Rd, T2222208, F2232343*. 7 rooms with attached bath (Rs

Going off with a bang

Esala Perahera (procession), Sri Lanka's greatest festival, is of special significance. It is held in the lunar month of Esala (named after the *Cassia fistula* which blossoms at this time) in which the Buddha was conceived and in which he left his father's home. It has also long been associated with rituals to ensure renewed fertility for the year ahead. The last Kandyan kings turned the Perahera into a mechanism for reinforcing their own power, trying to identify themselves with the gods who needed to be appeased. By focusing on the Tooth Relic, the Tamil kings hoped to establish their own authority and their divine legitimacy within the Buddhist community. The Sri Lankan historian Seneviratne has suggested that fear both of the king and of divine retribution encouraged nobles and peasants alike to come to the Perahera, and witnessing the scale of the spectacle reinforced their loyalty. In 1922, DH Lawrence described his experience as 'wonderful – midnight – huge elephants, great flares of coconut torches, princes... tom-toms and savage music and devil dances... black eyes... of the dancers'.

Today the festival is a magnificent 10-day spectacle of elephants, drummers, dancers, chieftains, acrobats, whip-crackers, torch bearers and tens of thousands of pilgrims in procession. Buddhists are drawn to the temple by the power of the Tooth Relic rather than by that of the King's authority. The power of the Relic certainly long preceded that of the Kandyan Dynasty. Fa Hien described the annual festival in Anuradhapura in 399 AD, which even then was a lavish procession in which roads were vividly decorated, elephants covered in jewels and flowers, and models of figures such as Bodhisattvas were paraded. When the tooth was moved to Kandy, the Perahera moved with it.

Following the Tree Planting Ceremony (Kap), the first five days, Kumbal Perahera, are celebrated within the grounds of the four devalas (temples) – Natha, Vishnu, Skanda and Pattini. The next five days are Randoli Perahera. Torch light processions set off from the temples when the Tooth Relic Casket is carried by the Maligawa Tusker accompanied by magnificently robed temple custodians. Every night the procession grows, moving from the Temple of the Tooth, along Dalada Veediya and DS Senanayake Mawatha (Trincomalee St) to the Adahanamaluwa, where the relic casket is left in the keeping of the temple trustees. The separate temple processions return to their temples, coming out in the early morning for the water cutting ceremony. Originally, the temple guardians went to the lake with golden water pots to empty water collected the previous year. They would then be refilled and taken back to the temple for the following year, symbolizing the fertility protected by the gods. On the 11th day, a daylight procession accompanied the return of the Relic to the Temple. The Day Perahera continues, but today the Tooth Relic itself is no longer taken out.

You don't necessarily need to buy tickets to watch the processions since you can get good views by standing along the street. A good vantage point is that opposite or near to the Queens Hotel as much of that area is slightly better lit (the Presidential vantage point is somewhere nearby) and can provide for slightly better photography.

1,200 with balcony, Rs 1,000 without – both including breakfast), Original guesthouse on this road but no longer the best.

E **McLeod Inn**, *65a Rajapihilla Mawatha, T2222832*. 8 rooms with bath and hot water (Rs 850), 2 with excellent views, restaurant has the best view of any in this area (can be patronised by non-residents with advance warning), friendly.

E **Tourmaline Guest House**, *Anniewatte, in same complex as Topaz and Tourmaline, T2224172, F2232073*. 7 excellent value rooms with bath, sharing facilities with big sister hotels.

E-F **Freedom Lodge**, *30 Saranankara Rd T2223506, freedom@sltnet.lk* 3 spotless rooms (Rs 750-950), super friendly and helpful owners, good food.

E-F **Lake Mount Tourist Inn**, *195a Rajapihilla Mawatha, T2233204, F2235522, hirokow@sltnet.lk* 8 spotless, modern though smallish rooms (Rs 600 shared bath, Rs 1,000 attached including breakfast), nets, meals, quiet, free pick up from station, friendly atmosphere.

E-F **Olde Empire Hotel**, *21 Deva Veediya, T2224284*. 15 rooms (Rs 1000 with attached bath, smaller rooms at back Rs 300-440) in rambling 150-year-old colonial building. Lovely veranda overlooking lake, excellent location close to Dalada Maligawa, cheap bar/restaurant, popular with backpackers, so book ahead. Recommended for atmosphere.

E-F **Sakura Hill Guest House**, *Anniewatta Rd*, (Buddha statue hill), good rooms with balcony in a delightful guesthouse, meals (Rs 150), will collect from station (arrange in advance) saving a 15-min walk uphill.

E-F **Star Light**, *15a Saranankara Rd, T2233573*. 5 clean rooms with attached bath (Rs 600), one larger bungalow (Rs 1,000) in peaceful gardens, good value, tasty food, can be pushy though.

E-F **Thambapanni Guest House**, *28 Sangaraja Mawatha (next to Hotel Suisse), T2223234*. 5 simple, large, moderately clean rooms (Rs 600-800), bar-cum-restaurant with virtual reality video games.

E-G **Travellers Nest**, *117/4 Anagarika Dharmapala Mawatha, T2232174*. 9 rooms, 1 dorm , upstairs better in very friendly guesthouse, homely atmosphere, excellent home cooking (owner will demonstrate recipes), quiet location, one of the first in Kandy, will pay for transport from station.

F **Green Woods**, *34a Sangamitta Mawatha, T2232970*. Quiet and rural location on edge of Udawattekele Sanctuary, doubles plus 1 family room, attached bath, friendly family, good food.

F **Paiva's**, *37 Yatinuvara Veediya, T2234493*. 7 simple but clean rooms (Rs 660), in centre but fairly quiet, bakery and restaurant downstairs.

F **Peace Haven**, *47/10 Louis Pieris Mawatha, T2232584*. 2 simple rooms, 1 spacious but sparsely furnished apartment in quiet location, great views, good food, 'exceptional hosts'.

F **The Glen**, *58 Saranankara Rd, T2235342*. 3 clean rooms with attached bath (Rs 700), nets, good food, fruit and spice garden, peaceful, friendly family home, good value.

F **Victory**, *Colombo St, T2222526*. 8 rooms (Rs 550), some rather cramped, but very central location, and popular restaurant/bar. Lunch packets available.

F-G **Lake Corner Rest Inn**, *9 Ampitiya Rd, T074-471444*. 8 small rooms (Rs 400 common bath, Rs 550 attached), discounts for long stay, good cheap café next door (room service available), free pick up from station, good value.

F-G **Lakshmi**, *56 Saranankara Rd, T2222154*, 10 simple, bright, clean rooms (Rs 400-500) in one of the road's originals.

F-G **YMCA**, *160a Kotugodale Veediya, T2223529*. 11 rooms, (doubles Rs 550), common bath. Dormitory accommodation for Rs 150. YMCA Sports Hall will allow visitors to sleep there for Rs 30 during the Perahera, together with 100s of mosquitoes.

G **Pink House**, *15 Saranankara Mawatha*. 9 basic but clean rooms with shared bath (Rs 300-400), pleasant garden, home cooking, friendly motherly hostess, popular with backpackers. There are also dormitories with shared facilities which may not be too clean.

G **Railway Retiring Rooms**, *Kandy station, T2234222*. Basic. Book ahead.

G **Thilini**, *60 Saranankara Rd, T2224975*. 2 rooms with attached cold bath (Rs 400),

For an explanation of the sleeping and eating price codes used in this guide, see the inside front cover.

homely atmosphere with charming family, very good food, non-residents often eat here (give advance notice), good value.

West of Kandy *p208, map p209*

A Citadel (Keells), *124 Srimanth Kuda, Ratwatte Mawatha, 5 km west on Mahaweli River, T/F2234365, htlres@keells.com* 121 large, comfortable a/c rooms (24 deluxe) with attractive door paintings, river views, 2 restaurants, large pool, terrace gardens, popular with groups (surcharge Christmas to Apr). Recommended if you can cope with monkeys jumping on the roofs!

A Le Kandyan, *Heerassagala, 7 km southwest (near Peradeniya), T2233521, cdchm@sltnet.lk* 100 very comfortable rooms (US$77) including 4 excellent **L** split-level suites in the most stylish hotel in Kandy based on a traditional Kandyan palace, excellent restaurant, tea room (40 varieties), good pool, superbly themed 'Le Garage' nightclub (Fri and Sat, Rs 400, ladies free), excellent views, well run.

D Peradeniya Rest House, *50 m east of the gardens entrance, T2386468, F2388299.* Former residence of Captain Dawson, 12 fairly basic rooms (Rs 1,350 including breakfast), next to the noisy main road, overpriced. Better as a lunch stop.

North of Kandy *map p209*

AL Mahaweli Reach, *35 PBA Weerakoon Mawatha, on river by Katugastota Bridge, 5 km north, T2232062, mareach@slt.lk* 115 large, well-furnished a/c rooms in striking building overlooking river, tubs, TV, balconies with excellent river views, superb food (including good buffet choice), very attentive service, Kandy's biggest and best pool, Ayurvedic health centre, extensive sports facilities, classic car collection in underground car park, family owned (started out as a 4-room guesthouse!). Highly recommended.

A Hunas Falls (Jetwing), *Elkaduwa, 27 km north of Kandy (1 hr drive), T2676402, hunasfalls@eureka.lk* 31 comfortable a/c rooms (2 suites, Scottish or Japanese styles), hot tubs, pool, boating, fishing, tennis, golf, games room for youngsters, many activities on offer, beautifully located in a tea garden by a waterfall with excellent walks, visits to tea estate, factory, farm (you can milk the cows!) and spice gardens. Excellent base for bird-watching.

A Tree of Life, *Yahalatenna, Werellagama, 11 km northwest (left off Kurunegala Rd at Barigama Junction), T2499777, F2499711, treelife@lanka.net* 38 well-furnished 'cottages', with 1 **AL** suite, tubs, balconies in new building, in natural surroundings, built around a century-old plantation bungalow frequented by Mountbatten (possibly), good restaurant, bar, pool, well-kept gardens (wealth of plants, herbs, spices), Ayurvedic health centre and aromatherapy.

C Grassmere Holiday Home, *Alupothuwala, Ukuwela, 19 km north (between Km 5 and 6 posts, on Wattegama-Matale Rd, take Bus 636), T2475947, grass@kandy.ccom.lk* 4 well-furnished, large rooms with bath (US$22) in a plantation bungalow, excellent (but expensive) home-cooked meals taken with hosts (popular with tour groups for lunch), beautiful 36-acre gardens (tea, coffee, fruit and spices), peaceful, homely, free pick- up from Kandy station (otherwise difficult to find). Recommended but up for sale.

East of Kandy *p209, map p209*

AL Earl's Regency (Aitken Spence), *4 km along A26, on Mahaweli River at Thennekum -bara, T2422122, ashmres@aitkenspence.lk* 84 rooms (standard US$100, plus several **L** suites), some with views overlooking Mahaweli River (and the road!) although the best views are to the rear, all facilities, good free-form pool although overall the site is rather characterless.

E Digana Village Resort, *Rajawella, 14 km east on Teldeniya Rd via Kundasale, T/F2374023.* 25 rooms in villas, restaurant, tennis, squash, pool, not far from Victoria.

South of Kandy *p210, map p209*

D-E Hantane Bungalow, *Hantane Tea Estate, 6 km south, T5743743.* 5 rooms (Rs 1,000- 1,700) in cottage with lovely gardens, beautiful peaceful spot high above Kandy with panoramic views over Knuckles and Hatton Hills, horse-riding possible, whole cottage available for Rs 1,500.

Eating

Colombo to Kandy *p196*
For options see Sleeping, p210. Restaurant, just inside entrance of the orphanage is useful for breakfast, omelettes and snacks.

Kandy *p199, map p200*
The top hotels in the town are good but can be expensive. Sri Lankan rice and curry is cheap but usually only available at lunchtime There are lots of excellent bakeries in town, many of which serve lunch packets too.
RsRsRs Rams, *87 Colombo St, T2236143, 1030-2200*. Excellent if pricey South Indian, first class service, attractive decor, immaculate. No alcohol.
RsRsRs Topaz Hotel does good buffets.
RsRs Devon, *main branch at 11 Dalada Veediya, T2224537, 0800-2100*, is a swiftly expanding chain with hotels, restaurants and bakeries all around town. It has 2 restaurants. The main restaurant has Sri Lankan rice and curry and Chinese, plus a new Indian restaurant (*open till 2200*), an excellent self-service area (*1000-2000*) for very cheap Sri Lankan/Chinese/seafood lunch and a fabulous bakery shop (*1100-1500*). Very popular with locals and foreigners, waiters are miserable but the food is worth the scowls.
RsRs Flower Song, *137 Kotugodalle Veediya (1st floor, a/c), 1100-2230*, serves excellent Chinese, good portions.
RsRs Lake Front, *0900-2100*, Chinese, noodles, fried rice, rice and curry (but no lake view).
RsRs Lyon's, *27 Peradeniya Rd, near the clocktower, T2223073, 0800-2000*, specializes in Chinese (big selection), but also does a 'full English breakfast' for Rs 180.
RsRs The Pub (see Bars below) also serves a range of variable western food.
RsRs Senani Restaurant, *30 Rajapihilla Mawatha, T2224833*. Good food in salubrious surroundings with excellent views.
Rs White House, *21 Dalada Veediya, T2223393*. Bakery, good Chinese food and Biryani (rice and curry 1100-1400), good coffee and very cheap lunch packets. Pleasant, old-fashioned feel and good value.
Rs Bake House, **Delight Bakery** and **Devon**, all on Dalada Veediya are all recommended, the latter 2 with branches on Colombo St too.

Around Kandy *p206*
For options see Sleeping, p215.

Bars and clubs

Kandy *p199, map p200*
There are traditional bars at **Pub Royale**, at **Queens Hotel**, usual beers available plus Three Coins' excellent Sando stout (Rs 125). Also **The Olde Empire**, both with good atmosphere.
The Pub, *Dalada Veediya (above the Bake House), T2234868, 1100-2300*, is a little more modern and serves draught Lion and Carlsberg (Rs 120 for 400g or Rs 485 for a pitcher), plus a good selection of spirits, as well as western food. There is a pleasant veranda overlooking street and a/c inside. Good atmosphere. An alcohol shop at the south end of DS Senanayake Veediya, masquerades as **Lanka Medicinal Wine City**! As far as clubs go there are 2 hotel nightclubs. One at **Swiss Residence** and the other at **Le Kandyan** (see Sleeping).

Entertainment

Kandy *p199, map p200*
There are performances of Kandyan dancing in several parts of the town, most starting between 1800 and 1900 and lasting 1 hr. Tickets Rs 300 (touts sell tickets around the lake but pay only the printed price). Many are disappointed by the shows, which are heavily geared towards the tourist market. The dances include snippets of several dances and the occasional fire walking, and thus lack authenticity. They include:
Kandyan Art Association, *72 Sangaraja Mawatha*, around 1800, interesting to see but some have complained that it is 'stale and routine'.
Kandy Lake Club Dance Ensemble, *7 Sangamitta Mawatha (off Malabar St), T2223505. Daily at 1900*. Performs dances of Sri Lanka.
Red Cross Building, performances includes fire dance, fire walk etc, simple but fine.
YMBA Hall, Kandyan and Low Country dancing, 1745, 1 hr, good value.

Festivals and events

Kandy *p199, map p200*
At the end of Jul/Aug is *Esala Perahera* for 10 days (see box, page213).

Shopping

Colombo to Kandy *p196*
The roads around Pinnawela Elephant Orphanage are lined with souvenir stalls selling a wide range of trinkets, not all elephant related. Bargaining is essential (a coconut shell animal priced at US$12 was bought for Rs 250!). Water is very expensive.

Kandy *p199, map p200*
Arts and crafts
Try the craft shops on Dalada Veediya near the Temple of the Tooth. Also several antique shops, many along the lake and on Peradeniya Rd.
Laksala, *near Lake Jetty, 0930-1700 (Sat till 1600)* and **Kandyan Art Association**, *72 Sangaraja Mawatha*, are government sales outlets where you can watch weavers and craftsmen working on wood, silver, copper and brass, and buy lacquer-ware and batik.
Crafts village set up with government help is at Kalapuraya, Nattarampota, 7 km away (see p209) .
Kandyan Handicrafts Centre, *10/4 Kotugodale Veediya*, has good metalwork.

Batiks and silks
Fresco, *901 Peradeniya Rd*. For good batiks. Also in curio shops on south Bandaranaike Mawatha, towards Botanical Gardens, just past railway station.
Senani Silk House, next to **Senani** Restaurant, has good range of quality silks.

Books
Mark Bookshop, *151/1 Dalanda Veediya*, has a good selection of books on local history.
Vijitha Yapa Bookshop, Kotugodella Veediya, with a wider range of books and magazines, and now open 7 days a week.
The Wheel, by lake, and **Buddhist Publications Centre**, see Directory below, for Buddhist literature.

Markets
Municipal Market, west of the lake, is well worthwhile even if you are
bargain for superb Sri Lank

Tea
Mlesna, *15 Dalada Veediy*
fine selection of teas and
very pleasant place to sho
outlets at **Ceylon Tea Museum** in Hantane.

Textiles
Junaid Stores, *19 Yatinuwara Veediya*. Outstanding made-to-measure western style clothes in quality fabrics, beautifully cut and sewn, and at reasonable prices. Shops along Colombo St sell material.

Sport and activities

Kandy *p199, map p200*
Cricket
Asgiriya Stadium, northwest of town, hosts Test matches and 1-day internationals, while a new international stadium at Pallekelle, east of town, is planned to open by 2005.

Golf
Victoria Golf Club, *Rajawella, 21 km east, off A26, T/F060-2800249, vgejew@sltnet.lk*
Excellently maintained 6,879 yd, par 73 course surrounded on 3 sides by Victoria Reservoir with the Knuckles Range providing a further attraction. A round, including green fees, caddy, club and shoe hire will cost around Rs 3,000 during the week, extra Rs 400 at weekends. Some larger hotels will provide free transfer for residents.

Riding
Victoria Saddle Club, *Rajawella, just before golf course, T072-2245707*, (evenings), offers lessons (Rs 350-750), pony rides for young children (Rs 150) and accompanied trail rides for experienced riders (Rs 1,000). Phone in advance for information and booking.

Swimming
Hotel Suisse has a large pool but during the peak season (Dec-Feb) it can be fairly crowded. **Queens Hotel** has a pool (no chlorine) is very clean and usually very quiet. **Tourmaline/Topaz**'s shared uncrowded pool is worth visiting for an afternoon for the spectacular hill-top views. **Thilanka** has good views over town. Non-residents pay

(includes use of towel) at these …ls. The best pool is at the **Mahaweli** …each, but it is out of town.

Tennis

Kandy Garden Club, *Sangaraja Mawatha, T2222675*. Rs 250 for 1 hr, including rackets and balls. Floodlit for evening use.

White-water rafting

There are opportunities for rafting on the Mahaweli river, starting from near the **Citadel Hotel**, and in the Dumbara Hills (see Tour operators below).

Tour operators

Kandy *p199, map p200*

Wildlife-Nature Trekking Tours, *c/o Expeditor Tourist Inn, 41 Saranankara Rd, T/F2238316, expeditorkandy@hotmail.com* Run by Mr Sumane Bandara Illangantilake who has 40 years experience in leading small groups on tours of the island. Specializes in trekking, nature (he can recognize over 200 bird calls) and wildlife tours as well as rafting. Trips arranged according to experience ranging from 'smooth' to 'adventure' lasting 4-14 days. Also starting nature conservation project for civet, pangolin and loris and organizing an 'eco-challenge' for late 2004 (Rs 500,000 first prize!).

Transport

Colombo to Kandy *p196*

Bus To Heneratgoda from **Colombo** and **Negombo** buses take 1 hr and 30 mins respectively. **Pinnawela** is 6 km northeast of Kegalla along the B32. Turn off at Udamalla if in car. Regular buses depart from **Kandy** (Goods Shed) to **Kegalla** (1 hr, Rs 11). Change at Kegalla clocktower for a (regular) **Rambukkana** bus, which stops at **Pinnawela** (10 mins). Some buses will drop you at the junction for Pinnawela on the A1.

Train For **Heneratgoda Botanical Gardens** most Colombo-Kandy trains stop at **Gampaha** and fromhere take a 3-wheeler (Rs 50). Trains from Kandy to **Rambukkana (Pinnawela)** (short bus or 3-wheeler ride from the orphanage) at 0645, 1030, 1415, 1540, 1650 and 1840 (1½ hrs). Enquire at station for return times. Trains continue to **Colombo Fort**, taking 2½-3 hrs.

Kandy *p199, map p200*

Air

Sri Lankan Airlines, *17 Deva Veediya, 2nd floor, T/F2232494. Mon-Fri 0830-1700, Sat 0830-1230.*

Bus

Clock Tower Bus Stand and Market Place Bus Stand are for government buses to 'local' destinations (including places near Kandy such as **Peradeniya**, **Katugastota** and **Hantane**, see below). Goods Shed Bus Stand near the railway station is for long-distance buses. Frequent buses to **Colombo**: regular Rs 41 (3½ hrs), last bus 2130; a/c buses (Intercity Expresses) leave from Station Rd and take 2½ hrs, Rs 100, but are often congested, nerve wracking and far less pleasant than the train. **Anuradhapura** on No 42 (1st bay on right), every 30 mins, 4 hrs, Rs 60, a/c 100, last bus 1630. Both CTB and private buses run approximately every half an hour to **Nuwara Eliya**,(4 hrs, last bus 1500), **Dambulla** (Rs 40) and **Badulla** (Rs 100). For **Polonnaruwa** (Rs 60), last bus 1630 and **Trincomalee** (5 hrs, Rs 70), buses leave every 1-2 hrs. There is 1 bus a day to **Sigiriya**.

Car hire

If time is very limited for sightseeing, it is possible to hire a car for the day to visit **Dambulla**, **Sigiriya** and **Polonnaruwa** (ask your hotel or guesthouse). While this is a very full day it can be very rewarding. Kandy Comforts, *118/6a Shanti Mawatha, Kalugula Rd, Katugastota, T4473430*, has been recommended as a cheap alternative to booking though guesthouses.

Taxis and three-wheeler

A 3-wheeler should cost around Rs 80 (after bargaining) to the Hotel Suisse area. A/c Radio cabs are very convenient, safe and reliable, Rs 25 per km, min Rs 50. Phone T2233322, giving location and allow 10 mins.

Train

Tickets on the Observation Car between Kandy and Colombo or Badulla should be reserved up to 10 days in advance (reservation charge Rs 50). Return tickets are valid for 10 days. Intercity express to **Colombo** at 0630 and 1500 (1st class Rs 172 including observation car fare, 2nd class

Rs 72, 2½ hrs), plus slower trains stopping at **Rambukanna** (for **Pinnawela**, see above) at 0130, 0525, 0645, 1030, 1540 and 1650 (2nd class Rs 68.50, 3rd class Rs 25, 3¼ hrs). For coastal destinations south of Colombo, such as **Hikkaduwa** and **Galle**, take the 0525, which travels on to **Matara** (2nd class Rs 157, 3rd class Rs 57, 7¼ hrs). For **Kurunegala**, **Anuradhapura** and other destinations north change at Polgahawela. Train to **Badulla** (Rs 181.50/Rs 104/Rs 38, 7¾ hrs) leave at 0855 and 2310, via **Nanu Oya** (for **Nuwara Eliya**, Rs 97.50/Rs 57/Rs 21, 4 hrs), **Haputale** (5½ hrs, Rs 137, Rs 79, Rs 28.50), **Banda-rawela** (6 hrs, Rs 149, Rs 85.50, Rs 31) and **Ella** (6½ hrs, Rs 161, Rs 97, Rs 33.50). Observation car fee Rs 50 extra. Trains to **Matale** (Rs 6, 1¼ hrs) at 0545, 0715, 1005, 1435, 1720 and 1855.

Around Kandy *p206*
Bus Regular buses to **Peradeniya** from the Market Place Bus Station, which stop outside the entrance, Rs 6, or 3-wheelers charge Rs 150 1-way.
Buses from Clocktower bus stand drop visitors nearby the **Gadaladeniya Temple**. There are hourly buses between Kandy and **Embekke village**, a short walk away from the devale.
Nattarampota Bus 655 from the Market Bus Stop drops you at the suspension bridge across the river from the **Degaldoruwa Cave Temple**.
For **Medawela**, bus 603 departs from the Clock Tower Bus Stop near the Central Market in Kandy.
For the **Ceylon Tea Museum** take bus 655 (Uduwela bus), from the Clocktower bus stand. Get off at the 4th mile post about 30 mins later. 3-wheelers charge around Rs 250. This bus runs on to **Hindagala Temple**.

Directory

Colombo to Kandy *p196*
Banks There is a branch of the Hatton National Bank opposite the Orphanage.
Communications There are a couple of **internet** places on the Elephant Bath Rd, Pinnawela.
Useful address Tourist police are next to the Orphanage, Pinnawela.

Kandy *p199, map p200*
Ayurvedic massage Shakthi Ayurveda Spa, *1 Mahamaya Mawatha, T4473678*. New, many different massage options, clean, friendly, eager to please.
Wedagedara, *76b Deveni Rajasingha Mawatha, T2226790, nawae@hotmail.com, 0800-2000*. Authentic treatments, 1-hr head, body massage and steam bath, Rs 1800, 1-hr full body massage, Rs 1,400.
Wedamedura, *7 Mahamaya Mawatha, T4479484, ayurvedawedamedura@ lankae.com* 1-hr full treatment Rs 1,300, 2½-hr treatment plus pedicure/reflexology Rs 3,200. Also henna treatment and pedicure.
Banks Plenty of banks are in town, most of which have ATMs and foreign exchange desks. ATMs at Bank of Ceylon, Commercial Bank, Hatton National Bank, HSBC, Nations Trust, People's Bank and Sampath Bank.
Buddhist institutes Buddhist Publication Centre, *54 Sangharaja Mawatha, T2223679*. Good library, a book shop and information on courses on Buddhism and meditation where serious visitors are welcome.
Theruwan Meditation Centre, *Uduwela (take Bus 655, then walk 2 km).*
Nilambe, *T2225471*, is beyond Galaha, south of Kandy.
Communications Many hotels and guesthouses have **internet** access but are not the cheapest. Kotugodale and Kande Veediyas are good for comfortable and cheap internet cafés. British Council (see below) has a free service on membership.
Cyber Cottage, *154 Kotugodale Veediya, T4479479, 0800-2000*. Rs 66 per hr (first 15 mins Rs 20). ISPnet, *77 Kotugodale Veediya, T2201610*, Rs 60 per hr off-peak. Sivaram, *65 Kotugodale Veediya, T2222417, 0800-2300*. Rs 60 per hr, new machines in separate booths.
Post office, *opposite the Railway Station, 0700-2100*, speedpost, EMS (before 1000), internet Rs 3 per min, Poste Restante, Philatelic Bureau. Branch on Senanayake Veediya (crossing with Kande Veediya).
Telephones outside hotels are cheaper. Some, including Matsui Communications, *3A Deva Veediya, T2232647, F2232343*, will receive fax messages. There are plenty of Metrocard and Lanka payphones phonecard boxes. Couriers DHL Keells, *7 Deva Veediya, T2232215, tracing@cmb.co.lk*

Embassies and consulates Assistant High Commissioner of India, *31 Rajapihilla Mawatha, T2222652, ahciknd@telenett.net, Mon-Fri 0830-1030*, will issue Indian visas in a day. Pakistan High Commissioner, *30 Colombo St, T2232346*.

Libraries and cultural centres Alliance Française, *412 Peradeniya Rd, T2224432*. Has a library and also shows films (*Mon-Sat, 1100-1700*). British Council, *178 DS Senanayake Veediya, T2222410*. Has a library plus 2-week old British papers (*Tue-Sat, 0930-1700, closed Sun, Mon and public holidays*). Reading rooms are open to non-members, and internet is available.

Medical services General Hospital, *T2222261*. New Kandy Dispensary, *Brownearigg St*.

Central Highlands

Steep mountain passes snake up through the brooding highland landscape south of Kandy, reaching their pinnacle in the Peak Wilderness Sanctuary, where the plateau of the Horton Plains represents the island's last stretch of high montane forest. It was not until the 19th century, and the coming of the British, that wild and impenetrable rainforest gave way to the familiar, intensively cultivated tea plantations of today. The British legacy has lingered longer here, most notably in the anachronistic hill station

The Highlands

of Nuwara Eliya, nicknamed 'Little England'. Equally distinctive is the Indian Tamil culture, which dates back to the same era when migrant plantation workers were brought in from Southern India. But the area's greatest appeal lies in the natural beauty of its scenery, carved by mountain streams and powerful waterfalls, and its cool, crisp air.

Kandy to the Central Highlands

By either rail or road, the journey up into the Central Highlands offers some spectacular views, climbing through tea estates and passing nearby some magnificent waterfalls. From Kandy you can either follow the direct route to Nuwara Eliya along the A5, or take the much longer but very scenic road over the Ginigathena pass to Hatton, from which a couple of hours drive takes you to Dalhousie, the most practical base for climbing Adam's Peak, Sri Lanka's holiest mountain. Both the main routes into the Highlands start by crossing the Mahaweli ganga, passing through Peradeniya and then following the river valley to the pleasant town of Gampola, a mediaeval Sinhalese capital. The Niyamgampaya *vihara* which has some interesting stone carvings, is built on the original 14th-century temple which was mostly built of brick and wood and largely disappeared. ▸▸ *For Sleeping, Eating and other listings, see pages 232-238.*

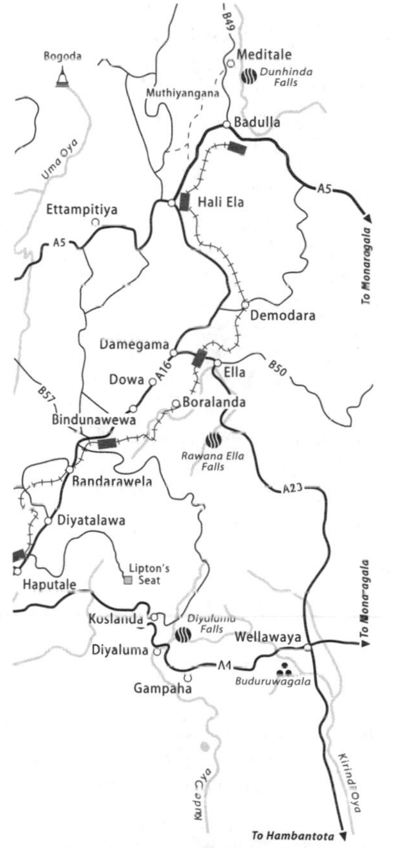

To Nuwara Eliya

From Gampola a road leads off towards the Ginigathena pass for the alternative Adam's Peak route through the tea estates of the Hatton-Dickoya region (see below), but most people continue on the more direct A5. Shortly after Gampola the road crosses the river and starts the long climb of almost 1,000 m up through some of the highest tea gardens in the world to Nuwara Eliya.

Pussellawa is a busy shopping centre and has a rest house where you can stop for a meal or a drink. The tea gardens begin just below Pussellawa. The craggy hill **Monaragala** appears to the south. Legends tell that this is where King Dutthagamenu hid in a rock while escaping from his father, who had imprisoned him.

Some 5 km later the road passes the Helbodda Oya. By Ramboda, you have climbed to 1,000 m. There is a fine 100-m waterfall with a twin stream on the **Puna Ela**, a tributary of the Mahaweli River, just off the road which can be seen from the bazaar. It may be possible to visit the **Rang Buddha tea estate**.

After 54 km from Kandy the road climbs through a series of hairpins to the Weddamulla Estate, with great views to the west over Kothmale Reservoir. The area is covered with pine trees and ferns.

A superior cup

Many concur that Sri Lankan tea, with its fine, rich flavour and bright, golden colour, is the best in the world. After textiles, tea remains Sri Lanka's second biggest export, and you will notice the distinctive cropped bushes all across the hill country. Although introduced by the British, the tea industry is a source of immense national pride, and recent years have seen some ingenious methods of capitalising on the country's heritage. Near Nuwara Eliya, an old factory has been converted into a magnificent hotel, retaining its original features, while the world's first tea museum has opened up near Kandy. A visit to a working tea factory is also recommended.

Tea famously originated in China (though one legend suggests it was introduced by an Indian missionary) but it was not until 1833 that the Chinese monopoly on exporting tea was abolished, and the East India Company began to grow tea in Assam in India. In Sri Lanka, the first tea bushes were planted in 1849 by James Taylor on a cleared hill slope just southeast of Kandy. It was an attempt at experimenting with a crop to replace the unfortunate diseased coffee. The experiment paid off and Sri Lanka today is the world's third biggest producer of tea, and the largest exporter, with a 20% share of global demand. The bushes now grow from sea level to the highest slopes, though the lush 'low-grown' variety lacks the flavour, colour and aroma which characterise bushes grown above 1,000 m. The slow-growing bushes at greater heights produce the best flavour and aroma when picked carefully by hand – just two leaves and bud.

The old 'orthodox' method of tea processing produces the aromatic lighter coloured liquor of the Golden Flowery Orange Pekoe in its most superior grade. The fresh leaves are dried by fans on 'withering troughs' to reduce the moisture content and then rolled and pressed to express the juices which coat the leaves. These are then left to ferment in a controlled humid environment in order to produce the desired aroma. Finally the leaves are dried by passing them through a heated drying chamber and then graded – the unbroken being the best quality, down to the 'fannings' and 'dust'.

The more common 'crushing, tearing, curling' (CTC) method produces tea which gives a much darker liquor. It uses machinery which was invented in Assam in 1930. The process allows the withered leaves to be given a short, light roll before engraved metal rollers distort the leaves in a fraction of a second. The whole process can take as little as 18 hours.

Despite its name and heritage, the Ceylon tea industry (as it is still called) has lost some of its dominance in the world market, cheaper producers having wrestled away traditional export markets. Britain, for example, which once absorbed 65% of total production, now only represents 3%, importing much of its lower grade tea from East Africa. Today Russia and the Middle East are the industry's biggest customers. In recent years however, privatisation and advances in production techniques have improved yields, and producers have responded to trends in the market, beginning to embrace the vogue for green, organic and flavoured teas. In 2003, a new Tea Association was created in order to transform the industry once again into *the* global brand, with investment plans of Rs 200 million in the industry over next five years.

The 415-ha **Labookellie estate**, ⓘ *T052-2235146, tours 0830-1810*, one of the island's largest, follows the twisty road for miles along the hillside. Teams of women pluck the tea on fairly steep slopes, picking in all weathers – the women using plastic sacks as raincoats. The women labourers are all Tamils, descendants of the labourers who migrated from Tamil Nadu before independence. They are keen to pose for photographs, and as they earn very little, tipping is customary. The tea factory, an enormous corrugated iron building, welcomes visitors to drop in to the delightful tea centre and sample a free cup of tea, and perhaps to buy a packet or two though there is no pressure to do so. The tour is quite informative – all stages of the process from picking, drying, oxidation and grading are shown if you go in the morning. There are free guided tours of the factory, available in English, German, French and Italian, which run every 20 minutes. You are also offered free tea and cake!

From the Labookellie Estate it is a short climb through more tea gardens to the narrow pass above Nuwara Eliya, and the road then drops down into the sheltered hollow in the hills now occupied by the town.

Kandy to Hatton and Adam's Peak

The alternative, much longer, route to Nuwara Eliya takes you close to the holy mountain of **Adam's Peak**, running close to the railway line for much of the way. It is a full day's journey, for which the train, despite its snail-like pace, offers a relaxing alternative.

From Gampola, the B43 branches to the right towards Nawalapitiya and then joins the A7, the main Colombo-Nuwara Eliya road, at the Ginigathena Pass (38 km). There are magnificent views at the top, although they are often obscured by cloud, for the pass is in one of the wettest areas of Sri Lanka. **Ginigathena** itself is a small bazaar for the tea estates and their workers. A right turn here takes you west on the A7 down to the attractively set village of Kitulgala (see page 231), or into the highlands where the road winds up through a beautiful valley, surrounded by green, evenly picked tea bushes to **Watawala** (10 km) and past the **Carolina Falls** nearby, which are spectacular in the wet season. It then follows the left bank of the Mahawelia Ganga to Hatton. The air becomes noticeably cooler, and occasionally there are views right across the plains to Colombo and the Kelaniya Valley. For details of the route from Hatton to Nuwara Eliya (in reverse), see page 229.

Nuwara Eliya → *Phone code: 052. Colour map 3, grid A5. Population: 26,000. Altitude: 1,990 m.*

Nuwara Eliya (pronounced Noo-ray-lee-ya) is one of those curiosities of history – a former British hill station. Vestiges of colonial rule are found everywhere, from the fine golf course threading through town to the creaking grand hotels, complete with overboiled vegetables and leaky roofs. Today, Sri Lanka's highest (and coolest) town remains a popular escape from the plains at long weekends and especially during the April 'season'. Visitors respond to Nuwara Eliya's fading appeal in different ways, some delighted by the tongue-in-cheek revelry in its colonial past, others are turned off by the town's lack of civic pride, depressed by its English climate (nights can get very cold), or simply confused by its archaism. For most though Nuwara Eliya represents nostalgic fun. This is also excellent walking country and a useful base for visiting Horton Plains. ▸▸ *For Sleeping, Eating and other listings, see pages 232-238.*

Ins and outs → *Never go out without an umbrella.*

Getting there The train is a scenic though time consuming alternative to the bus. Booking is essential for the Observation Car, especially during busy periods. During the pilgrimage season it is often full as far as Hatton. The train station is 6 km away at

Nuwara Eliya

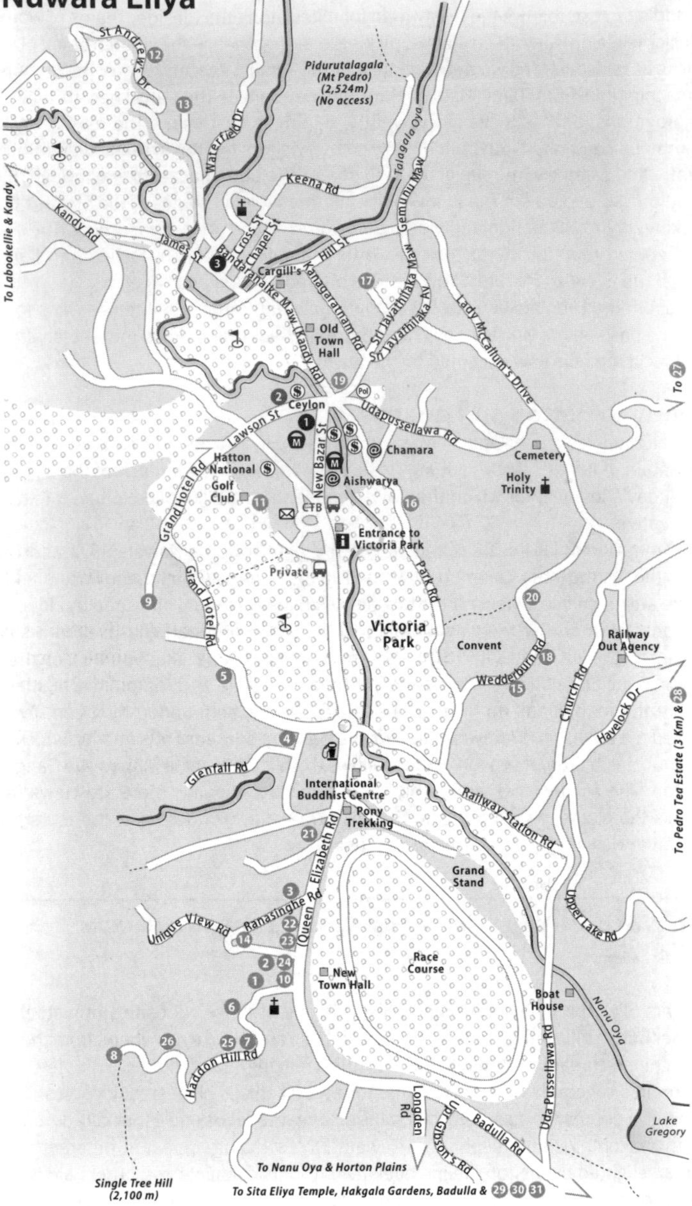

Sleeping
Alpine **1**
Ascot **22**
Carnation Rest **2**
Chalet du Lake **29**
Collingwood **3**
Galway Forest Lodge **28**
Glendower & King Prawn **4**
Golf Club **11**
Grand **5**
Green Garden **23**
Grosvenor **6**
Haddon Hill Inn **7**
Haddon Hill Lodge **8**
Haddon Hill View **26**
Heritage **21**
Hill Club **9**
Humbugs **31**
Maggie's Cottage **10**
Meena Ella Estate Bungalow **30**
Oatlands **12**
Princess Guest House **20**
Single Tree **25**
St Andrew's **13**
Sunhill **14**
Tea Factory **27**
Travelodge **24**
Tree of Life **15**
Victoria Inn **16**
Wattles Inn **17**
Wedderburn Rest **18**
Windsor **19**

Eating
Devon Food City **3**
Milano **1**

Bars & clubs
Lion Pub **2**

Nanu Oya, a short bus or taxi ride away (avoid the touts who will offer free transport
provided you go to a hotel of their choice – buses are always available). Ask to be dropped near the Town Hall if you are planning to stay in the southern part of town where most of the hotels are clustered up the hillside opposite the racecourse. Buses arrive in the centre of town.

Getting around The town is fairly compact, so it is easy to get around on foot but carry a torch at night to avoid holes in the pavement leading to the sewers.

Best time to visit The town really comes alive during the April 'season' (see box page 233) though accommodation is very expensive and hard to find. It is often cold at night, especially during January and March, when there may be frosts, though these are also the driest months.

Tourist information Tourist Information Centre, *next to Victoria Park entrance, 1000-1730*, free map and leaflets. Also an information counter, with internet access, at **Alpine Hotel** (see page 234).

Background

In 1846, when Samuel Baker first visited the semi-enclosed valley surrounded by hills on the west and overlooked by Pidurutalagala, the island's highest peak, he singled it out as an ideal spot for a hill country retreat. Today, with its television aerials, the highest on the island, and modern hotels, golf course and country walks, his rural idyll has been brought into the modern world.

'The City of Light' was a favourite hill station of the British and it still retains some distinctive features. The main street is the usual concrete jungle of small shops with the pink post office being an obvious exception. One of the distinctive features of Baker's plans was the introduction of European vegetables and fruit. Flowers are extensively cultivated for export to Colombo and abroad. The road out of Nuwara Eliya towards Hakgala passes through intensively cultivated fields of vegetables and a short walk up any of the surrounding hillsides shows how far intensive cultivation methods have transformed Nuwara Eliya into one of Sri Lanka's most productive agricultural areas.

The key to Nuwara Eliya's prosperity lay in the railway connection from Colombo to the hills. The line was extended from Talawakele to Nanu Oya in 1885, and a very steep narrow gauge line right into Nuwara Eliya was opened in 1910, but subsequently closed to passenger traffic in 1940 as buses began to provide effective competition.

Without the pretensions or political significance of the Raj hill stations in India, Nuwara Eliya nonetheless was an active centre of an English-style social life, with country style sports including a hunt, polo, cricket and tennis. It has retained all the paraphernalia of a British hill station, with its colonial houses, parks, an 18-hole golf course and trout streams (there are brown trout in the lake for anglers). The real clue to its past perhaps lies in its extensive private gardens where dahlias, snap-dragons, petunias and roses grow amongst well-kept lawns.

Sights

There are attractive walks round the small town, which has lawns, parks, an Anglican church and the nostalgic **Hill Club**. To the south of town are the racecourse and Lake Gregory (about 1 km from the town centre), for which boats which can be hired from Chalet du Lake.

Nuwara Eliya is popular bird-watching country, and there are two excellent areas close to town. **Galway's Land Bird Sanctuary**, ⓘ *0600-1730, Rs 10 entry for foreigners*, covers 60 ha to the north of Lake Gregory, while in **Victoria Park**, in the centre of town, 38 species have been identified. The park is pleasant, well kept and

Frond farewell

In 1911 Hermann Hesse wrote an evocative description of his climb to the top of Pidurutalagala at the end of a journey round India and Ceylon. He wrote, "To bid India a proper and dignified farewell in peace and quiet, on one of the last days before I left I climbed alone in the coolness of a rainy morning to the highest summit in Ceylon, Pidurutalagala.

The cool green mountain valley of Nuwara Eliya was silvery in the light morning rain, typically Anglo-Indian with its corrugated roofs and its extravagantly extensive tennis courts and golf links. The Singhalese were delousing themselves in front of their huts or sitting shivering, wrapped in woollen shawls, the landscape, resembling the Black Forest, lay lifeless and shrouded.

The path began to climb upward through a little ravine, the straggling roofs disappeared, a swift brook roared below me. Narrow and steep, the way led steadily upward for a good hour. The rain gradually stopped, the cool wind subsided, and now and again the sun came out for minutes at a time.

I had climbed the shoulder of the mountain, the path now led across flat country, springy moor, and several pretty mountain rills. Here the rhododendrons grow more luxuriantly than at home, three time a man's height.

I was approaching the last ascent of the mountain, the path suddenly began to climb again, soon I found myself surrounded once more by forest, a strange, dead, enchanted forest where trunks and branches, intertwined like serpents, stared blindly at me through long thick, whitish beards of moss; a damp, bitter smell of foliage and fog hung between.

Then the forest came to an end; I stepped, warm and somewhat breathless, out onto a gray heath, like some landscape in Ossian, and saw the bare summit capped by a small pyramid close before me. A high, cold wind was blowing against me, I pulled my coat tight and slowly climbed the last hundred paces.

What I saw there was the grandest and purest impression I took away from all Ceylon. The wind had just swept clean the whole long valley of Nuwara Eliya, I saw, deep and immense, the entire high mountain system of Ceylon piled up in mighty walls, and in its midst the beautiful, ancient and holy pyramid of Adam's Peak. Beside it at an infinite depth and distance lay the flat blue sea, in between a thousand mountains, broad valleys, narrow ravines, rivers and waterfalls, in countless folds, the whole mountainous island on which ancient legend places paradise."

provides a pleasant escape from the congested New Bazaar, but take care when walking along the outside of the park where the metal fence is in poor repair and has some sharp, rusty spikes.

Pidurutalagala (Mount Pedro), the island's highest peak at 2,524 m, is currently off limits to climbers for security of the island's first TV transmitter though some visitors have been able to obtain permits from the army. **Single Tree Hill**, at 2,100 m, is an alternative. The path to it winds up from Haddon Hill Road, beyond **Haddon Hill Lodge** (southwest of town), towards the transmission tower, through cultivated terraces and woods. You then follow the ridge along towards the north, through Shantipura, a small village and the island's highest settlement, eventually returning close to the golf course. This walk gives excellent views across Nuwara Eliya and beyond and takes three to four hours.

Pedro Tea Estate, ① *T2222016*, at Boralanda, 3 km away, still uses some original machinery and is less commercialized than other estates. There are some very pleasant walks through the plantations here, especially down to the tank and to Warmura Ella (ask at the Tea Centre). The estate can be visited on a Boralanda bus or it is a Rs 300-350 taxi ride away. Alternatively, for those feeling active it is a very attractive walk. The **Tea Factory**, at Kandapola, which, as well as having been innovatively converted into an award-winning hotel, see page 232, still retains a small working unit, is well worth a visit. The original oil driven engine, now powered by electricity, is still in place and switched on occasionally. It is a 30-minute taxi ride away and is a good place for lunch. **Labookellie Tea Estate** is only 15 km away, see page 223.

Excursions

On the route to Hakgala Gardens you pass **Sita Eliya Temple**, a temple to Rama's wife which is thought to mark the spot where she was kept a prisoner by King Ravana. There are magnificent views.

Hakgala Botanical Garden, ① *0730-1800, Rs 300, students and children, Rs 200, Sri Lankans Rs 20*, is 10 km from Nuwara Eliya. Established in 1861, it is located within a Strict Natural Reserve, and was once a Cinchona plantation. This delightful garden is now famous for its roses. The name Hakgala or 'Jaw Rock' comes from the story in the epic *Ramayana* in which the Monkey god takes back a part of the mountainside in his jaw when asked by Rama to seek out a special herb! There are monkeys here which are quite used to visitors. The different sections covering the hillside include a plant house, Japanese garden, wild orchid collection, old tea trails, arboretum, fruit garden, rock garden and oaks. Buses bound for Welimada or Bandarawela pass the entrance.

Horton Plains can be visited on a day trip if you have a car, but involve an early start (breakfast at 0600) as the plains have a reputation for bad weather after midday (see below). A jeep costs around Rs 1,500, though they are now accessible by car.

Randenigala Reservoir is good for bird-watching and in the early morning, elephants. It can easily be visited as a day trip, but is also a good camping spot. See page 293.

Horton Plains National Park → *Colour map 3, grid B5. Altitude: 2,130 m.*

32 km from Nuwara Eliya, 38 km from Haputale.

The island's highest and most isolated plateau is contiguous with the Peak Wilderness Sanctuary. Bleak and windswept, the landscape is distinctive and unlike any other on the island. It has been compared to both the Scottish highlands and the savannah of Africa. Most people come on a day trip to see the spectacular views from the sheer 700-m drop at World's End though there is more to see within the sanctuary. In recent years, park fees have spiralled and budget travellers are increasingly choosing to forego a visit. » *For Sleeping, Eating and other listings, see pages 232-238.*

Ins and outs → *Carry food and water.*

Getting there Horton Plains is accessible by car from Nuwara Eliya and Haputale. Both journeys take around 1½-2 hours – taxis cost around Rs 1,500. Ohiya, 11 km away, is the nearest train station from which you can take a taxi or walk to the park entrance. By train, Haputale is the closest base for a day trip though World's End will probably have clouded over by the time you arrive. If you are prepared to hire transport, Nuwara Eliya may be the most convenient option for day trips. Trekkers can come from Talawakale on the Agrapatana-Diyagama track or from Belihuloya via Nagarak, though this requires serious preparation.

 Getting around Horton Plains is unique amongst Sri Lanka's national parks as walking is permitted. Keep to the footpaths, especially if misty. A number of people go missing each year.

Best time to visit The best months to visit are April and August. The winter months tend to be the driest, with the best visibility, though can be very cold. The weather can be foul at any time and it can get cold at night so come prepared. For World's End it is essential to arrive by 0930-1000, after which the area usually clouds over for the day.

Tourist information *0600-1830*. Charges for foreigners add up to around US$17, children under 12 and students with ISIC US$8.50. Sri Lankans Rs 20. Tickets are checked at the park entrance 100 m away. The ticket office, below the car park, is open 0530-1600. Leaflet and maps are available, Rs 12. A new information centre is planned at **Farr Inn**, close to the park entrance but they've been saying that for years!

Background

Horton Plains' conservation importance lies in its role as the catchment area of most of the island's major rivers. Covering 3,160 ha, the area was declared a national park in 1988, though had received some protection since 1873 when logging above 5,000 ft was prohibited. The plains are named after former British governor Sir Robert Horton.

There is a mixture of temperate montane forest and wet patana grassland. The prominent canopy tree is the keena, its white flowers contrasting with the striking red

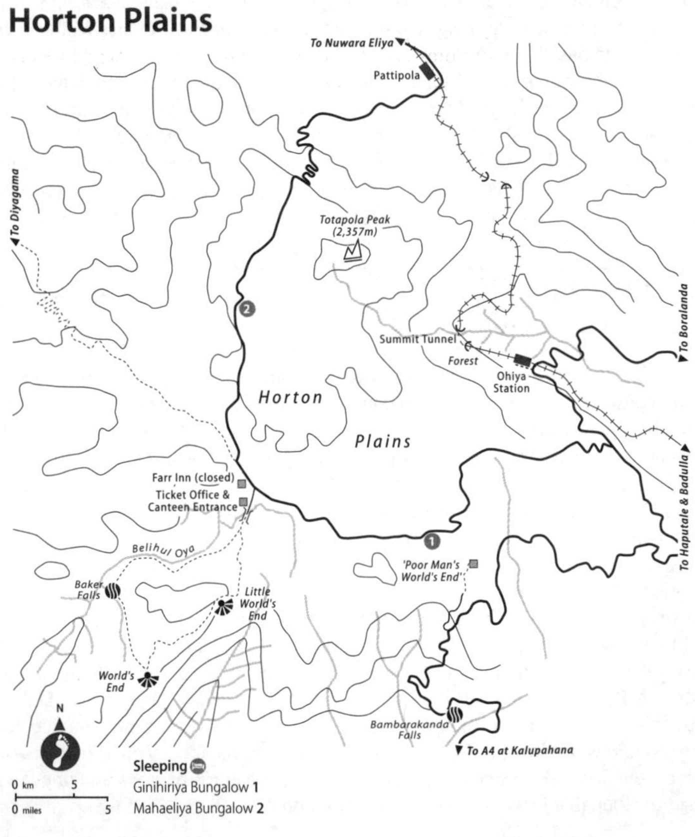

rhododendrons lower down, which makes them in some ways reminiscent of a Scottish moor. In other ways, the gently undulating grassland has an almost savannah-like feel with stunted forest on the hill tops. There is widespread concern about the condition of the forest which appears to be slowly dying. Blame seems to be attached to the acidification of rain.

The bleak and windswept area harbours many wild animals, including a few leopard though no longer the elephant. You may see sambar (sambhur), especially at dawn and dusk close to the entrance, and possibly toque macaques, purple-faced leaf monkeys and horned lizards. Wildlife has suffered at the hands of tourism though, with visitors' discarded plastic bags responsible for the death of large numbers of sambar. There is a rich variety of hill birds, and a number of endemics, including the dull blue flycatcher, Sri Lanka white-eye, and yellow-eared bulbul as well as a good range of butterflies. Some are disappointed by how difficult it is to see the wildlife; it is not impossible to visit and spot little more than the invasive crow. However by being attentive and patient an interesting variety of flora and fauna can be observed.

Sights

Most people will take the well-trodden 4.5 km bridle path to World's End, returning in a loop via the scenic Baker Falls. The walk takes three to four hours and it is essential to visit early in the morning before the looming mists close in, after which only a wall of cloud is visible.

World's End The 4½-km walk takes from 40 minutes to 1½ hours depending on how many times you stop to admire the view. You cross a small stream with lots of croaking frogs before passing across the grassland and then descending a few hundred metres through the forest. You first come to Little (or Small) World's End (2½ km), a mere 260 m cliff overlooking a ravine (more a wide valley) with a tiny village 700 m below. You can look along the sheer cliff face to the big green rock which marks (Big) World's End about 1 km away. The path continues another 2 km up the escarpment to the astonishing (Big) World's End, a spectacular precipice with a 1,050m drop. On a clear day, you can apparently see the coast, but more realistically, it is the blue-green lake of the Samanala Wewa reservoir project. Once at Big World's End, take the small path up the hill. After only a few yards, there is a split in the rock which gives an excellent view of the valley below.

Baker's Falls Return to the main path, and a track drops down to a valley along which a 2-km walk leads to a small forested escarpment. A climb and then a scrambling descent (very slippery for the last few metres so take care) take you to the picturesque Baker's Falls. The water here is deliciously cool and refreshing, though it is said to be unsafe to swim. From Baker's Falls it is an easy 3-km walk back along the river, passing the attractive Governor's Pool (again prohibited to swim) on the way.

Poor Man's World's End If you object to paying US$15 to view World's End, there is a free alternative to visit – what is now nicknamed Poor Man's World's End, accessible by several routes via the local tea plantations. Ask locally for directions, or at guesthouses in Haputale.

Nuwara Eliya to Adam's Peak

→ *For details of the route from Kandy, see page 221.*

From Nuwara Eliya many travellers continue east to Badulla or Ella via Welimada, see page 239, or southeast from the Horton Plains to Haputale and Bandarawela, see page 237. Alternatively you can head west to Adam's Peak, and then return to Kandy, or back to Colombo, via Kitulgala. The road to Adam's Peak takes you past some spectacular waterfalls and winds through the heart of some of the finest tea-growing country in the world. For much of the way it is above 2,000 m.

From Nuwara Eliya, the A7 runs through dryer country in the rain shadow of hills to the southwest and northeast. It climbs to Nanu Oya and Lindula, where a right turn leads up a beautiful mountain road to Agrapatana. In Talawakele, **Sri Lanka's Tea Research Institute** has played a major role in improving Sri Lanka's tea production (visits are possible if you get a permit from the Institute's office). The road drops as it crosses the railway line and winds through the tea estates of Dimbula.

Along this stretch, there are some magnificent views from the road. You first spy the 80-m **St Clair Falls**, dropping in three cascades down to the valley below. Opposite the viewpoint for the 98-m **Devon Falls**, an enormous bronze tea boiler introduces you to the St Clair Tea Centre, a good place to stop for a brew.

Hatton is one of the major centres of Sri Lanka's tea industry, and the base from which most pilgrims trek to the top of Adam's Peak, but the town itself is dirty and uninspiring.

It is a tortuously winding route from Hatton through Norwood up to Maskeliya at 1,280 m, skirting the attractive Castlereagh reservoir, an enormous HEP programme. If open it is worth stopping by the immaculately kept small stone **Anglican Church** (1878) at Warleigh in a picturesque setting overlooking the tank (give a donation). As you cross the dam, which is protected by the military, and pass through the new town of Maskeliya (the old one was flooded to make way for the tank), the pyramid shape of Adam's Peak begins to loom into view, looking for all the world like the Paramount Pictures logo. The air is already strikingly fresh, and the higher road is lined with tropical ferns. Stalls selling food and souvenirs for the pilgrims line the road as you descend into the makeshift settlement of Dalhousie. ▸▸ *For Sleeping, Eating and other listings, see pages 232-238.*

Adam's Peak (Sri Pada) → *Colour map 3, grid B4. Altitude: 2,260 m.*

Sacred to devotees of three of Sri Lanka's major religions, Adam's Peak is one of the island's most important pilgrimage sites. The giant 'footprint' on the summit is believed to be an imprint left by either the Buddha (hence 'Sri Pada', or 'Sacred Footprint') or Siva (Sivan Adipadham) by Hindus, or Adam by Muslims. Regardless of belief, the perfectly conical shaped mountain is worth the climb, both for the buzz and for the magnificent views, especially in the first rays of dawn. ▸▸ *For Sleeping, Eating and other listings, see pages 232-238.*

Ins and outs

Getting there The shorter (7 km) and more frequently used route is from the north, starting at Dalhousie (pronounced Dell-house). Much steeper, more difficult and more meritorious (for pilgrims) is the southern route from the Ratnapura side (11 km), starting from Palabadelle. See page 123. The really intrepid and fit could climb from Dalhousie and then walk down towards Ratnapura, a long but rewarding day.

Best time to visit The pilgrimage season runs from *Unduwap poya* (December) to *Wesak poya* (May), reaching its peak mid-season at *Medin poya*. At this time, there is a constant stream of pilgrims and the top can get very crowded. The climb is still quite possible at other times of year though you will need a torch at night as the path is not lit. It often rains in the afternoon here, especially in the off-season.

Tourist information Further reading, Markus Akland, *The Sacred Footprint: A Cultural History of Adam's Peak* (Bangkok: Orchid Press, 2001).

History

Each religion has its own myths describing the creation of the mountain's famous footprint. By far the most powerful is the Buddhist tradition, which states that the Buddha visited the mountain on his third visit to Sri Lanka on Wesak eight years to the day after Enlightenment, and was invited by the god Saman to leave an imprint. For Hindus, this is Siva's footprint, or Vishnu's in the form of the Buddha, while some Muslims believe that this was where Adam first landed on Earth after the Fall.

The mountain has been climbed for at least 1,000 years. King Vijayabahu (1055-1110) built shelters along its route, work continued by Parakaramabahu II (1225-69) who cleared jungle and built a road and bridges to the mountain. Marco Polo commented on the chains provided for pilgrims in the 13th century, while Muslim traveller Ibn Battuta visited in the 14th century and described the two approach routes still used, labelling them the Adam and Eve tracks. He warned that "anyone who goes by [the Adam – ie northern – route] is not considered...to have made the pilgrimage at all"! He also mentioned the leeches which can still be a problem to this day.

The climb → *For the climb itself, it is best to base yourself in Dalhousie.*

Most people do the walk by moonlight, setting off from Dalhousie around 0300, and arriving in time to see the dawn when the sun rises behind the conical peak, casting an extraordinary shadow across the misty plains to the west. Alternatively, you could climb up the previous evening and sleep on top of the mountain, though it is very cold up here until well after sunrise so it is essential to take warm clothing and sleeping bags. Either way, it is worth ordering breakfast in advance at the **Green House** or **Yellow House**.

For the devout, there are many significant stopping points en route where rituals are performed. Legend states that any woman who successfully climbs by this route that will be re-born in the next life as a man!

It takes about three hours to reach the top (though allow an hour either way depending on your fitness). The path is clearly marked throughout, beginning fairly gently but rapidly becoming steeper, with constant steps from about halfway. The climb is completely safe, even the steepest parts being protected, and lined with teashops and stalls if you need a break. In the company of pilgrims the trek is particularly rewarding but it can be very crowded. You may notice the first-timers with white cloth on their heads.

At the top, there are some breathtaking views across the surrounding hills, though the peak itself, only 50 m square, is not particularly impressive. Steps lead up to the sacred footprint, on top of a 4-m rock, which is covered by a huge stone slab in which has been carved another print. Pilgrims cluster round, throwing offerings in to the 1-m hollow, before moving to the Saman shrine up another flight of stairs where thanks are given. Pilgrims who have made the trip more than three times then ring one of the two bells at the summit, each chime representing a successful ascent. There are three official processions a day – at dawn, midday and dusk – with music, offerings and prayers, though many people perform their own ceremonies at other times.

Many are dismayed by how littered the route is, recently prompting a campaign for a clean-up. In 2003, plastic bags were banned from the trek, with returnable cloth bags dispensed to pilgrims at the bridge as an alternative.

Kitulgala → *Phone code: 036. Colour map 2, grid A3. 95 km from Colombo.* *For the route from Hatton to Kitulgala (in reverse) see page 221; for the road to Colombo (in reverse), see page 120.*

Kitulgala is a small, peaceful village lining the main road descending gently from the highlands to Colombo. It lies on the banks of the Kelaniya River and is known as a centre for *kitul* honey production. Aside from its beautiful setting, it has two other claims to fame which makes it well worth lingering. The first is that it provided the main location for the filming of David Lean's Oscar-winning film, *Bridge on the River Kwai*. You can wander down to the banks of the river to the original site of the bridge, signposted about 1 km before the Plantation Hotel (where you can pick up an interesting history of the filming, though you may be accosted by Mrs Perera, whose husband Samuel was an extra in the film; she will want to guide you for a fee. The area is surprisingly small, compared to the real bridge in Kanchanaburi, Thailand, and there is not much to see now, except for the concrete foundations of the bridge hewn into two rocks either side of the ganga, but for those familiar with the film the area will be recognizable. The sandbar from which the bridge was blown up has now been reclaimed by the jungle.

The other major reason to visit Kitulgala is that it is the base for the country's best **white-water rafting**, which can be arranged at the local hotels or in Colombo. The rapids are grade 3 (grade 4 during floods) and tend to start 5 to 6 km upriver, passing through 6 rapids to the 'bridge' area, where you can stop for a swim. There are some excellent places to stay in Kitulgala, so it is well worth a stop on the way from Colombo.

Some 5 km inland, near **Edurella Royal River Resort** (see page 235), at **Beli Lena**, are some part-excavated caves. Lying beneath a waterfall, under which you can bathe in the dry season, the caves are a wonderful place to watch butterflies and birds. Several skeletons and prehistoric tools have been found dating back 30,000 years. An old man looks after the site and will show you around (translation needed) but is so full of the dangers of the cave (vipers, cobras, even flying pigs – three once fell down the waterfall to their doom) that it's a wonder anyone survives a visit! The site is signposted off the main road. After 5 km, a track leads right at the sign for Kitulgala Tea Estate. The cave is 1 km walk along the path from here. » *For Sleeping, Eating and other listings, see pages 232-238.*

Sleeping

Kandy to Nuwara Eliya *p221*

B-C **Estate bungalows**, *Labookellie*. Available for hire at around Rs 2,500 including a cook.

C **Ramboda Falls**, *Rock Fall Estate, Ramboda, T/F052-2259582, info@rambodafalls.com* 16 rooms with hot bath and excellent views, good restaurant, bar, natural pool.

D **Rest House** (CHC), *Pussellawa, T081-2478397, reservations T011-2503497, F2503504*. In an attractive location, 4 rooms with bath in a colonial bungalow that are a little dated. However, pleasant (though steep) terrace garden at back with good views across the valley compensates. Seating under large permanent sun umbrellas covered with the exotic 'ladies slipper' vine.

Nuwara Eliya *p223, map p224*

Only a selection is listed here – there are more, especially on St Andrew's Drive. Some hotels are in the Raj style, well kept, with working fireplaces, good restaurants and plenty of atmosphere, and there are also a few good value 'budget' places, mainly in the southern end of town. However, prices can rise by as much as 3 times during the April New Year rush while long weekends can see prices double even if demand is low. It always pays to bargain. Usually bathrooms have hot water, though it may not always be on, and rooms have blankets provided. Avoid hotels introduced to you by touts, especially on the edge of town. Solo female travellers are advised to avoid **Glenfall Inn**.

AL **Tea Factory** (Aitken Spence), *Kandapola, T2229600, ashmres@aitkenspence.lk* Winner of numerous awards, including UNESCO Heritage Award, superbly inventive conversion of old British factory retaining original features, 57 comfortable rooms (best on top floor) including 4 suites, amidst 25-acre tea plantation with magnificent views, 2 restaurants (eat at the 'TCK6685' restaurant – in a railway carriage!), 9-hole putting green, riding, games, gym. Highly recommended for setting and originality.

A **St Andrew's** (Jetwing), *10 St Andrews Drive, T2222445, standrew@eureka.lk* 52 good rooms in beautiful century old building retaining a more homely colonial atmosphere than its rivals, good restaurant

Blooms, bets and beauty pageants

Throughout April, and particularly over Sinhalese and Tamil New Year, Nuwara Eliya is invaded by the Colombo set. A banner across the road proudly announces 'Nuwara at 6,128 ft: Welcome to the salubrious climate of Nuwara Eliya: cultured drivers are welcomed with affection!'

For several weeks, the normally sedate town throngs with visitors. Many come for a day at the one of the five races, beloved by all betting mad Sri Lankans, which culminate in the nine-furlong Governor's Cup. Motor-racing also draws the crowds. Over a hundred Formula Three cars hare around the hills at the Mahagastota Hill Climb, while the Fox Hill supercross at the nearby Diyatalawa circuit can be very exciting. Back in town, there are dances and beauty pageants, all culminating in the judging of the all-important flower show at the end of the month.

The town of course gets packed. Prices become inflated (tripled) and it is virtually impossible to find accommodation. Stallholders, mostly selling food and drink, pay vast amounts of money to rent a pitch alongside the main road by Victoria Park. Most hotels run all night discos (the best is said to be at the Grand Hotel) and the crowds roam the streets for much of the night.

with show kitchen, attractive and pleasant garden, tubs, English style country bar, good snooker room.

A-B **The Grand**, *Grand Hotel Rd, T2222881, F2222265, thegrand@sltnet.lk* 155 rooms in 2 wings – Golf Wing (US$60) larger, carpeted, more comfortable than Governor Wing (US$42), plus 2 Presidential suites, 2 restaurants (1 ballroom sized catering for package tour buffets), considerable colonial character in Victorian former governor's residence, efficient but can lack personal touch.

B **Hill Club**, *up path from Grand Hotel, T2222653, F2222654*. Now fully restored and oozing colonial atmosphere, 36 well furnished, comfortable rooms with fireplaces (hot water bottles in bed), including 2 A suites in 'modernized' 1930s Coffee Planter's Club, formal restaurant (jacket and tie for dinner, which can be borrowed!), 2 bars (1 men only – note the side entrance originally used by women who were banned from using the main entrance). Good public rooms (leaf through the magazines in the faded leather armchairs of the library), excellent snooker room, tennis courts. Recommended, though some feel the 'tongue-in-cheek fogeyism' has now gone a bit too far.

B **Galway Forest Lodge**, *89 Upper Lake Drive (1½ km from town), T2223728, info@galway.lk* 52 well-furnished, carpeted, comfortable rooms with TV, heater, some with king-size beds, public areas rather utilitarian, large restaurant, 'Fox and Hounds' pub, billiard room, quiet location close to Galway Forest Reserve, lovely walks through tea plantations, popular with tour groups.

B **Windsor**, *1 Kandy Rd, T2222554, F2222889*. Modern hotel despite 1930s appearance, 50 comfortable rooms in the heart of town (US$43-56, plus one impressive suite US$95) though quiet inside, tastefully decorated, good restaurant though lacking ambience, attractive plant-filled inner garden.

C **Glendower**, *5 Grand Hotel Rd, overlooking the 2nd Tee of the golf course, T2222749*. 6 airy, comfortable rooms with teak floors (Rs 1,900), plus 3 suites (Rs 2,800), stylishly decorated, attractive modern half-timbered bungalow-style hotel, pleasant lounge with good satellite TV, superb snooker table (Rs 120 per hr), 19th Hole Pub, excellent Chinese restaurant (big portions), friendly and efficient service, convenient for town.

C **Heritage** (was **Cey Bank Rest**), *96 Badulla Road, opposite racecourse, T2223053, hritage@sltnet.lk* Fine colonial house recently bought and restored, 18 large, ebony furnished rooms (US$20-23) in 2 wings (old wing better), including beautiful suite with art deco fireplace, fine sweeping staircase, restaurant, bar, open-air café outside for lunch packets. Ask for extra blankets at night.

C **Tree of Life**, *2 Wedderburn Rd, T2223685, F2223127*. Offshoot of hotel in Kandy, lovely old colonial bungalow with award-winning garden in quiet located, 5 rooms (Rs 1,950 with breakfast) clean but sparsely furnished, poor reports about food.

C-D **Alpine**, *4 Haddon Hill Rd, T2223500, alpinene@sltnet.lk* Recently refurbished, 25 spotless, warm, very comfortable rooms, all with bath tubs and TV (Rs 1,500-2,500), plus characterful 3-room suite with attic room (for up to 8, Rs 6,000), excellent tours (see below), friendly.

D **Chalet du Lake**, *Gregory Lake, Badulla Rd, T2234967*. 10 rustic wooden cabanas on the lakeside (Rs 1,500), hot bath, electric blankets (extra Rs 100), boat shaped restaurant, fishing (bring own equipment), canoes (Rs 225 per hr) and paddle boats (Rs 125), friendly, in need of some upkeep but good setting.

D **Grosvenor**, *6 Haddon Hill Rd, T2222307*. 10 comfortable rooms (Rs 1,320-1,650 including breakfast) in old colonial house, fireplaces or heaters, hot water, well furnished, good value.

D **Haddon Hill Lodge**, *29 Haddon Hill, T2222345, dholiday@sri.lanka.net* Under substantial renovation at time of visit but usually 8 clean rooms, 1 with tub, excellent views from pleasant garden on the hill, good food, homely atmosphere.

D **Wedderburn Rest**, *23 Wedderburn Rd, T/F2234965*. 7 rooms with excessively ornate ebony furniture (Rs 1,400), some with TV, minibar, hot bath with tubs, restaurant, but overall in rather poor taste.

D-E **Golf Club**, *T2222835, negolf@stlnet.lk* Nuwara's best-kept accommodation secret (but only if you play a round). 11 cosy, comfortable rooms (US$8-12), new wing better, well-furnished, good beds, plenty of atmosphere.

D-E **Haddon Hill View**, *8b Haddon Hill Rd, T078-60668*. 12 rooms with fireplaces, 1 with balcony and 4-poster bed (Rs 700-1,400), self-catering possible, jeeps to Horton Plains Rs 1,400.

D-E **Oatlands**, *124 St Andrew's Drive, T2222572*. Charming old bungalow, and equally charming host, 2 rooms attached bath, 2 rooms shared bath, all with washbasins, plus 4 simple **E** rooms, dining room, lounge, peaceful location in pleasant garden, homely atmosphere.

D-E **Sunhill**, *18 Unique View Rd, T2222878, F2223770, sunhill@itmin.com* 20 good, carpeted rooms (Rs 900-1,500), though some a little damp, upstairs with balcony, attached hot bath, TV in some, good Chinese food, bar, laundry, friendly and helpful management, jeep tours, good value.

D-F **Collingwood**, *112 Badulla Rd, T2223550, F2234500*. 12 variable rooms (Rs 600-1,400) in old planter's house with some old-world British character, some rooms with fireplace, a few a little damp (inspect first), one reader complained of 'tap dancing rats'!, needs a coat of paint, poor restaurant.

E **Green Garden**, *16 Unique View Rd, T2223609*. 8 carpeted rooms (Rs 900-1,150) with balcony, hot bath, restaurant, family run.

E **Meena Ella Estate Bungalow**, *Hakgala, menaka@kandyan.net* 5 simple rooms (being painted at time of visit) in attractive if faded 1912 colonial-style bungalow still owned by original family, well-kept vegetable garden, some fine old furniture. Meals.

E **Princess Guest House**, *12 Wedderburn Rd, T2222462*. Former government agent's house with faded charm, 7 rooms with fireplaces and original (and looking their age) bath tubs (Rs 950), 2 with bay windows, more planned in new building and due for renovation, friendly.

E **Travelodge**, *T2222733*. Large rooms in characterful old bungalow with period furniture (Rs 800-1,000), though management has rather given up the ghost.

E **Wattles Inn**, *17 Srimath Jayatilleke Mawatha, T2222804*. 9 dark but reasonable, wood panelled rooms (Rs 1,000), in half-timbered house, restaurant, bar, pleasant garden, though seen better days.

E-F **Carnation Rest**, *1 Unique View Rd, T072-859850, prasanna076@yahoo.com* 6 clean rooms (Rs 700-800) with reliable hot shower in friendly family run guesthouse, good value, quite cosy.

E-F **Haddon Hill Inn**, *Haddon Hill Rd, T2223304*. 10 basic but clean and comfortable rooms (Rs 650-950), hot water, reasonable value.

E-F **Humbugs**, *100 m beyond entrance to Hakgala gardens, T2222709, meenella@slt.lk* 5 quite attractive rooms (Rs 750-800), carpeted, hot water, balconies, quiet.

Restaurant serves good snacks including strawberries and cream in season (Rs 75)! Extensive views across the Uva basin, particularly attractive in the early morning mist.

E-F Maggie's Cottage, *Haddon Hill Rd, T2223826*. 5 rooms in family guesthouse, prices negotiable, food available.

E-F Single Tree, *1/8 Haddon Hill Rd, T2223009*. 10 clean wood-panelled rooms (Rs 750-850), some with balcony, large beds, good views, under refurbishment at time of visit, good food (dinner Rs 150-250), friendly, excellent tours (ask for Santha), good value.

F Victoria Inn, *15/4 Park Rd, T2222321*. Attractive ivy-clad building, 10 clean rooms, upstairs lighter (Rs 550), hot showers, restaurant, friendly, though caution about tours.

F-G Ascot, *120 Badulla Rd, T2222708*. 11 large but shabby and rather damp rooms, (hot water Rs 750, without Rs 450-500), restaurant, friendly and the cheapest option.

Horton Plains National Park *p227, map p228*

For all park accommodation, call the Wildlife Conservation Dept, *T2694241, wildlife@slt.lk*

C Ginihiriya Bungalow (formerly **Anderson Lodge**), *Haputale Rd, 3 km from park entrance*. Pleasant lodge, sleeps 10-12, caretaker cooks meals, minimum US$24.

E Mahaeliya Bungalow, *3 km along Pattipola Rd*, sleeps 10-12, more basic. There are also dormitories.

F 3 campsites near the river close to **Farr Inn**. Recommended, but if you camp inside the park, you'll have to pay for 2 days' admission. Overnight fees are US$6.

F Rangers' Huts have been offered to some travellers for Rs 250-400 (depending upon negotiating skills). They are very basic and you'll need your own sleeping bag and provisions.

Nuwara Eliya to Adam's Peak *p229*

Hatton is the main centre (see below) however there is basic accommodation available in Maskeliya. Dickoya, 6 km south of Hatton on the Maskeliya Rd, has 2 estate bungalows managed by the **Bank of Ceylon** (Colombo T2447845), each at Rs 1,200:

D Lower Glencairn, *T051-2222342*. 5 large rooms with bath tub and hot water, no food and looking its age but good views.

D Upper Glencairn, *T051-2222348*. Beautiful 100-year old bungalow in lovely gardens high on hill, good views, 5 well-furnished rooms, food available, very characterful.

D-F Hatton Rest House, *1 km away from Hatton on Colombo Rd, T051-2222751*. 7 spartan rooms (Rs 800), locals' bar, rundown but good location overlooking valley.

F Ajantha Guest House, *83 Park Rd, Hatton, 300 m off main road, across railway line, eastern edge of town, T051-2222337*. 9 reasonably clean rooms with hot water (Rs 750), restaurant.

Adam's Peak (Sri Pada) *p230*

For accommodation at Ratnapura, see p127.

D-G River View Wathsala Inn, *1 km before bus stand in Dalhousie, T051-2277427*. Smartest in town, 14 rooms (most with hot bath), upstairs large and clean with balcony and good views of lake (Rs 1,500), downstairs more basic (Rs 850), dorm available (Rs 200), restaurant.

F-G Green House, *just beyond first step, T051-2223956*. 11 clean rooms (Rs 400-600) with shared bath, excellent food (massive breakfast!), snacks before climb and herbal bath afterwards (Rs 100), very friendly, welcoming and homely.

G Sri Pale Guest House, next to **Wathsala Inn**, (no phone), 2 simple but respectable rooms, very cheap.

G Yellow House, *due to move Dec 2003, T051-2223958, gayanta@yahoo.com* New guesthouse to have 10 rooms with attached bath (Rs 440).

Kitulgala *p231*

B Edurella Royal River Resort, *6 km inland*, turning for Beli Lena (small sign) between 38 and 39 km post, reservations at **Plantation Hotel** (below). Environmentally harmonious small hotel, built around mini-HEP system from waterfall. 4 beautiful rooms (double US$45), homely (antiques, opera posters, working fireplaces), wonderfully refreshing natural swimming pool (you can drink the water!) built into rock. Wonderful secluded setting with local walks through tea and rubber plantations, good for birders. Excellent service.

B Plantation Hotel, *at 39 km post, T2287575, F2287574*. Owned by one of the world's

leading Acupuncture doctors (note the vintage cars in the garage), a fine refurbished colonial bungalow. 8 very comfortable rooms with antique furniture, TV, hot water (US$42). Excellent riverside restaurants a popular lunchtime stop for tour groups (good buffet Rs 390). Rafting trips organized (Rs 1,800 for 1½ hrs, up to 8 people).
C **Kitulgala Rest House** (CHC), *on riverbank before 37 km post, T2287528*. 20 pleasant, comfortable rooms, fan, net, hot water, with porches overlooking river (US$28). Restaurant (Rs 350 for lunch time buffet), bar, and exchange. Rafting trips arranged with **Adventure Lanka** (see below).

Eating

Kandy to Nuwara Eliya
For options see Sleeping, p232.

Nuwara Eliya *p223, map p224*
There are numerous cheap restaurants along Old and New Bazar Rds.
RsRsRs Hill Club, *up path from Grand Hotel, T2222653*, gets mixed reviews for its food, but it's a unique dining experience: dress code after 1900 (jacket and tie though fewer constraints for women), 4-course meal served promptly at 2000 (US$12), courteous service.
RsRsRs The Grand, *Grand Hotel Rd, T2222881*, has 2 restaurants – lunch (1230-1500) US$11, dinner (1830-2200), US$14.
RsRsRs King Prawn, *Glendower, open 1200-1500 and 1900-2200*. Good Chinese.
RsRs Grand Indian, new canteen at **The Grand**. Mainly South Indian, such as dosas, vindaloo and Goan fish curry.
RsRs Milano, *24 New Bazaar St, T2222763, open 0800-2200*. First Halal restaurant here, tasty seafood, Chinese and Sri Lankan (about Rs 140), good portions, tempting wattapalam dessert, sales counter, no alcohol. Several similar restaurants nearby.
RsRs Sunhill, *18 Unique View Rd*. For excellent Chinese.
Rs Devon Food City, *49 Kandy Rd, 0630-2000*. Small branch of the excellent Kandy-based bakery, small seating area inside.

Horton Plains National Park *p227, map p228*
For further options see Sleeping, p235.
Rs Canteen near the entry gate does superb rotties, wadais and dhal for breakfast (careful though as they charge by the rotty!), tea and simple snacks at other times.

Nuwara Eliya to Adam's Peak *p229*
For further options see Sleeping, p235.
Rs Devon Bakery, *Main St, Hatton*, for snacks. There are a couple of Chinese restaurants in Hatton.

Adam's Peak (Sri Pada) *p230*
Teashops and foodstalls selling food line the approach to the mountain and the steps themselves. Good food at the **Green House** and **Yellow House**, see p235.

Kitulgala *p231*
For options see Sleeping, p235.

Bars and clubs

Nuwara Eliya *p223, map p224*
Glendower, **The Grand**, **St Andrew's**, and most atmospherically, **Hill Club**, for old-fashioned ambience. Women however are only allowed into 1 of the 2 bars at **Hill Club**.
Lion Pub, *Lawson St, open 1100-2200*. Serves draught stout and lager (Rs 35 per mug) as well as bottled beer (Rs 50+). Busy local bar, inside is an English style pub whilst outside has a more European terrace feel. Snacks are also available, but check your bill.

Shopping

Nuwara Eliya *p223, map p224*
Warm jackets, including some well-known brands, can be picked up at the market to the west of New Bazaar St. Bargain hard.
Cargill's, *Kandy Rd*, branch of this super-market with café and laundrette.
Co-op City, *Lawson St*, too.
Mlesna, Cargill's, sells excellent tea as do the surrounding estates.

Nuwara Eliya to Adam's Peak *p229*
St Clair Tea Centre, *opposite Devon Falls*, has a good selection of teas and china available and a patio area for a cuppa.

Sport and activities

Nuwara Eliya *p223, map p224*
Beautiful and superbly maintained **golf**

course. 5,550 yds, par 70. Rs 2,800 including club hire, Rs 2,300 with own clubs, Rs 1,350 for 6 holes if you are pushed for time, membership Rs 100 per day, with bar, snooker, badminton etc available.

Pony-trekking available from large hotels (eg St Andrew's), and at the northwestern edge of the golf course, Rs 1,500 for 1-hr ride, T2235066.

Snooker at the **Hill Club** (Rs 75 plus Rs 60 temporary membership fee), though those who play like Alex Higgins may like to note the '1 million rupees first tear' sign (presumably the second one is free!). Three excellent tables at the **Grand**, Rs 200 a go, plus at **St Andrew's** and an antique table at **Glendower** .

Good **tennis** courts at the **Hill Club**, Rs 150 (plus membership).

Kitulgala *p231*

White-water rafting trips cost Rs 1,800-2,200. Can be arranged at local hotels, or better, from Colombo. Try **Eco Adventure Travels**, *T011-285601, www.ecotourismsrilanka.com*

Tour operators

Nuwara Eliya *p223, map p224*

Alpine Adventurers, *Mr Mahinda Kumara, c/o Alpine Hotel (see Sleeping), T077-726898 (mob), alpineeco@sltnet.lk* Established 19 years, jeep tours to Horton Plains (Rs 1,500), camping trips, '15 waterfalls' tours, fishing, rafting, island tours, bird-watching in Victoria Park (Rs 500) and further afield, mountain bikes for hire (Rs 500 per day), van hire. Also night transport to Adam's Peak, pick up at 2300 and return or drop elsewhere (Rs 3,500). Friendly, honest.

Santha, *c/o Single Tree, see Sleeping*, is an excellent driver/guide (ask for Aruna to call him), especially for the Highlands, though island tours also. Safe and reliable.

Transport

Nuwara Eliya *p223, map p224*

A new stand on Kandy Rd for all buses is under construction.

Bus To **Nanu Oya** every ½ hr, Rs 9. Frequent long-distance buses from both bus stands to **Badulla** (via Hakgala, Rs 30, 2½ hrs). For **Haputale** and **Bandarawela**, change at Welimada. Plenty of buses to **Hatton** (intercity Rs 40, 1½ hrs, normal bus Rs 26, 2½ hrs) and to **Kandy** (every half an hour, 3-4 hrs). Several a day to **Colombo** (Rs 80, 6 hrs) including faster a/c intercity buses (Rs 155, 5 hrs).

Car To Colombo, the most direct route is the A7 via Ginigathena and Avissawella.

Train New arrivals are besieged by touts actually on the train and at the station and will offer free transport to the hotel of their choice. You will end up paying heavily for this service in commissions. Better to take the bus which waits for the arrival of trains or take a taxi (if none at the station walk a few hundred metres to the main road). *Railway Out Agency* in town sells tickets. To **Colombo**, Udarata Menike, 0935, 6 hrs. Podi Menike, 1255, 7¼ hrs. Mail, 2140. Night Express, 2305. To **Kandy** (via Hatton), 0600, 5 hrs, Podi Menike 1255 (4 hrs), 1730 (7 hrs). To **Badulla** (3½-4 hrs), via **Haputale** (1½-2 hrs), **Bandarawela**, **Ella** (2½-3 hrs), 0255, 0510, 1000, 1300, 1540.

Horton Plains National Park *p227, map p228*

For details of the route by road from Kandy to Adam's Peak see p221.

Car From **Nuwara Eliya**, follow the A5 past Hakgala, after which a paved road leads from the Warwick tea estate to Ambewela and, close to the railway line, climbs to Pattipola. It passes between Mount Totapola (2,357 m, 7,730 ft) and Mount Kirigalpotta (2,396 m, 7,860 ft) to the gate. The 32-km journey takes 1½ hrs. Vans and jeeps can be hired in Nuwara Eliya for around Rs 1,500.

From **Haputale** (1½-2 hrs) turn on to the B805 from the A4, and then towards Ohiya from Boralanda, after which a good road winds up through wooded slopes up to the Udeira/Ohiya estate and to the plains. You may see bear monkeys (purple-faced langur) on this route. Transport again should cost around Rs 1,500.

Train Ohiya is the nearest train station. The Udarata Menike leaves **Haputale** at 0755 (40 mins), or **Ella** at 0653 (1¾ hrs) or **Bandarawela** at 0726, (1¼ hrs) – but check times. You can catch the 1636 back. If you're desperate to travel by train and want to see the view from World's End, take the Night Mail from Colombo, which leaves **Nanu Oya** (near Nuwara Eliya) at 0255, arriving at 0348. There may also be a 0510 (arrives 0606) – check.

From Ohiya you can walk or take a taxi. The walk along the road via the Ginihiriya bungalow (8 km) to the park entrance is scenic and straightforward, taking around 3 hrs. Locals may encourage you to take alternative shortcuts (and get in without paying) but be aware it is very easy to get lost.

Nuwara Eliya to Adam's Peak *p229*
Bus Intercity buses run from **Hatton** to **Colombo** (Rs 110, 4½ hrs) and normal buses to **Kandy** and **Nuwara Eliya** (each 3 hrs), with more during the pilgrimage season.
Train They run from **Hatton** (on the Colombo- Badulla line), with several trains a day to **Colombo** (6½ hrs), most (not all) via **Kandy** (2½ hrs), and to **Nanu Oya** (1½ hrs) and destinations further east.

Adam's Peak (Sri Pada) *p230*
Bus Run regularly to Dalhousie direct during the pilgrimage season from **Colombo**, **Kandy** and **Nuwara Eliya**. You may have to change in Hatton or Maskeliya during the off-season.
Taxi From **Hatton** (around Rs 700).
Train To **Hatton** (see above), then bus.

Kitulgala *p231*
Bus Between **Colombo** and **Hatton** or **Nuwara Eliya** pass through Kitulgala. From Ratnapura you must change in Avissawella.

Directory

Nuwara Eliya *p223, map p224*
Banks Bank of Ceylon, *on the corner of Kandy Rd and Lawson St*, has a Visa ATM and foreign exchange counter. Hatton National Bank, just up from post office, accepts Mastercard. Other banks congregate on Park Rd, including Commercial Bank (Cirrus ATM), People's Bank and Seylan Bank which cashes TCs.
Buddhist centre International Buddhist Centre, *Badulla Rd, T2235244*.
Communications Internet is expensive. Aishwarya Communications, *New Bazar St, Rs 10 per min, 0800-2000*. Chamara Computer Centre, *Park Rd, open 0830-1830*, Rs 7 per min. Three new terminals at Alpine Hotel. Post office, *opposite the CTB bus station, Mon-Sat 0700-2100, Sun 0800- 2100*. Salika Communications, *Old Bazar St*, offers discount IDD calls (0730-2100). TNT courier service, *36 Park Rd, T2222697*.
Medical services Chemists available at Cargills.

Nuwara Eliya to Adam's Peak *p229*
Banks Hatton has several banks. Friendly at Hatton National Bank!
Communications IDD and sometimes internet at the Swedish Jex Shop (sic) opposite Hatton station.

Uva Province

East of the Central Highland ridge are the picturesque hills of Uva Province. In contrast to the comparatively recently populated Highland region, Uva, which stretches across the plains as far south as Kataragama, is sometimes held to be the original home of the Kandyan civilization, whose people would have used the river valleys draining into the Mahaweli ganga as a natural migration route into the hills. Protected from the Wet Zone rains by the Highland massif, it has a sunny, dry climate and a relatively bare landscape. In the hills, there are some impressive waterfalls, and some of the best views on the island.

South of the provincial capital Badulla, whose festival draws Buddhist pilgrims from across the island, the climate of the triangle formed by Ella, Haputale and Welimada is regarded by many Sri Lankans as the most favourable on the island. This is marvellous walking country, where views, particularly at Ella and Haputale, formed by spectacular 'gaps' in its precipitous ridges come without the price tag of Horton Plains. There is a wonderful circular route from Nuwara Eliya which makes for a rewarding day tour, or there are plenty of attractive places to stay if you don't want to rush.

Nuwara Eliya to Badulla

From Nuwara Eliya, the A5 goes southeast across Wilson's Plains then east to Badulla. This is the market garden area where carrots, bean, brassicas and many other fresh vegetables are grown, much of it for export to the Middle East. Some 10 km past the Hakgala Botanical Gardens, see page 227, is a superb view southeast across the hills of Bandarawela and over the baked plains of the east coastlands. The road passes through **Keppetipola**, where you can pick up information about local attractions as it drops rapidly through to Welimada on the Uma Oya River.

Istripura Caves, north of Welimada, are a pot-holer's delight. They are reached by a path from Paranagama, which is 10 km along the road north from Welimada. The maze of damp caves holds a large lake.

From Welimada, a right turn on to the B51 leads to Bandarawela, see page 243, past terraced fields of paddy and across occasional streams. At Hali-Ela, the A5 goes to Badulla. This area is already in the rain shadow of the hills to the west, sheltered from the southwest monsoon and much drier than Nuwara Eliya. Rubber plantations cover some of the slopes before Badulla. ▸▸ *For Sleeping, Eating and other listings, see pages 245-250.*

Badulla → *Phone code: 055. Colour map 3, grid A6. Population: 42,000. Altitude: 675 m.*

The capital of Uva Province is surrounded by paddy fields along the banks of the river Gallanda Oya and has an old fort against a backdrop of mountains and a small lake.

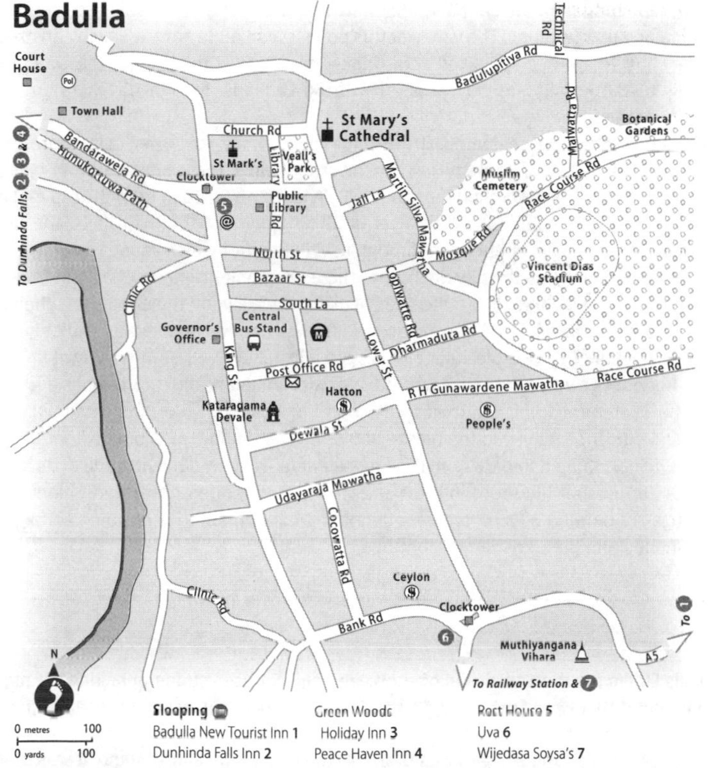

 It is one of the oldest towns in Sri Lanka though there are no traces of the earlier settlement. The Portuguese once occupied it but set the town on fire before leaving. At one time it was an extremely active social centre for planters, with a racecourse, golf, tennis and cricket clubs, long since fallen into disuse. » *For Sleeping, Eating and other listings, see pages 245-250.*

Sights → *Dunhinda Road is also known as Mahiyangana Road.*

Veall's Park was once a small botanical garden – some impressive specimens remain, such as the huge Australian pine. Notice the little stone grey Methodist church where Major Rogers, an elephant hunter who died from a lightning strike, is commemorated on a plaque.

Muthiyangana Vihara, attributed to Devanampiya Tissa, the first Buddhist convert on the island, is thought to have a 2,000-year old ancient core. There is a small provincial museum behind. The Hindu **Kataragama Devale** was built in the 18th-century highland style in thanksgiving for King Vimaladharma's victory over the Portuguese. Note the plaster-on-wood statues and wooden pillars of the 'throne room'. There is also a revered Bo tree.

Next to the stadium, in a pleasant four-acre park are the **Botanical Gardens**, ⓘ *Rs 10, free for under 12s*, welcome relief from the bustle of Badulla town.

Excursions → *Good mangoes are on sale in season at the falls.*

The island's highest perennial waterfalls, **Dunhinda Falls**, ⓘ *Rs 25*, can be spectacular. Some 6 km from town, there is a small car park on a bend in the road about 2 km from the falls, which takes about 25 minutes on foot. Buses from Badulla leave every half an hour and stop about a 10-minute walk away. The path to the falls is across the road from the car park. It is quite rough and steep in places, so take care and wear suitable shoes. The valley at this point is also quite narrow which can make it very hot. Numerous stalls sell cold drinks, herbs etc at the start of the walk and along it. As the falls are very popular with Sri Lankans, foreign travellers are not hassled too much.

Shortly after the beginning of the path you can see the lower falls (more of a cascade really), quite a long way down in the valley below. These are only about 15 m in height and much broader than the main falls. A ledge about 10 m from the top makes for a spectacular 'spurt' when the river is running high. At the main falls, the river plunges in two stages about 63 m through a 'V' in the rock which causes a misty haze (*dunhind*) which gives the falls its name. There are granite cliffs on either side and a large pool at the bottom. It is quite spectacular and well worth the effort. Here there is also a large, kidney shaped observation platform where concrete tables and benches have been built to give a pleasant picnic spot. It can, however, be very busy at times.

Bogoda is a very peaceful place with a small monastery and rock temple. It is well off the beaten track, off the road to the north of Hali Ela, 13 km from Badulla. The attractive 16th-century wooden bridge across the Gallanda Oya is built without nails (the original claimed to date from the first century). The only surviving one of its kind, it has an unusual tiled roof in the Kandyan style supported on carved pillars. The railings are painted with natural lacquer. **Raja Maha Vihara** rock temple nearby has old murals and pre-Christian inscriptions.

Ella → *Phone code: 057. Colour map 3, grid A6. Altitude: 1,043 m.*

Ella is little more than a handful of shops and guesthouses strung out along the main road, but it has an almost perfect climate and occupies a very scenic vantage point, with views on a fine day stretching right across to the south coast. A traveller writes, 'The view through the Ella gap was probably the best in the entire island. It was quite early and the isolated hills on the plain popped up like islands in the mist.' Most visitors go to the Grand Ella Motel garden to get the best view. The town is also a useful base from which to visit some local tea plantations, waterfalls and rock temples. This is excellent walking country. ▸▸ *For Sleeping, Eating and other listings, see pages 245-250.*

Sights

Rawana Ella Cave, in the massive Ella Rock, can be seen from the **Grand Ella Motel** to the right of the Ella Gap. It is associated with the *Ramayana* story, in which the demon king of Lanka, Ravana, imprisoned Rama's wife Sita. The cave, which is of particular interest to palaeontologists, has a small entrance which scarcely lets light in, and then a long drop to the floor. It is filled with water from an underground stream which has hindered exploration but excavations here have unearthed prehistoric remains of human skeletons and tools dating from 8,000 to 2,500 BC. The skeletons are believed to belong to *Homo sapiens Balangodensis*. They are said to show evidence of a culture superior to that of the present-day Veddas (Wanniya-laeto). To reach the caves you walk downhill beyond the **Ella Rest House** for 10 minutes until you reach

Ella area

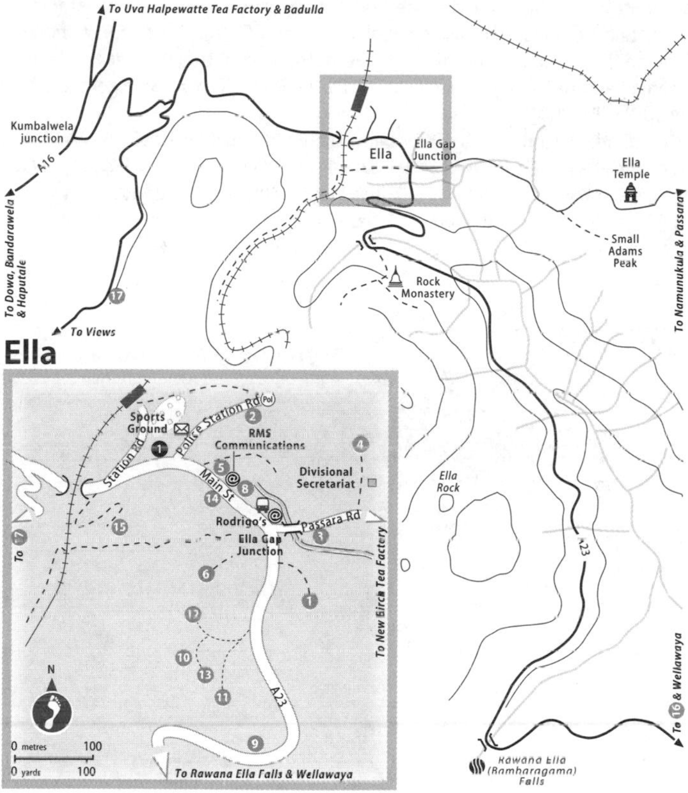

To Uva Halpewatte Tea Factory & Badulla
Kumbalwela junction
A16
To Dowa, Bandarawela & Haputale
To Views
Ella
Ella Gap Junction
Ella Temple
Small Adams Peak
Rock Monastery
To Namunukula & Passara
Ella Rock
A23
To 16 & Wellawaya
Rawana Ella (Bambaragama) Falls

Ella

Sports Ground
Station Rd
Police Station Rd
RMS Communications
Divisional Secretariat
Main St
Rodrigo's
Passara Rd
Ella Gap Junction
To 17
To New Birch Tea Factory
A23
To Rawana Ella Falls & Wellawaya
N
0 metres 100
0 yards 100

Sleeping
Ambiente 17
Beauty Mount Tourist Inn 1
Country Comfort Inn 2
Ella Adventure Park 16
Ella Gap Tourist Inn 3
Forest Paradise Guest Home 4
Garden View Inn 8
Gimhaniee Rest Inn 5
Grand Ella Motel 11
Highest Inn 15
Hill Top Guest House 6
Ravana Heights 9
Rawana Holiday Resort 10
Rock View Guest House 12
Tea Garden Holiday Inn 13
Udayanga Guest House 14

Eating
Ella View 1

the road bridge, then branch up the track to the right which climbs to a rock monastery. A young monk will happily show you the temple and hope for a few rupees' donation. There is often someone who will be pleased to accompany you on a very steep and difficult path up to the cave. He may not ask for payment but Rs 50 seems a fair reward for his trouble.

Rawana Ella Falls can be quite dramatic and the 1½-hour walk from the Rawana Ella Cave to reach them can be enjoyable: the road isn't usually busy and there are some fine views over fire-affected forest/savannah. From the cave return to the main road, near the bridge, and walk downhill to the falls. You will pass the small Rawana Ella Wildlife Sanctuary. The 90-m high Rawana Ella (or Bambaragama) Falls are to the right (west) of the road just beyond a bridge. You can climb over the rocks up the falls for quite a way, along with the monkeys who can often been seen scampering up and down the rocks. There is also a path to the right hand side of the bathing area, and you can climb up quite far. Local 'guides' are always keen to show you the route though the way (up) is fairly obvious. The Rawana Falls Restaurant sells expensive snacks and drinks at the bottom. At the falls themselves there is an intriguing small business in coloured stones gathered from the foot of the falls. A few enterprising vendors sell them to passing tourists. A handful of small stones should not cost much more than Rs 30 but a common method of transaction is to swap the stones for a foreign coin or coins. The stone seller then waits for the next tourist, hoping to exchange the foreign coins with a native of the relevant country at the prevailing exchange rate! The falls are 6 km south of Ella on the A23 so you can get there by bus (towards Wellawaya).

There are several other walks which command magnificent views. A short walk east on the Passara Road takes you to a track, after the 1 km post, which you follow to climb **Small Adam's Peak**. Some 10 km further east, and more strenuous, is the climb through tea plantations to **Namunukula**, which, at 2,036 m, is one of Sri Lanka's highest mountains. You will need a guide for this walk.

Bandarawela

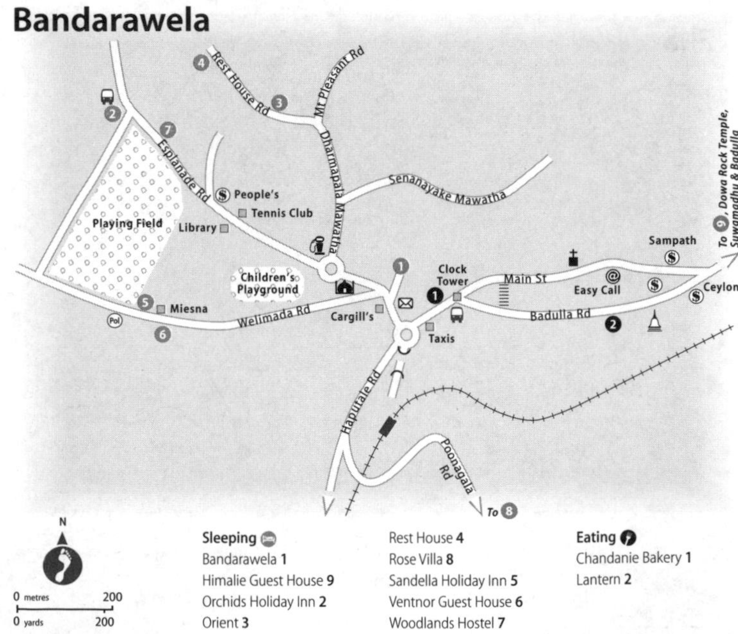

Several **tea factories** are nearby, including the Uva Halpewatte factory off the Badulla Road. Catch a bus travelling towards Bandarawela, change at Kumbalawela Junction, on to a Badulla bound bus. At 27 km post, take the track on the left leading uphill, and then turn left where it forks about 2 km from main road.

Dowa Rock Temple can also be visited from Ella, see below.

Bandarawela → *Phone code: 057. Colour map 3, grid A5. Altitude: 1,230 m.*

At the centre of the Uva 'health triangle', many Sri Lankans regard Bandarawela's climate as the most favourable on the island. Averaging around 21ºC, it is invariably dry and sunny, and the air clean and fresh. A centre for tea and fruit-growing, the town is pleasantly small, with a bustling market-town feel, and is good for picking up supplies. Market days are Wednesday and Sunday. Though there is little in the way of sights, the town is used mainly as a good base for walks and for exploring the Uva basin. » *For Sleeping, Eating and other listings, see pages 245-250.*

Sights → *For details of Bandarawela's Ayurveda and herbal therapy centres, see page 250.*

Dowa Rock Temple, 6 km from Bandarawela, is squeezed between the road and the stream in the bottom of the valley. It is a pleasant walk if you follow the attractive valley down. The cliff face has an incomplete carving of a large standing Buddha with an exquisitely carved face, while inside the cave there are murals and first century BC inscriptions. The inner cave has a 'House of the Cobra' which is usually locked (ask a monk to let you in) and said to be still inhabited by serpents. Take a Badulla bus and ask the bus driver to let you off at the temple. A guidebook on the temple (Rs 100) is available from Woodlands Network.

Woodlands Network, ⓘ *0800-1800. 38/1C Esplanade Rd, T2232328, www.woodlandsnetwork.org*, is worth if you plan to spend any time at all here. Set up by the late Father Harry Haas, a Dutch pastor, in 1994, this is a non-profit organization which works towards sustainable tourism by engaging the local community in tourism projects. Good advice is available on local walks and treks (knowledgeable guides are available), or meditation or Ayurveda, or drop in for a Sri Lankan cooking demonstration (recipe books for sale). There is basic accommodation, see page 247, or homestays can be arranged with local families. Volunteers can help out for a few days on the Network's own small tea plantation or working organic farm, or arrange three-month stays, see page 25. Sadly Father Harry died in 2002, though work continues under Sarojanie Ellawela. Highly recommended for those who wish to explore the culture and landscape of Uva in more depth.

Haputale → *Phone code: 057. Colour map 3, grid B5. Altitude: 1,400 m.*

Haputale, from its ridge-top position, has superb views at dawn over the Low Country to the east. On a clear day you can see the saltpans at Hambantota to the south, and the horizon is the sea. To the north, in magnificent contrast, are the hills. A small town with a busy shopping street, it is surrounded by great walks and the town itself, with plenty of cheap guesthouses, provides a good base in which to explore the area. The lively Sunday morning market is worth a stroll and to see a curious sight, walk down the main street from the Station Road crossing, and watch the apparent disappearance of the road over the cliff! Away from town, several tea plantations are happy to receive visitors – just stop and ask. Some estates have accommodation. » *For Sleeping, Eating and other listings, see pages 245-250.*

Sights

The **Dambetenne Road**, from the town towards the Kelburne Tea Estate, must rate as one of the most spectacular **walks** in the whole island with breathtaking views across five provinces, several tea plantations and down to the plains. It is possible to walk the length of the road, which is not busy, or alternatively take the regular bus which ferries plantation workers the 10 km from town to the Dambetenne (Lipton) Tea Factory. Along the way you will pass a number of tea factories (see below).

Some 7 km beyond the tea factory it is a short uphill walk following a clear trail up to **Lipton's Seat** from where, on a clear day, it is possible to see up to 60% of the island. This walk is highly recommended, but it's best to visit in the morning as mist tends to descend by about 1030.

Greenfields Bio Plantations, ⓘ *T/F 2268102, for a tour call first, 3 km on the Dambatenne Rd*, is one of the few organic tea producers in the country, where you can ask for a tour demonstrating the various processes involved. It's a very pleasant walk or hourly buses run.

The more traditional **Dambetenne Tea Factory** ⓘ *Visit between 0700 and 1200 to see the factory in full production, Rs 100 for a 30-min tour*, has the air of a philanthropic Victorian works, which indeed is what it is. Note the quote from Ruskin at the entrance, "Quality is no accident. It is the result of intelligent effort." Built in 1890 by Sir Thomas Lipton, the 20,000 sq ft factory employs 1,600 workers, 90% of which are resident, and accommodates over 4,000 people. Most of the tea is now exported to Europe, Japan and South Africa. There are hourly buses to Dambatenne.

Adisham monastery, ⓘ *0930-1230 and 1330-1700 Sat and Sun, Rs 60*, 3 km up a hill to the west, borders the Tangamalai bird sanctuary which is good for spotting jungle and highland species. It is worth walking up to at the weekend. A quirky stone-built anachronism dating from the 1930s, it houses a Benedictine novitiate which has interesting period features. Modelled on Leeds Castle (Kent, England), it has attractive rose gardens and orchards. A few spartan rooms with cold water in an annexe are open to visitors. Reserve ahead by post or call, T2268030. It takes about an hour to walk or is a bus ride away, no 327.

Excursions

The 170-m **Diyaluma Falls** drop in two stages over a huge convex outcrop. They are perhaps not as spectacular as the Dunhinda falls, mainly because the stream is much smaller, but it is quite peaceful here and although there are no official picnic areas, there are several large rocks to sit on. Beware of the monkeys though! You

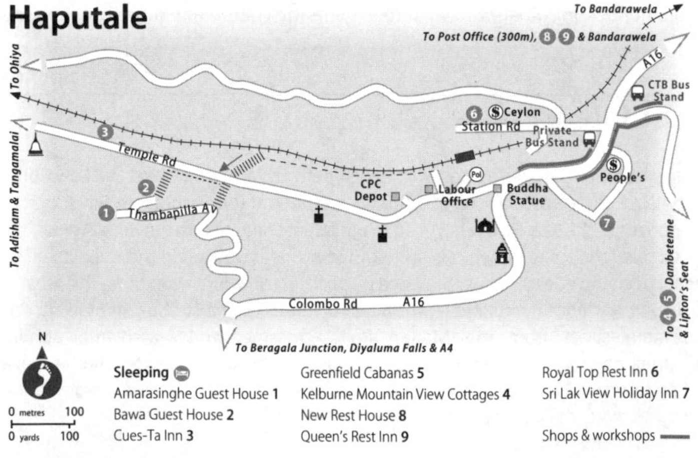

can buy drinks at a store nearby. You can climb up to some cool bathing pools about half way up the fall – walk about 500 m (back towards Haputale) to a minor road which winds up through rubber plantations – best to ask the way. The steady climb takes about an hour. Take any Wellawaya or Moneragala bus from Haputale, getting off at Diyaluma after a 1¼-hour journey. It is best to go in the morning as afternoon buses are scarce.

If using public transport, Haputale is probably a better base than Nuwara Eliya for visiting **Horton Plains National Park** and World's End since you can make a round trip by train/on foot in one day. However, by the time you arrive the plains will be covered in cloud, which normally sweeps up the valleys by midday. There is a train leaving at 0756 to the nearest station, Ohiya, taking about 40 minutes. You can return on the 1636. For further details, see page 237.

From Haputale

From Haputale the A16 goes west, past the Stassen Bio Plantation, to Beragala (10 km) where it joins the A4, the main road to Colombo which hugs the southern rim of the highlands. West of Beragala is some of the most rugged scenery in Sri Lanka. Black rocks tower above the road towards Belihuloya, see page 126, and much of the route is very windy, not steep but with many blind bends. The A4 continues west to Ratnapura, see page 125.

Travelling east from Beragala, the fine views through the Haputale Gap continue, and the road leads through a marvellous area of flora – teak, rubber, pepper, cacao and coffee trees – to Koslande and past the Diyaluma waterfall to Wellawaya, see page 186.

If you wish to return to Nuwara Eliya from Haputale, the B48 goes directly through Boralanda and Nawela, and Welimada, where it rejoins the A5 to Nuwara Eliya. Alternatively you can take the slower route via Horton Plains, see page 237.

Sleeping

Nuwara Eliya to Badulla *p239*

Forest Park, *3 km from Keppetipola Junction*, T072-2666608. Part of the Woodlands Network, there is simple accommodation, or you can just stop for tea or typical homemade Sri Lankan food.

Badulla *p239, map p239*

D-E Green Woods Holiday Inn, *301 Bandarawela Rd, 2.5 km before town, T2231358, F2232076*. 8 reasonable rooms (Rs 850) with hot bath in quiet location (although can get busy with local people), good restaurant, views would be good if you could open the childproof windows!

E Rest House (UDA), *800 m from railway station, T2222299*. 17 rooms (Rs 800 watch bills) with saggy beds around central courtyard, simple meals, central location.

E-F Dunhinda Falls Inn, *35/10 Bandaranaike Mawatha, 1.5 km from town centre, T222-3028, F2222406*. Respectable (local Rotary club meets here) despite disconcerting one-eyed leopard in entrance. 10 large rooms of very varying standards (Rs 500-990), restaurant, bar, exchange, car/cycle hire, visits to tea gardens.

F Badulla New Tourist Inn, *22 Mahiyangana Rd (towards Dunhinda Falls), T/F2223423*. 30 rooms (Rs 500-700), variable so check first, restaurant, courteous service, no hot water, delicious rice and curry. May see birds nesting in light fittings!

F Peace Haven Inn, *18 Old Bede's Rd, opposite General Hospital (3 km west of town), T2222523*. 8 rooms (Rs 600) quiet but a bit musty, restaurant, bar.

F-G Uva Hotel, *Station Rd, T2222306*. Colonial building (1881) with garden in shaded position, 12 basic rooms, 2 with attached bath (Rs 350-600), rundown at the moment but new ownership plans renovation and redecoration.

G Wijedasa Soysa's, *5/2 Malla Gastenne, T2222105, southeast of town*. One of a few local families who take in paying guests and offer good home cooking

Ella *p240, map p241*
There is an undercurrent of animosity between the different guesthouse owners, and each may have a bad story to tell about one of the others! Ignore any bad-mouthing. Most accommodation is very good. All hotels listed are on the Main St, unless listed, and most have hot water though check beforehand for the cheapest rooms.

A-B **Ella Adventure Park**, *12 km south of Ella on Wellawaya Rd, T011-5559709, wholiday@sri.lanka.net* Impressively environmentally sensitive lodge in forest setting spanning both banks of Kirindi Oya (river). 10 very comfortable 'rooms', comprising eco-lodges, tree-house (with own ropeway!), deluxe cabanas and camping tents (US$40-65 with breakfast), plus tree-top bar/restaurant. Full array of adventure sports offered, including rock-climbing, paragliding, canoeing and abseiling.

B-C **Grand Ella Motel** (CHC), *overlooking Ella Gap, 1 km south from railway station, T2228655, chc@slt.net* 14 large, attractive if new-looking rooms, TV, US$55 in new wing, US$30 in old. Wonderful garden, with own *Ficus religiosa*, still the best views in Ella.

C **Ravana Heights**, *opposite 27 km post, Wellawaya Road, T/F2231182*. 3 classy rooms (US$24) with good views in intimate guesthouse just outside town, classical music, personal attention, reasonable food. Recommended though a bit pricey.

C-E **Country Comfort Inn**, *Police Station Rd, T2228500, info@hotelcountrycomfort.com* 12 luxury rooms in new wing, very attractive teak furniture, TV, spotless (Rs 1,500-2,000), 8 clean rooms (Rs 850) in old wing, still good value if a little dark, good restaurant, reasonable but adds the highest service charge in Sri Lanka at 15%! Well worth bargaining with Shanthi (owner) as you can get up to 25% off the price.

D **Ambiente**, *2 km up Kitalella Road, high above the Ella town near Kinellan Tea Plantation, T055-2231666, kanta@telenett.net* 8 very clean spacious rooms (Rs 1,400-1,700), 5 in new block (can be noisy), magnificent views, friendly, free pick up from station. Pricey breakfast but setting compensates.

D-E **Ella Gap Tourist Inn**, *near Ella Gap Junction, T2228528*. 9 clean rooms (Rs 950), (2 with giant beds, Rs 1,350) set amongst lovely foliage. Good restaurant, friendly, one of the longest running guesthouses in Ella backed up by a consistently favourable visitor book, a bit pricey but worthwhile.

D-E **Tea Garden Holiday Inn**, *on top of the hill above the Grand Ella Motel, T2222915*. 9 good, clean rooms (Rs 900-1,300), good views of the gap, food available, starting price may depend on how wealthy you look, but otherwise all right.

E-F **Hill Top Guest House**, *off Main St, T2228780*. 8 good, clean rooms (Rs 650-800), better upstairs with excellent views, popular, good food, useful returnable walking maps, internet Rs 6 per min. Good choice.

F **Forest Paradise Guest Home**, *Passara Rd, T/F2228797*. Real frontier feel on edge of pine forest. 3 clean rooms (Rs 770), with private seating area, nets, friendly, rooms a bit pricey but recommended for setting.

F **Gimhaniee Rest Inn**, *T2222127*. 5 large, clean rooms (Rs 500), restaurant, friendly staff, good value.

F **Highest Inn**, *turn left before railway bridge, or take short cut through tea plantation, T2223308*. Under renovation at time of visit but good views all around, so worth a look. 3 rooms, Rs 500-750.

F **Rawana Holiday Resort**, *T2228794, nalankumara@yahoo.com* 4 fresh and absolutely spotless rooms (cleaned about 3 times a day!), nice home from home touches, Rs 500-600, good terrace with great views across forest, good food. Friendly.

F **Rock View Guest House**, *T2222661*. Good views of Rock! 4 large rooms (Rs 700), large popular restaurant (curry Rs 200, Sri Lankan breakfast Rs 140), friendly.

F-G **Beauty Mount Tourist Inn**, *off Main St, T2228799*. 1 bungalow (Rs 750) plus Rs 300-550 rooms.

G **Garden View Inn**, *previously Mount View Inn – name changed for reasons that become clear!), T2228792*. 3 very cheap if slightly grim rooms (Rs 350), 2 more to come.

G **Udayanga Guest House**, *T2228938*. 6 simple but good value rooms (Rs 300), restaurant.

Bandarawela *p243, map p242*
Budget options are along Welimada Rd, as well as Tea Estate Bungalows which are worth looking at if you have your own wheels.

A-B **Rose Villa**, *2 km along Poonagala Rd, T2222329, loshan@sltnet.lk* Peaceful family-owned villa with 4 rooms (US$40-65), secluded spot, organic vegetables grown in beautiful gardens, good food and service, rent whole house.

B-C Bandarawela Hotel (Aitken Spence), *14 Welimada Rd, near Cargill's supermarket, T2222501, ashmres@aitkenspence.lk* Old tea planters' club (1893) full of colonial charm, 35 rather cramped rooms, including 1 deluxe and 1 suite with attached hot tubs, retaining period furniture, rooms built around central courtyard (look for tortoises), good gardens, passable restaurant, residents' bar with fireplace, good tours to Horton Plains (ask for Mohidane), popular with groups but still recommended, though the noisy mosque will ensure you won't waste the day!

C Orient, *10 Dharmapala Mawatha, T2222377, orient@eureka.lk* 50 large, refurbished rooms (US$30), good views from top floor, some deluxe with TV and hot tub, restaurant, billiard room, fitness centre, English-style bar and beer garden, nightclub.

D Ventnor Guest House, *23 Welimada Rd, T2222511*. 4 large, carpeted rooms (Rs 1,250), well furnished, hot tub, restaurant.

E Rest House, *Rest House Rd, just beyond Orient Hotel, T2222299*. 9 large, simple rooms (Rs 1,000) in pleasant location though no views from rooms, nets, bar, restaurant.

E-F Himalie Guest House, *off Badulla Rd, Bindunuwewa, 3 km east (8 km from Ella), T2222362*. 7 large, furnished rooms (Rs 650-850), attached hot bath, quiet, attractive bungalow in a 5-acre tea estate, excellent views, restaurant (dinner Rs 200-250), very friendly, good value.

E-F Orchids Holiday Inn, *32/9 Esplanade Rd, T2222328*. 7 clean, rather starchy rooms with antique furniture (Rs 500-800).

F Sandella Holiday Inn, *50/5 Welimada Rd, T2222593*. 9 variable, basic rooms (Rs 600) close to sports ground.

F Woodlands Hostel, see p243. 4 simple double rooms, Rs 600, longer stays preferred.

Haputale *p243, map p244*

There is a good choice of cheap guest-houses with hot water being provided by most. The owners can usually advise on good walks in the area.

There is a short cut from the railway station to Temple Rd and nearby guesthouses. Walk west along the tracks, climb the steps to Temple Rd, then follow signposts down steps on the other side.

B Kelburne Mountain View Cottages, *2 km down Dambetenne Rd, T2268029*. 3 wonderfully furnished cottages (Rs 4,500-5,000), sleeping 4 or 6, 2 with fireplaces, at least 2 bathrooms in each, meals on order, spectacular views, unique hand-painted open-air visitors book! Superb place to unwind.

D Greenfield Cabanas, *Dambetenne Rd, T/F2268102, durk@sri.lanka.net* 5 new eco-lodges being built above the tea factory using local materials, with plans for a restaurant, herbal clinic, information centre, meditation centre, superb location.

E-F Queen's Rest Inn, *68 Badulla Rd, T2268268*. Variable rooms (decent-sized and fairly clean Rs 900, basic Rs 650), hot water, restaurant, bar with a wide selection of beers.

F Cues-Ta Inn, *Temple Rd, T2268110*. 5 clean rooms (Rs 500) although a bit run down, hot water, excellent views, restaurant.

F Diyaluma Falls Inn, *on the A4, 12 km west of Wellawaya, T057-2268491*. If you really like waterfalls – 8 rooms (Rs 500-750) with good views (if they've cleaned the windows). Otherwise a useful lunchtime spot (rice and curry Rs 200).

F New Rest House, *100 Bandarawela Rd (1 km), T2268099*. 6 simple but comfortable rooms (Rs 750) with hot bath although a bit musty, could do with a lick of paint, nets, good food in quiet location with garden.

F Royal Top Rest Inn, *22 Station Rd, T2268178*. 6 rather musty rooms (Rs 550 shared bath – better, Rs 750 attached), good restaurant, close to buses and trains, pleasant garden, inspect first.

F Sri Lak View Holiday Inn, *48 A Sirisena Mawatha, 200 m from bus stand, T2268125,* srilakv@sltnet.lk 11 clean rooms (Rs 650-750), some with views, hot water (solar powered), restaurant and breakfast room with excellent views, good food, free pick up from station, much expansion planned, Internet, friendly.

F-G Amarasinghe Guest House, *Thambapillai Av, T2268175, agh777@sltnet.lk*

For an explanation of the sleeping and eating price codes used in this guide, see the inside front cover.

Cosy family house with homely atmosphere, 7 good, clean, comfortable rooms, very good value at Rs 660 including some on first floor with excellent views, plus 2 rooms in separate block (Rs 440). Good food, friendly and knowledgeable owner. Best place in town, though no driver accommodation. Internet Rs 8 per min.
G Bawa Guest House, *32 Thambapillai Av, above Amarasinghe Guest House, T2268260.* 5 clean, bright rooms (Rs 400 with attached bath and view, single rooms in house cheaper and more basic), in family guesthouse, friendly owners 'urging you to eat more and more!', good vegetarian food (Sri Lankan breakfast Rs 100).

Eating

Nuwara Eliya to Badulla *p239*
For options see Sleeping, p245.

Badulla *p239, map p239*
For options see Sleeping, p245.

Ella *p240, map p241*
RsRs Grand Ella Motel, *overlooking Ella Gap, T2228655.* You come for the unrivalled setting but the food's good too.
RsRs Ella Gap Tourist Inn, *near Ella Gap Junction, T2228528.* Unimpressive surroundings, expensive but tasty food. Smallish servings but can be topped up.
RsRs Ella View Restaurant and Bar, *Main St.* Popular bar with locals and tourists alike, serves inexpensive food.
Rs Numerous places on the Main St do curd and honey, a local speciality.

Bandarawela *p243, map p242*
For futher options see Sleeping, p246.
Rs Chandanie Bakery, *Main St*, has an appealing array of cakes and patisseries.
Rs Pastry Shop, *Bandarawela Hotel.*
Rs Lantern, *Badulla Rd, T2232520*, 'chilly pheast' for Rs 85, rice and curry Rs 40. One of several cheap Chinese and rice and curry places on Badulla Rd.
Rs Woodlands Network for good rice and curry (Rs 100-125).

Haputale *p243, map p244*
For further options see Sleeping, p247. The home cooking at most of the guest houses is hard to beat. Several provide cheap lunch packets. No real restaurant here but you can buy rotties and snacks in food stalls, and good groceries along the road between the rail and bus stations. The bakery at the bus station does plenty of hot milk tea.

Festivals and events

Badulla *p239, map p239*
May-Jun, *Wesak and Poson* full moon festivals take place with drummers, dancers and elephants. In **Sep**, *Esala Perehera* at Muthiyangana Vihara when Veddas participate.

Shopping

Ella *p240, map p241*
Shops on Main St near the rest houses are overpriced. Walk up the street and pay half the price for water and provisions.

Bandarawela *p243, map p242*
Cargill's, opposite **Bandarawela Hotel**, the branch of the supermarket chain.
Mlesna, *184a Welimada Rd, T2231663*, a branch of this shop selling tea.
Prana Holistic Food, *Prana Retreat*, sells superb organically grown honeys, jams and conserves (try the Angel's Kiss) using traditional (and largely forgotten) preservative methods.

Tour operators

Badulla *p239, map p239*
Namunukula Mountaineering, *T2294762*, (ask for Indika) for exploring the Namunukula (nine mountains) Range between Ella, Passara and Badulla.

Ella *p240, map p241*
JP Wimalasooriya, *T071-2240376*, is a good local guide, with excellent English. Particularly recommended are his trips to Handapangala Tank, south of Wellawaya, see p186. Ask for him at **Garden View** or **Rawana Holiday Resort**.
Rodrigo's, *Main St, T2228615, tourinfo@sltnet.lk, 0700-2230.* Sooresh Rodrigo will give free map and local advice on transport and walks in area. Also tours for night-caving, jungle-trekking, rubber plantations and tea factories 'not in any guidebook'. Internet too (see below).

Transport

Badulla *p239, map p239*
Air Sri Lankan Airlines, *18/A Lower King St, T2232015.*
Bus Bus stand, with private and CTB buses, is about 200 m south of the **Rest House** along King St. No 296 every 20 mins to **Bandarawela**; no 99 to **Colombo** (hourly, 0600-2200) with several Intercity Express; CTB and private buses (no 21) to **Kandy** until 1400 (every 40 mins); no 47 every 30 mins to **Nuwara Eliya** until 1650; hourly to **Wellawaya**, via **Ella**; 1 bus a day (no 34) at 0630 to **Pottuvil**; 0630 (no 31) to **Galle**, via **Matara**.
Car hire From **Sugimal Fast Foods**, opposite Muthiyangana Vihara and Railway station, or **Dunhinda Falls Inn**, T2223028.
Three-wheeler Line up on the south side of the bus stand.
Train To **Colombo** via **Demodera** (look out for the Loop!), **Ella**, **Bandarawela**, **Haputale**, **Ohiya** (for Horton Plains) on Udarata Menike, 0555, 9¾ hrs, Podi Menike Exp, 0910, 11¼ hrs or Mail, 1745, 12 hrs, and 1915, 10½ hrs. To **Kandy**, Podi Menike Exp, 0910, 8 hrs. Local trains run as far as **Ohiya** at 0715, and to **Bandarawela** at 1415.

Ella *p240, map p241*
Persistent hotel touts besiege those arriving by train. Ignore them and go to the hotel of your choice, preferably with an advance reservation.
Bus Direct buses to **Nuwara Eliya** (5 a day, 2½ hrs) and **Kandy**, though more frequently if you change in Badulla. For **Colombo**, go to Kumbalawela Junction, 3 km north on the Haputale-Badulla Rd, where buses go every half an hour. For the south coast, direct buses go to **Matara**. Frequent buses to **Wellawaya** for connections to Okkampitiya (for Maligawila, see p185), and to **Bandarawela** (change for Haputale, 45 mins). Buses are infrequent for **Badulla** – you may have to go to Kumbalawela Junction.
Train Udarate Menike depart 0653, Podi Menike at 1008, mail train 1846; and Night Express 2015, calling at **Bandarawela** (30 mins), **Haputale** (1 hr), **Ohiya** (for Horton Plains), 1¾ hrs, **Nanu Oya** (for Nuwara Eliya, 2¾ hrs), **Hatton** (for Adam's Peak, 4 hrs) and **Colombo** (8½-11 hrs). For **Kandy** (6 hrs), take the 1008 or 1846. Several trains a day north to **Badulla** (1 hr).

Bandarawela *p243, map p242*
Bus The main stand is to the west of town, close to the playing field. Buses every 20 mins to **Badulla**, **Wellawaya** (via Haputale) and **Colombo** (from Haputale Rd). 6 buses a day for **Matara** and the south coast, or change at Wellawaya. 4 buses direct to **Nuwara Eliya**, or change at Welimada.

> *The hill railway from/to Kandy, Nuwara Eliya and particularly Haputale is highly recommended. Reserve the observation car to Colombo well in advance.*

Train To **Colombo** at 0726, 1042 and 1921 and 2050 (1042 and 1921 via Kandy). **Badulla** trains via Ella at 0500, 0728, 1210, 1415, 1500, 1740, 1812.

Haputale *p243, map p244*
Bus There are separate CTB and private bus stands with several early morning buses for **Colombo** (6 hrs), and some to **Nuwara Eliya**, but you may have to change at Welimada. Buses leave for **Bandarawela** every half an hour, while express buses run to **Badulla**. There is an early morning express bus to **Matara** (via **Hambantota** and **Tangalla**), though to get to the south coast you usually have to change at Wellawaya (every 2 hrs).
Train For **Colombo** (7½-10 hrs), Udarate Menike departs at 0756, Podi Menike, 1113, mail train, 1957; and Night Express, 2124, calling at **Ohiya** (for Horton Plains), **Nanu Oya** (for Nuwara Eliya), **Hatton** (for Adam's Peak). For **Kandy** (5½-6 hrs), the 1113 or 1957 are best, though the latter gets in around 0100. Faster trains north to **Badulla** (1¾ hrs), via **Bandarawela** (30 mins) and **Ella** (1 hr) at 0428, 0628, 1433 and 1714.

Directory

Badulla *p239, map p239*
Banks Bank of Ceylon, *Bank Rd*, has a Visa ATM. Hatton National Bank, *Ward St.*
Communications **Internet** available next to the Rest House. **Post office** faces the south side of the bus stand.

Ella *p240, map p241*

Communications **IDD calls** and **internet** (Rs 5 per min), fast (for Sri Lanka) at RMS Communications, *0730-2030*. Rodrigo's, *Main St, T2228615*, internet Rs 5 per min.

Bandarawela *p243, map p242*

Ayurveda and herbal therapies

Suwamadhu, *Bindunuwewa, 3 km east, T/F2222504, open 0800-2000*, is a popular herbal treatment centre, and produces its own creams and oils. Steam bath with 18 herbal medicines (Rs 2,200), full body massage (Rs 1,600), both together (Rs 3,400); longer courses available. AM Asha Priyadarshni also teaches Sri Lankan dance here (Sat and Sun). D rooms planned for students and Ayurveda patients.

Prana Retreat, *on hill 4 km from Bandarawela, ophelia1@sltnet.lk* 2 cosy cabanas with attached bath (half board US$55) in 2-acre forest setting with magnificent views. Spice, herb and rose garden, organic meals. Also 'Stress relief' packages run by Ophelia using yoga, meditation, reflexology, aromatherapy and Ayurveda, 2 day treatments, Rs 6,000, 3 days, Rs 9,500. Also on site Prana Holistic Food, see Shopping p248.

Banks People's Bank, *Esplanade Rd*, has an exchange counter. Most banks congregate at the bottom of Main St and Badulla Rd. Sampath Bank has Cirrus and Visa ATM, Bank of Ceylon has Visa and Electron ATM and Seylan Bank is very efficient.

Communications **Internet** and **IDD** at Easy Calls, *3 USC, Main St, open 0700-2100*, Rs 8 per min.

Haputale *p243, map p244*

Banks Bank of Ceylon, *Station Rd*, and People's Bank, change currency and TCs.

Ancient Cities

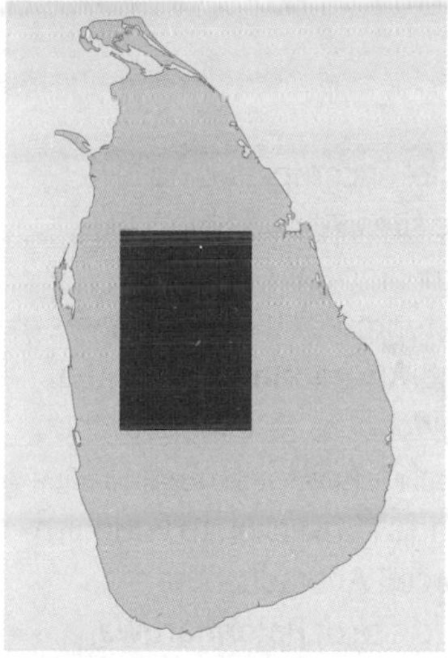

Introduction

This phenomenal 'Cultural Triangle' encompasses no fewer than five UNESCO World Heritage sites. At two points of the triangle (Kandy is the third), the ancient cities of Anuradhapura and Polonnaruwa represent the early phases of the nation's cultural development. **Anuradhapura** was the capital for 1,500 years, its soaring *dagobas* testament to the lofty ambitions of its kings, while an auspicious meeting at nearby **Mihintale** sealed the island's conversion to Buddhism. Repeated invasions from India forced Anuradhapura's abandonment for the less exposed site of **Polonnaruwa**, whose city walls today encircle the island's most rewarding archaeological complex, its unmissable highlight the serene rock-cut recumbent Buddha at the Gal Vihara.

But some of the region's most inspiring treasures lie outside the ancient capitals. Most spectacular of all is the astonishing **Sigiriya** rock, atop which lie the remains of a sort of fifth-century playboy's palace, complete with pin-ups in the form of its famous frescoes of semi-clad women. No less remarkable are some nearby Buddhist sites – the cave paintings at **Dambulla**, **Aukana's** sublime monolithic Buddha, and the ancient monastery at **Ritigala**, hidden deep within the jungle.

The area's appeal extends beyond archaeology though. In this distinctive landscape, occasional boulders of granite break the surface of the flat plains, with rice fields appearing as pockets of bright green in the widespread forest. Quiet roads make it excellent cycling country – just watch out for elephants! At the heart of the government's conservation scheme to re-establish their original migration corridors, two new national parks around the tanks at **Minneriya** and **Kaudulla** are welcoming jumbos and tourists alike.

★ Don't miss...

1. **Sigiriya** Enter the Lion's Paws and climb up the sheer sides of the 200m high rock to the sky palace of King Kasyapa, page 274.
2. **Polonnaruwa** Cycle around the forested ruins in the ancient walled city, and marvel at the serenity of the Gal Vihara, page 284.
3. **Anuradhapura** Take a tour of the mighty dagobas, each larger than the last, at Sri Lanka's first capital, page 260.
4. **Aukana** Stand in awe at the fearless symmetry of the massive Aukana Buddha, carved out of a single rock, page 256.
5. **Dambulla** After scaling the heights at the cave temple, go for lunch and a refreshing swim at the Kandalama Hotel, pages 254 and 258.

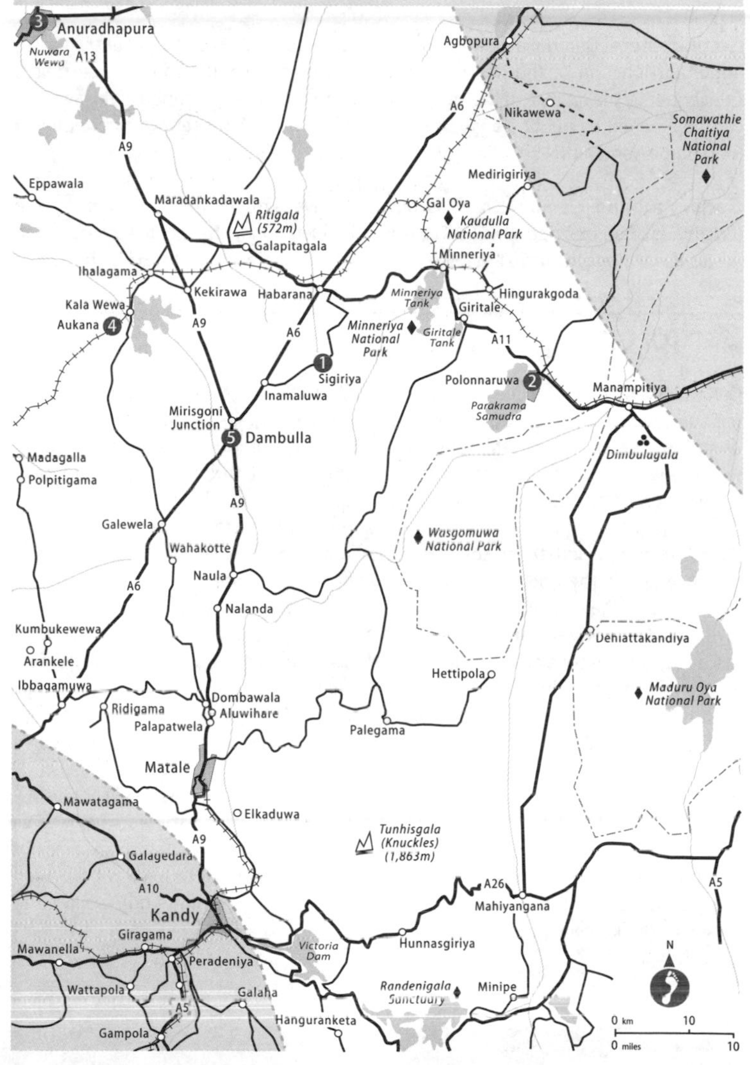

Dambulla and around

→ *Phone code: 066. Colour map 2, grid B4/C4.*

The richly painted cave temples at Dambulla which lie atop a vast rocky outcrop date to the first century BC and form one of Sri Lanka's World Heritage sites (designated in 1991). Though the site is now privately run by wealthy monks, it is still considered to be part of the cultural triangle. Nearby, you can visit the massive rock-cut Aukana Buddha and the monastery at Sasseruwa, while Sigiriya rock is only 19 km away. Those coming from Kandy can visit the rock monastery at Aluwihare, near Matale, and the Nalanda gedige (part of the Cultural Triangle round ticket) en route. » *For Sleeping, Eating and other listings, see pages 258-260.*

Ins and outs

Getting there Dambulla lies almost in the dead centre of the country on an important junction of the Kandy-Anuradhapura and Colombo-Trincomalee roads. Consequently the town, and the sights south and northwest described in the section, can be reached by public transport with the exception of Sasseruwa where private transport is required.

Getting around Dambulla itself is tiny. The cave temples lie 2 km south of the junction (a short bus ride or Rs 50 in a three-wheeler). Most cheaper accommodation is strung out along the main road. Sights around Dambulla are best reached by bus.

Background

Dambulla is sited on a gigantic granite outcrop which towers more than 160 m above the surrounding land. The rock is more than 1.5 km around its base and the summit is at 550 m. The caves were the refuge of **King Valagambahu** (Vattagamani Abhaya) when he was in exile for 14 years. When he returned to the throne at Anuradhapura in the first century BC, he had a magnificent rock temple built at Dambulla. The site has been repaired and repainted several times in the 11th, 12th and 18th centuries. In 2001, the temple authorities completed work on an enormous gold Buddha, said to be the largest in the world, which greets you from the car park.

The caves have a mixture of religious and secular painting and sculpture. There are several reclining Buddhas, including the 15-m long sculpture of the dying Buddha in Cave 1. The frescoes on the walls and ceilings date from the 15th to 18th centuries. The ceiling frescoes show scenes from the Buddha's life and Sinhalese history. Cave 2 is the largest and most impressive, containing over 150 statues, illustrating the Mahayana influences on Buddhism at the time through introducing Hindu deities such as Vishnu and Ganesh.

There is little evidence of monks who are housed in monasteries in the valley below where there is a monks' school. Some monasteries and sacred sites receive large donations from Buddhists overseas (particularly Japan) and so are not dependent on government sponsorship. Gifts and your entrance fee have provided the monks here with a four-wheel drive and many other comforts not available to others of similar calling.

Sights

Buddhist Museum

ⓘ *0730-2200. Rs 100.*

Beneath the big gold Buddha, you reach the bizarre new Buddhist Museum inside the Golden Temple (as distinct from the Rock Temple), through a fantastically gaudy dragon's mouth. Inside are exhibited statues gifted from around the Buddhist world, *ola* leaf manuscripts and copies of some of the cave paintings. Its air conditioning and piped music give it the atmosphere of a shopping mall.

Behind the museum, a flight of steps lead up into the new temple, and you can climb the new Buddha, in a *dhamma chakka* pose. It is already popular with monkeys and bees.

The Caves

ⓘ *0600-1900 (last ticket 1830). Rs 500 from the ticket booth at the entrance to the complex. Bags, shoes and hats are not allowed into the complex but they can all be left with the 'shoe keepers'. Carry a torch if you wish to view the cave paintings in detail. It is difficult to dodge the touts and beggars who line the steps leading to the caves and the guides as they stand in the temple doorway.*

The climb From the car park, it can be a hot and tiring climb. It is quite steep at first, almost 100 m across at times bare granite, after which there are about 200 steps in a series of 18 terraces, some longer and steeper than others. It is not too difficult to get to the top but try to avoid the heat in the middle of the day. In any case it is best visited in the early morning. There are panoramic views from the terrace of the surrounding jungle and tanks, and of Sigiriya. The caves are about half way up the hill and form part of a temple complex.

There are five overhung cliff caves. Monastic buildings have been built in front, complete with cloisters, and these in turn overlook a courtyard which is used for ceremonial purposes and has a wonderful view over the valley floor below. Some of the other subsidiary caves which were occupied by monks contain ancient inscriptions in Brahmi.

Cave I (Devaraja Viharaya) Contains the huge lying *Parinirvana* Buddha which is 14 m long and carved out of solid rock.

 The frescoes behind the Arahat Ananda (a disciple) are said to be the oldest in the site, though unrestored they lack the lustre of those in other caves. 'Devaraja' refers to the Hindu god Vishnu. The deity may have been installed here in the Kandyan period though some believe it is older than the Buddha images. There is a Vishnu temple attached.

Cave II (Rajamaha-Viharaya) This much bigger cave is about 24 sq m and 7 m high and was named after the two kings whose images are here. The principal Buddha statue facing the entrance is in the *Abhaya mudra*, under a *makara torana* (or dragon arch). The cave has about 1,500 paintings of the Buddha – almost as though the monks had tried to wallpaper the cave. The paintings of his life near the corner to the right are also interesting – you can see his parents holding him as a baby, various pictures of him meditating (counted in weeks, eg cobra hood indicates the sixth week); some have him surrounded by demons, others with cobras and another shows him being offered food by merchants. The other historical scenes are also interesting with the battle between Dutthagamenu and Elara particularly graphic, illustrating the decisive moment when the defeated falls to the ground, head first from an elephant. Here, in the right hand corner, you can see the holy pot which is never empty. Drips are collected into a bucket which sits in a wooden fenced rectangle and is used for sacred rituals by the monks.

You will notice that some paintings clearly show other older ones underneath.

Cave III (Maha Alut Viharaya) This cave is about 30 sq m and 18-m high. It was rebuilt in the 18th century and has about 60 images, some under *makara toranas*, and more paintings of thousands of the seated Buddha on the ceiling. This cave was a former storeroom and the frescoes are in the Kandyan style.

Cave IV (Pascima Viharaya or 'western' cave) The smallest cave and once the westernmost: it had the fifth cave constructed later to its west. It contains about 10 images though unfortunately the stupa here was damaged by thieves who came in search of Queen Somawathie's jewels. One image in particular, at the back of the cave, needed restoration. Unfortunately it is now painted in a very strong Marge Simpson yellow which jars with the rest of the cave.

Cave V (Devana Alut Viharaya) The newest, it was once used as a storeroom. The images here are built of brick and plaster and in addition to the Buddha figures, also includes the Hindu deities, Vishnu, Kataragama and Bandara (a local god).

Further reading A Seneviratna, *Golden rock temple of Dambulla*, (Colombo: Sri Lanka Central Cultural Fund, 1983). A good booklet in English and German is on sale, Rs 250.

Around Dambulla

→ *Aukana and Sasseruwa can be visited en route to Anuradhapura, whilst Matale, Aluwihare and Nalanda can be visited on the way from (or to) Kandy.*

Aukana

ⓘ *0700-1900. Rs 150 (includes photography). A few stalls sell drinks.*

One of the island's most elegant and perfect statues, the Aukana Buddha, to the west of the large Kala Wewa Tank, has gained even greater significance to Buddhists since the destruction of the similar (but much larger) statues at Bamiyan in Afghanistan (toponymical research suggests that in ancient times Bamiyan, in the region where Mahayana Buddhism originated, was known as Vokkana or Avakana). Here is a magnificent, undamaged 12-m high free-standing statue of the *Abhayamudra*

Buddha, showing superhuman qualities, carved out of a single rock. The right hand is raised toward the right shoulder with the palm spread, signifying a lack of fear, while the position of the left draws the worshipper to Buddha for release from earthly bonds. It has been ascribed to King Dhatusena (459-77) who was responsible for the building of several tanks, including the one here. When you walk down to the base, note the small lotus flower in between the Buddha's feet. The carving is so perfectly symmetrical that when it rains the water drops from his nose down to the centre of the 10-cm flower. » *For Sleeping, Eating and other listings, see pages 258-260.*

Sasseruwa → *Colour map 2, grid B3. 13 km west of Aukana. Allow 45 minutes to explore – best visited early in the morning.*

This extensive complex, ⓘ *Rs 150*, has an ancient monastery site with over 100 cave cells, remains of stupas, moonstones and inscriptions, and dates back to the second century BC. Here too, there is a similar standing Buddha framed by the dark rock, though it is either unfinished or lacks the quality of workmanship. It was possibly carved at the same time as Aukana, although some believe it to be a later copy. One legend is that the two images were carved in a competition between master and student. The master's Buddha at Aukana was completed first, so the Sasseruwa statue was abandoned. Its location, halfway up a rocky hillside, requires climbing nearly 300 steps. » *For Sleeping, Eating and other listings, see pages 258-260.*

Nalanda → *Colour map 2, grid B4. 49 km north of Kandy, 19 km south of Dambulla.*

ⓘ *Entrance to the gedige is covered by the Cultural Triangle Ticket. Or US$5 (ISIC and children under 12, US$2.50).*

This small reconstructed *gedige* (Buddha image house) shares some features in common with Hindu temples of southern India. Standing on the raised bund of a reservoir, it was built with stone slabs and originally dates from the seventh to the 10th centuries. Some tantric carvings have been found in the structure which combines Hindu and Buddhist (both Mahayana and Theravada) features. Note the *Karmasutra* bas-relief. It is the only extant Sri Lankan *gedige* built in the architectural style of the seventh-century Pallava shore temples at Mamallapuram near Chennai in India. The place is very atmospheric and has comparatively few visitors, which adds to its appeal. From the rest house where the bus drops visitors off there is a 1 km road, now tarred, leading east to the site. » *For Sleeping, Eating and other listings, see pages 258-260.*

In season, the mangoes available along the route from Kandy to Dambulla are some of the best in the country.

Aluwihare → *Colour map 2, grid C4. 32 km north of Kandy, 36 km south of Dambulla. Lying on a main tourist route, you will continually be asked for donations, which can get tiresome.*

Aluwihare has the renovated ruins of ancient shrines carved out of huge boulders. In the first and second century BC, the site was associated with King Vattagamani Abhaya (103-77 BC). The *Mahavansa* (Buddhist chronicle of the island) was inscribed here in Pali. The original manuscript, inscribed on palm leaves prepared by 500 monks, was destroyed in the mid-19th century, and replacements are still being inscribed today. With the expectation of a Rs 100 'contribution' to the temple (for which you are given a receipt) you are guided first into the small museum, where you will be shown the technique of writing on palmyra palm.

The palmyra palm strips were prepared for manuscripts by drying, boiling and drying again, and then flattened and coated with shell. A stylus was used for inscribing, held stationary while the leaf was moved to produce the lettering or illustration (the rounded shape of some South Asian scripts was a result of this technology). The inscribed grooves would then be rubbed with soot or powdered charcoal while colour was added with a brush. The leaves would then be stacked and sometimes strung together and sometimes 'bound' between decorative wooden 'covers'.

The path up the boulders themselves is quite steep and can be slippery when wet (a newspaper cutting in the museum commemorates how the Duke of Edinburgh "nearly had a nasty fall" during the royal visit in 1956). Four of the 10 caves have ancient inscriptions. The curious 'Chamber of Horrors' has unusual frescoes vividly illustrating punishments doled out to sinners by eager demons, including spearing of the body and pouring of boiling oil into the mouth. The sculptures in another cave show torture on a 'rack' for the wrongdoer and the distress of having one's brains exposed by the skull being cut open. The impressive painted reclining Buddhas include one about 10 m long. The stupa on top of the rock just beyond the cave temples gives fine views of the Dry Zone plains and pine covered mountains. ▸▸ *For Sleeping, Eating and other listings, see pages 258-260.*

Matale → *Phone code: 066. Colour map 2, grid C4. Population: 37,000. 24 km north of Kandy, 44 km south of Dambulla.*

The small but bustling town surrounded by hills has some interesting short walks as well as some longer treks into the Knuckles Range, see page 210. The British built a fort here at the beginning of the 19th century (of which only a gate remains) while the branch railway line opened in 1880. Tour groups often stop at the Sri Muthumariamman Thevasthanam temple here.

A large number of **spice gardens** line the road out of Matale towards Dambulla, as well as plantations of coffee, cocoa and rubber. While most are genuine, some so-called spice gardens which are open to visitors have very few plants and are primarily there to sell commercially grown spices and Ayurvedic herbal products. ▸▸ *For Sleeping, Eating and other listings, see pages 258-260.*

Sleeping

Dambulla *p254, map p255*

L-AL Kandalama (Aitken Spence), *head along Kandalama Rd for 4.5 km, take right fork, follow road, then cinder track for 8 km, T2284100, kandalama@aitkenspence.lk* Winner of many awards including Asia's first Green Globe. 162 plush a/c rooms in 2 wings. Unique design by Geoffrey Bawa, built between massive rock and peaceful tank and indistinguishable from its jungle surrounds. Resort style complex (at 968 m Sri Lanka's longest hotel!) with excellent cuisine and full facilities, 3 pools including one of the most spectacularly sited swimming pools in the world with crystal clear water (filtration system based on ancient Sri Lankan technology). Magnificent views across undisturbed forest, magical details, exceptional service.

A Culture Club Resort, *follow Kandalama Rd for 4.5 km, take left fork, then follow lake around for 4.6 km, T2231822, F2231932, cdchm@sltnet.lk* 92 very attractive, comfortable split-level a/c chalets with a village theme, many local touches (village drum beat beckons you to breakfast, flute and singing serenade at sundown), good pool in large gardens, restaurant, Ayurvedic health centre, very attractive setting on edge of lake, bullock cart trips, very relaxing.

C Gimanhala Transit, *754 Anuradhapura Rd, 1 km north of Colombo Junction, T2284864, F2284817, gimanhala@sltnet.lk* 17 comfortable, clean a/c rooms, upstairs with hot water, good restaurant overlooking lovely large and very clean pool (non-residents Rs 150), pleasant grounds with deer and friendly horse, bar, free bike hire, branch of Sri Lankan Airlines here. Best of the town hotels, good value.

C Pelwehera Village, *Bullagala Junction, 3 km northeast of Dambulla, T2284281*. 10 rather bare but spotless rooms (US$30, plus extra US$5 for a/c), hot water, excellent food, good service.

E Sunray Inn, *156 Kandy Rd,T2284769.* 7 clean rooms, 5 with veranda, good restaurant, bar, friendly management.

F Chamara Tourist Inn, *121 Matale/Kandy Rd, T2284488.* 7 simple, moderately clean rooms (Rs 750), nets, fan, bath, restaurant, pleasant communal terrace, relaxed.

G Freddy's Holiday Inn, *62 Missaka Rd, opposite Police Station, T2284780.* Clean, basic rooms (Rs 500), friendly owners, not bad value.

G Little Dream, close to tank along road to **Culture Club**, *T072-893736*. 5 simple rooms (Rs 300-400), cheaper with squat lavatory in peaceful, laid-back spot (Bob Marley, hammocks) close to Kandalama tank with swimming hole nearby. No electricity or hot water and concerns have been raised over its safety for female travellers.
G Oasis Tourist Welfare Centre, *T2284388*. Friendly and homely though very basic. 6 dark rooms (Rs 350), with one shared bathroom you won't want to spend much time in, herbal massage and bath.

Around Dambulla *p256*
D Clover Grange, *95 Kings St, Matale, 500 m north of bus station, T2231144, F2230406*. 6 large, well-furnished comfortable rooms with bath tubs (Rs 1,200), good restaurant, back from main road in pleasant garden, friendly and knowledgeable owner can advise on walking and trekking in the area.
D Country Side Restaurant and Holiday Cottages, *2 km south of gedige, Nalanda, T2246241, sanjeewar@yahoo.com* Popular lunch stop, 20 fairly clean cottages with fan in attractive spice garden (Rs 1,500 with breakfast), peaceful spot.
E Rest House, *Park Rd, at crossroads south of town centre, Matale,, T2222299, F2232911, thilanka@ids.lk* Now privately owned by **Thilanka** in Kandy, 14 clean, spacious rooms with balcony (Rs 1,000), plus one with a/c and TV, friendly and efficient.
F Rest House, *1.5 km from the gedige, Nalanda, T2246199*. Old rest house in good position, 5 basic rooms (Rs 600) with clean attached bath.

Eating

Dambulla *p254, map p255*
For further options see Sleeping, p258.
RsRs Dambulla Rest House, *Matale/Kandy Rd, T2284488*, good lunchtime rice and curry for Rs 300-350. Also **D** rooms available.
Rs Eco-Lodge, *Matale/Kandy Rd, 500 m south of site entrance, T/F2284803*. Good food (curry, Chinese) in open-air restaurant, friendly. Some small basic rooms.

Around Dambulla *p256*
The roadside places on the Kandy-Dambulla road in Aluwihare usually serve a limited selection of bland westernized food for the tour groups on the way up from Kandy.
RsRs Aluwihare Kitchens, *The Walauwe, 33 Aluwihare, T2222404*. This is the exception to the above. For parties of 6 or more is the promise of 'the biggest rice and curry in Sri Lanka' (25 separate curries). Superb location next to the home of Ena de Silva (see Shopping, below) with stunning views of the surrounding countryside. Booking essential.

Shopping

Dambulla *p254, map p255*
Branch of the **Buddhist Bookshop** in the new Buddhist museum complex.

Around Dambulla *p256*
Matale Heritage Centre, *The Walauwe, 33 Aluwihare, 2 km north of Matale, T2222404*. This community-based enterprise, the brainchild of renowned designer Ena de Silva, is a rewarding stop for those with a serious interest in tapestries, batiks, furniture and brassware. Much of the work is used by architects such as Geoffrey Bawa (see p367). Phone in advance.

Tour operators

Dambulla *p254, map p255*
Robert Gunasekara, *T2285263*, (or ask at **Sunray Inn**), has been recommended as a driver for ancient cities tours. He speaks English, French and German.

Transport

Dambulla *p254, map p255*
Air Sri Lankan Airlines, *at Gimonhale Transit, T2285444*.
Bus A new bus stand is under construction. Most long-distance buses stop at Colombo Junction, about 2 km north of the cave site. Local buses run to the site entrance, as do Kandy buses. Regular services from **Colombo** (4 hrs), **Anuradhapura**, **Kandy** and **Polonnaruwa** (about 2½ hrs each) and frequently to/from **Sigiriya** (30 mins).

Around Dambulla *p256*
To reach **Sasseruwa** you will need your own transport. The minor road from Aukana continues to the Sasseruwa via Negampaha. The surface is poor.

Bus To **Aukana** from Dambulla, there are occasional direct buses. More practical may be to take a bus to **Kekirawa** (45 mins, Rs 12), and change on to a Galnewa bus, getting off at Aukana Junction (Rs 15). From here it is a 500-m walk to the site. From Anuradhapura, buses to **Kekirawa** take 1½ hrs (Rs 20). You will need to take your own transport from Habarana.
There are frequent buses to **Nalanda** that run between Dambulla and Kandy stopping near the turn off opposite the rest house.
To **Aluwihare** buses run between Matale and Dambulla and stop on the main road – the caves are on the westside.
To get to **Matale** from Kandy no 636 runs every 15 mins (non-stop, Rs 25, CTB Rs 10.50). From Dambulla it costs Rs 40 (CTB Rs 11.50).
Train Stop at **Aukana** which lies on the Colombo-Batticaloa line but they stop more frequently at **Kala Wewa** (8 km from the site), where a 3- wheeler will charge Rs 300 to 'go and come'.
Matale's railway station, in the centre of town 100 m east of the A9, is the terminus of a branch line from **Kandy**. Several slow trains run daily (Rs 6, 1½ hrs).
Three-wheeler From Matale to Aluwihare it costs Rs 50.

Directory

Dambulla *p254, map p255*
Banks Trading at the 24-hr dedicated economic centre, north of the temple complex, means that banks have longer hours than usual. Plenty of banks with ATMs in town: **Commercial Bank**, **Hatton National Bank**, **Seylan Bank** and **Bank of Ceylon**.
Communications **Golden Temple**, very expensive internet, Rs 100 for first 15 mins, then Rs 10 per min, open 0730-2330. Several IDD places near Colombo Junction.
Medical centre Opposite **Commercial Bank**, *T2284735.*
Useful addresses **Police**, *Missaka Rd.*

Around Dambulla *p256*
Banks There are branches of all the main banks in Matale town.

Anuradhapura and Mihintale

→ *Phone code: 025. Colour map 2, grid A3/4. Population: 58,000.*

Anuradhapura is Sri Lanka's most sacred city. Along with Mihintale, it represents the first real home of Buddhism in Sri Lanka, and thus contains some of the island's most sacred Buddhist sites. It is here that the Sri Maha Bodhi tree was planted from a cutting from the original Bo under which the Buddha received Enlightenment, to this day drawing thousands of pilgrims from around the world. Today, Anuradhapura's ruins and monuments are widely scattered which makes a thorough tour exhausting and time-consuming, but for those with more than a passing interest in the island's past it more than repays the effort. Nearby Mihintale, where King Tissa received the Emperor Asoka's son Mahinda and converted to Buddhism, makes an excellent day-trip away from the bustle and noise, and can even be used as an alternative base. ▸▸ *For Sleeping, Eating and other listings, see pages 272-274.*

Ins and outs

Getting there

Anuradhapura's airport is 4 km south east of town, though flights had not resumed at the time of writing. Many visitors arrive from Dambulla to the southeast, along the A9/A13. Others come from Colombo via Kurunegala and Yapahuwa (see page 112), though the quickest route from the capital is along the A12 from Puttalam (see page 109). From Trincomalee, the route is via Horowupatana giving you the opportunity to visit Mihintale first. Anuradhapura and Mihintale are also now accessible from the north, from Jaffna via Vavuniya (see page 324). Buses are available in all directions. By train, Anuradhapura lies on the Northern line, and all trains between Colombo and Vavuniya stop here. From Kandy, you need to change at Polgahawela. Mihintale, 11 km east of Anuradhapura, is a short bus or cycle ride east from the city.

Getting around → *A high police presence remains in Anuradhapura, following damage in a 1998 LTTE attack.*

A three-wheeler from the train or bus station to your accommodation, assuming you are staying in the New Town, should cost around Rs 50. The New Town is about 2 km southeast of the central sites. If you want a full day tour, consider hiring a car or three-wheeler since the ruins, especially to the north, are very spread out and without cover can be exhausting under a hot sun. Many people use a bicycle (available from guesthouses) to get around but you should be prepared to park it and walk when told to. Bear in mind also that unless you follow a prescribed route (and even if you do!) it is easy to get lost, as there are many confusing tracks and signposting can be poor. Unlike Polonnaruwa, the monuments are not clustered into convenient groups so planning an itinerary can be difficult. The order of sites below follows a 'figure-of-eight' pattern, starting in the central area, then heading 3 km north and then east to Kuttan-Pokuna, before returning south to the Jetavanarama *dagoba*, and looping across to explore the museums and lakeside monuments south of the central area.

Best time to visit

There are several festivals during the year. In April, *Snana puja* at Sri Maha Bodhi. In June, at the full moon in Poson, the introduction of Buddhism to Sri Lanka is celebrated with huge processions when many pilgrims visit the area. In July-August, during *Daramiti Perahera*, locals bring firewood in a procession to the Bodhi tree, commemorating a time when bonfires were lit to keep away wild animals.

Tourist information

Anuradhapura tourist information office, *T2224546, 0900-1700 (till 1300 Sat, closed Sun)*, has moved from the New Town to a more central site on Sri Maha Bodhi Mawatha, the best approach road to the ancient city. Here you can pick up a local map and planning advice. There are four ticket offices: one at the Tourist Information Counter, another at the Archaeological Museum, a third at the Jetavanarama Museum, and finally one towards the Dalada Maligawa. The site is covered by the 'Cultural Triangle Round Ticket' (US$32.50, see page 35) though it does not cover all sights in the city. A single ticket for the main site costs US$15 (half-price for children). It is worth getting a guide: Rs 300-400 for three to four hours should suffice. There are lots of drink stalls around; the ones near the *dagobas* tend to be expensive. The souvenir sellers can be very persistent and unpleasant, so be firm. Mihintale is not covered by the Round Ticket; there is a Rs 250 charge for visiting the sacred centre.

Anuradhapura → *Allow a full day to explore the area.*

History

From origins as a settlement in the sixth century BC, Anuradhapura was made Sri Lanka's first capital in 377 BC by King Pandukhabhaya (437-367 BC) who started the great irrigation works on which it depended, and named it after the constellation Anuradha. The first era of religious building followed the conversion of King Devanampiya Tissa (ruled 250-10 BC). In his 40-year reign these included the Thuparama Dagoba, Issurumuniyagala, and the Maha Vihara with the Sri Maha Bodhi and the Brazen Palace. A branch of the Bodhi tree (see below) under which the Buddha was believed to have gained his Enlightenment was brought from Bodhgaya in India and successfully transplanted. It is one of the holiest Buddhist sites in the world.

Anuradhapura remained a capital city until the ninth century AD, when it reached its peak of power and vigour. At this time it may have stretched 25 km. Successive waves of invasion from South India however finally took their toll. After the 13th century it almost entirely disappeared, the irrigation works on which it had depended falling into total disuse, and its political functions were taken over first by Polonnaruwa, and then by capitals to the south. 'Rediscovered' by Ralph Backhaus, archaeological research, excavation and restoration was started in 1872, and has continued ever since. In 1988, it was designated a World Heritage Site. The New Town was started in the 1950s, and is now the most important Sinhalese city of the north. It houses the headquarters of the Sri Lanka Archaeological Survey.

Approach

Anuradhapura rivals Milton Keynes for its roundabouts. If you are staying in the New Town, the best approach to the ancient city is to cycle northwest across Main Street and the railway line, to Jayanthi Mawatha where you turn right, past the two rest houses, up to **Lion Pillar**. Here you turn left on to Sri Maha Bodhi Mawatha, continue past the Tourist Information Office (where you can pick up a ticket if necessary) up to the barrier, beyond which the road leads to the **Sri Maha Bodhi**. You are not allowed to cycle past this point, and you will be asked to park your bike in the car park (*Rs* 5!). Don't do this, as you will leave yourself with a long walk back from the central area to pick up your bike, though there are sometimes buses. Instead, continue past the car park for almost 1 km, heading up Nandana Mawatha (or path) towards the huge white **Ruvanwelisiya Dagoba**. Here you can park your bike (for free) close to the central area. There is a wide pedestrian walkway which leads from the *dagoba* to the Sri Maha Bodhi.

Ruvanwelisiya Dagoba

Begun by King Dutthagamenu (Dutugemunu) to house relics, this is one of the most impressive of all Sri Lanka's *dagobas*. Built with remarkable opulence, the king, who was said to have great luck, found a rich vein of silver from Ridigama to cover the expenses. Monks from as far away as Alexandria were recorded as being present at the enshrinement of the relics in 140 BC. The king however fell ill before the *dagoba*'s completion, so he asked his brother Saddhatissa to complete the work for him. Saddhatissa covered the dome with bamboo reeds and painted them with lacquer and imitation gold so that the king could witness the 'completion' of his magnum opus on his deathbed. Today, the dome is 80 m in diameter at its base and 53 m high. Apart from its sheer size, you will notice first the frieze on the outer wall of hundreds of life-size (and life-like) elephants, most of which are modern replacements. The *dagoba* is surrounded by the remains of sculptural pieces. You can see the columns often no more than 500 cm in height dotted around in the grass underneath huge rain trees where monkeys play. A small passage leads to the relic chamber. At the cardinal points are four 'chapels' which were reconstructed in 1873, when renovation started. The restoration has flattened the shape of the dome, and some of the painting is of questionable style, but it remains a remarkably striking monument. Today, you may find watching the *dagoba* being 'whitewashed' an interesting spectacle.

Brazen Palace

ⓘ *The site is open only on Poya Day.*

Follow the pedestrian walkway south towards to the Sri Maha Bodhi. Just before reaching the tree, you will see the many pillars of the Brazen Palace on your left. The name refers to the first monastery here and its now-disappeared roof, reputedly made of bronze. Built originally by Dutthagamenu, it was the heart of the monastic life of the city, the Maha Vihara. Described in the *Mahavansa* as having nine storeys, there were

White lines

The ubiquitous *dagoba* is one of the most striking features of the island, ranging in size from tiny village structures to the enormous monuments at Ruvanwelisiya in Anuradhapura and Mahaseya at Mihintale. Even in nature the stone of the canonball tree fruit is a perfectly formed white *dagoba*.

There are of course many reasons why they stand out in a landscape – partly for their position, partly their size but mostly for their colour – a dazzling white. Most are beautifully maintained and are often repainted before important Buddhist festivals.

It is no easy job to paint a large *dagoba*. A lime whitewash is used. Elaborate bamboo scaffolding cocoons the spire linked to the base by rickety bamboo ladders. Bamboo is ideal as it can be bent to conform to the shape of the dome and the lightness makes the ladders easily moveable. A team of about five painters assembles on the ladder which is about 20 m in height. Four men are deployed with ropes attached at the top and midpoints to give it some form of stability. At each stage, a painter is responsible for about 3 m of the surface in height, and an arm's width. The topmost 1.5 m of the painter's patch is covered first. Then he takes three steps down the ladder to cover the bottom 1.5 m. Once completed, the bamboo structure is moved an arm's width round and the whole process starts again.

You'll notice that not all the *dagobas* have yet been restored – their red brick or plain plastered surface are dull in comparison with those that have been returned to their original condition.

1,600 pillars, each just under 4 m high, laid out over an area 70 sq m. Above, each storey was supposed to have 100 windows, with 1,000 rooms overall, the building adorned with coral and precious stones. This requires imagination these days, though now a wooden first floor has been erected, aiming to recreate the monastery's top storey. Originally destroyed by Indian invasion, the monastery was rebuilt several times, much of what is visible today being the reconstruction of King Parakramabahu I in the last quarter of the 11th century, making use of the remnants of former buildings.

Sri Maha Bodhi tree → *This is one of Sri Lanka's most sacred sites.*

ⓘ *Rs 50. Shoes must be removed on entering the terrace – there is a booth at the eastern entrance.*

The 'Bo' ('Bodhi') tree or Pipal (*Ficus religiosa*) was planted as a cutting brought from the tree in Bodhgaya in India under which Buddha found Enlightenment, brought by Emperor Asoka's daughter, the Princess Sanghamitta, at some point after 236 BC. Guardians have kept uninterrupted watch over the tree ever since, making it, all tourist literature will proudly tell you, the oldest historically authenticated tree in the world. Today, in keeping with tradition, it is the Army who guard the tree, while the Director of the Peradeniya Botanical Gardens tends to its health. Nowadays, you can only see the top of the Bo tree, on the highest terrace, which is supported by an elaborate metal structure and is surrounded by brass railings. There are other Bo trees around the Sri Maha Bodhi which are bedecked with colourful prayer flags and smaller strips of cloth which pilgrims tie in expectation of prayers being answered. In April a large number of pilgrims arrive to make offerings during the *Snana puja*, and to bathe the tree with milk. Every 12th year the ceremony is particularly auspicious.

Archaeological and Folk museums

This is convenient place to visit these two museums which are both worth taking a look around. The **Archaeological Museum,** ⓘ *0800-1700, closed Tue and public holidays*, is in the old colonial headquarters. It is an excellent small museum, with a

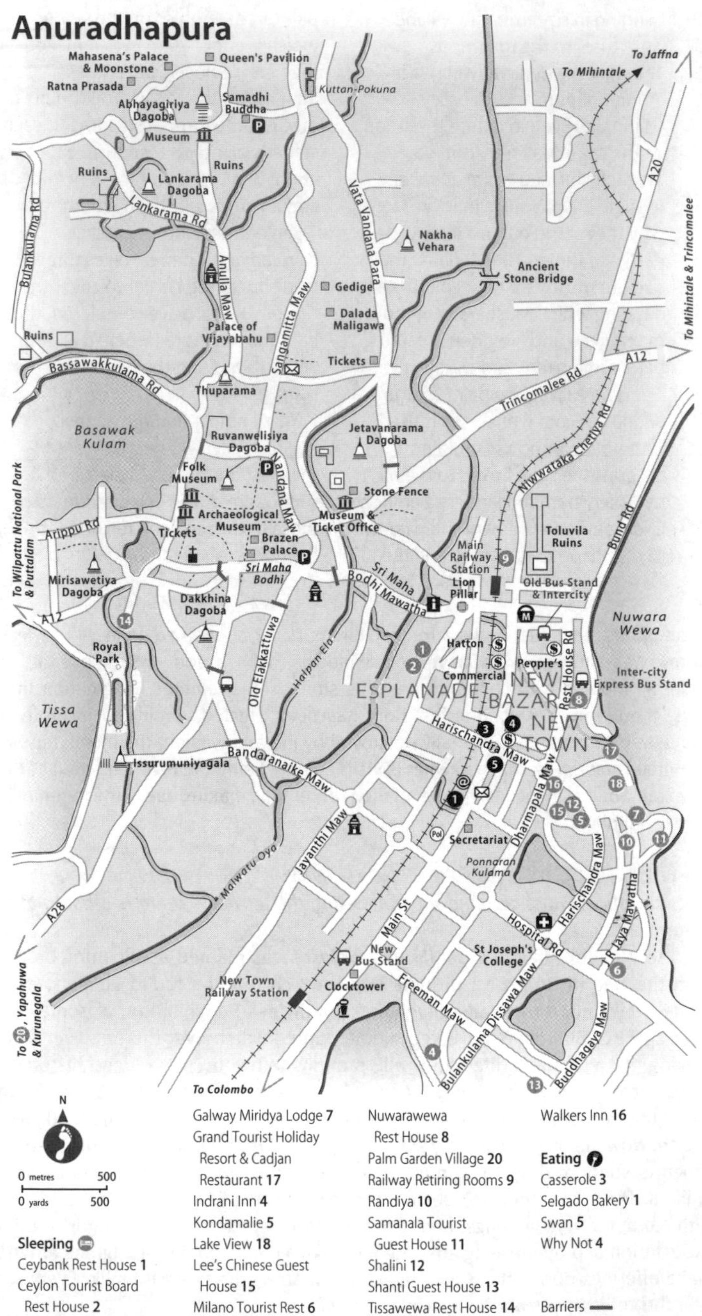

Five of the best sites not to miss in Anuradhapura

Sri Maha Bodhi – one of the holiest trees in the world.
Ruvanwelisiya dagoba – impressive *dagoba* with elephant wall.
Samadhi Buddha – serene statue beloved by Jawarhalal Nehru.
Jetavananarama dagoba – simply enormous!
Issurumuniyagala – bats, reclining Buddha and 'the lovers'.

large collection from all over the island, Including some beautiful pieces of sculpture and finds from Mihintale. It is well laid out, with occasional informative labels and some fascinating exhibits. There are statues from several sites, moonstones, implements, and a model of Thuparama *vatadage*. Outside in the garden, there are beautifully sculpted guard stones and an array of meticulously designed latrines. Separate latrine plinths were used for urinals, solid waste and bidets. Under each immaculately carved platform was a succession of pots containing sand, charcoal and limestone to purify the waste.

The **Folk Museum**, n *0900-1700, closed Thu, Fri. Rs 40, camera Rs 135 (not strictly enforced)*, nearby, is a collection that reflects rural life in the North Central Province with a large display of vessels used by villagers in Rajarata, and handicrafts.

Thuparama

Return to the Ruvanswelisiya *dagoba* to pick up your bike. Continuing north, turn left at the crossroads to the site's oldest *dagoba*, said to house the right collar-bone of the Buddha. Built by Devanampiya, the 19-m high *dagoba* was originally in the shape of a 'paddy-heap' – its beautiful bell shape dates to renovation work completed in 1862. It is surrounded by concentric circles of graceful granite monolithic pillars of a *vatadage* which was added in the seventh century, possibly originally designed to support an over-arching thatched cover. It is a centre of active pilgrimage, decorated with flags and lights.

Abhayagiriya Dagoba

Left from the first crossroads, 2 km north along Anulla Mawatha to the Abhagiriya Dagoba. First, a detour to the west takes you to the restored **Lankarama Dagoba**. Built in the first century BC it bears some similarities to the earlier Thuparama. Some columns remain of its *vatadage*.

The Abhayagiriya Dagoba was the centre of one of Anuradhapura's largest and oldest monastic complexes. It is 400 m round and was supposedly 135 m high in its original form (part of the pinnacle has disappeared). It is now about 110 m high. Built in 88 BC by Vattagamani (and later restored by Parakramabahu I in the 12th century), it has two splendid sculpted *dwarapalas* (guardians) at the threshold. The *dagoba* and its associated monastery were built in an attempt to weaken the political hold of the Hinayana Buddhists and to give shelter to monks of the Mahayana school. It was considered an important seat of Buddhist learning and the Chinese traveller/monk Fa Hien, visiting it in the fifth century, noted that there were 5,000 monks in residence. He also points out a 7-m jade Buddha, sparkling with gems, while the *dagoba* itself was said to have been built over a Buddha footprint.

Abhayagiriya (Fa Hien) Museum

Abhayagiriya (Fa Hien) Museum, just south of the Abhayagiriya Dagoba, was built by the Chinese. The collection includes further examples of latrine plinths as displayed in the Archaeological Museum. There is also an extensive display detailing the excavation of the Abhayagiriya site.

Ratna Prasada

To the west of the Abhayagiriya Dagoba are the ruins of the monastery. The area had once been the 'undesirable' outskirts of Anuradhapura where the cremation grounds were sited. In protest against the King's rule, an ascetic community of monks set up a *tapovana* community (see box) of which this is an architectural example. This type of monastery typically had two pavilions connected by a stone bridge within a high-walled enclosure which contained a pond. The main entrance was from the east, with a porch above the entrance. Here the Ratna Prasada, or 'gem palace', did not remain a peaceful haven but was the scene of bloody massacres when a rebellious group took refuge with the monks and were subsequently beheaded by the King's men. Their turn to have their heads roll in the dust followed another bloody revolt.

Mahasena Palace

The nearby Mahasena Palace has a particularly fine carved stone tablet and one of the most beautifully carved **moonstones**, see page 365, though the necessary protective railing surrounding it makes photography a little tricky. Note also the flight of steps held up by miniature stone dwarfs! You can return to the Archaeological museum by taking the Lankarama Road to the south.

Samadhi Buddha

Continue east from the Abhayagiriya Dagoba to this superb statue of the serene Buddha, probably dating from the fourth century AD. With an expression depicting 'extinction of feeling and compassion', some used to think the expression changes as the sun's light moves across it. Sadly though it has now been roofed to protect it from the weather.

Kuttan-Pokuna

A new road through the forest leads to these two ponds – recently restored eighth and ninth-century ritual baths with steps from each side descending to the water. They were probably for the use of the monastery or for the university nearby. Though called 'twin' ponds, one is over 10 m longer than the other. You can see the underground water supply channel at one end of the second bath.

South to Jetavaranama Dagoba

There are two routes south from here. Sangamitta Mawatha leads back to the central area through the site of the 11th-century palace of **Vijayabahu I**, and close to the original **Dalada Maligawa** where the Tooth Relic was first enshrined when it was brought to Ceylon in AD 313. Only the stone columns remain. Alternatively, a 2-km cycle down Vata Vandana Para takes you straight to the vast Jetavanarama Dagoba.

Jetavanarama Dagoba

This *dagoba*, looming impressively from the plain, is said to be the highest brick-built *dagoba* of its kind in the world. Started by King Mahasena (AD 275-92), its massive scale was designed in a competitive spirit to rival the orthodox Maha Vihara. The paved platform on which it stands covers more than 3 ha and it has a diameter of over 100 m. In 1860 Emerson Tennent, in his book *Ceylon*, calculated that it had enough bricks to build a 3-m high brick wall 25 cm thick from London to Edinburgh, equal to the distance from the southern tip of Sri Lanka to Jaffna and back down the coast to Trincomalee. The *dagoba* is being renovated with help from UNESCO, though work periodically stops as there is a dearth of bricks!

The size of the image house here shows that Mahasena had an enormous Buddha image, similar to (though larger than) the one at Aukana, installed here facing the *dagoba*. There is a huge lotus pedestal, with large mortices for the feet of the statue. The image would have been destroyed by fire.

Forest finery

The *Pansukulika* or *Tapovana* sect of ascetic Buddhist hermits who lived a simple life of deep meditation in forests and caves around the seventh to the 11th centuries are associated with Arankale, Mihintale and Ritigala. The monks were expected to wear ragged clothing and to immerse themselves in seeking the Truth, devoid of ritualistic forms of worship associated with Buddha images, relics and relic chambers. Such communities often won the admiration and support of Kings, such as Sena I (831-51).

The sites had certain features in common. There was a porched entrance, ambulatories, a water pool for cleansing and the *padhanag-hara*. Another similarity was an open terrace, possibly intended as a 'chapter house' connected to a smaller section which was usually roofed. These 'double platforms' were aligned east to west; the two raised stone-faced platforms were connected by a narrow walkway or bridge. An interesting contradiction of the austere life was the beautifully carved latrines or urinal stones the monks used, examples of which can be seen in the Anuradhapura Archaeological Museum, see page 264.

Jetavanarama Museum

This museum, well worth a visit, houses some interesting objects from the surrounding 300-acre site, including some fine guardstones and an amazingly intricate 8 mm gold chain with 14 distinguishable flowers. Udaya Prasad Cabra is a helpful and knowledgeable Information Officer who will show you around the museum for no fee.

To the lakeside monuments

Continuing west across the main site towards Tissawewa, you might visit the Archaeological and Folk museums at this point. West of here is the **Basawak Kulam Tank**, the oldest artificial lake in the city, built by King Pandukabhaya in the fourth century BC. The dried-up southern side is good for walks and bird-watching, and there are excellent sunset views from the eastern shore.

Alternatively, head south to stop off for lunch or a drink at the Nuwarawewa Rest House. The Miraswetiya Dagoba is close by.

Mirisawetiya Dagoba

This was the first monument to be built by Dutthagemunu after his consecration, enshrining a miraculous sceptre which contained a Buddha relic. The sceptre which had been left here by the king when he visited the tank, could not on his return be removed by any means. After a Chola invasion, the *dagoba* was completely rebuilt during the reign of King Kasyapa V in 930 AD. Surrounded by the ruins of monasteries on three sides, there are some superb sculptures of *Dhyani* Buddhas in the shrines of its chapels.

Tissawewa and Royal Park

This tank was built by King Devanampiya Tissa, and was associated with the bathing rituals of newly crowned kings. You can walk/jog on the east and south sides along the raised tank bund and continue all round using local tracks on the west and a tarmac road on the north. The park just below the lake is very pleasant as it has few visitors. You can wander undisturbed across large rocks among ruined buildings and remains of bathing pools.

Issurumuniyagala Monastery

ⓘ *0800-1930. Rs 100. Ask for permission to take photos.*

This small group of striking black rocks is one of the most attractive and peaceful places in town. It also has some outstanding sculpture. The temple, carved out of solid rock, houses a large statue of the reclining Buddha. There is a cleft in the rock which is full of bats which are fascinating to watch. On the terraces outside is a small square pool. Don't miss the beautifully carved elephants, showing great individual character, just above the water level as if descending to it. The small **museum** is to the left of the entrance. Some of the best sculptures in Anuradhapura are now housed here, including perhaps the most famous of all – 'the lovers', which may represent Dutthagemunu's son Saliya and his girlfriend Asokamala, for whom he forsook the throne.

Behind the temple, you can climb up steps to the top of the rock above the temple to get a good view of the countryside and tank. Here there is a footprint carved into the rock, into which money is thrown.

Nuwara Wewa

Nuwara Wewa, which lies to the east of the New Town, is the largest of Anuradhapura's artificial lakes (1,000 ha). It was probably built by Gajabahu I in the second century AD.

Mihintale

→ *Colour map 2, grid A3. 11 km east of Anuradhapura.*

Mihintale (pronounced Mihin-taalay), named as Mahinda's Hill, is revered as the place where Mahinda converted King Devanampiya Tissa to Buddhism in 243 BC, thereby enabling Buddhism to spread to the whole island. The legend tells how King Tissa was chasing a stag during a hunting expedition. The stag reached Mihintale and fled up the hillside followed by the King until he reached a place surrounded by hills, where the animal disappeared and the frustrated King was astonished to find a gentle person who spoke to him the Buddha's teachings. It was Mahinda, Asoka's son, who had come to preach Buddhism and was able to convert the King with 40,000 followers. As well as being important historically, it is an important religious site and is well worth visiting as it is a pleasant place to just stroll around away from the crowds at the more famous ancient sites. Mihintale town is little more than a junction and a few shops. It is however an important centre for pilgrims during the June festival. » *For Sleeping, Eating and other listings, see pages 272-274.*

Approach

→ *If visiting in the heat of the day it is worth bringing socks to protect your feet against the hot floor.*

Mihintale is close to the Anuradhapura-Trincomalee Road. The huge *dagoba* can be seen from miles around, and is especially striking at night. At the junction with the village road, where you turn off for the main site, there are statues of six of the principal characters of the site. Follow the minor road leading to the site. On the right are the ruins of a ninth-century **hospital**, which appears to have had an outer court where medicines were ground and stored, and stone tanks for oil and herbal baths. The inner court appears to have had small treatment rooms. A 10th-century stone inscription mentions the use of leeches in treatment. There is a small archaeological museum nearby (see below).

On the left at the foot of the steps, there is evidence of the **quincunx vihara** of a monastery (*arama*). You can avoid about half of the steps by driving round to the upper car park, which takes you straight to the second (refectory) level.

The Climb

There are about 1,840 granite **steps**, some carved into the rock, to the top but they are very shallow and it is much less of a climb than it first looks. The width of the steps indicate the large number of pilgrims who visited the sacred site on special occasions in the past. The climb starts gently, rising in a broad stairway of 350 steps shaded by frangipani trees which lead to the first platform. Further steps to the right take you up to an open area with Kantaka Chetiya.

The first terrace

Kantaka Chetiya is the earliest *stupa* here. Excavated in 1932-35, it had been severely damaged. Over 130 m in circumference, today it is only about 12m high compared with its original height of perhaps 30 m. There is some unique stonework in the four projecting frontispieces at the cardinal points, especially to the eastern and southern points. Note the marvellously detailed friezes of geese, dwarves and a variety of other animals, flanked by *stelae* with floral designs. Around the Kantaka Chetiya are 68 caves, where the first monks here resided.

Returning to the first platform, steeper steps lead to a large refectory terrace. As you climb up (it takes under 10 minutes from the car park, at a gentle pace) you can see the impressive outer cyclopean wall of the complex. As an alternative to the steps to get to the refectory level, take a faint footpath to the left between the second and third flights. This crosses an open grassy area. Walk to the end and you will see the lake, green with algae. A path to the left takes you towards the Giribandhu Chetiya Kiri Vehara, though it is largely ruined and grassed over on the north side. You can look down on the lower car park and the quincunx. To the right, the path approaches the refectory from the rear and you pass a massive stone trough.

The second terrace

The Refectory Immediately on the left is the **Relic House** and the rectangular **Bhojana Salava** (Monks' refectory). There is a stone aqueduct and two granite troughs, one probably used for rice, the other for gruel. The square **Chapter**

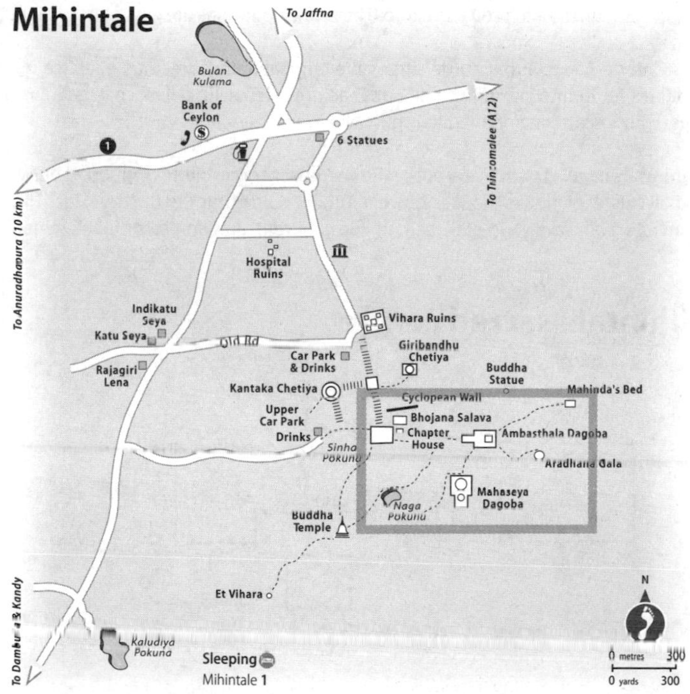

 House/'Conversation Hall' with signs of 48 pillars and a 'throne' platform, immediately to the north, is where the monks and lay members met. This has the bases of a series of evenly spaced small brick *dagobas*. At the entrance, stone slabs covered in 10th-century inscriptions on granite give detailed rules governing the sacred site.

The flat grassy terrace which can also be approached by car from the south up the old paved road or steps down from the Kantaka Chetiya, is dotted with trees and the outlines of three small shrines.

Sinha Pokuna (Lion Bath) To the west of the terrace, a short distance down the old road, this is about 2 m sq and 1.8 m deep and has excellent carvings in the form of a frieze around the bottom of the tank of elephants, lions and warriors. The finest, however, is the 2 m high rampant lion whose mouth forms the spout. Water was gathered in the tank by channelling and feeding it through the small mystic gargoyle similar to the one that can be seen at Sigiriya.

The main path up to the Ambasthala Dagoba up the long flight of steps starts by the 'Conversation Hall' in the square. After a five-minute climb a path leads off to the right, round the hillside, to the Naga Pokuna, which you can visit on the way back down (see below). Continuing to climb, you pass a beautifully inscribed rock on the right hand side listing in second-century AD script lands owned by the king.

The sacred centre → *Rs 250, plus tip for shoes.*

Ambasthala Dagoba At the top of the steps, you come to the ticket office, where you must leave your shoes (and hat). Straight ahead at the heart of the complex is the 'mango tree' *dagoba*, the holiest part of the site, built at the traditional meeting place of King Tissa and Asoka's son Mahinda. The monk in his office makes frequent loud-speaker announcements for donations from pilgrims – these donations have funded the erection of a large white Buddha statue on a rock overlooking the central area in 1991, up to which you can climb. The bronze Buddhas are gifts from Thailand.

Sela Cetiya A rock stupa at the site of the original mango tree has a replica of the Buddha's footprint. It is quite small and is surrounded a gilt railing covered in prayer flags, with a scattering of pilgrims' coins.

Mahinda's cave A path leads out of the northeast corner of the compound between a small cluster of monks' houses down a rough boulder track to the cave, less than a 10-minute walk away. A stall selling local herbal and forest product remedies

Mihintale sacred centre

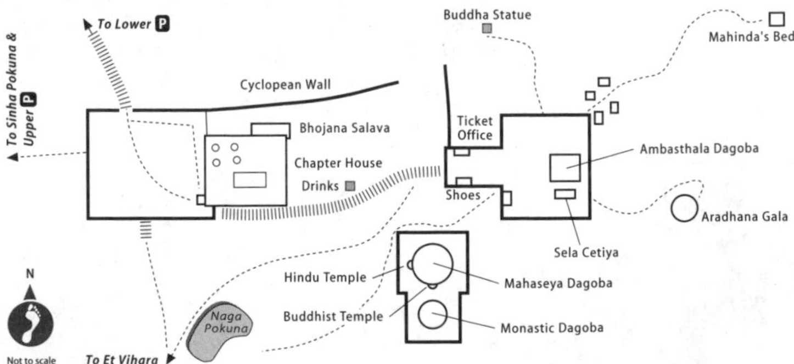

(including 'a cure for arrack!') is sometimes set up halfway. The cave is formed out of an extraordinary boulder, hollowed out underneath to create a narrow platform at the very end of a ridge above the plain below. From the stone 'couch', known as **Mahinda's bed**, there are superb views to the north across the tanks and forested plains of the Dry Zone. You have to retrace your steps to the Ambasthala compound.

Aradhana Gala From the southeast corner of the compound a path with rudimentary steps cut in the bare granite rock leads to the summit of the Aradhana Gala (Meditation Rock). It is a very steep climb, and if you have no socks, very hot on the feet. A strong railing makes access quite secure. There is nothing much to see on the rock but there are superb views from the top, especially across the compound to the Mahaseya Dagoba, which is at the same height.

Mahaseya dagoba A short flight of steep steps from the southwest corner of the compound, just beyond a small temple with a modern portrayal of Mahinda meeting King Tissa at the mango tree, leads up to the summit (310 m) with the Mahaseya Dagoba. According to legend this was built on the orders of King Tissa as a reliquary for a lock of the Buddha's hair or for relics of Mahinda. The renovated *dagoba*, which dominates the skyline, commands superb views back towards Anuradhapura to the southwest. Another monk may ask for donations here (anything above Rs 100 is recorded in a book).

On the south side of the main *dagoba* is a smaller brick *dagoba* while abutting it on its south side is a small Buddhist temple. To the west side is a Hindu temple with modern painted images of four Hindu deities *Ganesh*, *Saman*, *Vishnu* and *Kataragama*.

Descent

Naga Pokuna After collecting your shoes, and immediately below the rock inscription (see above) is a small path which leads through cool forest to the Naga Pokuna. This 'Snake Pond', which has a five-headed cobra carving which you can still make out, is a 40 m pool carved out of solid rock which stored water for the monastery and, some believe, is where King Tissa would have bathed. At one end is a very small tank, now without water. Apparently this was where the Queen would bathe. It is a peaceful and beautiful place.

Et Vihara If you still have energy, a flight of 600 steps from the Naga Pokuna leads up to this inner temple, at the highest elevation in Mihintale. Though the small stupa is not very impressive, there are some magnificent views from here.

After descending and exiting the main complex, head west to the Kandy Road (accessible from either car park). Close to the junction are the remains of a monastery complex with two *dagobas*, of which the **Indikatu Seya** on a raised stone square platform to the north, is the larger. It shows evidence that the monks were devotees of Mahayan Buddhism in the ninth century. South of here, inscriptions in the **Rajagiri Lena** (Royal Rock Caves) suggest that they may represent the first living quarters of Sri Lanka's earliest Buddhist monks.

Archaeological Museum

This small, free museum is close to the lower car park. Displays include some terracotta dwarves, a couple of fine Ganadevi statues and a model of the middle chamber of the Mahaseya *dagoba*. There are some labels in English.

Sleeping

Anuradhapura *p261, map p264*
Anuradhapura has a good selection of reasonably priced hotels and guesthouses, but is rather lacking at the top end. Except for the wonderfully atmospheric Tissawewa Rest House, all are in the New Town, 2-3 km from the ancient site. The main cluster is around the junction of Harischandra Mawatha and JR Jaya Mawatha. The guest-houses on Freeman Mawatha are much closer to the 'New' bus station and the 'New Town' railway station, though even further away from the ruins. Nearly all rent out bicycles (usually Rs 150-200 per day) and can arrange guided tours. Alternatively opt for the good rest house in Mihintale, see below.

A **Palm Garden Village**, *Post 42, Puttalam Rd, Pandulagama, 2.5 km from the sites, T2223961, pgvh@pan.lk* 50 stylish a/c rooms with king-size beds in upmarket Italian-owned hotel (from US$90), 50 acre gardens with deer, full facilities including large pool, Ayurvedic centre, open-sided restaurants.

B **Galway Miridya Lodge**, *Wasaladantha Mawatha, T2222112, info@galway.lk* 39 comfortable a/c rooms, some with TV (US$40 with breakfast), attractive bathrooms, some with view over Nuwara Wewa, restaurant, bar, exchange, pool (non-residents pay Rs 100), pleasant atmosphere and attractive gardens with ponds overlooking tank ideal for a sunset stroll.

C **Nuwarawewa Rest House**, *Rest House Rd, near New Town, T2222565, F2223265, quiktur@lanka.com* Modern block, 70 a/c rooms (US$26) with balcony, some with tank views, modern bathrooms, public areas rather shabby, good restaurant, bar, clean pool (non-residents pay Rs 100, and the occasional monkey has a dip too!), attractive garden, friendly and helpful staff. Doesn't compare for atmosphere with **Tissawewa Rest House** though.

C **Tissawewa Rest House**, *near the tank, T2222299, F2223505, hotels@quickshaws.com* Former Dutch Governor's house with bags of colonial character, wooden floorboards and ceilings, some period furniture and fittings, beautifully situated in secluded parkland with lots of monkeys. 25 rooms, a few with a/c (US$24, plus US$2.50 for a/c), which vary – downstairs a bit dark so inspect first – but slight grubbiness seems to add to charm. Restaurant, bike hire (Rs 150 per day), guests can use pool at Nuwarawewa Rest House, reasonable value, closest to archaeological sites.

D-E **Randiya**, *off JR Jaya Mawatha, T/F222-2868, randiya@globellk.net* 10 comfortable rooms, all with balcony in modern house (Rs 1,050) including 2 a/c (extra Rs 275), hard beds, restaurant, bar, plans to go upmarket, good value.

D-E **Shalini**, *41/388 Harischandra Mawatha (opposite Water Tower Stage 1), T/F2222425, hotelshalini@hotmail.com* 13 large, clean, comfortable rooms, more under construction, in modern house (Rs 1,000-1,200), some with hot bath, very good food in attractive roof-top restaurant, well kept, keen owner, cycle hire, free transfer from/to station, internet café to come.

E **Ceybank Rest House**, *Jayanthi Mawatha, T/F2235520*. 26 large rooms with small balconies (Rs 720) and some family rooms (Rs 1,130), clean, mainly for local pilgrims.

E **Grand Tourist Holiday Resort**, *Lake Rd (off Harischandra Mawatha), T2235173*. 4 rooms in pleasant house with good views very close to tank (Rs 800), **Cadjan Restaurant** serves good food.

E **Kondamalie**, *388/42 Harischandra Mawatha, T2222029*. 31 clean rooms, new rooms best (Rs 850, a/c extra Rs 350) now in hands of original owner, good terrace restaurant, bike hire (Rs 200), friendly.

E-F **Ceylon Tourist Board Rest House**, *Jayanthi Mawatha, T2222188. Book on T011-243 7059.* Set in extensive grounds, 35 large rooms in attractive neo-colonial building (a/c Rs 1,150, non a/c Rs 730), fan, attached bath, slightly grubby, reasonable value though service rather slow, popular in the pilgrimage season, restaurant with very cheap food.

E-F **Lake View**, *4C4 Harischandra Mawatha, T2221593*. 10 rooms, some comfortable and clean with hot water, others a bit dingy so inspect first, a/c Rs 1000 (negotiable), fan only Rs 550-600, pleasant owner, Mihintale *dagoba* visible from here.

For an explanation of the sleeping and eating price codes used in this guide, see the inside front cover.

E-F Milano Tourist Rest, *Stage One, JR Jaya Mawatha, T2222364*. 8 variable rooms (from Rs 650), good restaurant, bar, better rooms good value, tours offered to Wilpattu National Park (2 hrs drive), Rs 4,500 for vehicle.
E-F Samanala Tourist Guest House, *4N/2 Wasala Daththa Mawatha, T2224321*. 4 large, clean rooms (Rs 700-800), quiet location next to lake (boating can be arranged), pleasant garden, cycle hire, excellent home cooking.
F Indrani Inn, *745 Freeman Mawatha, along a lane south, 1 km from New bus stand, T2222478*. 2 clean rooms, cycle hire.
F Lee's Chinese Guest House, *388/28 Harischandra Mawatha, T2235476*. 3 rooms (Rs 500, 1 a/c, 1 triple), basic but clean, good value, volleyball court.
F Walkers Inn, *387 Harischandra Mawatha, T2222100*. New guesthouse owned by son of **Samanala** owner, with 3 rooms (Rs 550) quiet, close to town, friendly owner with good English.
F-G Shanti Guest House, *981 Mailagas Junction, Freeman Mawatha, T2235876*. 10 basic but large rooms of varying standards (Rs 200-500) although 5 are occupied by long-stay guests, friendly, good food, free map, tour and bike hire (Rs 150) arranged, popular with backpackers, free pick up from station.
G Railway Retiring Rooms, *T2222571*. 10 basic rooms, not too clean but only 1 train at night so quiet, security-conscious caretaker, rooms available for non-passengers.

Mihintale *p268*
B-C Hotel Mihintale (CHC), *Anuradhapura Rd, 600 m west of the crossroads, T2266599*. 10 well furnished a/c rooms (US$31), those upstairs far lighter (extra US$10), 2 good-value family rooms (US$51), pleasant atmosphere, good value, decent rice and curry lunch (Rs 300).

Eating

Anuradhapura *p261, map p264*
The north end of town lacks restaurants but has some friendly food stalls. Most of the below are eateries in guesthouses etc. See Sleeping for location and contact details.
RsRs Tissawewa Rest House has the best atmosphere and the only restaurant close to the main sites: rice and curry Rs 235-305, plus a range of sandwiches, salads and snacks, though no alcohol.
RsRs Galway Miridya Lodge and the **Nuwarawewa Rest House** offer reasonable food and pleasant seating. Book ahead at the three listed above as they are popular with package groups.
RsRs Kondamalie has pleasant, open-air seating (take mosquito repellent!), popular with budget travellers.
RsRs Milano Tourist Rest (rice and curry Rs 150+, Western dishes slightly more) is also recommended.
RsRs Lee's Chinese Guest House has a Chinese cook. Recommended.
RsRs Shalini serves excellent food (breakfast, eg good rotties, Rs 225, fried lake fish Rs 350) on terrace restaurant in tree-tops. Recommended.
RsRs Swan, *Harischandra Mawatha*, popular bar sometimes serving good food, generous portions, reasonable prices.
Rs Casserole, *above Family Bakers, T2235441*, a/c offers welcome respite from the heat, with good value Chinese (eg pork with black bean sauce Rs 120), but has the atmosphere of a school gym.
Rs Selgado, *opposite Post Office*, cheap bakery, good for short eats and drinks.
Rs Why Not, *opposite Casserole, T4581020*. Lunchtime rice and curry buffet (1130-1500, Rs 65), Chinese and devilled dishes in the evening but lack of ventilation means it can get unbearably hot.

Festivals

Mihintale *p268*
Poson at full-moon in **Jun** is of particularly importance to Buddhists who commemorate the arrival of Buddhism on the island. Tens of thousands flock to climb to the sacred spot, chanting as they go: *Buddham saranam gachchaami. Dhammam saranam gachchaami. Sangam saranam gachchaami*, meaning 'In the Buddha I seek refuge, In Dhamma I seek refuge, In the Sangha I seek refuge'.

Shopping

Anuradhapura *p261, map p264*
Gunasena, *just north of the Main St-*

Harischandra Mawatha roundabout, has a small selection of books in English.

Transport

Anuradhapura *p261, map p264*
Bus There is a frequent bus service between Old and New Bus Stands. For long distance services there are 2 bus stations. New Bus Station, Main St, south end of town, serves most destinations except Colombo and Kandy. Departures for **Polonnaruwa** are frequent from 0515 to 1400, Rs 35, 3 hrs; **Trincomalee** (3½ hrs); **Vavuniya** (Rs 20, 1 hr); **Mannar** (3 hrs). Buses to **Mihintale** buses can be picked up on the main road (frequent, Rs 8.50, 30 mins). **Old Bus Station**, Rest House Rd, has CTB buses to **Colombo** (hourly, 5 hrs). **Kandy** via **Dambulla** (hourly, 4 hrs). **Intercity express buses** leave from diagonally opposite the Old Bus Station, and offers a/c express services to **Colombo** (hourly, 4 hrs), **Kandy** (hourly, 3½ hrs) and to **Kurunegala** and **Negombo**.
Car hire Available for hire from guesthouses and hotels in New Town.
Cycle hire From most guesthouses and hotels in the New Town (about Rs 150-200 per day). To get to **Mihintale** it is an 11 km easy ride along a flat road.
Motorbike hire Available in guesthouses/hotels, New Town, Rs 500 per day.
Three-wheeler From train station to Main St about Rs 30, and to Freeman Mawatha hotels Rs 70. From Archaeological Museum to Main St Rs 100. From New Bus Stand to Freeman Mawatha Rs 30, and to Main St, about Rs 50. To **Mihintale** it costs about Rs 500 for a half day trip.
Train From the main station include Intercity to **Colombo** (4-5 hrs, Rs 277/141/110) at 0640, 1430, 2310. Also slow trains (5 hrs+, Rs 220/116/42) at 0500 (on to **Matara**, Rs 205/75, no first class, 10 hrs), 0855, 1040. Change at **Polgahawela** for **Kandy**. For **Habarana**, **Polonnaruwa** and other destinations east change at Maho Junction (0855 best but bus is much quicker). North to **Vavuniya** (for **Jaffna** buses) at 0310, 1030, 1745, 1915, 2030 (Rs 1¼ hrs, 30/10.50). Note that the branch line to **Mihintale** only runs at festival time in Jul. Be aware that the hotels around Freeman Mawatha are closer to the New Town station (south of the main station). though intercities do not usually stop here.

Mihintale *p268*
Bus Regular between Mihintale and **Anuradhapura**'s New Bus Station (Rs 8.50, 20 mins).
Cycle/motorbike For the easy ride of 11 km along a flat road from Anuradhapura.
Train Trains only run on the branch line from Anuradhapura during the Jun festival.

Directory

Anuradhapura *p261, map p264*
Banks Most major banks are represented on Main St in New Town, all of which have foreign exchange facilities. For ATM users, Commercial Bank, Sampath Bank and Seylan Bank are best.
Communications **Post office** is on Main St, south of the Harischandra Mawatha junction. **Internet** can be found opposite the post office at **Hi-Lite**, Rs 6 per min, 0800-2100.

Sigiriya

→ *Phone code: 066. Colour map 2, grid B5.*

The bloody history of the vast flat-topped 200-m high Lion Rock, a tale of murder and dynastic feuding, is as dramatic as its position, rearing starkly from the plain beneath. An exceptional natural site for a fortress, the rock dominates the surrounding countryside of the central forest and from the top offers views that stretch as far as the Dry Zone and south to the Central Highlands. Deriving its name (Sinha-Giri) from the lions which were believed to occupy the caves, for many visitors this impressive site is their favourite in the whole of Sri Lanka. The rewards of Sigiriya (pronounced See-gi-ri-ya), with its palace, famous frescoes and beautiful water gardens, justify the steep climb. Frequently labelled the 'Eighth Wonder of the World', it was designated a World Heritage Site in 1982. ▸▸ *For Sleeping, Eating and other listings, see pages 279-280.*

Ins and outs → *Allow at least two hours for a visit. Evenings bring out armies of mosquitoes, so take precautions and cover up.*

Getting there and around

The main bus stop is close to the bridge by the exit (at the south of the Rock) so those without their own transport have to undertake the 10 minute walk round to the entrance (to the west) to buy their ticket (the track is signposted off the road 1 km west from the bus stand, past the rest house). Those visiting by car are dropped at the entrance – the driver will then drive round to the car park at the exit. Be careful in Sigiriya at night, especially if a lone female.

Best time to visit

Very early morning is beautiful, the site very quiet until 0730, but the late afternoon light is better for the frescoes. Avoid the high sun around noon. There can be long queues on public holidays and the rock can be very crowded from mid-morning. If you wish to make an early start (avoiding groups which start arriving by 0800) buy your ticket on the previous day if you arrive in time.

Tourist information

The ticket office is near the entrance. US$15 (half price for ISIC holders and children), and Cultural Triangle Tickets (US$32.50) can also be bought here. The round ticket (see page 35) is only for a single entry at each site. The ticket office is open 0700-1530, but those holding the round ticket can enter as soon as it is light. It is advisable not to take food as the site is over-run by dogs who will follow you around. Worse still are the phenomenally aggressive monkeys who will probably pinch it off you before you get to the top! A new road has been built right to the base of the rock for ease of access for disabled visitors.

There is a tourist information counter east of the bus stand near the tank, 0800-2100 (theoretically). At the site there are many touts – if you would like a guide you needn't pay more than Rs 300 (check if he is certified). There are over 60 licensed guides here so competition is fierce. Raja Abeykoon, T2233314, has been recommended as knowledgeable and multilingual (English, French and German). *Sigiriya*, by RH De Silva, Ceylon, Department of Archaeology, 1971, is recommended for further information.

History

Hieroglyphs suggest that the site was occupied by humans from times long before the fortress was built. The royal citadel, built between 477-485 AD, was surrounded by an impressive wall and a double moat. As well as the palace, the city had quarters for the ordinary people who built the royal pavilions, pools and fortifications.

The engineering skills required to build the palace, gardens, cisterns and ponds become even more extraordinary when you realise that the entire site was built over a period of seven years and effectively abandoned after 18 years. For the famous frescoes Kasyapa gathered together the best artists of his day.

Water, a scarce commodity in the Dry Zone, was conserved and diverted cleverly through pipes and rock-cut channels to provide bathing pools for the palace above, and to enhance the gardens below with pools and fountains. The water pumps are thought to have been powered by windmills. On the islands in the two pools in the water garden near the entrance stood pavilions, while the shallow marble pools reflected the changing patterns of the clouds. Excavations have revealed surface and underground drainage systems.

Legends of Sigiriya

The romance of Sigiriya, the playboy's palace in the sky, has provided inspiration for many books, plays and even films, with more than one legend to explain its origins. All theories hinge around the cult of King Kasyapa.

The *Mahavansa* records that King Kasyapa (reigned 477-495 AD) killed his father, King Dhatusena, by plastering him alive to a wall, in order to gain the throne, after which he lived in terror that his half brother, Moggallana, who had taken refuge in India, would return to kill him. He did come back, after 18 years, to find that Kasyapa had built a combination of pleasure palace and massive fortress. Kasyapa came down from the hill to face his half brother's army on elephant back. Mistakenly thinking he had been abandoned by his supporters, he killed himself with his dagger.

A conflicting, if equally bloody alternative theory, propounded by historian Senarat Paranavitana, is claimed to have been deciphered from inscriptions by a 15th-century monk. In this, Dhatusena is told that he can obtain imperial status by becoming a *Parvataraja*, or mountain king, ruling from a palace built on a rock summit. In the struggle for succession, Kasyapa on return from exile in India mistakenly attacks and defeats his father's army, believing it to belong to his brother, at which Dhatusena beheads himself. Remorseful as the cause of his father's death, Kasyapa, now king, attempts to put his father's dream into reality. In order to be accepted by overseas merchants, he proclaims himself as *Kubera*, the God of Wealth, and attempts to recreate his legendary palace on earth. He issues a gold coinage and establishes free ports, which accrue great wealth for the kingdom. In this theory Kasyapa dies in his palace after Moggallana persuades his wife to poison him.

When the citadel ceased to be a palace after Moggallana's reign, it was inhabited by monks till 1155, and then abandoned. It was rediscovered by archaeologists in 1828.

Sights

Approach

Entering the site across the moat from the west, you will pass the fifth-century water gardens (restored by the Central Cultural Fund with UNESCO sponsorship) with walks, pavilions, ponds and fountains which are gravity fed from the moats as they were 1,500 years ago. You can see the secret changing room doors. Legend states that Kaspaya used to watch his concubines bathe here from his palace.

A straight path leads through the group of four fountain gardens with small water jets (originally fifth century), some with pretty lotuses attracting a number of water birds. Finally you reach the flower garden with colourful beds and flowering trees. To the right as you walk up to the rock is a **miniature water garden**. The whole area (including the moat and drive) is immaculate. It is difficult to visualize the winter palace as there are no visible foundations.

The Rock

The top of the rock has a surface area of 1.5 ha. It is easy to forget that the site was in fact developed as a massive defensive fortress. Lookout points were located on ledges clinging to the rock. Mind the aggressive monkeys in this area.

Base of the rock Before reaching the steps the path goes through the boulder garden where clusters of rocks, including the **preaching rock** with 'seats', are marked with rows of notches and occasional 'gashes'. These may have been used for decorating the area with lamps during festivals. To the right at the start of the climb, under a natural overhang, is the **Cobra Hood** rock which has a drip ledge inscription in Brahmi script dating from the second century BC. The floor and ceiling have lime plaster, the latter is decorated with paintings and floral patterns. A headless Buddha statue is placed horizontally. It is thought to have been a monk's cell originally. The **Cistern** and the **Audience Hall** rocks are parts of a single massive boulder which had split, and half of which had fallen away. The exposed flat surface had a 'throne' at one end and came to be called the Audience Hall while the upper part of the standing half retained the rectangular cistern. A second set of steps is under construction from the end of the new road to the Lion Terrace.

The climb This begins in earnest with steps leading through the Elephant Gate on well-maintained brick-lined stairways. These lead up to the second checkpoint immediately below the gallery containing the frescoes. Steps continue up to the **Fresco gallery**, painted under an overhanging rock and reached by a spiral staircase which was built in 1938. A second staircase for descent was added in 2003 to ease congestion. Of the original 500 or so frescoes, which vie with those in Ajanta in Western India, only 21 remain. They are remarkably well preserved as they are sheltered from the elements in a niche. In the style of Ajanta, the first drawing was done on wet plaster and then painted with red, yellow, green and black. The figures are 'portraits' of well-endowed *apsaras* (celestial nymphs) and attendants above clouds – offering flowers, scattering petals or bathing. Here, guides are keen to point

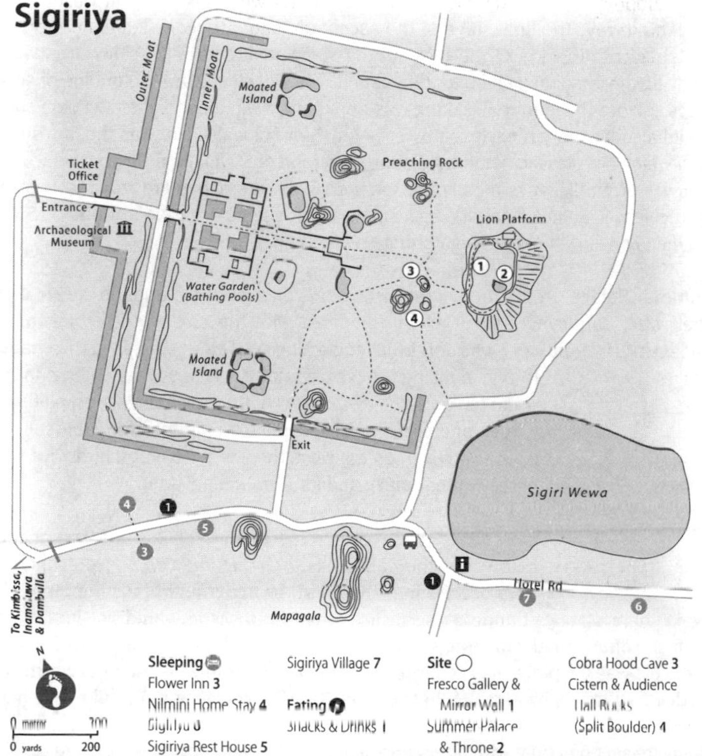

out the girl with three hands and another with three nipples. Note the girls of African and Mongolian origin, proof of the kingdom's widespread trade at this time. Some paintings were destroyed by a madman in 1967 and you can see pictures of this in the small museum, and others may be cordoned off because the rusty walkway may be unsafe. You may photograph the frescoes but a flash is not permitted. A 'fast' film (ISO 400), or a steady hand, is recommended.

Mirror wall Immediately beyond the foot of the spiral staircases the path is protected on the outer side by the 3-m high, highly polished plaster wall believed to have been coated with lime, egg white and wild honey. After 15 centuries it still has a reflective sheen. Visitors and pilgrims (mostly between seventh and 11th century) wrote verses in Sinhalese – 'graffiti' prompted by the frescoes and by verses written by previous visitors. Some, today, find this section a little disappointing. Despite the threat of a two-year jail sentence, there is plenty of modern graffiti to obscure the originals and it can be difficult to stop and study because of the pressure of people when the rock is busy. As you continue to climb, note the massive rock, close to the Guard House, wedged with stone supports which could be knocked out to enable it to crash on the enemy far below.

Lion Terrace Here, the giant plaster-covered brick paws of the lion become visible. Originally, the entire head and front part of the body would have awed visitors. Though the remainder of the structure has disappeared, the size of the paws gives some clue to the height of the lion's head. The terrace marks the halfway point of the climb where cool drinks (Rs 50) are available. The wire cage is apparently to protect people from wild bees. You can see their nests under the metal staircase.

Final stairway The final stage of the ascent on the north ledge leads through the lion's paws to the top of the rock up the steep west and north sides. It is worth studying the remaining climb to the summit. You can clearly see the outline of small steps cut into the granite. The king was apparently scared of heights so these steps would also have been enclosed by a 3-m high mirror wall. Here was the lion's gate after which the place is named: *Si* (shortened form of *Sinha*, lion) *Giriya* (throat). The stairway of 25 flights is mostly on iron steps with a small guard rail and is steep (particularly in one place where a small flight resemble a ship's ladder!). Small children can find this quite frightening.

Summer Palace At the top are the ruins of the palace. The foundations reveal the likely size, surprisingly small when compared with the size of the stone throne underneath it, although it was only built for the King and Queen. There was the granite throne, dancing terraces, a small pool fed by rain water, drinking water tanks, sleeping quarters of the concubines, a small flower garden and precariously positioned platforms for guards. If you walk to the sign on the west, there is a very good birds-eye view of the winter palace and its surrounding moat.

As you descend you can see steps cut into the rock for soldiers to guard the palace. The King apparently feared attack not only from his half-brother but also from enemies within his palace.

Descent Retrace your steps to the second checkpoint. Just below this, the path splits to the left from where you can get a view of the king's audience chamber and his anteroom. Once again, there is a huge throne in a semicircle where his advisors would sit – justice was swift and often brutal. Immediately below the audience chamber was another granite slab: this was the place of execution. Again to the left is the ante-chamber which was cooled by a tank of water cut into the rock above the ceiling. It too would have been covered in frescoes. Much of the construction is in brick, faced with lime plaster but there are sections built with limestone slabs which would have been carried up. The upper structures which have disappeared were probably wooden. Finally you exit through the cobra gate – a huge, overhanging rock.

Other sights

These include the **Mapagala Rock** with evidence of dressed stone work, a *dagoba* and other ruins on the roadside just over a kilometre away. **Pidurangala Royal Cave Temple** and Buddhist Meditation centre are 1½ km away and signposted from the car park. The cave on the rock Pidurangala, where there had been an ancient monastery, still has a stupa with a 10th-century reclining Buddha and an inscription dating from the first century BC. These, and other finds of early settlement in **Rama Kale** nearby, point at the ancient nature of the spot chosen by Kasyapa for his palace fortress. The small **Archaeological Museum,** hitherto not particularly impressive, was closed for renovation at the time of visiting. It's usually open 0730-1730.

Sleeping

Sigiriya *p274, map p277*

Inamaluwa and Kimbissa, 4-6 km west of the rock, are good options for mid-price accommodation, which tends to be expensive or basic in Sigiriya itself. Regular buses leave from these villages to the site from early morning onwards.

LL-L **Elephant Corridor**, *Inamaluwa, T2283333, hotel@elephantcorridor.com* Sri Lanka's newest luxury 'boutique' hotel, so exclusive they initially wouldn't let us in! Marketed under slogan *pic cit* (mahout's command to 'let go'), 200-acre site overlooking tank with stunning views of the rock. 24 suites in 5 categories (from deluxe to presidential, US$150-1,000). Each room has private plunge pool, DVD player/hifi, dressing room, individual garden and lots of gadgets (eg night-vision binoculars, painting easel). Sports facilities include stables and 3-hole golf course. Not all rooms have good views but blend of details and beauty of setting make it a surefire success.

A **Sigiriya Village**, *Sigiriya, T/F2231803, hotelssv@sltnet.lk* 120 tastefully furnished rooms (US$65-85) with small terraces, including 80 a/c, good open-sided restaurants, beautifully planted 33-acre site with carefully landscaped gardens and theme clusters of cottages (eg King's Arbour in Sigiriya rock style), each with its own colour scheme and accessories, good Ayurvedic centre, own farm, friendly and efficient management.

B **Sigiriya**, *Sigiriya, T2284811, sigiriya@slt.lk* 80 well-decorated, comfortable a/c rooms (from US$54), started as a small guesthouse, arranged around 2 terraces, reasonable food, large pleasant garden, bird-watching walks, attractive wooded setting, cultural shows, good freshwater pool, good value.

C **Eden Garden**, *Sigiriya Rd, Inamaluwa, T2284635, F2285230.* 25 large, clean rooms (Rs 2,300), including 15 a/c (extra Rs 550), pool, attractive gardens, restaurant.

C **Sigiriya Rest House** (CHC), *Sigiriya, T2231899.* 17 rooms, 4 refurbished with a/c and new bathrooms. Rest are rather musty and smelly and all are overpriced at US$25-35 (including breakfast). Pleasant dining area and terrace with great view of the rock though, site tickets available here.

E **Ancient Villa**, *Kimbissa, T2285322, saarcair@sltnet.lk* Excellent value cabanas (Rs 900) in 12 acre jungle site, good for nature walks, elephants visible at night. Poor food and management can be pushy but recommended for location.

E **Globetrotter Inn**, *Inamuluwa, T077-7801818, rajaguna8@sltnet.lk* 3 clean tiled rooms (Rs 1,000) in brand new lodge near open jungle, coconut thatch restaurant.

E **Grand Tourist Holiday Resort**, *Kimbissa, 5 km from site, T077-7384723.* Not grand (or for grand tourists) but large, well-furnished, good value rooms (Rs 800) in 2 small Dutch-style bungalows in attractive gardens.

E **Inamaluwa Inn**, *Inamuluwa, T2284533.* 10 reasonable rooms with attached bath, upstairs better (Rs 800-1,000), 1 a/c (Rs 1,800), pricey restaurant.

For an explanation of the sleeping and eating price codes used in this guide, see the inside front cover.

F Flower Inn, *Sigiriya, (no phone)*. 3 rooms (Rs 500, negotiable), a little frayed round the edges, table fans, attached bath, good food, friendly owner.
G Nilmini Home Stay, *opposite Flower Inn, Sigiriya, T2233313*. 3 simple rooms (Rs 250 shared bath, Rs 400 attached) in rather dilapidated house, good food, very friendly, free bicycle hire.

Eating

Sigiriya *p274, map p277*
RsRs Cadjan Restaurant, *at Grand Tourist Holiday Resort*, is one of several restaurants on the way into town.
RsRs Sigiriya Rest House, *Sigiriya*, is the best option for lunchtime rice and curry.

Shopping

Sigiriya *p274, map p277*
Shops in the village sell bottled water and film.
Kottegoda Batik, *Inamaluwa*, for batik.
Silk Shop, *2 km before the site on the Inamawula-Sigiriya road*, for good saris.

Transport

Sigiriya *p274, map p277*
The journey by car from **Colombo** takes about 4 hrs and from **Kandy** about 2½ hrs.
Bus The main stop is close to the exit from the site. Non-stop bus from **Colombo** to **Dambulla** (3 hrs), then hourly local buses to Sigiriya (30 mins) or a 3-wheeler/taxi, Rs 400. Frequent buses between **Kandy** and **Dambulla** or **Matale** and connections to Sigiriya (total 3½-4 hrs), though fewer in the afternoon. From **Kandy**, 1 direct morning bus to Sigiriya, 3 hrs (check times). From **Sigiriya**, there is a direct bus to **Colombo** at 0415, at least 2 buses to **Kandy** (0830, 1145), and buses to **Dambulla** (30 mins) about every 30 mins (last at about 1830).

Directory

Sigiriya *p274, map p277*
Banks None; money change at hotels.
Useful addresses **Tourist police**, T2231808, near the entrance to the Rock, though only during office hours.

Sigiriya to Polonnaruwa

From Sigiriya, a right turn at Moragaswewa leads east through low forest clad hills, skirting the picturesque tanks at Minneriya and Giritale, to the ancient city of Polonnaruwa. Elephants migrate across this route in the late afternoon. To the north of Habarana lies the Kaudulla tank, around which Sri Lanka's newest national park has been formed, while northwest of town, the remote hermitage of Ritigala, buried deep within the jungle, is well worth the detour off the Anuradhapura road.

Habarana → *Phone code: 066. Colour map 2, grid B5.*

Habarana is an important crossroads, with roads extending southwest to Colombo or Kandy, northwest to Anuradhapura and Jaffna, northeast to Trincomalee, and southeast to Polonnaruwa and Batticaloa. Tour groups often spend a night here, though apart from a scattering of hotels and rest houses and its accessibility, it has little to offer. It is however a good base for visiting **Kaudulla** or **Minneriya National Parks**, both close by, though shop around for jeeps. Elephant 'safaris' are also available though they are expensive at US$20 (for one hour). Nearby there is an attractive **Buddhist temple** with excellent paintings. Behind the tank, next to the temple, you can climb a rock for superb views over the forest to Sigiriya. ▸▸ *For Sleeping, Eating and other listings, see pages 283.*

66 99 To experience something of the thrill of 'discovering' a remote site in a jungle, Ritigala is well worth visiting.

Ritigala → *Colour map 2, grid B4.*

ⓘ *US$5, covered by the Cultural Triangle Permit. There is a local guide who you are obliged to follow though he speaks no English, so it helps to have your own guide to translate. He expects a tip. From Habarana the return trip by car costs around Rs 1,500.*

The 366-acre archaeological site is located within a 3,878-acre Strict Nature Reserve, where wildlife includes elephants, sloth bear and leopard and varied bird life. The area, rich in unusual plants and herbs, is associated with the *Ramayana* story in which Hanuman dropped a section of herb-covered Himalaya here, see page 154.

The forest hermitage complex here was occupied by the ascetic *Pansakulika* monks. The structures found here include the typical double platforms joined by stone bridges, stone columns, ambulatories, herbal baths filled by rain water, sluices and monks' cells. There are many natural caves on the mountain slopes, some quite large, in which priests would meditate. Brahmi inscriptions here date the site from the third and second centuries BC.

As you enter the site, you will clamber over ruined steps leading down to the now overgrown two-acre bathing tank, the **Banda Pokuna**. Over an original stone bridge, follow a part-restored pathway, laid with interlocking ashlar, to the first major clearing, the monastery hospital, where you can see the remains of a stone bed, oil bath and medicine grinder. The next set of ruins is believed to be a library, now partly restored, perched atop a rock with magnificent views across to the jungle below. Beyond here, you come to the monastery, with a remarkably well-preserved urinal which would have had three clay pots beneath, of charcoal, sand and *kabok* for filtration. Here are the distinctive raised double-platforms, characteristic of Ritigala and other forest monasteries, see box, page 267. The platforms were probably for congregational use.

Platform 17 marks the end of the excavated territory – special permission is required from the Wildlife Department to venture further, and guides are in any case fearful of wild animals (workers have been maimed or killed in this area by elephants). Though in the Dry Zone, the Ritigala summit has a strange cool, wet micro-climate, with vegetation reminiscent of Horton Plains, see page 227.

You need your own vehicle to reach Ritigala. From Habarana, follow the A11 for 22 km west towards Maradankadawala, taking a right turn at Galapitagala for 5 km into the forest, then turn left along a track (suitable for a two-wheel drive) for about 3 km where an ancient rock-cut path leads to the site. ▸▸ *For Sleeping, Eating and other listings, see pages 283.*

Kaudulla National Park → *Colour map 2, grid A4. Best time to visit: April-August.*

ⓘ *US$6 plus service charge, tracker etc.*

Sri Lanka's newest national park was opened to the public in September 2002, partly as another step in establishing protection for the elephants' ancient migration routes. It completes a network of protected areas around the Polonnaruwa area, comprising Minneriya National Park, Minneriya-Giritale Nature Reserve and Wasgomuwa National Park to the south, and Flood Plains and Somawathie to the east and north.

The 6,936 ha park acts mainly as a catchment to the Kaudulla Tank, which dates back to the 17th century. Its most prominent feature is its large herds of elephant (up to 250), which can be seen at the tank during the dry season (April to August) when water is scarce elsewhere. The vegetation, which consists of semi-mixed evergreen, grasslands and riverine forest, supports a small population of leopard and sloth bear, while birdlife is excellent.

Outside the dry season, elephants are easier to see from the main Habarana-Trincomalee Road (on the left coming from Habarana) than in the park itself. These are their preferred feeding grounds due to the lushness of the vegetation. Jeeps in Habarana are keen to take you to this area in these months but if you already have a vehicle there is little point getting a jeep since they feed very close to the road.

Facilities are currently limited. There are no places to stay and the road system is poor, though new stretches are planned for 2004. The turn-off for the park is 17 km north of Habarana at Hatarasgoduwa from where it is a 5 km ride to the park office and entrance at the 'Nine Doors' bridge. Jeeps from Habarana will usually charge Rs 2,500 (up to six people) for a three-hour 'safari', leaving 1500-1600. » *For Sleeping, Eating and other listings, see pages 283.*

Minneriya National Park

→ *Best time to visit: April-August. 26 km west of Polonnaruwa. Keep a look out for wild elephants on the Minneriya-Giritale Road, and don't drive this route at night.*

ⓘ *US$12 plus service charge, tracker etc.*

A sanctuary since 1938, Minneriya was upgraded to national park status in 1997. Here is King Mahasena's magnificent Minneriya Tank (fourth century AD) covering 3,000 ha, which dominates the park. It is an important wetlands, feeding around 8,900 ha of paddy fields, and supporting many aquatic birds, such as painted storks, spot-billed pelicans, openbill storks and grey herons. At the end of the dry season there is little evidence of the tank which gets covered in weeds, the vegetation on its bed becoming a vital source of food for many animals. Around September and October, an influx or local migration of elephants takes place in a spectacular wildlife event. The high forest canopy also provides ideal conditions for purple-faced leaf monkey and toque monkey, while the short bushes and grasslands provide food for sambhar and chital. There are small populations of leopard and sloth bear. Mugger crocodiles and land and water monitors can also be seen. The park entrance is at Ambagaswewa, east of Habarana on the Batticaloa Road. Jeeps charge the same as to Kaudulla (see above). » *For Sleeping, Eating and other listings, see pages 283.*

Giritale

→ *Phone code: 027. Colour map 2, grid B5.*

Giritale also has a fine tank, which dates from the seventh century AD, and occupies a site which was once a wealthy suburb of ancient Polonnaruwa. Legend has it that King Parakramabahu met his future bride, the daughter of his uncle Girikandasiva, here, to whom he donated the tank and from whom it derives its name. There is little reason to stay here other than its position and its proximity to Minneriya and Polonnaruwa – the hotels here are more upmarket than in the ancient city itself. The road that skirts the tank south leads to Wasgomuwa National Park (see page 293), to which hotels also arrange trips (as well as to Minneriya and Kaudulla). As you drive out of town towards Polonnaruwa you will see a copy of the Aukana Buddha by the tank, erected in 2001. If you haven't made it to Aukana, you will get an idea how impressive is the real thing. » *For Sleeping, Eating and other listings, see pages 283.*

Sleeping

Habarana *p280*
Habarana is usually used as a base for visiting the national parks

AL The Lodge (Keells), *T/F2270011, htlres@keells.com* 150 tastefully decorated a/c rooms in bungalows, some deluxe with tubs and TV, excellent facilities and lush grounds with woods, good pool, good service.

B The Village (Keells), *T/F2270046, htlres@keells.com* 106 'rustic' cottages including 25 a/c (US$10 extra), on the banks of the lake, extensive gardens, small boomerang shaped pool, excellent food, reception inefficient.

E Rest House, *Habarana Junction, T2270003.* 4 large clean rooms (Rs 1,021 taxes included) back from the road.

F-G Habarana Rest (or Habarana Inn), *south of Habarana Junction, T2270186, tuduwaka@hotmail.com* 7 simple rooms on main road (can be noisy), 4 very clean and good value at Rs 750, other Rs 450 mainly designed for locals. Have proved to be dishonest in running safaris though – shop elsewhere.

Giritale *p282*
The upmarket hotels in Giritale, just off the main road overlook the tank in beautiful settings, can make a convenient base for Polonnaruwa. Other cheaper hotels are all on the Habarana-Polonnaruwa Rd.

A B Deer Park, *T2246272, deerpark@jinasena.com.lk* 76 luxurious cottages in jungle style overlooking Giritale Tank. Some with open-air showers, plus 4 excellent suite villas. Upmarket facilities with 3 restaurants, business centre, gym, herbal health centre, split-level pool. Also **LL Private villas** with own swimming pool and butler. Magnificent.

B Giritale Hotel, *T2246311, maya@carcumb.com* 42 good a/c rooms (US$41) high above the Giritale Tank, small pool, unattractive public areas but good facilities and superb views from the restaurant and terrace. Plenty of wildlife within hotel grounds, including chital and monkeys.

B Royal Lotus, *T2246316, royallotus@jinasena.com.lk* 56 comfortable a/c rooms plus 4 cottages, fine views over Giritale Tank, pool, good food, friendly and efficient staff.

E Himalee, *Polonnaruwa Rd, T/F2246257.* 18 large, basic rooms (Rs 1,100), helpful staff but overpriced.

E Village, *T2247275.* Not to be confused with hotel of the same name in Polonnaruwa. 5 spotless rooms well back from the road (Rs 900). Also good roadside: authentic rice and curry (11 curries), Rs 320, very good service.

F Woodside Tour Inn, *Polonnaruwa Rd, T2246307.* 10 large and clean rooms (Rs 600).

Eating

Habarana *p280*
Most groups choose to stop in Habarana, where local restaurants compete with each other to impress tourists with the number of curries they can serve at lunchtime. Prices are usually Rs 300-350. Best of the bunch are:

RsRs Acme Transit Hotel, *1 km east of Habarana Junction, T2270016.* 11 curries (Rs 350) with friendly management. Rooms available, though not well maintained and at Rs 1,700, grossly overpriced.

RsRs Rukmali Rest, *1 km further east, T2270059.* A mighty 17 curries (Rs 300).

Transport

Habarana *p280*
Bus Habarana Junction is a good place to pick up buses in all directions: **Dambulla** (Rs 8, 20 mins), **Trincomalee** (Rs 40, 2 hrs), **Polonnaruwa** (Rs 25, 1 hr), **Batticaloa** (Rs 140, 3 hrs), **Colombo** (Rs 70, 5 hrs). For **Anuradhapura**, take a bus to **Maradankadawala** (Rs 12, 45 mins) and change (45 mins).

Train The station is 2 km north of Habarana Junction and is on the Colombo-Batticaloa line. 1 train a day to **Colombo** (5 hrs, Rs 203/119/43.50) and **Trincomalee** (Rs 80/49/18), 2 to **Polonnaruwa** (Rs 49.50/28.50/10.50).

Directory

Habarana *p280*
Ayurvedic treatment Sigiri Dasuna, *Audangawa (south of Habarana), T072-2565394, 0830-2000.* New branch of respected **Suwamadhu** in Bandarawela. 1½-hr herbal treatment (45-min massage, 20-min steam bath, 20-min herbal sauna) Rs 2,000, and other treatments available.

Banks Branch of **People's Bank** just south of Habarana junction.

Polonnaruwa

→ *Phone code: 027. Colour map 2, grid B5. Population: 12,500.*

Polonnaruwa, the island's medieval capital between the 11th and 13th century, is for many visitors the most rewarding of the ancient cities. Flowering principally under three kings over a short period of less than 100 years, it is, in contrast to Anuradhapura, historically as well as geographically compact, and so it feels easier to assimilate. Today, the ruins, built alongside the vast and beautiful Parakrama Samudra, stand witness to a lavish phase of building, culminating in the sublime Gal Vihara. In its imperial intentions, and the brevity of its existence, Polonnaruwa may be compared to the great Mughal emperor Akbar's city of Fatehpur Sikri, near Agra in India. » *For Sleeping, Eating and other listings, see pages 290-291.*

Ins and outs

→ *Allow at least three hours but a whole day is better to get some impression of this ancient site.*

Getting there

Trains and buses arrive at Kaduruwela, 4 km east. From here, local buses run frequently (Rs 4) to Polonnaruwa, or take a three-wheeler (Rs 100).

Getting around

Under a hot sun the site is too spread out to walk around. Even if you have a car, cycling is the most practical and fun way to explore the town (Rs 100 per day, available from most hotels), though take it easy as brakes are a luxury and the tracks are rough in places – you'll do well if you get round without a puncture! It is best to get your bearings before starting a tour. The ruins can be split broadly into five groups, though your ticket is only needed for three. Close to the entrance and within the old walls are the Royal Citadel Group to the south and the Quadrangle to the north. The Northern Monuments, which include the magnificent Gal Vihara, spread out over 3 km north of here. Across the main road from the main site, close to the museum and bund is the small Rest House Group, and finally, the Southern Group is about 3 km south of town. The museum, unless you arrive early morning, is a good place to start. The entrance to the main site is 500 m from here though you may wish to see the Rest House Group first as it is closest to the museum. Once in the main site, there is a one-way route through the sacred site that is generally quite well signed.

There are far fewer mosquitoes here than elsewhere in the Dry Zone. Instead red ants test your pain/patience threshold.

Best time to visit

As ever, early morning or late evening is best, out of the heat. To visit many sites you will need to remove your shoes – even in the blazing sun when the stones are scorching so taking socks is a good idea. Avoid visiting more remote ruins late in the day, as attacks on lone tourists have been known.

Tourist information

Tickets are available from the counter at the Archaeological Museum, close to the Rest House, which also acts as an information desk and sometimes sells maps of the city. Though the museum itself doesn't open till 0900, the desk is open from 0730. Tickets cost US$15, or you can also buy a Cultural Triangle Round Ticket (US$32.50, students and children half price). A book on Polonnaruwa is available from the nearby bookshop for Rs 75.

Background

The Sinhalese kings of Anuradhapura in 369 AD used Polonnaruwa as their residence but it did not rank as a capital until the eighth century. The Cholas from South India

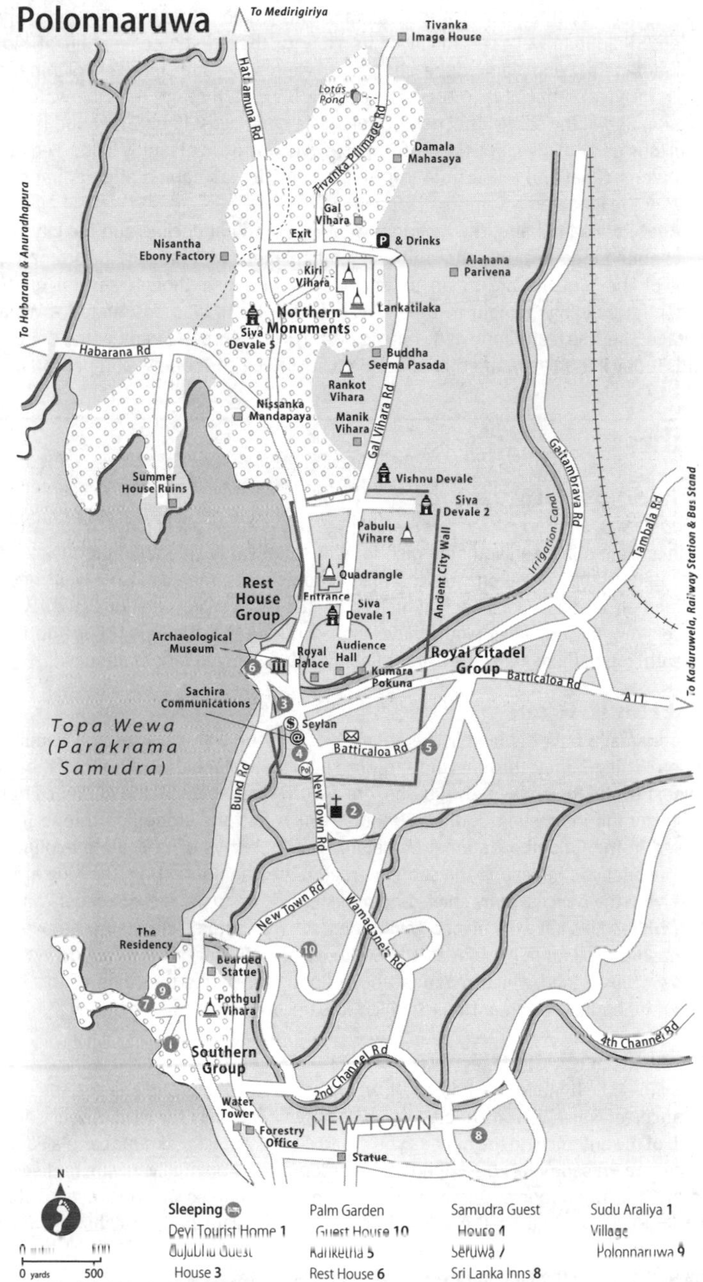

 destroyed the Sinhalese Kingdom at the beginning of the 11th century, and taking control of most of the island, they established their capital at Polonnaruwa. In 1056 King Vijayabahu I defeated the Cholas, setting up his own capital in the city. It remained a vibrant centre of Sinhalese culture under his successors, notably Parakramabahu I (1153-86) who maintained very close ties with India, importing architects and engineers, and Nissankamalla (1187-96). The rectangular shaped city was enclosed by three concentric walls, and was made attractive with parks and gardens. Polonnaruwa owes much of its glory to the artistic conception of King Parakramabahu I who planned the whole as an expression and statement of imperial power. Its great artificial lake provided cooling breezes through the city, water for irrigation and at the same time, defence along its entire west flank. The bund is over 14 km long and 1 m high, and the tank irrigates over 90 sq km of paddy fields. Fed by a 40 km long canal and a link from the Giritale tank, it was named after its imperial designer the Parakrama Samudra (Topa Wewa).

After Parakramabahu, the kingdom went into terminal decline and the city was finally abandoned in 1288, after the tank embankment was breached. Fortunately, many of the remains are in an excellent state of repair though several of the residential buildings remain to be excavated. In 1982, it was designated a World Heritage Site. The restoration at the site is by the UNESCO sponsored Central Cultural Fund. Today it attracts numerous water birds, including cormorants and pelicans.

Sights

Archaeological Museum

ⓘ *0900-1830. Entry is covered by the site ticket.* This is an excellent place to start a tour of the ancient ruins, and you may wish to return afterwards. In addition to the clearly presented exhibits found on site, and many photographs, there is also a well-written commentary on Sri Lanka's ancient history. Scaled down representations give you an idea of how the buildings would have looked during the city's prime. In the final (seventh) room, there are some extraordinarily well-preserved bronze statues.

Rest House Group

Nissankamalla built his own 'New' Palace close to the water's edge in a beautiful garden setting. Today, the ruins are sadly in a poor state of repair. Just north of the rest house, beyond the sunken royal baths, are a stone 'mausoleum', the Audience Hall, and lastly the interesting Council Chamber which had the stone lion throne (now housed in the Colombo National Museum). The four rows of 12 sculpted columns have inscriptions indicating the seating order in the chamber – from the King at the head, with the princes, army chiefs and ministers, down to the record keepers on his right, while to his left were placed government administrators, and representatives of the business community. Across the water, to the northwest, the mound on the narrow strip of land which remains above flood water, has the ruins of the King Parakramabahu's 'Summer House' which was decorated with wall paintings.

Royal Citadel Group

Cycle along the bund to the main road, where stalls sell drinks and snacks. The main entrance, for which you will need a ticket, is opposite, across the road. About 200 m south of the entrance (to the right as you enter), stands King Parakramabahu's Palace (Vejayanta Prasada). It is described in the Chronicles as originally having had seven storeys and 1,000 rooms, but much of it was of wood and so was destroyed by fire. The large central hall on the ground floor (31 m x 13 m) had 30 columns which supported the roof. You can see the holes for the beams in the 3 m thick brick walls. It has porticoes on the east and west and a wide stairway.

The Council Chamber (sometimes called Audience Hall) is immediately to its east. It has fine, partly octagonal, granite pillars and friezes of elephants, lions and dwarves, which follow the entire exterior of the base. Nearby, outside the palace wall, is the stepped Kumara Pokuna (Prince's Bath), restored in the 1930s. You can still see the spouts where the water is channelled through the open jaws of crocodiles.

Quadrangle

Turning left from the entrance, you come first to the Siva Devale I, a Hindu Temple (one of the many Siva and Vishnu temples here), built in about 1200 AD, which has lost its brick roof. An example of the Dravidian Indian architectural style, it shows exceptional stone carving, and the fine bronze statues discovered in the ruins have been transferred to the Colombo Museum.

Some 50 m further on, steps lead up to the Quadrangle, the highlight of the ruins within the ancient city wall. Though the structures here are comparatively modest in size, they are carved in fine detail. This is still regarded as a sanctuary and shoes and hats have to be removed.

The **Vatadage** ('hall of the relic') to the left as you enter the Quadrangle is a circular building with a *dagoba* on concentric terraces with sculptured railings, the largest with a diameter of 18 m. A superbly planned and executed 12th-century masterpiece attributed to Nissankamalla (1187-96), the Vatadage has modest proportions but remarkably graceful lines. It was almost certainly intended to house the Tooth Relic. There are impressive guard stones at the entrances of the second terrace and wing stones with *makaras* enclosing lion figures. The moonstone to the north entrance of the top terrace is superb. The *dagoba* at the centre has four Buddhas (some damaged) with a later stone screen.

The **Hatadage**, with extraordinary moonstones at its entrance (see page 365), is

Polonnaruwa Quadrangle

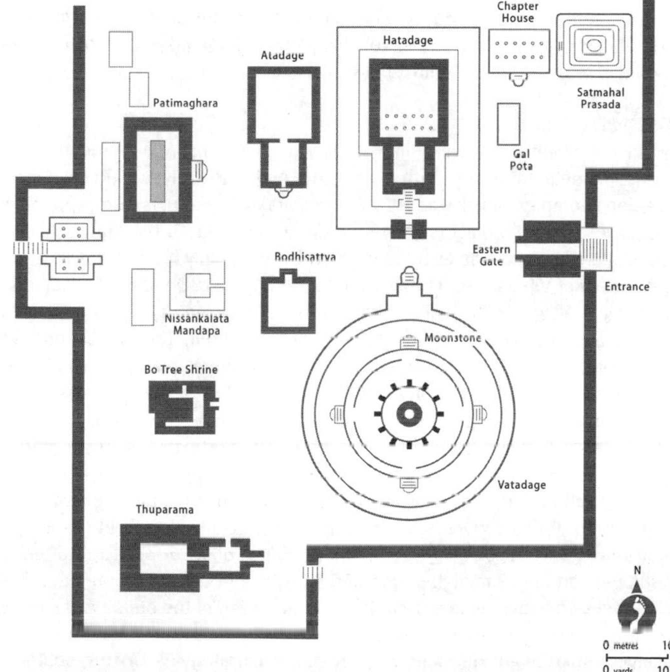

 the sanctuary built by Nissankamalla and is also referred to as the Temple of the Tooth, since the relic may have been placed here for a time. See the Buddha statue here framed by three solid doorways, and then look back at one of the Buddha statues in the Vatadage, again beautifully framed by the doorways.

Gal Pota, to the east of the Hatadage, the 'Book of Stone' is to the side of the path and can easily be missed. According to the inscription it weighs 25 tons, and was brought over 90 km from Mihintale. It is in the form of a palm leaf measuring over 9 m by 1.2 m, over 60 cm thick in places, with Sinhalese inscriptions praising the works of the King Nissankamalla including his conquests in India. The **Chapter House** nearby dates from the seventh century. The ziggurat-like **Satmahal Prasada** (originally seven-storeyed) in the northeast corner, decorated with stucco figures, has lost its top level. The 9-m sq base decreases at each level as in Cambodian *prasats*.

West of the Hatadage, the **Atadage** ('house of eight relics') was the first Tooth Relic temple, constructed by Vijayabahu when the capital was moved here. There are some handsome carved pillars. The ruins of the **Patimaghara**, west of here, reveal the remains of a reclining Buddha.

The **Bo Tree shrine** is to the west of the main Vatadage. The **Nissankalata (Lotus Mandapa)** nearby was built by King Nissankamalla (1187-96) for a *dagoba*. This small pavilion has the remains of a stone seat (from which the King listened to chanting of scriptures), steps and a stone fence imitating a latticed wooden railing with posts. The ornamental stone pillars which surround the *dagoba* are in the form of thrice-bent lotus buds on stalks, a design which has become one of Sri Lanka's emblems. A statue of a *Bodhisattva* is to its east. The impressive **Thuparama**, in the south of the Quadrangle, is a *gedige* which was developed as a fusion of Indian and Sinhalese Buddhist architecture. This has the only surviving vaulted dome of its type and houses a number of Buddha statues. It has very thick plaster-covered brick walls with a staircase embedded in them. Exiting the Quadrangle by the same steps that brought you in, 500 m to the northeast are two temples which belong to different periods. If you walk past the **Pabulu Vihare**, a squat stupa up to the north wall of the ancient city, you come to one of the earliest temples with Tamil inscriptions, **Siva Devala 2**. Built of stone by the Indian Cholas in a style they were developing in Tamil Nadu (as at Thanjavur), but using brick rather than stone, it is almost perfectly preserved.

Northern monuments

Beyond the original city wall, another group of scattered monuments stretches several kilometres further north. First, the **Alahana Parivena** (Royal Crematory Monastery) Complex, which was set aside by Parakramabahu, is worth exploring. The UNESCO restoration project is concentrated in this area. At the **Manik Vihara**, the squat cloistered stupa was restored in 1991. This originally housed precious gems.

The **Rankot Vihara**, further on, is the fourth largest *dagoba* on the island with a height of 55 m. It was built by Nissankamalla in the 12th century. See the perfection of the spire and the clarity of the statues round the drum. The tall **Buddha Seema Pasada** was the Chapter House or convocation hall where you can still make out the central throne of the chief abbot, which was surrounded by monks' cells.

The large *gedige* **Lankatilaka** ('ornament of Lanka'), the image house with a Buddha statue, had five storeys. It has walls which are 4 m thick and still stand 17 m high, although the roof has crumbled. The design illustrates the development in thinking which underlay the massive building, for it marks a turning away from the abstract form of the *dagoba* to a much more personalized faith in the Buddha in human form. The building is essentially a shrine, built to focus the attention of worshippers on the 18 m high statue of the Buddha at the end of the nave. Though built of brick and covered in stucco, the overall design of the building shows strong Tamil influence. The exterior bas-relief sculpture, most of which is impressively well preserved, sheds light on contemporary architectural styles. To the south of the

Queen Subhadra is believed to have built the 'milk white' **Kiri Vihara** stupa next to it, so named because of its unspoilt white plaster work when it was first discovered. It remains the best preserved of the island's unrestored *dagobas*. The plasterwork is intact although the whitewash is only visible in place, such as around the relic box. There are excellent views from the Chapter House which has the foundations only just visible.

The **Gal Vihara** (Cave of the Spirits of Knowledge) is rightly regarded as one of the foremost attractions of Sri Lanka and has great significance to Buddhists. It forms a part of Parakramabahu's monastery where a Buddha seated on a pedestal under a canopy was carved out of an 8-m high rock. On either side of the rock shrine are further vast carvings of a seated Buddha and a 14 m recumbent Buddha in *Parinirvana* (rather than death), indicated, in part, by the way the higher foot is shown slightly withdrawn. The grain of the rock is beautiful as is the expression. Near the head of the reclining figure, the 7-m standing image of banded granite with folded arms was once believed to be his grieving disciple Ananda but is now thought to be of the Buddha himself. The foundation courses of the brick buildings which originally enclosed the sculptures, are visible. Sadly, the presentation of the magnificent carved Buddhas is rather disappointing. An unattractive, protective canopy now shields the seated Buddha, which is caged in with rusty metal bars and a scratched plastic 'viewing window' making clear viewing and photography impossible.

A path continues north to rejoin the road. The **Lotus Pond**, a little further along, is a small bathing pool, empty in the dry season, with five concentric circles of eight petals which form the steps down into the water. The road ends at the **Tivanka Image House** where the Buddha image is in the unusual 'thrice bent' posture (shoulder, waist and knee) associated with a female figure, possibly emphasizing his gentle aspect. This is the largest brick-built shrine here, now substantially renovated (though work continues). There are remarkable frescoes inside depicting scenes from the *Jatakas*, though not as fine as those in Sigiriya. Under the 13th-century frescoes, even earlier original paintings have been discovered. The decorations on the outside of the building are excellent with delightful carvings of dwarves on the plinth. The image house actually has a double skin, and for a small tip the guardian will unlock a door about half way inside the building. You can then walk between the outer and inner walls. The passage is lit from windows high up in the wall. It is an excellent way of seeing the corbel building technique. The guardian may also unroll the painted copies of the frescoes, which eventually will be repainted onto the walls.

Southern Group

This group is quite separate from the rest of the ruins, though it makes sense to start here if you are staying nearby. It is well worth walking or cycling down here along the bund as the view is lovely, though the main entrance is from the main road. You will first see the giant 3.5 m high **statue** of a bearded figure, now believed to be King Parakramabahu himself, looking away from the city he restored, holding in his hand the palm leaf manuscript of the 'Book of Law' (some suggest it represents 'the burden of royalty' in the shape of a rope). Sadly, the statue is covered by an ugly canopy.

To its south is the part-restored **Pothgul Vihara**, which houses a circular *gedige* (instead of being corbelled from two sides), with four small solid *dagobas* around. The central circular room, with 5 m thick walls, is thought to have housed a library.

Other sights

Once you've exhausted the ruins, a few peaceful hours can be spent cycling along the bund and attractive tree-lined **canals**, perhaps catching sight of a giant water monitor. The water system is so well planned it is hard to believe it is almost 1,000 years old. Some 4 km south past the Southern Group along the east bank of the tank you come to a weir, a popular spot for bathing. If you have a 4WD, you can drive down to the dam at Angamedilla, a beautiful spot where the tank is fed by the Amban Ganga. Here is an (unofficial) entry point for **Wasgomuwa National Park** (see below), though make sure you're with someone who knows the way.

At **Medirigiriya,** ⓘ *US$5, covered by the Cultural Triangle ticket*, 30 km north of Polonnaruwa is **Mandalagiri Vihara**, a seventh to eighth-century *vatadage* almost identical in measurement and construction to that in the ancient city's Quadrangle. The circular image house with concentric pillared terraces is located up a flight of granite steps on a hilltop site. It has lost its facing and, despite its atmospheric location, is less impressive than Polonnaruwa. The site it best reached by bus from Kaduruwela to Hingurakgoda, 15 km from the site, from which you can take another bus or three-wheeler.

Sleeping

Polonnaruwa *p284, map p285*
There are some good choices right in the centre, near the tank and entrance to the ruins. For hotels near the New Town you can get a bus from the railway station or the Old Town bus stop, and take the path signposted beyond the Statue, for 1 km to the east. Hotels in the complex west of the Pothgul Vihara by the tank, near the Southern Group, are 3 km from the old town so transport is essential. Bikes are available.

B **Sudu Araliya**, *near the Southern Group, T2224849, hotelaraliya@mail.ewisl.net* Attractive light open spaces, 30 very comfortable carpeted a/c rooms (US$43), TV, minibar, some with tank view, bar, pool, herbal treatment etc.

C **Rest House** (CHC), *by Parakrama Samudra, T2222299, chc@sltnet.lk* Magnificent setting by the the tank. Modernized and extended for Queen's visit in 1954, HM's **A** suite is spacious with TV, minibar and own garden overlooking tank (US$60). Other rooms US$27-35 depending on old or new wing – new wing a/c, larger with tank view. Slightly ageing and austere, but good lunch spot.

C **Seruwa** (CHC), *near the Southern Group, T2222411, chc@sltnet.lk* 40 clean if rather dark, cramped rooms, all with private lake-facing balcony, US$27 a/c, US$21 non-a/c. Restaurant, well-located bar, large pool, popular with tour groups.

D **Village Polonnaruwa**, *near the Southern Group, T2223366, villapol@sltnet.lk* 37 rooms, Rs 1,710 a/c, less Rs 500 without, small pool, restaurant, bar, unattractive building (dark public areas), but reasonable value given the amenities.

D-E **Gajabha Guest House**, *opposite museum, near tank, T2222394, F2222268.* 25 comfortable rooms (Rs 1,200) including some with hot bath, not always clean. TV lounge, good restaurant, free bike hire, usually friendly though some have found management overbearing. Watch your bills.

E **Palm Garden Guest House**, *5/1 2nd Channel Rd, New Town, T2222622, a-mahavitana@hotmail.com* New, spotless if rather clinical rooms, bath, fan, nets (too small), amongst paddies near town (Rs 900), free pick-up.

E **Sri Lanka Inns**, *2nd Channel Rd, New Town, T2222403*. 17 pricey rooms (Rs1,000), around a pleasant courtyard, meals to order, beautiful walks along waterways, clean.

E-F **Devi Tourist Home**, *Lake View Garden Rd, off New Town Rd, T2223181*. 4 very comfortable rooms with attached bath (Rs 500-800), very clean, extremely welcoming family, excellent vegetarian home cooking, bike hire (expensive at Rs 150/day), free pick-up from Old Town, peaceful location.

E-F **Ranketha**, *160 Kaduruwela Rd, T2222080*. Very variable rooms, some dirty and depressing (Rs 750, or Rs 850 with a/c), others large and cool (Rs 1,200), so inspect first. Rural style theme, with open-air restaurant overlooking rice fields.

G **Samudra Guest House**, *Habarana Rd, T2222817*. 8 variable rooms with wall fan (Rs 250-350) including 1 wooden cabana (good value) and 1 cottage. Grotty bathrooms, but friendly and popular with backpackers. Restaurant and laundry service available, recommended for the price.

Eating

Polonnaruwa *p284, map p285*
RsRsRs **Rest House**, *Parakrama Samudra*, is a popular lunch spot, overlooking the tank with a welcome breeze, though you pay for

the (magnificent) location. Set lunch (eastern or western) is Rs 450-600.
RsRs Gaiabha, *opposite museum*, offers good food at a more reasonable price with many guests from other hotels dining here.
Rs There are several cheap eating places (Chinese/Sri Lankan) along Habarana Rd.

Transport

Polonnaruwa *p284, map p285*
Bus When leaving Polonnaruwa, it pays to get on at Kaduruwela to get a seat. The out-of-town bus stop is near the railway station in **Kaduruwela**. Hourly buses to **Colombo** (Rs 75, 6 hrs), via **Dambulla** (Rs 28, 1½ hrs), 7 a day to **Anuradhapura** (Rs 40, 3 hrs), regular buses to **Kandy** (Rs 50, 3 hrs), and plenty to **Habarana** (Rs 20, 1 hr).
For **Sigiriya**, travel to Sigiriya Junction in Inamaluwa, and change to a CTB/private bus. Buses leave for **Batticaloa** along the Batticaloa Road (Rs 40), via Valaichchenai for **Passekudah**. For **Trincomalee**, (Rs 63, 4 hrs), there are direct buses or travel to Habarana Junction and change.
Train The station is in Kaduruwela, 4 km east of the Old Town on Batticaloa Rd. To **Colombo**: 0942 and 2118 (Rs 245/147/75.50), to **Trincomalee** 0942 (Rs 59/25.50 – no first class). Trains have also resumed east to **Batticaloa**, via Valaichchenai (check).

Directory

Polonnaruwa *p284, map p285*
Banks Seylan Bank, *corner of Habarana Rd and road to Rest House*, has Visa ATM and will change TCs. More choice in Kaduruwela, where there are branches of the **Commercial** (nearest to the Old Town), **Hatton** and **Sampath** banks, all with ATMs.
Communications Internet at Sachiri Communications, *0830-2130*. Rs 6 per min.
Useful addresses **Tourist police**, *junction on Habarana Rd, Batticaloa Rd, New Town Rd, T2223099*. Also near the Gal Vihara at the main site.

Polonnaruwa to Kandy via Mahiyangana

Only 15 km longer than the Dambulla road, though rarely used by tourists, this route takes you through wild and isolated country, across the vast Dry Zone plains irrigated by the enormously ambitious Mahaweli Ganga Project. The road comes close to some rarely visited archaeological sites and national parks which are worth breaking the journey for. The route also provides respite from the hordes attracted by the many 'star' attractions in the area.

South to Mahiyangana

East of Polonnaruwa, the A11 follows the railway line towards the coast, leading ultimately south to Batticaloa. Road and rail converge at the impressive Manampitiya iron bridge to cross the wide Amban Ganga, after which there is an important turn-off for Maduru Oya National Park and Mahiyangana (see below). Elephants are often sighted feeding close to the road here. » *For Sleeping, Eating and other listings, see page 294.*

Dimbulagala → *Colour map 2, grid B6.*

Dimbulagala archaeological complex is a spread out series of over 100 caves carved into an imposing rock, also known as Gunner's Quoin. The caves have been in continuous use for thousands of years, first by the Veddas, while scattered ruins have been found from various periods between 300 BC and AD 1200. Parts of the complex are still used as a forest hermitage. One Brahmi inscription shows that the caves were once used by Queen Sundari, the daughter-in-law of King Vijayabahu I of

 Polonnaruwa. Follow the signs for 8 km and you will reach first the sign for Namal Pokuna, where a 1 km climb brings you to a small complex with a restored *dagoba*, a *gedige* and *bodhigaraya* (wall around a Bo-tree). Nearby is a lily pond (the Namal Pokuna itself), and an ancient stone bridge. Another climb brings you to a perfectly clear drinking pool and a set of meditation caves. Some 4 km south of here, past the **Ahasmaligawa** ('sky palace'), a recent stupa built high on a steep rock, you come to **Pulligoda**, where there is a 12th-century cave fresco depicting five gods, four in the *anjali mudra* (palms together showing obeisance) position, seated on an embroidered scarf. They are painted using the plaster and lime method of Sigiriya, though nowhere near as impressive.

Maduru Oya National Park → *Colour map 4, grid C1.*

ⓘ *US$12. Main entrance is 25 km south of Manampitiya.*

The Mahiyangana road turns back towards the hills with Wasgomuwa National Park to the right (see below). The 58,850 ha Maduru Oya National Park is to the left. It was designated a national park in 1983 to protect the catchment of the reservoirs in its neighbourhood and also to conserve the natural habitat of the large marsh frequenting elephant which is found particularly in the Mahaweli flood plain. It is proposed to link the park with Gal Oya to the southeast via the Nilgala jungle corridor. Deer, sambar and the rare leopard and bear can be spotted and there is abundant, varied bird life.

Vedda lands

The area to the east of Mahiyangana is one of the few areas left where Veddas, or Wanniya-laeto, the original inhabitants of Sri Lanka, are found. They live on the edge of the Maduru Oya forest and, transformed from hunter-gatherers to 'poachers' overnight by the park's creation, have since successfully fought for rights to hunt in some areas of the Park (though bows and arrows may have been superseded by the gun). On this route guides are often keen to take tourists to the meet the chief of the local Vedda village at **Dambane**, where you can witness some of their remarkable skills and dexterity, and buy ornaments and honey, though some visitors feel uncomfortable at this incursion of the privacy of this fragile community. If you choose to visit Dambane, note that the traditional Vedda greeting (men only) is to grasp forearms. Money is not requested but will be accepted.

Mahiyangana → *Phone code: 055. Colour map 2, grid C5.*

This is a bustling town with a long history. In legend it is associated with the Buddha's first visit to Sri Lanka, while the late President Premadasa had a new temple built here to resemble the famous Buddhist temple at Bodhgaya in Bihar, India. Opposite the temple, north of Kandy Road, six statues of symbolically important Sri Lankan leaders have been erected: three ancient kings, Devanampiya Tissa, Dutthagamenu and Parakramabahu; Kirti Sri who reigned over an 18th-century Buddhist revival (see page 202); and two modern political figures – first Prime Minister DS Senanayake, and son Dudley, who oversaw the Mahaweli Ganga Project, the source of the town's importance and prosperity.

Rajamaha Dagoba, 1.5 km m south from the main Kandy road, is of special importance since the Buddha was supposed to have visited the spot and preached to the tribal people. The large *dagoba*, which was expanded by Dutthagemunu and has been restored many times, is said to enshrine a fistful of the Buddha's hair. The area is very attractive – the park with the *dagoba* in it is well kept and is overlooked by the hills on the far bank of the Mahaweli.

Sorabora Wewa is just on the outskirts of Mahiyangana on the road to Bibile. According to legend a giant is said to have created the dam. You will probably have to

The island's original people

There are few remaining homes for the Veddas. Living in isolated pockets (in particular in the Nilgala and Dambane jungles), normally out of sight, these aboriginal peoples can still occasionally be seen. Once hunter-gatherers, the matrilineal Veddas worshipped ancestral spirits, but most have lost their old hunting grounds and have been forced to find alternative methods of survival by adopting local Sinhalese ways, and with that many of their tribal beliefs and customs. Those in the Eastern Province, around Gal Oya, have become assimilated into the local Tamil community.

The government's resettlement schemes have been strongly resisted by some, who have remained on the forest edge carrying out subsistence farming by the *chena* ('slash and burn') method, having abandoned their customary bow and arrow. Under increasing pressure to allow some Vedda groups to return to their old settlements, the government has set aside 'reserved' areas for them and given them hunting rights.

ask someone to find the road for you. You can see two enormous outcrops (the Sorabora Gate) through which the run off from the lake is channelled. » *For Sleeping, Eating and other listings, see pages 294.*

Mahiyangana to Kandy

There are three possible routes. This first route goes via a little visited national park and then traverses what is often referred to as Sri Lanka's most dangerous road. West of Mahiyangana, at Hasalaka you can turn off the main road for **Wasgomuwa National Park**, ⓘ *US$12, plus taxes*, created in 1984 to conserve wildlife displaced by the Mahaweli project. From Hasalaka it is 45 km north to the park entrance at Handungamuwa. The park's isolation, hemmed in on three sides by rivers, and the lack of human disturbance, have made it a rich feeding ground with a population of around 150 elephants. There is a belt of woodland on both sides of the river but otherwise the vegetation consists of grass, scrub and low bushes.

After Hasalaka, the A26 climbs into the hills through a series of 18 hairpin bends between 62 and 57 km from Kandy. For anyone familiar with mountain roads in the Himalaya the relatively gentle climb and forested slopes present little sense of hazard but buses often take the bends too fast for safety. There are spectacular views across the plains of the Dry Zone, now irrigated by the Mahaweli Ganga Project. Don't forget to stop near the top to look back on the glistening Mahaweli crossing the plains below. Approaching Kandy the road passes the dolomite quarries of Rajooda and the Kandy Free Trade Zone before crossing to the west bank of the Mahaweli Ganga.

These two pleasant alternatives to the A26 go through the **Randenigala Sanctuary**. The slightly shorter route crosses the Mahaweli Ganga at Mahiyangana and then goes due south to Weragantota immediately after crossing the river. The road climbs to the south side of the Randenigala Reservoir, then crosses the Victoria Dam to rejoin the A26 about 20 km from Kandy. To take the second alternative, you have to take the B road out of Mahiyangana to the southeast to Pangarammana, then join the road which also climbs to the southern edge of the Randenigala Reservoir. Here elephants can often be seen roaming along the shores of the lake. The irrigation development has created an area of intensive rice production and during the *maha* harvest (April-May) you will come across farmers winnowing and the stalks being constructed into quite large circular walls. After passing through **Minipe** the road follows the 30 km long Minipe Right Bank Canal, then slowly starts to rise. It crosses the river at the base of the Randenigala Reservoir Dam, which straddles the last gorge before the Mahaweli Ganga plunges to the plains. Its crest is 485-m long and 94-m high. The road then winds spectacularly around the southern side of the upper lake. Notice too the 'contour lines' on the lakeside as the water level drops during the dry season. The road continues to climb over a small pass – you see paddy fields in the valley below. Once over the pass you can see the **Victoria Dam**. There are a couple of vantage points from which you can take photographs. Over 120 m high, the dam is a massive structure, even bigger than the Randenigala Dam. There is a restaurant and look out place on the dam's north side. Not surprisingly both dams are quite heavily guarded and there are several checkpoints. ▸▸ *For Sleeping, Eating and other listings, see pages 294.*

Sleeping

South to Mahiyangana *p291*
At Maduru Oya National Park there is a circuit bungalow, dormitory and campsite. *Contact the Wildlife Department for details, T011-2694241, wildlife@slt.lk*

Mahiyangana *p292*
All accommodation is along Rest House Rd, 750 m west of the clocktower. Ask the bus to drop you at the Old Rest House stop. For eating the best option is at the New Rest House. There are also small food stalls and 'bakeries' in the bazaar.
C-F **New Rest House**, *500 m south of A26, T2257304*. 10 rooms with bath (Rs 700), 2 a/c (Rs 2,000), restaurant serving good food (meals Rs 150), rooms are large but not of a particularly good standard, nice position overlooking the river, pleasant garden, quiet (the river is dangerous for bathing).
F-G **Venjinn Guest House**, *east of New Rest House, T2257151*. 10 large, fairly clean if darkish rooms (Rs 350-650, a/c Rs 750), pleasant gardens, good value.
G **(Old) Rest House**, *closer to the main road, T2257299*. 3 rooms at the back (Rs 350), meals in dining room, fairly clean, basic but good value for the price.

Mahiyangana to Kandy *p293*
At Wasgomuwa National Park there are 5 bungalows and 5 campsites in or on the edge of the park. *Contact the Wildlife Department for details, T011-2694241, wildlife@slt.lk*
Safari Village, *10 mins from park, T066 2232816, T011-2591728, kinjou@dialogsl.net* Has cabanas on the lake front. There are also jeeps available for hire.

Eating

For options see Sleeping above.

Transport

Mahiyangana *p292*
Bus Regular private and government buses to **Kandy** up to 1730 (a/c private bus Rs 74, 2½-3 hrs). Also to **Colombo** (a/c bus Rs 160, 5 hrs), normal buses frequently to **Badulla** (Rs 32) and **Bibile** (Rs 20); and 2-3 a day to **Batticaloa** (3-3½ hrs) and **Polonnaruwa** (3½-4 hrs). You will need to have your own transport to visit **Dimbulagala**, the **national parks** and **Dambane village**. It is also best to have your own transport to visit sites en route between Mahiyangana and Kandy.

Directory

Mahiyangana *p292*
Banks Several close to the new temple west of Clocktower Junction, parallel with Kandy Rd. **Commercial Bank** has a talking ATM!

The East

Introduction

While elsewhere the island's magnificent beaches have begun to fall prey to commercialism, the remote and beautiful beaches of the east coast have lain almost forgotten, isolated for long periods due to the ethnic fighting. As word spreads that the area is no longer off-limits, curious visitors are beginning to be drawn by its lack of tourist paraphernalia. Though bleak reminders of the conflict continue to scar the landscape, the province may yet derive some benefits from its years without development.

Located entirely within the dry zone, Sri Lanka's Eastern Province has always been one of its most sparsely populated areas. Its coastline, dotted with hamlets along its lagoon-fringed shore, supports Tamil and Muslim fishing communities, while pockets of Sinhalese have traditionally eked out a hard existence in the forested interior.

The main focuses of interest are the idyllic beaches of **Nilaveli** and **Uppuveli**, just north of the magnificent natural harbour at **Trincomalee**, while to the south of the province, surfing centre **Arugam Bay** is Sri Lanka's latest hotspot. All along the coast, there is great potential, largely unexplored, for diving and snorkelling on reefs unaffected by the 'bleaching' elsewhere on the island, while the opportunities for whale watching are only now being assessed.

Inland is some of Sri Lanka's wildest country, where a short trip off the main roads, often requiring a four-wheel drive and plenty of patience, will be rewarded with a sense of discovery. Here are some the island's most impressive national parks, some of which are yet to reopen, which form an elephant corridor allowing the animals a free passage right across the region.

★ Don't miss...

1. **Trincomalee** Survey the harbour, sometimes compared with Sydney, and join the evening pilgrimage up to the sacred Swami Rock, page 300.
2. **Pigeon Island** Snorkel across the coral garden in the inviting waters off Pigeon Island, page 304.
3. **Nilaveli** Soak up the rays on these pristine sands, page 304.
4. **Arugam Bay** Ride the waves on the surfing points here and then relax with the crowds at Siam View or a peaceful dinner at Stardust, page 309.
5. **Batticaloa** Paddle out on a full moon night to the picturesque lagoon with a prawn fisherman to listen for the unusual 'singing fish', page 316.
6. **Kumana Sanctuary** Pick up a four-wheel drive at Arugam and head south into the deserted wilderness, visiting abandoned jungle hermitages en route to the recently reopened sanctuary at Kumana, page 310.

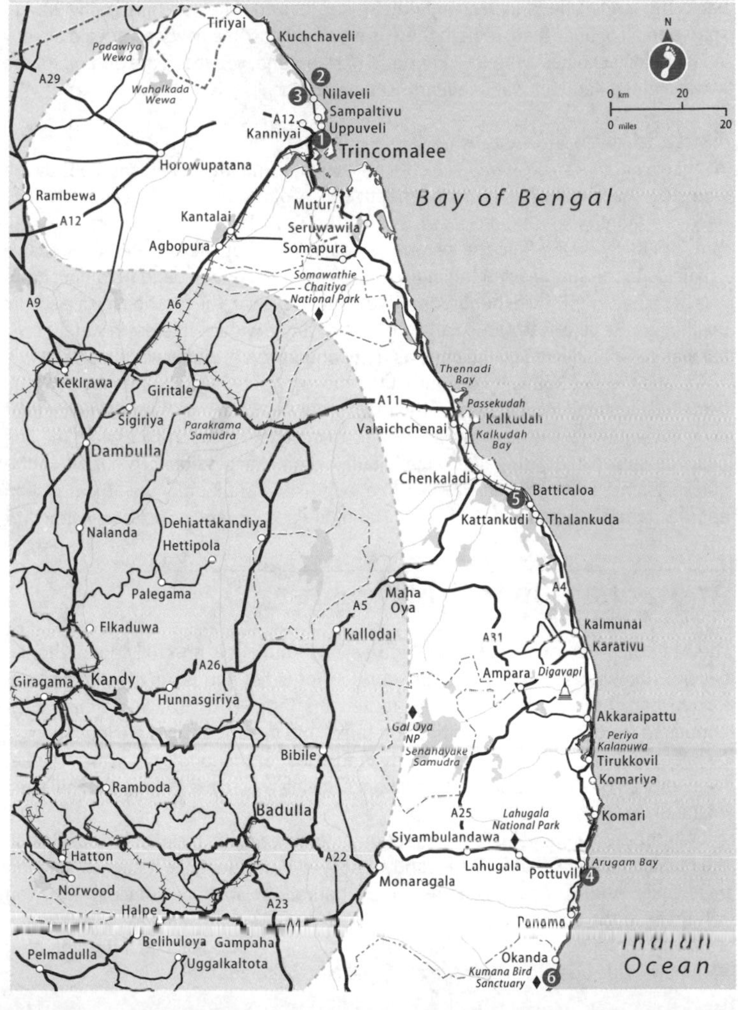

To Trincomalee

There are two routes east across the dry zone plains to Trincomalee. The coastal routes north and south of the city, which involve numerous ferry crossings where shallow lagoons flow into the sea, have had no work on them for years. They remain virtually impassable and may be unsafe. » *For Sleeping, Eating and other listings, see page 299.*

Habarana to Trincomalee

The road now relaid, this is the fastest and most frequently used route to Trincomalee. The ceasefire has triggered the removal of nearly all barriers and checkpoints, and Trincomalee is now accessible within two hours. The effects of the war are still visible – for long stretches you will see where the forest has been cleared on each side of the road to provide a clear firing zone for military bunkers. It is now beginning to grow back. The landscape is increasingly bleak and barren, forested hills giving way to sparse areas of bush land, though there is evidence of some new western aid agency led irrigation schemes. About 18 km north of Habarana, you reach the turn-off for the newly-created Kaudulla National Park, see page 281.

Kantalai → *Phone code: 026. Colour map 2, grid A5.*

At Agbopura, the large Kantalai tank become visible, and there are many stalls by the side of the road selling fresh curd in attractive clay pots. Kantalai is the centre of a very intensive farming area made possible from the irrigation provided by its beautiful tank, originally dating from the seventh century, which provides water to extensive rice fields to the southeast of the main road. The restored tank bund (retaining dam) was breached in 1987 with hundreds killed. Before the war, the rest house, in a scenic position by the lake, was particularly enjoyed by those with an interest in water birds, but was commandeered by the army as a headquarters. The army withdrew in March 2003, and the rest house is once again the property of the CHC, but it may be years before it is restored. About 3 km off the main road, Kantalai town has little going for it except a turn-off for the coast which is likely to increase in importance when the fine beaches south of Trincomalee once again become accessible. This road is the quickest land route to **Seruwawila** (see page 305). At Somapura it passes an approach road to Somawathie Chaitiya National Park, currently closed to visitors.

Anuradhapura to Trincomalee

The A12 from Anuradhapura to Trincomalee via Mihintale is now fully open, though beyond Horowupatana has had little work on for years and takes at least an hour longer than the Habarana road. The route runs through one of Sri Lanka's least populated regions. Abandoned irrigation tanks and marshy ground are interspersed by forest and occasional fields of paddy land. Most of the journey is across the flat plain, broken by a few isolated granite blocks, giving way to the low range of hills just inland of the coast.

Northeast of Mihintale, in the direction of **Rambewa**, an ancient stone bridge on the Mahakanadarawa tank was recently discovered accidentally. It suggests a road once linked Anuradhapura with the ancient harbour at Gokanna (Trincomalee). You can break at the dusty crossroads town of **Horowupatana**, 42 km east of Mihintale, where an attractive road leads northwest to Vavuniya (see page 324). A turn-off after Rathmale leads up to the *vatadage* at **Tiriyai** (see page 304).

Tourist paradise or military asset?

Since the ceasefire in 2002, Trincomalee has become the focus of plans to regenerate the troubled east. Having caught the imagination of government and business, which plan to redevelop the port and industrial wasteland, the town, coastal area and hinterland have been opened up for foreign investment, with a particular focus on 'ecotourism'.

As resorts at Nilaveli and Uppuveli begin to draw crowds again, the beaches of Marble Bay, Sweat Bay and Dead Man's Cove have been leased to the Sri Lankan Tourist Board for development; Powder Bay is said to be ideal for a yachting marina; infrastructure for wildlife tourism in the region's forests is being encouraged; and last but not least, Trinco could become one of the world's hotspots for whale-watching, with pods of Sperm and Blue Whales known to live off east coast waters.

All this is a long way off and much is likely to depend on a convincing peace settlement. Meanwhile, the big bucks for Sri Lanka lie in Trinco's harbour, arguably the island's most valuable natural resource, and its military and economic importance is not lost on two of the world's major powers. In 2002, Indian Oil Corporation (IOC) negotiated a Rs 200 million deal to refurbish the 99 mostly dormant oil tanks in China Bay, a dominant feature of the seascape. Meanwhile since the inception of their war on terror the US have shown renewed military interest in Trincomalee as an important staging post for its naval assets in Southeast Asia. The financial benefits for this little country may prove irresistible.

About 8 km before Trincomalee is a turn-off to the hot wells at **Kanniyai,** ⓘ *Rs 2 (parking Rs 10)*. This is a popular spot with locals who perform certain rites following the death of friends or family here. Hindu legend states that Vishnu appeared to Rawana here to tell him that his mother, after whom the wells are named, had died in order to prevent him from embarking on a foolish project. Vishnu then disappeared, touched his sword to the ground and the wells burst forth in his place. There are seven springs here, each formed into small bathing pools enclosed in tiled tubs. You can only splash the water over yourself with a bucket (the tubs are not big enough to bathe in) but the water is a perfect temperature (from 37 to 41ºC) and very refreshing. The wells are located 1 km south of A12 (signposted).

Sleeping

Habarana to Trincomalee *p298*

F Larkhchein Gest, *50 m off main road, Kantalai, T2234748*. Reasonable rooms with grimy attached bath (Rs 650), Chinese restaurant, chiefly services local weddings.

Anuradhapura to Trincomalee *p298*

G Rest Houses, *Kahatagasdigiliya (22 km east of Mihintale), and Horowupotana*. Very basic. The latter, despite its attractive position overlooking a lotus pond, is mainly a local bar and best avoided by single women.

Eating

For options see Sleeping above.

Transport

For transport to Trincomalee, see p307. Buses leave for Kanniyai Hot Wells from Trinco Rs 6.

For an explanation of the sleeping and eating price codes used in this guide, see the inside front cover.

Trincomalee and around

→ *Phone code: 026. Colour map 4, grid A1.*

Easily accessible from the south once again, Trincomalee, the largest city in Eastern Province, is undergoing something of a renaissance. Trinco's fame – and perhaps one day its fortune – lies in its magnificent natural harbour, described by Nelson as the finest in the world. Fiercely contested for centuries, it was a crucial naval base for the British during the Second World War. Today, after a recent past it would rather forget, this dusty port, still heavily militarized and displaying the scars of war, is for most tourists the gateway to the magnificent deserted northern beaches. Buoyed by an influx of investment. The city itself, a uniquely balanced ethnic blend, is too worthy of some time spent exploring.

Leaving the city behind most visitors take the route north to the famous white sand beaches at Uppuveli and, especially, Nilaveli. As the area slowly begins to draw back tourists, two resort hotels have reopened, plus numerous guesthouses, though some can find the debris of war and continued high military presence rather off-putting. Further afield, some important religious sites are once again accessible, but on terrible roads require a four-wheel drive and infinite patience.

Trincomalee

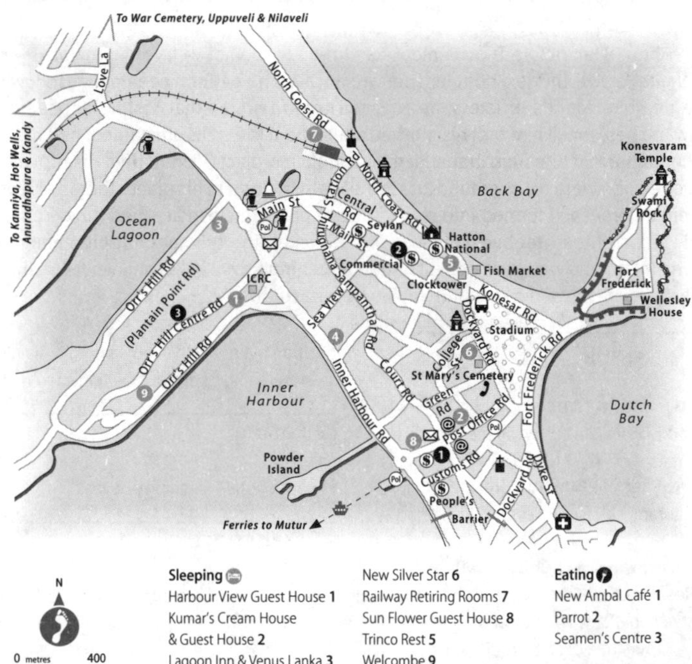

Sleeping
Harbour View Guest House **1**
Kumar's Cream House & Guest House **2**
Lagoon Inn & Venus Lanka **3**
Medway **4**
New Silver Star **6**
Railway Retiring Rooms **7**
Sun Flower Guest House **8**
Trinco Rest **5**
Welcombe **9**

Eating
New Ambal Café **1**
Parrot **2**
Seamen's Centre **3**

Ins and outs

→ *For information regarding safety whilst travelling in this area, see page 325.*

Getting there

At the time of writing, the resumption of flights from Colombo to the airport at China Bay, 10 km south of Trinco, was in the pipeline but no date was fixed. However, Trincomalee is easily reached by bus from Colombo and Kandy via Habarana, and from Anuradhapura via Horowupatana. The coastal route from Batticaloa involves numerous ferry crossings and is very slow. There is a daily train from Colombo via Gal Oya.

Getting around

The centre of Trincomalee is quite compact, though you will need to take a bus or three-wheeler to get to the beaches north of town. Orr's Hill, 15 minutes walk from the centre, is the main ex-pat area, with NGO offices and the town's only luxury hotel. Kanniyai hot wells, the Commonwealth War Cemetery and the beaches north of Trinco can easily be visited from the city but north of Nilaveli the coastal road deteriorates. If heading south you will find that the road is good as far as Kinniyai. Beyond here it worsens rapidly and to reach Mutur involves four ferry crossings – it is better to catch a boat across the bay from the jetty on Inner Harbour Road. ▸▸ *For further details, see page 307.*

Best time to visit

Trincomalee and its surrounding beaches are best visited between April and October, when the area is at its driest. Between November and March, the east is sometimes battered by strong wind and rains, and the sea in unsuitable for swimming during these months.

Background

Originally known as Gokanna, Trincomalee was one of the earliest settlements of Indian Tamils in Sri Lanka, and later was used as a port by the Kandyan kings. The scale of its advantages was however only fully realized by successive European invaders.

The town is a remarkable exception to the typical pattern of colonial ports which, once established, became the focal points for political and economic development of their entire regions. In India, Madras, Calcutta and Bombay each owed their origin to colonial development and succeeded in re-orienting the geography and economy of their entire regions. However, Trincomalee was established as a colonial port purely for its wider strategic potential: the finest natural harbour in Asia, dominating the vital navigation lanes between Europe and Asia, especially significant from the late 19th century when steam power saw a massive increase in the size and draught of naval ships. Trincomalee was home to the South East Asia Command of the British Navy during the Second World War, and its bombing by the Japanese in 1942 was seen as a major threat to the Allies' lifeline to Australasia and the Pacific.

Despite the port's global strategic importance it had virtually no impact on its immediate hinterland. Barren and thinly populated, the region around the city saw no development, and economically Trincomalee District remained one of Sri Lanka's most backward regions. The town itself has never been very important, but that reflects its location in Sri Lanka's dry northeastern region, where the interior has been difficult to cultivate and malaria-infested for centuries. Only today, with the completion of the Victoria Dam and the re-settlement scheme of colonizers using irrigation from the Mahaweli Ganga Project, is the area inland developing into an important agricultural region.

Jane Austen's younger brother Charles is buried in St Stephen's Cemetery in Trincomalee.

Torn by political strife since 1983, the future for the town is at last beginning to brighten. A resurgence in tourism offers one opportunity for increasing revenue, and the possibility of a return to peace remains the best hope of stimulating significant economic development in its hinterland (see box). Despite the ceasefire, however, at the time of writing the cessation of talks and continued skirmishes between the Navy and the LTTE's Sea Tigers off Trinco's waters had put the prospect of a settlement in the balance.

Sights

The main town is built on a fairly narrow piece of land between Back Bay and the Inner Harbour, and, while much of the harbour remains off-limits, Fort Frederick provides the main point of tourist interest. At any one point it is only possible to see sections of the magnificent bay which gives the harbour its reputation, but there are some good views from Orr's Hill. One of the town's more unusual features is its many spotted deer which can be seen grazing throughout the city, including on the beach.

Fort Frederick

Situated on a rocky headland, this is still an active army base but visitors may enter. It is especially worthwhile to go up to the **Swami Rock** and the Konesvaram temple built on the cliffs high above the sea. The fort was originally built by the Portuguese in 1623 who destroyed the original and ancient Siva temple. Entering through the gate, which dates from 1676, a noticeboard on the left gives a short history of the fort's complex vacillating fortunes: it was continually handed back and forth between the Dutch, British and French, a result of wars in Europe, until finally taken by the British in 1796. It was christened Fort Frederick after the Duke of York, son of George III, who was stationed here.

Inside, in a cordoned off military zone, there are two cannons, a howitzer and a mortar. To the right of the path is **Wellesley House**, now the home of the Kachcheri. The house has a remarkable role in changing the course of European history. In 1800 the Duke of Wellington convalesced here from an illness after his South India campaign, missing his ship which subsequently went down with all hands in the Gulf of Aden. Nearby there are four British and Dutch gravestones from the early 18th century.

The modern Hindu **Konesvaram Temple**, one of the five most sacred Saivite sites in Sri Lanka, stands at the farthest end of **Swami Rock** in the place of the original. It has a lingam, believed to be from the original shrine, which was recovered from the waters below by a diver. Only a couple of stone pillars from the original temple have survived. The new temple is highly decorated and painted; regular services are held with the one on Friday evening particularly colourful. Leave your shoes at the entrance, for which a small donation will be requested. Go behind the temple to find **'Lovers Leap'**, apparently so-called after the legend according to which the daughter of a Dutch official, Francina van Rhede, threw herself from the rock after her lover sailed away. The truth seems to be more prosaic than the fiction, however, for according to government archives she was alive and well when the Dutch memorial was placed here! A memorial stands on an old temple column on the rock summit though is now sealed off to prevent others following the same fate. Nearby, on a precarious ledge on the cliff side a tree has typical strips of coloured cloth tied on its branches, left there by devotees of the temple in the hope of having their prayers answered.

The terrace around the temple offers fine views to the north across Back Bay and the Inner Harbour, and from vantage points on the rock cliff you can sometimes see turtles swimming in the transparent blue-green sea over 100 m below.

The market

North of the stadium and clocktower, Main Street, Central Street and North Coastal (NC) Road form a thriving shopping area where small single-storey shops and pawnbrokers, many Muslim-run, sell all sorts of goods. Just by the clocktower is a busy fish market, where you can watch tuna, rays and swordfish change hands.

Other sights

Sadly, many of Trinco's interesting buildings, such as Admiralty House, the British Dockyard and Fort Ostenburg, built on a hill east of Inner Bay, are not open to visitors. There is little left of the British naval days apart from vivid and graphic names on the map: Marble Bay, Sweat Bay, Yard Cove, Deadman's Cove, Powder and Sober Islands. French Pass marks the passage where the French fleet escaped.

North of Trincomalee

Commonwealth War Cemetery

→ *Colour map 4, grid A1*

At **Sampalthivu**, about 5 km north of Trinco, just before the road crosses the Uppuveli creek, is the Commonwealth War Cemetery. During the Second World War, Trinco was an important naval and air force base and the harbour was the focus of Japanese air raids in April 1942. Five Blenheim bombers were shot down, and the aircraft carrier HMS *Hermes*, along with the destroyer *Vampire* and corvette HMS *Hollyhock*, were sunk off Kalkudah and Passekudah bays to the south; many graves date from this time. As the island was a leave recuperation centre, still more died as a result of their wounds.

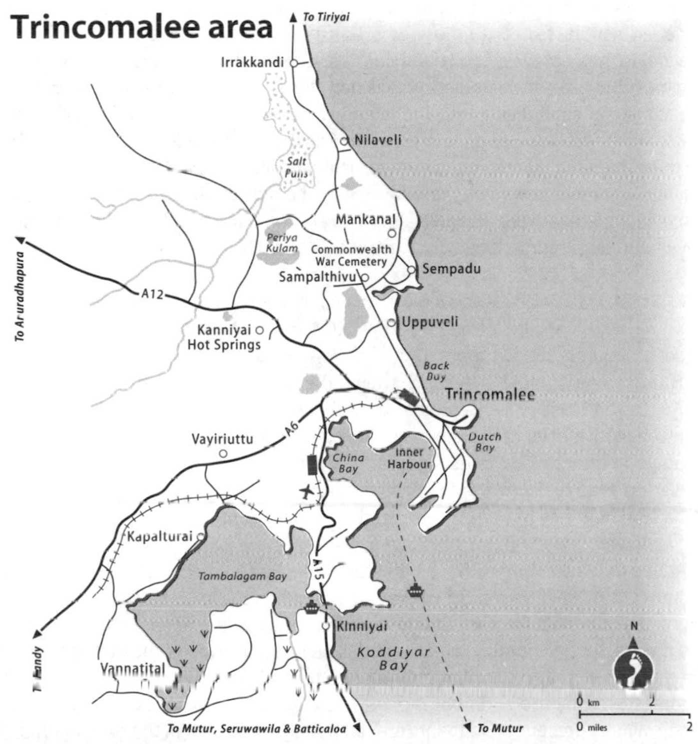

The cemetery was damaged by bombing during Sri Lanka's civil war in the late 1980s. The damaged headstones have now been replaced and the garden is beautifully maintained in the tradition of Commonwealth War cemeteries. HRH Princess Anne visited in 1995 and planted a *margosa* tree. The cemetery has great sentimental value for many whose families were stationed at the naval base, and a visit is a sobering experience for anyone. The custodian has a register of the graves and will show the visitor some interesting documents relating to Trincomalee.

Uppuveli → *Phone code: 026. Colour map 4, grid A1.*

For those without transport, Uppuveli beach, 4 km north of Trinco, is probably a better option than its more famous northerly neighbour. It is more convenient for trips into town with buses and three-wheelers running regularly, and the main road is more accessible from the beach. While most buildings were destroyed, there is also a little more evidence of some post-war recovery, making the beach experience a little less surreal. The reopening of a major resort hotel has meant that parts of the beach, suitable for swimming from March to December, are now well maintained.

Nilaveli → *Phone code: 026. Colour map 4, grid A1.*

Nilaveli, 16 km north of Trincomalee, is Sri Lanka's longest beach, and before the war was one of the island's most popular. It is not hard to see why. The straight wide strip of inviting white sand, backed by screw pines and palmyras which provide shade, stretches for miles, and the beach's gentle waters are safe for swimming outside the period of the northeast monsoons. The collapse of tourism through the war years has token its toll, though. Two minutes' walk from the beach's only surviving resort hotel is the sad and depressing sight of the bombed remains of its resort neighbours, while away from the Nilaveli Beach, the beach is strewn with litter. The situation will improve however as tourists return.

Most visitors, especially those who stay in the northern part of the beach, hire a boat out to the narrow **Pigeon Island**, just a few hundred metres offshore. It is covered with rocks but has some sandy stretches and offers snorkelling to view corals and fish. There is some good diving too. The island is named after Blue Rock pigeons which breed here (the island was once used by the British Fleet for target practice!). Their eggs are prized by Sri Lankans. There are no facilities and little shade, so go prepared. Hotels run trips to the island from Rs 550, while local fisherman often approach tourists direct, undercutting hotel prices. The area around the **Nilaveli Beach Hotel** is the best place to leave from – trips are quickest and cheapest from here.

North of Nilaveli → *Colour map 1, grid C6. Take local advice before making this trip.*

This area has a stark and desolate beauty. White sandy beaches are backed by inland lagoons though detritus from the civil war is found everywhere. Few pre-war structures remain; most are empty shells. The majority of local people have yet to return. Beyond Nilaveli, the coastal road deteriorates rapidly and you will need a four-wheel drive beyond Kuchchaveli. Bring plenty of drinking water and expect to be stopped frequently for questions at the many checkpoints and army camps. Foreigners are usually allowed to pass through unhindered, but slow right down and make sure that they have acknowledged you before continuing.

At **Tiriyai**, 35 km north of Nilaveli, there are the part-restored remains of an eighth-century *vatadage* with a small stupa inside and fine guardstones atop a hill, reminiscent of Medirigirya. Sri Lanka's first temple is said to have been built here during the Buddha's lifetime, enshrining a hair relic he gave to two Indian merchants as a reward, though nothing remains of this period. At the top of the hill there are fine views across to sea, 4 km away, and inland. The modern temple at the foot of the hill was destroyed by the LTTE, but monks returned here in May 2002 protected by a strong military presence. Elephants are often seen in this area in the evening. The site can be reached directly from Trinco or it is also accessible from a turn-off on the Anuradhapura-Trinco Road near Pankulam via Gomarankadawela, though the road is again said to be poor.

South of Trincomalee

Mutur → *Colour map 4, grid A1. 12 km from Trincomalee.*

Sri Lanka's longest river, the Mahaweli Ganga, drains into the sea at Mutur. Here, there is also a stone memorial under a tree to Sir Robert Knox, see page 381, who was captured here by King Rajasinha II in 1660, taken upriver and imprisoned for almost 20 years. Knox's *An Historical Relation of Ceylon* was one of the inspirations for Defoe's *Robinson Crusoe*.

Seruwawila → *Colour map 4, grid A1.*

Seruwawila Raja Maha Vihara, close to Allai tank, was originally built by King Kavantissa in the second century AD in an attempt to extend his authority to the ancient kingdom of Seru here. The small restored *dagoba* is said to enshrine the Buddha's frontal bone, around which several ancient structures remain. Nearby are two caves housing Buddha figures under the cobra hood of a Naga king.

Sleeping

Trincomalee *p300, map 300*

The possibility of a lasting peace has resulted in a mini-spate of hotel renovation, giving travellers the option of staying comfortably in Trinco itself, rather than needing to press on to Nilaveli. The grotty beachfront guest houses on Dyke St are not recommended.

B **Welcombe**, *Orr's Hill, T2222373, welcombehotel@sltnet.lk* Trinco's first luxury hotel! Complete refurbishment and redesign of the former 7 **Islands Hotel** has resulted in an architecturally interesting boat design. 25 stylishly furnished and spacious rooms, all with balconies (those at 'stern' and 'bow' best) and harbour views, rooftop terrace restaurant, naval themed wood-panelled bar, pool planned.

C **Medway**, *250 Inner Harbour Rd, T2227655, F2222582, jrstrinc@slt.lk* Large, spotless, comfortable if characterless rooms (US$30) with TV, good showers (hot water) and snazzy a/c units in motel-style building.

D-F **Lagoon Inn**, *208 Plantain Point Rd, T/F2221037*. 15 rooms, more to come, 2 a/c (Rs 1,750), rest fan (Rs 700), bar, restaurant.

E **Sun Flower Guest House**, *154 Post Office Rd, T2222963*. 7 clean rooms with fan and attached bath (Rs 1,000) in friendly new guesthouse, bakery downstairs for breakfast.

F **Harbour View Guest House**, *22 Orr's Hill Lower Rd, T2222284*. Good position overlooking the harbour but unattractive rooms (Rs 650-750), a local watering hole, only if you're desperate.

F **Kumar's Guest House**, *102/2a Post Office Rd, T2227792*. 5 small, clean rooms (Rs 650), nets, ice cream parlour downstairs.

F **New Silver Star**, *27 College St, T2222348*. Fairly clean rooms (Rs 600) around a central courtyard, quiet, restaurant.

F **Railway Retiring Rooms**, 6 rooms with fan, shower, some with nets, all share a sitting area with balcony, eats downstairs.

F **Venus Lanka**, *206 Plantain Point Rd (Orr's Hill Lower Rd), T2222555*. 5 basic rooms (Rs 500) in enormous building used mainly for weddings, pleasant location on Yard Cove, meals available.

G **Trinco Rest**, *opposite clocktower, 497 Dockyard Rd, T2227545*. Very basic small rooms (Rs 300-400), pungent smell of fish but may be useful if you have an early bus.

North of Trincomalee *p303*

A-B **Club Oceanic**, *on beach 4.5 km north of Trinco, 600 m off road, (and 300 m before war cemetery), T2222307, htlres@keells.com* Substantially refurbished in 2003, 40 comfortable rooms, all with a/c, some with TV and sea-view balcony (US$48-60), plus 16 excellent, well-designed beachfront 'luxury chalets' (US$85). Good location right on curved bay with superb sandy beach, open-sided restaurant, pool, nightclub.

A-D **Nilaveli Beach (NBH)**, *11th mile post, 4 km north of Nilaveli Village, T2232295, tangerinetours@eureka.lk* The only place to remain open throughout the conflict, 85 rooms, most now renovated, covering a broad spectrum of budgets from luxury suites with TV, huge beds, great views and private roof sun-terrace (US$55), through standard a/c (US$38) to unrenovated but good value 'garden view' rooms (Rs 1,700); also homely chalets with 2 bedrooms, kitchen and dining room. Good evening buffets (with cheesy entertainment), large pool, densely shaded beachfront garden, excellent location on best part of beach. PADI diving school (open Apr-Oct), trips to Pigeon Island (Rs 550 for 2), fishing (Rs 990 first hr), tennis and badminton.
D **Nema Beach House**, *on main road, Uppuveli, T2227613*. 4 fairly clean rooms with attached bath (Rs 1,250 including breakfast), 400 m from beach.
D **Nilaveli Garden Inn**, *near NBH, Nilaveli, T2232228*. 15 simple but clean rooms with terrace (overpriced at Rs 1,400-1,500 but big reductions off-season). 200 m from beach, set amongst lovely gardens, restaurant. 26 more rooms to come.
D-F **French Garden Pragash**, *Uppuveli, T2221705*. Cleanish, small, basic rooms, sea view Rs 750, no view Rs 500, plus 1 a/c (Rs 1,350, not worth it), excellent location right on the beach, fan, nets, attached bath, good seafood restaurant (dinner Rs 150-250, breakfast Rs 150-200), boat for hire.
E **Shahira**, *10th mile post (1.5 km south of NBH), Nilaveli, T2232224*. 20 clean rooms with fan (Rs 800) around shady garden, attached bath, restaurant, bar, exchange, 200 m from beach, friendly, good value.
E-F **Coral Bay**, *389 Fisherman's Lane, first hotel on beach in Nilaveli village, T2232272*. 10 clean, good value rooms (a/c Rs 850, non-a/c Rs 750) overlooking well-kept garden in front of beach, though variable food.
F **Anton Tourist Guest House**, *near French Garden Pragash, Uppuveli, no phone*. Dark dingy rooms with horrid bathrooms (Rs 500) but friendly (brother of owner of French Garden).
F **Golden Beach Cottages**, *next to Club Oceanic, Uppuveli*. 10 small, dark but fairly clean rooms with attached bath (Rs 600). Lovely setting on fine beach, restaurant.
F **H & U Guesthouse**, *100 m from NBH towards road, Nilaveli, T2226254, vetri@sltnet.lk* 5 clean rooms with fan (Rs 500), restaurant, IDD and internet (Rs 10 per min). Owner is a licensed tour guide with good English and German.
F **Seayard**, *2 km south of NBH, Nilaveli, no phone*. Just 2 mins from beach, 7 basic but clean rooms, fan and own terrace, Rs 770 (including taxes), restaurant.

Eating

Trincomalee *p300, map 300*
RsRs **Welcombe Restaurant**, magnificent position overlooking Inner Harbour.
RsRs **Seaman's Centre**, *20c Central Rd, Orr's Hill, T2224782, open 1030-1430, 1730-2200*. A/c restaurant with large menu of seafood, Sri Lankan and Chinese specialities.
Rs **Parrot Restaurant and Bar**, *96 Main St, open 0900-2130*. Cheap Chinese, devilled dishes, string hoppers.
Rs **New Ambal Café**, *79 Post Office Rd*, does good dosai and short eats. One of several good cheap eateries at the junction of Post Office and Court Rds. There are others by the bus stand.
Rs **Kumar's Cream House**, ice cream and snacks, open 0900-2100.

Bars and clubs

Trincomalee *p300, map 300*
Welcombe Restaurant, see Eating above, is a stylish place for a drink, or the guesthouses on Dyke St in Dutch Bay serve alcohol.

North of Trincomalee *p303*
Nilaveli Beach has 3 bars though drinks are expensive (Carlsberg Rs 220); the evening's entertainment varies in quality.
Toddy Tavern, *on the main road just after Shahira turn-off*, no-nonsense drinking den full of belching one-eyed old fishermen but toddy is cheap at Rs 25 per plastic jug.

Entertainment

Trincomalee *p300, map 300*
There are an enormous number of cinemas showing abysmal US action and 'adults only' films (*Killer Babe of the CIA* was popular at the time of visit).

⚽ Sport and activities

North of Trincomalee *p303*
Nilaveli Beach Hotel (Apr-Oct) runs diving and snorkelling trips to Pigeon Island, and Red Rocks, both of which are good for coral and exotic fish, and trips to nearby wrecks.

Transport

Trincomalee *p300, map 300*
Bus CTB and private bus stations are adjacent to each other. To **Colombo** private buses (via **Habarana** and **Dambulla**) depart when full during the morning and early afternoon (5-6 hrs). CTB buses leave every 30 mins-1 hr (5½-7 hrs, semi-luxury Rs 125, normal Rs 85). Fairly frequent buses to **Kandy** (5 hrs, Rs 54). To **Habarana** hourly until 1630 (semi-luxury Rs 40, normal Rs 40). To **Polonnaruwa** 3 buses a day (3½ hrs, Rs 45) or change in Habarana. Fairly regular buses to **Anuradhapura** (3 hrs, Rs 37) and **Vavuniya**, or change in **Horowupatana**. One bus daily to **Batticaloa** (5½ hrs, Rs 76); for **Passekudah** beach change at Valaichchenai.
Train The station is at the north end of town about 800 m northwest of the clocktower. To **Colombo Fort**, 0845 and 2000, (8 hrs, 2nd class Rs 168, 3rd class Rs 61). Change at Habarana for **Polonnaruwa** and destinations east.

North of Trincomalee *p303*
Bus Crowded buses run to **Uppuveli** (Rs 4) and **Nilaveli** (Rs 12) hourly until 1830 from Trincomalee or you can take a 3-wheeler (Rs 100 to Uppuveli, Rs 300 to Nilaveli).
Tiriyai is a 2- to 3-hr drive. Buses run from Trincomalee at 0545 and 1230 which take 4 hrs – it is easier to take a 4WD. Between Kuchchaveli and Tiriyai a ferry transports vehicles and cars across the lagoon.

South of Trincomalee *p305*
Ferry They leave Inner Bay for **Mutur** at 0730, 1030, 1430 and 1700, returning at 0745, 1045, 1430 and 1645 (Rs 40, 1½ hrs).
Bus 2 a day take the long land route from Trinco (5 hrs, Rs 54). Occasional from Mutur to **Seruwawila**, or take a 3-wheeler (1½ hrs).

Directory

Trincomalee *p300, map 300*
Banks Plenty of banks in the centre of town, including **Commercial Bank**, Central Rd and **Hatton National Bank**, NC Rd.
Communications **Post office**, *corner of Power House and Court rds*. Also, plenty of **Metrocard** and **Lanka Payphones** cardphones around town, or make discount IDD calls at **Votre Maison**. There are several **internet** cafés with fast connections near the post office, *Court Rd*, all charging Rs 60 per hr: **Cometnet**, *0800-2200*, **JSP Internet Cafe**, *0600-2330*, and **PC Home**, *0700-2300*.

North of Trincomalee *p303*
Banks People's Bank changes foreign currency and TCs in Nilaveli village or exchange at the **Nilaveli Beach Hotel**.
Communications **Post office** in Nilaveli village. **Friends Communication** near the Toddy Tavern provides IDD. **Internet** at H&U Guesthouse Rs 10 per min; cheaper in Trinco.

Arugam Bay and around

Even while civil war has raged through the beach resorts along the coast to the north, a small but persistent body of travellers has always been drawn to the surfer's paradise of Arugam Bay. But if this laid-back little village invitingly set between a picturesque lagoon and a magnificent sandy bay has something of a reputation as a long-stay hippie hideaway, the opening up of the surrounding area should attract a different crowd. The growing range of good value (and sometimes quirky) accommodation here make an excellent base for exploring some of the wildest countryside in Sri Lanka. This feels like frontier territory, largely deserted during the civil war, and ideal for those tired of the commercialism of the west coast. ▸▸ *For Sleeping, Eating and other listings, see pages 312-316.*

Ins and outs

Getting there

There are few direct buses to Arugam Bay – one early morning from Colombo. Badulla and Wellawaya are the best starting points, though you may need to change in Monaragala. For details of these routes, see below, East to Arugam Bay. The main bus stand is in Pottuvil, about 3 km north of the accommodation at Arugam Bay – a few buses a day make the trip across the lagoon, or a three-wheeler costs around Rs 60.

Getting around

The roads around Arugam Bay are quiet and flat, so cycling (available from guesthouses) is a convenient way to get around the local area. For excursions further afield and to the national parks, you will need a jeep or motorbike.

Best time to visit

Most travellers come for the surfing season from April to October, when it is dry and there are constant breezes. Off-season many guesthouses close, though the area still has its attractions: from January to March windsurfing, fishing and swimming are good, and bird-watching is most rewarding when winter migrants arrive.

Tourist information

The long-established hotels, **Stardust** and **Siam View**, are valuable resources with good websites: www.arugambay.com and www.arugam.com respectively.

East to Arugam Bay

Routes to Monaragala

There are two routes to Arugam Bay from the west. The quickest is the A4 from Wellawaya, via Buttala, and Okkampitiya, where there is open-pit garnet and sapphire mining. At Kumbakkana, a turn-off leads to the ancient site at Malagawila, see page 185. The alternative longer but more scenic route descends from the hills on the A22 from Badulla, passing Mount Namunukula and through tea country. It joins the A4 at Hulanduwa, which takes you to on to Monaragala.

Monaragala → *Phone code: 055. Colour map 5, grid B4. 71 km from Pottuvil.*

Most people pass through the small town of Monaragala ('Peacock Rock'), backed by forested hills, in the rush for the coast. But this small district headquarters, deep within the Dry Zone, is surprisingly lush and verdant owing to its own Wet Zone micro-climate. There's little to do in Monaragala itself but it has a laid-back appeal and is both a useful stop halfway to Arugam Bay and an excellent base from which to explore the surrounding countryside, rich in wildlife and unfairly ignored by tourists.

To the north are the remains of the 12th-century palace of **Galabedda**, with a fine bathing pool reminiscent of the Kumara Pokuna in Polonnaruwa, while to the south there are some attractive walks into the cool **Geelong Hills**.

Monaragala to Arugam Bay

The road surface is good until **Siyambalanduwa**, a former major checkpoint at which all vehicles travelling west would be searched. There is a still a large police presence but now little fuss. The A25 here leads north to Ampara and Batticaloa. East of here, potholes begin to appear and the pace of life (never very fast) slows still further. Ox-pulled cart becomes a common mode of transport and it is a peaceful drive through the dappling, the road lined with jack, margosa and tamarind trees. The road passes through **Lahugala**

National Park, and elephants are frequently seen from the road in the afternoon. For details of Lahugala and the nearby Magul Mahavihara See page 310.

Arugam Bay → *Phone code: 063. Colour map 5, grid D6.*

The Bay

Arugam Bay's wonderful wide sweep of sandy beach is usually deserted, except at the southwest corner, where some fishing boats and thatch huts reveal the tiny fishing village of **Ulla**, just to the south of the guesthouse area. This is also the safest area for swimming, which has led to a tussle between local hoteliers and fishermen (only ever one winner, the boats will probably relocate to the next beach). The lack of tourists, especially in the off-season, means that the beach can be dirty in some places, strewn with plastic bags and bottles.

The bay lies between two headlands and is excellent for surfing. **Arugam Point**, to the south, is the main break, regarded by many as the best in the country, with a clean wall of surf allowing a ride of up to 400 m. In season it can get crowded. In contrast, **Pottuvil Point** at the northern end of the bay, is often deserted and is popular with more experienced surfers. The journey to the beach here takes you across some attractive meadows teeming with wildlife. From Arugam Bay three-wheeler drivers charge Rs 350-400 return to Pottuvil Point, including waiting time.

There are various opportunities for wreck diving in the bay with five pre-1850 ships within 5 km of each other.

Pottuvil & Arugam Bay

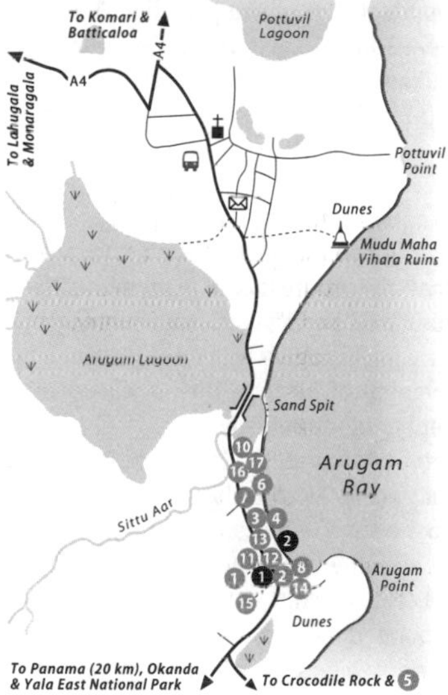

Sleeping
Aloha Cabanas 13
Arugambay Beach Resort 6
Arugam Bay Hillton 2
Beach Hut 7
Galaxy Beach 16
Hang Loose 15
Hideaway 1
Kudakkallya Bungalow 5
Mid Bay 3
Rupa's Beach 14
Sea Shore 17
Siam View Beach 8
Stardust Beach 10
Sun Rise 12
Tri-Star 11
Tsunami Beach 4

Eating
A-Bay & Surf Shop 1
Hanif's Food Garden 2

Not to scale

Lagoons → *For boat trips, see page 315.*

Arugam's picturesque lagoon divides Ulla village from Pottuvil town. The bridge is an excellent vantage point for the sunset, and at night you can watch prawn fishermen throwing, gathering and emptying their nets. Pottuvil lagoon, north of town, supports a wide variety of wildlife including crocodiles, monkeys, water snakes and plenty of birds, though partial destruction of the lagoon's mangrove forest has had a negative effect on wildlife. There are re-planting schemes afoot.

Pottuvil

The dusty Muslim town of Pottuvil, 3 km north of Ulla, has little of interest, except for the ruins, half-submerged amongst the sand-dunes, of the **Mudu Maha Vihara**, where a Buddha statue and two Avalokiteswara figures, around ninth or 10th century, can be found in a pillared structure, along with the boundary wall of an image house.

Crocodile Rock

The Crocodile Rock is 2 km south of Arugam Point along another deserted beach to **Kudakalliya**. Scrambling across the dunes and fording the lagoon where it joins the sea, you reach the rock, at the top of which there are magnificent views inland across the paddies and lagoon. Eagles swoop overhead, and you can sometimes spot elephants. There is another good surf point nearby. Do be careful getting here though. Currents sometimes render it impossible to cross the lagoon to the rock, and beware of large mugger crocodiles and the occasional elephants that attempt to climb the rock! Take advice first.

Around Arugam Bay

Lahugala National Park → *Colour map 5, grid B5. 14 km west of Pottuvil.*

This small national park (15 sq km) is good for watching birds and large elephant herds. Though it remains officially closed, in practice trips are often organized from Arugam Bay. Lying between Gal Oya and Yala, the park is part of the 'elephant corridor' for the elephant population to move freely across the south-eastern part of the island.

The **Lahugala, Mahawewa** and **Kitulana tanks** here attract numerous species of water birds, while in the dry season (especially July to August) herds of 100 or more elephants are drawn to the *beru* grass that grows in the shallow tanks. The best time to watch them is in the late afternoon. The climbing perch fish is said to slither across from the Mahawewa to Kitulana tanks when the former runs dry!

Magul Mahavihara → *8 km west of Pottuvil along the A4.*

An inscription plate here testifies that the extensive 200-acre monastery complex here (of which 50 have now been excavated) is a 14th-century reconstruction, though the site was originally constructed by King Dhatusena in the sixth century. There is an unrestored *dagoba*, a *vatadage* with an unusual moonstone, a *bodhigara* (for enclosing a bo tree) and several pavilions. A kilometre south, a circular structure with dressed slabs of stone may be an elephant stable. Excavations are due to start again in late 2003.

South to Kumana

The coastal scenery south of Arugam Bay is highly distinctive. Rising from the flat landscape are giant boulders in bizarre formations, at the foot of many of which are abandoned now overgrown cave monasteries and hermitages, some dating back almost 2,000 years. Cultivated paddy fields are interspersed with open parkland and scrub jungle, all supporting a remarkable variety of birdlife. This is wild country, largely abandoned during the war, where elephants roam freely.

The paved road ends 12 km to the south at **Panama**, the last inhabited village before Yala. Turtles can be seen in the attractive lagoon here, and crocodiles sometimes bask on its banks. A track leads to the sand dunes approaching Panama's seemingly endless beach, with its pink rocks shimmering in the distance.

At **Okanda**, 28 km south of Arugam Bay, there is an ancient Skanda shrine at the foot of a rocky outcrop. There are several associated legends. Ravana was supposed to have stopped here on his way to Koneswaram, while Skanda (Kataragama) landed here in a stone boat, with consort Valli, in order to fight Sooran. She is venerated by the Valli Amman kovil at the top of the rock. Kataragama-bound pilgrims usually stop at the shrine for the 15-day festival in July. Some 2 km inland, around Helawa lagoon, the large **Kudimbigala** rock houses a forest hermitage with a part-restored stupa and drop-ledge caves from the second century BC at its base.

Yala East National Park (Kumana Bird Sanctuary)

→ *Colour map 5, grid B6.*

The park entrance is at Kumana, ⓘ *US$6 plus extra charges. Jeeps can be hired in Arugam Bay.* Yala East National Park reopened to the public in March 2003 after 18

Pada Yatra

The traditional annual Pada Yatra from Nagadipa in the Jaffna peninsula to Kataragama is one of the world's great pilgrimages, on a par with the trip to Mount Kailasa in Tibet. Though ethnic strife nearly put an end to the trek in the 1980s, the foundation of the Kataragama Devotees Trust in 1988 has sparked a revival in recent years. Each *Wesak Poya*, an increasing band of pilgrims, predominantly but not exclusively Hindu, set out on the perilous six-week journey down the east coast along the country's ancient tracks. Dressed as beggars (*antis*) and formed into small groups (*kuttams*), they cover 8-10 km a day, bathing in rivers, sleeping in camps, and worshipping at over 70 temples en route where they are offered alms. The final section from Pottuvil, via Okanda and through Yala National Park (the only occasion on which people are allowed on foot in the park), is the most popular and dangerous. Some get lost, and even die en route, which is said to be the ultimate distinction and a sign of Kataragama's grace. The goal is the flag-hoisting ceremony at Kataragama which marks the beginning of *Esala Perahera*.

years of closure owing to the war. As at Wilpattu, see page 110, there has been some despoliation of the park's habitats and wildlife population in the intervening years. The focus is the wetland formed by the Kumana *villu*, fed by a channel from the Kumbukkan-oya when a sandbar forms at the mouth of the river in the dry season. In recent years, the tank has been unable to fill with sufficient water killing off part of the mangrove, though it has recently been reconstructed and is said to be filling up.

Large flocks of painted storks may be seen, while many birds can be spotted along the Kumbukkan-oya. The park still supports an elephant population, though herds are smaller, and it is evident that deer and wild boar have been poached, though some arrests have recently been made.

Arugam Bay to Batticaloa → *Despite the ceasefire, this is area is still prone to bouts of violence – check the local situation before venturing here.*

The quiet but well-laid coastal road north of Arugam Bay passes through alternating Hindu and Muslim fishing villages on its way to Batticaloa, now accessible within three hours. Though the sea is rarely in sight, this is a beautiful drive rich in bird life. Rice paddies and lagoons dominate the landscape, though cultivation can be affected by frequent cyclones and flooding. There is evidence of numerous income-generating projects developed by western aid agencies, and much new construction in some of the larger towns, such as **Akkaraipattu**, **Kalmunai** and **Kattankudi**, much of it an Islamic style. The Danish government is planning a harbour at Oluvil, with a new industrial zone, which will help regenerate the local area. The places of interest to visitors however lie a short distance inland.

Digavapi → *Colour map 5, grid A6.*

ⓘ *Donations requested (part of the complex was destroyed during the war).*

The enormous part-restored *dagoba* here, originally 98 m high, built by King Saddhatissa in the first century BC. Is one of the sixteen holiest Buddhist sites in Sri Lanka. The site is said to have been visited by Buddha on his third visit. Amongst the scattered remains of this ancient complex are shrine rooms, monastic quarters, *bodhigaras* and hospitals. Three gold caskets were also found during excavations. There is a small archaeological museum nearby. From the A4, take the B607 towards Ampara and turn right at the village of Varipathanchenai.

Ampara → *Phone code: 063. Colour map 5, grid A5.*

The modern district headquarters of Ampara has a recent bloody history, though is well-connected and if safe could be a used as a base for Gal Oya National Park, with accommodation, restaurants and banks. Near the Kandavatavana tank on the road to Inginiyagala is the gleaming white *dagoba* of a peace pagoda, donated by the Japanese government in 1988.

Gal Oya National Park → *Colour map 5, grid A5.*

This magnificent park was established to protect the catchment area of the Senanayake Samudra, an enormous reservoir created in 1948 by damming the Gal Oya. It remains testament to one of the most ambitious development schemes to irrigate the barren lands of the east and resettle Sinhalese from the west. Backed by sheer forested slopes, the lake is the largest in Sri Lanka, and highly impressive. The park extends over 540 sq km of rolling country most of which is covered in tall grass (*illuk* and *mana*) or dry evergreen forest which escaped being submerged. The hilly country to the west was one of the last strongholds of the Veddas, and certain areas of the park still harbour medicinal herbs and plants which are believed to have been planted centuries ago. Recent reports however suggest extensive illicit logging as well as poaching during the period of the park's closure. Gal Oya is famous for its elephants and a variety of water birds which are attracted by the lake. Crocodiles and birds such as the white-bellied sea-eagle are also often seen.

The best way to view the wildlife is by boat in the early morning, when elephants and buffaloes come down to the water.

At the time of writing there were few facilities for visitors and nowhere to hire motorboats. Contact the Wildlife Department before setting out, *T011-2694241, wildlife@sltnet.lk* A good road leads southwest from Ampara to Inginiyagala where you enter the park, or alternatively turn north from the A4 at Siyambalanduwa. The few tracks inside however are overgrown and in a poor state.

Sleeping

East to Arugam Bay *p308*

D-F **Wellassa Inn Rest House**, *500 m before bus stand, Monaragala, T2276815.* 6 simple rooms, 1 a/c, set in attractive well-maintained gardens, restaurant with good rice and curry lunch (Rs 175).

D-F **Victory Inn**, *65 Wellawaya Rd, Monaragala, T2276082, F2276100.* Under expansion, rooms of variable quality – best upstairs, brand new, clean with balcony (though not much to see), a/c available, restaurant, bar.

F **Kanda Land**, *1 km before bus stand (signposted), opposite Roman Catholic church, Monaragala, T2276925.* Has accommodation and also arranges homestays with local families. They also arrange tours, see p315.

G **Asiri Holiday Inn**, *8 Pottuvil Rd (behind service station), Monaragala, T2276618.* 6 clean, simple rooms, restaurant, decent option 2 mins walk from bus stand.

There are some simple roadside places serving local food near the bus stand.

Arugam Bay *p309, map p309*

Some guesthouses close in the off-season. Many original guesthouse owners are returning from the west and south coasts to restore their derelict properties, though the 5 or 6 well-established places that have carried on through the war years tend to have the best local knowledge. Prices, for years much lower than the national average, are beginning to rise, though it is still possible to get a basic cabana for as little as Rs 150.

LL-G **Siam View Beach Hotel**, *T2248195, arugambay@aol.com* Run by a syndicate of 5 people from 5 continents (and it shows), Arugam's party centre in a – loosely – Thai setting. Outside are 2 red British phone

Elephas maximus maximus

Cumbersome yet capable of remarkable grace, full of charisma yet mortally dangerous if rankled, universally revered yet critically endangered, the Asian variety of the world's largest land mammal has a complex relationship with man.

Once widespread across the country, elephants have been tamed for over 2,000 years. Their massive power was harnessed by the ancient Sinhalese in wars against invaders, used to construct ancient palaces, temples and reservoirs, while some were exported as far afield as Burma and Egypt. Seemingly without paradox, they also possess a mythical and religious status: the *Jataka* tales refer to the birth of Buddha in the body of an elephant, while a caparisoned elephant carries the Buddha's Tooth in Kandy's Esala Perahera; for Hindus, they represent Lord Ganesh.

Yet, despite protection, Sri Lanka's wild elephants, now mainly confined to the Dry Zone, are in crisis, numbers falling from around 10,000 at the turn of the 18th century to between 3,000 and 4,000 today. The population was drastically reduced by the British, who shot them for sport and declared them an agricultural pest, and the hill country was all but cleared of herds to make way for tea plantations. Yet after a period of recovery aided by the establishment of protected areas, numbers since the 1960s have again declined rapidly: almost 1,400 elephants were killed in the 1990s, 162 in 2001 alone, or the equivalent of around 5% of the total population in one year. Sri Lanka's ethnic troubles have been a contributory factor.

The problem lies of course in what is termed the 'human-elephant conflict'. Given the rarity of tuskers ivory is not a major issue, but deforestation, agricultural expansion and the explosion of the human population (set to double by 2035) have all deprived the elephants of their natural habitat. And while there is a growing network of protected reserves, buffer zones and elephant corridors (three national parks – Lunugumvehera, Minneriya and Kaudulla – have been established in the last decade), in practice these areas are usually too small to accommodate these enormous animals which require 200 kg of food and 200 litres of water per day, and are forced to push into adjacent agricultural lands.

Yet life is hard too for the farmer who may have his entire annual staple crop destroyed in one night, or who may even have to defend his own life from a marauding bull. Various solutions have been tried for this seemingly intractable problem – in periodic elephant 'drives' the animals are immobilized and transferred to a national park, while electric fences are a common management tool. Some suggest that compensation should be introduced for crop damage (to counter the heavy fines and/or imprisonment for killing an animal). But many experts agree the real key is in attempting to converge of the interests of people and elephants by encouraging compatible land use, such as grazing. One way forward is for farmers to derive economic benefits from elephant products such as manure for organic farming.

boxes (with authentic BT 'out of order' signs). Inside, the rooms are an extraordinary range, a real curate's egg: from a Taj Mahal themed 'Royal Suite' with personal butler, hi-fi, Jacuzzi and whirlpool (US$250); semi-detached 2-bedroom solar- powered stilt bungalows (US$75); a/c rooms with waterbed (US$15); to the cheapest en suite cabana in Arugam (Rs 300) (and everything in between)! Own generator for power cuts, restaurant and well-stocked bar, latest movies on DVD, AVH bikes now available. Eccentric, democratic, audacious.

B **Kudakkaliya Bungalow**, *2 km south of Arugam Bay, 20 mins walk from Elephant Rock, T071-2733630, jpfernando@eureka.lk* Attractive villa in secluded position with own beach and surf point, choice of bedroom or sleeping *al fresco* on (protected) veranda, cook provided or self-cater, water tank with veranda with magnificent views. From US$50 to rent whole house.

B-D **Stardust Beach Hotel**, *T/F2248191, sstarcom@eureka.lk* Danish-run, Arugam's original hotel is in beautiful location where the beach meets the lagoon and has been for many years a traveller's oasis. Choice of beach cabanas with private terrace, bungalows and new luxury rooms (US$47, with TV and phone), very clean, pleasant beach garden, excellent if pricey restaurant, cycle hire, attentive service, good source of local info, quiet, civilized.

C **Tri-Star**, *T/F2248404*. Completely renovated in 2003, 20 rooms (half a/c) flanking pool, with hot water, TV, mini-bar, plus bar, restaurant, pool, 4-person jacuzzi and steam bath, limited architectural merit but unheard of luxury for Arugam Bay!

D **Sea Shore**, *T2248410*. 4 large, clean rooms with spotless bath, plus 2 cabanas, restaurant, good position at northern end of beach.

E **Aloha Cabanas**, *T/F2248379*. Swiss-run, 5 rooms and 4 cabanas (some with ingenious extra roof compartment accessed by ladder for sitting/sleeping) in attractive plot with hanging baskets, open-air bathrooms, surf shop planned for 2004.

E **Arugambay Beach Resort**, *T2248405, orient@eureka.lk* Good, clean rooms with balcony, chalets and cabanas, friendly service.

E **Hideaway**, *T/F2248259, tissara@eureka.lk* Beautiful house with 5 rooms with veranda overlooking garden plus 4 excellent, cool cabanas, tastefully decorated, pleasant restaurant, satellite TV, peaceful location, relaxed atmosphere.

E **Rupa's Beach Hotel**, *T2248258*. 4 rooms with attached bath (Rs 1,000, more in 2004), plus 5 cabanas (Rs 350-400).

E-G **Tsunami Beach**, *T2248038, tsunami@slt net.lk* 11 simple, cleanish rooms, nets, fan, some with terrace (Rs 1,000) plus wooden cabanas (without bath, Rs 400) in shaded palm garden (with hammocks!) on beach, small restaurant.

F **Arugam Bay Hillton**, *T/F2248189, raheemhilton@yahoo.com* 9 spotless rooms with good beds, restaurant, satellite TV, internet available, organize ecotrips on lagoon (see above).

F-G **Beach Hut**, *T2248202*. Wide range of good-value accommodation (Rs 150-500) especially popular with long-termers: coconut-thatch and *kadjan* cabanas, tree-house, simple beach huts, basic rooms with 'Sri Lankan'-style shower; good cheap vegetarian food, run by Ranga, a lovely man and one of the best sources of local information in town.

F-G **Mid Bay**, *T2248390, surfcity@itmin.com* 2 rooms with bath, net, fan (Rs 500), plus 3 simple wooden cabanas (Rs 350).

F-G **Sun Rise**, *T2248200*. 5 small rooms, with or without bath, seafood restaurant, friendly.

G **Galaxy Beach Hotel**, *T2248415*. 3 beach cabanas (shared bath) plus 4 rooms with attached bath, simple, clean, popular, friendly, good vegetarian food. Good value.

G **Hang Loose**, *T2248225*. 10 clean, small rooms with attached bath (Rs 200-300) back from road, friendly.

Arugam Bay to Batticaloa *p309*

B **Inginiyagala Safari Inn**, *Inginiyagala, T011- 2693189, shasun@eureka.lk* Superb picturesque site, 10 min walk to Samudra tank, 10 rooms under renovation at time of visit (due to reopen late 2003 but ring before making the trip), day trips to Arugam Bay, Gal Oya and Lahugala to be arranged.

D-F **Gal Oya Lake Front Rest**, *106 Kandy Rd (500 m from clocktower), Ampara, T2222295.* Large but grubby a/c and non-a/c rooms (a/c way overpriced) but attractive garden and pleasant position.

F-G **Electricity Board Circuit Bungalow**, *on lake west of Ampara, T011-2451098*. 5 rooms (2 large a/c with balcony, 3 smaller non-a/c), attractive position overlooking lake, won't expect foreigners.

Eating

East to Arugam Bay *p308*

For options see Sleeping, p312.

Arugam Bay *p309*
Basic places spring up along the guesthouse draq in season. Service can be a little slow. Order food well in advance.
RsRsRs Siam View Beach Hotel, see Sleeping above. 3 chefs – Thai, Chinese and Sri Lankan – and a noisy, fun atmosphere. Sunday's all-you-can-eat buffet is popular.
RsRsRs Stardust Beach Hotel, see Sleeping above. First-class western dishes (chefs and most ingredients imported from Denmark) cooked to perfection in a laid-back setting. Expensive but worth it.
RsRs A-Bay (see Surfing below). Australian haute cuisine – beach barbies with burgers and whole BBQ fish.
RsRs Hanif's Food Garden is in a great setting on the beach for seafood dishes.
Rs Beach Hut is very popular for authentic Indian vegetarian food and has 'awesome' banana lassis.

Bars and clubs

Arugam Bay *p309*
As a Muslim area, Arugam Bay is officially 'dry' and you won't see alcohol on the menu in many places: so you'll be accosted in the street with it instead! In season, there are full-moon beach parties.
Siam View is currently the only place with a licence and has an excellent selection of beers, including Three Coins' *Riva* (wheat beer). Check Happy Hour times. Latest movies are also shown on pirated DVDs, or there is a full-size snooker table.

Sport and activities

Arugam Bay *p309*
Diving Is only possible May to July. Ask at **Stardust** in season. Fishermen run boat trips out to a black coral garden for snorkelling. Lobster fishermen will take you night fishing; ask at **Siam View**.
The **surfing** season runs from Mar to Oct. Equipment is widely available. **A-Bay Surf Shop**, *T2248187*, is Australian-run, with up to the minute equipment at Oz prices (ie cheaper than Europe), board rental Rs 300 a day.

Tour operators

East to Arugam Bay *p308*
Kanda Land, see Sleeping p312, is part of Woodlands Network. C Vasanthan is a certified local guide, offering treks into the wilderness buffer zone with Yala (3-5 days, Rs 2,500 per person per day), to the Geelong Hills and other ideas for exploring the local area.

Arugam Bay *p309, map p309*
A fishermen's cooperative society, with support from NGO Sewa Lanka, *T2248189*, runs 2-hr trips in outrigger canoes on Pottuvil lagoon in season at 0700 and 1600 (except Fri am). Rs 1,200 per canoe (2 people).

Around Arugam Bay *p310*
Guided trips to Lahugala National Park are organized by guesthouses in Arugam Bay, usually leaving around 1530-1600.

Transport

East to Arugam Bay *p308*
Bus From Monaragala, hourly buses to **Colombo**. CTB bus at 0930 and 1230 for **Pottuvil** (Arugam Bay). For the highlands it is best to change at **Wellawaya**, though there are infrequent direct buses to **Badulla**. Direct buses also go to **Kataragama** and **Matara**.
Three-wheeler They will run to Arugam Bay if you miss the bus (asking for Rs 1,000), but this is dangerous as there may be elephants on the road.

Arugam Bay *p309, map p309*
Bus A **Colombo**-bound CTB bus originating in Panama passes through Pottuvil at 0630 each morning (Rs 150, 9-10 hrs), or private bus leaves at 1700 (Rs 250). There may also be buses between Pottuvil and **Wellawaya**, though generally you have to change at Monaragala (Rs 30-35). To **Batticaloa** at 1230, plus several buses a day to **Akkaralpattu**, where you can change.

Around Arugam Bay *p310*
Bus Occasionally run to **Panama**, or you can take a 3-wheeler.
Three-wheeler Can (just!) manage the track to **Okanda** (Rs 800), but a 4WD is safer and more comfortable.

Directory

East to Arugam Bay *p308*
Banks Bank of Ceylon and People's Bank at north end of Monaragala town.

Arugam Bay *p309, map p309*
Banks Siam View now has a foreign exchange counter, or there is a Bank of Ceylon in Pottuvil town.
Communications **Post office** in Pottuvil. There are numerous places for IDD on Main Rd in Arugam. **Internet** costs Rs 5 per min off-peak at Siam View.
Tourist police By main Police Checkpoint in Pottuvil, *T2248002*.

Batticaloa and around

Until late 2002, the Tamil town of Batticaloa, along with its two famous beaches, Passekudah and Kalkudah, was well off the tourist map. Accessible once more, curious locals and foreigners are beginning to visit this remote part of the coast, and have found not a war-ravaged shell but a likeable town cautiously coming to terms with its recent troubles. Batticaloa (or 'Batti' as it is frequently called), famous for the 'singing fish' in its picturesque lagoon, has few sights but the friendliness of its people, who are genuinely pleased that you came, can make a stop on the way through to Arugam Bay or Polonnaruwa a rewarding experience. It is a relaxed place, with bicycle the chief mode of transport, making walking a pleasure. To the north, the deserted former resort of Passekudah is a bleak testament both to the ravages of war and the fragility of package tourism. Vacated by the army, however, there are the first, tentative murmurings of a return to its former lifeblood – tourism. ▸▸ *For Sleeping, Eating and other listings, see pages 319-320.*

Ins and outs

Getting there

Buses run from to Batticaloa from Colombo and Kandy via Habarana and Polonnaruwa, although it is also possible to travel from Badulla and the eastern hill country via Bibile, see page 318. From Pottuvil and Arugam Bay, you may need to change in Ampara or Kalmunai. From Trincomalee, you will need to take the inland route via Habarana. At the time of writing, the train service from Colombo terminated at Valaichchenai, close to the beaches at Passekudah and Kalkudah but check.

Getting around

Batticaloa is small enough to walk or cycle around, but you will need your own transport or to take a bus to reach the beaches north of town.

Batticaloa → *Phone code: 065. Colour map 4, grid C2.*

The fort area

The coast to the south of Batticaloa was the first landing point of the Dutch in Sri Lanka in 1602, who were welcomed by the Kandyan king to help drive out the Portuguese. They subsequently captured the Portuguese fort here in 1638, which was later rebuilt. Although overgrown and neglected, the ramparts remain intact and it is possible to walk most of the way round them – the barbed wire and armed troops will tell you when not to go any further! The area is now shared between the Kachcheri and the Army, who also occupy the Weber Stadium (once a Dutch cemetery), Town Hall, Rest House and Esplanade.

Enter from Court House Road. Take a look at the tunnel, now sadly shut off and clogged up with rubbish, which ran parallel to the lagoon, formerly providing access to a jetty. At the eastern side of the fort is a VOC gate which has been widened to let in traffic, flanked by two cannons facing out to the lagoon. A small museum, ⓘ *0900-1630*, in the complex holds various artefacts from the Portuguese, Dutch and British periods.

The lagoon → *April to October at full moon is said to be the best time to hear the fish.*

At 48 sq km, this is Sri Lanka's longest navigable lagoon, and is home of course to the **singing fish**. Numerous theories abound to the cause of this strange phenomenon, sometimes likened to a single sustained note on a guitar, one being that it is the courting call of mussels resonating against the rocks beneath. It is usually only possible to hear the fish around full moon and clearest if you go out at night with a local fisherman, who will know where to find the rocks, and for maximum effect put an oar into the lagoon with the other end to your ear.

Other sights

Batticaloa's most impressive sight lies 60 m under water, 5 km off-shore, and unless you are very experienced diver, you are very unlikely to see it. It is the gargantuan wreck of **HMS *Hermes***, the British aircraft carrier sunk in 1942 by the Japanese. Several dive teams from Hikkaduwa explored the wreck in 2002-03 and reported it to be in good condition.

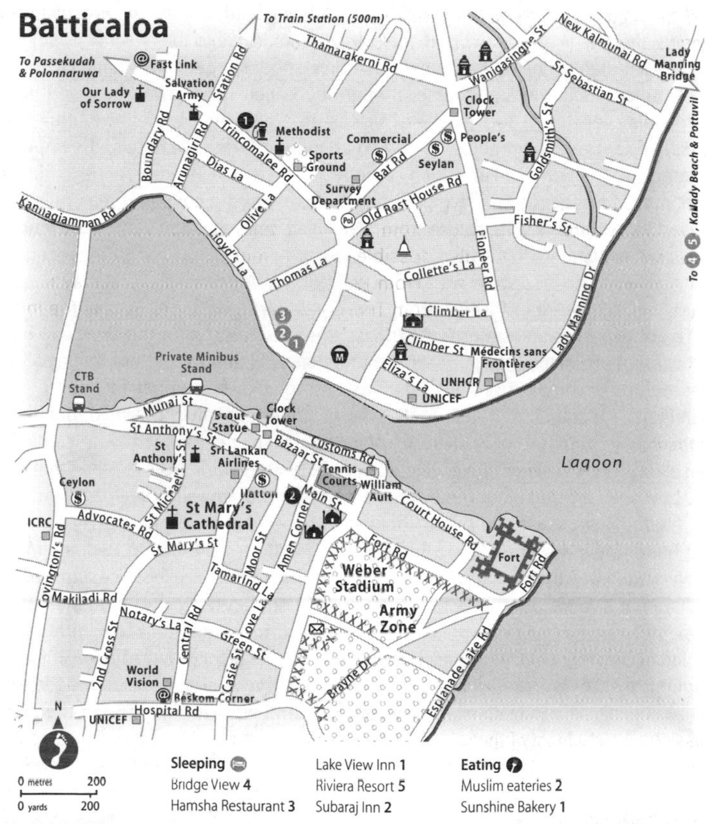

The nearest beach to Batti is at **Kallady**, 3 km from the centre of town, though those at Passekudah and Kalkudah, see below, are better. Kallady beach has fine sand though the seas are rough, it needs a bit of a clean-up and is not suitable for swimming. There are no facilities but you'll have it to yourself. To get to Kallady beach, cross Lady Manning Bridge and turn left. Otherwise, buses take 20 minutes (Rs 4).

There are some fine restored kovils and churches around town, as well as a couple of curious recently erected monuments: one an unexpected statue of a boy scout by the clocktower, commemorating the 80th anniversary of Baden-Powell's movement, the other near the fort is a bronze statue of William Ault, a pioneer of education on the East Coast. Taking you out of town to the south is the British-period iron **Lady Manning Bridge**, open to traffic with a pedestrian walkway alongside. It's just too small for two sets of traffic, so crossing by vehicle can be a bruising experience.

Around Batticaloa

Passekudah and Kalkudah beaches

➔ *Phone code: 065. 32 km north of Batticaloa.*

In peaceful times, the resorts at Passekudah and Kalkudah were one of the honey pots of east coast tourism, drawing large crowds each day to their gentle waters, safe for swimming year-round, and glorious sandy beaches. At the time of writing Kalkudah, which is protected by an off-shore reef, remained off-limits and its rest house was still occupied by the army (though there were plans to move out), but the road to Passekudah, 1 km north, was open. A few guesthouses have optimistically opened, though an army edict prevents construction close to the beach.

Passekudah's fine 4-km sweep of horse-shoe shaped bay, reminiscent of Unawatuna, is still there of course, though the beach is narrower, hemmed in by encroaching vegetation and in need of a clean-up. Lining the bay are the bombed out husks, ridden with bullet holes, of its two abandoned package hotels, the **Imperial Oceanic** and the **Sun and Fun** which is pretty shocking. Life is however beginning to stir – part of the beach is active with fishing boats, and a couple of tea stalls had opened at the time of writing. The water itself is crystal-clear and very shallow up to 500 m out to sea.

West from Batticaloa

There are two possible routes west across the scrub jungles of the Dry Zone from Batticaloa, both relaid and each with the option of visiting some hot springs. This passes through some LTTE controlled areas, and you may be stopped for papers to be examined. The quickest route to the north continues on the A15 through the depressingly bombed out town of **Valaichchenai**, near which you can visit Passekudah beach (see above). From here, Polonnaruwa is accessible within two hours, or you can stop off at **Dimbulagala** cave complex en route, see page 291.

Alternatively, a left turn off at Chenkaladi heads southwest on the A5 across a vast barren plain towards Kandy (via Mahiyangana), or via Bibile to Badulla. Maha Oya junction, 40 km on, is a good place to stop for lunch. Excellent rice and curry is available at a roadside café, after which, 2 km along a gravel road from Maha Oya town, you can visit some impressively **hot sulphuric springs**, rather unattractively pooled in concrete pots. After passing southeast of the 687-m Kokagala hill, the road is joined by the A26 at Padiyatalawa. The A5 continues south through Bibile and climbs steeply to Lunugala and Tennugewatta, and west to Badulla. For the route along the A26 to Mahiyangana and Kandy, see page 291.

For an explanation of the sleeping and eating price codes used in this guide, see the inside front cover.

Sleeping

Batticaloa *p316, map p317*
There aren't many places to stay in Batticaloa. Most can be found on the north bank of the lagoon off Trinco Rd, or 2 km out of town across the bridge in Kallady. A/c comes at a high premium.

C **C G Riviera Resort**, *New Dutch Bar Rd, Kallady, T2222165, riviera@sltnet.lk* 10-acre garden in beautiful position overlooking bridge and lagoon, a range of rooms – 3-room bungalow suite (Rs 2,000), another 3 with terrace near water's edge (Rs 600), or sleep in the water-tank (Rs 450)! Tennis court (rackets available), restaurant.

D-F **Bridge View**, *63/24 New Dutch Bar Rd, Kallady (500 m from beach), T2223723.* Near lagoon, 5 rooms including 2 a/c, clean, comfortable, restaurant.

D-F **Lake View Inn**, *6b Lloyds Ave, T2222339.* Longest-running, best-known and least clean option, rooms vary from OK (a/c, Rs 1,200) to grimy (Rs 500-750), manager barks orders in style of Basil Fawlty, passable food and popular rooftop bar but check your bill.

D-G **Subaraj Inn**, *6/1 Lloyds Ave, T2225983.* 10 large, spotless, recently redecorated rooms (a/c Rs 1,375, non-a/c Rs 550, shared bath Rs 440). Restaurant with good food.

E-F **Hamsha Restaurant**, *4 Lloyds Ave, T2223632.* 5 clean and bright rooms (Rs 500), 2 a/c (Rs 950). Indian/Chinese restaurant downstairs.

Around Batticaloa *p318*
Accommodation in Passekudah/Kalkudah is some way from the beach.

E **New Pearl Inns**, *Valaichchenai Rd, Kalkudah.* 6 rooms in large rambling house, attached bath, cool, clean, food available.

F **Ethan Inn**, *Passekudah village, T2226313.* 2 basic rooms with attached bath, seafood restaurant.

F **Gloria Inn**, *Rest House Rd, Kalkudah (500 m from beach).* 4 rooms in need of a paint but owner speaks good English.

F-G **Simla Inn**, *Station Rd, Kalkudah (from the south, cross railway line and turn right at crossroads).* Family-run guesthouse continuously open since 1981 (the last comments book lasted 19 years!), 3 simple rooms with net, fan (Rs 400-500), outside shower or draw water from well, organic food from own garden (a medicine cabinet of plants!), very friendly, basic.

Eating

Batticaloa *p316, map p317*
There are numerous Muslim eateries on Main St which are a friendly stop for lunch or a cup of tea, though hygiene may not be high on the agenda.

RsRs **Subaraj Inn** has a full English breakfast for Rs 150, Chinese dishes and good desserts (caramel pudding Rs 40).

Rs **Sunshine Bakery**, *136 Trinco Rd, T222-5159*, is a life-saver for ex-pats, with excellent cheap rolls and samosas, good lunch packets (Rs 45-80, 1100-1400), enticing cakes, seating area at back of bakery.

Bars and clubs

Batticaloa *p316, map p317*
Lake View Inn, *6b Lloyds Ave*, (Lion lager Rs 100) has a small roof-top terrace overlooking the lagoon and is popular with ex-pats.
Riviera Resort, *New Dutch Bar Rd*, is a lovely place for a sunset drink.

Shopping

Batticaloa *p316, map p317*
The market on the north side of the lagoon is a noisy and fascinating place to pick up clothes, fresh produce etc, or for range you might consider a visit to the busy modern Muslim town of Kattankudi to the south.

Transport

Batticaloa *p316, map p317*
Bus CTB and private bus station in Batticaloa are situated next to each other on Munai St, south of the lagoon. Buses leave for **Passekudah** 4 times a day (Rs 15, 1-1½ hrs), and **Kalmunai** every half an hour. To get to **Passekudah** you can also take a Kandy bus and get off at Valaichchenai. CTB buses run to **Colombo** (0645 and 1200, Rs 95-140, varying with comfort, 7½-8 hrs); **Trincomalee** (0630, Rs 70, 6 hrs); **Pottuvil** (0645, Rs 38, 4 hrs); **Badulla** (0500, Rs 65, 7 hrs) and **Kandy** via **Polonnaruwa** and **Dambulla**. Private buses also cover the major routes. Buses can be

picked up in all directions on the main road near Passekudah.

Train At the time of writing, trains on the Batticaloa line from Colombo terminated at **Valaichchenai**. They had resumed as far as Batticaloa in April 2003, only to be suspended again in July following a dispute between the government and LTTE. Check at Colombo Fort for an update, see p95.

Directory

Batticaloa *p316, map p317*

Airlines **Sri Lankan Airlines**, Central Rd (opposite Hatton Bank).

Banks Plenty of banks in town, especially on Bar Rd. **Commercial Bank**, Cirrus, Mastercard, Visa ATM, **Seylan Bank** has 24-hr Visa ATM.

Communications **Post office** is south of Weber Stadium just outside the army zone is open 0900-1700. **Internet** is available here for Rs 4 per min. IDD calls and fax are available from numerous places on Trinco Rd. **Beskom Corner**, corner of Central and Hospital Road, is open until 2130, and has internet (Rs 6 per min) and postal facilities. **Fast Link**, 34 Trinco Rd, 0830-2000. Internet Rs 5 per min, good connection. Also van hire.

Jaffna & the North

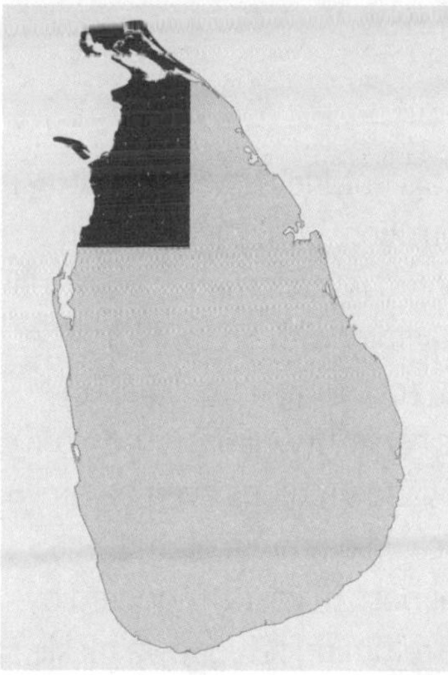

Introduction

Sri Lanka's Northern Province has for centuries been the cultural heartland of the island's Tamil population. With the northern and western tips of the province only a few kilometres boat ride from the coast of southwest India, affinity with Sri Lanka's larger neighbour has always been strong. Yet owing to its isolation from the rest of the country and its harsh, dry climate, the North was one of the least visited of the island's regions even before the vicious ethnic fighting which sealed off much of the province to the outside world for almost 20 years. Triggered by the ceasefire of 2002, amongst the returning refugees, a trickle of tourists is now beginning to unearth the region's almost forgotten attractions. Tragically, the worst fears have been confirmed; little remains untouched by the destruction of conflict. There are few tourist facilities here, and those available are basic.

A visit to the North provides rewards precisely because of its contrasts to the rest of the island. The main focus of interest, north of the desolate and largely barren Wanni region, is the densely populated **Jaffna peninsula**. Here, amongst the war detritus, some of the flat landscape remains cultivated despite the arid climate, while fishing continues in the peninsula's shallow lagoons and along its coastline. Jaffna town's historic centre has taken a pounding but its rebuilt temples and churches are flourishing, and colourful festivals across the peninsula are once again beginning to pack in enormous crowds. Away from town are some curious natural phenomena: a desert of dunes and a bottomless well. Further afield, Jaffna's abandoned islands possess some truly deserted beaches and, at **Nainativu**, a pilgrimage site of national importance. Further south, recent evidence shows that off **Mannar island**, the narrow finger of land pointing towards India, are the remains of a causeway almost two million years old.

★ Don't miss...

1. **Nallur** Join the company of thousands at the colourful chariot festival at Nallur's Kandaswamy Temple each August, page 329.
2. **Nainativu** Take a ferry to this sacred island for the colourful *puja* at the Ambal kovil, followed by a temple lunch eaten off a banana leaf, page 335.
3. **Manalkadu** Wander amongst the dunes of the mini-Sahara searching for the half-buried church of St Anthony's, page 333.
4. **Mannar Island** Visit the largest tree in Asia and then hire a fishing boat to explore the two-million year old causeway from Sri Lanka to India, page 337.

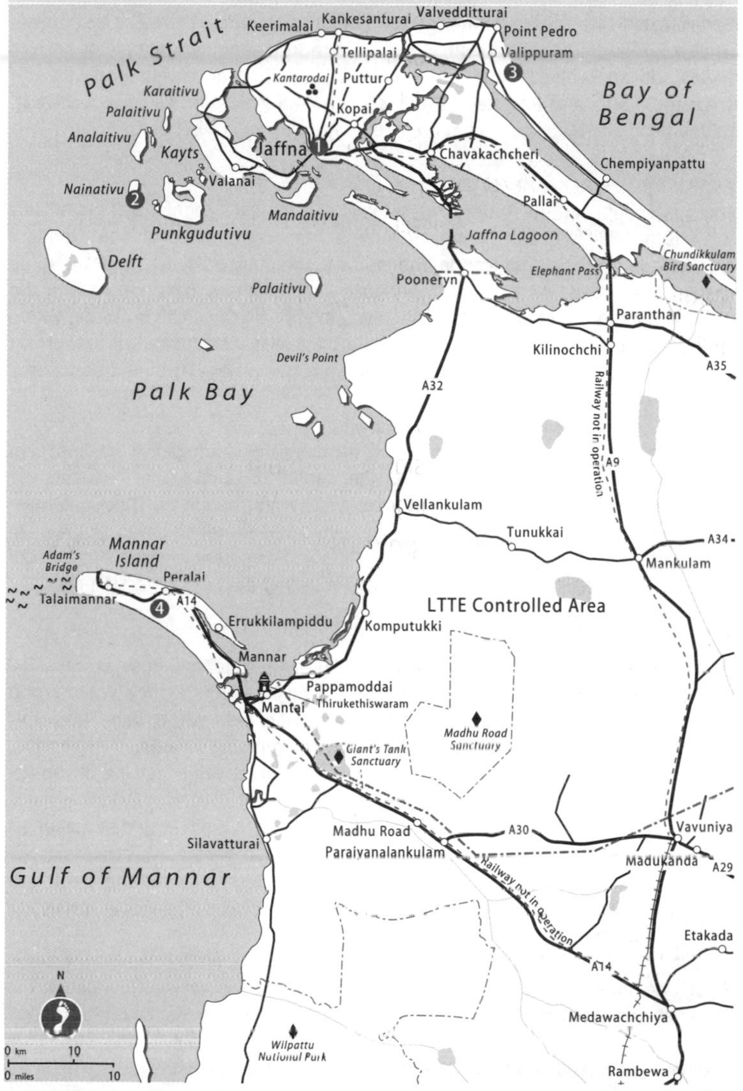

Jaffna & the north

Anuradhapura to Jaffna

The hot, arid Wanni region is at the heart of Sri Lanka's ethnic conflict, and remains under Liberation Tigers of Tamil Eelam (LTTE) control. Ravaged by fighting, it is a desolate wasteland of war detritus – cleared forest and uncleared minefields, military bunkers and shelled homes. As you travel north, uncultivated scrub takes over the flat landscape. The Wanni swelled with refugees after the Tamil exodus from Jaffna in 1995, though many are now returning home. Except for Kilinochchi and Vavuniya, there is little settlement along the A9. ▸▸ *For Sleeping, Eating and other listings, see pages 325-326.*

North to Vavuniya

Heading northeast from Anuradhapura, the A20 joins the A9 at Rambewa. **Medawachchiya** is the last Sinhalese town of any size, where there is a rest house. Some 2 km north, on top of **Issin Bessa Gala rock**, is a modern temple of ancient origins, with an elephant frieze and restored *dagoba*. There are excellent views south to Anuradhapura and Mihintale. The A14 leads northwest from Medawachchiya to Madhu Road and Mannar, though the A30 from Vavuniya is a better road.

Vavuniya → *Phone code: 024. Colour map 1, grid C4.*

About 1½ hours north of Anuradhapura, Vavuniya, now the terminus of the railway line, has the feel of a bustling frontier town. That it marks the start of disputed territory is evident in its heavy fortification and enormous military presence, and due to its strategic crossroads position its importance and prosperity have grown with the conflict. There is little to do here, though you might visit the small **museum**, where there are some ancient Buddha statues. About 4 km east at **Madukanda** is a *vihara* on the spot where the Tooth Relic was said to have rested on its way to Anuradhapura.

Kilinochchi → *Phone code: 024. Colour map 1, grid B3.*

Close to the large, modern Iranamadu tank, the dusty uninspiring town of Kilinochchi is currently the LTTE's headquarters, or the 'capital of Tamil Eelam', housing the Tigers' court complex, police HQ and other government buildings. There has been some investment in the town and there are banks and accommodation. Some 5 km west of the A9 at Kanagapuram is a **Tamil Tiger war cemetery**, where almost 2000, cadres are interred. A three-minute silence is observed daily at 1755 (LTTE time).

North to Jaffna → *Colour map 1, grid A2/3.*

Separating the Jaffna peninsula from the mainland, **Elephant Pass** is so-called because elephants were once driven through its shallow waters on their way to export from Jaffna. Strategically important since the Dutch built a fort here, it is now notorious as the site of one of the army's most humiliating defeats: in April 2000, groups of LTTE cadres stormed into the heavily fortified camp, forcing an abrupt capitulation from the 15,000-strong military garrison. The shell of an army tank remains by the side of the road as you enter the peninsula. The area is still mined so do not get out of your vehicle.

Chundikkulam Bird Sanctuary at the southeastern edge of the peninsula traditionally attracted a large winter flamingo population, and migrants in spring and autumn, though remains off-limits.

After Elephant Pass, Jaffna's distinctive palmyras become the dominant feature, though around the Pallai checkpoint even these have been reduced to stumps. The sizeable town of **Chavakachcheri** was retaken by the LTTE for several months in 2000 and reduced to rubble. After crossing numerous restored colonial bridges over the shallow lagoons, you approach the eerily quiet suburbs of Jaffna town.

Word of warning

Between 1983 and 2001, most of Northern Province, including the Jaffna peninsula, and much of Eastern Province was off-limits to travellers due to intermittent fighting between the Sri Lanka government's military forces and the Liberation Tigers of Tamil Eelam (LTTE). Many roads were sealed off by military checkpoint. However, following the signing of a formal ceasefire agreement, the Memorandum of Understanding (MoU), between the two sides in February 2002, most roads have reopened and flights to Jaffna have resumed. Basic infrastructure is being rebuilt, the humanitarian situation is much improved, and many displaced people have returned to their homes. While there remains a threat of local skirmishes, we regard travel in the North and East as safe providing travellers are aware of the local situation and take precautions. Much of the landscape of the Jaffna peninsula and the Wanni region remains inaccessible due to land-mines and unexploded ordnance not all of which is accounted for and sealed off with warnings. You are advised not to step off roads, and in particular travel off the main A9 route into the interior of the Wanni region is not recommended. Moreover, a high military presence remains throughout the region, and the Peninsula has a number of army High Security Zones which are normally inaccessible to travellers. And while to date there have yet to be any major breaches of the ceasefire, it is advisable to check the latest situation locally first.

Sleeping

Anuradhapura to Jaffna *p324*
The main place to stay on this route is Vavuniya. Lots of places to stay and eat near the bus and rail stations, though all are quite basic.
D-E **1-9 Lodge**, *167 Kandy Rd, Kilinochchi, T071-2345629*. 8 rooms, 2 with attached bath (Rs 850-1,250), clean, nets, fan, restaurant fried rice, noodles, devilled dishes).
E **Rest House** (CHC), *Medawachchiya, T025-2245699*. Comfortable, clean rooms (though saggy beds), useful stopover.
E-F **Vanni Inn**, *Gnanavairavar Kovil Lane, off 2nd Cross St, Vavuniya, T2221406*. Better from outside than in, but quiet and the best of the bunch, functional rooms (a/c Rs 1,000, non-ac Rs 500), restaurant.
E-F **Kanathenu Lodge**, *Kilinochchi, T021-222 3954*. 14 rooms (Rs 500-1,000), some with attached bath, spartan but fairly clean, food on request.
E-G **Rest House**, *Station Rd, Vavuniya, T2222299*. 9 basic rooms (Rs 450), a/c Rs 1,000, unattractive, mainly a local bar.
The comfortable-looking **Tank View Guest House** on the Iranamadu tank south of town is only available for official guests of the LTTE!

Eating

Anuradhapura to Jaffna *p324*
For further options see Sleeping above.
Rs **Prince Hotel**, *111 Kandy Rd, Vavuniya*, serves good short eats.

Transport

Anuradhapura to Jaffna *p324*
Vavuniya is the transport hub for the region.
Bus Buses leave for **Colombo** (5 hrs) regularly. Normal (Rs 72), semi-luxury (Rs 120) and luxury (Rs 150). For **Anuradhapura**, take a Kandy or Colombo bus. Many buses to **Omantai** (for Jaffna, Rs 15, 30 mins), 0530-1630 but best to leave early. To **Mannar**, every 2 hrs, Rs 28; to **Trincomalee**, 7 a day 0630-1530, Rs 48; to **Batticaloa**, 0600 and 1000, Rs 77.
Private van For **Jaffna** can be picked up here along Kandy Rd in Vavuniya. **Westar Travels**, *Prince Hotel, T024-2222731*, charges Rs 600 to Jaffna, Rs 800 back.
Train To **Colombo** (intercity Rs 326.50/ 144/52.50), via **Anuradhapura** (1 hr 20 mins, Rs 49.50/28.50/10.50, local train also at 0720) at 0315 (7 hrs to **Colombo**, then on to

Borders, bureaucracy and bumps

In March 2002, the main land route from the south on the A9 to Jaffna reopened for civilian traffic. The trip takes you through the isolated Wanni region, which remains the stronghold of the LTTE and functions as a separate state.

By public transport, the trip from Vavuniya to Jaffna is a gruelling journey, taking around eight hours on the dusty, pot-holed track. The best way to do it is to spend the night in Anuradhapura, and leave early in the morning to be sure of reaching the final checkpoint before it closes at 1700, or you will have to spend the night in Kilinochchi. You will effectively cross two border controls, from SLA (Sri Lankan Army) owned land to LTTE-controlled territory, and back again once on the peninsula. The border controls, monitored by the ICRC (International Committee of the Red Cross) are quite efficient, but will involve four ID checks and baggage searches. Whilst as a foreigner the SLA will usually wave you through, the LTTE's unsmiling border guards will require you to buy a registration form (Rs 2 for a foot passenger, in Tamil only), which needs to be completed and kept throughout your stay in 'Tamil Eelam'. Some items, such as binoculars, video cameras and alcohol are technically forbidden in Tiger territory.

From Vavuniya, you will need to change buses several times, first at the army checkpoint at Omantai (30 minutes from Vavuniya, Rs 15), after which another bus (Rs 5) will take you to the LTTE border control near Puliyankulam. Here, you may face a long wait for another bus for the three-hour journey to the Muhamalai checkpoint near Pallai (Rs 150). You can buy snacks at the stalls in Murikandy, where all vehicles stop to pray at the small Hindu temple. From here you pass straight through Kilinochchi across Elephant Pass to Pallai, where the LTTE will check your paperwork again. After another bus trip across no man's land, the SLA will wave you through and you change again for the final stretch to Jaffna town (1½ hours, Rs 30).

If this sounds exhausting (and it is), you may opt to join a private Jaffna bus service, which can be picked up in Colombo (Rs 1,000, advertised all around Wellawatta) or in Vavuniya (Rs 700). This will still involve security checks but removes the scramble for buses along the way. Or, simplest of all, you can charter your own vehicle and driver (usually around Rs 5,000), though Sinhalese drivers may be reluctant to undertake the journey. The driver will take care of paperwork, as a foreigner you will usually be catapulted through the checkpoints, and though the vehicle will be searched, border guards probably won't concern themselves with your luggage. Or, if you're reading this in Colombo, you might take that flight after all!

Matara), 0545 (intercity, 5 hrs), 1315 (6 hrs) and 2130 mail train (7½ hrs), plus Sun only **Matara** express at 1500. Buses 0315, 1315 and 2130 call at **Kurunegala** (4 hrs) and Polgahawela for **Kandy** (4½-5 hrs, 1315 best for connections).

Directory

Anuradhapura to Jaffna *p324*

Banks Vavuniya has branches of most major banks, with ATMs.

Communications **Internet** at Infonet, 28 Station Rd (close to railway), Vavuniya, Rs 60 per hr.

Jaffna

→ *Phone code: 021. Colour map 1, grid A2.*

As the centre of Sri Lankan Tamil culture, and, in peaceful times, the country's second most populous city, Jaffna has been the greatest pawn, and the greatest victim, of the 20-year ethnic conflict of the north. Devastated by shelling, much of the town today resembles a depressing post-apocalyptic wasteland. However, the ceasefire and the reopening of the land route to the south have brought a glimmer of hope: month by month, Jaffna's displaced citizens are beginning to return home, and whilst many houses remain uninhabitable, lacking roofs and basic facilities, and widespread mines will render the surrounding lands inaccessible for years to come, many of the town's schools, temples, churches and mosques have been rebuilt, a testament to the spirit of this proud community, as well as to its support from abroad. With most of its heritage and 'sights' destroyed, Jaffna may be no place for a holiday, but those who do make the trip are often unexpectedly charmed. The city can throw up some surprises from its lively festivals and glorious old cars to its distinctive cuisine and famous ice cream parlours. The most lasting memories however are of its people. Despite, or perhaps because of, the scars of battle they are amongst the warmest and most genuine on the island. »» *For Sleeping, Eating and other listings, see pages 330-331.*

Ins and outs

→ *For details of the bus route from the south, see page 326.*

Getting there By far the easiest way to reach Jaffna is by air from Ratmalana airport, south of Colombo. Three airlines fly several times a day to Palaly airport (KKS) in the north of the peninsula. Since it is located within a HSZ, there is an army check and police escort. All airlines offer a free bus service to town (1½ hours). The main bus stand is in Hospital Road, about 2 km (a Rs 50 three-wheeler ride) west of Chundikuli, the main guesthouse and ex-pat area. The bus route passes along Kandy Road – you can ask to be let off before the terminus.

Getting around The city is quite spread out, and walking around it can be tiring in the heat. There is a good local bus network but cycling is the best way to get around. At the time of writing however there was nowhere to hire them! You may be able to borrow one from your guesthouse.

Best time to visit April to May can be unbearably hot when the southwest monsoon and heatwaves from South India conspire to drive up temperatures towards 40ºC; August to September is also very hot. December and January is the coolest time. The biggest festival is at Nallur in August (see below).

Tourist information Further reading: Philippe Fabry, *Essential Guide for Jaffna and its region* (Negombo: Viator Publications, 2003).

Background

→ *See page 345 for the political history.*

There are few archaeological or literary clues to the early period of Jaffna's history, but the peninsula's proximity to India ensured that when Tamil settlers came to Sri Lanka 2,000 years ago Jaffna was one of their earliest homes. Ruins at Kantarodai suggest that Buddhism was once the dominant religion of the peninsula, then known as Nagadipa, or the island of the Naga people, who may have had links to Greece and Rome. The period of the Kingdom of Jaffna, often invoked by nationalists today, began in the 13th century under the Indian King Kalinga, lasting, except for a brief period of Sinhalese occupation in the 15th century, until the execution of King Sankili by the Portuguese in 1620.

Over the centuries Jaffna's Tamils built a wholly distinctive culture. Despite the unsuitability of much of the thin red soil for agriculture, Tamil cultivators developed techniques of well irrigation which capitalized on the reserves of groundwater held in the limestone, making intensive rice cultivation the basis of a successful economy. Diversity was provided by coconut and palmyra palms, tobacco and a wide range of other crops, but the Tamil population was also international in its outlook. It maintained trading links not only with the Tamil regions across the Palk Straits but also with Southeast Asia.

The Dutch captured Jaffna from the Portuguese in 1658, losing it to the British in 1796. It was not until 1833 however that they politically unified Tamil regions with Sinhalese for administration purposes, ending the separateness of Tamil identity. From the mid-19th century Jaffna Tamils took up the educational opportunities which came with an extended period of British rule, and rapidly became numerically dominant in a range of government services and jobs both inside and outside Sri Lanka. In the early 1970s, this led to the 'quota' systems for education and employment which aimed to reduce Tamil influence, another contributory factor to today's conflict (see page 346).

Sights

Historic centre

Jaffna's historic centre has been devastated by the fighting. The 20-ha **Dutch fort**, built on the site of an earlier Portuguese building to control the trade route to India, was arguably the strongest fortification in Asia. Though the black coralline walls surrounded by a huge moat remain intact, all buildings inside, including the fine Groote Kerk, took a pummelling in 1990 when the army camp was shelled. Once taken by the LTTE, the Dutch buildings, regarded as a symbol of oppression, were demolished to prevent reoccupation. Though the approach road to the fort is open, the entrance is sealed off by barbed wire and guarded by sentries, who claim that it is mined. Nearby the town hall, rest house and post office have all been destroyed.

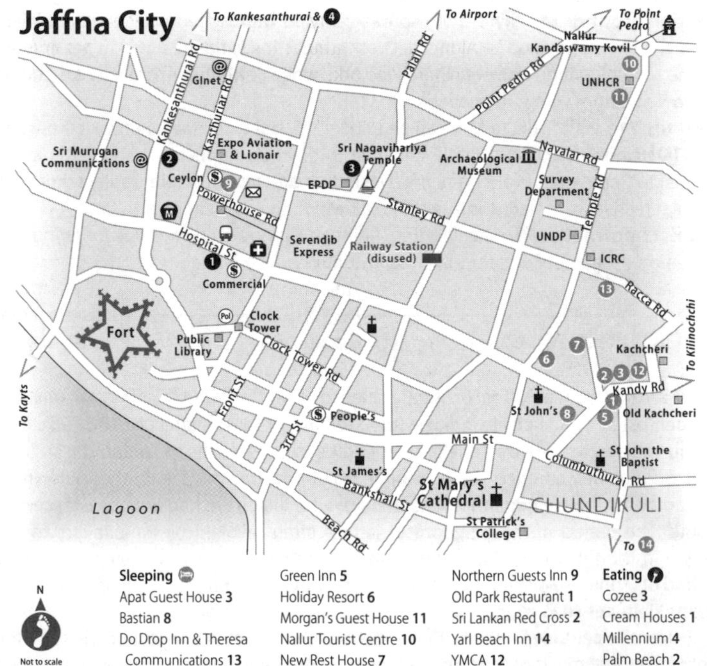

Vintage survivors

For fans of old British cars Jaffna is an unlikely Mecca. Fleets of Morris Minors, Austin Cambridges and Morris Oxfords still rattle around the town's dusty streets, preserved for posterity by Jaffna's unique situation. Their lifeline came in the late 1980s when owners of newer vehicles were forced to turn them in for the war effort, leaving the sturdy old beauties as kings of the road. The peninsula cut off since then, their owners were forced to find ever more ingenious methods of keeping them on the road, hammering out spare parts in local metal shops, and, when fuel costs spiralled out of control, by feeding these vintage survivors on a steady diet on kerosene, the carburettors fooled by just a drop of petrol. Today, Sri Lanka does a roaring trade in exporting parts to enthusiasts worldwide. Of around 70,000 Morris Minors on the road in Britain, it is estimated that more than half are sustained by the metalworkers of Sri Lanka.

In contrast, across the stadium to the east is the gleaming, restored Moghul-style **public library**, still empty at the time of visiting. The original building was torched by an anti-Tamil mob in June 1981, tragically destroying almost 100,000 books and priceless *ola* leaf manuscripts. Thousands of volumes have been donated to the new library from abroad, particularly France and India. In the library garden is a statue of its founder, Reverend Long, said to have died on hearing the news of the original library's demise. Jaffna's restored **clocktower** reopened in June 2002, with clocks donated by HRH the Prince of Wales.

Commercial centre

Life has returned to a semblance of normality in the busy **market area** between Stanley and Hospital roads. Along Kankasanthurai (KKS) Road, it is still possible to pick up some traditional palmyra craftwork, while jewellery shops cluster along Kasturiya Road.

Temples and churches

Some 3 km northeast of the fort, the ornate **Kandaswamy Temple** at Nallur hosts a spectacular 25-day festival in July/August, which in peacetime can attract up to a million devotees. The festival reaches its zenith on the 24th day, when decorated *ratham* (chariots) are paraded from dawn until midnight in honour of the god. The current temple dates from the 19th century, the original, which is believed by some to be dated from 10th-century, like most others in Jaffna having been razed by the Portuguese. *Puja* takes place seven times a day. Men must remove shirts before entering and photography in the inner sanctum is not allowed.

The legacy of successive waves of proselytising Christians from Europe, most notably Roman Catholics, is visible in Jaffna's many churches, some of which, like the Goan-style **St Mary's Cathedral** and **St James's**, are enormous edifices. Post-war restoration, aided by donors abroad, has been speedy though not always of great architectural merit. The **Sri Nagaviharaya** with its restored *dagoba* and 'elephant wall' is Jaffna's only active Buddhist temple.

Archaeological museum

This museum contains various artefacts excavated from Kantarodai, though anti-royalists may enjoy best the portrait of Queen Victoria with a bullet-hole through her! The museum is found on Navaly Road behind the Navalar Maddapam Hall.

Sleeping

Jaffna *p327, map p328*
Most accommodation is in the ex-pat area of Chundukuli-Old Park, 2 km east of the bus stand. Unsurprisingly for a city with few tourists for two decades, the choice is limited, basic and overpriced in comparison to the rest of the island, if friendly and helpful. It is worth booking early as options are frequently full. The city's hotels were taken over by the police and army during the war, and so guesthouses are the only option. New places are beginning to open up.
C **Morgan's Guesthouse**, *Nallur Rd, next to UNHCR building, T077-7262698*. Brand new, run by NGO, clean a/c rooms Rs 3,000. Bar, garden. Smartest option in town.
C-E **Old Park Restaurant**, *40 Kandy Rd, T2223790*. 4 new, spacious, well-furnished a/c rooms (Rs 2,500, Rs 1,000 for 3rd person), fan, nets, attached bath, clean, friendly and helpful, good restaurant, small garden, comfortable, popular so book ahead.
C-E **Green Inn**, *60 Kandy Rd, T2223898, F2222298*. 8 basic rooms, ranging from a/c with attached bath (Rs 2,200) to fan only with shared bath (Rs 800). Restaurant, a/c van and driver Rs 4,000 a day, pick-up from airport can be arranged (though there is a free bus), can be pushy.
C-E **Yarl Beach Inn**, *8 Old Park Rd, T2225490*. 8 clean rooms with attached bath, some with tub, a/c Rs 2,000, non Rs 1,000, friendly.
C-F **Bastian Hotel**, *37 Kandy Rd, T/F2222605*. 8 rooms (Rs 2,000 a/c attached bath, Rs 1,000, bath separate, fan, Rs 500 single), no nets, restaurant, helpful.
D-E **New Rest House**, *19 Somasundarum Ave, T2225928*. 4 rooms with fan (Rs 1,250 attached bath and net, Rs 1,000 attached bath squat toilet, Rs 850 separate bath), breakfast Rs 60, lunch and dinner Rs 90.
D-F **Holiday Resort**, *859/15 Hospital Rd, opposite St John's Church, T2225643*. 4 rooms (Rs 1,500 with a/c, separate bath, Rs 1,000 with attached bath, fan only, Rs 500 separate bath), basic but clean, friendly owner. Meals to order – breakfast Rs 30, dinner Rs 100.
F **Apat Guest House**, *43(75) Kandy Rd, T077-7559717*. 3 rooms, fan, nets, bath separate, clean, friendly, good option.
F **Do Drop Inn**, *Theresa Communication, 72 Racca Rd, T/F2222597, brendonj@sltnet.lk* 3 clean rooms, 1 with balcony (often on long-term rent to NGOs), internet, TV, very friendly and helpful.
F **Nallur Tourist Centre**, *431 Temple Rd, T077-7170072*. Basic rooms with attached bath (Rs 500).
F **Northern Guests Inn**, *20 Kannathiddy Lane*. 10 rooms (Rs 600) bath separate, clean, friendly, helpful, quiet. Plans for 2 more.
G **Sri Lankan Red Cross**, *73 Kandy Rd, T2222561*. Beds available in very basic dorms (Rs 250), dirty bathrooms and fairly grim.
G **YMCA**, *109 Kandy Rd, at the corner with Kachcheri Rd, T2222499*. 18 rooms (Rs 350), common bath, basic, meals at canteen, noisy.

Eating

Jaffna *p327, map p328*
RsRs **Cozee**, *15 Sirambiyadi Lane (off Stanley Rd)*. South Indian specialists (cook from Chennai), smart, clean, new restaurant, kebabs recommended! Rooms planned.
RsRs **Old Park Restaurant** and **Yarl Beach Inn** do similar Sri Lankan and Chinese fare (Rs 100-200 per dish). Popular with ex-pats.
RsRs **Palm Beach**, *10/11 Stanley Rd, T077-7733316, 1130-2230*. A/c restaurant and takeaway, large menu of South Indian curries, dosai, noodles (Rs 100-200), even pizzas (Rs 500-700), though often need to order the day before.
Rs There are plenty of cheap 'hotels' close to the market. Jaffna's cream houses are legendary. Serving delicious wadais and other short eats as well as ice cream, they are busy with local families throughout the day. They cluster on Hospital Rd.

Entertainment

Jaffna *p327, map p328*
Centre for Performing Arts, *238 Stanley Rd, cpajaffna@eureka.lk* Open-air theatre.

Festivals and events

Jaffna *p327, map p328*
Nallur kovil has the biggest Hindu festival in the North (Jul-Aug) but there are many others – ask locally. *Easter* is widely celebrated with passion plays performed in churches and at Jaffna's open-air theatre.

Shopping

Jaffna *p327, map p328*
Palmyra handicrafts can still be picked up in the market area, as can Jaffna wine, arrack and jaggery. The wine, along with nelli crush, is produced by the **Rosarian sisters**, *123 Main St*. For provisions, **Amrai Naga Food City**, Jaffna's first a/c supermarket is useful.

Transport

Jaffna *p327, map p328*
Air Regular services between Jaffna and **Colombo**, 1 hr, Rs 3,500 1-way, Rs 6,250 return. **Lionair**, *1T Stanley Rd, T2226026, lionairsales@sierra.lk*, is recommended. Other companies include: **Expo Aviation**, *1E Stanley Rd, T/F2223891, jaffna@expoavi.com* and **Serendib Express**, *13 New Market Building, Power House Rd, T2223916, serendibexpres@sltnet.lk*
Bus Good bus network around town, across the peninsula, and to **Kayts**, **Karaitivu** and **Pungudutivu**. Public buses leave regularly for **Muhamalai** (for the Palali checkpoint) (1 hr, Rs 20). Private bus to **Vavuniya** (Rs 800) or **Colombo** (Rs 1,000) available all over town - look around the bus station. You can also charter a bus across the Wanni from around Rs 4,000.
Three-wheeler Can be hired for about Rs 1,500 per day.
Van Can hired for around Rs 2,500 per day.

Directory

Jaffna *p327, map p328*
Banks Most banks can be found on Hospital St in town; those with ATMs include Commercial and Seylan banks.
Communications **Internet** at **Gl@netcafé**, *379 Kasthuriar Rd (corner with Navalar Rd), open 0930-2100*, and **Sri Murugan**, *303 KKS Rd, open 0700-2200*. Closer to Kandy Rd try **Theresa Communications** at Do Drop Inn (see Sleeping), but it is pricey.
Post office in a lane just north of the bus stand. **Telephones** on Kandy Rd for IDD available from **Palan's Communication** Centre. Most mobiles now work in Jaffna.
Useful addresses Survey Department, behind UNDP, Temple Lane.

Peninsula and islands

An extensive road grid criss-crosses the low, flat Jaffna landscape. Areas of sandy scrubland with palmyras alternate with intensively cultivated tobacco, banana and manioc plantations, although large areas remain mined. Another obstacle is the presence of High Security Zones (HSZs), areas regarded as strategically important in which security is high and movement restricted. At least you won't need to struggle with Tamil's legendarily unpronounceable names – most major towns have a user-friendly three-letter short form. The coastal road from Thondamanaru through Valvedditturai to Point Pedro is a pleasant cycle ride. ▸▸ *For Sleeping, Eating and other listings, see pages 335-336.*

Northeast to Point Pedro

Thirunelveli

Poongani Solai, or Poonkanichcholai, ⓘ *T2222976, Ramalingam Rd, Mudamayadi, Rs 10*, about 1 km west of Nallur temple, offer some light relief. These small pleasure gardens, impeccably kept, feature some imaginative fountains, brightly painted statues and a grotto, though the enjoyment is marred by the shackled animals on show. On some days around 1500-1600, locals come dressed up to have photos or videos taken. The gardens are 3 km northeast of town. Follow Temple Road going west and the gardens are found on the right hand side.

Kopai

The immaculately maintained **LTTE war cemetery** at Kopai, is a sobering experience. Over 1,700 cadres are buried here in row upon row of neatly laid out graves. In the corner is a display of remains of LTTE monuments destroyed by the army on re-taking Jaffna in 1995. Buses bound for Point Pedro pass nearby.

Nilavarai

The square **tidal well** at Nilavarai, 10 km from Jaffna town, near Puttur, is an interesting natural phenomenon. Legend states that Rama plunged his arrow into the soil here, quenching his thirst from its 'bottomless' spring. The water, fairly fresh at the surface, increases in salinity with depth, and a fissure in the limestone probably connects it directly to the sea. You can walk down to the well, though locals warn against swimming here.

Valvedditturai

Valvedditturai (VVT) is a small fishing town with a reputation as a centre for **smuggling** from India and beyond. The **festival** at the large Muthumari Amman kovil here, featuring processions and fire-walking, was resurrected in 2003 and draws enormous crowds each April, but the town is now most famous as the birthplace of the leader of the LTTE. A board outside his childhood home, now abandoned and overgrown, 100 m west of the Amman temple, introduces you to **'Honoured Velupillai Prabakaran's House**, the President of Tamil Eelam'. Unsurprisingly, it has become a popular local graffiti spot.

Point Pedro

Bustling little Point Pedro (PPD), 8 km east, is the peninsula's second largest town. In peaceful times, a local challenge was to swim to India from here. As well as several large churches, there is a fishing harbour, a beach and a lighthouse, which marks the most northerly point of Sri Lanka (see also page 159), though these are located within an High Security Zone. A 20-25-km tunnel built in the 10th century is said to connect Point Pedro to Nallur.

Jaffna Peninsula & Islands

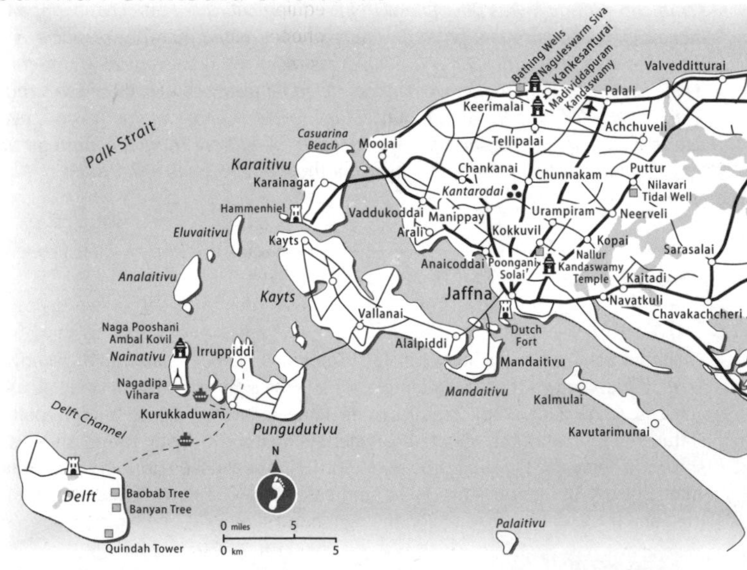

Manalkadu desert

Off the main road south of Point Pedro, is an area of **white sand dunes** known as the Manalkadu desert. Some 15 m high in places, the dunes are formed by sand blown onshore from South India by the winds during monsoons. There are the remains of the old **St Anthony's Church** here, atmospherically half-submerged in the sand. The small village of **Valippuram**, 6 km from Point Pedro, was once the capital of Jaffna and has a thriving temple, second in size on the peninsula only to Nallur. Vishnu was said to have appeared here as a fish. An inscription on a gold plate discovered here suggests that a *vihara* existed here during the reign of King Vasaba in the first century.

Road to Kankesanthurai → *Bring your passport to visit Keerimalai.*

Kantarodai

At Kantarodai, about halfway to Kankesanthurai (KKS), are the remains of around 30 squat Buddhist stupas, most between 2 to 4 m in height, crammed into a small plot. Excavations in 1918 discovered ancient Indian coins here, suggesting a 2,000-year history. Some commentators have likened the stupas in form and origin to those in the upper platform at Borobodur in Indonesia. Though no theories for their existence have proved conclusive, many agree that they represent a monastic burial ground. Kantarodai is 2 km left off the KKS road at Chunnakam junction, then another left (300 m), and then right at the junction. The site is on the left, 600 m from here.

Tellipalai

Sri Durga Devasthanam here is a fine Durga temple with an enormous *gopuram*. There is a two-week festival in August with a water-cutting ceremony. The temple is especially active on Tuesdays.

North of Tellipalai

The area north of Tellipalai lies within an army HSZ, and is inaccessible by public transport. Travelling to Kankesanthurai and Keerimalai may involve a lengthy wait for security clearance. You will be required to hand in your passport, and any equipment such as cameras, mobile phones etc. and will receive an armed escort throughout your visit.

Kankesanthurai (KKS) was during the time of the ancient Jaffna kingdom the peninsula's most important port, though is now in ruins and almost completely abandoned.

Naguleswaram Siva Kovil at **Keerimalai** is one of the earliest and most venerated Hindu temples in Sri Lanka. Largely destroyed in an aerial attack in 1990, and subsequently stripped of its antiquities, it was not until 1996 that worshippers were allowed to return. At the time of visiting, new deities by Indian craftsmen were being carved. Close to the beach behind the kovil, spring water flows up through a rock fissure to form two popular **bathing wells** (one male, one female), associated with the visit by the

Tree of Life

Jaffna's palmyras are as much the dominant feature of the northern landscape as the southern coconut, and are a cornerstone of the local economy. These tall, straight trees, which can grow up to 30 m in height, have an astonishing variety of uses. The leathery, fan-shaped leaves can be worked into mats, baskets and roof thatch, while the fruits, which grow in clusters on the stem when young, can be punctured with a finger and the water sucked out; when mature the pulp is roasted and sun-dried. The sap ferments a few hours after sunrise (just in time for the fishermen's return from their catch!), and the toddy is often drunk from an attractive cup (*pila*) ingeniously shaped from a frond and tied at one end. Alternatively it is distilled into arrack. The sap also makes jaggery, a more nutritious alternative to cane sugar. The seedlings can be eaten fresh or are used in cooking, while all parts of the plant may be used in local medicines. The trees also have an important ecological role – their drought-resistant roots help retain water in the soil, paramount in this driest of regions, and the tall trunks act as natural barriers during strong winds common to the north.

Predictably, the conflict has been a ecological disaster for the north's palmyras. Over 2.5 million trees have been uprooted, not only for firewood and to create military bunkers, but 500 m of land either side of the region's major arteries was bulldozed in order to deter ambushes. A recent ban on felling palmyras may aid re-forestation programmes.

Chola Princess Sangamittha in the seventh century, whose disfigured face looked like a horse's head. She was cured, legend states, by bathing in its healing waters, and in gratitude constructed the Madividdapuram Kandaswamy Kovil, 2 km south, which has a tall *gopuram* and a festival in July/August. The water in the wells is very pleasant, though the large military presence can be disconcerting. Swimming in the sea at Keerimalai is forbidden.

The islands

The religious site of Nainativu (Nagadipa), sacred to both Buddhists and Hindus, is the only place in this area that receives a significant amount of visitors – the site is increasingly thronged with day-trippers from around the country. Kayts and Karainagar are linked to the mainland by separate causeways, while a third which cuts seemingly endlessly through dazzling blue sea, joins Kayts to Punguditivu, at the southwestern corner of which ferries can be caught to the outlying islands. The islands are rich in birdlife. Watch out for flamingos on the causeway to Kayts.

Kayts

To the north of the island, the nearest to Jaffna town, is Kayts town, once a wealthy and sought-after area – look out for the ruins of beautiful villas lining the approach road. The road ends at a jetty for boats to Karaitivu Island, but is closed off by an army checkpoint. Here you can see Indian fishing boats impounded for fishing in Sri Lankan waters, and to the west, the well-preserved island fort of **Hammenheil**, a long-term navy base and one-time prison. At the south of Kayts island, Velanai is a popular beach.

“” Relentlessly flat open grasslands interspersed with shallow lagoons, Jaffna's largely deserted islands are eerie places to visit.

Karaitivu

The road to the Karaitivu causeway passes through Vadukoddai, where there is a large Portuguese church. Behind the church are 27 gravestones, predominantly Dutch, rescued from the Groote Kerk in Jaffna's fort. To the east at **Chankanai**, are the overgrown remains of another Portuguese church, constructed of coral in 1641. At the north end of Karaitivu, is **Casuarina beach**, the most popular in Jaffna, where swimming is safe in the calm, shallow waters. A few stalls sell drinks and snacks. The beach is so-called after the beefwood (*Casuarina*) trees found here.

Nainativu

Accessed by ferry from the deserted **Punguditivu**, the tiny island of Nainativu has great religious importance to both Buddhists and Hindus. For the former it is Nagadipa, the point at which the Buddha set foot on his second visit to the island, four years after the first, in order to settle a quarrel between two Naga kings over a throne, said to be enshrined here. A *vihara*, with a restored silver *dagoba* and image house, guarded by a large military presence (your battered sandals will line up against many neat pairs of shiny black boots at the entrance to the temple), marks the spot. There is a bo tree opposite. The *vihara* is a 10-minute walk along the road leading left from the jetty point.

In a Hindu-dominated area however, the **Naga Pooshani Ambal kovil** at the jetty point is the livelier temple, and can be the focus of a day-trip. Regular *pujas* are taken, with colourful processions, clattering drums, bells and pipes, and gasps as the inner sanctum of the temple is revealed. In its 15-day festival in June, a 30-m Ambal is paraded. In order to take advantage of Ambal's generosity, it is a good idea to arrive for the important *puja* at 1300, after which crowds of several hundred line up in the hall behind the temple for rice and curry, ladled out on to a banana leaf. Lunch is usually finished in time to catch the 1430 boat back to Punguditivu.

Delft

The windswept and bleak landscape of Delft, the outermost inhabited island, has been less affected by the conflict and contains various reminders of the Portuguese and Dutch periods. Famous for its wild ponies, which come from a Portuguese breeding stock, there are also the remains of a coral fort, fairly tumbledown but still recognisable, behind the hospital. South of the jetty is a single baobab tree (see Mannar below) and, further, a large banyan, while at the southern tip the Quindah tower is an ancient navigational landmark.

Sleeping

Peninsula and islands *p331*

Jaffna must be used as a base if travelling in this area as there is little accommodation.

Eating

Peninsula and islands *p331*

Choices are limited. To be on the safe side take provisions from Jaffna.

For an explanation of the sleeping and eating price codes used in this guide, see the inside front cover.

RsRs **Millennium**, *76/60 Ramanathan Rd (Campus Rd), Kaladdy, T2222810*. A bit off the beaten track, but attractive beer garden popular with locals and ex-pats, with tasty snacks (eg devilled prawns Rs 150), relaxed.

Transport

The peninsula and islands can easily be visited on a day trip from Jaffna town. All buses originate from Jaffna town.

Northeast to Point Pedro *p331*
Bus For **Nilavarai** take an Achchuveli bus (no 986). 4 a day leave from the main bus stand, Rs 13. For **Valvedditturai** no 751 which runs hourly, costs Rs 18.50. For **Point Pedro** regular nos 2, 750 and 751. For **Manalkadu desert** catch no 755 at PPD.

Road to Kankesanthurai *p333*
Bus For **Kantarodai** hourly buses (no 768, Rs 9) from Jaffna to Alveddi, from where you can take a three-wheeler. For **Tellipalai** bus no 769 (every 30 mins, Rs 10) terminates close to the temple. North of Tellipalai is inaccessible by public transport.

The islands *p334*
Bus and ferry For **Kayts** hourly buses (nos 777 and 780) to Kayts town (Rs 18). For **Karaitivu** several buses a day direct to Casuarina, or take an (hourly) bus to Karainagar and get a three-wheeler. For **Nainativu** take the 776 bus, which crosses Kayts island to the jetty point at Kurukkaduwan on Pungudutivu (every 30 mins to 1 hr, Rs 19). Boats for the 20-min crossing leave hourly from 0800-1830. For **Delft** ferries leave the KKD jetty at 0700 and 1330, returning at 1030 and 1530. There is also a boat from Nainativu at 0530, returning at 1700. A bus traverses the island, or you might hire a tractor.

Mannar

→ *Phone code: 023. Colour map 1, grid B1.*

Mannar Island is one of the driest and most barren places in the country, yet is also one of the most intriguing. Linked by a 3-km road dam and iron bridge to the mainland it is quite remote from the rest of Sri Lanka. Mannar's historical importance lies in its proximity to India to which it is linked by an an ancient causeway. » *For Sleeping, Eating and other listings, see pages 338.*

Anuradhapura to Mannar

The remote island of Mannar is accessible by road from Medawachchiya (86 km along the A14), though the relaid A30 from Vavuniya (78 km) is the faster route. Both roads run through elephant country, and meet at Paraiyanalankulam, where the A30 continues northwest past the turning for Madhu Road and Giant's Tank. Palmyras and umbrella thorns are increasingly visible in this barren, open landscape interspersed with some paddy cultivation. Frequent army bunkers line the route.

Madhu Road

→ *Colour map 1, grid C2. 12 km northeast of the A30 from Madhu Road Junction.*

The rebuilt **church** at Madhu Road is the most important Catholic pilgrimage site in Sri Lanka. Its altar houses the sacred **Our Lady of Madhu statue**, which was brought here in 1670 by 20 Catholic families fleeing persecution by the Dutch at Mantai, near Mannar. Amongst the fugitives was Helena, the daughter of a Portuguese captain, who was sanctified and founded the first church here. The Madhu statue is venerated throughout the country for its miracles, especially the cure of snakebite, and major festivals are held here throughout the year. The largest, on 15 August, attracts up to half a million visitors. Though reopened in 2002, the road (poor but accessible by car) lies within LTTE-controlled territory, and you will pass through a full security check, with baggage search and examination of all personal and vehicle documents.

Giant's Tank → *20 km east of Mannar Town.*

Possibly built by King Parakramabahu I, Giant's Tank, is rich in scrub and shore birds. There are a couple of vantage points along the A14, though the tank is often empty.

Thiruketthiswaram kovil

A short distance inland from the Mannar causeway, the restored Saivite Thiruketthiswaram kovil near Mantai is one of five ancient temples in Sri Lanka said to pre-date the arrival of Buddhism. Around the 1,500-year old inner sanctum are various statues of deities in scenes from stories. Apparently, after bathing in the adjacent Palavi tank childless women bring a pot of water to pour over Siva's lingam and drink. With most of its worshippers still refugees living in India, the temple was, at the time of visiting, usually deserted except on Fridays when there is a big *puja* at 1200. There is also a 40-day festival in July with a water-cutting ceremony. Remove shoes and shirts. If arriving from the east, turn right off the A14 5 km before the Mannar causeway.

Mannar Island

The island's distinctive character has been forged by its settlers, who first crossed Adam's Bridge from India almost two million years ago, while nearby Mantai was the ancient port of Mahatittha, which pre-dates Sinhalese times and brought at various times traders and invaders. Arabs brought Islam, the baobab tree and the ubiquitous donkey, rare elsewhere in the country, while Portuguese influence is also strong, the Catholic Church claiming the majority of islanders. The Dutch developed their fort into one of the strongholds of the north. Historically famous for its long-abandoned pearl banks to the south, Mannar today is an impoverished and marginalized backwater, its ferry route across to India and railway inland victims of the conflict. At the time of writing, over 40,000 of the district's inhabitants were displaced to refugee camps in India. Yet its isolation has also helped preserve the island – sealed off for seven years when its road bridge was blown up in 1990, it has avoided much of the destruction elsewhere in the region.

Mannar town

The town is dominated by its mosques and churches. The Goan-style St Sebastian's has ornate latticework giving it a Moorish appearance. It is impossible to miss Mannar's **fort**, which stands proudly on the right as you cross the mudflats to enter the town. Constructed by the Portuguese in 1560, it was taken by the Dutch in 1658 and rebuilt. The fort's ramparts and four bastions, part surrounded by a moat, are intact, although most buildings inside have been blasted. There is an ornate Dutch stone tablet close to the main gate. A tunnel is said to connect Mannar's fort to the remains of another at Arippu, two hours south. The police occupy the fort, though permission for visits is usually granted.

Mannar is famous for its baobab trees and 2 km south at Pallimunai is what is claimed to be the largest tree in Asia. With a circumference of 19.5 m, a board states that it was probably planted in 1477. Other baobabs on the island have been radio-carbon dated to 1,000 years old. Bus no 946 travels to Pallimunai, Rs 3.

Around the island

The A14 continues, following and at one point crossing the old railway line, through the sandy wastes and jungle scrub to Talaimannar, the westernmost point of the island. The Muslim village of **Erukkulampiddu**, 15 km from Mannar (turn right at Toddaveli) along the A14, is known locally for its mat-weaving.

Pesalai is a Catholic fishing village with one of the largest churches in Sri Lanka (rebuilt in 1999), where there is an image of Christ under a mosquito net! A passion

New time, old time

You may find that different parts of Northern Province operate on different time zones, a curiosity caused by uncertainty in the political climate. Some businesses in Jaffna, for example, hang two separate clocks, one showing 'new' time (matching the rest of Sri Lanka), the other 'old' time (half an hour earlier). This dates from 1996, when, during a drought, Sri Lanka's clocks were wound forward in order to save daylight and electricity. Officially, Jaffna changed with the rest of the country but in a rebel-dominated area, many were reluctant to adhere.

play is performed at Easter here using life-size dolls. Sadly, there have been some ugly clashes here in recent years with Indian fishermen, whose superior trawlers have encroached on local waters.

A left-turn at **Talaimannar** takes you to South Point, close to which begins **Adam's Bridge**, a series of rocks, sandbanks and shallows which links Mannar to Rameswaram in India. In 2002, NASA space images revealed the crossing to be man-made because of its composition and curvature, proving that settlers arrived in Sri Lanka at least 1,750,000 years ago. This sheds light on the *Ramayana* legend in which Hanuman constructed a causeway in his attempt to rescue Sita from the demon-god Ravana. The prospect of peace and closer relations with India have prompted talks of developing a modern bridge to Rameswaram from here, but in the fraught internal political climate this is likely to be years away. The toddy tavern here serves good toddy from traditional palmyra cups. Fishermen will offer to take you to for a 30-40 minute boat ride to the 'fourth island' of Adam's Bridge for Rs 1,500, though the going rate is around Rs 500.

A kilometre north of Talaimannar town is the old pier from which, until 1984, ferry boats crossed to India. There is an attractive but abandoned and rather forlorn lighthouse on the mined beach here – take care. Even so, the beach buzzes with fishermen (and women) in the morning. Close to Talaimannar is a Muslim shrine which, a legend states, is the burial place of Adam and Eve.

Sleeping

Mannar *p336*

F **Manjula Inn**, *2nd Cross St, Mannar, T223-2037*. Clean and comfortable rooms with common bath, good home-cooked food.

F-G **Mannar Rest Inn**, *Moor St, Mannar*. Clean rooms with or without attached bath, quiet, close to small lagoon, meals available, very friendly.

F-G **Sinnathambi's Restaurant**, *2 km from town along Thavulpadu Rd, T2232748*. 3 rooms (2 with attached bath), clean and friendly, (sea)food available.

Eating

Mannar *p336*

For options see Sleeping above.

Transport

Mannar *p336*

Bus For **Madhu Road Church** private and CTB buses leave from Vavuniya and Mannar (Rs 20, 2 hrs). For **Thiruketheeswaram** bus no 944/1 from Mannar (Rs 12, 45 mins). From Mannar town buses run every 2 hrs to **Vavuniya** (no 83/2, Rs 28); 4 a day to **Colombo** (7 hrs); daily buses to **Anuradhapura**, **Trincomalee** and **Kalpitiya**. For **Pesalai** bus no 948 leaving from the main bus stand (Rs 10). For **Talaimannar** bus no 948 leaves Mannar town regularly, Rs 16.

Directory

Mannar *p336*

Banks Several banks in Mannar town including Hatton National Bank.

Background

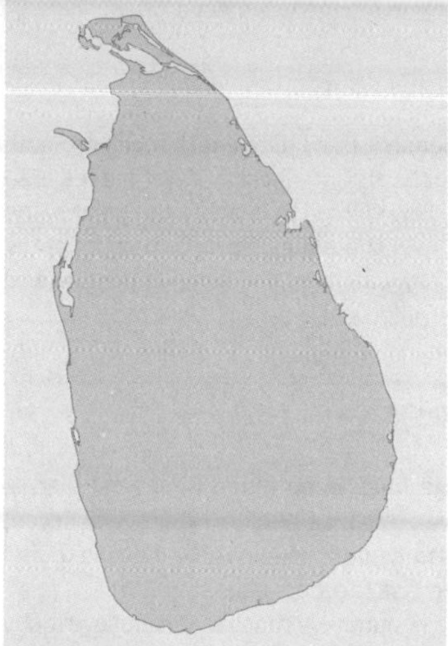

History

Sri Lanka has a rich cultural history. In this sense it is no different to much of South Asia where religion and the migraton of people are interlocked. What makes it so interesting to the traveller is its accessibility. Few will fail to imagine the great battle involving kings atop elephants as they look over the plains from the heights of the fortress at Sigiriya. Others will be moved as they watch the sun set over the Sun and Moon bastions at the colonial fortification in Galle.

Settlement and early history

Stone tools from the Middle Palaeolithic Age have been found in several places, evidence of settlement in Sri Lanka perhaps as much as 500,000 years ago. Recent genetic research however suggests that *Homo sapiens* may not have evolved until very much later, and spread from Africa in the last 100,000 years.

The early record of settlement in Sri Lanka is scanty. Archaeologists believe today that the first *Homo sapiens* arrived perhaps 75,000 years ago, bringing with them a life of hunting and gathering centred on open-air campsites. Evidence of their activity has been found in a variety of habitats. However, no Neolithic tools have been found, and no tools from the Copper Age, which is so well represented in peninsular India from the second millennium BC.

The picture changes with the arrival of the Iron Age, for the megalithic graves, associated with black and red pottery, suggest that Sri Lanka had direct contact with South India well before the Aryans immigrated from North India from around 500 BC. Sri Lanka's archaeological record remains comparatively sparse, with barely any evidence with which to date the development of Stone Age cultures or the later spread of domesticated animals and cultivation. At some point in the first millennium BC rice cultivation made its appearance, though whether as a result of migration from either North India or South East Asia remains controversial.

The earliest aboriginal settlers, of Australoid, Negrito and Mediterranean stock, have now been almost entirely absorbed in the settled populations. The earliest named culture is that of **Balangoda**, distributed across the whole island between 5000 and 500 BC. The **Veddas** are the only inhabitants today whose ancestors were in Sri Lanka before the Aryan migrations. Related to the Dravidian jungle peoples in South India, they dwelt in caves and rock shelters, and lived by hunting and gathering. They practised a cult of the dead, communicating with ancestors through reincarnated spirits. Today the Veddas have been largely absorbed into the Sinhalese community and have virtually ceased to have a separate existence. Their numbers have shrunk to just a few hundred. See the box on page 293 for further details.

Migration from India

The overwhelming majority of the present population of Sri Lanka owes its origins to successive waves of migration from two different regions of India. Most people are of Indo-Aryan origin and came from North India. The earliest migrations from North India may have taken place as early as the fifth century BC. Although these migrants brought with them a North Indian language which had its roots in the Sanskrit tradition, they were not yet Buddhists, for Buddhism did not arrive in Sri Lanka until the third century BC. It is most likely that the Sinhalese came from India's northwest, possibly Punjab or Gujarat, and it seems probable that Gujarati traders were already sailing down India's west coast by this time. The origins of Tamil settlement are unclear, but are thought to go back at least to the third century BC, when there is clear evidence of trade between Sri Lanka and South India.

Today the **Sinhalese** make up 74% of the total population. Sri Lanka's **Tamil** population comprises the long settled Tamils of the north and east (12.6%) and the migrant workers on the tea plantations in the Central Highlands (5.5%) who settled in Sri Lanka from the late 19th century onwards. At the height of the conflict, up to 750,000 Tamils had repatriated abroad, though many have since returned. The so-called **'Moors'**, Tamil speaking Muslims of Indian-Arab descent, were traders on the east coast and now number over 1.1m (7.7%). A much smaller but highly distinct community is that of the **Burghers**, numbering about 50,000. The Dutch (mainly members of the Dutch Reformed Church) and the Portuguese intermarried with local people, and their descendants were urban and ultimately English speaking. There are similar numbers of Malays and smaller groups of Kaffirs. The Malays are Muslims who were brought by the Dutch from Java. The Kaffirs were brought by the Portuguese from Mozambique and other parts of East Africa as mercenaries.

A literate society

With the development of agriculture came the origins of a literate and complex society. Tradition associates the founding of Sri Lanka's first kingdom with Devanampiya Tissa (250-221 BC), who was converted to Buddhism by Mahinda, son of the great Indian Emperor Asoka. Myth and legend are bound up with many of the events of South Asian history, but the Sri Lankan historian KM de Silva has noted that the historical mythology of the Sinhalese "is the basis of their conception of themselves as the chosen guardians of Buddhism". The basic text through which this view of the island's history has been passed on by successive generations of Buddhist monks is the **Mahavansa** (*Great Dynasty* or *Lineage*), which de Silva suggests possibly goes back to the sixth century AD, but is probably much more recent. It is the epic history from Prince Vijaya, the legendary founder of Sri Lanka, to King Mahasena (died 303 AD) and is a major source on early history and legend. It was continued in the 13th-century text by the *Culavansa*, which gives a very full account of the medieval history of the island. These works were compiled by **bhikkus** (Buddhist monks) and inevitably they have the marks of their sectarian origins.

Interpretation of Sri Lanka's early history does not depend entirely on the writings of the Buddhist monks who ultimately wrote the *Mahavansa*. The first known writings are inscriptions discovered near caves in several parts of the island. Written in the Brahmi script (which was also used in India on the great inscriptions of the Emperor Asoka to express his principles of government and to mark out the limits of his territorial power), in Sri Lanka the inscriptions are brief epigraphs, testifying to the donation of caves or rock shelters to Buddhist monks. Written in an early form of Sinhala, rather than in the Prakrit which was the language used by Asoka, they give vivid testimony to the existence of prosperous, literate agricultural societies. The alphabet and the language were common right across the country, and even from early times it is clear that wet rice cultivation using sophisticated irrigation technology was the basis of the economy. Settlement spread steadily right through to the 13th century. A notable feature of this early settlement and culture was its restriction to the Dry Zone and to altitudes below 300 m.

From the origins of this agricultural civilization in the third century BC there was a progressive economic and social evolution. The economy and the culture developed around the creation of extraordinarily sophisticated irrigation systems, using the rivers flowing from the Central Highlands across the much drier northern and eastern plains. Traditional agriculture had depended entirely on the rainfall brought by the retreating monsoon between October and December. The developing kingdoms of North Sri Lanka realized the need to control water to improve the reliability of agriculture, and a system of tank irrigation was already well advanced by the first century BC. This developed into possibly the most advanced contemporary system of hydraulic engineering in the world by the end of the fifth century AD. Many of these developments were quite small-scale and today it is impossible to identify their creators. Others however were of a previously unparalleled size and are clearly identified with powerful kings, for example King Mahasena (274-302 AD) and the 15-m high dam which impounded the Kantalai Tank, covering 2,000 ha and is served by a 40-km long canal. King Dhatusena (460-78 AD) constructed the Kalawewa Lake in Anuradhapura, then by far the largest tank in Sri Lanka, to be surpassed in the late 12th century by King Parakramabahu's Parakrama Samudra ('Sea'), retained by an embankment 14-km long.

Political developments in pre-colonial Sri Lanka

Proximity to India has played a permanent part in Sri Lanka's developing history. Not only have the peoples of the island themselves originated from the mainland, but through more than 2,000 years, contact has been an essential element in all Sri Lanka's political equations.

According to the *Mahavansa*, the Buddha commanded the king of the gods, Sakra, to protect Lanka as the home in which Buddhism would flourish. In recent years, much has been read into both the text and to more recent history to suggest that the Sinhalese have always been at war with the Tamils. The truth is far more complicated. The earliest settlement of the island took place in the northeast, the area now known as the Dry Zone. Until the 13th century AD this was the region of political and cultural development for Sinhalese and Tamil alike.

The political history of the island after the establishment of the first recorded kingdom was not as smooth as might be inferred from the steady expansion of settled agriculture and the spread of sophisticated irrigation technology. Before the 13th century AD three regions played a major role in the island's political life. **Rajarata** in the north-central part of the island's plains grew into one of the major core regions of developing Sinhalese culture. To its north was **Uttaradesa** ('northern country'), while in the southeast, **Rohana** (Ruhunu) developed as the third political centre.

Periodically these centres of Sinhalese power came into conflict with each other, and with Tamil kings from India. The *Mahavansa* records how the Rohana Sinhalese King Dutthagamenu defeated the Chola Tamil King Elara, who had ruled northern Sri Lanka from Anuradhapura, in 140 BC. Dutthagamenu's victory was claimed by the chroniclers as a historic assertion of Buddhism's inalienable hold on Sri Lanka. In fact it is clear that at the time this was not a Tamil-Sinhalese or Buddhist-Hindu conflict, for the armies and leadership of both sides contained Sinhalese and Tamils, Buddhists and Hindus. By that time Buddhism had already been a power in the island for two centuries, when the king Devanampiya Tissa (307-267 BC) converted to Buddhism.

Buddhism became the state religion, identified with the growth of Sinhalese culture and political power. The power of the central kingdom based at Anuradhapura was rarely unchallenged or complete. Power was decentralized, with a large measure of local autonomy. Furthermore, provincial centres periodically established their independence. Anuradhapura became one of Asia's pre-eminent cities, but from the 11th century AD, Polonnaruwa took over as capital.

The Tamil involvement

Although Buddhist power was predominant in Sri Lanka from the first century BC, Sri Lankan kings often deliberately sought Tamil support in their own disputes. As a result Sri Lanka was affected by political developments in South India. The rise of the expansionist Tamil kingdoms of the Pandiyas, Pallavas and Cholas from the fifth century AD increased the scope for interaction with the mainland. In de Silva's words, "South Indian auxiliaries became in time a vitally important, if not the most powerful element in the armies of the Sinhalese rulers, and an unpredictable, turbulent group who were often a threat to political stability. They were also the nucleus of a powerful Tamil influence in the court."

It was not a one way flow. Occasionally the Sinhalese were themselves drawn in to attack Tamil kings in India, as in the ninth century when to their enormous cost they joined with their beleaguered allies the Pandiyans and attacked the Cholas. The Chola Emperor **Rajaraja** I defeated them in India and then carried the war into Sri Lanka, adding Jaffna and the northern plains, including Anuradhapura, to his empire.

The Cholas ruled from Polonnaruwa for 75 years, finally being driven out by the Rohana king **Vijayabahu I** in 1070 AD. He established peace and a return to some prosperity in the north before civil war broke out and disrupted the civil administration again. Only the 33 year rule of **Parakramabahu I** (1153-86) interrupted the decline. Some of Sri Lanka's most remarkable monuments date from his reign, including the Parakrama Samudra at Polonnaruwa. However, it was the collapse of this kingdom and its ultimate annihilation by the Tamils in the 13th century that left not only its physical imprint on the North Sri Lankan landscape, but also an indelible psychological mark on the Sri Lankan perception of neighbouring Tamil Hindus.

Sinhalese move south

Other factors, such as the spread of malaria which occurred with the deterioration in maintenance of the irrigation system, may have led to the progressive desertion of the northern and eastern plains and the movement south of the centre of gravity of the Island's population. Between the 12th and 17th centuries Sinhalese moved from the dry to the Wet Zone. This required a change in agriculture from irrigated to rain fed crops. Trade also increased, especially in cinnamon, an activity controlled by the rising population of Muslim seafarers. A **Tamil Kingdom** was set up in Jaffna for the first time, briefly coming back under Sinhalese power (under the Sinhalese king **Parakramabahu VI**, 1412-67, based in his capital at **Kotte**), but generally remaining independent, and a frequent threat to the power of the Sinhalese kingdoms to the south. Other threats came from overseas. As early as the 13th century, a Buddhist king from Malaya invaded Sri Lanka twice to try and capture the Tooth Relic and the Buddha's alms bowl. In the early 15th century the island was even invaded by a fleet of Chinese junks sent by the Ming Emperors.

The Kandyan kingdom

Between the southern and northern kingdoms, Kandy became the capital of a new power base around 1480. Established in the Central Highlands, it became fully independent by the end of the 15th century. By the early 16th century the Sinhalese kingdom of Kotte in the south was hopelessly fragmented, giving impetus to Kandy's rise to independent power. Its remote and inaccessible position gave it added protection from the early colonial invasions. Using both force and diplomacy to capitalize on its geographical advantages, it survived as the last independent Sinhalese kingdom until 1815. It had played the game of seeking alliances with one colonial power against another with considerable success, first seeking the help of the Dutch against the Portuguese, then of the British against the Dutch. However, this policy ran out of potential allies when the British established their supremacy over all the territory surrounding the Central Highlands in 1796, and by 1815 the last Kandyan King, a Tamil Hindu converted to Buddhism, was deposed by his Sinhalese chiefs, who sought an accord with the new British rulers in exchange for retaining a large measure of their own power.

Colonial power

The succession of three colonial powers, the Portuguese, Dutch and the British, finally ended the independent Sinhalese and Tamil rule. Expanding Islam, evidenced in the conversion of the inhabitants of islands on the Arab trading routes such as the Maldives and the Laccadives as well as significant numbers on the southwest coast of India, had also been making its presence felt. The Portuguese arrived in Sri Lanka in 1605 and established control over some of the island's narrow coastal plains around Colombo. They were responsible for large-scale conversions to Roman Catholicism which today accounts for 90% of the island's Christians, leaving both a linguistic legacy and an imprint on the population, evidenced today in many names of Portuguese origin. During this period the rest of the island was dominated by the rulers of Sitavaka, who overpowered the Kotte Kingdom in 1565 and controlled the whole of the southwest apart from Colombo. For 10 years they occupied Kandy itself, nearly evicted the Portuguese and came close to reasserting Sinhalese power in the far north.

By 1619 the Portuguese had annexed Jaffna, which thereafter was treated by the Dutch, and more importantly the British, as simply part of the island state. They were less successful in subjugating Kandy, and in 1650 the Portuguese were ousted by the Dutch. The Dutch extended their own colonial control from Negombo (40 km north of Colombo) south, right round the coast to Trincomalee, as well as the entire northern peninsula, leaving the Kandyan Kingdom surrounded in the Central Highlands. Because the Portuguese and Dutch were interested in little other than the spice trade, they bent most of their efforts to producing the goods necessary for their trade. The British replaced the Dutch in 1795-96 when British power was being consolidated in South India at the expense of the French and the Mysore Muslim Raja, Tipu Sultan. Their original purpose was to secure the important Indian Ocean port of Trincomalee. Initially the British imported administrators and officials from Madras, but as BH Farmer points out, by 1802 'it was apparent that Madras-trained officials were, apart from other disabilities, quite unable to understand the language and customs of the Sinhalese, and Ceylon became a Crown Colony.'

When the British came to control the whole island after 1815 they established a quite distinctive imprint on the island's society and economy. This was most obvious in the introduction of plantation agriculture. During the British period coffee took over from cinnamon, but by the beginning of the 20th century, even though coffee had largely been wiped out by disease, plantation agriculture was the dominant pillar of the cash economy. Rice production stagnated and then declined, and Sri Lanka became dependent on the export of cash crops and the import of food. In 1948 it was only producing about 35% of its rice needs.

The colonial period also saw major social changes take place. Under the Portuguese and then the Dutch the development of commercial activity in the coastal lowlands encouraged many 'low-country' Sinhalese to become involved in the newly emerging economic activity. In a process which continued in the early British colonial period, the Low Country Sinhalese became increasingly westernized, with the widespread adoption of an English education and the rise of an urban middle class, while the Kandyan Sinhalese retained far stronger links with traditional and rural social customs. Despite British reforms in 1833 which introduced a uniform administrative system across the whole of Ceylon, wiping out the Kandyan political system, a contrast between Kandyan and Low-Country Sinhalese persisted into the modern period.

However, an even more significant change took place in the 19th century. British commercial interests saw the opportunities presented for the cultivation of cash crops. Cinnamon and coconuts had been planted by the Dutch and become particularly important, but after 1815 coffee production was spread to the Kandyan hills. Despite ups and downs production increased dramatically until 1875, when a catastrophic attack of a fungus disease wiped out almost the entire crop. It was replaced, particularly in the higher regions, by tea.

Labour had already begun to prove a problem on the coffee plantations, and as tea spread the shortage became acute. Private labour contractors were recruited to persuade labourers to come to Ceylon from the Tamil country of South India. Between 1843-59 over 900,000 men, women and children migrated to work as indentured labour. The cost of their transport was deducted from their wages after they arrived, and they could not leave until they had repaid their debt. Immigration on that scale created a massive change in the ethnic mix of the Highlands, with a particularly significant effect on the Kandyan farmers, whose land was increasingly hemmed in by the spread of estates. The Indian Tamils however remained entirely separate from the Sinhalese, returning to South India whenever possible and sending cash remittances home.

The moves to independence

Dominated by Buddhists and Sinhalese in its early stages, no one in the Independence movement at the beginning of the 20th century would have believed that British rule would end within 50 years – nor would many have wanted it to. The **Ceylon National Congress**, formed in 1919, was conservative and pragmatic, but the pressures of imminent democratic self-rule made themselves felt throughout the 1930s, as minority groups pressed to protect their position. Universal suffrage came in 1931, along with the promise of self-rule from the British Government. It had the positive benefit of encouraging the development of welfare policies such as health care, nutrition and public education. However, it also had the immediate impact of encouraging a resurgence of nationalism linked with Buddhist revivalism.

Independence came with scarcely a murmur on 4 February 1948, six months after that of India and Pakistan. Ceylon's first Prime Minister was **Don Stephen Senanayake**. His son **Dudley Senanayake**, who followed, was identified with a pragmatic nationalism. The heart of his programme was the re-colonization of the deserted Sinhalese heartlands of the Dry Zone. It was a programme deliberately calculated to recapture the glories of the past while laying the groundwork for post-Independence prosperity. In the event, its results have proved far more complex than even its critics fully recognized.

Modern Sri Lanka

Sri Lanka is a parliamentary democracy with an elected president and freely contested elections. Sri Lankans enjoy a long life expectancy, a high literacy rate that belies its low per capita income, and generally an advanced health system. Over the last 50 years the island has continued to see rapid economic and social change. The old plantation economy remains important though no longer as dominant as it was during the colonial period, while newer industries, including tourism, have taken on the prime role.

In the early post-independence years, Sri Lanka was regarded as a 'model colony'. The country started on a strong economic footing with a strong sterling balance and little internal division. Within the new constitution there was also a commitment to religious neutrality. Both the island's main languages, Sinhala and Tamil, had been declared national languages and equitable access to political and administrative positions to be guaranteed. However, successive governments failed to maintain commitment to either equality or economic development in the face of greater welfare spending and a rapidly growing young and literate population. The pattern of the early post-independence governments was to manipulate disaffection within the electorate in an effort to gain votes, with the effect of stirring up communal emotions between racial and religious groups. Within 10 years the seeds had been sown for the faction fighting of the last two decades which threatened to tear the country apart.

Between 1983 and 2001, Sri Lanka was involved in a bitter internal ethnic conflict, predominantly in the North and East, between the government and separatist Tamil rebels, the **Liberation Tigers of Tamil Eelam (LTTE)** or **'Tamil tigers'**. After the election of a new government in December 2001 however a formal ceasefire agreement was signed in February 2002 between Prime Minister Ranil Wickremasinghe and LTTE leader Vellupillai Prabhakaran, to be monitored by the Norwegian government. This Memorandum of Understanding (MoU) successfully put a stop to hostilities and prompted several rounds of peace talks between September 2002 and March 2003, but the LTTE pulled out of the talks in April 2003 after accusing the government of failing to deliver on promises agreed during the peace talks. At the time of writing (September 2003) they had yet to resume, although there haven't been any major breaches of the ceasefire. The LTTE has however continued a programme of systematic assassination of the political leaders of opposition parties and informants.

The origins of Sri Lanka's ethnic conflict are complex. Here, a brief sketch of significant post-war events is offered which aims to elucidate some of the immediate causes. Sri Lanka's first government was formed by the **United National Party (UNP)**, a broad union of conservative ideologies led by **DS Senanayake**, Minister of Agriculture during the last years of British rule. Senanayake saw Sri Lanka's pluralism as its strength, thwarting any divisive forces. He concentrated on economic progress, particularly in agricultural policy, including the setting up of the massive Gal Oya project in the east of the country, designed to increase rice production, as well as planting subsidies on rice. The party however was wrought by internal divisions with the first serious break occurring in 1951 when its left bloc broke away under the leadership of **SWRD Bandaranaike**, to form the **Sri Lanka Freedom Party (SLFP)**. After Senanayake's death in a riding accident in 1952, his son Dudley succeeded him but failed to maintain the UNP's popularity when it became clear that the country faced significant economic problems. Senanayake's massive spending on welfare (up to 35% of budget) forced him to reduce the government rice subsidy, leading to massive protests and his resignation.

Against this background, the SLFP emerged as the main opposition party. Bandaranaike, part of a wealthy Sinhalese family, had been educated – and discriminated against – at Oxford. Returning to Sri Lanka, he rejected western values and embraced Buddhism. His election campaign of 1956 sought to provoke the nationalist passions of the Buddhist majority in order to eradicate traces of colonial rule. While this was initially targeted at Christian influence, it coincided with a greater awareness amongst Sinhalese that they had 'lost out' at independence. During the British colonial period, a disproportionate number of government and administrative positions had been given to the traditionally hardworking Tamils, who tended to be better educated than the Sinhalese and occupied a greater number of university places, a trend which continued after independence. English had been, and continued to be, the main language of administration, and since the Tamils tended to have greater mastery, Bandaranaike chose to fight the 1956 election on a platform making Sinhala the only official language. After winning the election, Bandaranaike successfully passed the **Sinhala Only Act**, which led to widespread Tamil resentment and, within two years, the first violent clashes in which hundreds, mainly Tamils, died.

Education has been one of the triumphs, with the country achieving high adult literacy figures. It has the sixth highest pupil-teacher ratio in the world, with 14 primary pupils per teacher (Asiaweek).

Bandaranaike pursued popular but economically unfeasible nationalisation policies, expanding the public sector and draining the nation's resources. By the time he was assassinated by a Buddhist monk in 1959, the country faced grave instability. The SLFP however maintained popular support, and in July 1960 his widow, Sirimavo Bandaranaike swept to power, becoming the world's first female Prime Minister. She continued her husband's socialist-style legislation, nationalizing significant sectors of the economy, including foreign-controlled industries such as petroleum, and forced a government takeover of denominational schools. This soured relations with the country's many Catholics, while her aggressive reinforcement of Sinhala as the only official language led to Tamil disobedience in the North and East, whose political activity was subsequently curtailed in a state of emergency. In 1965, Dudley Senanayake and the UNP regained power, but despite improving relations with the US (who had suspended aid in 1963) and doubling private sector investment, the economy failed to show any significant improvement, and the government was blighted by greater civil violence and states of emergency.

Mrs Bandaranaike returned to power in 1970 under the banner of the **United Front**, a three-party coalition, promising land reform and further nationalization, and extending diplomatic relations to countries such as the GDR, Vietnam and North Korea. The radical left mobilized at this time, and in 1971 a Sinhalese Maoist youth movement, the JVP (Janatha Vimukthi Peramuna or People's Liberation Front) attempted a blitzkrieg, with fierce fighting in the North Central and Southern Provinces leaving over 1,000 dead. Ruthlessly repressed by the military, the uprising gave the government reign to force through a new constitution in May 1972, verging on the authoritarian. The military were given greater powers, while Sinhala was enshrined as the official language and the country was given a new name, Sri Lanka, invoking the ancient Sinhalese kingdoms. The constitution lacked any hint of federalism, which dismayed Tamils. Instead, it removed many minority rights, conferring greater status on Buddhism. Even more irksome to Tamils was the 'standardization' policy on university admissions, which lowered the standard required by Sinhalese to gain university places. With many Tamils disenfranchised and disillusioned, this iniquitous change in the system, combined with heavy handed treatment by the army, was the fundamental cause of the breakdown of ethnic relations in the 1970s and the radicalization of Tamil politics. The proportion of Tamils in public service had fallen from 60% in 1956 to 10% by 1970, and from 40% to 1% in the military, while the percentage of university places held by Tamils almost halved between 1970 and 1975. In 1976, the Tamil leadership (the newly formed Tamil United Liberation Front, or TULF) for the first time advocated a separate Tamil state. The **LTTE** at this time emerged as the most powerful of a number of underground separatist groups. They first gained notoriety in 1975 when they assassinated the Mayor of Jaffna, and from a handful of guerrilla fighters in the early years, they grew with the help of funding and military training from abroad (notably from Tamil Nadu) into a well-disciplined military unit.

Indispensable coconut

The coconut, so much a part of the coastal scene on the island, particularly to the west, is the country's third most important crop, and sometimes called the 'money tree'.

The inland palm is often short enough to be harvested by cutting bunches of mature nuts with a sharp knife tied to the end of a long bamboo pole which the 'picker' skilfully manipulates from the ground. The coastal palm is too tall to be harvested this way so the nuts must be collected by climbing each tree.

Every bit of the palm is put to use. The green fruit produces an excellent refreshing 'milk' which is on tap when the top is cut off. The 'shell' is split open to expose the soft white kernel which is edible. The outer fibrous coir, just under the skin, is removed and soaked in tanks before being woven into mats, twisted into rope or used as mattress filling and even exported for agricultural and garden use to improved soil texture.

The dry, older nut yields a white layer of 'flesh' or kernel, which is grated or pounded for cooking while some of the best is turned into desiccated coconut (a small industry which employs women) for use at home and abroad.

The fresh sap which is 'tapped' from a proportion of trees is prized by most Sri Lankans who drink the fermented toddy or the more alcoholic arrack. The sweet juice is also turned into jaggery or treacle. See also the box on page 131.

During this period support for the UNP had declined but when political divisions between left and right began to split the United Front, the UNP under a new leader, **JR Jayawardene**, actively improved their image and won a convincing victory at the polls in 1977. Promising a fairer society, he radically altered the constitution the following year, replacing the Westminster style of governance with a French style presidential system, the democratically elected president to appoint a prime minister, with parliamentary approval. While the new constitution also included concessions to the Tamils, including giving Tamil the status of a 'national' language and abrogating the 'standardisation' policy for universities, it was a case of too little too late. The country's worst rioting in 19 years had greeted the new government's inception, and in 1979 the government passed an act, condemned by international groups, to attempt to curb the rapid proliferation of Tamil terrorist groups. The possibility of an effective solution became increasingly distant when the TULF boycotted the 1982 presidential elections (which saw a confirmation of Jayawardene's presidency whose economic advances had proved popular with the Sinhalese). When TULF members were expelled from parliament for refusing to recite allegiance to the constitution, Tamil hopes of a political solution effectively ended.

Sporadic rioting had continued to increase, notably over a three-month period in 1981 during which Jaffna's historic library was destroyed, but it was during 'Black July' in 1983 that the country descended into turmoil. In retaliation for an ambush of an army patrol, organized Sinhalese mobs went on the rampage, first in Colombo, where Tamil areas were devastated and hundreds were killed, and then spreading throughout the country. Over 150,000 Tamils fled as refugees to India, many ultimately finding new homes in Europe and North America.

Between 1983 and 1987 the LTTE waged an increasingly successful battle for control of 'Eelam' – roughly Sri Lanka's Northern and Eastern Provinces. Brutal acts were perpetrated on both sides. The conflict began to assume an international dimension when the Sri Lankan government accused India of supporting the Tamil cause, and as the situation reached deadlock, Indian leader Rajiv Gandhi agreed to intervene. On 29 July 1987, Gandhi and Jayawardene signed the Indo-Lanka accord, under which the Sri Lankan government made a number of concessions to the Tamils, including some devolution of power to the provinces and a merger of the Northern and Eastern provinces. Fifty thousand troops, the Indian Peace Keeping Force (IPKF), were sent in to disarm the rebels. Most groups agreed to surrender their weapons. Within weeks, however, the LTTE announced their intention to continue the fight for Eelam, entering into a bloody battle with the Indian peacekeepers. The government pressed on with reform, holding council elections, but a return to peace was complicated when Sinhalese nationalism, opposed to concessions to the Tamils and an Indian presence on Lankan soil, rose again and the JVP, which had been quiet since the early 1970s, began to reassert itself. There followed one of the ugliest periods in Sri Lankan history. The JVP embarked on a systematic attempt to bring down the government, through strikes, sabotage, closure of schools and hospitals, assassination of politicians and the murder of hundreds of government supporters. The government, relieved of its burden in the North, responded violently. By the time the JVP insurrection was finally quashed in 1990, many thousands of suspected insurgents had been killed or 'disappeared'. The systematic abuse of human rights by the government and military at this time drew widespread condemnation from the international community.

Meanwhile, presidential elections in 1988 had been won by **Ranasinghe Premadasa**. He promptly demanded that Indian troops leave and opened up discussions with the LTTE, who agreed to a ceasefire and talks in order to speed up the Indian withdrawal. Within three months of their eventual departure in March 1990, the LTTE had resumed hostilities, 'Eelam War II', at one point murdering 600 police officers in the North whom they had promised free passage. Having been pushed back to Jaffna in 1987, they now took control of large sections of the North and East. Vendettas were also pursued. In 1991, they assassinated Rajiv Gandhi in Madras and two years later at a May Day rally, Premadasa himself. With the UNP weakened after 17 years of rule, tainted by corruption, political scandal and continued failure to solve the conflict, new president Dingiri Banda Wijetunga called elections in August 1994. Chandrika Kumaratunga, daughter of Sirimavo Bandaranaike, had by now assumed the leadership of the SLFP and led a loose coalition of parties, the People's Alliance (PA), to a narrow victory over the UNP. After appointing her mother as prime minister, she entered into negotiations with the LTTE. Once again these broke down when the LTTE's Black Sea Tigers sank two naval gunboats off the coast of Trincomalee. But in launching 'Eelam War III' it soon became evident that the LTTE had themselves miscalculated. In a huge gamble, the army launched 'Operation Riviresa' (Sunshine), a successful attempt to retake Jaffna in October 1995, preceded by a mass evacuation of its residents. Jaffna has remained narrowly under government control ever since.

Between 1996 and 2000, the LTTE achieved a series of military victories. Chased out of Jaffna, they regrouped to the East, assuming control of vast sections of Trincomalee and Batticaloa districts as well as the Wanni. In April 1996, they killed over 1,200 soldiers and police in retaking Mullaitivu, and successfully continued their campaign of attacking key civilian targets, including, in January 1996, a bomb at Colombo's Central Bank which killed over 100 people. In May 1997 the army launched Operation Sure Victory which saw almost 30,000 troops attempt to reopen the vital northern highway to Jaffna. The Tigers resisted fiercely, retaking Kilinochchi in September 1998 and forcing the government forces to abandon its programme. By late 1999, the army had been forced back to Vavuniya, while in April 2000 it launched

The name Sri Lanka, first recorded in the Ramayana, means 'Resplendent Land' in Sanskrit. It reverted to its original name from Ceylon on 22 May 1972.

a massive and successful onslaught on the strategic Elephant Pass garrison, located on the isthmus between the Jaffna peninsula and the mainland. This was one of the bloodiest periods of the war, with thousands killed on both sides.

Kumaratunga herself was the target of a suicide bomber in December 1999 whilst on the campaign trail for re-election. She survived, though lost the sight of one eye, and won the election with 62% of the vote. Prior to 2000's parliamentary elections, in August the government presented parliament with a modified constitutional package with far greater autonomy for Tamil majority regions, but it failed to pass parliament. The PA was narrowly re-elected in October, but it was hardly a vote of confidence. Successive attempts to achieve a constitutional and political solution to the confrontation had met with repeated failure, and alienated not just the LTTE but much of the Sinhalese majority.

With all other options exhausted, Kumaratunga accepted the Norwegian government's proposal to act as a facilitator with the LTTE, even though the LTTE refused to give up its claim to Eelam. The first meeting took place in November 2000 but it was not until the snap elections of December 2001, and the re-election of the **UNP** under **Prime Minister Ranil Wickremasinghe** that serious strides could be made towards peace. Wickremasinghe had been secretly negotiating with the LTTE for peace whilst in opposition. By now, all sides, as well as public opinion, were exhausted by war, the economy had slowed down, and the government faced bankruptcy. Two earth-shattering events precipitated discussions. The first was the LTTE's overrunning of the massively guarded international airport at Katunayake in July 2001. A crack unit of Tiger commandos destroyed almost half the national airline's fleet, as well as eight military planes and helicopters. It exacerbated economic ruin for the government and was the death-knell for the PA. The second was the events of September 11, which turned worldwide attention on terrorist groups, leading to the closing down of many of the LTTE's foreign sources of revenue, and greater US support for the government.

The situation remains in the balance. On one hand, the LTTE have broken off peace discussions, and their future plans are unclear, though there is progress towards a federal solution, with the government formally presenting a set of proposals to grant political, administrative and financial authority to the LTTE in July 2003. Several factors may yet muddy the waters. There is an uneasy relationship between prime minister and president, on opposite political sides. The influential politics of Sinhalese nationalist groups in the south present a further threat, with many objecting to foreign influence, whilst there are also groups who have benefited from the war. But overwhelmingly public opinion in Sri Lanka supports continued peace initiatives. The costs of the war have been enormous, estimated at over Rs 1,400 billion, with as many as 1 million people displaced, and around 65,000 deaths. The government and humanitarian services continue with the rebuilding of the shattered North and East. Each month, thousands of civilians continue to return to their homes and basic infrastructure, with international aid, is being restored, albeit slowly. Crucially, tourism, fundamentally important to the national economy is growing fast. It offers particular hope to the North and East.

Economy

Key statistics

Main agricultural products in 2001: tea 295,000 tonnes, rubber 86,000 tonnes, paddy 2,695 tonnes, coconut 2,905 billion nuts. Major exports: textiles and garments Rs 208,602 million, tea Rs 61,602 million, rubber Rs 2,129 million, coconuts Rs 3,639 million, petroleum products Rs 6,053 million, gems Rs 7,276 million.

Fact file

Official name Sri Lanka Prajatantrika Samajawadi Janarajaya (Democratic Socialist Republic of Sri Lanka).
Capital Sri Jayawardenepura Kotte (Legislative); Colombo (Commercial).
Population 19.4 million (2001 census).
Annual growth rate 1.3%.
Crude birth rate 1.9%.
Crude death rate 0.6%.
Urban population 22%.
Life expectancy at birth 72.3 (female 76 and male 71).
Adult literacy 91.9% (male 94% and female 89% (in comparison to India: male 69% and female 42%).
Area 66,000 sq km.
Population density 299 per sq km.
GDP US$15.9 billion.
GDP per capita US$849 (UN real GDP per capita: US$3,180).
Unemployment 14.2% (2001 estimate).
Average annual growth rate 3%, 2002
HDI (Human Development Index) 99 (UNDP)

Agriculture and fishing

About 25% of Sri Lanka's area is cultivated by sedentary farmers or under cultivated forests, a further 15% being under shifting cultivation. About half is under forest, grassland, swamp and waste land. In the Wet Zone virtually all the cultivable land is now taken up.

Sri Lanka has not produced enough food to meet the needs of its population since the 18th century, yet in many respects it has been the most obviously prosperous state in South Asia. In the 1970s more than half the money earned from the export of tea, rubber and coconuts was spent on importing food grains, leaving little for investment. In 1999, for the first time for over a decade, agriculture grew as fast as the rest of the economy. In 2002 it grew by 2.4%, compared to the overall growth of 3%. A high proportion of Sri Lanka's farmers remain poor, and 25% of the total population is below the government's poverty line.

Sri Lanka has two main **rice** growing seasons. The *Maha* crop is harvested between January and March, the *Yala* crop between August and September. Attempts to increase rice production have ranged from land reform to the introduction of high yielding varieties (hyv). By the early 1980s there was virtually a 100% take-up of new varieties. Yields have increased significantly, and by 2000 Sri Lanka was producing over 80% of its domestic needs despite the speed of population growth. In addition to the intensification programme the government has also carried out major colonization schemes, bringing new land under rice cultivation though these were stalled by the ethnic conflict.

The **cash crops** of tea, rubber and coconuts continue to contribute the lion's share of Sri Lanka's foreign exchange earnings with approximately 15% of foreign exchange earnings still came from these three products alone. The **coconut** palm (*Cocos nucifer*) grows easily along the south and west coast and in the Kurunegala District. Kernel products rather than fresh nuts remain more important for export. See page 348. **Tea** suffered for many years from inadequate investment and fierce competition from expanding production in other countries of cheaper, lower quality tea. The area cropped under tea fell steadily, though production improved between 1948 and 1965, only to decline again. Since the mid-1980s there has been a remarkable turnaround though exports have wobbled during the recent global recession. The Iraq war in 2003 triggered a 10% decline in tea earnings (see also page 222). The commercially important **rubber** tree, a native of Brazil, is cultivated in plantations in areas of high rainfall. New clones

Growing on trees

Third in importance after tea and coconuts as a crop, the first rubber trees were introduced to Sri Lanka from their native Brazil via Kew gardens in London in the last quarter of the 19th century. In the decade after 1904 Sri Lanka experienced a rubber boom, the Wet Zone land between the sea and the Central Highlands being found particularly well-suited. The apparently sparsely populated land, combined with an ideal climate, encouraged widespread planting. In fact the shifting cultivation which had dominated much of the region around Kalutara, now one of the most important centres of the rubber industry, was severely curtailed by the planting of rubber trees, which spread up the valley sides, leaving paddy the dominant crops in the valley bottoms.

The pale cream sap (latex) of the rubber plant is gathered (or 'tapped') from a fine cut in the bark, renewed two or three times a week. The latex is collected in a tin cup or coconut shell hung beneath the cut. You can ask to be shown round a rubber estate and the processing plant, where you can see the latex being mixed with water, strained and hung out to dry after having been rolled into sheets.

have been developed which are disease resistent and high yielding. See box above. **Spices** (cinnamon, pepper, clove, nutmeg/mace and cardamom), coffee and cocoa also contribute a significant percentage of earnings from export.

The potentially rich **fishery resources** have yet to be fully developed. Fresh water stocking programmes have increased the yield of rivers and lakes, and brackish water fishing is becoming increasingly commercialized. However, nearly 40% of households which depend on fishing have no boats or equipment, and despite the potential of the export market production does not meet domestic demand. Political uncertainty has been a major barrier to expansion in the North and East, though fishing has now resumed.

Resources and industry

Sri Lanka has few fossil fuels or metallic minerals. Gemstones, graphite (crystalline carbon) and heavy mineral sands are the most valuable resources. Gemstones include sapphires, rubies, topaz, zircon, tourmaline and many others. Gem bearing gravels are common, especially in the southwest. The greatest concentration of heavy mineral sands – ilmenite, rutile and monazite – is north of Trincomalee, where deposits are 95% pure. High evaporation rates make shallow lagoons, suitable for salt manufacture especially around Hambantota.

Due to the lack of fossil fuel resources, 95% of the island's electricity is now generated by hydro power. The first HEP project was opened in the 1930s, but firewood still accounts for over half of all energy used. Supplies are under increasing pressure, and the Mahaweli Project undertaking has meant that most of the HEP is now developed.

Sri Lanka had very little industry at Independence, manufacturing accounting for less than 5% of the GDP. Since then however a number of new industries have developed – cement, mineral sands, ceramics and most importantly textiles. These were all planned originally in the state controlled sector. The socialist government under Mrs Bandaranaike envisaged public ownership of all major industries, but the United National Party government elected under President Jayawardene's leadership in 1977 reversed this policy, moving towards a free trade economy.

Among the leading sectors of the new policy was **tourism**. Although tourism has been seriously affected by the political unrest, most recently by the LTTE attack on Katunayake airport in 2001, the ceasefire has triggered a significant recovery. During the first half of 2002, it recovered to the levels of before the attack, and has posted substantial gains ever since. It was showing a 30% increase on 2002 by July 2003. Shipping is also staging a strong recovery as a direct result of the improved political climate.

Current indicators

The overall economic performance has been remarkably strong in recent years. Despite a decline the previous year, GDP grew by 3% in 2002 and by 5.5% in the first quarter of 2003, which is set to continue into 2004. Services were growing by 7.6% in the same period, contributing to 71% of overall growth, while agriculture and industry both recorded gains, the latter growing at 6-7% per annum. Exports floundered in a sluggish global economy in 2002, falling by 2.4% to US$4.7 billion, after a fall of 12% the previous year, which widened Sri Lanka's already sizeable trade deficit. Textiles, dependent on the US and EU markets, were particularly hard hit. However, as the global economy improves, the dollar value of export growth was expected to reach 6.5% in 2003, according to the Asian Development Bank. The economy is however particularly vulnerable to fluctuating oil prices. Moreover, unemployment remains high, with 9% growth in 2002 despite a recovery in production. Inflation is running at around 10%.

Much of this projected growth however is dependent on the internal political situation. The end of hostilities has meant the relief of a crippling drain on the country's resources, but in order to maintain investor confidence and aid from abroad, the island desperately needs not just real progress in the peace talks but continued co-operation between the government and presidency.

Religion

The white stupas of Anuradhapura and the serene stillness of the Buddha's image captured in stone across the island testify to the interweaving of Buddhism with Sinhalese life. Yet Sri Lanka has always been a diverse society. Hinduism has been the dominant religion of Tamils in the north for over 2,000 years and of many of the tea plantation workers today. Islam arrived with the Arab traders across the Indian Ocean over a thousand years ago, and the three main colonial powers – the Portuguese, Dutch and British – brought Catholicism and Protestant Christianity to the island from the 17th century onwards. In Colombo these religions all have a visible presence, and Buddhists, Christians and Muslims live peacefully side by side in many parts of the island, despite present-day political conflicts. Statistically the population is split: Buddhists 69%; Hindus 15%; Christians 7.5%; Muslims 7.5%; Others 1%.

Buddhism

In Sri Lanka Buddhism is the most widespread religion of the majority Sinhalese community. Although India was the original home of Buddhism, today it is practised largely on the margins of the sub-continent, and is widely followed in Ladakh, Nepal and Bhutan as well as Sri Lanka.

Buddha's life

Siddharta Gautama, who came to be given the title of the Buddha – the Enlightened One – was born about 563 BC in the Nepal/India foothills of the Himalaya. A prince in a warrior caste, he was married at the age of 16 and his wife had a son. When he reached the age of 29 he left home and wandered as a beggar and ascetic. After about six years he spent some time in Bodh Gaya in the modern Indian state of Bihar. Sitting under the Bo tree, meditating, he was tempted by the demon Mara, with all the desires of the world. Resisting these temptations, he received Enlightenment.

These scenes are common motifs of Buddhist art. The next landmark was the preaching of his first sermon on 'The Foundation of Righteousness' and set in motion the *Dharma Chakra* (Wheel of the Law) in the deer park at Sarnath near Benaras (Varanasi) to his first five disciples. This was followed by other sermons during his travels when he gathered more disciples. Ananta (his closest disciple) was a cousin. Another cousin, Devdutta, opposed the Buddha and made three attempts to have him killed but failed – a hired assassin was converted, a boulder rolled downhill split in two and finally the wild elephant sent to crush the Buddha underfoot was calmed by his sermon. By the time he died the Buddha had established a small band of monks and nuns known as the *Sangha*, and had followers across North India. The male monks were divided into *sramana* (ascetics), *bhikku* (mendicants), *upasaka* (disciples) and *sravaka* (laymen); the nuns were known as *bhikkuni*.

On the Buddha's death or *parinirvana* (Parinibbana or 'final extinction') at the age of 80, his body was cremated, and the ashes, regarded as precious relics, were divided up among the peoples to whom he had preached. Some have been discovered as far west as Peshawar, in the northwest frontier of Pakistan, and at Piprawa, close to his birthplace.

Sri Lankan Buddhism

The recent history of Sri Lanka's **Theravada** Buddhism may conceal the importance of the cultural and historical links between Sri Lanka and India in the early stages of its development. The first great stupas in Anuradhapura were built when Buddhism was still a religious force to be reckoned with in mainland India, and as some of the sculptures from Sigiriya suggest there were important contacts with Amaravati, another major centre of Buddhist art and thought, up to the 5th century AD.

The origins of Buddhism in Sri Lanka are explained in a legend which tells how King Devanampiya Tissa (died 207 BC) was converted by Mahinda, widely believed to have been Asoka's son, who was sent to Sri Lanka specifically to bring the faith to the Island's people. He established the Mahavihara monastery in Anuradhapura. Successors repeatedly struggled to preserve Sri Lankan Buddhism's distinct identity from that of neighbouring Hinduism and Tantrism. It was also constantly struggling with Mahayana Buddhism, which gained the periodic support of successive royal patrons. King Mahasena (276-303AD) and his son Sri Meghavarna, who received the famous 'Tooth of the Buddha' when it was brought to the island from Kalinga in the fourth century AD, both advocated Mahayana forms of the faith. Even then Sri Lanka's Buddhism is not strictly orthodox, for the personal character of the Buddha is emphasized, as was the virtue of being a disciple of the Buddha. Maitreya, the 'future' Buddha, is recognized as the only Bodhisattva, and it has been a feature of Buddhism in the island for kings to identify themselves with this incarnation of the Buddha.

The Sinhalese see themselves as guardians of the original Buddhist faith. They believe that the scripture in Pali was first written down by King Vattagamani Abhaya in the first century BC. The Pali Theravada canon of scripture is referred to as *Tipitakam Tripitaka* ('three baskets'), because the palm leaf texts on which they were written

Sri Lanka's flag, adopted in 1978, is based on the ancient flags of the Kandyan kings, with a lion clutching the sword of authority. The four leaves are from a Bo tree, under which the Buddha meditated. To the left, the green and orange panels represent the two sizeable minorities, Tamils and Muslims, while the whole is surrounded by a saffron yellow border, signifying the nation's protection by Buddhism.

were stored in baskets (*pitakas*). They are conduct (*vinaya*), consisting of 227 rules binding on monks and nuns; discourses (*sutta*), the largest and most important, divided into five groups (*niyakas*) of basic doctrine which are believed to be the actual discourses of the Buddha recording his exact words as handed down by word of mouth; and metaphysics (*abhidhamma*) which develop the ideas further both philosophically and psychologically. There are also several works that lack the full authority of the canon but are nonetheless important. Basham suggests that the main propositions of the literature are psychological rather than metaphysical. Suffering, sorrow and dissatisfaction are the nature of ordinary life, and can only be eliminated by giving up desire. In turn, desire is a result of the misplaced belief in the reality of individual existence. In its Theravada form, Hinayana Buddhism taught that there is no soul and ultimately no God. *Nirvana* was a state of rest beyond the universe, once found never lost.

The cosmology

Although the Buddha discouraged the development of cosmologies, the Hinayana Buddhists produced a cyclical view of the universe, evolving through four time periods.

Period 1 Man slowly declines until everything is destroyed except the highest heaven. The good go to this heaven, the remainder to various hells.
Period 2 A quiescent phase.
Period 3 Evolution begins again. However, 'the good *karma* of beings in the highest heaven' now begins to fail, and a lower heaven evolves, a *world of form*. During this period a great being in the higher heaven dies, and is re-born in the world of form as Brahma. Feeling lonely, he wishes that others were with him. Soon other beings from the higher heaven die and are reborn in this world. Brahma interprets these people as his own creation, and himself as The Creator.
Period 4 The first men, who initially had supernatural qualities, deteriorate and become earthbound, and the period fluctuates between advance and deterioration.

The four-period cycles continue for eternity, alternating between 'Buddha cycles' – one of which we live in today – and 'empty cycles'. It is believed that in the present cycle four Buddhas – *Krakucchanda*, *Kanakamuni*, *Kasyapa*, and *Sakyamuni* – have already taught, and one, *Maitreya*, is still to come.

In Sri Lanka the scriptures came to be attributed with almost magical powers. Close ties developed between Buddhist belief and **Sinhalese nationalism.** The Sinhalese scholar *Buddhaghosa* translated Sinhalese texts into Pali in the fifth century AD. At the beginning of the 11th century Sri Lankan missionaries were responsible for the conversion of Thailand, Burma, Cambodia and Laos to Theravada Buddhism. Subsequently, in the face of continued threats to their continued survival, Sri Lanka's Buddhist monks had to be re-ordained into the valid line of Theravada lineage by monks from Southeast Asia. Buddhist links with Thailand remain close.

Buddhist practice

By the time Buddhism was brought to Sri Lanka there was a well developed religious organization which had strong links with secular authorities. Developments in Buddhist thought and belief had made it possible for peasants and lay people to share in the religious beliefs of the faith. As it developed in Sri Lanka the main outlines of practice became clearly defined. The king and the orders of monks became interdependent; a monastic hierarchy was established; most monks were learning and teaching, rather than practising withdrawal from the world. Most important, Buddhism accepted a much wider range of goals for living than simply the release from permanent rebirth.

The most important of these were 'good rebirth', the prevention of misfortune and the increase in good fortune during the present life. These additions to original Buddhist thought led to a number of contradictions and tensions, summarized by Tambiah as: the Buddha as a unique individual, rather than a type of person (*Bodhisattva*) coming into the world periodically to help achieve release from *samsara* (rebirth), or rebirth into a better life; Buddhism as a path to salvation for all, or as a particular, nationalist religion; Buddhism as renunciation of the world and all its obligations, in contrast with playing a positive social role; and finally, whether monasteries should be run by the monks themselves, or with the support and involvement of secular authorities. These tensions are reflected in many aspects of Buddhism in Sri Lanka today, as in debates between monks who argue for political action as against withdrawal from the world.

Sects Until the 16th century Buddhism in Sri Lanka enjoyed the active support of the state. It remained longest in Kandy, but was withdrawn steadily after the British took control in 1815. The 18th-century revival of Buddhism in the Wet Zone was sponsored by the landowning village headmen, not by royalty, and castes such as the *Goyigama* and *Salagama* played a prominent role. Through the 19th century they became the dominant influence on Buddhist thought, while the remaining traditional Buddhist authority in Kandy, the *Siyam Nikaya*, suffered permanent loss of influence.

The *Siyam Nikaya*, one of the three sects of Sri Lankan Buddhism today, originated in the 18th mission of the Kandyan kings to Ayuthya in Thailand (Siam) to re-validate the Buddhist clergy. By a royal order admission to the sect's two branches was restricted to high caste Sinhalese. Today their monks are distinguished by carrying umbrellas and wearing their robe over one shoulder only. The exclusion of lower castes from this sect however bred resentment, and in 1803 a new sect, the *Amarapura Nikaya*, was established to be open to all castes, while in 1835 the third contemporary sect, the *Ramanya Nikaya*, was set up in protest at the supposedly excessive materialism of the other two. Both these sects wear robes which cover both shoulders, but while the *Amarapura* sect carry umbrellas the *Ramanya* carries a traditional shade. Sri Lankan monks wear orange robes and take the vows of celibacy and non-possession of worldly wealth, owning only the very basic necessities including two robes, begging bowl, a razor, needle and thread. They do not eat after mid-day and spend part of the day in study and meditation. The order of nuns which was introduced in Sri Lanka in the early days was shortlived.

This new, independent Buddhism, became active and militant. It entered into direct competition with Christians in proselytizing, and in setting up schools, special associations and social work. After Independence, political forces converged to encourage State support for Buddhism. The lay leadership pressed the government to protect Buddhists from competition with other religious groups. The Sinhalese political parties saw benefits in emphazising the role of Buddhism in society.

Buddhist worship

The Buddha himself refuted all ideas of a personal God and of worshipping a deity, but subsequent trends in Buddhism have often found a place for popular worship. Even in the relatively orthodox Theravada Buddhism of Sri Lanka personal devotion and worship are common, focused on key elements of the faith. Temple complexes (*pansalas*) commonly have several features which can serve as foci for individual devotion. Stupas or *dagobas*, which enshrine personal relics of the Buddha, are the most prominent, but Bodhi or Bo trees and images of the Buddha also act as objects of veneration.

Sri Lankan Buddhists place particular emphasis on the sanctity of the relics of the Buddha which are believed to have been brought to the island. The two most important are the sacred Bo tree and the tooth of the Buddha. The Bo tree at Anuradhapura is believed to be a cutting from the Bo tree under which the Buddha

Four Noble Truths

The Buddha preached Four Noble Truths: that life is painful; that suffering is caused by ignorance and desire; that beyond the suffering of life there is a state which cannot be described but which he termed *nirvana*; and that nirvana can be reached by following an eightfold path.

The concept of nirvana is often understood in the West in an entirely negative sense – that of 'non-being'. The word has the rough meaning of 'blow out' or 'extinguish', meaning to blow out the fires of greed, lust and desire. In a positive sense it has been described by one Buddhist scholar as 'the state of absolute illumination, supreme bliss, infinite love and compassion, unshakeable serenity, and unrestricted spiritual freedom'. The essential elements of the eightfold path are the perfection of wisdom, morality and meditation.

himself achieved Enlightenment at Bodh Gaya in modern Bihar. The Emperor Asoka is recorded as having entrusted the cutting to Mahinda's sister Sanghamitta to be carried to Sri Lanka on their mission of taking Buddhism to the island. As the original Bo tree in Bodh Gaya was cut down, this is the only tree in the world believed to come directly from the original tree under which the Buddha sat, and is visited by Buddhists from all over the world. Many other Bo trees in Sri Lanka have been grown from cuttings of the Anuradhapura Bo tree.

The tooth of the Buddha, now enshrined at the Dalada Maligawa in Kandy, was not brought to Sri Lanka until the fourth century AD. The Portuguese reported that they had captured and destroyed the original tooth in their attempt to wipe out all evidence of other religious faiths, but the Sinhalese claimed to have hidden it and allowed a replica to have been stolen. Today pilgrims flock from all over the island, queuing for days on special occasions when special access is granted to the casket holding the tooth in the Dalada Maligawa.

In ordinary daily life many Buddhists will visit temples at least once a week on *poya* days, which correspond with the four quarters of the moon. Full moon day, a national holiday, is a particularly important festival day (see page 59). It is also an opportunity for the worship of non-Buddhist deities who have become a part of popular Buddhist religion. Some have their origins explicitly in Hinduism. The four Guardian Deities seen as future Buddhas, include Natha, Vishnu, Skanda and Saman. **Skanda**, described below, the Hindu god of war, is worshipped as Kataragama, and **Vishnu** is seen as the island's protector. It is not surprising, therefore, to see the Hindu deities in Buddhist temples. Other deities have come from the Mahayana branch of Buddhism, such as **Natha**, or *Maitreya*, the future Buddha. Thus in worship as in many other aspects of daily life, Sinhalese Buddhism shares much in common with Hindu belief and practice with which it has lived side by side for over 2,000 years.

A final feature of Buddhist worship which is held in common with Hindu worship is its individualism. Congregational worship is usually absent, and individuals will normally visit the temple, sometimes soliciting the help of a *bhikku* in making an offering or saying special prayers. One of the chief aims of the Buddhist is to earn merit (*punya karma*), for this is the path to achieving nirvana. Merit can be earned by selfless giving, often of donations in the temple, or by gifts to *bhikkus*, who make regular house calls early in the morning seeking alms. In addition merit can be gained by right living, and especially by propagating the faith both by speech and listening.

Caste system

Some elements of the caste system were probably present in pre-Buddhist Sri Lanka, with both the priestly caste of Brahmins and a range of low caste groups such as scavengers. Although Buddhism encouraged its followers to eradicate distinctions based on caste, the system clearly survived and became a universal feature of social structures among Buddhists and subsequently Christians, despite their beliefs which explicitly condemn such social stratification. However, the complexities and some of the harsh exclusiveness of the caste system as practised in India was modified in Sri Lanka.

Sinhalese Buddhism has no Brahmin or Kshatriya caste, although some groups claim a warrior lineage. The caste enjoying highest social status and the greatest numbers is the Goyigama, a caste of cultivators and landowners who are widely seen as roughly equivalent to the Vellala caste among Jaffna Tamils. The Bandaras and the Radalas comprise a sub-caste of the Goyigamas who for generations have formed a recognizable aristocracy. Among many other castes lower down the social hierarchy come fishermen (*Karavas*), washermen (*Hena*), and toddy tappers (*Durava*).

Some caste groups, such as the **Karava**, have achieved significant changes in their status. Ryan suggests for example that the original Karava community came from South India and converted to Buddhism and began to speak Sinhalese while retaining their fishing livelihoods. Subsequently many converted to Roman Catholicism, located as they were in the heart of the coastal region just north of modern Colombo controlled by the Portuguese. Through their conversion many Karavas received privileges reserved by the Portuguese for Christians, enabling them to climb up the social ladder. Thus today, unlike the fishing communities of Tamil Nadu who remain among the lowest castes, the Karava are now among Sri Lanka's upper caste communities.

Hinduism

Hinduism in northern Sri Lanka was brought over by successive Tamil kings and their followers. It has always been easier to define Hinduism by what it is not than by what it is. Indeed, the name Hinduism was given by foreigners to the peoples of the sub-continent who did not profess the other major faiths, such as Muslims, Christians or Buddhists. The beliefs and practices of modern Hinduism began to take shape in the centuries on either side of the birth of Christ. But while some aspects of modern Hinduism can be traced back more than 2,000 years before that, other features are recent. Hinduism has undergone major changes both in belief and practice. Such changes came from outside as well as from within. As early as sixth century BC the Buddhists and Jains had tried to reform the religion of Vedism (or Brahmanism) which had been dominant in some parts of South Asia for 500 years.

Modern Hinduism

A number of ideas run like a thread through intellectual and popular Hinduism, some being shared with Buddhism. Some Hindu scholars and philosophers talk of Hinduism as one religious and cultural tradition, in which the enormous variety of belief and practice can ultimately be interpreted as interwoven in a common view of the world. Yet there is no Hindu organization, like a church, with the authority to define belief or establish official practice. Although the Vedas are still regarded as sacred by most Hindus, virtually no modern Hindu either shares the beliefs of the Vedic writers or their practices, such as sacrifice, which died out 1,500 years ago. Not all Hindu groups believe in a single supreme God. In view of these characteristics, many authorities argue that it is misleading to think of Hinduism as a religion at all.

Be that as it may, the evidence of the living importance of Hinduism is visible among Hindu communities in Sri Lanka as well as in India. Hindu philosophy and practice has also touched many of those who belong to other religious traditions, particularly in terms of social institutions such as caste.

Four human goals

For many Hindus there are four major human goals: material prosperity (*artha*), the satisfaction of desires (*kama*), and performing the duties laid down according to your position in life (*dharma*). Beyond those is the goal of achieving liberation from the endless cycle of rebirths into which everyone is locked (*moksha*). It is to the search for liberation that the major schools of Indian philosophy have devoted most attention. Together with *dharma*, it is basic to Hindu thought.

Dharma

Dharma (dhamma to Buddhists) represents the order inherent in human life. It is essentially secular rather than religious, for it doesn't depend on any revelation or command of God but rather has 10 'embodiments': good name, truth, self-control, cleanness of mind and body, simplicity, endurance, resoluteness of character, giving and sharing, austerities and continence. In *dharmic* thinking these are inseparable from five patterns of behaviour: non-violence, an attitude of equality, peace and tranquillity, lack of aggression and cruelty, and absence of envy.

Karma

According to *karma*, every person, animal or god has a being or self which has existed without beginning. Every action, except those that are done without any consideration of the results, leaves an indelible mark on that self. This is carried forward into the next life, and the overall character of the imprint on each person's 'self' determines three features of the next life. It controls the nature of his next birth (animal, human or god) and the kind of family he will be born into if human. It determines the length of the next life. Finally, it controls the good or bad experiences that the self will experience. However, it does not imply a fatalistic belief that the nature of action in this life is unimportant. Rather, it suggests that the path followed by the individual in the present life is vital to the nature of its next life, and ultimately to the chance of gaining release from this world.

Rebirth

The belief in the transmigration of souls (*samsara*) in a never-ending cycle of rebirth has been Hinduism's most distinctive and important contribution to the culture of India and Sri Lanka. The earliest reference to the belief is found in one of the Upanishads, around the seventh century BC, at about the same time as the doctrine of karma made its first appearance. By the late Upanishads it was universaly accepted, and in Buddhism there is never any questioning of the belief.

Ahimsa

AL Basham pointed out that belief in transmigration must have encouraged a further distinctive doctrine, that of non-violence or non-injury – *ahimsa*. Buddhism campaigned particularly vigorously against the then-existing practice of animal sacrifice. The belief in rebirth meant that all living things and creatures of the spirit - people, devils, gods, animals, even worms - possessed the same essential soul.

Hindu philosophy

It is common now to talk of six major schools of Hindu philosophy. The best known are yoga and Vedanta. Yoga is concerned with systems of meditation that can lead ultimately to release from the cycle of rebirth. It can be traced back as a system of thought to at least the third century AD. It is just one part of the wider system known as Vedanta, literally the final parts of the Vedantic literature, the *Upanishads*. The basic texts also include the *Brahmasutra of Badrayana*, written about the first century AD, and the most important of all, the *Bhagavadgita*, which is a part of the epic the *Mahabharata*.

Hindu worship

Some Hindus believe in one all-powerful God who created all the lesser gods and the universe. The Hindu gods include many whose origins lie in the Vedic deities of the early Aryans. These were often associated with the **forces of nature**, and Hindus have always revered many natural objects. Mountain tops, trees, rocks and above all rivers, are regarded as sites of special religious significance. They all have their own guardian spirits. You can see the signs of the continuing lively belief in these gods and demons wherever you travel. Thus trees for example are often painted with vertical red and white stripes and will have a small shrine at their base. Occasionally branches of trees will have numerous pieces of thread or strips of coloured cloth tied to them – placed there by devotees with the prayer for fulfilment of a favour. Hilltops will frequently have a shrine of some kind at the highest point, dedicated to a particularly powerful god. Pilgrimage to some important Hindu shrines is often undertaken by Buddhists as well as Hindus.

For most Hindus today worship (often referred to as 'performing **puja**') is an integral part of their faith. The great majority of Hindu homes will have a shrine to one of the gods of the Hindu pantheon. Individuals and families will often visit shrines or temples, and on special occasions will travel long distances to particularly holy places such as Kataragama. Acts of devotion are often aimed at the granting of favours and the meeting of urgent needs for this life – good health, finding a suitable wife or husband, the birth of a son, prosperity and good fortune. In this respect the popular devotion of simple pilgrims of all faiths in South Asia is remarkably similar when they visit shrines, whether Hindu, Buddhist or Jain temples, the tombs of Muslim saints or even churches. Performing *puja* involves making an offering to God, and darshan – having a view of the deity. Although there are devotional movements among Hindus in which singing and praying is practised in groups, Hindu worship is generally an act performed by individuals. Thus Hindu temples may be little more than a shrine in the middle of the street, housing an image of the deity which will be tended by a priest and visited at special times when a darshan of the resident God can be obtained. When it has been consecrated, the image, if exactly made, becomes the channel for the godhead to work.

The **image** of the deity may be in one of many forms. Temples may be dedicated to Vishnu or Siva, for example, or to any one of their other representations. The image of the deity becomes the object of worship and the centre of the temple's rituals. These often follow through the cycle of day and night, as well as yearly life cycles. The priests may wake the deity from sleep, bathe, clothe and feed it. Worshippers will be invited to share in this process by bringing offerings of clothes and food. Gifts of money will usually be made, and in some temples there is a charge levied for taking up positions in front of the deity in order to obtain a darshan at the appropriate times.

Hindu sects

Today three Gods are widely seen as all-powerful: **Brahma**, **Vishnu** and **Siva**. Their functions and character are not readily separated. While Brahma is regarded as the ultimate source of creation, Siva also has a creative role alongside his function as destroyer. Vishnu in contrast is seen as the preserver or protector of the universe. There are very few images and sculptures of Brahma, but Vishnu and Siva are far more widely represented and have come to be seen as the most powerful and important. Their followers are referred to as Vaishnavite and Saivites respectively, the majority in Sri Lanka today being Saivites.

Caste

One of the defining characteristics of South Asian societies, caste has helped to shape the social life of most religious communities in South Asia. Although the word caste (meaning 'unmixed' or 'pure') was given by the Portuguese in the 15th century AD, the main features of the system emerged at the end of the Vedic period. In Sri Lanka the Tamils of Jaffna have a modified form of the caste social structure typical of neighbouring Tamil Nadu. Brahmins occupy the same priestly position that they hold in India, and have also played an important role in education. Beneath them in ritual hierarchy but occupying a dominant social and political position, until recent times at least, were the cultivating and landlord caste known as the *vellalas*. Below them in rank was a range of low and outcaste groups, filling such occupations as washermen, sweepers and barbers, such as the Pallas and Nallavas. The tea plantation workers are all regarded as low caste.

Virtually all Hindu temples in Sri Lanka were destroyed by the Portuguese and the Dutch. Those that have been rebuilt never had the resources available to compare with those in India. However, they play a prominent part in Hindu life. De Silva suggests that Arumuga Navalar's failure to argue for social reform meant that caste – and untouchability – were virtually untouched. The high caste Vellalas, a small minority of the total Hindu population, maintained their power unchallenged until after Independence. Removal of caste disabilities started in the 1950s. The civil war over the demand for a separate Tamil state, Tamil Eelam, during which the Liberation Tigers of Tamil Eelam (LTTE) took complete control of social and political life in Jaffna and the north, may have changed the whole basis of caste far more thoroughly than any programme of social reform.

Islam

Islam was brought to Sri Lanka by Arab traders. Long before the followers of the Prophet Mohammad spread the new religion of Islam, Arabs had been trading across the Indian Ocean with southwest India, the Maldives, Sri Lanka and South East Asia. When the Arab world became Muslim the newly converted Arab traders brought Islam with them, and existing communities of Arab origin adopted the new faith. However, numbers were also swelled by conversion from both Buddhists and Hindus, and by immigrant Muslims from South India who fled the Portuguese along the west coast of India. The great majority of the present Muslim population of Sri Lanka is Tamil speaking, although there are also Muslims of Malay origin. Both in Kandy and the coastal districts Muslims have generally lived side by side with Buddhists, often sharing common interests against the colonial powers. However, one of the means by which Muslims maintained their identity was to refuse to be drawn into colonial education. As a result, by the end of the 19th century the Muslims were among the least educated groups. A Muslim lawyer, *Siddi Lebbe*, helped to change attitudes and encourage participation by Muslims.

In 1915 there were major Sinhalese-Muslim riots, and Muslims began a period of active collaboration with the British, joining other minorities led by the Tamils in the search for security and protection of their rights against the Sinhalese. The Muslims have been particularly anxious to maintain Muslim family law, and to gain concessions on education. One of the chief of these is the teaching of Arabic in government schools to Muslim children. Until 1974 Muslims were unique among minorities in having the right to choose which of three languages - Sinhala, Tamil or English - would be their medium of instruction. Since then a new category of Muslim schools has been set up, allowing them to distance themselves from the Tamil Hindu community, whose language most of them speak.

Muslim beliefs

The beliefs of Islam (which means 'submission to God') could apparently scarcely be more different from those of Buddhism or Hinduism. Islam has a fundamental creed; 'There is no God but God; and Mohammad is the Prophet of God' (*La Illaha illa 'llah Mohammad Rasulu 'llah*). One book, the Qur'an, is the supreme authority on Islamic teaching and faith. Islam preaches the belief in bodily resurrection after death, and in the reality of heaven and hell.

The idea of heaven as paradise is pre-Islamic. Alexander the Great is believed to have brought the word paradise into Greek from Persia, where he used it to describe the walled Persian gardens that were found even three centuries before the birth of Christ. For Muslims, Paradise is believed to be filled with sensuous delights and pleasures, while hell is a place of eternal terror and torture, which is the certain fate of all who deny the unity of God.

Islam has no priesthood. The authority of Imams derives from social custom, and from their authority to interpret the scriptures, rather than from a defined status within the Islamic community. Islam also prohibits any distinction on the basis of race or colour, and there is a strong antipathy to the representation of the human figure. It is often thought, inaccurately, that this ban stems from the Qur'an itself. In fact it probably has its origins in the belief of Mohammad that images were likely to be turned into idols.

Muslim sects

During the first century of its existence Islam split in two sects which were divided on political and religious grounds, the Shi'is and Sunnis. The religious basis for the division lay in the interpretation of verses in the Qur'an and of traditional sayings of Mohammad, the *Hadis*. Both sects venerate the Qur'an but have different *Hadis*. They also have different views as to Mohammad's successor.

The **Sunnis** – always the majority in South Asia – believe that Mohammad did not appoint a successor, and that Abu Bak'r, Omar and Othman were the first three caliphs (or vice-regents) after Mohammad's death. Ali, whom the Sunni's count as the fourth Caliph, is regarded as the first legitimate Caliph by the Shi'is, who consider Abu Bak'r and Omar to be usurpers. While the Sunni's believe in the principle of election of caliphs, **Shi'is** believe that although Mohammad is the last prophet there is a continuing need for intermediaries between God and man. Such intermediaries are termed Imams, and they base both their law and religious practice on the teaching of the Imams.

From the Mughal Emperors in India, who enjoyed an unparalleled degree of political power, down to the poorest fishermen in Sri Lanka, Muslims in South Asia have found different ways of adjusting to their Hindu or Buddhist environment. Some have reacted by accepting or even incorporating features of Hindu belief and practice in their own. Akbar, the most eclectic of Mughal Emperors, went as far as banning activities like cow slaughter which were offensive to Hindus and celebrating Hindu festivals in court.

Muslim year

The first day of the Muslim calendar is 16 July 622 AD. This was the date of the Prophet's migration from Mecca to Medina, the Hijra, from which the date's name is taken (AH = Anno Hijrae). The Muslim year is divided into 12 lunar months, alternating between 29 and 30 days. The first month of the year is *Moharram*, followed by *Safar*, *Rabi-ul-Awwal*, *Rabi-ul-Sani*, *Jumada-ul-Awwal*, *Jumada-ul-Sani*, *Rajab*, *Shaban*, *Ramadan*, *Shawwal*, *Ziquad* and *Zilhaj*.

Significant dates

New Year's Day – 1st of *Moharram*
Anniversary of the killing of the Prophet's grandson Hussain, commemorated by Shi'i Muslims – 9th and 10th of *Moharram*
Birthday of the Prophet (Milad-ul-Nabi) – 12th of *Rabi-ul-Awwul*
Start of the fasting month – 1st of *Ramadan*
Night of prayer (Shab-e-Qadr) – 21st of *Ramadan*
Three-day festival to mark the end of Ramadan – 1st of *Shawwal: Id-ul-Fitr*
Two-day festival commemorating the sacrifice of Ismail; the main time of pilgrimage to Mecca (the Haj). An animal (goat) is sacrificed and special meat and vermicelli dishes are prepared – 10th of *Zilhaj: Id-ul-Ajha*

Christianity

Christianity was introduced by the Portuguese. Unlike India, where Christian missionary work from the late 18th century was often carried out in spite of colonial government rather than with its active support, in Sri Lanka missionary activity enjoyed various forms of state backing. One Sinhalese king, Dharmapala, was converted, endowing the church, and even some high caste families became Christian. When the Dutch evicted the Portuguese they tried to suppress Roman Catholicism, and the Dutch Reformed Church found some converts. Other Protestant denominations followed the arrival of the British, though not always with official support or encouragement. Many of the churches remained dependent on outside support. Between the two World Wars Christian influence in government was radically reduced. Denominational schools lost their protection and special status, and since the 1960s have had to come to terms with a completely different role in Sri Lanka.

Christian beliefs

Christian theology had its roots in Judaism, with its belief in one eternal God, the Creator of the universe. Judaism saw the Jewish people as the vehicle for God's salvation, the 'chosen people of God', and pointed to a time when God would send his Saviour, or Messiah. Jesus, whom Christians believe was 'the Christ' or Messiah, was born in the village of Bethlehem, some 20 km south of Jerusalem. Very little is known of his early life except that he was brought up in a devout Jewish family. At the age of 29 or 30 he gathered a small group of followers and began to preach in the region between the Dead Sea and the Sea of Galilee. Two years later he was crucified in Jerusalem by the authorities on the charge of blasphemy – that he claimed to be the son of God.

Christians believe that all people live in a state of sin, in the sense that they are separated from God and fail to do his will. They believe that God is personal, 'like a father'. As God's son, Jesus accepted the cost of that separation and sinfulness himself through his death on the cross. Christians believe that Jesus was raised from the dead on the third day after he was crucified, and that he appeared to his closest followers. They believe that his spirit continues to live today, and that he makes it possible for people to come back to God.

The New Testament of the Bible, which, alongside the Old Testament, is the text to which Christians refer as the ultimate scriptural authority, consists of four 'Gospels' (meaning 'good news'), and a series of letters by several early Christians referring to the nature of the Christian life.

Christian worship

Although Christians are encouraged to worship individually as well as together, most forms of Christian worship centre on the gathering of the church congregation for praise, prayer the preaching of God's word, which usually takes verses from the Bible as its starting point. Different denominations place varying emphases on the main elements of worship, but in most church services today the congregation will take part in singing hymns (songs of praise), prayers will be led by the minister, priest or a member of the congregation, readings from the Bible will be given and a sermon preached. For many Christians the most important service is the act of Holy Communion (Protestant) or Mass (Catholic) which celebrates the death and resurrection of Jesus in sharing bread and wine, which are held to represent Christ's body and blood given to save people from their sin. Although Christian services may be held daily in some churches most Christian congregations in Sri Lanka meet for worship on Sunday, and services are held in Sinhala and Tamil as well as in English. They are open to all.

Denominations

Between the second and the fourth centuries AD there were numerous debates about the interpretation of Christian doctrine, sometimes resulting in the formation of specific groups focusing on particular interpretations of faith. One such group was that of the Nestorian Christians, who played a major part in the theology of the Syrian Church in Kerala. They regarded the Syrian patriarch of the east their spiritual head, and followed the Nestorian tradition that there were two distinct natures in Christ, the divine and human. However, although some believe that St Thomas and other early Christians came to Sri Lanka as well as South India the early church left no real mark on the island.

Today Roman Catholics account for 90% of the island's Christians. The Roman Catholic church believes that Christ declared that his disciple Peter should be the first spiritual head of the Church, and that his successors should lead the Church on earth. Modern Catholic churches still recognize the spiritual authority of the Pope and cardinals.

The reformation which took place in Europe from the 16th century onwards resulted in the creation of the Protestant churches, which became dominant in several European countries. They reasserted the authority of the Bible over that of the church. A number of new denominations were created. This process of division left a profound mark on the nature of the Christian church as it spread into South Asia. The Dutch brought with them their Dutch Reformed faith and left a number of churches, and subsequently during British colonial period the Anglican Church (Church of England) also became established, and several Protestant missionary denominations including Baptist and Methodist, established small churches. The reunification of the Protestant Christian churches which has taken significant steps since 1947 has progressed faster in South Asia than in most other parts of the world.

Architecture

Sri Lankan architecture has many elements in common with Buddhist and Hindu Indian traditions, but the long period of relative isolation, and the determined preservation of Buddhism long after its demise in India, have contributed to some very distinctive features.

Buddhist architecture

Buddhist and Hindu architecture probably began with wooden building, for the rock carving and cave excavated temples show clear evidence of copying styles which must have been developed first in wooden buildings. The third and second century BC caves of the Buddhists were followed in the seventh and eighth centuries AD by free standing but rock-cut temples.

Stupas

Stupas were the most striking feature of Buddhist architecture in India. Originally they were funeral mounds, built to house the remains of the Buddha and his disciples. The tradition of building stupas was developed by Sri Lanka's Sinhalese kings, notably in the golden age of the fourth and fifth centuries AD, and the revival during the 11th and 12th centuries. In Sri Lanka, a stupa is often referred to as *'dagoba'* (from Sanskrit *dhatu* – relic, *garbha* – womb chamber) and sometimes named *'saya'* (from *cetiya* - funeral mound) or *'wehera'* (from *vihara* – monastery). Some of the stupas (*dagobas*) are huge structures, and even those such as the fourth century *Jetavana* at Anuradhapura, now simply a grassed-over brick mound, is impressively large.

Few of the older Buddhist monuments are in their original form, either having become ruins or been renovated. Hemispherical mounds built of brick and filled with brick and rubble, they stand on a square terrace, surmounted by three concentric platforms. In its original or its restored form, the brick mound is covered with plaster and painted white. Surrounding it on a low platform (*vahalakadas*) is the ambulatory, or circular path, reached from the cardinal directions by stone stairways. Around some of the *dagobas* there are fine sculptures on these circular paths at the head of each stairway.

The design is filled with symbolic meaning. The hemisphere is the dome of heaven, the axis of the cosmos being represented by the central finial on top, while the umbrella-like tiers are the rising heavens of the gods. Worshippers walk round the stupa on the raised platform in a clockwise direction (*pradakshina*), following the rotational movement of the celestial bodies.

Many smaller stupas were built within circular buildings. These were covered with a metal and timber roof resting on concentric rows of stone pillars. Today the roofs have disappeared, but examples such as the Vatadage at Polonnaruwa can still be seen. King Parakramabahu I also built another feature of Sri Lankan architecture at Polonnaruwa, a large rectangular hall in which was placed an image of the Buddha. Most of Sri Lanka's early secular architecture has disappeared. Made of wood, there are remnants of magnificent royal palaces at both Anuradhapura and Sigiriya.

Moonstones

Sri Lanka's moonstones (not the gem) are among the world's finest artistic achievements. Polished semi-circular granite, they are carved in concentric semi-circular rings ('half-moons', about 1 m in radius) portraying various animals, flowers and birds, and normally placed at the foot of flights of steps or entrances to important buildings. There are particularly fine examples in Anuradhapura and Polonnaruwa.

The moonstones of pure Buddhist art at Anuradhapura comprise a series of rings and are often interpreted in the following way. You step over the flames of fire, through which one must pass to be purified. The next ring shows animals which represent the four stages of life: 1 Elephant - birth; 2 Horse - old age; 3 Lion - illness; 4 Bull – death and decay. These continue in an endless cycle symbolizing the continuous rebirths to which one is subject. The third row represents the twisting serpent of lust and desire, while the fourth is that of geese carrying lotus buds, representing purity. The lotus in the centre is a symbol of nirvana.

The steps have on either side beautifully carved **guard stones** with *makaras* designed to incorporate features from eight symbolically significant creatures: the foot of the lion, the crocodile's mouth and teeth, an elephant's tusk, the body of a fish, the peacock's feather, the serpent inside the mouth and the monkey's eyes.

Hindu architecture

Hindu temple building

The principles of religious building were laid down in the *Sastras*, sets of rules compiled by priests. Every aspect of Hindu and Buddhist religious building is identified with conceptions of the structure of the universe. This applies as much to the process of building – the timing of which must be undertaken at astrologically propitious times – as to the formal layout of the buildings. The cardinal directions of north, south, east and west are the basic fix on which buildings are planned. The east-west axis is nearly always a fundamental building axis.

Hindu temples were nearly always built to a clear and universal design, which had built into it philosophical understandings of the universe. This cosmology, of an infinite number of universes, isolated from each other in space, proceeds by imagining various possibilities as to its nature. Its centre is seen as dominated by **Mount Meru** which keeps earth and heaven apart. The concept of separation is crucial to Hindu thought and social practice. Continents, rivers and oceans occupy concentric rings around the mountain, while the stars encircle the mountain in another plane. Humans live on the continent of **Jambudvipa**, characterized by the rose apple tree (*jambu*).

The *Sastras* show plans of this continent, organized in concentric rings and entered at the cardinal points. This type of diagram was known as a **mandala**. Such a geometric scheme could then be subdivided into almost limitless small compartments, each of which could be designated as having special properties or be devoted to a particular deity. The centre of the mandala would be the seat of the major god. Mandalas provided the ground rules for the building of stupas and temples across India, and provided the key to the symbolic meaning attached to every aspect of religious buildings.

Temple design

Hindu temples developed characteristic plans and elevations. The focal point of the temple lay in its sanctuary, the home of the presiding deity, known as the womb-chamber (*garbhagriha*). A series of doorways, in large temples leading through a succession of buildings, allowed the worshipper to move towards the final encounter with the deity himself and to obtain *darshan* – a sight of the god. Both Buddhist and Hindu worship encourages the worshipper to walk clockwise around the shrine, performing *pradakshina*.

The elevations are designed to be symbolic representations of the home of the gods, the tallest towers rising above the *garbagriha* itself, symbolizing the meeting of earth and heaven in the person of the enshrined deity. In both, the basic structure is usually richly embellished with sculpture. When first built this would usually have been plastered and painted, and often covered in gems. In contrast to the extraordinary profusion of colour and life on the outside, the interior is dark and cramped. Here is the true centre of power.

Hindu architecture on the island bears close resemblances with the Dravida styles of neighbouring Tamil Nadu. Although all the important Hindu temples in Sri Lanka were destroyed by the Portuguese, the style in which they have been re-built continues to reflect those southern Indian traditions.

Grand designs

In May 2003, Sri Lanka mourned the death of Geoffrey Bawa, the island's best known, most prolific and most influential architect. Amongst his many projects Bawa was the creative visionary behind some of the Sri Lanka's most spectacular hotels, from the austerity of the 1-km long camouflaged jungle palace of Kandalama near Dambulla, to the colonial-influenced Lighthouse at Galle. He also constructed Sri Lanka's first purpose built tourist complex, the Bentota Beach in 1968.

Bawa's work blends traditional Sri Lankan architecture and use of materials with modern ideas of composition and space. Hallmarks include a careful balance, and blurring of the boundaries, between inside and outside, the creation of vistas, courtyards and walkways that offer a range of perspectives, and an acute sensitivity to setting and environment. His work builds on Sri Lanka's past, absorbing ideas from the west and east, while creating something innovative and definably Sri Lankan.

Born in 1919 to wealthy parents, Bawa went to England in 1938, where he studied English at Cambridge and took up the law. Soon tiring of this, he spent some years drifting and it was not until 1957, at the age of 38, that he qualified as an architect. On his return to Ceylon, he gathered together a group of talented young artists who shared his interest in the island's forgotten architectural heritage, including batik artist Ena de Silva (see page 259) and designer Barbara Sansoni (see page 91). The prolific practice he established set new standards in design over the next 20 years for all styles of buildings, from the residential and commercial to the religious and the educational.

Bawa's fame was sealed in 1979 when he was invited by President Jayawardene to design the new parliament building in Kotte. The result, which required the dredging of a swamp to create an artificial lake and island, itself symbolising the great irrigation of the ancient period, was a series of terraces with copper domed roofs rising from the water, with references to monastic architecture, Kandyan temples and South Indian palace architecture, all within a Modernist framework. Other high profile buildings followed including the Ruhuna University near Matara, dramatically arranged on two rocky hills overlooking the ocean.

In 1998 he suffered a massive stroke. Although it rendered him paralysed his colleagues completed his projects with a nod of assent or shake of the head from the bed-ridden master. In the same year he was honoured privately by his friend the Prince of Wales who snuck away from the official 50th anniversary celebrations to pay him tribute; official recognition followed in 2001 when he was awarded the prestigious Chairman's Award for Lifetime Achievements by the Aga Khan.

Tamil Nadu has been at the heart of southern Indian religious development for 2,000 years. Temple building was a comparatively late development in Hindu worship. Long before the first temple was built shrines were dotted across the land, the focus of **pilgrimage**, each with its own mythology. Even the most majestic of South Indian temples have basic features in common with these original shrines, and many of them have simply grown by a process of accretion around a shrine which may have been in that spot for centuries. The **myths** that grew around the shrines were expressed first by word of mouth. Most temples today still have versions of the stories which were held to justify their existence in the eyes of pilgrims. There are several basic features in common. David Shulman has written that the story will include 'the (usually miraculous) discovery of the site and the adventures of those important exemplars (such as gods, demons, serpents, and men) who were freed from sorrow of one kind or another by worshipping there'. The shrine which is the object of the story nearly always claims to be supreme, better than all others. Many stories illustrate these claims of superiority: for example, we are often told that the **Goddess Ganga** herself is forced to worship in a South Indian shrine in order to become free of the sins deposited by evil-doers who bathe in the river at Benares. Through all its great diversity Hindu temple architecture repeatedly expresses these beliefs, shared though not necessarily expressed, by the thousands of Sri Lankan Hindus who make visiting temples such a vital and living part of their life.

Today the most striking external features of Hindu temples in Sri Lanka are their elaborately carved towering gateways (*gopurams*). These were first introduced by the **Pandiyas** in the 10th century, who succeeded the Cholas a century later. The *gopuram* took its name from the 'cow gate' of the Vedic village, which later became the city gate and finally the monumental temple entrance. This type of tower has an oblong plan at the top which is an elongated vaulted roof with gable ends. It has sloping sides, usually 65°, so that the section at the top is about half the size of the base. Although the first two storeys are usually built solidly of stone masonry, the rest is of lighter material.

By the 15th century the Vijayanagar kings established their empire across much of South India. Their temples were built on an unprecedented scale, with huge *gopurams* studding the outside walls. None of the Sri Lankan temples were built on a scale anywhere near that of the 16th and 17th-century Vijayanagar temples of South India. Furthermore, all Hindu temples were destroyed by the Portuguese during the period in which Vijayanagar architecture was flourishing across the Palk Straits. Thus contemporary Hindu temples in Sri Lanka, while retaining some of the elements common to Hindu temples in Tamil Nadu, are always on a much smaller scale.

Art

Sculpture

Early Sri Lankan sculpture shows close links with Indian Buddhist sculpture. The first images of the Buddha, some of which are still in Anuradhapura, are similar to second and third century AD images from Amaravati in modern Andhra Pradesh. The middle period of the fifth to 11th centuries AD contains some magnificent sculptures on rocks, but there is a range of other sculpture, notably moonstones. There are decorated bands of flower motifs, geese and a variety of animals, both Anuradhapura and Polonnaruwa having outstanding examples. While the moonstones are brilliant works in miniature, Sri Lankan sculptors also produced outstanding colossal works, such as the 13-m high Buddha at Aukana, now dated as from the ninth century, or the 13th-century reclining Buddha at Polonnaruwa.

Painting

Sri Lanka's most famous art is its rock paintings from Sigiriya, dating from the sixth century AD. The *apsaras* (heavenly nymphs), scattering flowers from the clouds, are shown with extraordinary grace and beauty (you may notice the absence of the black pigment). Polonnaruwa saw a later flowering of the painting tradition in the 12th and 13th centuries. The Thivanka murals depict tales from the *Jatakas* and the Buddha's life, some elaborating and extending the strictly religious subject by introducing scenery and architectural elements. The wall paintings of Dambulla are also noteworthy (although many of the original paintings were covered by later ones), but thereafter classical Sri Lankan art declined though the folk tradition of scroll painting carried on.

The mid-18th century saw a new revival of painting in the Kandyan Kingdom, this time based on folk art which were inspired by traditional tales instead of religious themes. Many survive in temples around Kandy and elsewhere in the southwest.

Crafts

Local craft skills are still practised widely in households across the country. Pottery, coir fibre, carpentry, handloom weaving and metalwork all receive government assistance. Some of the crafts are concentrated in just a few villages. **Brasswork**, for example, is restricted to a small area around Kandy, where the 'city of arts', Kalapura, has over 70 families of craftsmen making superb brass, wood, silver and gold items. Fine **gold and silver chain work** is done in the Pettah area of Colombo. **Batiks**, from wall hangings to *lungis* (sarongs), and a wide range of cotton **handloom**, in vibrant colours and textures are widely available. **Silver jewellery** (also from Kandy), trays, ornaments and inlay work is a further specialization. **Masks** are a popular product in the southwest of the island, especially around Ambalangoda, based on traditional masks used in dance dramas, while Galle is famous for pillow **lace** and crochet. **Reed**, cane, rattan are fashioned into attractive household goods, while fine **wood-carving** and colourful **lacquer ware** can reach a high standard.

Language

Sinhala

Sinhala (or Sinhalese), the language of the Sinhalese, is an Indo-European language with North Indian affinities, unlike the Dravidian language, Tamil. Brought by the North Indian migrants, possibly in the fifth century BC, the language can be traced from inscriptions dating from the second century BC onwards which show how it had developed away from the original Sanskrit. The spoken language had changed several vowel sounds and absorbed words from the indigenous races and also from Tamil. Sinhala language had acquired a distinct identity by the beginning of the first century.

Although at first glance the **script** might suggest a link with the South Indian scripts, it developed independently. The rounded form was dictated by the use of a sharp stylus to inscribe on palm-leaf which would later be filled in with 'ink' instead of the North Indian technique of writing on bark.

The early verse and later prose **literature** were religious (Buddhist) and apart from inscriptions, date from the 10th century although there is evidence of some existing 300 years earlier. Non-religious texts only gained prominence in the last century.

Tamil

Like Sinhala, Tamil is also one of South Asia's oldest languages, but belongs to the Dravidian language family. It originated on the Indian mainland, and although Sri Lankan Tamil has retained some expressions which have a 'pure', even slightly archaic touch to them, it remains essentially an identical language both in speech and writing to that found in Tamil Nadu.

The first Tamil literature dates from approximately the second century AD. At that time a poets' academy known as the **Sangam** was established in Madurai. The poetry was devoted to religious subjects. From the beginning of the Christian era a development began to take place in Tamil religious thought and writing. Krishna became transformed from a remote and heroic figure of the epics into the focus of a new and passionate devotional worship – *bhakti*. Jordens has written that this new worship was 'emotional, ardent, ecstatic, often using erotic imagery'. From the seventh to the 10th century there was a surge of writing new hymns of praise, sometimes referred to as 'the Tamil *Veda*'. Attention focused on the 'marvels of Krishna's birth and infancy and his heroic and amorous exploits as a youth among the cowherds and cowherdesses of Gokula'. In the ninth century Vaishnavite Brahmans produced the *Bhagavata Purana*, which, through frequent translation into all India's major languages, became the vehicle for the new worship of Krishna. Its tenth book has been called 'one of the truly great books of Hinduism'. There are over 40 translations into Bengali alone. These influences were transmitted directly into Hindu Tamil culture in Sri Lanka, which retained intimate ties with the southern Tamil region.

Cinema

As in India, cinema is a favourite pastime in Sri Lanka, and while Hindi and Tamil films are predictably popular, there is a Sri Lankan tradition, which is worth searching out.

Although Sri Lanka is credited with opening, in 1903, the first film society in Asia, it was not until 1947, and the release of *Kadawunu Poronduwa* (Broken Promise) that Sinhalese dialogue was first heard in cinemas. Like most of Sri Lanka's early movies it was produced in India and though it began a spate of film-making in India using Sri Lankan actors, most followed formulaic South Indian storyline and acting styles. The post-independence creation of a **Government Film Unit** however established a breeding ground for a national style, and in 1956 British-trained director Lester James Pieris became the father of a new wave in Sri Lankan cinema with his first feature, *Rekawa* (Line of Destiny). Shown at Cannes, and receiving awards at three international festivals, it was the first to portray Sri Lankan culture realistically, using amateur actors and shooting in natural light. His subsequent film *Gamperaliya* (Changing of the Village) (1963), based on a story by novelist Martin Wickremasinghe, was successful both critically and commercially abroad, and was a great influence on a new breed of Sri Lankan directors in the 1960s. More recent Pieris films include *Beddegama* (1981), based on Leonard Woolf's *Village in the Jungle*, *Kaliyugaya* (1982, the second in his Wickremasinghe trilogy), and, in 2003, *Wekande Walauwa* (Mansion by the Lake), depicting an upper-class Buddhist family in the late 1980s and part-based on Chekhov's *The Cherry Orchard*. Pieris received a Legion d'Honneur in 1997 and a UNESCO Fellini Gold Medal (alongside Clint Eastwood!) at Cannes in 2003.

In 1970, the SLFP nationalized the film industry, with an aim of fostering an indigenous style, giving rise to a decade of experimentation from directors such as Dharmasena Pathiraja (Ahas Gauwa and *Bambaru Avith*), who introduced social realism, HD Premaratne (*Sikuruliya*, 1975) and Vasantha Obeysekera (Wesgaththo, 1970). The eighties were a mixed decade – Tissa Abeysekara's *Viragaya* (1987) regarded as a high spot – but by the end of the decade and throughout the 90s, the film industry was in decline, a victim of the government monopoly's restrictive policies and lack of investment.

There are however some significant films of recent years, often made with the help of foreign investment. The ethnic conflict has been a subject of a number of films, Prasanna Withanage's *Purahanda Kaluwara* (Death on a Full Moon Day) (1997), which was initially banned in Sri Lanka, is perhaps the most notable of these. Set in the quintessentially Buddhist North Central Province, the film exposes the chauvinism of the modern-day institution of Buddhism by focusing on a naïve father who refuses to believe that his son, a soldier in the SLA, has been killed. *Saroja* (Somaratne Dissanayake, 1999) sets the innocent friendship between a Sinhalese and a Tamil child against a backdrop of racial hatred and violence, with fateful consequences. *Punchi Surunganavi* (Little Angel) (2001) has a similar theme.

The film industry was liberalized in 2000 with the removal of the government's monopoly, giving rise to a brighter future.

Land and environment

Geography

Sri Lanka is practically on the equator so there is little difference between the length of night and day, both being about 12 hours. The sun rises around 0600 and it is completely dark by 1900. Its position has meant that Sri Lanka is at the heart of the Indian Ocean trading routes. The opening of the route round the Cape of Good Hope by Vasco da Gama in 1498 brought the island into direct contact with Western Europe. The opening of the Suez Canal in 1869 further strengthened the trading links with the West.

Origins

Only 100 million years ago Sri Lanka was still attached to the great land mass of what geologists call 'Pangaea', of which South Africa, Antarctica and the Indian Peninsula were a part. Indeed, Sri Lanka is a continuation of the Indian Peninsula, from which it was separated less than 10,000 years when sea level rose to create the 10-m deep and 35-km wide **Palk Straits**. It is 432 km long and at its broadest 224 km wide. Its 1,600 km of coastline is lined with fine sandy beaches, coral reefs and lagoons.

Many of the rocks which comprise over 90% of Sri Lanka and the Indian Peninsula were formed alongside their then neighbours in South Africa, South America, Australia and Antarctica. Generally crystalline, contorted and faulted, the Archaean rocks of Sri Lanka and the Indian Peninsula are some of the oldest in the world.

The fault line which severed India from Africa was marked by a north-south ridge of mountains. These run north from the Central Highlands of Sri Lanka through the Western Ghats, which form a spine running up the west coast of India. Both in Sri Lanka and India the hills are set back from the sea by a coastal plain which varies from 10 km to over 80 km wide while the hills are over 2,500-m high.

The oldest series are the **Charnockites**, intrusive rocks named after the founder of Calcutta and enthusiastic amateur geologist, Job Charnock. These are between 2,000 and 3,000 million years old. In Sri Lanka they run like a broad belt across the island's heart, important partly because they contain most of Sri Lanka's minerals, including gems, though these are found largely in the gravelly river deposits rather than in their original rocks.

Unlike the central Himalaya to their north which did not begin to rise until about 35 million years ago, the highlands of Sri Lanka have been upland regions for several hundred million years. The island has never been completely covered by the sea, the only exception being in the far north where the Jaffna peninsula was submerged, allowing the distinctive Jaffna limestones to be deposited in shallow seas between seven million and 26 million years ago.

Today the ancient crystalline rocks form an ancient highland massif rising to its highest points just south and southwest of the geographical centre of the pear-shaped island. The highlands rise in three dissected steps to Piduratalagala (Sri Lanka's highest mountain at 2,524 m) and the sacred Adam's Peak (2,260 m). The steps are separated from each other by steep scarp slopes. Recent evidence suggests that the very early folding of the ancient rocks, followed by erosion at different speeds, formed the scarps and plateaus, often deeply cut by the rivers which radiate from the centre of the island. Even though the origin of these steps is not fully understood the steep scarps separating them have created some beautiful waterfalls and enormous hydro-electric power potential. Some of this has now been realized, notably through the huge Victoria Dam project on the Mahaweli Ganga, but in the process some of the most scenic waterfalls have been lost.

Rivers lakes and floods

By far the largest of the 103 river basins in Sri Lanka is that of the Mahaweli Ganga, which covers nearly one fifth of the island's total area. The river itself has a winding course, rising about 50 km south of Kandy and flowing north then northeast to the sea near Trincomalee, covering a distance of 320 km. It is the only perennial river to cross the Dry Zone. Its name is a reference to the Ganga of North India, and in Sri Lanka all perennial rivers are called Ganga, while seasonal streams are called *oya* (Sinhalese) or *aru* (Tamil). A number of the rivers have been developed both for irrigation and power, the Victoria project on the Mahaweli Ganga being one of the biggest in Asia – and one of the most controversial. It has created island's largest lake, the Victoria Reservoir.

The short rivers of Sri Lanka's Wet Zone sometimes have severe floods, and the Kelani, which ultimately reaches the sea at Colombo, has had four catastrophic floods in the last century. Others can also be turbulent during the wet season, tumbling through steamy forests and cultivated fields on their short courses to the sea.

Climate

Sri Lanka's location, just north of the equator, places it on the main track of the two monsoons which dominate South Asia's weather systems. Derived from the Arabic word *mausim* (meaning season), the 'monsoon' is now synonymous with 'rains'. Strictly however it refers to the wind reversal which replaces the relatively cool, dry and stable northeasterlies, characteristic from October to May, with the very warm and wet southwesterlies from May to October. However, the northeasterlies, which originate in the arid interior of China, have crossed over 1,500 km of the Bay of Bengal by the time they reach Sri Lanka, and thus even the northeast monsoon brings rain, especially to the north and east of the island.

Rainfall

Nearly three quarters of Sri Lanka lies in what is widely known as the 'Dry Zone', comprising the northern half and the whole of the east of the country. Extensively forested and with an average annual rainfall of between 1,200-1,800 mm, much of the region does not seem unduly dry, but like much of southeast India, virtually all of the region's rain falls between October and January. The rain often comes in relatively short but dramatic bursts. Habarana, for example, located between Polonnaruwa and Anuradhapura received 1,240 mm (nearly 50 in) of rain in the three days around Christmas in 1957. These rains caused catastrophic floods right across the Dry Zone.

The Wet Zone also receives some rain during this period, although the coastal regions of the southwest are in the rain shadow of the Central Highlands, and are much drier than the northeast between November and January. The southwest corner of Sri Lanka, the Wet Zone, has its main wet season from May to October, when the southwest monsoon sweeps across the Arabian Sea like a massive wall of warm moist air, often over 10,000 m thick. The higher slopes of the Central Highlands receive as much as 4,000 mm during this period, while even the coastal lowlands receive over 500 mm.

Agriculture in the north and east suffers badly during the southwest monsoon because the moisture bearing winds dry out as they descend over the Central Highlands, producing hot, drying and often very strong winds. Thus June, July and August are almost totally rainless throughout the Dry Zone. For much of the time a strong, hot wind, called *yal hulunga* by the Sinhalese peasantry and *kachchan* by the Tamils, desiccates the land.

From late October to December cyclonic storms often form over the Bay of Bengal, sometimes causing havoc from the southern coast of India northwards to Bangladesh. Sri Lanka is far enough south to miss many of the worst of these, but it occasionally suffers major cyclones. These generally come later in the season, in December and January and can cause enormous damage and loss of life.

The Wet Zone rarely experiences long periods without rain. Even between the major moonsoon periods widespread rain can occur. Convectional thunderstorms bring short cloudbursts to the south and southwest between March and May, and depressions tracking across the Bay of Bengal can bring heavy rain in October and November.

Temperatures

Lowland Sri Lanka is always relatively hot and humid. On the plains temperature reflects the degree of cloud cover. Colombo has a minimum of 25°C in December and a maximum of 28°C in May. At Nuwara Eliya, over 2,000 m up in the Central Highlands, the average daytime temperatures hover around 16°C, but you need to be prepared for the chill in the evenings. Only the northeast occasionally experiences temperatures of above 38°C.

Wildlife

For one small island Sri Lanka packs an enormous variety of wildlife. This is largely because in that small space there is a wide range in altitude. The Central Highlands rise to over 2,500 m with damp evergreen forests, cool uplands and high rainfall. Within 100 km there are the dry coastal plain and sandy beaches. The climatic division of the island into the larger, dry, mainly northern and eastern region, and the smaller, wet, southwestern section is of importance to observers of wildlife. In the Dry Zone remnants of evergreen and deciduous forests are interspersed with cultivation, and in the east of this region the savanna grasslands are dominated by the metre high grass, *Imperata cylindrica*, widely regarded as a scourge. The whole vegetation complex differs sharply from both the Central Highlands and the Wet Zone of the southwest. These different areas support very different species. Many species occur only in one particular zone, but there are some, often the ones associated with man, which are found throughout. See the booklist on page 382.

Mammals

The **Asiatic elephant** (*Elephas maximus*) has a sizeable population, some wild which can be seen in several of the national parks. The animals come down to the water in the evening, either in family groups or herds of 20 or so. The 'Marsh Elephants', an interesting, significantly larger sub-species, are found in the marshy basin of the Mahaweli River. Wild elephants increasingly come into contact with humans in the growing settlements along their traditional migration routes between the northwest and southeast of the island and so the Wildlife Conservation Department is attempting to protect migration corridors from development. Visitors travelling away from the coast may get a chance to see domesticated animals being put to work or watch them at Pinnawela near Kandy.

The solid looking **Asiatic wild buffalo** (*Bubalus bubalis*), with a black coat and wide-spreading curved horns, stands about 170 cm at the shoulder. When domesticated, it is known as the water buffalo.

The **leopard or panther** (*Panthera pardus*), the only big cat in Sri Lanka, is found both in the dry lowland areas and in the forested hills. Being shy and elusive, it is rarely seen. The greyish **fishing cat** (*Felis viverrina*), with dark spots and dashes with somewhat webbed feet, search for prey in marshes and on the edge of streams.

The **sloth bear** (*Melursus ursinus*), about 75 cm at the shoulder, can be seen in areas of scrub and rock. It has an unkempt shaggy coat and is the only bear of the island.

The deer on the island are widespread. The commonest, the **chital (or spotted) deer** (*Axis axis*), only about 90 cm tall, is seen in herds of 20 or so in grassy areas. The bright rufous coat spotted with white is unmistakable. The stags carry antlers with three tines. The magnificent **sambar** (*Cervus unicolor*) (150 cm tall) with its shaggy coat varying from brownish grey to almost black in older stags, is seen in wooded hillsides. The stags carry large three-tined antlers and have a mane-like thickening of the coat around the neck. The **muntjac or barking deer** (*Muntiacus muntjak*) is small and shy (60 cm at the shoulder). It is brown with darker legs with white underparts and chest. The **stag** carries a small pair of antlers. Usually found in pairs, their staccato bark is heard more often than they are seen.

The **wild pig** (*Sus scrofa*) is easily identified by its affinity to the domestic pig. It has a mainly black body sparsely covered with hair except for a thick line along the spine; the young are striped. Only the male (boar) bears tusks. Commonly seen in grass and light bush, near water, it can do great damage to crops.

The interesting **purple-faced langur** (*Presbytis senex*) is only found in Sri Lanka. A long-tailed, long-legged monkey about 125 cm in length, nearly half of it tail, it has a dark coat contrasting with an almost white head. Hair on the head grows long to form swept back whiskers, but the face itself is almost black. Usually seen in groups of a dozen or so, it lives mainly in the dense, damp mountain forests but is also found in open woodland.

Apart from animals that still live truly in the wild, others have adapted to village and town life and are often seen near temples. The most widespread of the monkeys is the **grey langur** (Presbytis entellus), another long-tailed monkey with a black face, hands and feet. The **tocque macaque** (*Macaca sinica*), 60 cm, is a much more solid looking animal with shorter limbs. It varies in colour from grey to brown or even reddish brown above, with much paler limbs and underparts. The pale, sometimes reddish, face has whorls of hair on the cheeks. On top of the head the hair grows flat and cap-like, from a distinct parting!

Look out for the **flying fox** (*Pteropus giganteus*) which has a wingspan of 120 cm. These are actually fruit-eating bats, found throughout, except in the driest areas. They roost in large, sometimes huge, noisy colonies in tree tops, often in the middle of towns or villages, where they look like folded umbrellas hanging from the trees. In the evening they can be seen leaving the roost with slow measured wing beats.

The **ruddy mongoose** (*Herpestes ismithii*) is usually found in scrub and open jungle. The **brown mongoose** (*Herpestes fuscus*) can also be seen in gardens and fields. The mongoose is well known as a killer of snakes, but it will also take rats, mice, chickens and birds' eggs.

Birds

Sri Lanka is also an ornithologist's paradise with over 250 resident species, mostly found in the Wet Zone, including the Sri Lanka myna, Sri Lanka whistling thrush, yellow-eared bulbul, red-faced malkoha and brown-capped babbler. The winter migrants come from distant Siberia and western Europe, the reservoirs attracting vast numbers of water birds – stilts, sandpipers, terns and plover, as well as herons, egrets and storks. The forests attract species of warblers, thrushes, cuckoo and many others. The endemic **jungle fowl** (*Gallus lafayetti*) is Sri Lanka's national bird. It is common to see large ornaments topped by a brass jungle fowl which has an honoured place in the home on special occasions. The recently reopened **Kumana** sanctuary in the southeast, and **Bundala** (famed for flamingoes) and **Kalametiya**

Holy but not wholly efficacious

The sal tree is one of the most widespread and abundant trees in the tropical and sub-tropical Ganges plains and Himalayan foothills; it was the tree under which Gautama Buddha was born. Like the pipal (*Ficus religiosa*), under which the Buddha was enlightened, the sal is greatly revered in Sri Lanka. It is often planted near temples, for example on the lawn close to the Temple of the Tooth Relic in Kandy. However, the sal in Sri Lanka is very different to the one found in northern South Asia, and the difference has been known to have serious consequences since extracts from the tree are widely used for medicinal preparations. The sal tree proper is *Shorea robusta* (*dipterocarpaceae*), whereas the sal of Sri Lanka is the tree known all over the tropics as the cannon ball tree (*Couroupita surenamensis*). Unfortunately, the difference is not widely known and it is not unknown for Auyurvedic medicinal preparations using the Sri Lankan sal but following recipes of Indian origin, to have been taken without any effect.

sanctuaries between Tissamaharama and Hambantota in the south, both with lagoons, are the principal bird sanctuaries.

Reptiles

Two species of crocodile are found in Sri Lanka. The rather docile **mugger (or marsh) crocodile** (*Crocodilus palustrus*), 3-4 m in length, lives in freshwater rivers and tanks in many parts of the island. The **estuarine (or saltwater) crocodile** (*Crocodilus porosus*) prefers the brackish waters of the larger rivers where it can grow to 7 m. Among the lizards, the large water **monitor** (*Varanus*), up to 2 m long, greyish brown with black and yellow markings, is found in a variety of habitats. They have become quite widespread and tame and can even be seen scavenging in the rubbish dumps and market places. The land monitor lacks the yellow markings.

Seashore and marine life

Among the living coral swim a bewildering variety of colourful fish. There are shoals of silvery **sardinella** and stately, colourful **angelfish** (*Pomacanthus*) often with noticeable mouths in a different colour. Butterfly fish (*Chaetodontidae*) are similar to small angelfish but their fins are rounded at the end. The **surgeon fish** (*Acanthuridae*) get their name from the sharp blades at the base of their tails. Rounded in outline, with compressed bodies and pouting lips, they are often very brightly coloured (eg 17 cm **blue surgeon**). Striped like a zebra, the **scorpion fish** (*Pteriois*) is seen among live coral, and sometimes trapped in pools of the dead reef by the retreating tide. Although it has poisonous dorsal spines it will not attack if you leave it alone.

Corals are living organisms and consist of two basic types: the typical hard coral (eg Staghorn) and the less familiar soft corals which anchor themselves to the hard coral – one form looks like the greyish pink sea anemone. The commonest shells are the **cowries** which you can find on the beach. The **ringed cowrie** (*Cypraea annulus*) has a pretty grey and pinkish white shell with a golden ring, while the **money cowrie** which was once used as currency in Africa, varies from greenish grey to pink, according to its age. The big and beautiful **tiger cowrie** (*Cypraea tigris*) (up to 8 cm), has a very shiny shell marked like a leopard. The spectacular **spider conch** (*Lambis*) and the common **murex** (*M. bicorreus*) can grow 15-20 cm. **Sea urchins** (*Echinoidea*), fairly common on sandy beaches and dead coral, are extremely painful to tread on, so be sure to wear shoes when beach combing.

Of the seven species of marine turtle in the world, five return to lay their eggs on Sri Lankan beaches but all are on the endangered list. One of the rarer species is the giant **leather-back turtle** (*Dermochelys coriacea*) which grows to 2 m in length, has a ridged leathery skin on its back instead of a shell. The smaller **olive ridley turtle** (*Lepidochelys olivacea*) has the typical rows of shields along the shell. The Turtle Conservation Project is carrying out a very worthwhile programme near Tangalla on the south coast, see page 160.

Watching Wildlife: A brief introduction

by Gehan de Silva Wijeyeratne, see www.jetwingeco.com

Classical biogeographic theory predicts that small islands do not have large animals. However, the largest terrestrial mammal, the elephant, roams the remaining wildernesses in Sri Lanka. You have the best chance of seeing the wild Asian elephant on this island than anywhere else on the globe. At Uda Walawe National Park, a sighting is virtually guaranteed. Other national parks such as Wasgomuwa National Park and Yala National Park are also good for seeing elephants. During August to September, probably the largest congregation of wild elephants in a single place occurs. As the waters of the Minneriya Lake recede in Minneriya National Park, grasses flourish on the exposed lake bed. At times over 300 elephants maybe gathered on the lake bed, in clusters of small family groups which coalesce into super units, at times numbering over a 100. It is one of the most impressive spectacles in the international wildlife calendar.

The coastal waters of Sri Lanka are rich in marine mammals and are particularly noted as being one of the best places in the world for observing a high diversity of marine mammals. These include the world's largest marine mammal, the blue whale. The humpback whale, another marine giant, is also found in good numbers. However, whale watching is yet in its infancy.

On land is a spotted predator. Glamorous and at times elusive, the leopard is the highlight of a big game safari. Largely nocturnal, with some good daytime sightings, the Sri Lanka leopard is one of potentially eight sub species and is unique to the island. Yala National Park is the best place in Asia for leopard watching. In Block 1 of the park, which is usually visited by tourists, the density is as high as one per 1.1 per sq km according to a study (see www.jetwingeco.com). This, combined with the stretches of open terrain and the leopard's position an emboldened top predator, makes it relatively easy to see. In 2003, Wilpattu National Park reopened after nearly two decades. Leopard enthusiasts are hopeful that over time the park will regain its glory as a destination for leopards and other wildlife.

Another largely nocturnal hunter is the sloth bear. During June and July, it gorges itself on the yellow berries of the Palu Tree found in the dry zone. The best chances of a diurnal viewing are during this time. The low country parks in the dry zone host a number of mammals which visitors have a good chance of seeing including spotted deer, sambar, wild pig, jackal, black-naped hare, ruddy, grey and stripe-necked mongoose, civet cat etc.

On the southern coastal line is the Kalametiya Sanctuary, Bundala National Park and Palatupana Salt Pans, famous for their wintering shorebirds. Every year, tens of thousands of migrant shorebirds and ducks from Asia and Europe winter in the estuaries, lagoons and wetlands in these areas. At times, clouds of pintail and garganey (ducks) or waders such as black-tailed godwit, take to the air. Soon after arrival, the migrants spread out. Many of the migrant shorebirds, also called waders, will be familiar to foreign visitors. What makes places such as Palatupana so special is the diversity and close proximity of the birds. Little stints, Temminck's stints, lesser and greater sand plover, redshank, broad-billed sandpiper, ruff, greenshank etc, crowd along the water's edge. Bird-watchers in search of birds such as black and yellow bitterns of freshwater wetlands should try the Talangama Wetland, near Colombo, or the Muthurajawela Wetland, close to the International Airport. Around Tissamaharama are a complex of inland, man-made lakes that is also popular with bird-watchers. In fact the island is dotted with hundreds of lakes that are refuges for wildlife.

Much of Sri Lanka's endemic bio-diversity is confined to what is known as the wet zone in the southwest of the island. The most visited and best known of these is the Sinharaja Man and Biosphere Reserve. Visitors to Galle could try the Kottawa Rainforest and Arboretum, or, less than half an hour's drive or about three hours away is the Kanneliya Forest Reserve. Kottawa has interesting endemic animals such as the hump-nosed lizard but is a relatively small forest patch, lacking the species diversity of larger rainforests such as Sinharaja and Morapitiya. Kanneliya Rainforest is vast, but was once heavily logged and has lost the richness of animal species of Sinharaja.

Sinharaja is the jewel in the crown and one of the best places for observing 'mixed species feeding flocks'. Birds of many species forage together to enhance security and feeding efficiency, combing through the rainforest like a giant vacuum cleaner. Bird-watchers should look out or more likely listen for clues from the garrulous orange-billed babbler which forms a 'nucleus species'. The crested drongo, a courageous bird, acts as sentinel to the flock and also utters far carrying calls. When a feeding flock is encountered, it is easy to be distracted by the commotion of babblers, drongos and barbets. Carefully observing the mid canopy will often reveal Malabar Trogon. The female is dull, but the male has a striking scarlet breast. In the canopy is the discrete and enigmatic red-faced malkoha. This relatively large bird can surprisingly go unnoticed. In the lowland streams gaudily coloured endemic paradise combtails swim. Shoals of cherry barbs may swim by. Endemic stone suckers cling to the stone bed, as currents swirl past them.

Even a short visit to Sinharaja will result in a number of butterflies and dragonflies being seen. The glamour set of the insect world. Endemic tree nymphs in black and white splotches look like Chinese art work. They float lazily on barely discernible air currents. Common bluebottles and commanders fly by more purposefully. Dragonflies, voracious predators hunt in adjoining paddyfields as well as in the gloomy forest interior. Eastern scarlet darters have their red set off vividly against green foliage.

The rainforests also harbour one of the most significant radiations of animal species to be discovered in the past few decades. It is believed that as many as 200 new species of tree frogs are awaiting scientific description. Sri Lanka could surpass countries like Costa Rica in the number of tree frog species, making it the frog capital of the world. A key to this extraordinary diversity is the evolution of 'direct development'. Most amphibians including frogs are usually dependent on water in which they lay their eggs. Sri Lanka frogs have developed an ability to lay their eggs in a moist, foam nest. The eggs develop into small frogs within the eggs and emerge as adults by passing the water dependent tadpole stage.

In Sri Lanka, designated National Parks are under the purview of the Department of Wildlife Conservation. The Horton Plains National Park, about 45 minutes drive from Nuwara Eliya, is the only National Park where visitors are allowed to travel on foot, subject to designated footpaths. The Horton Plains are characterized by wind swept grasslands interspersed with patches of cloud forest. Some species of plants and animals are confined to the cloud forests. Bird-watchers visit the plains to look for montane specialties such as the Sri Lanka whistling thrush, Sri Lanka wood pigeon and dull-blue flycatcher.

Despite its small size, the presence of a mountainous core and two monsoons create sharply defined climatic zones in Sri Lanka. As a result, sub species have evolved in different climatic zones. A good example is the highland race of the Purple-faced Leaf Monkey. This race, also called the Bear Monkey, on account of its thick coat, can be seen in the cloud forest.

Vegetation

From tropical thorn forest in the driest regions of the southeast and northwest, (generally with a rainfall of less than 1,200 mm) the vegetation ranges through to montane temperate forest of the Central Highlands and then to mangroves of some stretches of the coast. Today mangroves are restricted almost exclusively to a stretch of the west coast, north of Puttalam and of the southeast coast, east of Hambantota and in the northern peninsula.

None of the original forest cover has been unaffected by human activity, and much has now been either converted to cultivated land, or given over to a range of tree cash crops, notably coconut and rubber at low altitudes and tea at higher levels. Indeed most of the forest cover is now restricted to the Dry Zone. Here dry evergreen forest, with trees generally less than 12 m in height, and moist deciduous forest, whose canopy level is usually up to 20 or 25 m, provide an excellent habitat for wildlife, and continue to cover extensive tracts of land. Even here the original forest has been much altered, most having re-colonized land which was extensively cultivated until 500 years ago. Sri Lanka also has four different types of grassland, all the result of human activity.

Common trees

In addition to the endless lines of **coconut palms** (*Cocos nucifer*) along the coastal belt and the Kurunegala district, the **sago** or **fish-tail palm** (*Caryota urens*), locally called 'kitul', is a regular feature on the island. The leaves are large and distinctive consisting of many small leaflets, each shaped like a fish tail while the flowers hang down like horses' tails. Sago comes from the pith, toddy and jaggery from the sap and the fibres are used to make bristles in brushes, as well as rope.

The **rain tree** (*Samanea saman*) is a large tree from South America, with a spreading canopy, often planted as a roadside shade tree. The dark green feathery leaves are peculiar in that they become horizontal in the daytime, thus maximizing the amount of shade thrown by the tree. At night time and in the rain they fold downwards. The flowers are pale pink, silky looking tufts.

The **eucalyptus or gum tree** (*Eucalyptus grandis*), introduced from Australia in the 19th century, is now widespread and is planted near villages to provide both shade and firewood. All the varieties have characteristic long, thin leaves and the colourful peeling bark and fresh pleasant smell. **Bamboo** (*Bambusa*) strictly speaking is a grass which is found almost everywhere. It can vary in size from small ornamental clumps to the enormous wild plant whose stems are so strong and thick that they are used for construction and as pipes for irrigation in small holdings.

The **banyan** (*Ficus benghalensis*), featured widely in eastern literature, is planted by temples, in villages and along roads. Curiously its seeds germinate in crevices in the bark of other trees. It sends down roots to the ground as it grows until the original host tree is surrounded by a cage-like structure which eventually strangles it. So a single banyan appears to have multiple 'trunks' which are in fact roots.

Related to the banyan, the **peepal** (*Ficus religiosa*) is distinguishable by the absence of aerial roots, and pointed heart shaped leaves which taper into a pronounced 'tail'. It too is commonly found near temples and shrines where it cracks open walls and strangles other trees with its roots. The purplish figs it bears in abundance are about 1 cm across.

Flowering trees

Visitors to Sri Lanka cannot fail to notice the many flowering trees planted along the roadside. The **golden mohur** *(Delonix regia)*, a native of Madagascar, grows throughout the island. A good shade tree, it grows only to about 8 or 9 m in height and has spreading branches. The leaves are an attractive feathery shape, and a bright light green in colour. The fiery coloured flowers which appear after it has shed its leaves, make a magnificent display.

The **jacaranda** (*Jacaranda mimosaefolia*), originally from Brazil, though rather straggly in shape, has attractive feathery foliage. The purple-blue thimble-shaped flowers (up to 40 mm long) make a striking splash of colour.

The **tamarind** (*Tamarindus indica*) is an evergreen with feathery leaves and small yellow and red flowers which grow in clusters in its spreading crown. The noticeable fruit pods are long, curved and swollen at intervals.

The large and dramatic **silk cotton tree** (*Bombax ceiba*) can be up to 25m in height. The bark is often light grey with conical spines; the bigger trees have noticeable buttress roots. The wide spreading branches keep their leaves for most of the year, the cup-shaped fleshy red flowers appearing only when the tree is leafless. The dry fruit pod produces the fine silky cotton which gives it its name.

The **Ceylon ironwood** (*Mesua ferrea*) is often planted near Buddhist temples. Its long slender leaves, reddish when young set off the white four-petalled flowers with yellow centres.

The beautiful flowering **rhododendron** (*Rhododendron Zeylanicum*) is common in the highland regions. It grows as either a sprawling shrub or a tree up to 12-m high. In the wild, the flowers are usually crimson or pale purple.

Fruit trees

The **mango** (*Mangifera indica*), a fairly large tree ranging from 6 to 15-m high or more, has spreading branches forming a rounded canopy. The dense shade it casts makes it a very attractive village meeting place. The distinctively shaped fruit is quite delicious and unlike any other in taste.

The **jackfruit** (*Artocarpus heterophyllus*) is one of the most remarkable trees. A large evergreen with dark green leathery leaves, its huge fruit can be as much as 1-m long and 40 cm thick, growing from a short stem directly off the trunk and branches. The skin is thick and rough, almost prickly. The strong smelling fruit of the main eating variety is sickly sweet and an acquired taste.

The **banana plant** (*Musa*) is actually a gigantic herb arising from an underground stem. The very large leaves grow directly off the trunk which is about 5 m in height. The fruiting stem bears a large purple flower, which yields up to 100 fruit.

The **papaya** (*Carica papaya*) which often grows to 4 m has distinctive palm-shaped leaves. Only the female tree bears the shapely fruit which hang down close to the crown.

The **cashew nut** (*Anacardium occidentale*) tree, a native of tropical America, was introduced into Sri Lanka, but now grows wild as well as being cultivated. Usually less than 7 m in height, it has bright green, shiny, rounded leaves. The nut hangs from a fleshy bitter fruit called a cashew apple.

Originally from tropical America, the **avocado pear** (*Persea*) grows well in the Wet Zone. The broad-leaved tree up to 10m in height, with oval, pointed leaves, bear the familiar fruit at the ends of the branches.

Flowering plants

Many flowering plants are cultivated in parks, gardens and roadside verges. The **frangipani** (*Plumeria rubra*) is particularly attractive with a crooked trunk and regular branches which bear leaves with noticeable parallel veins which taper to a point at each end. The sweetly-scented waxy flowers are usually white, pale yellow or pink.

The **bougainvillea** grows everywhere as a dense bush or a strong climber, often completely covered in flowers of striking colours from pinks to purples, oranges to yellows, and brilliant white. If you look carefully you will see that the paper-thin colourful 'petals' are really large bracts.

The trumpet-shaped flowers of the **hibiscus** too, come in brilliant scarlet, pink and yellow or simply white. **Orchids** abound but sadly most go unnoticed because of their tiny flowers. The large flowered, deep mauve **Dendrobium macarthiae** can be seen around Ratnapura in May. From spring to summer you may find the varicoloured, sweet-scented **vanda tessellata** in bloom everywhere.

Books

Art and architecture

Archer, WG & Paranavitana, S *Ceylon, paintings from Temple Shrine and Rock* (1958) Paris: New York Graphic Soc.

Arumugam, S *Ancient Hindu temples of Sri Lanka* (1982) Colombo.

Basnayake, HT *Sri Lankan Monastic architecture* (1986) Delhi: Sri Satguru. A detailed account of Polonnaruwa.

Coomaraswamy, AK *Medieval Sinhalese Art* (1956) New York: Pantheon.

Godakumbure, CE *Architecture of Sri Lanka* (1963) Colombo: Department of Cultural Affairs Monograph.

Manjusri, LTP *Design elements from Sri Lankan Temple Paintings* (1977) Colombo: Archaeological Survey of Sri Lanka. A fine collection of line drawings from the 18th and 19th century, particularly of the Kandyan style.

Robinson, D *Bawa: the Complete Works* (2002) London: Thames & Hudson.

Seneviratna, A *The Temple of the Sacred Tooth Relic* (1987) Govt of Sri Lanka (State Engineering Corp). A well-illustrated survey of the various temples in ancient Sinhalese capitals that held the sacred relic, in addition to Kandy. Also *Ancient Anuradhapura* (1994) Colombo: Archaeological Survey Department. Readable but detailed guide to the archaeological sites, including Mihintale. Others on Kandy, Dambulla and Polonnaruwa.

Current affairs and politics

De Silva, KM *Reaping the Whirlwind* (1998) New Delhi: Penguin. Tirelessly researched but readable analysis of the origins of the ethnic conflict.

Little, D *Sri Lanka: the invention of enmity* (1994) Washington: United States Institute of Peace Press. An attempt to provide a balanced interpretation of conflict in Sri Lanka.

Moore, MP *The State and Peasant Politics in Sri Lanka* (1985) London. An academic account of contemporary Sri Lankan political development.

McGowan, W *Only man is vile: The Tragedy of Sri Lanka* (1983) Picador. An account of the background to the 1983 Tamil-Sinhalese conflict.

Narayan Swamy, MR *Tigers of Lanka* (2002) Colombo: Vijitha Yapa. Updated edition of a study of Tamil militancy and the Indian role from an Indian perspective.

History: pre-history and early history

Deraniyagala, SU *The Prehistory of Sri Lanka* (1992) Colombo: Department of Archaeological Survey of Sri Lanka, 2 Vols. An erudite and detailed account of the current state of research into pre-historic Sri Lanka, available in Colombo and at the Anuradhapura Museum.

History: medieval and modern

de Lanerolle, Nalini *A Reign of Ten Kings* (1990) Colombo: CTB.

de Silva, KM *A History of Sri Lanka* (1981) London: OUP. Arguably the most authoritative historical account of Sri Lanka.

de Silva, RK and Beumer, WGM *Illustrations and views of Dutch Ceylon* (1988). Superbly illustrated.
Geiger, W *Culture of Ceylon in Mediaeval times* (1960) Wiesbaden: Harrassowitz.
Knox, Robert *An Historical Relation of Ceylon* (1981) Dehiwala: Tisara Prakasayo. Fascinating seventeenth century account of the experiences of a British seaman imprisoned by a Kandyan king for 20 years.
Robinson, Francis (ed) *Cambridge Encyclopedia of India, Pakistan, Bangladesh, Sri Lanka* (1989). Excellent and readable introduction to many aspects of South Asian society.

Language

Dissanayake, JB *Say it in Sinhala.*
Pragnaratne, Swarna *Sinhala Phrasebook* (2002) Lonely Planet.

Literature

Clarke, Arthur C *View from Serendib (among many others)* (1977) New York: Random House. A personal view from the prolific author who has made Sri Lanka his home.
Goonetileke, HAI *Lanka, their Lanka* (1984) New Delhi: Navrang. Delightful cameos of Sri Lanka seen through the eyes of foreign travellers and writers.
Goonetilleke, DCRA (ed) *The Penguin New Writing in Sri Lanka* (1992).
Gunesekhara, Romesh *Monkfish Moon* (1998) Penguin. Evocative collection of short stories of an island paradise haunted by violent undercurrents; *Reef* (1994). The story of a young boy growing up in modern Sri Lanka; and *Heaven's Edge* (2003) Bloomsbury. College graduate returns to a (thinly disguised) Sri Lanka to connect with his dead father's memory.
Muller, Carl *The Jam Fruit Tree* (the first of a series) about the free-and-easy Burghers; other books from this prolific author include *Colombo*, and *A Funny Thing Happened on the Way to the Cemetery.*
Obeyesekere, R & Fernando, C, Eds *An anthology of modern writing from Sri Lanka.* (1981) Tucson.
Ondaatje, Michael Writing by modern novelist, including the amusing autobiographical, *Running in the family* (1983) Penguin, and *Anil's Ghost* (2000) Picador. Winner of the Irish Book Prize, a young forensic anthropologist returns to Sri Lanka to investigate the 'disappearances' of the late 80s, rich and evocative.
Reynolds, CHB, Ed *An anthology of Sinhalese Literature of the 20th century* (1987) London.
Selvadurai, Shyam *Funny Boy* (1995) Vintage. A Tamil boy comes to terms with his homosexuality and racism in 1980s Colombo. *Cinnamon Gardens* (2000) Anchor Books. A young school teacher is caught between her own and her parents' desires for her future.
Sivanandan, A *When Memory Dies* (1998) Arcadia. Explores racial tensions across three generations of one family.

People and places

Cordiner, James *A description of Ceylon*. An account of the country, inhabitants and natural productions (1807), now reprinted by Colombo: Tisara Prakasakayo (1983).
Beny, Rolf *Island Ceylon* (1971) London: Thames & Hudson. Large coffee-table book with some excellent photos and illustrative quotes.
Brohier, RL *Changing face of Colombo 1505-1972* (1984) Colombo: Lake House. Excellent history of Colombo.
Maloney, Clarence *Peoples of South Asia* (1974) New York: Holt, Rheinhart & Winston. A wide ranging and authoritative review, perhaps over-emphasising the Dravidian connection with Sri Lanka.

Religion

Malangoda, K *Buddhism in Sinhalese Society, 1750-1900* (1976) Berkeley.

Perera, HR *Buddhism in Ceylon, Past and Present* (1966) Kandy: Buddhist Publication Society.

Qureshi, IH *The Muslim Community of the Indo-Pakistan Sub-Continent* 610-1947 (1977) Karachi: OUP.

Travel

Handbook for the Ceylon Traveller, 2nd ed, (1983) Colombo: Studio Times. A good collection of essays from many writers (who live in and plainly love the island) about people, places and everything Sri Lankan. Now dated, but many interesting insights.

Hatt, John *The tropical traveller: the essential guide to travel in hot countries*, 3rd ed (1992). Excellent, wide ranging and clearly written common sense, based on extensive experience and research.

Leestemaker, J, and others *Trekkers' guide to Sri Lanka* (1994) Colombo: Trekking Unlimited. A well described selection of popular (and some off-the-beaten-track) treks and walks, pointing out wildlife and interesting features, and with maps to help.

Woolf, Bella Sidney *How to See Ceylon* (reprinted 2002) Boralesgamuwa: Visidunu Prakashakayo. Entertaining colonial era guidebook from the sister of Leonard Woolf.

Natural history

Department of Wildlife Conservation's Guide to the National Parks of Sri Lanka (2001) Colombo: DWLC. Useful practical guide to all the parks, including maps.

Bond, Thomas *Wild Flowers to the Ceylon Hills* (1953) OUP.

Harrison, John & Worfolk, Tim *A Field Guide to the Birds of Sri Lanka* OUP, and **Wijeyeratne, Gehan de Silva** *A Photographic Guide to Birds of Sri Lanka* (2000) London: New Holland. Excellent user-friendly pocket guide.

The Pica traveller Sri Lanka, Pica Press, UK. Covers wildlife in general and also cultural sites.

Henry, GM *Guide to the birds of Ceylon* (1978) 3rd ed. India: OUP.

Munro, Ian *Marine and Fresh water fishes of Ceylon* (1955) Canberra: Australian Department of External Affairs.

Oriental Bird Club's *A bird-watcher's guide to Sri Lanka* (1997) Basingstoke: Ruby Publications. A good, illustrated leaflet giving all you need to know about the numerous reserves on the island.

Wijesinghe, DP *Checklist of birds of Sri Lanka* (1994) Colombo: Ceylon Bird Club.

Woodcock, Martin *Handguide to Birds of the Indian Sub-Continent*, London: Collins.

Footnotes

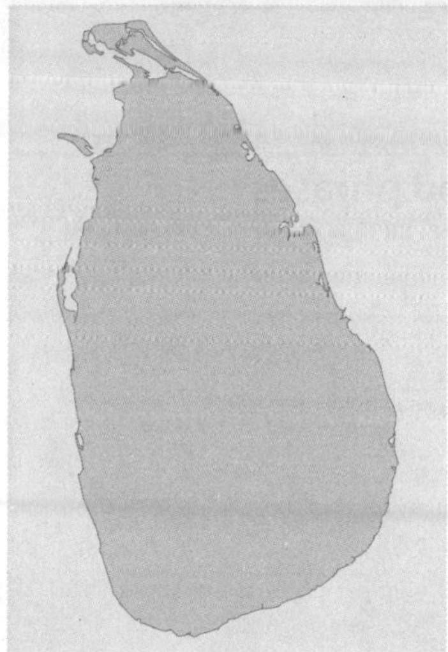

Language

Sinhalese useful words and phrases

Pronunciation

ah is shown **ā** as in car
ee is shown **ī** as in see
oh is shown **ō** as in old
These marks, to help with pronunciation, do not appear in the main text

General greetings	*Ayubowan*
Thank you / No thank you	*Es-thu-thee / mata epa*
Excuse me, sorry	*Samavenna*
Pardon?	*Ah?*
Yes/no	*Ou/na*
Nevermind/that's all right	*Kamak na*
Please	*Karunakara*
What is your name?	*Nama mokakda?*
My name is …	*Mage nama …*
How are you?	*Kohamada?*
I am well thanks	*Mama hondin innava*
Not very well	*Wadiya honda ne*
Do you speak English?	*Ingirisi kathakaranawatha?*

Shopping

How much is this?	*Mīka kīyada?*
That will be 20 rupees	*Rupial wissai*
Please make it a bit cheaper	*Karunakara gana adukaranna*

The hotel

What is the room charge?	*Kamarayakata gana kiyada?*
May I see the room please?	*Kamaraya karnakara penvanna?*
Is there an a/c room?	*A/c kamarayak thiyenawada?*
Is there hot water?	*unuwathura thiyenawada?*
… a fan/mosquito net	*… fan/maduru delak*
Please clean the room	*Karnakara kamaraya suddakaranna*
This is OK	*Meka hondai*
Bill please	*Karunakara bila gaynna*

Travel

Where is the railway station?	*Dumriyapola koheda?*
When does the Colombo bus leave?	*Colombata bus eka yanne kīyatada?*
How much is it to Colombo?	*Colombota kīyada?*
Will you go for 10 rupees?	*Rupiyal dahayakata yanawada?*
Left/right	*Wama/dakuna*
Staight on	*Kelin yanna*
Nearby	*Langa*
Please wait here	*Karunakara mehe enna*
Please come here at 8	*Karunakara mehata atata enna*
Stop	*Nawathinna*

Time and days

right now	*dang*	week	*sathiya*
morning	*ude*	month	*masey*
afternoon	*dawal*	Sunday	*irrida*
evening	*sawasa*	Monday	*sanduda*
night	*raya*	Tuesday	*angaharuwada*
today	*atha*	Wednesday	*badhada*
tomorrow	*heta*	Thursday	*brahaspathinda*
yesterday	*īye*	Friday	*sikurada*
day	*dawasa*	Saturday	*senasurada*

Numbers

1	*eka*	9	*namaya*
2	*deka*	10	*dahaya*
3	*thuna*	20	*wissai*
4	*hathara*	30	*thihai*
5	*paha*	40	*hathalihai*
6	*haya*	50	*panahai*
7	*hatha*	100/200	*sīayaī/desiyai*
8	*ata*	1000/2000	*dāhai/dedāhai*

Basic vocabulary

Some English words are widely used such as airport, bathroom, bus, embassy, ferry, hospital, stamp, taxi, ticket, train (though often pronounced a little differently).

bank	*bankuwa*
café/food stall	*kamata kadyak*
chemist	*beheth sappuwa*
clean	*sudda*
closed	*wahala*
cold	*sī thai*
dirty	*apirisidui*
doctor	*dosthara*
excellent	*hari honthai*
ferry	*bottuwa*
food/to eat	*kanda/kāma*
hospital	*rohala*
hot (temperature)	*rasnai*
hotel	*hōtalaya*
open	*aralu*
police station	*policiya*
restaurant	*kāmata*
road	*pāra*
room	*kamaraya*
shop	*kade*
sick (ill)	*asaneepai*
station	*istashama*
this	*meka*
that	*araka*
water	*wathura*
when?	*kawathatha?*
where?	*koheda?*

Useful words and phrases: Sri Lankan Tamil

general greeting	*vanakkam*
Thank you/no thank you	*nandri*
Excuse me, sorry, pardon	*mannikkavum*
Yes/no	*ām/illai*
never mind/that's all right	*paruvai illai*
please	*thayavu seithu*
What is your name?	*ungaludaya peyr enna*
My name is...	*ennudaya peyr*
How are you?	*ningal eppadi irukkirirgal?*
I am well, thanks	*nan nantraga irrukkirain*
Not very well	*paruvayillai*
Do you speak English?	*ningal angilam kathappirgala*

Shopping

How much is this?	*ithan vilai enna?*
That will be 20 rupees	*athan vilai irupatha rupa*
Please make it a bit cheaper!	*thayavu seithu konjam kuraikavuam!*

The hotel

What is the room charge?	*arayin vilai enna?*
May I see the room please?	*thayavu seithu arayai parka mudiyama?*
Is there an a/c room?	*kulir sathana arai irrukkatha?*
Is there hot water?	*sudu thanir irukkuma?*
...a bathroom?	*oru kuliyal arai...?*
...a fan/mosquito net?	*katotra sathanam/kosu valai...?*
Please clean the room	*thayavu seithu arayai suththap paduthava*
This is OK	*ithuru seri*
Bill please	*bill tharavum*

Travel

Where's the railway station?	*station enge?*
When does the Galle bus leave?	*eppa Galle bus pogum?*
How much is it to Kandy?	*Kandy poga evalavu?*
Will you go to Kandy for 10 rupees?	*paththu rupavitku Kandy poga mudiyami?*
left/right	*idathu/valathu*
straight on	*naerakapogavum*
nearby	*aruqil*
Please wait here	*thayavu seithu ingu nitkavum*
Please come here at 8	*thayavu seithu ingu ettu*
stop	*nivuthu*

Time and days

right now	*ippoh*
morning	*kalai*
afternoon	*pitpagal*
evening	*malai*
night	*iravu*
today	*indru*
tomorrow/yesterday	*nalai/naetru*
day	*thinam*
week	*vaaram*
month	*maatham*

Sunday	*gnatruk kilamai*
Monday	*thinkat kilamai*
Tuesday	*sevai kilamai*
Wednesday	*puthan kilamai*
Thursday	*viyalak kilamai*
Friday	*velli kilamai*
Saturday	*sanik kilamai*

Numbers

1	*ontru*	10	*pattu*
2	*erantru*	20	*erupathu*
3	*moontru*	30	*muppathu*
4	*nangu*	40	*natpathu*
5	*ainthu*	50	*ompathu*
6	*aru*	100/200	*nooru/irunooru*
7	*aelu*	1000/2000	*aiyuram/iranda iuram*
8	*ettu*		
9	*onpathu*		

Basic vocabulary

Some English words are widely used, often alongside Tamil equivalents, such as, airport, bank, bathroom, bus, embassy, ferry, hospital, hotel, restaurant, station, stamp, taxi, ticket, train (though often pronounced a little differently).

airport	*agaya vimana nilayam*
bank	*vungi*
bathroom	*kulikkum arai*
café/food stall	*unavu kadai*
chemist	*marunthu kadai*
clean	*suththam*
closed	*moodu*
cold	*kulir*
dirty	*alukku*
embassy	*thootharalayam*
excellent	*miga nallathu*
ferry	*padagu*
hospital	*aspathri*
hot (temp)	*ushnamana*
hotel/restaurant	*sapathu*
juice	*saru/viduthi*
open	*thira*
road	*pathai*
room	*arai*
shop	*kadi*
sick (ill)	*viyathi*
stamp	*muththirai*
station	*nilayam*
this	*ithu*
that	*athu*
ticket	*anumati situ*
train	*rayll*
water	*thannir*
when?	*eppa?*
where?	*enge?*

Glossary

A

aarti (arati) Hindu worship with lamps
abhaya mudra Buddha posture signifiying protection; forearm raised, palm facing outward fingers together
ahimsa non-harming, non-violence
ambulatory processional path
amla/amalaka circular ribbed pattern (based on a gourd) on top of a temple tower
Ananda the Buddha's chief disciple
anda lit 'egg', spherical part of the stupa
antechamber chamber in front of the sanctuary
apse semi-circular plan, as in apse of a church
arama monastery (as in Tissamaharama)
architrave horizontal beam across posts or gateways
Arjuna hero of the Mahabharata, to whom Krishna delivered the Bhagavad Gita
arrack spirit distilled from palm sap
aru river (Tamil)
Aryans literally 'noble' (Sanskrit); prehistoric peoples who settled in Persia and N India
asana a seat or throne; symbolic posture
ashlar blocks of stone
ashram hermitage or retreat
Avalokiteshwara Lord who looks down; Bodhisattva, the Compassionate
avatara 'descent'; incarnation of a divinity, usually Vishnu's incarnations

B

banamaduwa monastic pulpit
Bandaras sub-caste of the Goyigama caste, part of the Sinhalese aristocracy
bas-relief carving of low projection
basement lower part of walls, usually adorned with decorated mouldings
bazar market
beru elephant grass
Bhagavad-Gita Song of the Lord from the Mahabharata in which Krishna preaches a sermon to Arjuna
bhikku Buddhist monk
bhumi 'earth'; refers to a horizontal moulding of a shikhara (tower)
bhumisparasa mudra earth-witnessing Buddha posture
Bo-tree Ficus religiosa, large spreading tree associated with the Buddha; also Bodhi
Bodhisattva Enlightened One, destined to become Buddha
Brahma universal self-existing power; Creator in the Hindu Triad. Often represented in art, with four heads
Brahman (Brahmin) highest Hindu (and Jain) caste of priests
Brahmanism ancient Indian religion, precursor of modern Hinduism and Buddhism
Buddha The Enlightened One; founder of Buddhism who is worshipped as god by certain sects
bund an embankment; a causeway by a reservoir (tank)
Burghers Sri Lankans of mixed Dutch-Sinhalese descent

C

cantonment large planned military or civil area in town
capital upper part of a column or pilaster
catamaran log raft, logs (*maram*) tied (*kattu*) together (Tamil)
cave temple rock-cut shrine or monastery
chakra sacred Buddhist Wheel of Law; also Vishnu's discus
chapati unleavened Indian bread cooked on a griddle
chena shifting cultivation
chhatra, chatta honorific umbrella; a pavilion (Buddhist)
Chola early and medieval Tamil kingdom (India)
circumambulation clockwise movement around a stupa or shrine while worshipping
cloister passage usually around an open square
coir coconut fibre used for making rope and mats
copra dried sections of coconut flesh, used for oil
corbel horizontal block supporting a vertical structure or covering an opening
cornice horizontal band at the top of a wall
crore 10 million
Culavansa Historical sequel to Mahavansa, the first part dating from 13th century, later extended to 16th century

D

dagoba stupa (Sinhalese)
darshan (darshana) viewing of a deity
Dasara (dassara/dussehra/dassehra) 10 day Hindu festival (September-October)
devala temple or shrine (Buddhist or Hindu)
Devi Goddess; later, the Supreme Goddess; Siva's consort, Parvati
dhal (daal) lentil 'soup'
dharma (dhamma) Hindu and Buddhist concepts of moral and religious duty
dharmachakra wheel of 'moral' law (Buddhist)
dhyana meditation
dhyani mudra meditation posture of the Buddha, cupped hands rest in the lap
distributary river that flows away from main channel, usually in deltas
Diwali festival of lights (September-October) usually marks the end of the rainy season
Dravidian languages – Tamil, Telugu, Kannada and Malayalam; and peoples mainly from S India

Durga principal goddess of the Shakti cult; rides on a tiger, armed with weapons
dvarpala doorkeeper

E

eave overhang that shelters a porch or verandah
eri tank (Tamil)

F

finial emblem at the summit of a stupa, tower or dome; often a tier of umbrella-like motifs or a pot
frieze horizontal band of figures or decorative designs

G

gable end of an angled roof
garbhagriha literally 'womb-chamber'; a temple sanctuary
gedige arched Buddhist image house built of stone slabs and brick
gopura towered gateway in S Indian temples
Goyigama landowning and cultivating caste among Sinhalese Buddhists

H

Haj (Hajj) annual Muslim pilgrimage to Mecca (Haji, one who has performed the Haj)
hakim judge; a physician (usually Muslim)
Hanuman Monkey hero of the Ramayana; devotee of Rama; bringer of success to armies
Hari Vishnu
harmika the finial of a stupa; a pedestal where the honorific umbrella was set
Hasan the murdered eldest son of Ali, commemorated at Muharram
howdah seat on elephant's back
Hussain the second murdered son of Ali, commemorated at Muharram

I

illam lens of gem-bearing coarse river gravel
imam Muslim religious leader in a mosque
Indra King of the gods; God of rain; guardian of the East
Isvar Lord Sanskrit

J

jaggery brown sugar made from palm sap
jataka stories accounts of the previous lives of the Buddha
JVP Janatha Vimukhti Peramuna (People's Liberation Army) – violent revolutionary political movment in 1970s and 1980s

K

kadu forest (Tamil)
kalapuwa salty or brackish lagoon
Kali lit 'black'; terrifying form of the goddess Durga, wearing a necklace of skulls/heads
kalyanmandapa (Tamil) hall with columns, used for the symbolic marriage ceremony of the temple deity
kapok the silk cotton tree
kapurala officiating priest in a shrine (devala)
karandua replica of the Tooth Relic casket, dagoba shaped
Karavas fishing caste, many converted to Roman Catholicism
karma present consequences of past lives
Kataragama the Hindu god of war; Skanda
Kartikkeya/Kartik Son of Siva, also known as Skanda or Subrahmanyam
katcheri (cutchery, Kachcheri) public office or court
khondalite crudely grained basalt
kolam masked dance drama (Sinhalese)
kovil temple (Tamil)
kitul fish-tailed sago palm, whose sap is used for jaggery
Krishna Eighth incarnation of Vishnu; the cowherd (Gopala, Govinda)
Kubera Chief yaksha; keeper of the earth's treasures, Guardian of the North
kulam tank or pond (Tamil)

L

laddu round sweet snack
lakh 100,000
Lakshmana younger brother of Rama in the Ramayana
Lakshmi Goddess of wealth and good fortune, consort of Vishnu
lattice screen of cross laths: perforated
lena cave, usually a rock-cut sanctuary
lingam (linga) Siva as the phallic emblem
Lokeshwar 'Lord of the World', Avalokiteshwara to Buddhists and of Siva to Hindus
LTTE Liberation Tigers of Tamil Eelam, or "The Tigers", force rebelling against Sri Lankan Government
lungi wrap-around loin cloth

M

maha great; in Sri Lanka, the main rice crop
Mahabodhi Great Enlightenment of Buddha
Mahadeva literally 'Great Lord'; Siva
Mahavansa literally "Great Dynasty or Chronicle", a major source on early history and legend
Mahayana The Greater Vehicle; form of Buddhism practised in East Asia, Tibet and Nepal
Mahesha (Maheshvara) Great Lord; Siva
mahout elephant driver/keeper
Maitreya the future Buddha
makara crocodile-shaped mythical creature
malai hill (Tamil)
mandapa columned hall preceding the sanctuary in a Jain or Hindu temple
mandir temple
mantra sacred chant for meditation by Hindus and Buddhists
Mara Tempter, who sent his daughters (and soldiers) to disturb the Buddha's meditation
mawatha roadway
maya illusion
Minakshi literally 'fish-eyed'; Parvati, Siva's consort

Mohammad 'the praised'; The Prophet; founder of Islam
moksha salvation, enlightenment; lit `release'
moonstone the semi-circular stone step before a shrine; also a gem
mudra symbolic hand gesture and posture associated with the Buddha
Muharram period of mourning in remembrance of Hasan and Hussain, two murdered sons of Ali

N

Naga (nagi/nagini) Snake deity; associated with fertility and protection
Nandi a bull, Siva's vehicle and a symbol of fertility
Narayana Vishnu as the creator of life
Nataraja Siva, Lord of the cosmic dance
Natha worshipped by Mahayana Buddhists as the bodhisattva Maitreya
navagraha nine planets, represented usually on the lintel of a temple door
navaratri literally '9 nights'; name of the Dasara festival
niche wall recess containing a sculpted image or emblem,
nirvana enlightenment; (literally 'extinguished')

O

ola palm manuscripts
oriel projecting window
oya seasonal river

P

pada foot or base
paddy rice in the husk
padma lotus flower. Padmasana, lotus seat; posture of meditating figures
pagoda tall structure in several stories
Pali language of Buddhist scriptures
pankah (punkha) fan, formerly pulled by a cord
pansukulika Buddhist sect dwelling in forest hermitages
parapet wall extending above the roof
Parinirvana (parinibbana) the Buddha's state prior to nirvana, shown usually as a reclining figure
Parvati daughter of the Mountain; Siva's consort
pilimage Buddhist image house
potgul library
pradakshina patha processional passage or ambulatory
puja ritual offerings to the gods; worship (Hindu)
pujari worshipper; one who performs puja
punya karma merit earned through actions and religious devotion (Buddhist)

R

raj rule or government
raja king, ruler; prefix 'maha' means great
Rama seventh incarnation of Vishnu; hero of the Ramayana epic
Ramayana ancient Sanskrit epic
Ravana Demon king of Lanka; kidnapper of Sita
rickshaw 3-wheeled bicycle-powered (or 2-wheeled hand-powered) vehicle
Rig Veda (Rg) oldest and most sacred of the Vedas
rupee unit of currency in Sri Lanka, India, Pakistan and Nepal

S

sagar lake; reservoir
Saiva (Shaiva) the cult of Siva
sal hardwood tree of the lower mountains
sala hall
salaam greeting (Muslim); literally 'peace'
samadhi funerary memorial, like a temple but enshrining an image of the deceased; meditation state
samsara eternal transmigration of the soul
samudra sea, or large artificial lake
sangarama monastery
sangha ascetic order founded by Buddha
Saraswati wife of Brahma and goddess of knowledge; usually seated on a swan, holding a veena
Shakti Energy; female divinity often associated with Siva; also a name of the cult
shaman doctor/priest, using magic
Shankara Siva
sharia corpus of Muslim theological law
shikhara temple tower
singh (sinha) lion
Sita Rama's wife, heroine of the Ramayana epic.
Siva The Destroyer among Hindu gods; often worshipped as a lingam (phallic symbol)
Sivaratri literally 'Siva's night'; festival (February-March) dedicated to Siva
Skanda the Hindu god of war
sri (shri) honorific title, often used for 'Mr'
stucco plasterwork
stupa hemispheric funerary mound; principal votive monument in a Buddhist religious complex
Subrahmanya Skanda, one of Siva's sons; Kartikkeya in South India
sudra lowest of the Hindu castes
svami (swami) holy man
svastika (swastika) auspicious Hindu/ Buddhist emblem

T

tale tank (Sinhalese)
tank lake created for irrigation
Tara historically a Nepalese princess, now worshipped by Buddhists and Hindus
thali South and West Indian vegetarian meal
torana gateway with two posts linked by architraves
tottam garden (Tamil)
Trimurti Triad of Hindu divinities, Brahma, Vishnu and Siva

U

Upanishads ancient Sanskrit philosophical texts, part of the Vedas
ur village (Tamil)

V

Valmiki sage, author of the Ramayana epic

varam village (Tamil)

varna 'colour'; social division of Hindus into Brahmin, Kshatriya, Vaishya and Sudra

Varuna Guardian of the West, accompanied by Makara (see above)

vatadage literally circular relic house, protective pillard and roofed outer cover for dagoba

Veda (Vedic) oldest known religious texts; include hymns to Agni, Indra and Varuna, adopted as Hindu deities

vel Skanda's trident

Vellala Tamil Hindu farming caste

verandah enlarged porch in front of a hall

vihara Buddhist or Jain monastery with cells opening off a central court

villu small lake (Sri Lanka)

Vishnu a principal Hindu deity; creator and preserver of universal order; appears in 10 incarnations (Dashavatara)

vitarka mudra Buddhist posture of discourse, the fingers raised

W

Wesak Commemoration day of the Buddha's birth, enlightenment and death

wewa tank or lake (Sinhalese)

Y

yala summer rice crop

yoga school of philosophy concentrating on different mental and physical disciplines (yogi, a practitioner)

yoni female genital symbol, associated with the worship of the Siva Linga (phallus)

Food Glossary

Basic vocabulary	Sinhalese	Tamil
bread	*pān*	*rotti/pān*
butter		*butter/vennai*
(too much) chilli	*miris wadi*	*kāram*
drink	*bīma*	*kudi*
egg	*biththara*	*muttai*
fish	*malu*	*min*
fruit	*palathuru*	*palam*
food	*kama*	*unavu*
jaggery	*hakuru*	*sini/vellam*
juice	*isma*	*sāru*
meat	*mus*	*iraichchi*
oil	*thel*	*ennai*
pepper	*gammiris*	*milagu*
pulses (beans, lentils)	*parippu*	*thāniyam*
rice	*buth*	*arisi*
salt	*lunu*	*uppu*
savoury		*suvai*
spices	*kulubadu*	*milagu*
sweetmeats	*rasakevili*	*inippu pondangal*
treacle	*pani*	*pāni*
vegetables	*elawalu*	*kai kari vagaigal*
water	*wathura*	*thanneer*

Fruit		
avocado	*alkigetapera*	
banana	*keselkan*	*valaippalam*
cashew	*cadju*	*muruthivi*
coconut	*pol*	*thengali*
green coconut	*kurumba*	*pachcha niramulla thengai*
jackfruit	*(jak) kos ambul*	
mango	*amba*	*mangai*
orange	*dodam*	
papaya	*papol*	*pappa palam*
pineapple	*annasi*	*annasi*

Vegetables		
aubergine	*vambatu*	*kathirikai*
beans (green)	*bonchi*	*avarai*
cabbage	*gowa*	*muttaikosu*
gourd (green)	*pathola*	*pudalankai*
mushrooms		*kalān*
okra	*bandakka*	*vendikkai*
onion	*luunu*	*venkayam*
pea		*pattani*
pepper	*miris*	*kāram*
prawns	*isso*	*irāl*
potato	*ala*	*uruka kilangu*
spinach	*niwithi*	*pasali*
tomato	*thakkali*	*thakkali*

Meat, fish and seafood

chicken	*kukulmas*	*koli*
crab	*kakuluvo*	*nandu*
pork	*ōroomas*	*pantri*
potato	*ala*	*uruka kilangu*
spinach	*niwithi*	*pasali*
tomato	*thakkali*	*thakkali*

Ordering a meal in a restaurant: Sinhalese

Please show the menu	*menu eka penwanna*
sugar/milk/ice	*sini/kiri/ice*
A bottle of mineral water please	*drink botalayak genna*
do not open it	*arinna epa*

Order a meal in a restaurant: Tamil

Please show the menu	*thayavu seithu thinpandangal patti tharavum*
sugar/milk/ice	*sini/pāl/ice*
A bottle of mineral water please	*oru pothal soda panam tharavum*

Sri Lankan specialities

amblulthial sour fish curry

kaha buth kaha rice (yellow, cooked in coconut milk with spices and saffron/turmeric colouring) kiri rice is similar but white and unspiced, served with treacle, chilli or pickle

biththara rotti rotti mixed with eggs

buriyani rice cooked in meat stock and pieces of spiced meat sometimes garnished with boiled egg slices

hoppers (āppa) cupped pancakes made of fermented rice flour, coconut milk, yeast, eaten with savoury (or sweet) curry

lamprais rice cooked in stock parcelled in a banana leaf with dry meat and vegetable curries, fried meat and fish balls and baked gently

mallung boiled, shredded vegetables cooked with spice and coconut

pittu rice-flour and grated coconut steamed in bamboo moulds, eaten with coconut milk and curry

polos pahi pieces of young jackfruit (tree lamb) replaces meat in this dry curry

rotty or rotti flat, circular, unleavened bread cooked on a griddle

sambol hot and spicy accompaniment usually made with onions, grated coconut, pepper (and sometimes dried fish)

sathai spicy meat pieces baked on skewers (sometimes sweet and sour)

'short eats' a selection of meat and vegetable snacks (in pastry or crumbled and fried) charged as eaten.

string hoppers (indiappa) flat circles of steamed rice flour noodles eaten usually at breakfast with thin curry

thosai or ***dosai*** large crisp pancake made with rice and lentil-flour batter

vadai deep-fried savoury lentil dough-nut rings

Sweets (rasakavilis)

curd rich, creamy, buffalo-milk yoghurt served with treacle or jaggery

gulab jamun dark, fried spongy balls of milk curd and flour soaked in syrup

halwal aluva fudge-like, made with milk, nuts and fruit

kadju kordial fudge squares made with cashew nuts and jaggery

kaludodol dark, mil-based, semi solid sweet mixed with jaggery, cashew and spices (a moorish delicacy)

rasgulla syrup-filled white spongy balls of milk-curd and flour

thalaguli balls formed after pounding roasted sesame seeds with jaggery

wattalappam set 'custard' of coconut, milk, eggs and cashew, flavoured with spices and jaggery

Index

Shorts' index

Map index

Advertisers' index

Map symbols

Administration

- Capital city
- Other city/town
- Regional border

Roads and travel

- National highway
- Paved road
- Unpaved road
- Track
- Footpath
- Railway with station

Water features

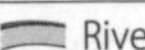

- River
- Ocean, lake, wewa (tank)
- Seasonal marshland
- Beach, sand bank
- Reef
- Waterfall
- Ferry

Cities and towns

- Sight
- Sleeping
- Eating
- Bars & clubs
- Building
- Main through route
- Main street
- Minor street
- Pedestrianized street
- Tunnel
- One way street
- Bridge
- Steps

- Fortified wall
- Park, garden, stadium
- Airport
- Bus station
- Fort
- Bank
- Hospital
- Market
- Museum
- Petrol
- Police
- Post office
- Tourist office
- Cathedral, church
- Mosque
- Hindu temple (kovil)
- Buddhist temple, dagoba
- Internet
- Telephone
- Golf
- Parking
- Detail map
- Related map

Topographical features

- Contours (approx), rock outcrop
- Mountain
- Mountain pass
- Escarpment
- Gorge
- Salt flat

Other symbols

- Archaeological site
- National park/wildlife reserve
- Viewing point
- Campsite

Credits

Footprint credits
Editor: Stephanie Lambe
Map editor: Sarah Sorensen
Proof reader: Avril Elhrich

Publisher: Patrick Dawson
Editorial: Alan Murphy, Sophie Blacksell, Sarah Thorowgood, Claire Boobbyer, Caroline Lascom, Felicity Laughton, Davina Rungasamy, Laura Dixon
Cartography: Robert Lunn, Claire Benison, Kevin Feeney
Series development: Rachel Fielding
Design: Mytton Williams and Rosemary Dawson (brand)
Advertising: Debbie Wylde
Finance and administration: Sharon Hughes, Elizabeth Taylor

Photography credits
Front cover: Alamy
Back cover: Alamy
Inside colour section: Hilary Emberton, Alamy

Print
Manufactured in Italy by LegoPrint
Pulp from sustainable forests

Footprint feedback
We try as hard as we can to make each Footprint guide as up to date as possible but, of course, things always change. If you want to let us know about your experiences – good, bad or ugly – then don't delay, go to www.footprintbooks.com and send in your comments.

Publishing information
Footprint Sri Lanka
4th edition

ISBN 1 903471 78 8
CIP DATA: A catalogue record for this book is available from the British Library

Published by Footprint
6 Riverside Court
Lower Bristol Road
Bath BA2 3DZ, UK
T +44 (0)1225 469141
F +44 (0)1225 469461
discover@footprintbooks.com
www.footprintbooks.com

Distributed in the USA by
Publishers Group West

Neither the black and white nor colour maps are intended to have any political significance.

Every effort has been made to ensure that the facts in this guidebook are accurate. However, travellers should still obtain advice from consulates, airlines etc about travel and visa requirements before travelling. The authors and publishers cannot accept responsibility for any loss, injury or inconvenience however caused.

Acknowledgements

There are many people without whose help and guidance this book would never have reached its present form. I am greatly indebted to Bob and Roma Bradnock who wrote the first three editions of the guide, and for their advice in the preparation of this, the fourth. Particular thanks must go to Gehan de Silva Wijeyeratne of Jetwing Eco Tours whose limitless knowledge and passion for Sri Lankan wildlife I have raided, and for his excellent piece, Wildlife reserves, in the Background chapter of this guide. The Sri Lanka Tourist Board's Charmarie Maelge (London) and Nizam Lantra (Colombo) were both very helpful in smoothing my path. Huge thanks too to Nilan Wickramasinghe at Lion Royal, and to my two excellent and very patient drivers, Wilbert (Matara) and Kusumsiri (Gamage) of Boralesgamuwa who became a trusted guide and friend. Hilary Emberton's updates, comments, photography and in particular her detailed research on Jaffna were invaluable. And warm thanks to Fergus Thomas whose enthusiasm for the peninsula really opened up my eyes (even though he hogged Angelina to himself!).

I am grateful also to the following: Hana Borrowman (Manchester) for tips before I left; Lyn and Peter (Bournemouth or Beruwela, depending on the time of year) for fixing my laptop; Sabri Khalid for his advice on the Galle area; Paddy Halton on Batticaloa; Rafael for putting me up (and up with me) in Jaffna; Anita and everyone at SLMM in Mannar; Fred Miller in Arugam Bay; Asela Pethiyagoda in Kandy; and various three-wheeler drivers who saved the day, including Jagi (Beruwela) and Sunil (Unawatuna). Thanks also to Catherine Lewis for proof-reading the third edition; Rachel Fielding for commissioning me to write the fourth; and Stephanie Lambe for her careful editing and encouragement.

And most important, many many thanks to the following readers and travellers who wrote in with their comments, corrections and updates. Apologies to anyone I've missed: Umayanga Abeysekara, Galle; David Acklam, by e-mail; Mannilla Bartels, The Netherlands; Harry and Nasja Berg, The Hague, Netherlands; Florence Blanchet, France; Don & Vicki Brewer, by e-mail; Diana Buff, Switzerland; DJ Butterworth, Poole, UK; Chris Carruthers, by e-mail; Louise Catling, Norwich, UK; Rod Daldry, by e-mail; Dave & Beck, by email; Jean-Paul Degen, Netherlands; Dr Randell Drum, USA; Johannah Fawthrop, by email; Jean Freed, Canada; Hilvie & Georg Fries, Brunsbüttel, Germany; Bob Geater, UK; Daragh Glynn, by e-mail; Lucy Goodman, by email; Peter de Groot, by e-mail; SFB Heaton, Great Missenden, UK; Geoff Hobbs, London, UK; Peter Jensen, Denmark; Damian Johnstone, by email; Mark Kininmonth, by email; Doron Lev, by e-mail; Linton, Kandy; Nirit Lotan, Hagolan, Israel; Fiona MacKay, London, UK; Gavin McCloskey, UK; Miranda McMinn; Walter Michel, Tangalle; Colette Milward, UK; Jennifer Moore, by email; Aravinth Raj Muthukrishnan, India; Peter Phillips, Shropshire, UK; Adrian Preston, Crowborough, UK; Daniela Rahn, Germany; Kurt Renold, Belgium; Lesley Rhodes, by email; Olivier Rosenthal, France; Bianca Schmid, by e-mail; AC Seneviratne, Negombo; Marianne and Bill Shakespeare, Salisbury, UK; Charles Shaw, by e-mail; Tal Shohan, Hagolan, Israel; Lisa Slapinski, by email; Anne Kristine Søvik, Oslo, Norway; Herman van der Steen, Belgium; A Verrycken, Belgium; Asoka Weerasinghe, Unawatuna; Sunil Wickremasinghe, Colombo; Philip & Bobby Williams, Stroud, UK; Sara Worman, London.

Complete listing

Footprint publishes travel guides to over 150 destinations worldwide. Each guide is packed with practical, concise and colourful information for everybody from first-time travellers to travel aficionados. The list is growing fast and current titles are noted below.

Available from all good bookshops and online

www.footprintbooks.com

(P) denotes pocket guide

Latin America and Caribbean
Argentina
Barbados (P)
Bolivia
Brazil
Caribbean Islands
Central America & Mexico
Chile
Colombia
Costa Rica
Cuba
Cusco & the Inca Trail
Dominican Republic
Ecuador & Galápagos
Guatemala
Havana (P)
Mexico
Nicaragua
Peru
Rio de Janeiro
South American Handbook
Venezuela

North America
Vancouver (P)
New York (P)
Western Canada

Africa
Cape Town (P)
East Africa
Libya
Marrakech & the High Atlas
Marrakech (P)
Morocco
Namibia
South Africa
Tunisia
Uganda

Middle East
Egypt
Israel
Jordan
Syria & Lebanon

N
NE
E
SE
SW
W
NW

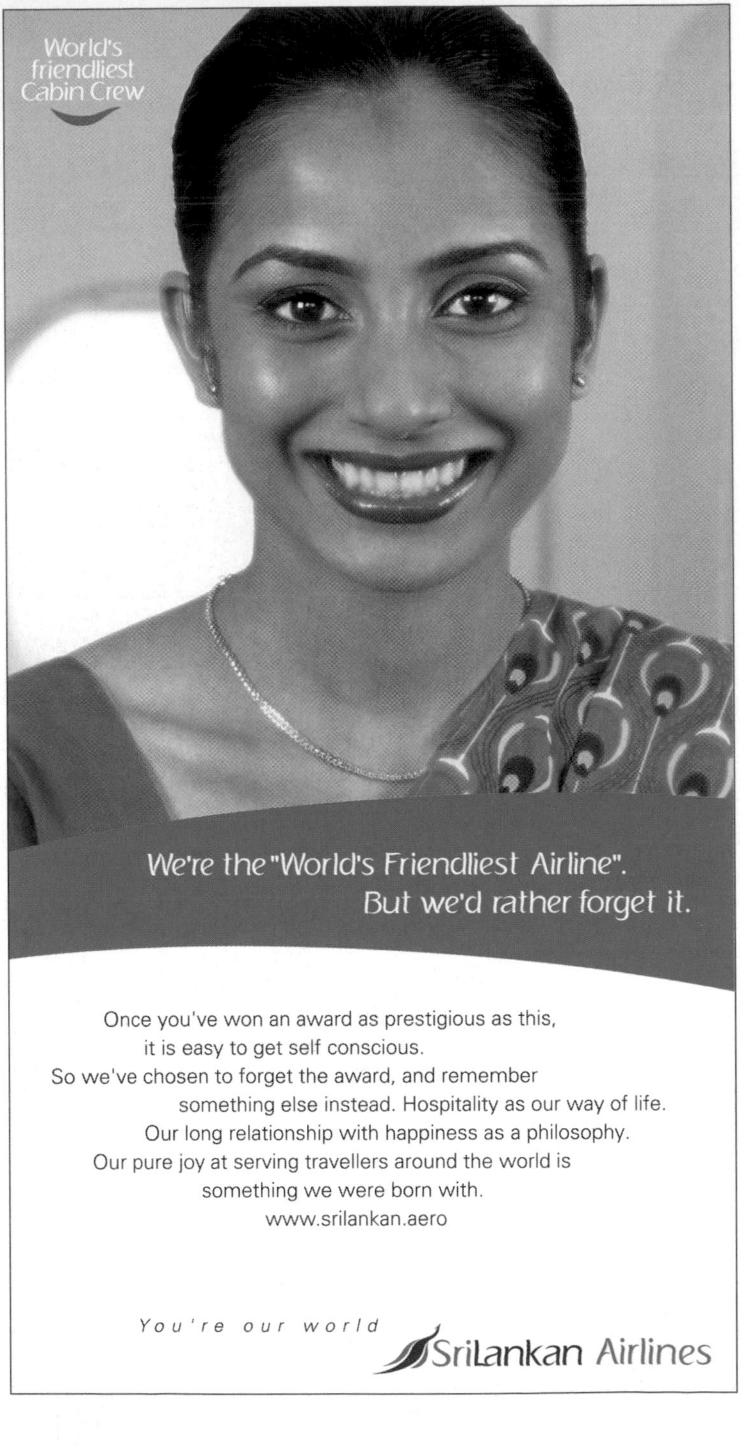
World's friendliest Cabin Crew
We're the "World's Friendliest Airline".
But we'd rather forget it.
Once you've won an award as prestigious as this, it is easy to get self conscious. So we've chosen to forget the award, and remember something else instead. Hospitality as our way of life. Our long relationship with happiness as a philosophy. Our pure joy at serving travellers around the world is something we were born with.
www.srilankan.aero
You're our world
SriLankan Airlines

Sri Lanka

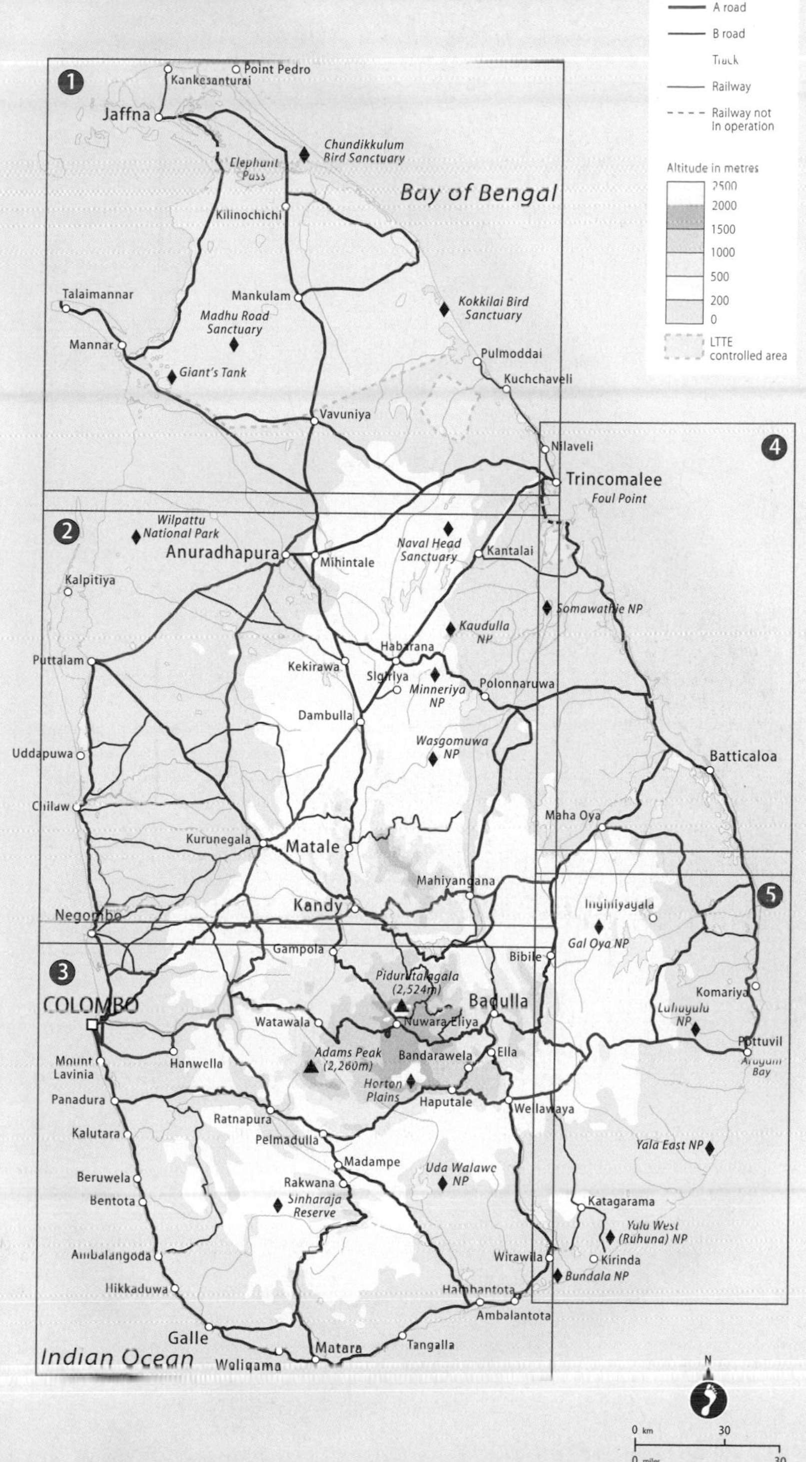
A road
B road
Track
Railway
Railway not in operation
Altitude in metres
2500
2000
1500
1000
500
200
0
LTTE controlled area
1
2
3
4
5
Point Pedro
Kankesanturai
Jaffna
Chundikkulum Bird Sanctuary
Elephant Pass
Bay of Bengal
Kilinochchi
Talaimannar
Mankulam
Madhu Road Sanctuary
Kokkilai Bird Sanctuary
Mannar
Pulmoddai
Giant's Tank
Kuchchaveli
Vavuniya
Nilaveli
Trincomalee
Foul Point
Wilpattu National Park
Naval Head Sanctuary
Anuradhapura
Mihintale
Kantalai
Kalpitiya
Somawathie NP
Kaudulla NP
Habarana
Puttalam
Kekirawa
Sigiriya
Minneriya NP
Polonnaruwa
Dambulla
Wasgomuwa NP
Uddapuwa
Batticaloa
Chilaw
Maha Oya
Kurunegala
Matale
Mahiyangana
Kandy
Negombo
Gampola
Gal Oya NP
Bibile
Pidurutalagala (2,524m)
COLOMBO
Badulla
Komariya
Watawala
Nuwara Eliya
Lahugala NP
Pottuvil
Arugam Bay
Adams Peak (2,260m)
Bandarawela
Ella
Mount Lavinia
Hanwella
Horton Plains
Panadura
Haputale
Wellawaya
Ratnapura
Kalutara
Pelmadulla
Yala East NP
Madampe
Uda Walawe NP
Beruwela
Rakwana
Bentota
Sinharaja Reserve
Katagarama
Yala West (Ruhuna) NP
Ambalangoda
Wirawila
Kirinda
Bundala NP
Hikkaduwa
Hambantota
Ambalantota
Galle
Tangalla
Matara
Indian Ocean
Weligama
N
0 km 30
0 miles 30

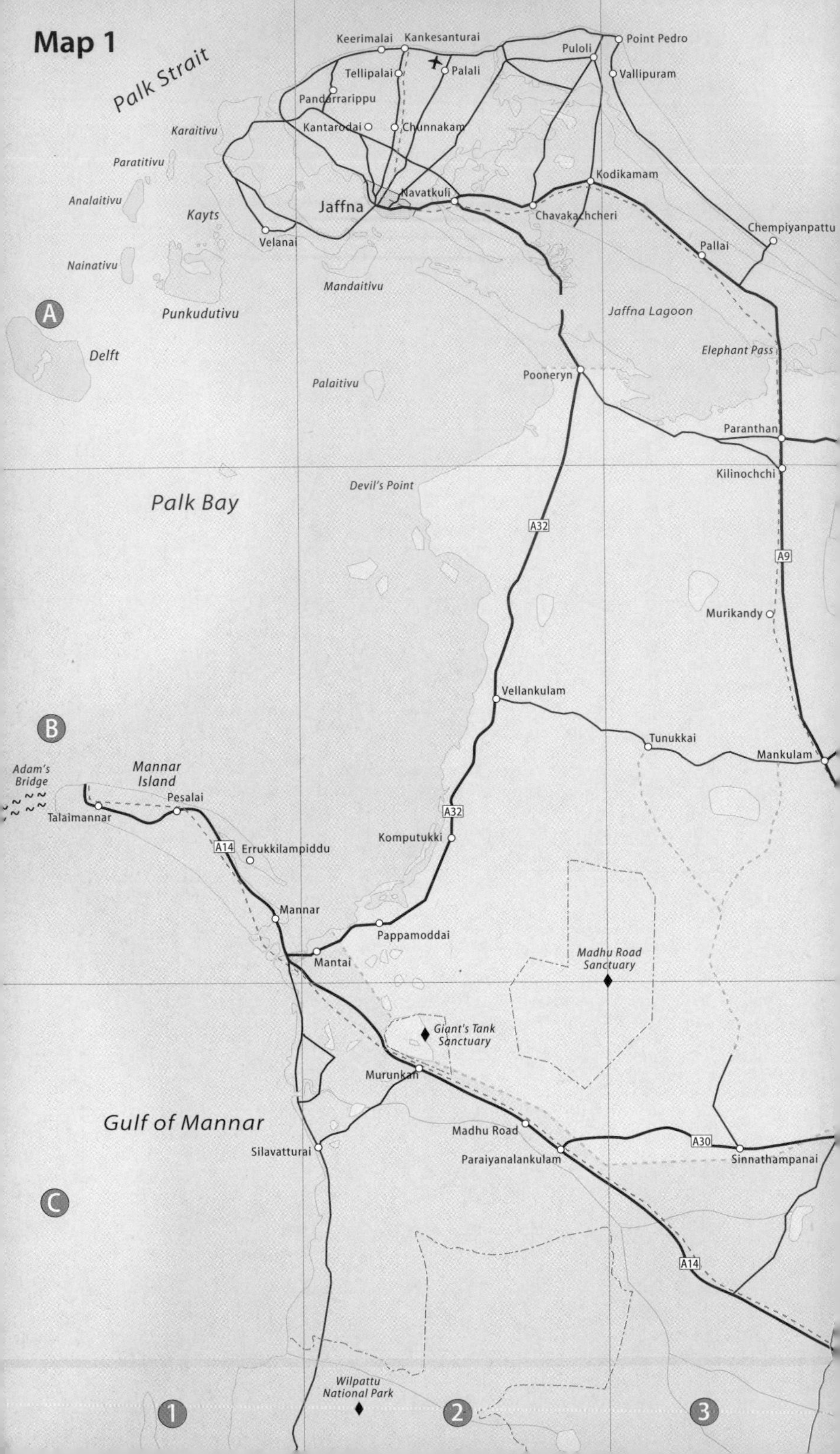

Map 1
Palk Strait
Keerimalai
Kankesanturai
Palali
Tellipalai
Pandarrarippu
Kantarodai
Chunnakam
Point Pedro
Puloli
Vallipuram
Karaitivu
Paratitivu
Analaitivu
Kayts
Jaffna
Navatkuli
Kodikamam
Chavakachcheri
Velanai
Nainativu
Mandaitivu
Chempiyanpattu
Pallai
Punkudutivu
Jaffna Lagoon
Delft
Elephant Pass
Pooneryn
Palaitivu
Paranthan
Kilinochchi
Palk Bay
Devil's Point
A32
A9
Murikandy
Vellankulam
Tunukkai
Mankulam
Adam's Bridge
Mannar Island
Pesalai
Talaimannar
A32
Komputukki
A14
Errukkilampiddu
Mannar
Pappamoddai
Mantai
Madhu Road Sanctuary
Giant's Tank Sanctuary
Murunkan
Gulf of Mannar
Madhu Road
Paraiyanalankulam
A30
Sinnathampanai
Silavatturai
A14
Wilpattu National Park
A
B
C
1
2
3

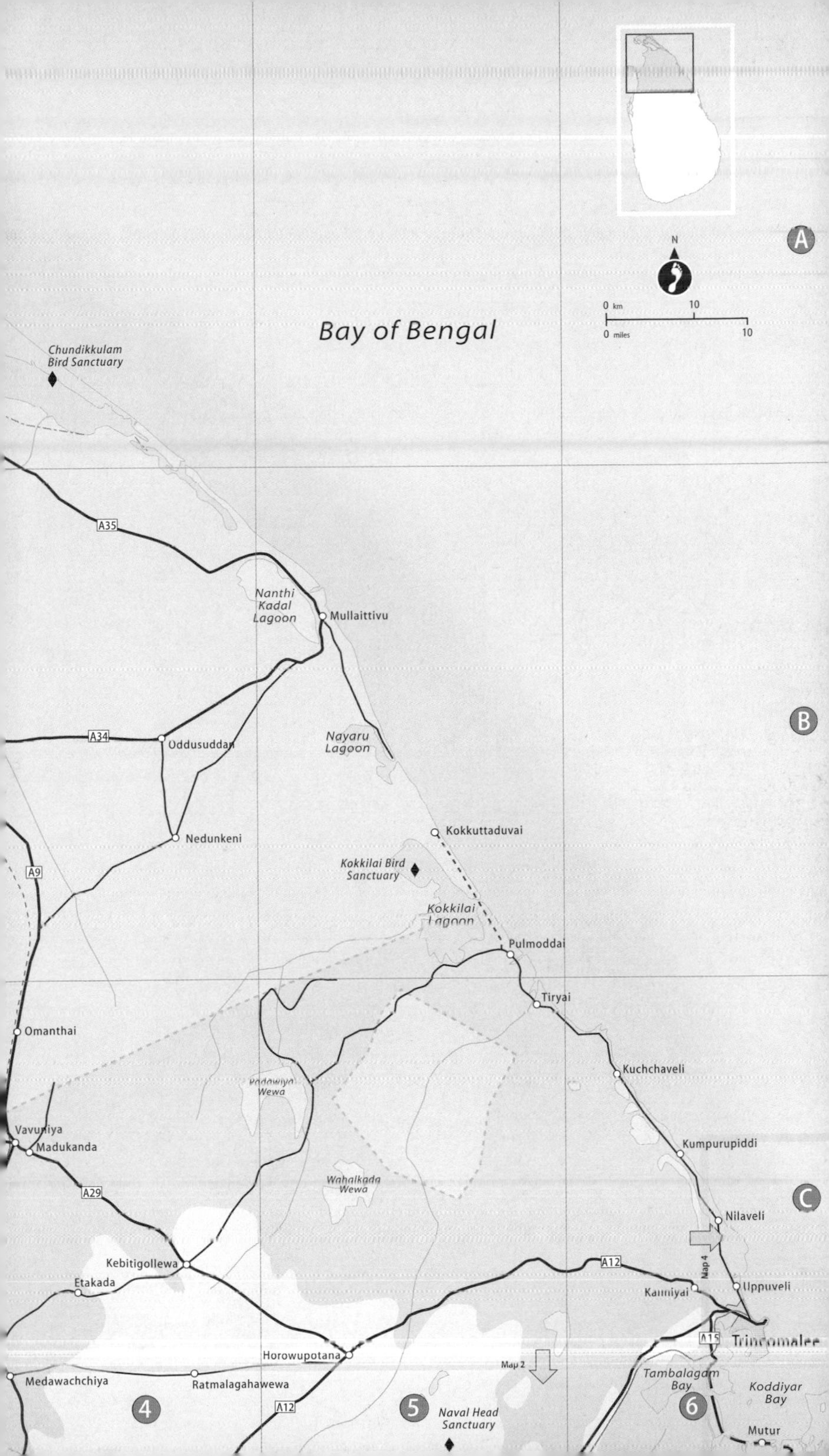

Bay of Bengal
N
0 km
10
0 miles
10
A
B
C
Chundikkulam Bird Sanctuary
A35
Nanthi Kadal Lagoon
Mullaittivu
A34
Oddusuddan
Nayaru Lagoon
Nedunkeni
Kokkuttaduvai
A9
Kokkilai Bird Sanctuary
Kokkilai Lagoon
Pulmoddai
Tiryai
Omanthai
Kuchchaveli
Padawiya Wewa
Vavuniya
Madukanda
Kumpurupiddi
Wahalkada Wewa
A29
Nilaveli
Kebitigollewa
A12
Map 4
Etakada
Kanniyai
Uppuveli
A15
Trincomalee
Horowupotana
Map 2
Medawachchiya
Ratmalagahawewa
Tambalagam Bay
Koddiyar Bay
4
A12
5
Naval Head Sanctuary
6
Mutur

Map 2

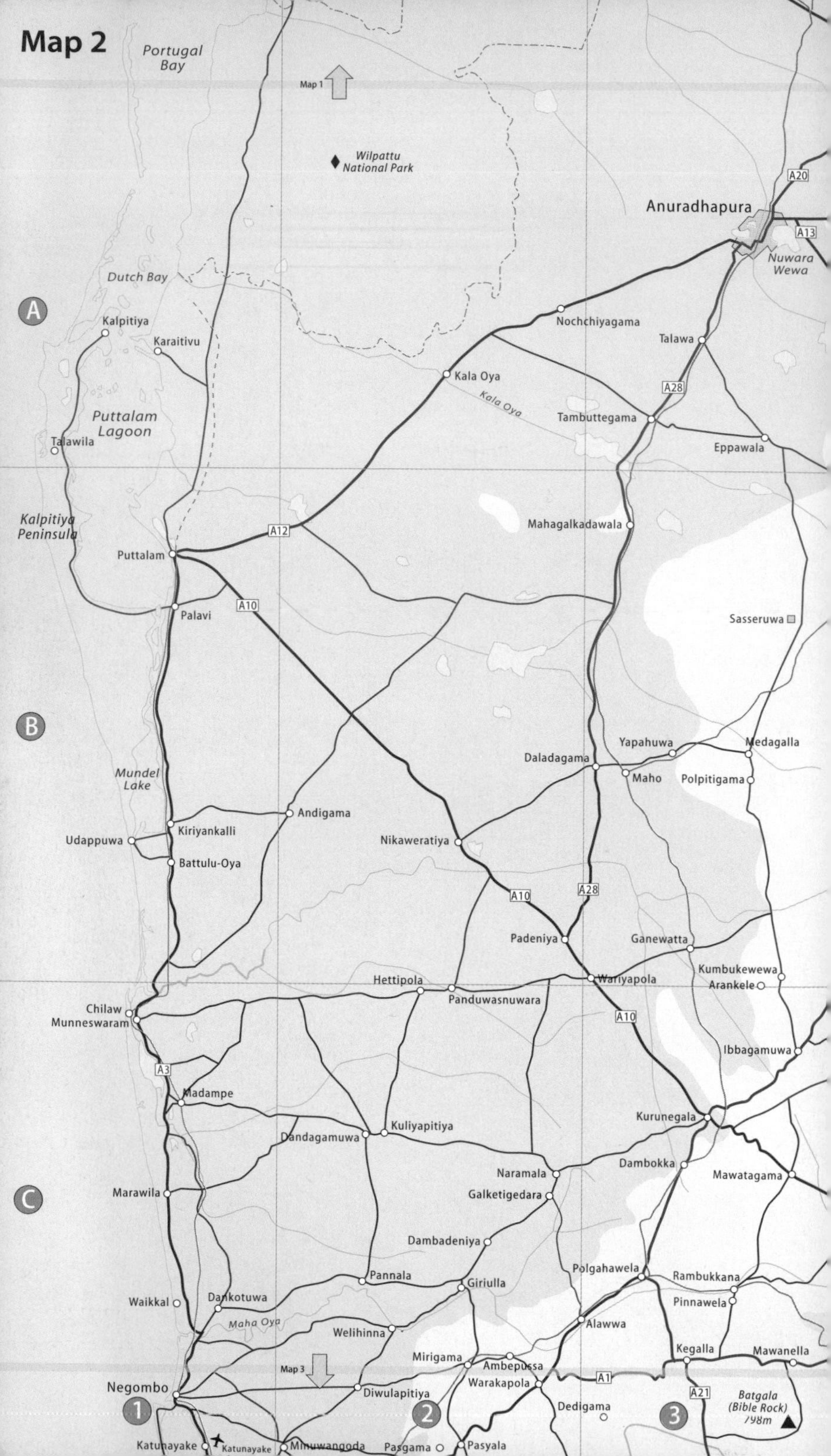

Portugal Bay
Map 1
Wilpattu National Park
A20
Anuradhapura
A13
Nuwara Wewa
Dutch Bay
A
Kalpitiya
Karaitivu
Nochchiyagama
Talawa
Kala Oya
Kala Oya
A28
Puttalam Lagoon
Tambuttegama
Talawila
Eppawala
Kalpitiya Peninsula
Mahagalkadawala
A12
Puttalam
A10
Palavi
Sasseruwa
B
Yapahuwa
Medagalla
Daladagama
Maho
Polpitigama
Mundel Lake
Andigama
Kiriyankalli
Udappuwa
Nikaweratiya
Battulu-Oya
A10
A28
Padeniya
Ganewatta
Kumbukewewa
Hettipola
Wariyapola
Arankele
Panduwasnuwara
Chilaw
Munneswaram
A10
Ibbagamuwa
A3
Madampe
Kurunegala
Kuliyapitiya
Dandagamuwa
Dambokka
Naramala
Mawatagama
Galketigedara
C
Marawila
Dambadeniya
Polgahawela
Pannala
Rambukkana
Giriulla
Waikkal
Dankotuwa
Pinnawela
Maha Oya
Alawwa
Welihinna
Kegalla
Mawanella
Mirigama
Ambepussa
Map 3
A1
Negombo
Warakapola
Diwulapitiya
A21
Batgala (Bible Rock) 798m
1
Dedigama
2
3
Katunayake
Katunayake
Minuwangoda
Pasgama
Pasyala

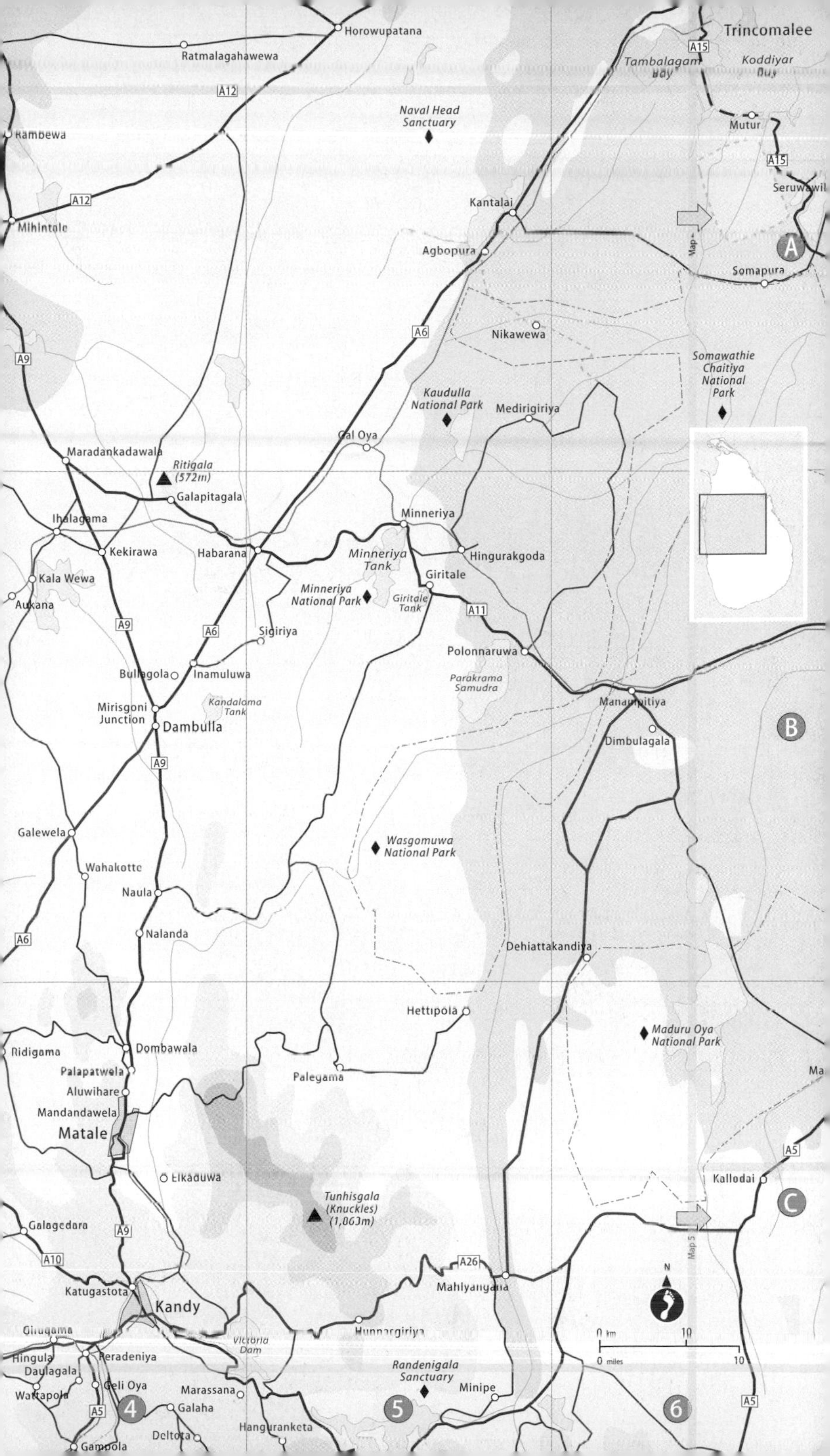

Trincomalee
Horowupatana
Ratmalagahawewa
A12
A15
Tambalagam Bay
Koddiyar Bay
Naval Head Sanctuary
Mutur
Rambewa
A15
Seruwawil
A12
Kantalai
Mihintale
Agbopura
A
Somapura
A6
Nikawewa
A9
Somawathie Chaitiya National Park
Kaudulla National Park
Medirigiriya
Gal Oya
Maradankadawala
Ritigala (572m)
Galapitagala
Ihalagama
Minneriya
Kekirawa
Habarana
Minneriya Tank
Hingurakgoda
Giritale
Kala Wewa
Minneriya National Park
Giritale Tank
Aukana
A11
A9
A6
Sigiriya
Polonnaruwa
Bullagola
Inamuluwa
Parakrama Samudra
Kandalama Tank
Manampitiya
Mirisgoni Junction
Dambulla
B
Dimbulagala
A9
Galewela
Wasgomuwa National Park
Wahakotte
Naula
A6
Nalanda
Dehiattakandiya
Hettipola
Maduru Oya National Park
Ridigama
Dombawala
Palapatwela
Palegama
Aluwihare
Mandandawela
Matale
A5
Kallodai
Elkaduwa
Tunhisgala (Knuckles) (1,863m)
C
Galagedara
A9
A10
A26
Mahiyangana
Katugastota
Kandy
N
Hunnargiriya
0 km 10
0 miles 10
Victoria Dam
Peradeniya
Hingula
Daulagala
Randenigala Sanctuary
Geli Oya
Minipe
Marassana
Wattapola
A5
4
Galaha
5
6
A5
Deltota
Hanguranketa
Gampola
Map 5

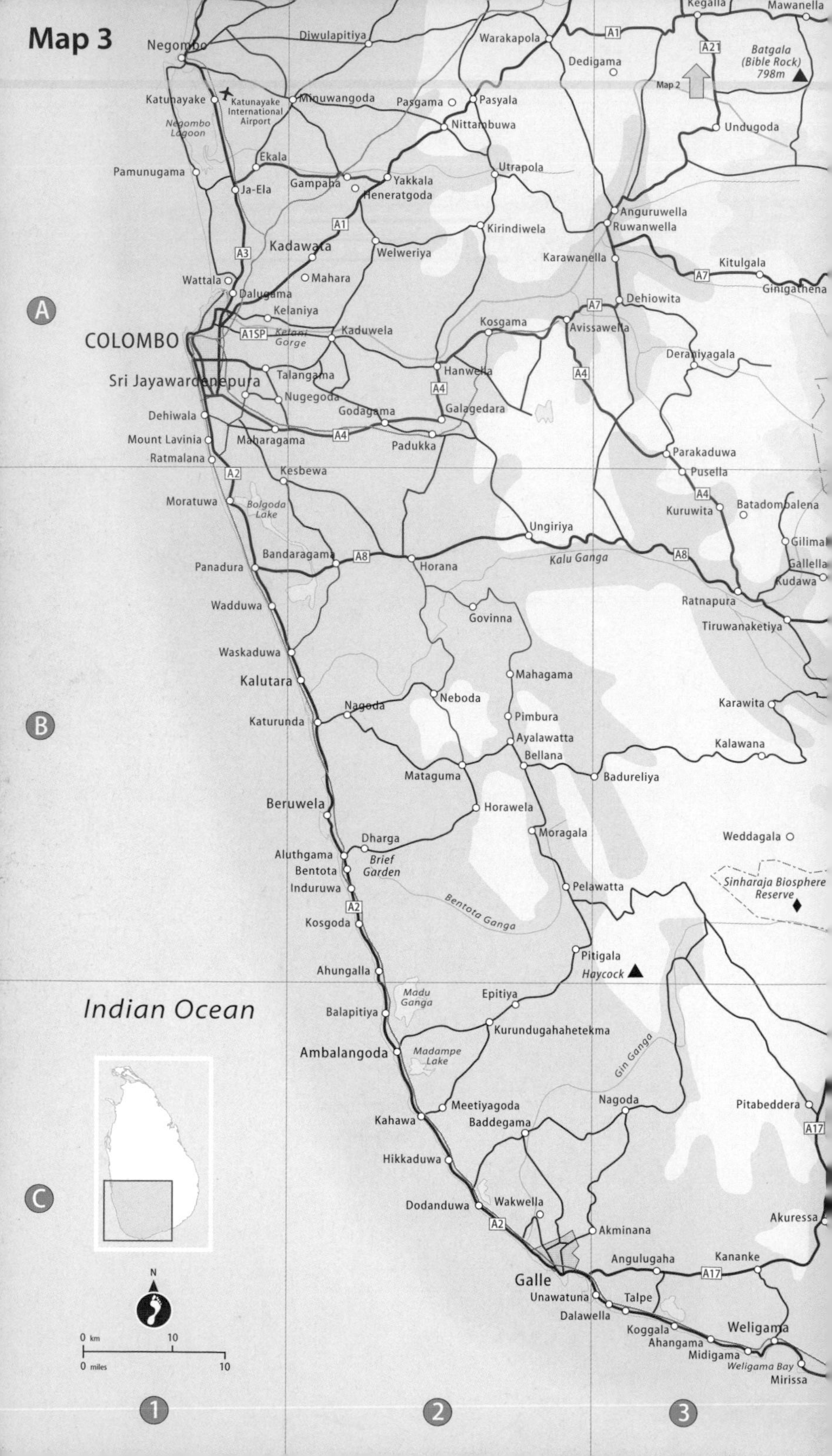

Map 3
Negombo
Diwulapitiya
Warakapola
Kegalla
Mawanella
A1
A21
Dedigama
Batgala (Bible Rock) 798m
Map 2
Katunayake
Katunayake International Airport
Minuwangoda
Pasgama
Pasyala
Negombo Lagoon
Nittambuwa
Undugoda
Ekala
Pamunugama
Utrapola
Gampaha
Yakkala
Ja-Ela
Heneratgoda
Anguruwella
Ruwanwella
A1
Kirindiwela
Kadawata
A3
Welweriya
Karawanella
Kitulgala
Mahara
A7
Wattala
Ginigathena
Dalugama
A7
Dehiowita
A
Kelaniya
Kosgama
Avissawella
A1SP
Kaduwela
Kelani Gorge
COLOMBO
Deraniyagala
Hanwella
Talangama
A4
Sri Jayawardenepura
A4
Nugegoda
Godagama
Galagedara
Dehiwala
Mount Lavinia
Maharagama
A4
Padukka
Parakaduwa
Ratmalana
Pusella
A2
Kesbewa
A4
Moratuwa
Bolgoda Lake
Kuruwita
Batadombalena
Ungiriya
Gilima
Bandaragama
A8
A8
Horana
Kalu Ganga
Gallella
Panadura
Kudawa
Ratnapura
Wadduwa
Govinna
Tiruwanaketiya
Waskaduwa
Mahagama
Kalutara
Neboda
Karawita
Nagoda
Pimbura
B
Katurunda
Ayalawatta
Kalawana
Bellana
Mataguma
Badureliya
Horawela
Beruwela
Moragala
Weddagala
Dharga
Aluthgama
Brief Garden
Bentota
Sinharaja Biosphere Reserve
Induruwa
Pelawatta
A2
Bentota Ganga
Kosgoda
Pitigala
Ahungalla
Haycock
Madu Ganga
Epitiya
Indian Ocean
Balapitiya
Kurundugahahetekma
Ambalangoda
Madampe Lake
Gin Ganga
Meetiyagoda
Nagoda
Pitabeddera
Kahawa
Baddegama
A17
Hikkaduwa
C
Wakwella
Dodanduwa
Akuressa
A2
Akminana
Angulugaha
Kananke
A17
Galle
Unawatuna
Talpe
Dalawella
Koggala
Weligama
Ahangama
Midigama
Weligama Bay
Mirissa
N
0 km 10
0 miles 10
1
2
3

Daulagala
Wattappola
Geli Oya
Marassana
Victoria Randenigala Sanctuary
Minipe
A5
Galaha
Deltota
Gampola
Hanguranketa
Bibile
Pussellawa
Hewaheta
Padiyapelella
Nawalapitiya
Ramboda
A
Pidurutalagala (2,524m)
Ragalla
Meditale
Dunhinda Falls
Kandapola
Udapassellawa
Badulla
Dimbula
Watagoda
Carolina
Watawala
Nuwara Eliya
Paranagama
Kandapola
Nanu Oya
Sita Ella
Ettampitiya
Hali-Ela
Kotagala
Talawakale
A7
Mount Namunukula
Hakgala
A16
Norton Bridge
Keppetipola
Welimada
Demodara
A22
Hatton
Mona
Ambewela
Ella
Hullanda
Norwood
Totapola (2,357m)
Pattipola
Bandarawela
Maskeliya
Boralanda
Kumbakkana
Bogawantalawa
Rawana Falls
Adam's Peak (Sri Pada) (2,243m)
Upcot
Kirigalpotta (2,395m)
Horton Plains
Ohiya
A16
A23
A4
Haputale
Okkampitiya
Kalupahana
Diyaluma Falls
Halpe
Haldumulla
Beragala
Buttala
Diyaluma
Wellawaya
Maligawila
Belihuloya
Gampaha
Buduruvagala
Rassagala
Balangoda
Uggalkaltota
Ellepola
Pelmadulla
Menik Ganga
Rajawaka
A2
A18
Diyainna
B
Map 5
Galge
Madampe
Handagiriya
Kuda Oya
Godakawela
Timirigahamankada
Rakwana
Uda Walawe National Park
Uda Walawe Reservoir
A17
Pallebedda
Suriyakanda
Karawila
Tanamalwila
Sella Katagarama
Kolonne
Timbolketiya
Malala Oya
Lunuganwehera Reservoir
Katagaram
Sittarama
Gongala (1,358m)
Lunuganwehera Sanctuary
Hayes
Deniyaya
Panamure
Embilipitiya
Padawkema
Lunuganwehera
Suriyawewa
A32
Kotapola
Tunkama
Pannegamuwa
Mahapelessa Hot Springs
Landajulana
Tissamaharama
Molakepupatana
Morawaka
Middeniya
Wirawila
Ridiyagama
Conoruwa
Andalla
Siyambalagoda
Weligatta
Tellula
Keligama
Walawe Ganga
Bundala
Godakoggolla
Bundala National Park
Udamalala
Wiraketiya
Ganegoda
Arrabokka
Godaraya
Mulgirigala
Kalametiya Bird Sanctuary
Ambalantota
A2
Hambantota
C
Hungama
Nonagama
Ranna
Hakmana
Kirinda
Beliatta
Tangalla
Mawella
Kudawella
Matara
A2
Dikwella
Dondra
4
5
6

Map 4

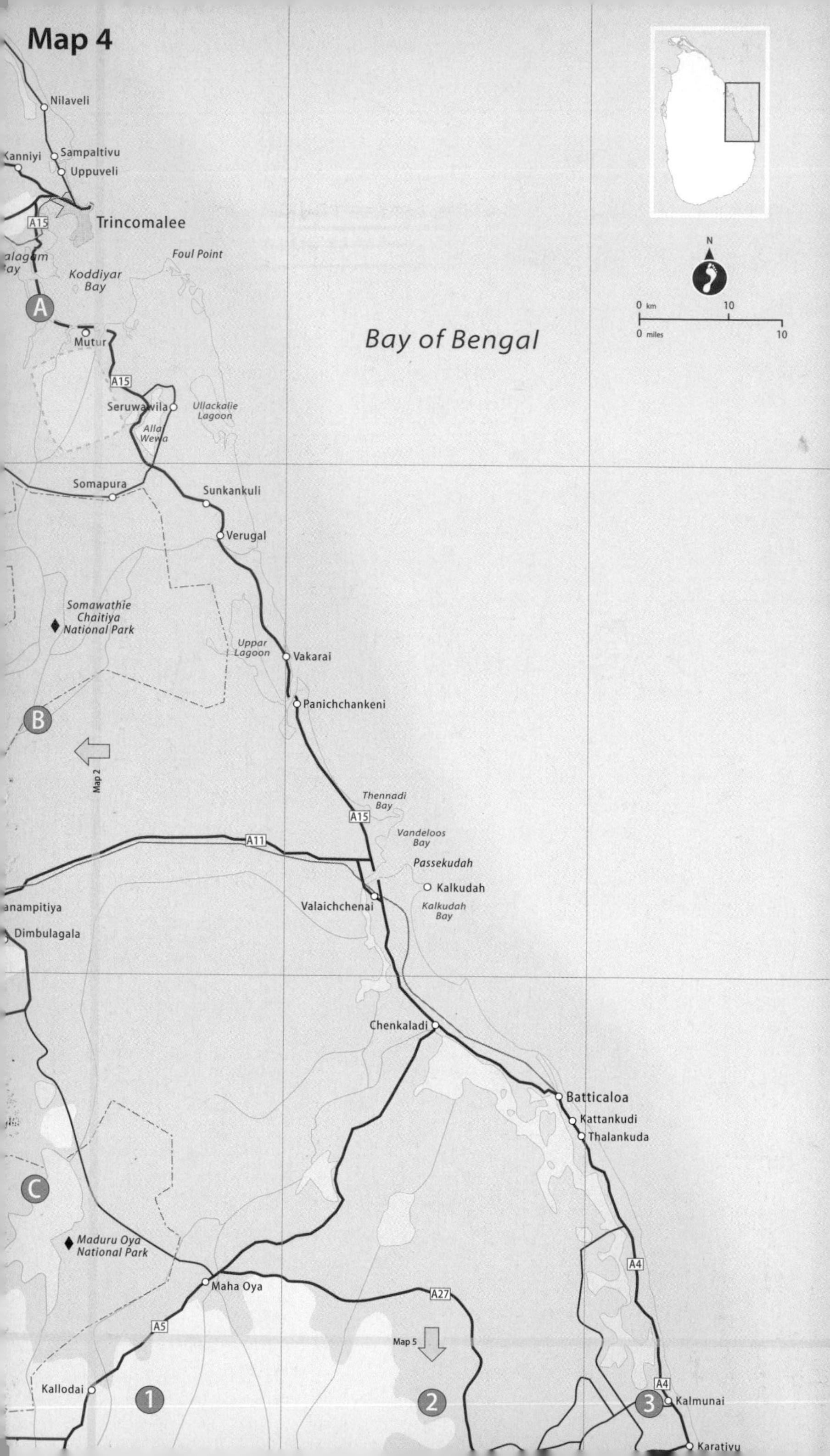

Nilaveli
Kanniyi
Sampaltivu
Uppuveli
A15
Trincomalee
Foul Point
Koddiyar Bay
A
Mutur
A15
Seruwawila
Ullackalie Lagoon
Alla Wewa
Bay of Bengal
N
0 km 10
0 miles 10
Somapura
Sunkankuli
Verugal
Somawathie Chaitiya National Park
Uppar Lagoon
Vakarai
Panichchankeni
B
Map 2
Thennadi Bay
A15
Vandeloos Bay
A11
Passekudah
Kalkudah
Valaichchenai
Kalkudah Bay
Dimbulagala
Chenkaladi
Batticaloa
Kattankudi
Thalankuda
C
Maduru Oya National Park
A4
Maha Oya
A27
A5
Map 5
Kallodai
1
2
A4
3
Kalmunai
Karativu

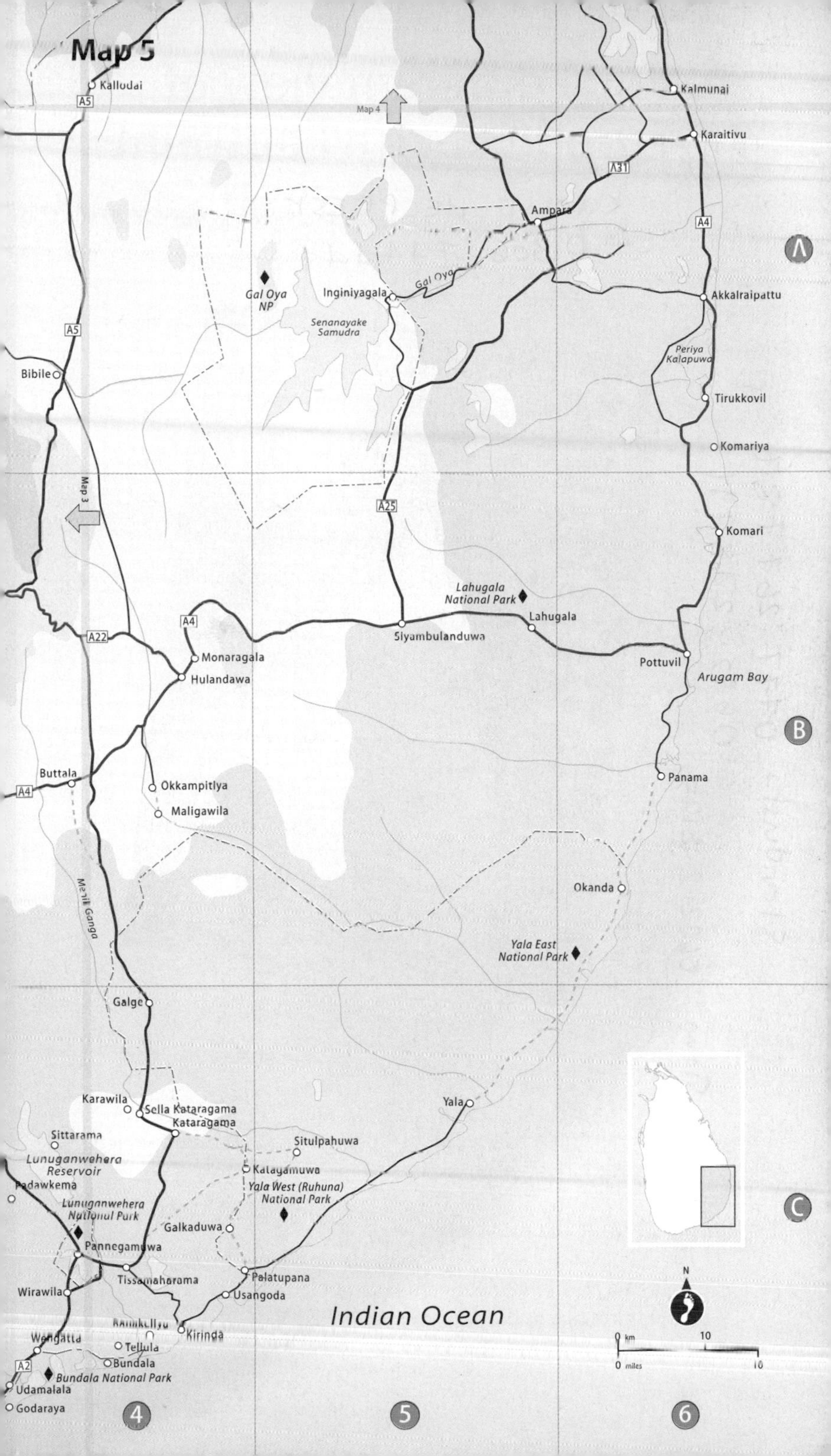

Map 5
Kallodai
A5
Map 4
Kalmunai
Karaitivu
A31
Ampara
A4
A
Gal Oya NP
Gal Oya
Inginiyagala
Senanayake Samudra
Akkalraipattu
A5
Bibile
Periya Kalapuwa
Tirukkovil
Komariya
Map 3
A25
Komari
Lahugala National Park
A4
Lahugala
A22
Siyambulanduwa
Monaragala
Hulandawa
Pottuvil
Arugam Bay
B
Buttala
A4
Okkampitiya
Maligawila
Panama
Menik Ganga
Okanda
Yala East National Park
Galge
Karawila
Sella Kataragama
Kataragama
Yala
Sittarama
Situlpahuwa
Lunuganwehera Reservoir
Katagamuwa
Padawkema
Yala West (Ruhuna) National Park
Lunuganwehera National Park
C
Galkaduwa
Pannegamuwa
Tissamaharama
Palatupana
Wirawila
Usangoda
Indian Ocean
N
Kirinda
Wengatta
Tellula
Bundala
A2
Bundala National Park
Udamalala
Godaraya
0 km 10
0 miles 10
4
5
6

For a different view of Europe, take a Footprint

"Superstylish travel guides – perfect for short break addicts."
Harvey Nichols magazine

Discover so much more...
Listings driven, forward looking and up to date. Focuses on what's going on right now. Contemporary, stylish, and innovative approach, providing quality travel information.